SAP PRESS e-books

Print or e-book, Kindle or iPad, workplace or airplane: Choose where and how to read your SAP PRESS books! You can now get all our titles as e-books, too:

- By download and online access
- For all popular devices
- And, of course, DRM-free

Convinced? Then go to www.sap-press.com and get your e-book today.

Sales and Distribution with SAP S/4HANA®: Business User Guide

SAP PRESS is a joint initiative of SAP and Rheinwerk Publishing. The know-how offered by SAP specialists combined with the expertise of Rheinwerk Publishing offers the reader expert books in the field. SAP PRESS features first-hand information and expert advice, and provides useful skills for professional decision-making.

SAP PRESS offers a variety of books on technical and business-related topics for the SAP user. For further information, please visit our website: *www.sap-press.com*.

Christian van Helfteren
Configuring Sales in SAP S/4HANA
2020, 766 pages, hardcover and e-book
www.sap-press.com/4907

Tritschler, Walz, Rupp, Mucka
Financial Accounting with SAP S/4HANA: Business User Guide
2020, 604 pages, hardcover and e-book
www.sap-press.com/4938

Karl Liebstückel
Plant Maintenance with SAP S/4HANA: Business User Guide
2021, 665 pages, hardcover and e-book
www.sap-press.com/5180

Bhattacharjee, Narasimhamurti, Desai, Vazquez, Walsh
Logistics with SAP S/4HANA: An Introduction (2nd Edition)
2019, 589 pages, hardcover and e-book
www.sap-press.com/4785

Janet Salmon, Stefan Walz
Controlling with SAP S/4HANA: Business User Guide
2021, 593 pages, hardcover and e-book
www.sap-press.com/5282

James Olcott, Jon Simmonds

Sales and Distribution with SAP S/4HANA®: Business User Guide

Editor Will Jobst
Acquisitions Editor Emily Nicholls
Copyeditor Julie McNamee
Cover Design Graham Geary
Photo Credit iStockphoto.com: 1210182359/© alvarez, 1203763961/© bernie_photo
Layout Design Vera Brauner
Production Graham Geary
Typesetting SatzPro, Krefeld (Germany)
Printed and bound in Canada

ISBN 978-1-4932-2080-9
© 2021 by Rheinwerk Publishing, Inc., Boston (MA)
1st edition 2021

Library of Congress Cataloging-in-Publication Data
Names: Olcott, James, author. | Simmonds, Jon, author.
Title: Sales and distribution with SAP S/4HANA : business user guide / by James Olcott and Jon Simmonds.
Description: 1st Edition. | Boston : Rheinwerk Publishing, 2021. | Includes index.
Identifiers: LCCN 2021009235 | ISBN 9781493220809 (hardcover) | ISBN 9781493220816 (ebook)
Subjects: LCSH: SAP HANA (Electronic resource) | Selling. | Customer relations--Data processing | Physical distribution of goods--Data processing.
Classification: LCC HF5438.25 .O4483 2021 | DDC 658.850285/53--dc23
LC record available at https://lccn.loc.gov/2021009235

All rights reserved. Neither this publication nor any part of it may be copied or reproduced in any form or by any means or translated into another language, without the prior consent of Rheinwerk Publishing, 2 Heritage Drive, Suite 305, Quincy, MA 02171.

Rheinwerk Publishing makes no warranties or representations with respect to the content hereof and specifically disclaims any implied warranties of merchantability or fitness for any particular purpose. Rheinwerk Publishing assumes no responsibility for any errors that may appear in this publication.

"Rheinwerk Publishing" and the Rheinwerk Publishing logo are registered trademarks of Rheinwerk Verlag GmbH, Bonn, Germany. SAP PRESS is an imprint of Rheinwerk Verlag GmbH and Rheinwerk Publishing, Inc.

All of the screenshots and graphics reproduced in this book are subject to copyright © SAP SE, Dietmar-Hopp-Allee 16, 69190 Walldorf, Germany.

SAP, ABAP, ASAP, Concur Hipmunk, Duet, Duet Enterprise, ExpenseIt, SAP ActiveAttention, SAP Adaptive Server Enterprise, SAP Advantage Database Server, SAP ArchiveLink, SAP Ariba, SAP Business ByDesign, SAP Business Explorer (SAP BEx), SAP BusinessObjects, SAP BusinessObjects Explorer, SAP BusinessObjects Web Intelligence, SAP Business One, SAP Business Workflow, SAP BW/4HANA, SAP C/4HANA, SAP Concur, SAP Crystal Reports, SAP EarlyWatch, SAP Fieldglass, SAP Fiori, SAP Global Trade Services (SAP GTS), SAP GoingLive, SAP HANA, SAP Jam, SAP Leonardo, SAP Lumira, SAP MaxDB, SAP NetWeaver, SAP PartnerEdge, SAPPHIRE NOW, SAP PowerBuilder, SAP PowerDesigner, SAP R/2, SAP R/3, SAP Replication Server, SAP Roambi, SAP S/4HANA, SAP S/4HANA Cloud, SAP SQL Anywhere, SAP Strategic Enterprise Management (SAP SEM), SAP SuccessFactors, SAP Vora, TripIt, and Qualtrics are registered or unregistered trademarks of SAP SE, Walldorf, Germany.

All other products mentioned in this book are registered or unregistered trademarks of their respective companies.

Contents at a Glance

Dear Reader,

Think about your favorite dish to cook (or bake, or grill!). At this point, you might be able to make it from memory, and have probably mentally even edited the recipe to make it suit your taste buds exactly.

But how'd you first find it? A family secret passed down for generations, a blog post on a hobbyist's website, or a page from your favorite chef's foundational book? A good recipe not only makes great food—it helps you understand *why the food is great*. By understanding the fullness of your dish's flavor, you unlock more possibilities for your meal, making you stronger in the kitchen (and more impressive at the dinner table!).

This book is a recipe book of a different sort. In these pages, authors James Olcott and Jon Simmonds provide the definitive cookbook for sales and distribution operations with SAP S/4HANA. Their combined expertise will show you the ins and outs of SD, expanding your repertoire and familiarity with key processes. Just like a good recipe is the product of a lifetime of tinkering, this book is the result of their extensive experience and collaboration in the proverbial kitchen.

Let's dig in!

Will Jobst
Editor, SAP PRESS

willj@rheinwerk-publishing.com
www.sap-press.com
Rheinwerk Publishing · Boston, MA

Contents

Preface

It's been four years since SAP PRESS last published an extensive guide to its Sales and Distribution module on the SAP ERP platform. A lot has changed in the intervening time, namely the rollout of SAP S/4HANA software over the past few years to replace the previous matured SAP ERP version for which support will start to sunset in 2027 (although further extension is possible).

What hasn't changed is the importance of sales and distribution to both SAP and its customers. The sales and distribution functionality focuses squarely on the customer: You write sales orders to them, ship them your goods (or sell services), and send them invoices, and they shower you with inbound cash that sustains your operations indefinitely. Contrast this with the vendor focus of the material management functionality in which you send money out.

Whichever module or version of SAP you use, the most important thing worth noting, and we do so right here at the very beginning, is that this is one solid piece of software. Ever notice how SAP applications never crash? Think about your other office applications for a moment. Remarkable in this day and age, isn't it?

Our user guide is an ideal reference for both business users and sales and distribution consultants who would benefit from an overview of the entire module from a high level. Consultants with extensive experience in SAP ERP will especially appreciate the delta discussions regarding what's new in SAP S/4HANA. Many consultants tend to work in one specific area of sales and distribution with little contact to others. For example, a sales and distribution consultant may work in a service industry and therefore have little exposure to logistics, outbound delivery processing, and handling units. This manual helps fill in those high-level details for all kinds of sales and distribution consultants.

The good news is that many of the processes in SAP S/4HANA are easily recognizable to the experienced SAP ERP user.

In addition to our focus on changes brought by SAP S/4HANA, we also offer a refreshed walkthrough of the core order-to-cash document flow in both SAP GUI and SAP Fiori.

What This Book Covers

Like the previous edition, our goal is to serve as both a tutorial and reference guide for all key processes as well as changes in sales and distribution.

This user manual starts with a look at the history of SAP as an organization, a detailed discussion of the changes from SAP ERP to SAP S/4HANA with a focus on customer master data. After a review of navigation basics, we take you from presales to billing.

We finish up by revealing what exactly happens afterward and cover some additional functionalities such as rebates and repairs.

Our explanation of sales and distribution flows as follows: **Chapter 1** introduces SAP S/4HANA and details the most significant changes, such as in business partner management, new data tables, and technical enhancements. In **Chapter 2**, we elucidate all the necessary prerequisites for running sales and distribution transactions, primarily the types of master data that must be present. **Chapter 3** covers the basics of navigating SAP S/4HANA screens; all SAP GUI and SAP Fiori transactions use familiar buttons and icons, and this is laid out for the benefit of new users. **Chapter 4** starts off the full-scale review of the sales and distribution document flow with the first presale activity, the inquiry. The presales flow continues with the next step in **Chapter 5** for the legally binding quotation document. **Chapter 6** is one of the main chapters of this manual in that sales documents are the workhorse of the entire sales and distribution flow. There are several different types to cover, and some of the logic underpinning the document functionalities are explained here. Following the sales document discussion, **Chapter 7** covers the logistics processes, including picking, packing, outbound delivery, and posting the goods issue. **Chapter 8** discusses billing, which is the culmination of the previous processes. What happens if you make a mistake? **Chapter 9** on reversals answers this question authoritatively, complete with a handy matrix to serve as a necessary reference going forward. **Chapter 10** provides step-by-step instructions for setting up and applying rebate and settlement functionality in SAP S/4HANA. **Chapter 11** introduces warranty and repairs management and provides a brief overview. **Chapter 12** explains what happens to your invoice to the customer after issuance.

The appendices that follow are intended as useful references. **Appendix A** provides lists of commonly used transaction codes for both SAP GUI and SAP Fiori, and **Appendix B** provides a list of new SAP Fiori apps.

Our goal is not only to give you an overview of the most important elements of sales and distribution as gleaned from our combined 40 years of experience but also to provide you with useful guides to which you can refer time and again. Accordingly, we hope that this book will be pulled down from your office bookcase often.

Acknowledgments

The authors would like collectively to extend their gratitude to our great senior acquisitions editor Emily Nicholls; without her encouragement and initiative, this book could not have been written. Our thanks as well to development editor Will Jobst for his tireless eye to details and requirements.

A special note is in order to Divyendra Purohit for generously contributing the rebates and settlements chapter. For much more information on this topic, please see

Divyendra's authoritative work *Introducing Rebate and Settlement Management with SAP S/4HANA* (SAP PRESS, 2020).

James first wishes to thank his father Bernard Olcott for having started an IT business in Manhattan in the 1960s. At a tender age, James recalls fondly all the accoutrements that fueled IT at the time like computer punch cards and terminals (available by the hour). At a tender age, James thought everything was IT related, and without that experience, this book could not have been written. James would like to extend special thanks to Kim Hoang from Laidon Consulting for her generous assistance on all things FI. Jon and I worked on a generic SAP S/4HANA box that had to be configured and set up soup to nuts. There were some persistent FI configuration items that needed an expert like Kim to adjust. We are grateful for her continuous availability to resolve those issues when needed.

James also thanks Ravi Srinivasan who, like Jon, is also a frequent contributor to EURSAP's SAP Blog, and is selfless in responding to detailed questions on SAP nomenclature and special features.

Finally, but not at all last, James needs to thank his coauthor Jon for his enthusiastic work ethic and his eye to detail on resolving periodic issues together. It was a pleasure to work with Jon, and he looks forward to repeating the experience in the future. James thanks his family Melissa, Celine, Grant, and Max, especially for their forbearance while overhearing endless SAP minutiae. Gratitude is also expressed to landlords Gino Garlanda, Jasper, Donna Zilkha, Sue and Andrew de Courcy-Ireland, and Mary and Steve Cohen, who kindly tolerated the writing of much of this text in their abodes under lockdowns and quarantines.

Jon firstly would like to thank his coauthor James for his tireless and relentless drive for perfection, for being flexible in his approach to sharing chapters, and for his honesty and creativity in proofreading efforts. If all colleagues were as easy and useful to deal with as James, the world would be a better place.

Finally, Jon would like to thank his family, particularly Susan, Ella and Charlie, for their never-ending patience with lost evenings and weekends to this book.

Chapter 1
Introduction to Sales and Distribution with SAP S/4HANA

SAP is the market-share leader in the enterprise resource planning (ERP) software category. The SAP software suite covers the essential business functions and processes required by an organization to run their businesses. This includes such functions as sales, distribution, manufacturing, warehousing, finance, service, quality management, and human resources, to name just a few.

In this chapter, we'll investigate the background of SAP as a company and how its technologies and applications grew into the globally recognized brand we see today. From here, we'll also investigate how sales and distribution has evolved from the hugely popular SAP ERP 6.0 version into the cutting-edge SAP S/4HANA version of today. This section of the book is a reference section only; much of the information that follows is for background purposes and isn't essential knowledge for the sales and distribution business user.

We'll then explore the structure of sales and distribution in SAP S/4HANA, from presales documents in the system, flowing right through to billing and accounting.

1.1 The SAP Ecosystem

This initial section provides a brief overview of the history of SAP and how the company moved from a small tech startup to the innovation giant it is today. The details cover the initial tentative steps in the early 1970s, through mainstream establishment in the 1980s to 2000s, and on to the innovative differentiation we see currently.

1.1.1 Origin Story

SAP has a long and successful history in the ERP industry, dating back as far back as 1972 in the early groundbreaking days in the IT sector. Back in those days, five IBM employees left their roles to start up their own company called SAP, initially meaning "Systemanalyse und Programmentwicklung" (System Analysis and Program Development). The first versions of SAP were developed and accepted very quickly at their first client,

Imperial Chemicals Industry, providing a standard for business application software featuring real-time data processing.

Initial progress of the fledgling company was slow, but after one year, SAP employed four new employees taking the total to nine, generating DM620,000 in revenue. Two offices were opened in Germany: the headquarters in Weinheim and a nearby office in Mannheim.

As the 1970s progress, SAP as we know it, begins to take shape, starting with the first module—a financial accounting system known as RF. Using DOS on IBM servers, new up-and-coming SAP modules became fully integrated with RF in the coming years to form SAP's first overarching solution under the name SAP R/1. This full integration of modules became the hallmark of the SAP solution, lending the company its competitive edge in the marketplace.

By 1976, SAP created a sales and support subsidiary—SAP GmbH "Systeme Anwendungen und Produkte in der Datenverarbeitung" (Systems, Applications, and Products in Data Processing). The partnership of SAP GmbH and the original SAP was dissolved eventually in 1981 in favor of SAP GmbH.

Further developments in the 1970s showed SAP moving into the international market, with the first non-German companies picking up the product in Austria in 1977 and the development of a French language version of the software in 1978, in partnership with John Deere, the farm equipment manufacturer. Around this time, SAP also moved its headquarters to Walldorf, Bavaria. By 1980, SAP modules included the original financial module RF, RM for materials management, and RV for sales and distribution. The upgrade of SAP's own servers in conjunction with the new fully integrated modules heralded the era of SAP R/2.

1.1.2 Progression from SAP R/2 to SAP R/3 to SAP ERP to SAP S/4HANA

The SAP R/2 era lasted for 10 years, throughout the 1980s, during which radical developments in ERP software were spearheaded by SAP. The early 1980s saw the creation of further integrated modules—RM-PPS for production planning, RK for controlling, and RP for personnel. This rapid expansion saw SAP reach 300 employees and DM100 million in revenue by the middle of the decade, but the unprecedented growth did not stop there. The late 1980s saw the shaping of the organization we know today: a new training facility was opened in Walldorf, SAP Consulting was established to support new customers in their implementations, multiple offices were opened across Europe, and SAP became a public limited company called SAP AG.

Furthermore, efforts to standardize across the ERP space paved the way for the next generation—SAP R/3. Further technical developments included SAP diving into the select industries sector by developing RIVA, a system specifically for utility companies.

A new graphical user interface (GUI) for R/2 was developed, but the look and feel of the solution was still a long way off from the SAP GUI of today. Projects such as the definition and development of the ABAP/4 programming environment were taking up large amounts of time in SAP research and development and were deeply embedded in the transition to SAP R/3.

By the end of the decade, SAP revenue had grown fivefold in four years, to DM500 million, and the company employed 1,700 people across Europe.

In 1991, SAP launched SAP R/3 to incredibly positive reviews—the new GUI was revolutionary at the time. Following successful pilot implementations in the early 1990s, SAP went from strength to strength, beginning by collaborating with Microsoft on integration with the Windows operating system as well as with IXOS to design an electronic archiving solution. Expansion to a US site near Silicon Valley as well as a Japanese version of the software with kanji characters saw SAP's footprint in the marketplace rocket to new heights. Large companies such as General Motors, Burger King, and Coca-Cola came on board to take advantage of technology innovations such as EnjoySAP (the strategy intended to simplify the SAP product from a user point of view) and mySAP.com (combining e-commerce solutions with existing SAP applications).

The strength of the SAP offering was underscored when, in 2001, after the dotcom bubble burst, SAP continued to show incredibly strong growth, realizing 17% revenue increases during the year.

The new millennium saw SAP technological advances carry on apace, with the launch of the technology platform SAP NetWeaver. Within the first year of the product, more than 1,000 customers had signed up.

In the mid-2000s, SAP launched SAP ERP, with the core Enterprise Central Component (ECC), known as SAP ECC 5.0, soon to be developed into SAP ECC 6.0, the most successful and widely used ERP system in history. As a part of this capability improvement, SAP expanded its offerings to encompass solutions specific to dozens of industries.

The latter part of the 2000s saw SAP expand aggressively in the market with new acquisitions such as Business Objects and new technology applications such as SAP Business One and SAP Business ByDesign in a move to break into the small and midsize organization market. Furthermore, a major milestone was the launch of SAP Business Suite 7—bringing together all the applications under one unified banner.

The 2010s began with a bang for SAP with the launch of its in-memory database SAP HANA in 2011. In the next three years, SAP HANA would be enabled on the entire SAP Business Suite, generating nearly €1.2 billion in revenue, making it the fastest-growing product in the history of enterprise software. Growth through acquisition was the hallmark of the 2010s for SAP, including major acquisitions of SuccessFactors, Ariba, Fieldglass, and Concur.

One of the most fundamental technological changes in the company's history took place in 2015 with the launch of SAP S/4HANA, built exclusively on the SAP HANA database, with a brand-new user experience (UX) called SAP Fiori, fully enabled for mobile devices. Almost immediately after the launch, SAP followed with SAP S/4HANA Cloud. Further cloud innovations have followed including SAP Cloud Platform, SAP's platform as a service (PaaS) offering.

The progression of SAP technology is shown in Figure 1.1.

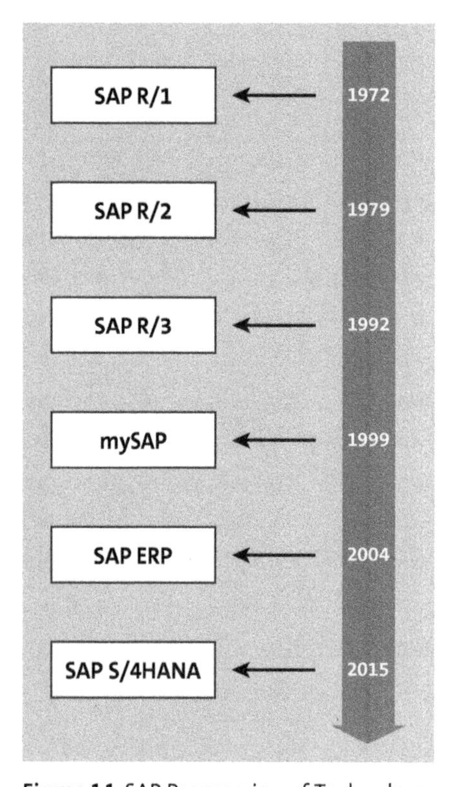

Figure 1.1 SAP Progression of Technology

1.1.3 On-Premise SAP S/4HANA and SAP S/4HANA Cloud

SAP S/4HANA can be deployed in two ways: on-premise or in the cloud. Let's examine the differences and what circumstances are considered when choosing between the two.

The main difference between the two approaches is around speed of implementation, total cost of ownership, and control over the solution. It's important to note, as displayed in Figure 1.2, that an SAP cloud deployment can take a number of different guises depending on the infrastructure and service requirements.

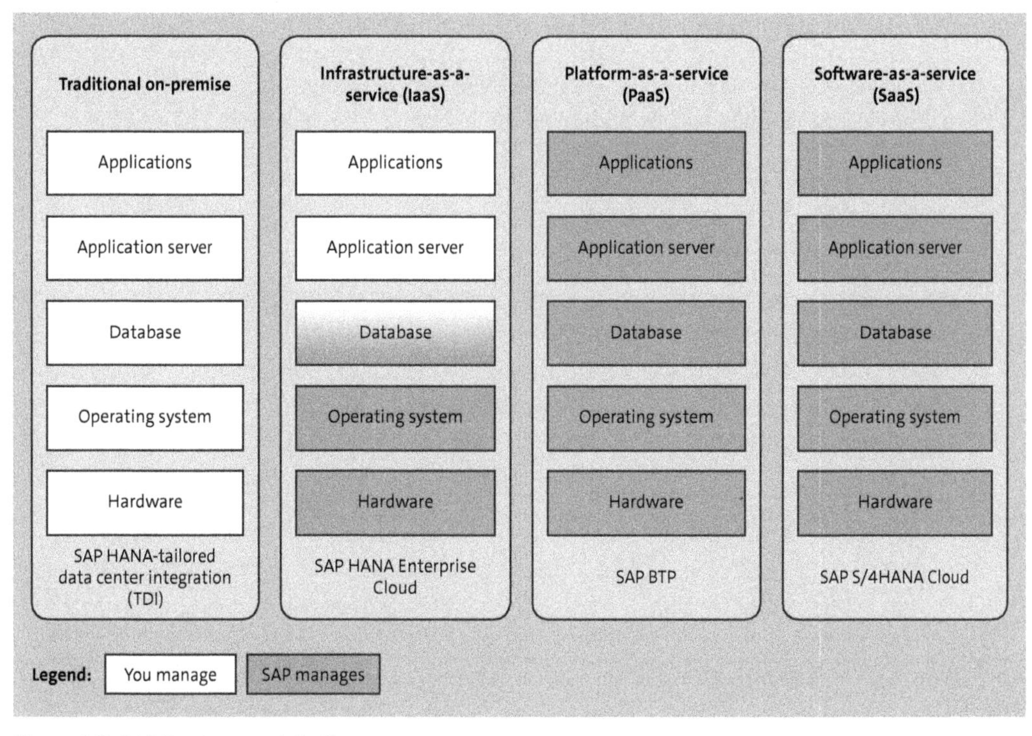

Figure 1.2 SAP Deployment Options

There are advantages and disadvantages of on-premise and cloud deployments that lead organizations to decide on one or the other. The considerations are given in Table 1.1 (in this table, "Cloud" refers to the PaaS and SaaS offerings).

Consideration	On Premise	Cloud
Full control over customization	Yes	No
Automated upgrades	No—annual version releases, but must be planned manually	Yes—every quarter
Licensing	Perpetual user licenses plus ongoing maintenance	Subscription
Business specificity	Can be customized to meet individual business requirements	Predefined best practice configuration deployed

Table 1.1 SAP Deployment Considerations

1.2 Changes from SAP ERP to SAP S/4HANA

For users that are accustomed to the SAP ERP way of doing things, there are some key differences that need to be explored when it comes to SAP S/4HANA, as we'll do in this section.

1.2.1 User Interface

Of all the changes heralded by the advent of SAP S/4HANA, the user interface (UI) is the most far reaching and important. The SAP GUI is a relatively old institution now, dating back to the 1990s, with a few minor tweaks in the intervening years, but starting to show its age recently. SAP has responded to this and associated criticisms from the industry by launching the new UX application: SAP Fiori.

> **Note**
>
> SAP Fiori is a web-based UX that replaces the need to log in to SAP via the logon pad. As a result, it can be used on any mobile device, with automatic screen resizing.

SAP GUI and SAP Fiori screens are, in many cases, very different. If you look at the SAP GUI landing page in Figure 1.3 compared to the SAP Fiori pages in Figure 1.4, you can see immediately the fresher, simplified, and more modern look that SAP Fiori offers.

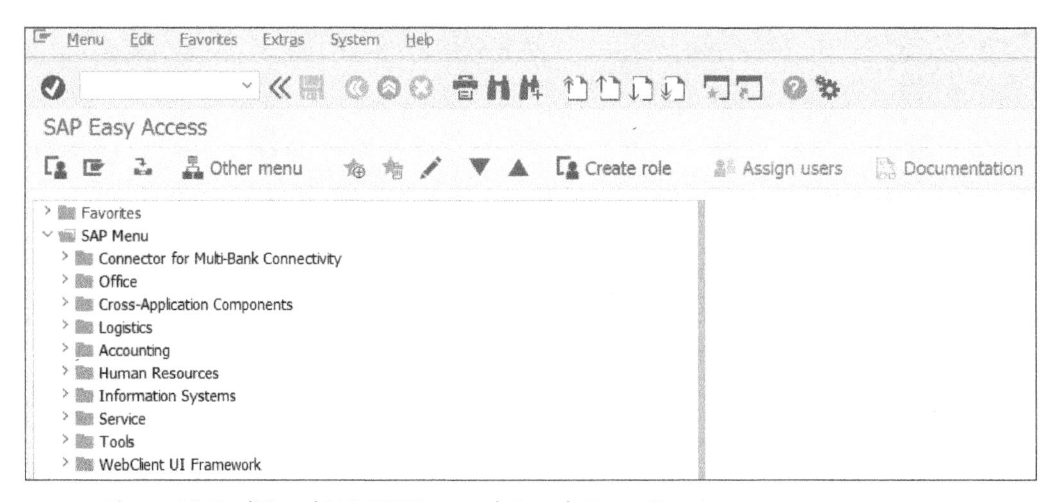

Figure 1.3 Traditional SAP GUI Tree-and-Branch Menu Structure

Figure 1.4 SAP Fiori UX

Having said that, many SAP Fiori screens are web representations of the GUI, so it isn't uncommon for organizations to implement SAP S/4HANA without SAP Fiori. This approach, however, is becoming less common as the benefits of SAP Fiori are being realized. These benefits include the following:

- The implementation of SAP Fiori is free of charge and included in your SAP licensing cost.
- SAP Fiori is where all SAP innovations will be in the future.
- Training is much easier using SAP Fiori due to the intuitive nature of the architecture (e.g., no need to remember transaction codes).
- Analytical apps in the sales and distribution area are extremely powerful and popular with end users.

For the purposes of this book, we'll be concentrating reasonably heavily on the SAP GUI as that is still the most common way to access the SAP functionality. However, at key points, it's useful to refer to SAP Fiori apps, so understanding how the SAP Fiori UX architecture is structured is helpful.

From the perspective of an SAP user logging on to the system, the structure of the landing page is very different from the traditional SAP GUI. The page itself is separated into *user groups* and then *tiles*.

User Groups

In Figure 1.5, the user groups are highlighted by the red box, and the tiles appear under each user group option when selected.

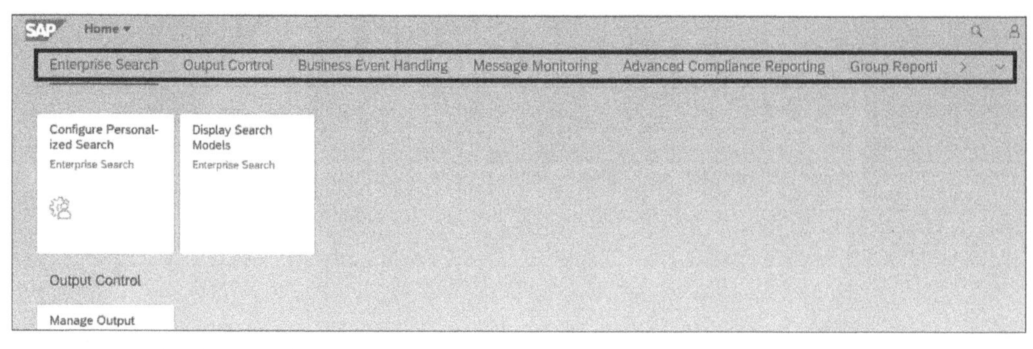

Figure 1.5 SAP Fiori User Groups

Sometimes the display of these user groups all on the same screen can give the screen a very busy look, and often SAP Fiori users would rather see one group at a time. This can be achieved by amending your SAP Fiori settings, as follows:

- Click the person icon and select **Settings** (see Figure 1.6).

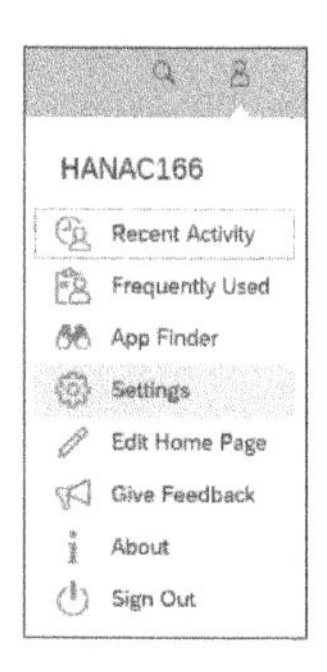

Figure 1.6 SAP Fiori Settings

- Select the **Home Page** option, and select either **Show all content** to display all the user group details on one screen or **Show one group at a time** to display only one user group's details (see Figure 1.7).

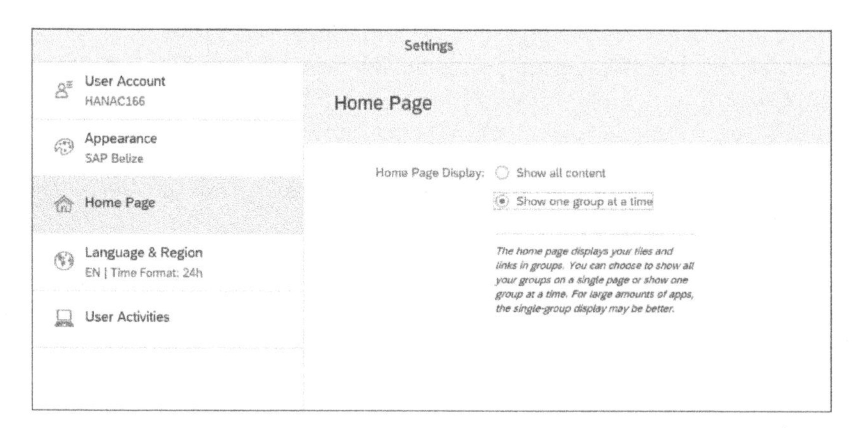

Figure 1.7 SAP Fiori Home Page Settings

Tiles

SAP Fiori tiles are the launching place for a specific SAP Fiori app. The front of these tiles often display dynamic data, which can often be configured. For example, in Figure 1.5, the second user group in the screen is **Output Control** and contains the tile **Manage Output Items** under it. This tile shows a **0** on the front of the tile to denote that there are no output items to be managed currently.

Clicking on the tile causes SAP Fiori to launch the Manage Output Items app.

Apps

There are three different types of SAP Fiori apps in SAP S/4HANA:

- **Transactional apps**
  These apps most closely represent your traditional SAP GUI transaction codes. An example of this kind of app is Create Sales Documents, which will take you to a SAP Fiori–style representation of Transaction VA01, as displayed in Figure 1.8.

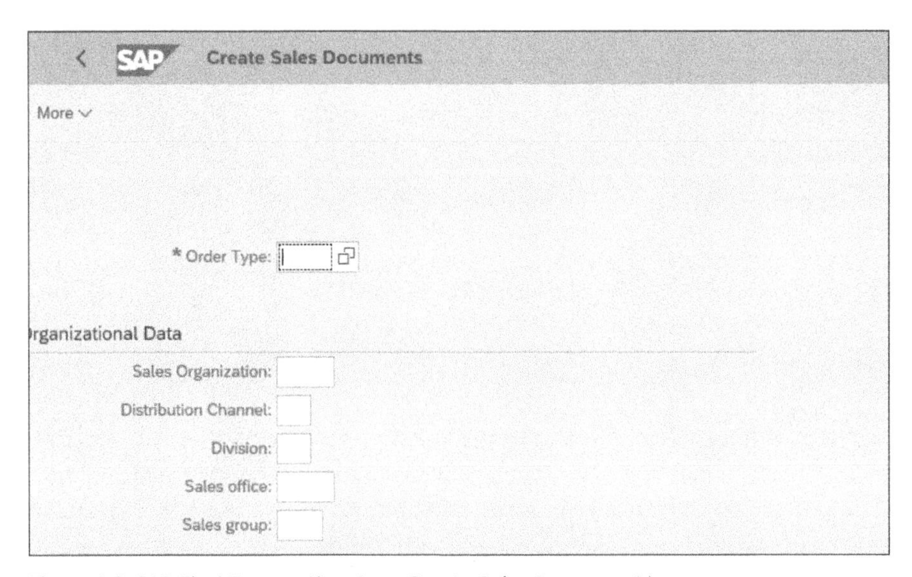

Figure 1.8 SAP Fiori Transaction App: Create Sales Documents

- **Analytical apps**
  These apps are the real game changers in SAP Fiori and can be extremely useful for providing insights into roadblocks. For example, the Sales Order Fulfillment app allows you to see issues with the progress of sales orders through to deliveries and billing, with specific options to resolve these issues. The data can be viewed in several different ways to amend the structure of your analysis. An example of the look and feel of an analytical app is shown in Figure 1.9. Many of these types of apps show key performance data on the tile, and the measures on the tile can often be configured (see Figure 1.10).

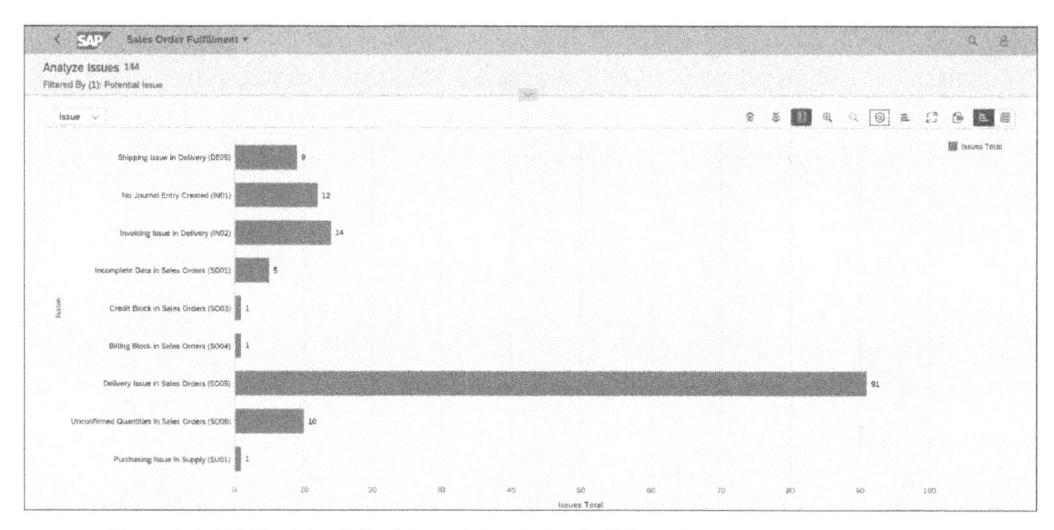

Figure 1.9 SAP Fiori Analytical App: Sales Order Fulfillment

Sales Order Fulfillment
Analyze Issues
Value 1 1550M
Value 2 219.2M
Value 3 66.46M

Figure 1.10 SAP Fiori: Sales Order Fulfillment with Dynamic Data

- **Factsheet apps**
  These apps provide you contextual information about the data you're looking at, all in one place, with specific drilldowns to key SAP objects. For example, with the Customer 360° View factsheet app, you can see all information (transactional and master data) relating to a given customer, as shown in Figure 1.11. Note that factsheet apps are normally only launched from within other apps.

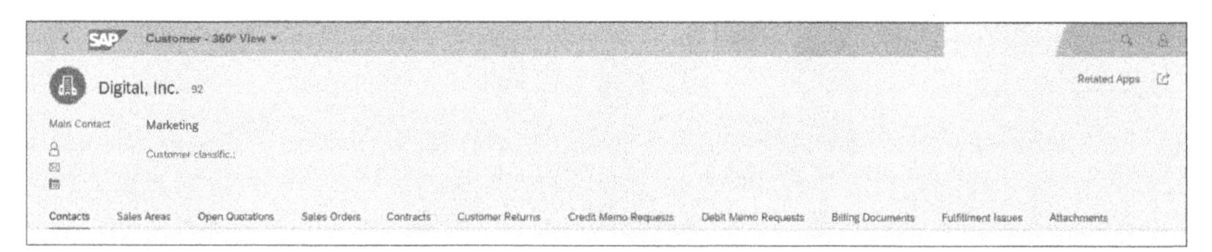

Figure 1.11 SAP Fiori Factsheet App: Customer 360° View

1.2.2 Table Management

While exploring differences between SAP ERP and SAP S/4HANA, there are a number of other background changes to be aware of. For users operating in sales and distribution in SAP S/4HANA, these table changes aren't essential knowledge, but after users become more familiar with SAP structures, the information becomes useful to their overall understanding.

All the SAP data—master data, transactional data, and Customizing data—is housed in database tables, which have been relatively static for years in the SAP landscape. However, SAP S/4HANA has introduced some key changes to these database tables for the purposes of improved performance and removal of redundant data.

Columnar Orientation and Indexes

The first change is related to how the SAP HANA database stores data in the tables. Traditionally, data has been stored in rows, which, by definition, means that any duplicated data in rows are eliminated, thus improving performance significantly.

As an example, let's view a table with entries, as shown in Table 1.2.

Country	Material	Sales per Year
US	1234	400
US	9876	900
MX	1234	500
GB	9876	600

Table 1.2 Example Database Table

In the preceding table, a row store of the data would look like Table 1.3.

Row 1	US
	1234
	400
Row 2	US
	9876
	900

Table 1.3 Row Store Database Table Example

Row 3	MX
	1234
	500
Row 4	GB
	9876
	600

Table 1.3 Row Store Database Table Example (Cont.)

However, a column store would look like Table 1.4.

Country	US
	US
	MX
	GB
Material	1234
	9876
	1234
	9876
Sales per Year	400
	900
	500
	600

Table 1.4 Column Store Database Table Example

As you can see, in the column store, there are only three entries (country, material, and sales per year) as opposed to four in the row store. Furthermore, the column store contains repeated adjacent entries for which the SAP HANA database can employ highly efficient compression methods.

Consider that you want to run a report on the data in your example database to determine your total sales per year. In the row store, each and every row would have to be read to fetch the total. In the column store, only one read is necessary because all the sales data is in the same store. This yields a very real enhancement in fetch times for big databases.

The use of column stores in the SAP HANA database also eliminates the need to store additional index structures, as the index is effectively built in to each column.

Pricing Tables

Additional to the overall architecture of data storage, SAP S/4HANA introduces a few new tables in the sales and distribution area, the most notable of which is in the sales pricing area. Table PRCD_ELEMENTS has been introduced to hold all the transactional data for sales pricing in the system. This table replaces the traditional SAP ERP 6.0 table KONV.

Order Restriction Tables and Other Sales and Distribution Tables

In SAP ERP 6.0, a common complaint was that any order reason and any rejection reason could be used for any sales order type. For example, there would be nothing to stop you using an order reason such as "Incorrect prices – credit" on a standard sales order type, rather than a credit memo request. SAP responded to this complaint by introducing a table that can restrict the use of order reasons as well as rejection reasons in later versions of SAP ERP 6.0 and then SAP S/4HANA. The use of order reasons can now be restricted based on the sales order type and sales organization. These restrictions are set up by the IT team in the Customizing tables TVAU_AUART_VKO and TVAG_AUART_VKO (see Figure 1.12).

Order reason depend on order type and sales organization

SaTy	SOrg.	OrdRs	Description

Figure 1.12 Order Reason Restriction Table

A similar table can be used to restrict the use of the rejection reasons according to sales order type and sales organization, as shown in Figure 1.13.

Reason for rejection depend on order type and sales org

SaTy	SOrg.	Rj	Description

Figure 1.13 Rejection Reason Restriction Table

A few additional tables have also been added into the SAP S/4HANA solution. For example, in Customizing, you can now control how updates to a purchase order linked to a sales order can automatically update settings in the sales order.

1.2.3 Master Data Management

Master data is critical to the operation of a successful SAP S/4HANA system. In this section, we'll discuss the crucial key master data objects and how they can be used.

Furthermore, we'll explore the best practice methods for searching for master data objects, as well as uploading master data as part of an implementation effort.

Customer

The concept of business partners isn't new to SAP S/4HANA. Business partners have been around in SAP ERP versions for a long time and in SAP Customer Relationship Management (SAP CRM) for even longer.

However, what is new is that SAP S/4HANA mandates the use of business partners, instead of using traditional methods of creating separate objects for customers, vendors, and contacts. In SAP ERP 6.0, these objects would be created by Transactions XD01, XK01, VD01, VAP1, and so on. All these transactions have been deprecated in SAP S/4HANA in favor of the unified business partner maintenance transaction—Transaction BP. If you try to use these transactions, you'll be forwarded automatically to Transaction BP, as shown in Figure 1.14.

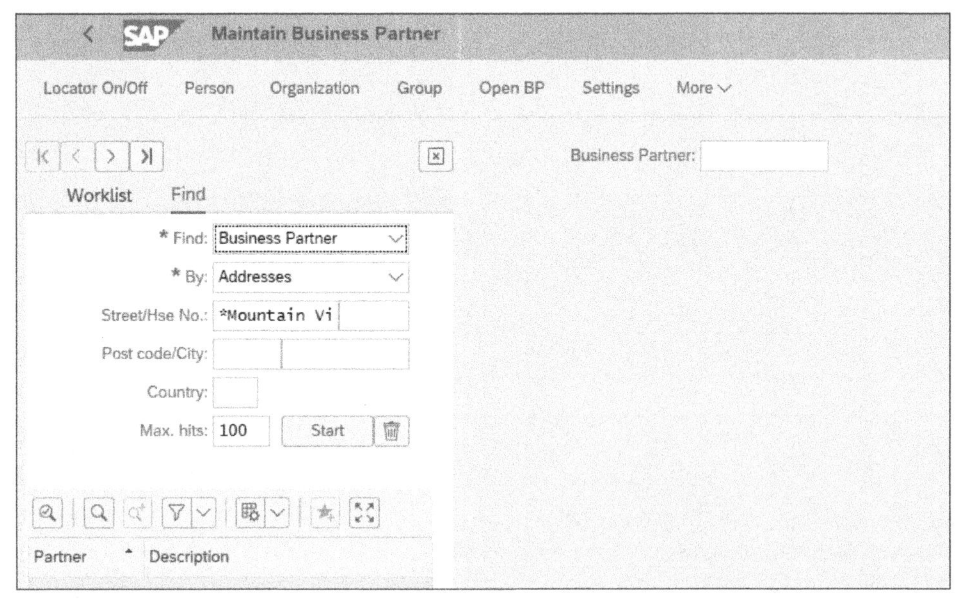

Figure 1.14 Transaction BP

> **Note**
> In addition to the central Transaction BP, Transactions BUP1, BUP2, and BUP3 can be used for creating, changing, and displaying business partners respectively.

A business partner can be defined as a one of the following:

- A person
- An organization
- A group of persons
- A group of organizations

The business partner is normally created and maintained in a central function and is used for a number of different business transactions.

Therefore, with the business partner approach, one business partner can be a customer, vendor, contact person, sales representative, and so on all at once—no need for separate master data objects.

For SAP Fiori users, the Manage Business Partner Master Data app or Maintain Business Partner app can be used, as shown in Figure 1.15.

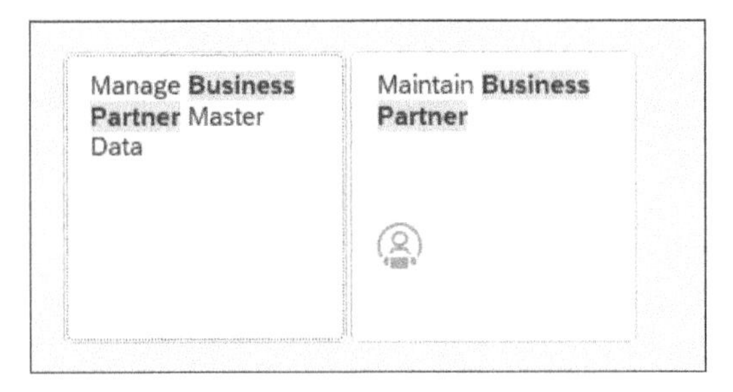

Figure 1.15 Business Partner Apps in SAP Fiori

The Manage Business Partner Master Data app can be used to open a number of factsheet apps to give you insights into the customer. For example, from the app's selection screen, if you select a business partner and click anywhere in the line details, the app will navigate directly to the Business Partner factsheet app, as shown in Figure 1.16 and Figure 1.17.

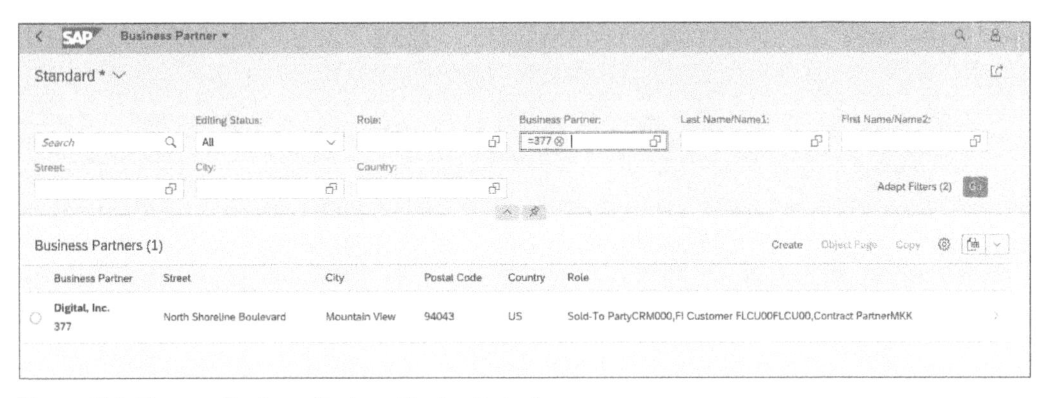

Figure 1.16 Manage Business Partner Master Data App

From within this factsheet app, you can edit the details of the business partner or even copy the details to a new business partner, amending as you go.

Using the Maintain Business Partner app will take you into the transactional app, which is a direct representation of Transaction BP in the SAP GUI.

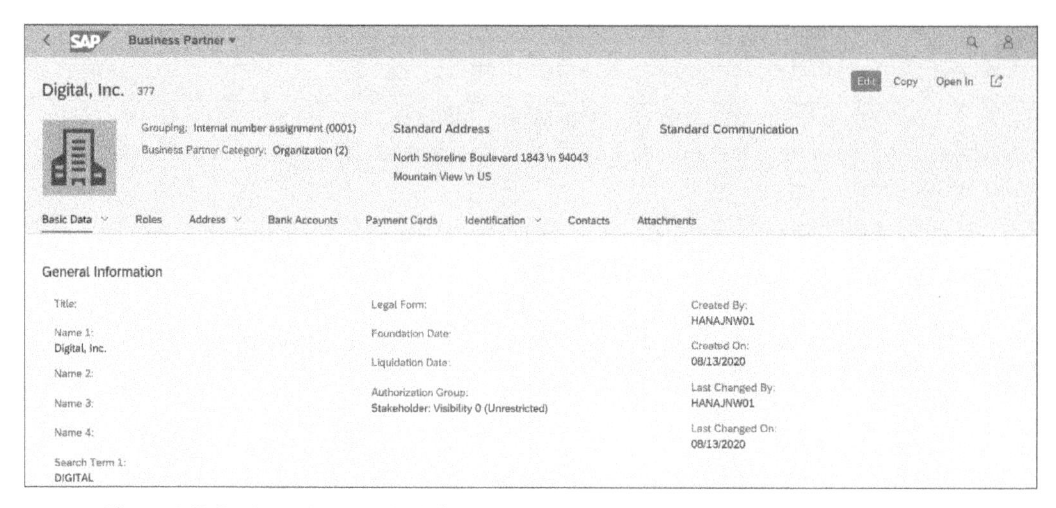

Figure 1.17 Business Partner Factsheet App

A business partner is created in SAP S/4HANA using a specific type—person, organization, or group. A further level of classification for business partners sees the creation separated by a specific role, such as customer, vendor, contact person, sales representative, tax collector, or many others delivered standard by SAP, as shown in Figure 1.18.

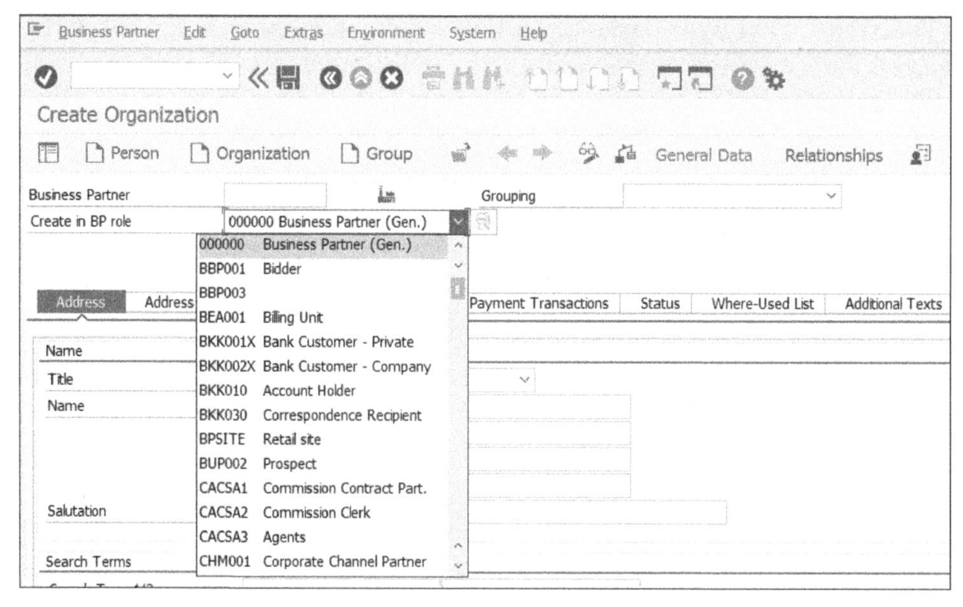

Figure 1.18 Business Partner Roles

Typically, a business partner will be created in the **Business Partner (Gen.)** role to house the name and address only, and then be extended to other roles as required, such as **Customer** or **Supplier**.

After the business partner is extended to the **Customer** role, all the relevant background customer master database tables are automatically filled by the system when the record is saved. More information on this is provided in Chapter 2, Section 2.2.

Searching for customers in SAP S/4HANA is slightly different from the traditional methods of searching in SAP ERP 6.0. First, a search can be executed as normal from any field where a customer is referenced. This is unchanged. Second, in Transaction BP, the *business partner locator* can be used to search for business partners using a variety of different criteria, as shown in Figure 1.19.

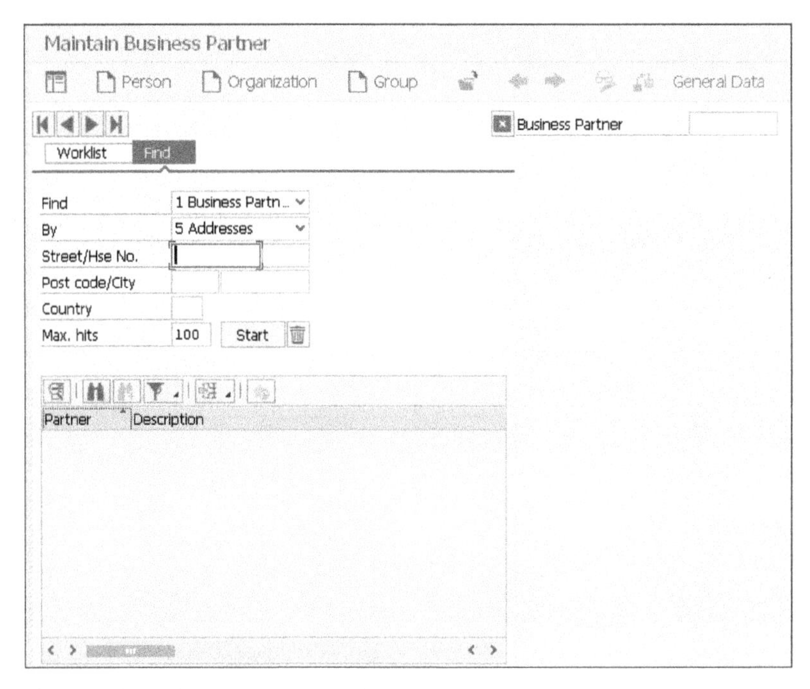

Figure 1.19 Business Partner Locator

Several options are available in the business partner locator to search by business partners, persons, organizations, or groups. Additionally, the **By** field can be used to narrow down the search based on any number of criteria (see Figure 1.20).

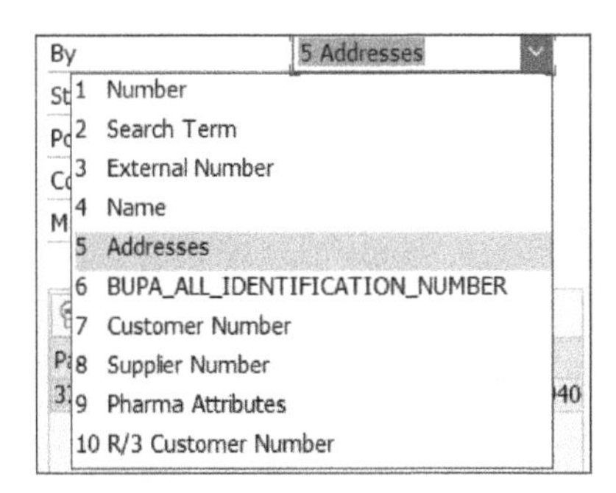

Figure 1.20 Business Partner Locator: Search By

After the search has been executed, results can be seen in the list at the bottom of the business partner locator. From there, you can navigate directly to the customer by double-clicking, or you can select **Add to My Objects**, making the customer a favorite that can be viewed at any time in the **Worklist** tab (see Figure 1.21 and Figure 1.22).

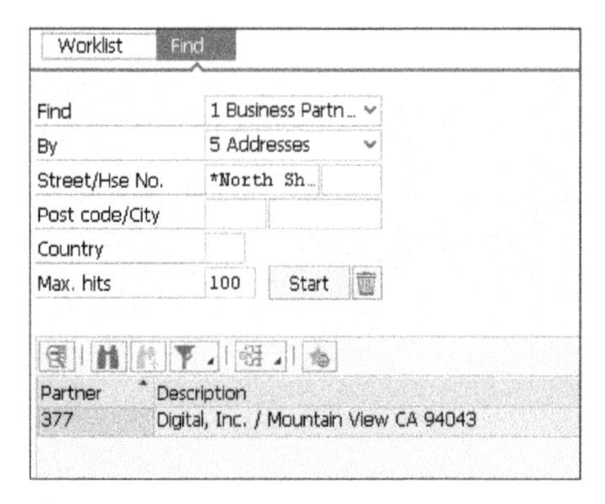

Figure 1.21 Business Partner Locator: Results

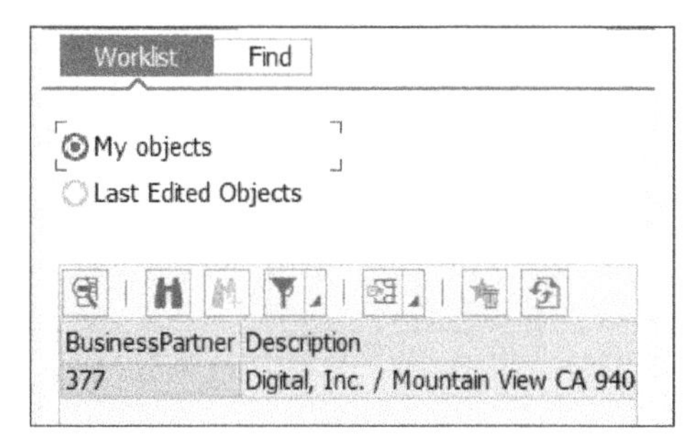

Figure 1.22 Business Partner Locator: Worklist Tab

Searching for customers in SAP Fiori opens a whole new level of functionality. SAP Fiori has introduced the Enterprise Search functionality, which allows you to utilize the SAP HANA database power for intelligent searches throughout the entire system. For example, you can choose **All** in the dropdown to search for a customer number or name (see Figure 1.23). This process can be used for anything in the system, not just customers.

SAP will generate a list of everything in the system with that number or name. The list will give you the results broken down in all categories; for example, Figure 1.24 shows an enterprise search for the word "Digital" returning **Contract Partner** and **Customer**.

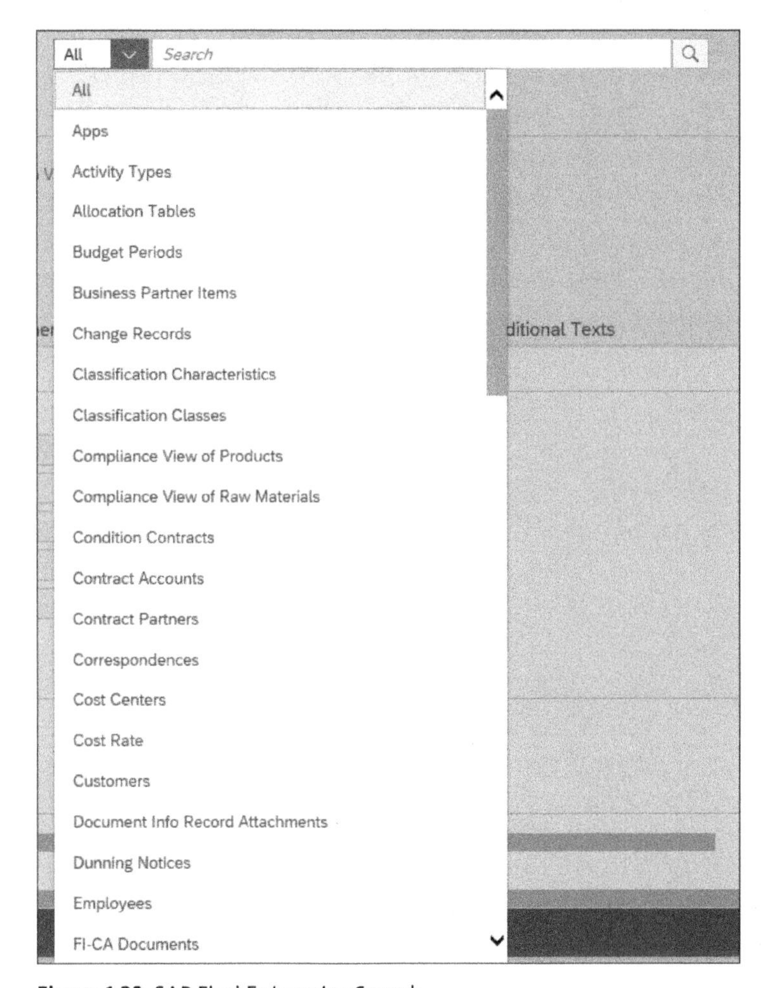

Figure 1.23 SAP Fiori Enterprise Search

Figure 1.24 SAP Fiori Enterprise Search Results

Related apps are listed below the customer number for navigating to **Display Customer Balances**, **Display Customer List**, and so on. Selecting one of these options will navigate you directly to that factsheet app.

An alternative to a full Enterprise Search is to narrow your search down by selecting **Customers** instead of **All**, as shown in Figure 1.25, to speed up the performance of the search.

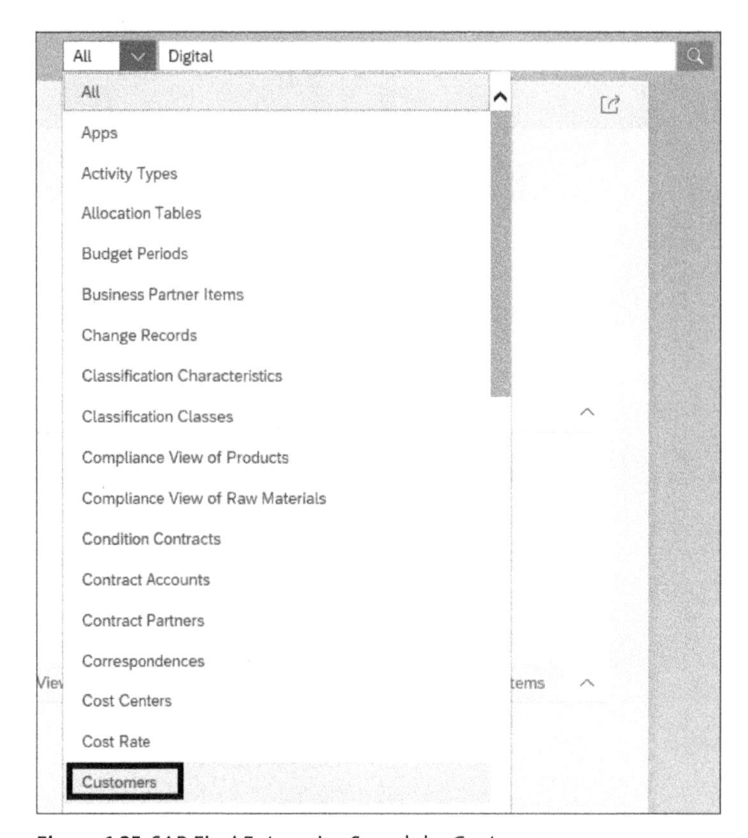

Figure 1.25 SAP Fiori Enterprise Search by Customer

Materials

In SAP ERP 6.0, the character length of the material number was 18 characters. This has sometimes led to difficulties with especially long material numbers in some industries and/or external numbering formats. As a result, with SAP S/4HANA, we now see the material number length increased from 18 characters to a maximum of 40 characters. This finalized length is a configurable attribute of the SAP S/4HANA system. Figure 1.26 shows the SAP ERP 6.0 material number length, and Figure 1.27 shows the character length in SAP S/4HANA.

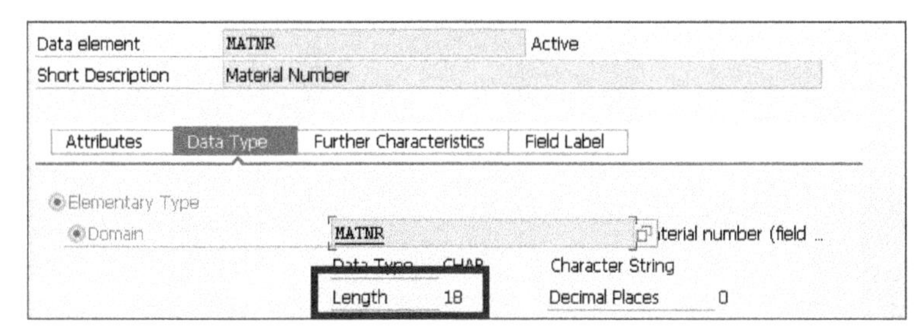

Figure 1.26 Material Data Object in SAP ERP 6.0

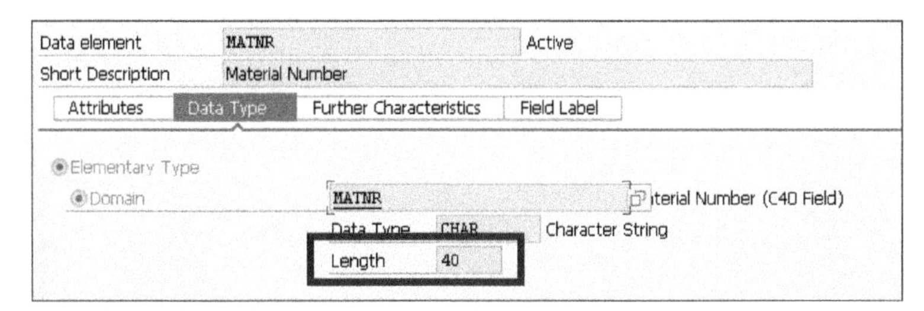

Figure 1.27 Material Data Object in SAP S/4HANA

Uploading with the Migration Cockpit

A major part of SAP implementation projects has always been data conversion exercises from your legacy ERP system into your SAP system. With traditional SAP ERP 6.0 systems, this has been handled using the Legacy System Migration Workbench (LSMW).

Loading through the Transaction LSMW required data conversion analysts to design and write specific scripts within LSMW. There were no standard methods or approaches, so the design approach was left entirely up to the analyst's discretion. This is a reasonably risky approach to take to data conversion, and SAP has addressed this by deprecating the use of LSMW in favor of the new SAP S/4HANA migration cockpit, accessed from the SAP GUI using Transaction LTMC.

SAP migrated to Transaction LTMC from Transaction LSMW for the following reasons:

- Elimination of the need to make batch data communication (BDC) recordings, essentially removing the need to record the user's screen keystrokes
- Theoretically, less training required for end users to use the migration cockpit
- More user friendly, with predelivered templates

With standard SAP-delivered templates for use with the migration cockpit, the risks associated with traditional LSMW methods of data conversion are eliminated. These templates can be seen in the web interface for the migration cockpit, as shown in Figure 1.28.

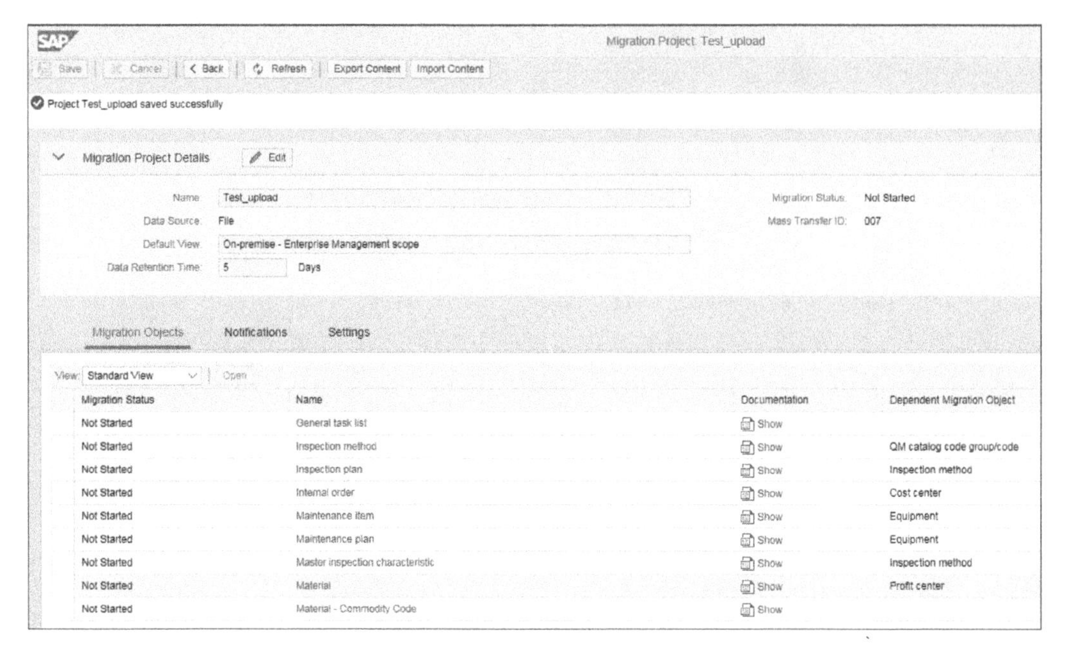

Figure 1.28 Migration Cockpit Templates

1.2.4 Functional Sales Related Changes

In terms of pure sales and distribution–related changes within the SAP S/4HANA system, there are many key differences from SAP ERP 6.0. These will be explored at a high level in this section. Again, it's important to illustrate that this section gives you an overview of the changes involved in moving to an SAP S/4HANA environment over SAP ERP 6.0 environment; the details of these changes aren't essential knowledge for the sales and distribution business users, but rather serves as background information.

Rebates and Settlement Management

Sales and distribution rebate processing was central to providing customers with rebates as a part of ongoing contracts. This has been overhauled, and the old sales and purchasing rebates mechanism has been replaced with settlement management, which will be explored in more detail in Chapter 10.

The overview of the settlement management process is shown in Figure 1.29.

You may ask why the change? Settlement management is a far more flexible tool for managing rebates, but it also has the added advantage that performance and database size isn't compromised in the same way it is with the old rebates process. Under the rebates approach in SAP ERP 6.0, the underlying database table VBOX could become huge and unwieldy. In SAP S/4HANA, table VBOX has been made redundant completely. All rebates now go through the condition contract management (CCM) process. Furthermore, redundant processes have been removed, allowing condition contracts to be placed with customers and vendors in the same process.

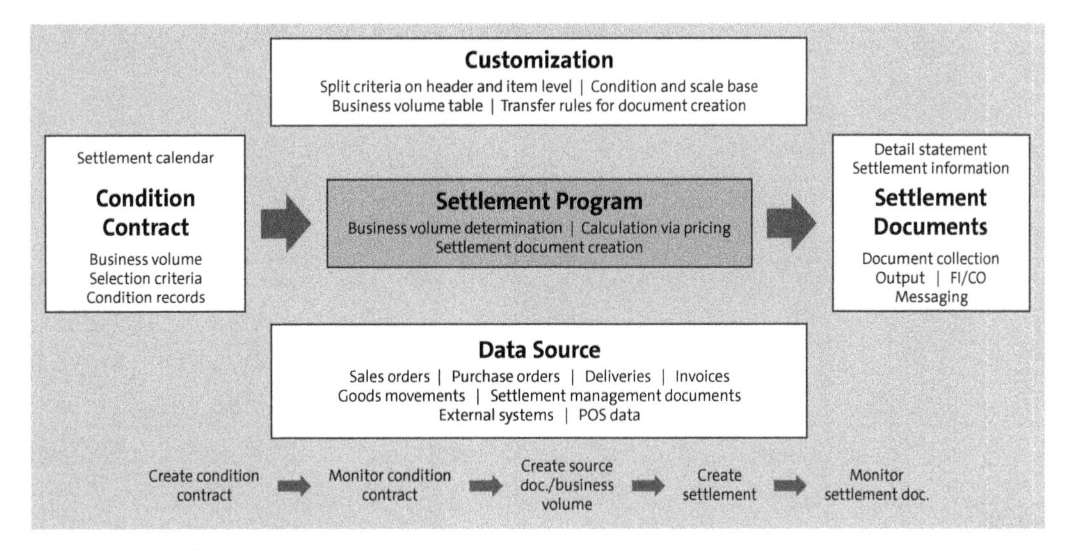

Figure 1.29 Settlement Management

Business Rule Framework

Business Rules Framework plus (BRFplus) has been around in SAP for many years, predating the advent of SAP S/4HANA. However, its use in output determination (the generation of print and email output forms, e.g., invoices to customers) is new to SAP S/4HANA. BRFplus isn't unique to output management and, in fact, can be used in many areas of SAP. It can be used as an alternative to coding in the SAP programming language—ABAP—by specifying rules and then calling those rules for specific business scenarios.

The rules are developed and deployed by your IT team within the BRFplus web-based engine, which can be accessed via Transaction BRF+ (see Figure 1.30).

Note

BRFplus is the default engine for driving outputs from SAP S/4HANA for sales and distribution. However, it isn't uncommon for SAP S/4HANA clients to switch off this default and use traditional output determination methods.

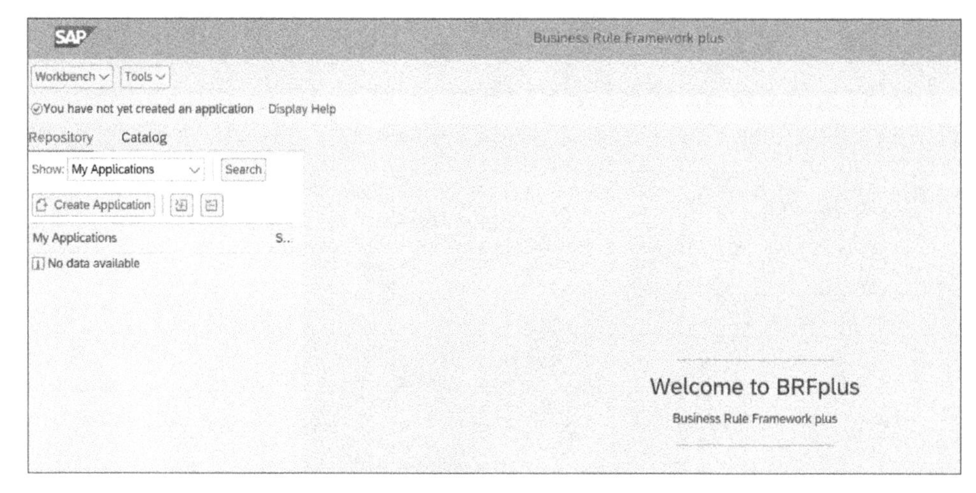

Figure 1.30 Business Rules Framework Plus Engine

Error handling through BRFplus can be accessed in SAP Fiori by using the Manage Output Items app. There is a dynamic number on the front of the tile showing how many failed outputs are present in the system (see Figure 1.31 and Figure 1.32).

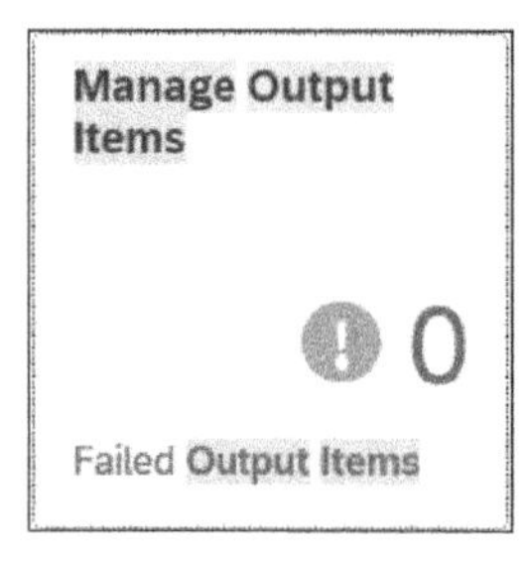

Figure 1.31 SAP Fiori: Manage Output Items Tile

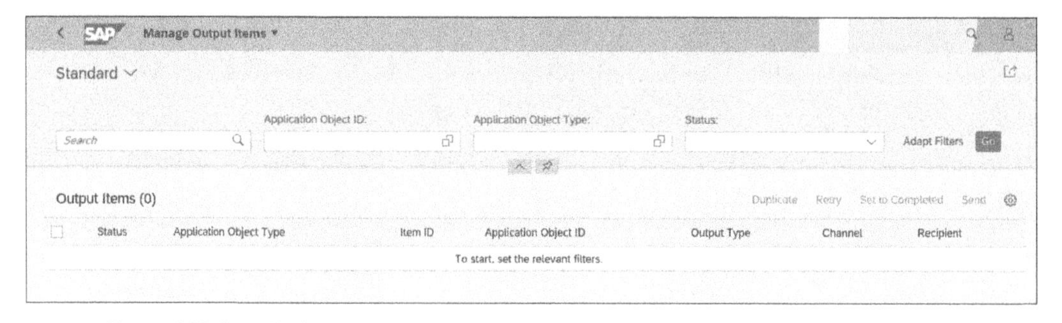

Figure 1.32 SAP Fiori: Manage Output Items App

Credit Management

Credit management is another area in SAP S/4HANA that is almost unrecognizable from the approach undertaken in SAP ERP 6.0. The credit limits were formally housed in the SAP Credit Management functions against the payer in a separate transaction. This has been merged in SAP S/4HANA so that these functions and settings are now housed within the business partner itself and can be seen under Transaction BP (see Figure 1.33).

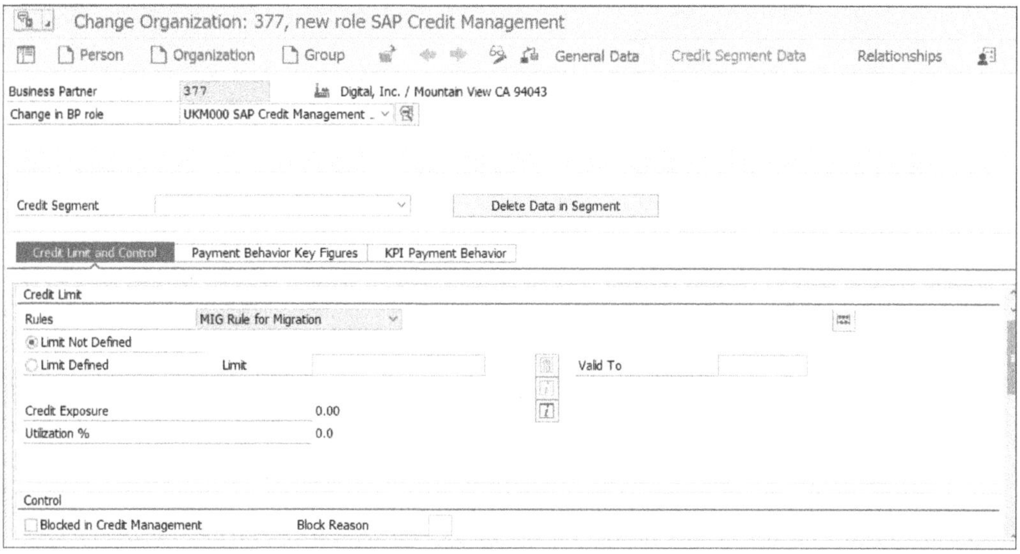

Figure 1.33 Credit Management Functions in a Business Partner

In SAP S/4HANA, the credit management functions are much more aligned with the financial supply chain and therefore truly become a function of the finance team within an organization. As a result, we'll just give a very brief overview here.

SAP overhauled credit management in SAP S/4HANA for the following reasons:

- Higher degree of automation with automated calculation of credit scores
- Documented credit decisions
- Accounts for relationships between business partners in calculation of credit limits
- Improved performance through elimination of redundant data
- Standardized integration with external credit agencies
- Additional options of automatic calculation of credit limits, automatic calculations of risk class, and internal scoring

Note

Those additional options (automatic calculation of credit limits and risk class, as well as internal scoring) can be provided by the Credit Rules Engine, but this requires the purchase of an additional license. Furthermore, a cloud-based standard link to external credit agencies, such as Dun & Bradstreet, is provided out of the box, but that also requires additional licensing.

Revenue Accounting and Reporting

In SAP ERP 6.0, when a contract was billed, the revenue had to be recognized for that contract over a given period of time or at given milestones over time. Interestingly, this can be at variance to when payments are actually received from the customer. This was carried out through revenue recognition within the Sales and Distribution module of the system.

Then in 2014, the International Financial Reporting Standards (IFRS) Foundation and the International Accounting Standards Board (IASB) introduced IFRS 15, and the US Generally Accepted Accounting Principles (GAAP) introduced its version, ASC 606 Revenue from Contracts with Customers. These principles became mandatory in the United States and much of Europe in 2018. With this in mind, SAP overhauled its revenue recognition offerings and introduced SAP Revenue Accounting and Reporting (SAP RAR).

SAP RAR is actually available in SAP ERP 6.0 now but is mandatory in SAP S/4HANA for revenue recognition purposes. Like credit management, its functionality resides within the financial supply chain, so a high-level view of the approach will suffice for the sales and distribution business user.

The IFRS 15 approach follows five steps, which are replicated in SAP RAR:

- **Step 1: Identify the contract.**
  The contract itself in SAP RAR can be a list of items combined from multiple systems, such as SAP CRM and any other non-SAP systems, all combined into one revenue accounting contract.
- **Step 2: Identify the performance obligations (POBs).**
  The POB is the level of the contract where the standard selling price is determined.
- **Step 3: Determine the transaction price.**
  The transaction price is the price derived from SAP pricing conditions in the document.
- **Step 4: Allocate the price to the POBs.**
  The transaction price is allocated to a POB of a contract.
- **Step 5: Recognize revenue as the POBs are fulfilled.**
  Completion can be defined over a specific time period or a specific event/set of events.

Many of these steps are automated by the process based on sets of definable rules in your system.

Advanced Available-to-Promise

Available-to-promise (ATP) has been around since the dawn of SAP and controls how inventory can be allocated against sales orders and deliveries in the system (this will be covered more later in this chapter). However, there has always been an undercurrent of dissatisfaction with ATP in that it wasn't completely flexible enough to meet the complex requirements of today's business needs, requiring clients to turn to other SAP tools such as SAP Advanced Planning and Optimization (SAP APO) or other external tools for assistance.

SAP S/4HANA has addressed this and replaced much of the ATP functionality in SAP APO with advanced available-to-promise (aATP) within the core system. This functionality does have an additional license cost, so not all SAP S/4HANA clients install it.

Within aATP, SAP S/4HANA has introduced a brand-new confirmation strategy that can classify your customers in to five different categories (see Figure 1.34):

- **Win**
  When demand exceeds supply, these customers will always be top of the pile for confirmation and fulfilment.
- **Gain**
  When demand exceeds supply, these customers will always keep their original confirmations and further orders will be confirmed if there is stock available after the Win group has had all its orders confirmed.
- **Redistribute**
  When demand exceeds supply, these customers may lose some original commitments to the Win or Gain groups. However, if there is stock available after these two groups have confirmations, then they will also be in the Win category.

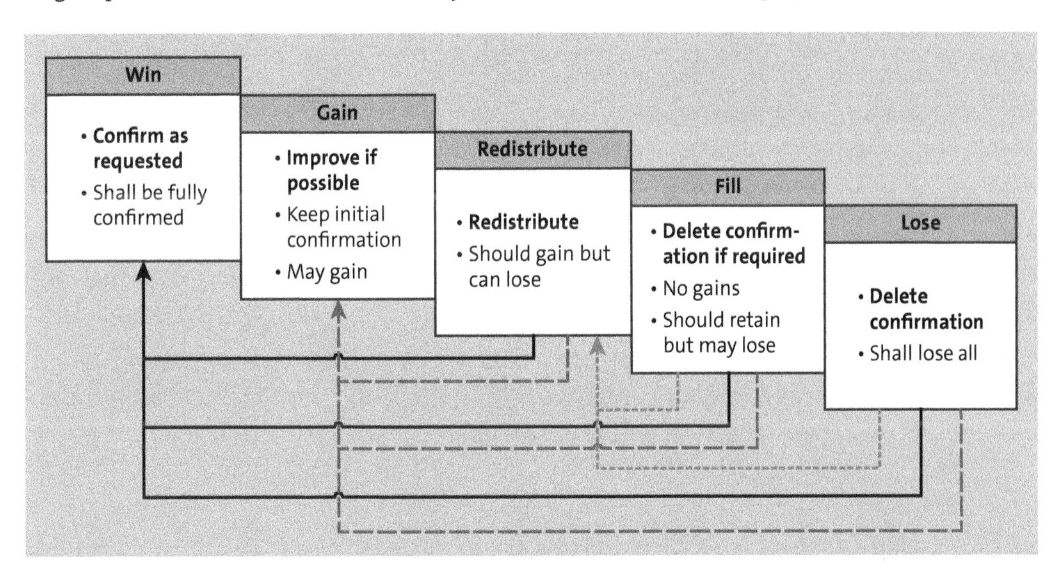

Figure 1.34 Advanced Available-to-Promise

- **Fill**
  When demand exceeds supply, these customers act as the Redistribute group, except they won't gain any confirmations.
- **Lose**
  When demand exceeds supply, these customers will lose their confirmations to the higher ranked groups.

The five categories are allocated to specific sales documents according to rules as set out in back order processing (BOP). These rules can be defined within the Configure BOP Segment app, which is one of a number of SAP Fiori apps that can be used to control aATP through configuring the rules, assigning them to specific strategies (Win, Gain, Redistribute, Fill, Lose), and then running and monitoring the BOP to allocate the sales documents accordingly (see Figure 1.35).

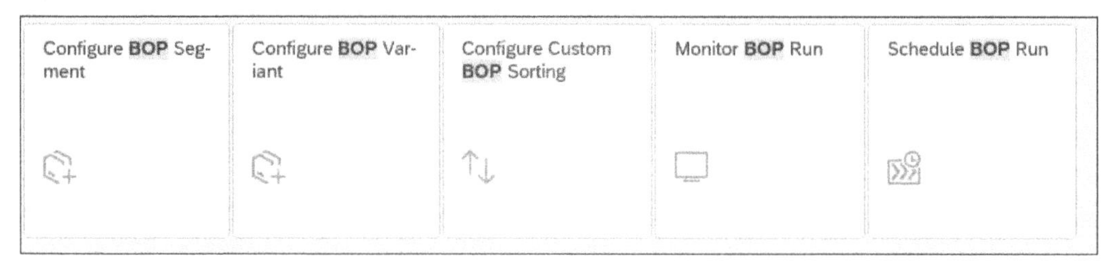

Figure 1.35 Configure BOP Segment App Tile

The most useful thing about BOP through aATP is that you have full flexibility over which orders/customers take priority over which others depending on any number of parameters, and that flexibility can be maintained at a business level and amended according to changes in business requirements over time.

Foreign Trade

In SAP ERP 6.0, foreign trade data was firmly a part of the Sales and Distribution landscape. This covered transportation data for sales documents, intrastat settings, and export compliance through license control.

All these settings have been deprecated in SAP S/4HANA. The current recommended approach is to implement SAP Global Trade Services (SAP GTS). This is SAP's most comprehensive solution for global trade, but it comes with additional licensing. Some of the functions, which are described here, have been moved to international trade in SAP S/4HANA.

With international trade, SAP S/4HANA allows you to do the following:

- Set classifications for materials, such as commodity codes, intrastat service codes, and custom tariff numbers.
- Control licenses for export purposes, including managing and releasing blocked documents.

- Block sales documents for countries under embargo.
- Manage intrastat declarations.
- Integrate with SAP Watch List Screening.

Note

The maintenance of international trade in SAP S/4HANA is carried out exclusively in SAP Fiori, not in the backend GUI.

The international trade solution relies heavily on setting classifications against materials, and here we come across another update in SAP S/4HANA. Unlike SAP ERP 6.0, it isn't possible to assign a commodity code to a material in the material master; this functionality is now carried out exclusively in SAP Fiori within the suite of international trade apps shown in Figure 1.36.

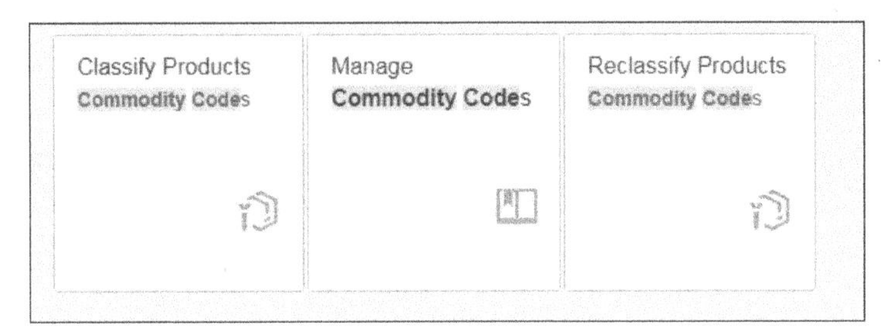

Figure 1.36 International Trade SAP Fiori Apps

The following apps are available for international trade:

- **Classify Products – Commodity Codes app**
  This app allows you to assign a specific material to a specific commodity code.
- **Manage Commodity Codes app**
  This app allows you to enter a new commodity code with validity dates and unit of measure settings for a specific language.
- **Reclassify Products – Commodity Codes app**
  This app allows you to amend assignments of commodity codes to materials.

There are very similar SAP Fiori apps for intrastat service codes too, which operate in exactly the same way as the commodity codes apps (see Figure 1.37).

International trade can also be used to carry out export control through embargoes and export licenses.

Figure 1.37 Intrastat SAP Fiori Apps

A suite of SAP Fiori apps are provided to control export licenses through legal control:

- Manage Control Classes
- Classify Products – Legal Control
- Reclassify products – Legal Control
- Manage Licenses
- Resolve Blocked Documents – Trade Compliance

The first three apps operate in the same way as the settings for commodity codes.

To create an export license, the Manage Licenses app can be used as shown in Figure 1.38.

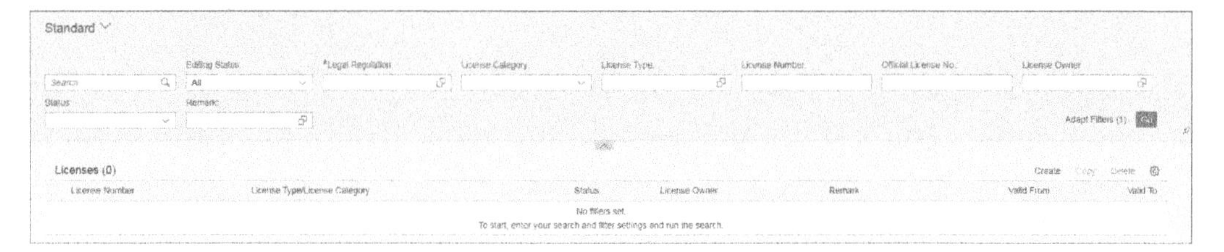

Figure 1.38 SAP Fiori App: Manage Licenses

A sales order that contains a control-relevant product will prompt SAP S/4HANA to go through the process of finding an active license which houses that material number (or commodity code or control class assigned to the material). If an active license isn't found, then the sales order will be blocked for any further action (e.g., delivery), as shown in the Resolve Blocked Documents – Trade Compliance app in Figure 1.39.

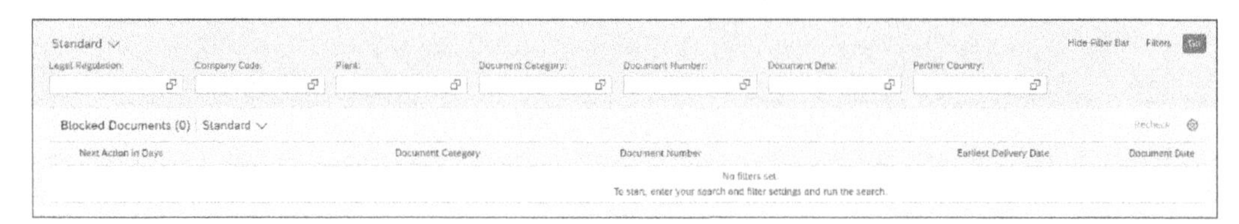

Figure 1.39 SAP Fiori App: Resolve Blocked Documents

1.3 Transactional Data

SAP S/4HANA houses two forms of data:

- **Master data**
  Data that is created centrally and can be used for a number of applications. Typical examples are business partners, materials, and prices.
- **Transactional data**
  Data created in the process of carrying out a business transaction. Typical examples include creation of a sales order or an invoice.

In the sales and distribution area of SAP S/4HANA, the basic transactional data can be broken down into five areas:

- Presales
- Sales orders
- Deliveries
- Billing documents
- Accounting

In this section, we'll explore the role of these five areas of transactional data in the SAP S/4HANA system.

1.3.1 Presales

The SAP S/4HANA order-to-cash flow is depicted in Figure 1.40. The presales section of the flow is highlighted.

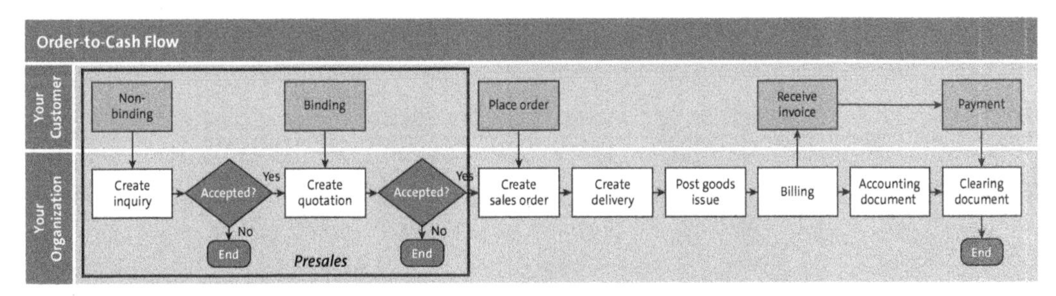

Figure 1.40 Order-to-Cash Flow: Presales

As can be seen, the presales section encompasses both inquiry documents as well as quotation documents. There is often some confusion as to the difference between the two documents, so let's explore the differences:

- **Inquiry**
  An inquiry is an informal request for price and availability from a customer. This document can be logged in the system for future reference and to expedite the

process of setting up a quotation. The inquiry document is a nonbinding informational document in SAP S/4HANA that provides the customer a way of receiving the information and storing the information internally. The creation of inquiries must, by its very nature, be a quick process. Inquiries are created in the SAP GUI using Transaction VA11.

- **Quotation**
  A quotation is a legally binding document offering the delivery of goods and services to a customer for a defined price by a specified date. The quotation document can be created with reference to an inquiry if needed, thus carrying through all the terms and conditions, but this isn't essential. The quotation is seen as the first legally binding step in the presales process. Quotations are created in the SAP GUI using Transaction VA21.

Both the inquiry document and the quotation document have validity dates inserted against them as to when the terms and conditions on offer are valid (see Figure 1.41 and Figure 1.42, respectively).

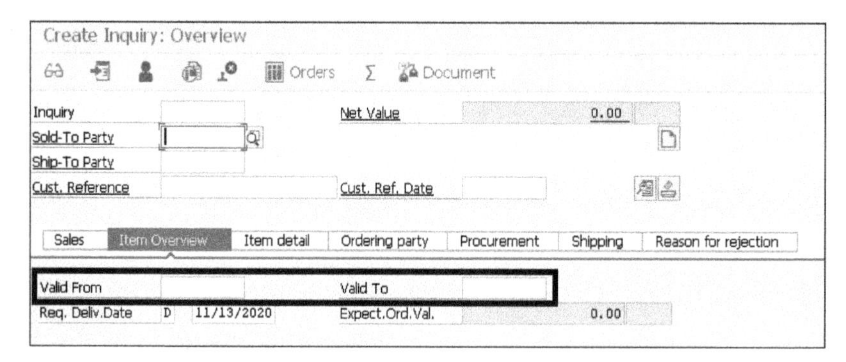

Figure 1.41 Inquiry Validity Dates

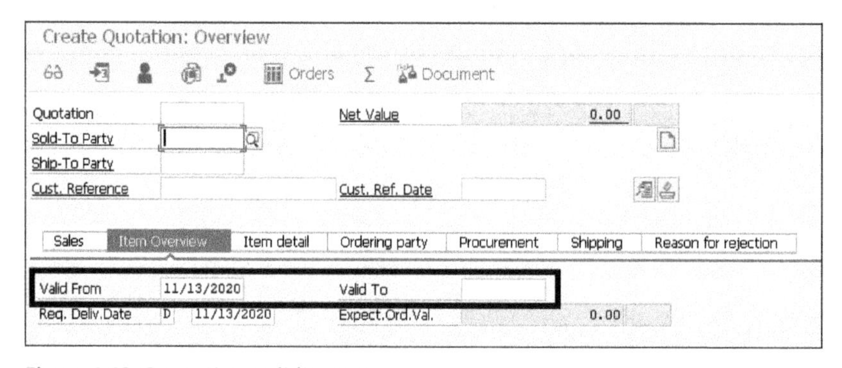

Figure 1.42 Quotation Validity Dates

Typically, an inquiry won't generate a formalized output to a customer, whereas a quotation will almost always produce a printed or emailed document to the customer confirming the price, availability, and validity dates.

1.3.2 Sales Documents

After a quotation has been accepted, the order-to-cash process moves into the sales section, as highlighted in Figure 1.43.

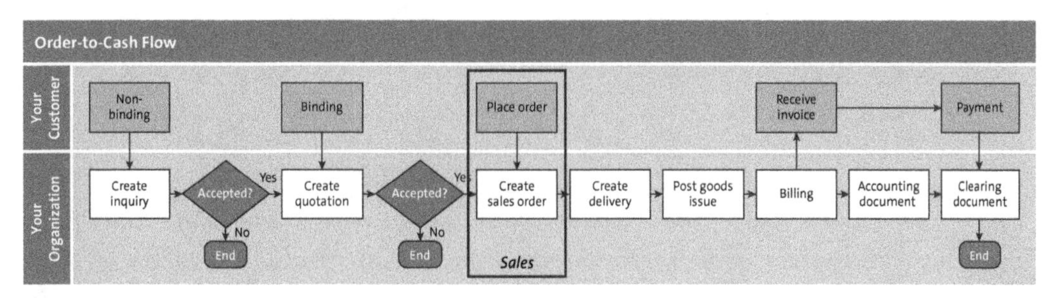

Figure 1.43 Order-to-Cash Flow: Sales

A sales document can come in many different guises in SAP S/4HANA, and it's worth exploring an introduction to each variation here.

Sales Order

A *sales order* is a catchall term to refer to a full list of variations of documents that can be created using the Transaction VA01 (Create Sales Order). Following is a descriptive list of the main sales order variations:

- **Standard order**
  This is the most basic version of a sales document, which records a customer's request for the supply of goods and services within a given time frame, for a given price. Information held in the sales order document refers to the terms and conditions of the trading agreement—such as the various business partners involved in the sale, payment terms, delivery terms, Incoterms, dates of supply, materials ordered, sales pricing, and so on. Much of this data is automatically populated from master data held in the customer, material, and pricing masters. Commonly, a sales order will generate a printed or emailed output document—usually an order confirmation or order acknowledgement—to the customer, confirming all this information.
- **Rush order**
  This is a specific sales order type within Transaction VA01 (Create Sales Order). The sales order type used for rush orders is SO. The behavior of a rush order is slightly different from a standard order in that as soon as you create the sales order and save it, the delivery document is automatically created in the background. This is to expedite the process and allow for either a customer pickup of the goods or same-day delivery. The invoice is generated from the delivery document as normal.
- **Cash sale**
  This is a specific sales order type within Transaction VA01 (Create Sales Order). The

sales order type used for cash sales is BV. Like the rush order, the cash sale order generates a delivery as soon as the sales order is saved. Furthermore, a cash invoice can also be generated from the sales invoice. Depending on your business scenario, the customer maybe already be in possession of the goods, or the goods may be relevant for picking in the warehouse immediately. After the customer has received the goods, the transaction is considered complete.

- **Credit memo request**
  This is a specific sales order type within Transaction VA01 (Create Sales Order). The sales order type used for credit memo requests is CR. The credit memo request is used for issuing a credit note to the customer in the event of a complaint. A credit memo request would be used, for example, if a customer has complained of being incorrectly charged too high a price. Typically, credit memo requests are created with reference to an earlier sales document such as an invoice document, but this isn't mandatory. The credit memo request can be defined in such a way as to be blocked for further processing automatically. In this way, an approval step is required to unblock the document and release the credit memo request to billing to create the credit note.
- **Debit memo request**
  This is a specific sales order type within Transaction VA01 (Create Sales Order). The sales order type used for debit memo requests is DR. This sales document is used in complaints processing to issue a debit note to charge the customer. A debit memo request would be used, for example, if a customer has been incorrectly charged too low a price. Like the credit memo request, the debit memo request can be set up in such a way as to block the document for further processing, awaiting an approval step to release to billing to create a debit note.
- **Returns**
  This is a specific sales order type within Transaction VA01 (Create Sales Order). The sales order type used for returns is RE. The sales order type for returns is the first step in the sales returns process, when a customer returns goods as a result of a complaint. Like a credit memo request and debit memo request, the return can be set up to be blocked for further processing, awaiting an approval step to release to the logistics steps (returns delivery and goods receipt, followed by credit note).
- **Consignment processing**
  These sales order types denote each step in the consignment process:
  - Consignment fill-up (sales order type KB): The fill-up process is used when moving your own inventory to the site of a customer while retaining ownership.
  - Consignment issue (sales order type KE): The issue process follows the fill-up and is used when your customer consumes some of the inventory and therefore requires an invoice for it.

- Consignment returns (sales order type KR): The return process is used when stock which has already been issued to your customer is returned back into consignment stock.
- Consignment pickup (sales order type KA): The pickup process is used to move stock from consignment stock back to your normal plant stock.

These processes are shown in Figure 1.44 and Figure 1.45.

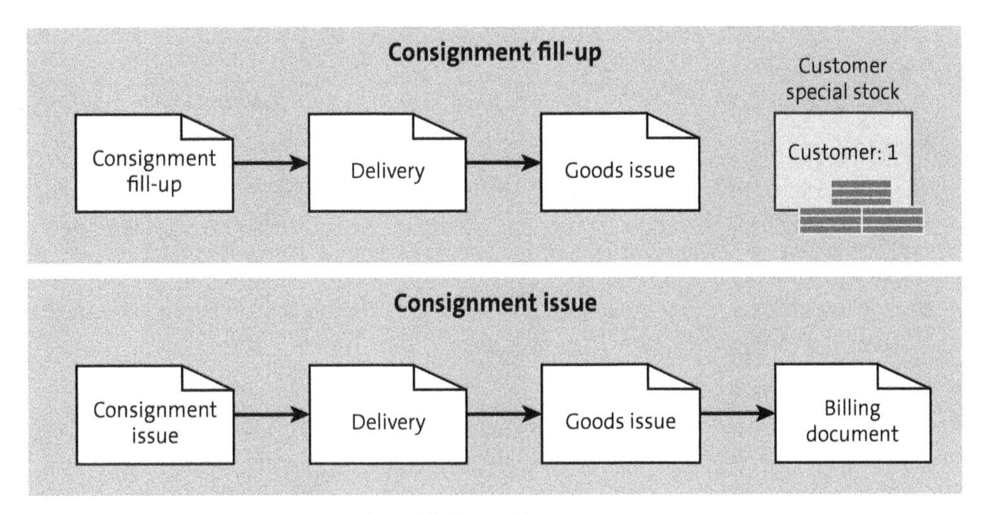

Figure 1.44 Consignment Processing: Fill-Up and Issue

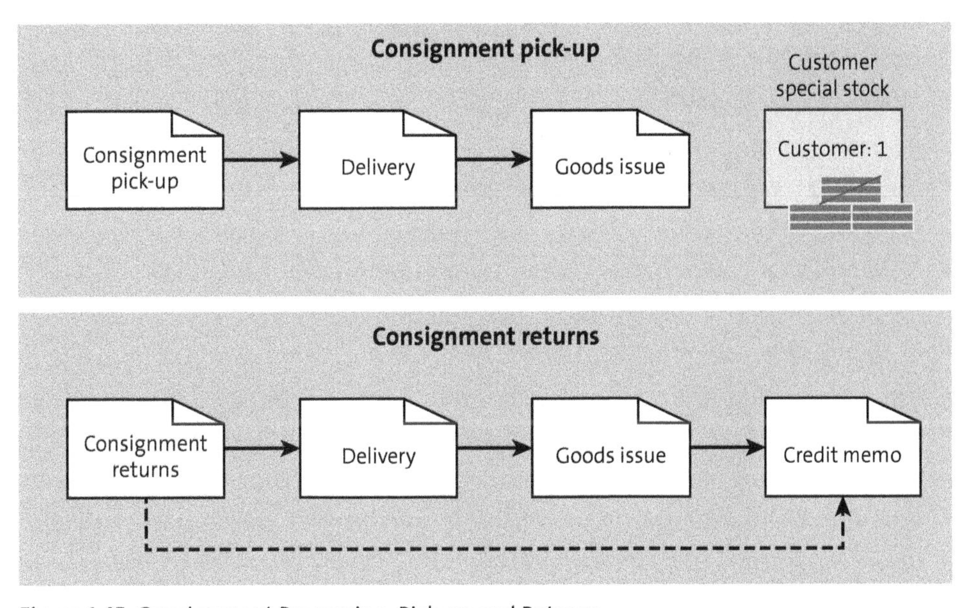

Figure 1.45 Consignment Processing: Pick-up and Returns

Scheduling Agreements

A *scheduling agreement* is an outline agreement between your organization and the customer that contains scheduled delivery dates and quantities into the future. Scheduling agreements are created using either document type LZ or document type LZM. Document type LZ creates a standard scheduling agreement from which deliveries can be created for supply of the goods to the customer. Document type LZM creates a scheduling agreement from which delivery orders are created for the individual supply items to trigger the deliveries to the customer. Scheduling agreements are created using Transaction VA31.

Contracts

A *customer contract* is an outline agreement for supply of goods or services to a customer within a given time frame. There are different types of contracts, as follows:

- **Master contracts**
  This is an overall document used to house many different types of contracts for the purposes of grouping them together under one document.
- **Quantity contracts**
  This is an agreement with your customer to supply a certain quantity of goods or services over a certain period of time. No dates or quantities are given.
- **Value contracts**
  This is an agreement with your customer to supply goods or services within a given time period up to a certain value.
- **Service contracts**
  This is an agreement to provide a specific service to your customer, and these can take the form of rental or maintenance contracts.

Contracts are created using Transaction VA41.

1.3.3 Deliveries

We've been through a high-level introduction to sales documents in SAP S/4HANA, and now it's clear that these documents represent a firm agreement with your customer to supply goods and services. However, where those goods are deliverable, the outbound delivery document is created to pull in all the details for a specific delivery to your customer.

The delivery itself is created with reference to one or more sales documents and has set rules around how and whether it can be combined into one document covering multiple reference documents. From the delivery document, warehouse activities such as picking, packing, and shipping can be carried out. It's also the basis for the creation of a dispatch note and shipping notification to the customer.

The delivery document can be created manually in SAP S/4HANA or can be created automatically as a background task.

For certain types of service industries, where there is no delivery of a physical good, these delivery documents are omitted. Invoicing is thus performed immediately after creation of the sales documents (otherwise known as *order-relevant billing* as opposed to *delivery-relevant billing*).

1.3.4 Billing

The final stage in the sales and distribution process flow is kicked off by the billing document in SAP S/4HANA. The most usual form of billing is a customer invoice, with associated printed, emailed, or electronic data interchange (EDI) output. However, the billing process can also encompass such documents as credit notes, debit notes, and pro forma invoices.

As with the delivery document, the billing document can be created manually or via a background task. Creation of the billing document is with reference to a preceding document, such as a sales order or a delivery.

After the billing is completed, the final step of the order-to-cash process is initiated: the interface to accounting.

1.3.5 Accounting

The accounting document represents the interface between the sales and distribution functionality and the finance functionality within SAP S/4HANA. After the accounting document is saved, credits and debits are posted to specific general ledger accounts. The posting of the accounting document is normally an automated task, but this can be done directly from the billing document.

1.4 Summary

In this chapter, you've seen the development of SAP from a small software company in the early 1970s to the global brand and industry leader you know today. From promising beginnings in Germany through various iterations of the software, we now stand in a position to exploit the functional and technical capabilities of SAP S/4HANA to achieve radical business outcomes.

Many of the changes that have come about with the advent of SAP S/4HANA are listed in this chapter, but be aware that these are solely focused on sales and distribution. There are many innovations in other functional areas in SAP S/4HANA that aren't covered here at all.

The exploration of the transactional documents as set out in Section 1.3 follows a rational flow from inquiries, quotations, sales orders, deliveries, and billings, all the way through to accounting documents in the financial accounting functionality. This flow can be seen in the document flow of the sales and distribution process in SAP S/4HANA. More details will be provided for the document flow in later chapters.

After reading through this chapter, hopefully you now have an introductory understanding of some of the key concepts in sales and distribution in SAP S/4HANA. These concepts will be explored in greater detail in the coming chapters.

In Chapter 2, we'll work our way through more in-depth concepts around the methodologies used to initiate a brand-new SAP S/4HANA system, as well as explore much more detail around the critical area of master data. We'll close the chapter with a look at different types of transactional processes, namely order-related billing and delivery-related billing.

Chapter 2

System Prerequisites

SAP S/4HANA is a complex and far-reaching system that requires many prerequisites to run effectively. We'll explore those prerequisites in depth in this chapter.

You'll hear or have heard many times that master data is essential to the effective use of SAP applications, and, in this chapter, we'll explore how master data can help you get the most out of your sales and distribution functionality in SAP S/4HANA. We'll touch on some key configuration topics as concepts and explore how the sales and distribution master data is used to drive the transactional data we uncovered at the end of Chapter 1, such as inquiries, quotations, sales orders, deliveries, and invoices.

Initially, however, we'll begin at a high level, by understanding how the SAP S/4HANA system is built through an implementation project.

2.1 Configuration Tools in SAP S/4HANA

SAP implementation projects have undergone radical changes in recent years. The most important changes to discuss here revolve around the SAP Activate implementation methodology and the SAP Model Company approach.

2.1.1 SAP Activate Methodology

SAP Activate is the most up-to-date methodology for implementing SAP S/4HANA. It was developed around 2015 in response to the mindset shift from "waterfall" approaches to "agile" approaches to implementation. In traditional waterfall implementations, specific phases were defined for each step in the project. These phases typically followed this path:

- **Discover**
  This phase is used to run the discovery assessment, which involves defining any benefits and business value for the implementation project. By doing this, the business can also define its overall strategic roadmap.

- **Prepare**
  This phase is used to onboard all the relevant teams and agree on team structure, roles, and responsibilities. From a technology point of view, the prepare phase sees the deployment of the basic SAP S/4HANA system with embedded best practice solutions.
- **Explore**
  This phase sees the fit-gap analysis carried out against the best practices defined solution. From this exercise, nonstandard requirements are identified for implementation.
- **Realize**
  This phase is the main event in the implementation project and takes up the bulk of the time. During this phase, agile sprints are run to configure, build, and test the solutions. These agile sprints can be seen in crude terms as mini "design" and "test" phases within one SAP Activate phase. During this phase, data is also loaded, and training of end users can begin.
- **Deploy**
  This phase is the initiation of go-live, including the final setup of the production system and the business "go/no-go" decision based on business readiness.
- **Run**
  This phase sees the business live on the new system, with the driving of new efficiencies via the adoption of the new solution across the business.

SAP Activate follows the agile methodology, where the implementation project is broken down into six distinct phases, as shown in Figure 2.1.

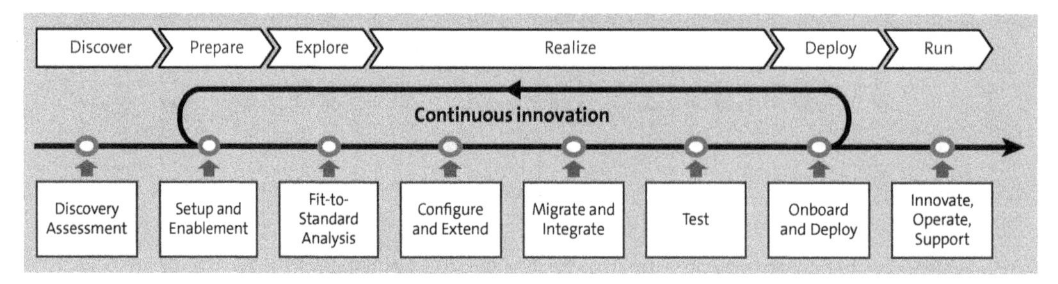

Figure 2.1 SAP Activate Phases

2.1.2 SAP Model Company

Many SAP clients these days begin their journey to SAP S/4HANA with a deployment based on the SAP Model Company solution. So, what exactly is SAP Model Company? SAP Model Company is a predelivered, prepackaged reference solution for SAP S/4HANA. It includes business content (e.g., process flows and test data) and preconfigured end-to-end processes designed to fit into specific industries, such as Banking, Life

Sciences, Oil and Gas, or Automotive. In total, SAP offers 30 industry solutions within the SAP Model Company approach; within those 30 industries, there are 29 SAP Model Company solutions.

The industries and SAP Model Company solutions are selected from the SAP website under the SAP Model Company navigator. The industries available are shown in Figure 2.2.

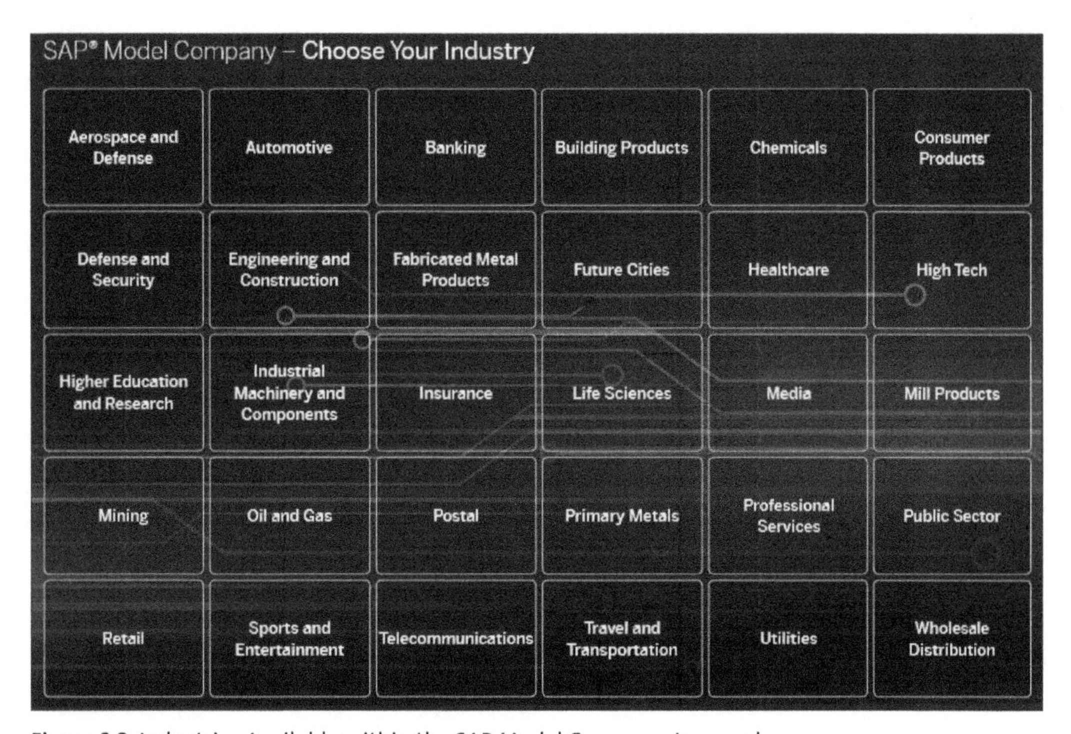

Figure 2.2 Industries Available within the SAP Model Company Approach

After the industry has been selected, the SAP Model Company solutions available for that industry are shown, as in Figure 2.3, where Aerospace and Defense is selected as the industry.

After the industry and SAP Model Company solutions are established, they can be downloaded and installed, providing an extremely useful base for the overall SAP solution, in which SAP has harnessed all of its years of experience with its clients in industry to tailor a specific solution designed to meet most needs out of the box.

Increasingly, SAP Model Company is being used by clients as the starting point for their SAP S/4HANA implementations, driving down implementation costs by as much as 80% and drastically shortening project lead times.

Figure 2.3 SAP Model Company Solutions Available for a Specific Industry

2.2 Master Data

It's no exaggeration to say that bad master data has the capacity to break an SAP S/4HANA implementation or make a very good solution look very bad. In Chapter 1, we defined master data as data created centrally to be used for a number of applications. Typical examples of master data are business partners, materials, and prices. Let's look at master data in a bit more detail.

Master data resides within your SAP S/4HANA system and normally remains unchanged for long periods of time, which separates it from transactional data that relates to day-to-day operations. As an example, a sales order is transactional data, whereas the customer, material, and price used to create the sales order are master data.

The picture becomes clearer as we delve into specific master data objects. In this chapter, we'll look at the key sales and distribution master data objects of customer, material, and sales pricing.

2.2.1 Customer Master

In SAP S/4HANA, customers are created within the framework of the overall business partner, which was discussed in more depth in Chapter 1, Section 1.2.3. In this section, we'll build on the business partner concept to explore its use in the context of a customer in the sales and distribution process. This necessitates looking at the roles a business partner can play, the sales area the partner will operate in, the functions the partner can be used for, any financial data relating to the company code, and additional relationships between business partners.

Roles

Essentially, a business partner is a named person, organization, or group, along with an address and some basic attributes and characteristics. From this shell, the business partner can be extended to become a customer, vendor, contact person, or any number of other roles.

When creating these roles in Transaction BP, the role is selected from a list of standard roles in the **Change in BP Role** dropdown menu, as shown in Figure 2.4.

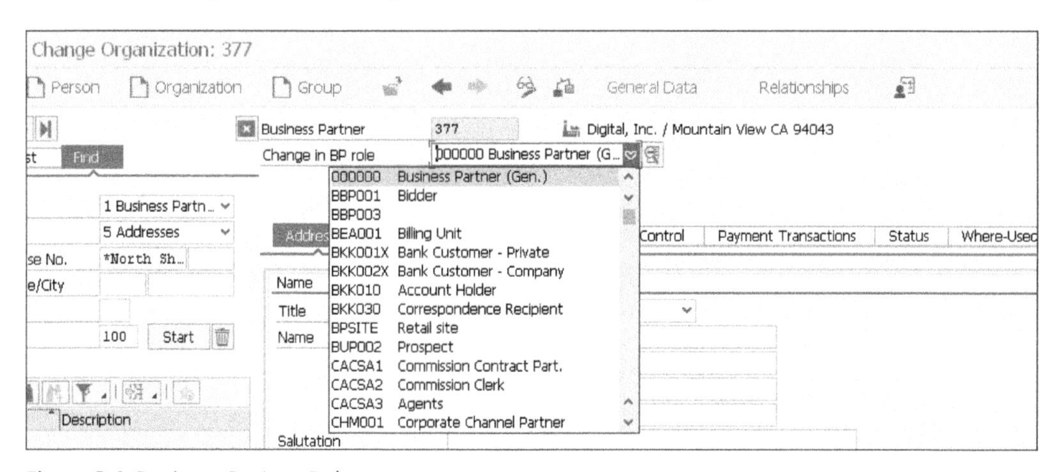

Figure 2.4 Business Partner Roles

To create a business partner as a customer, the role **FLCU01 Customer** should be selected. In Figure 2.5, this is suffixed with **(Maintained)** to denote that this role has already been maintained for this business partner number.

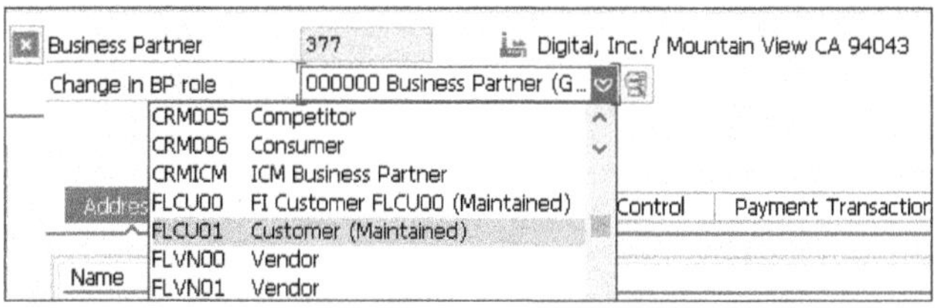

Figure 2.5 Business Partner Roles: Customer

After the customer role is selected, more tabs become visible in the business partner data with more available fields, such as industry codes and freely definable attributes under the **Customer: Additional Data** tab.

Additionally, a new **Sales and Distribution** button appears at the top of the screen, as shown in Figure 2.6.

Figure 2.6 Customer Master: Sales and Distribution Button

By selecting this button, a new set of data appears—this is the data used in all your sales transactions, such as inquiries, quotations, sales orders, deliveries, and billing documents This data is shown in Figure 2.7.

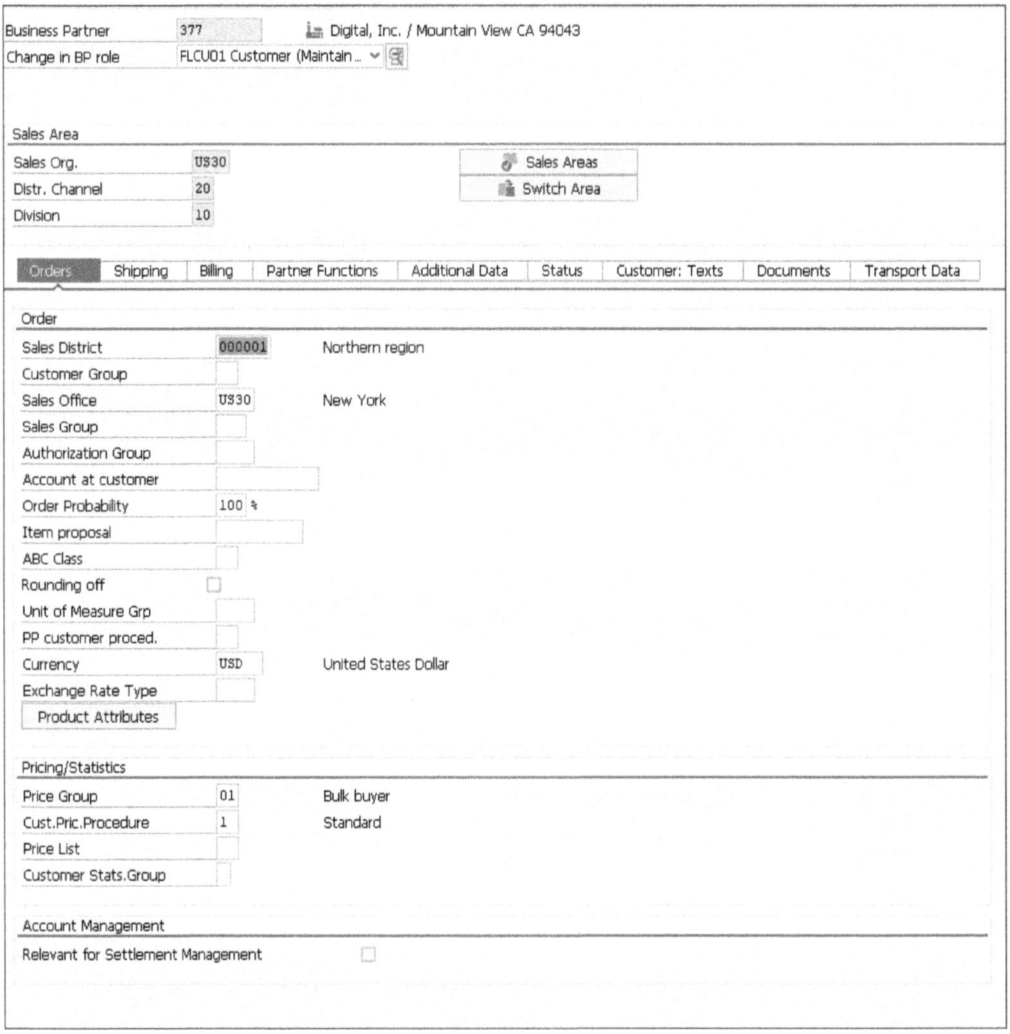

Figure 2.7 Customer Master: Sales and Distribution Data

Sales Area

The data contained in these screens is specific to the sales area defined in the screen. A sales area in SAP S/4HANA is composed of a combination of three organizational objects:

- **Sales organization**
  The sales organization is fully responsible for all sales activities. For a specific legal entity, a sales organization is the organizational object to which all sales and logistical transactions belong.
- **Distribution channel**
  The distribution channel is an organizational representation of the channel by which goods and services are delivered to customers. Standard SAP distribution channels include wholesale, retail, and direct sales, but additional channels usually are configured according to business requirements.
- **Division**
  The division is the organizational unit used to group together a range of products. Each material is allocated to one division only.

When combined, all three of these organization units are referred to as the sales area. Each sales transaction must be assigned to a specific sales area.

> **Note**
>
> The relationship between the individual organizational objects can be described as follows:
>
> - Sales organization to distribution channel is a one-to-many relationship.
> - Distribution channel to division is a many-to-many relationship.

An example sales area is shown in Figure 2.8.

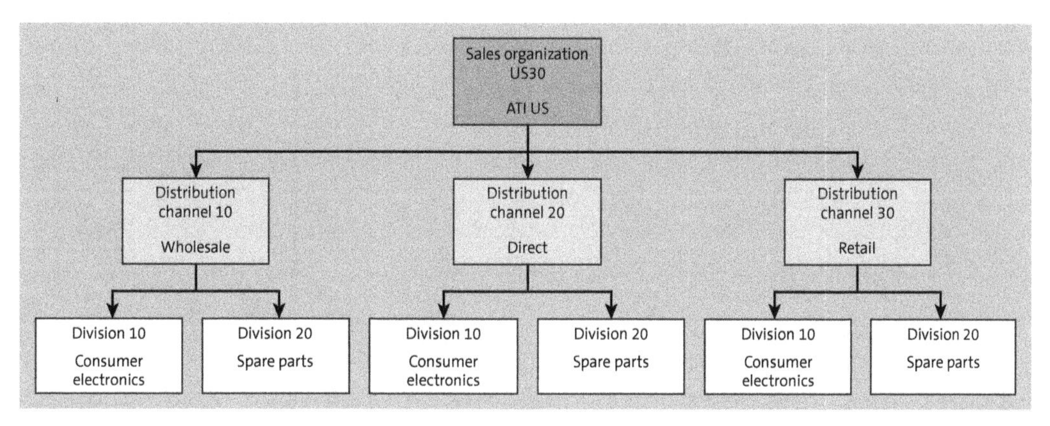

Figure 2.8 SAP Sales Area

Customers in SAP S/4HANA can be assigned to multiple sales areas, allowing the flexibility within the system to share master data across organizations. However, specific key data objects are unique to each sales area. Let's explore which data is general data and which data is sales area-specific data.

General data is specific to the business partner but can be shared across any number of roles for which the business partner is created. For example, name and address data is the same whether the business partner is transacting as a supplier or a customer. This is also true of other attributes such as identification numbers, taxation data, banks, and credit cards. As a result, this data is housed at the central business partner level under general data.

When first using Transaction BP to open a business partner, the general data is the initial data to be seen, as shown in Figure 2.9.

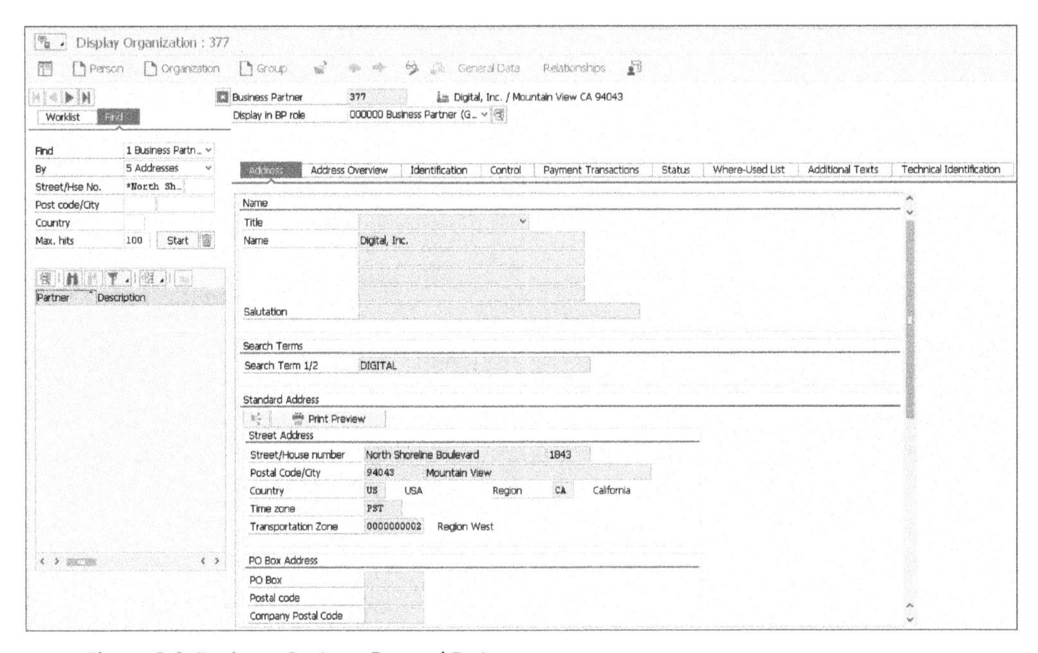

Figure 2.9 Business Partner General Data

At the top of the screen, the **General Data** button is grayed out because the screen is already showing that data. However, when viewing a customer's sales and distribution data, the **General Data** button is available for selection, navigating you back to the general data of the business partner (see Figure 2.10).

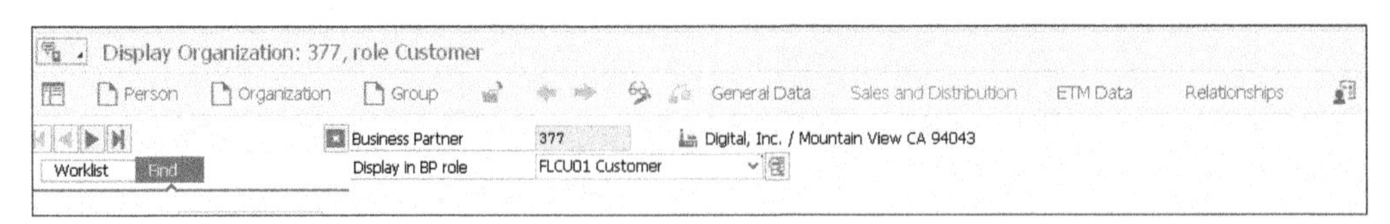

Figure 2.10 Business Partner Sales and Distribution with the General Data Button

Sales and distribution data, as already mentioned, is data specific to the sales area specified. As all sales transactions are created for a given sales area, this data is key to accurate sales document creation. The kind of data held here includes customer groupings and classifications such as sales district, customer group, sales office, and sales group, as well as preferred currency. The sales area data also includes shipping data such as delivery priority, shipping conditions, and settings denoting whether multiple orders for the same customer should be combined into one delivery, whether partial deliveries are allowed (and, if so, how many), and whether the customer allows over- or under delivery quantities.

From a billing perspective, the data found for the sales area of the customer can include scheduling of invoices so they are always produced on a given day of the week/month, incoterms, and payment terms.

Partner Functions

Probably the most essential information maintained for the customer's sales area data is related to partner functions.

From the point of view of sales, customers in SAP S/4HANA represent four basic, standard functions (see Figure 2.11):

- Sold-to party
- Ship-to party
- Bill-to party
- Payer

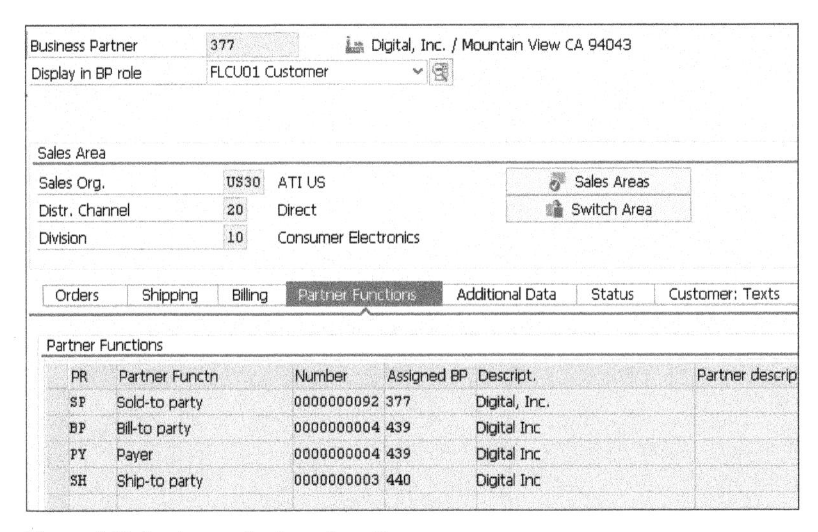

Figure 2.11 Customer Partner Functions

To examine each of these, consider the following example: An order is received into your organization from Digital Inc., and because Digital placed the order, it is the sold-to party. However, the purchase order makes it clear that the goods should be sent to Goods Inwards at a given address—this customer, therefore, is the ship-to party. Furthermore, the purchase order also makes it clear that the invoice should be sent to the Purchasing department, who would also pay the invoice. Therefore, this customer is the bill-to party and the payer.

All these can be specified individually in the sales order or specified by default in the customer master **Partner Functions** tab in the sales and distribution area. If they are set within the customer master, then those partner functions will automatically be pulled into any sales document such as an inquiry, a quotation, or a sales order. They can, of course, also be amended within the document manually.

Note

Any sales document created will pull in the partner functions that are assigned to the sold-to party.

Most of the terms and conditions held at the sales document level, such as delivery options and customer classifications, are derived directly from the sold-to party. There are some exceptions to this. A prime exception is payment terms, which are always derived from the payer. Furthermore, any credit limits are read from the payer record, not the sold-to party.

Company Code

All the sales information for a customer is housed within the sales and distribution option, but there are other key data points that should be considered for customers, namely financial data, such as credit limits and credit risk categories. For information such as this, you need to switch roles from **FLCU01 Customer** to **UKM000 SAP Credit Management**, as shown in Figure 2.12.

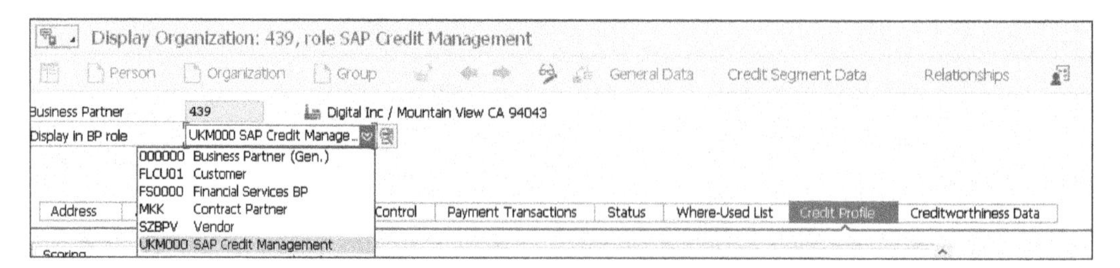

Figure 2.12 Business Partner SAP Credit Management Role

After this role is opened, new tabs open as well, such as **Credit Profile** and **Creditworthiness Data**, as shown in Figure 2.13.

A new **Credit Segment Data** button appears too, as shown in Figure 2.14.

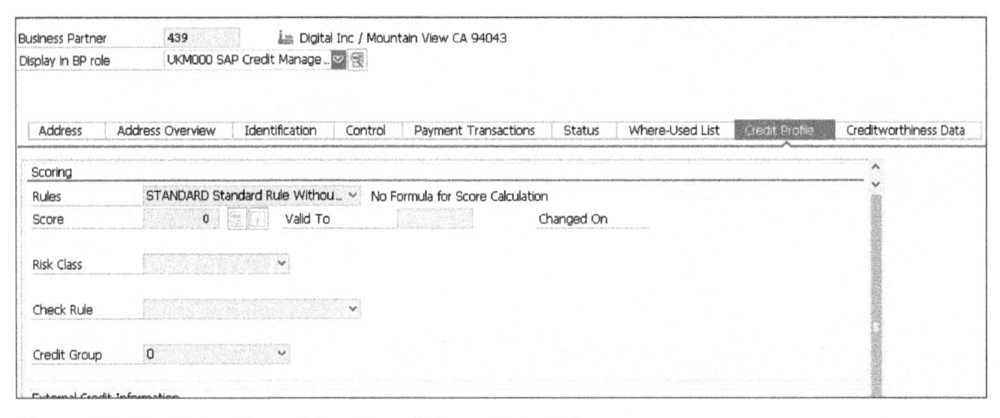

Figure 2.13 Credit Profile and Creditworthiness Data Tabs

Figure 2.14 Credit Segment Data Button

By selecting this button, you can view credit limits for a given credit segment (a financial organizational unit). This data is completed by the finance team for the customer who acts as the payer. The data is shown in Figure 2.15.

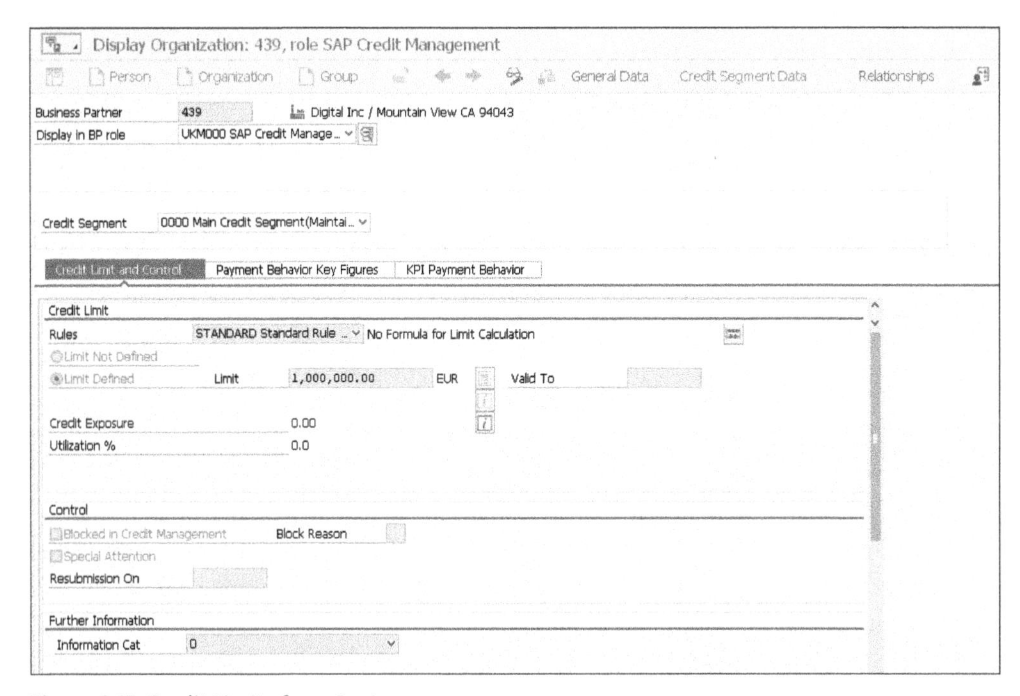

Figure 2.15 Credit Limits for a Customer

Relationships and Customer Hierarchy

An additional important setting for the customer is to link customers with other business partners through the **Relationships** tab, as shown in Figure 2.16.

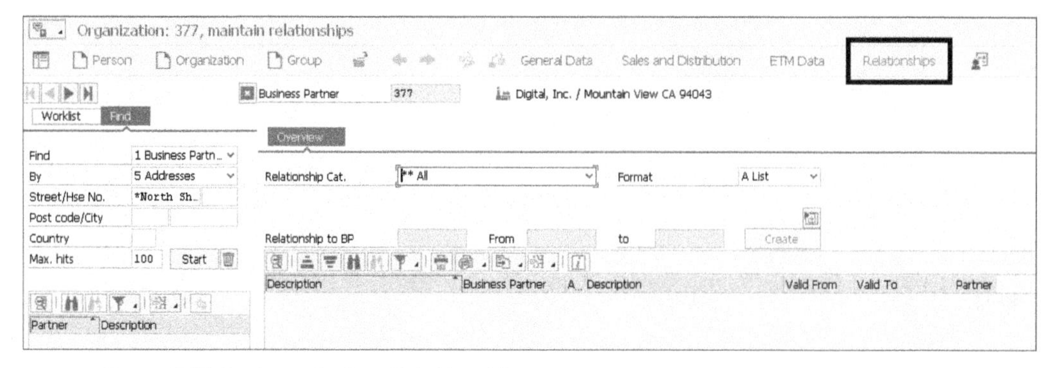

Figure 2.16 Business Partner Relationships

Through this section of the customer master, you can establish relationships between business partners by selecting the appropriate category from the **Relationship Cat.** dropdown list shown in Figure 2.17.

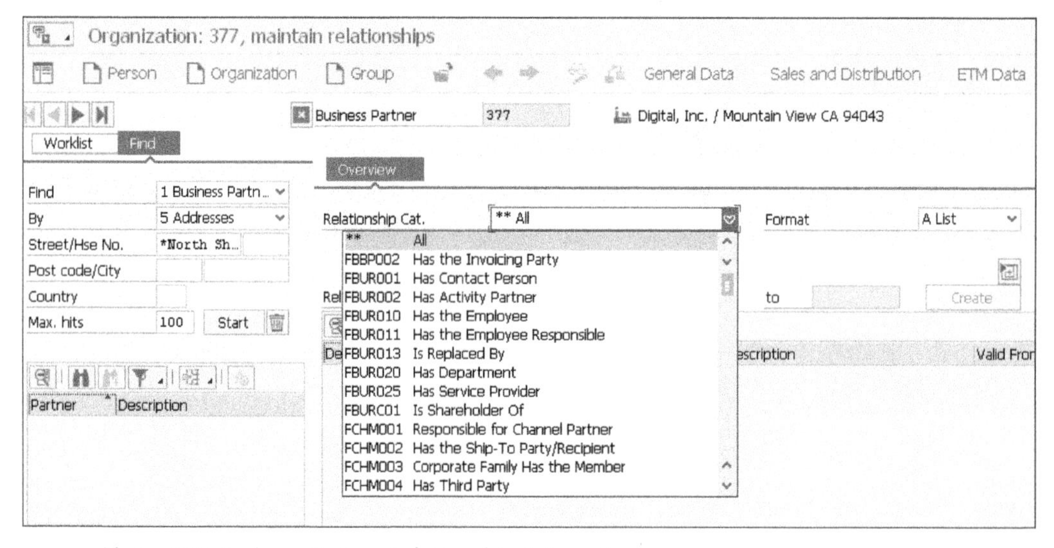

Figure 2.17 Business Partner Relationship Categories

These relationships can be validity date restricted for maximum flexibility.

It's also worth noting that additional customer relationships can be housed within the customer hierarchy, accessible through the SAP GUI Transaction VDH1N or Process Customer Hierarchy app in SAP Fiori. With this option, customers can be linked together through a defined hierarchy of customer hierarchy nodes. Nodes are set up as master data in Transaction BP, as with any other customer, except they are normally set up as groups as shown in Figure 2.18, with a separate **Grouping** designation, which gives them a different number range, as shown in Figure 2.19.

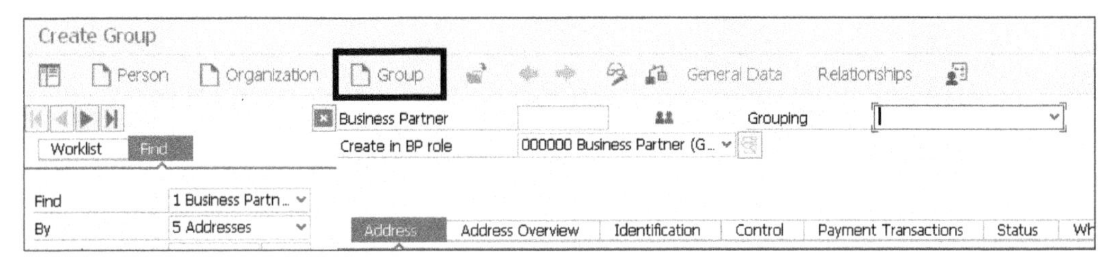

Figure 2.18 Create Group

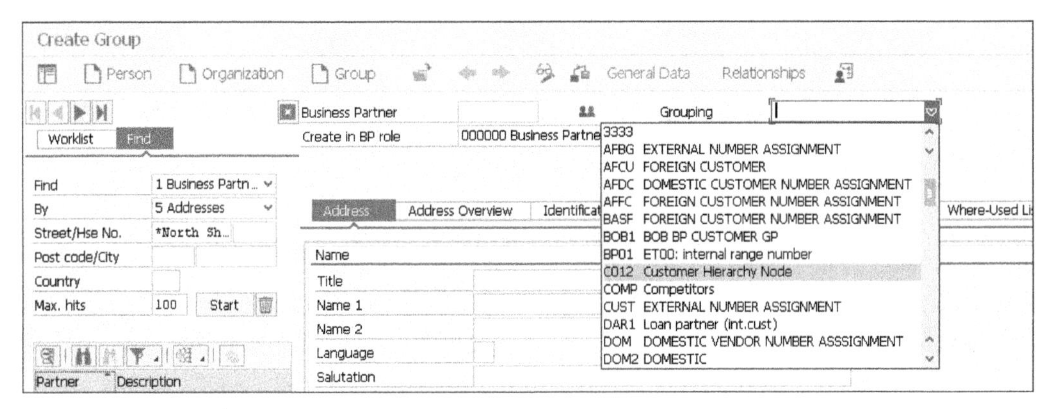

Figure 2.19 Customer Hierarchy Grouping

After the nodes are created, then customers can be assigned to them in Transaction VDH1N. Initially, a customer hierarchy type must be specified. SAP S/4HANA only provides one standard customer hierarchy type, but this option is provided so that more entries can be added to give business flexibility where required (see Figure 2.20).

Process Customer Hierarchy

Hierarch.parameters

Customer hierarchy type	A			
Validity date	11/14/2020			

More selection criteria

Customer	92	to		
Sales organization	US30	to		
Distribution channel	20	to		
Division	10	to		

☐ Limit display to paths

Figure 2.20 Customer Hierarchy Processing

After the hierarchy type is selected, customers can be added to a hierarchy in unlimited levels, using the **Higher-level customer** option, as shown in Figure 2.21.

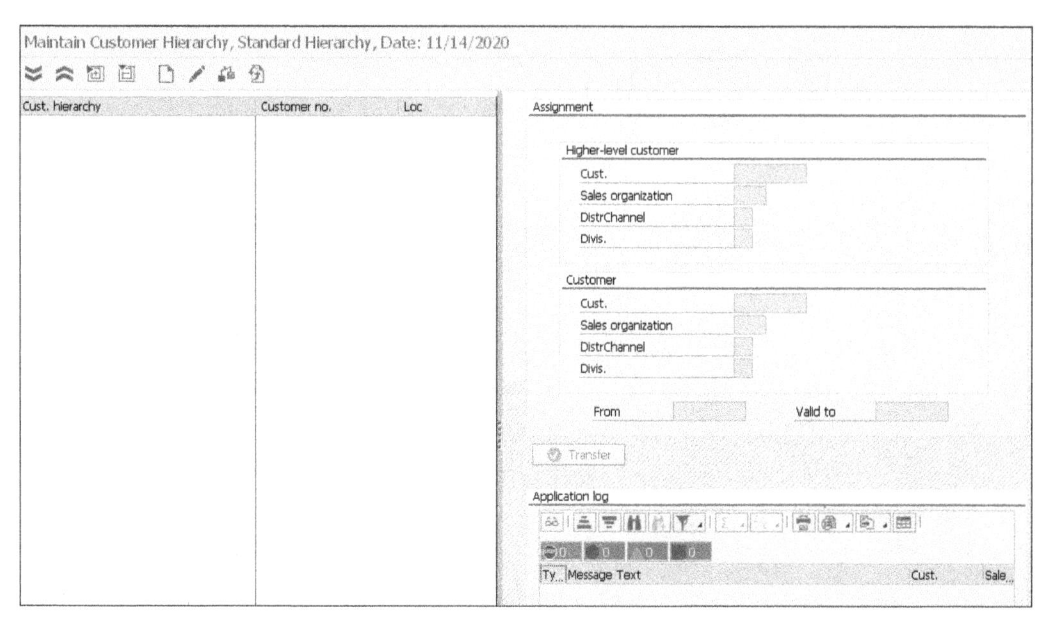

Figure 2.21 Customer Hierarchy Maintenance

Additionally, customers can also be created from within the Transaction VDH1N screen by following the menu path in Figure 2.22 to navigate to Transaction BP.

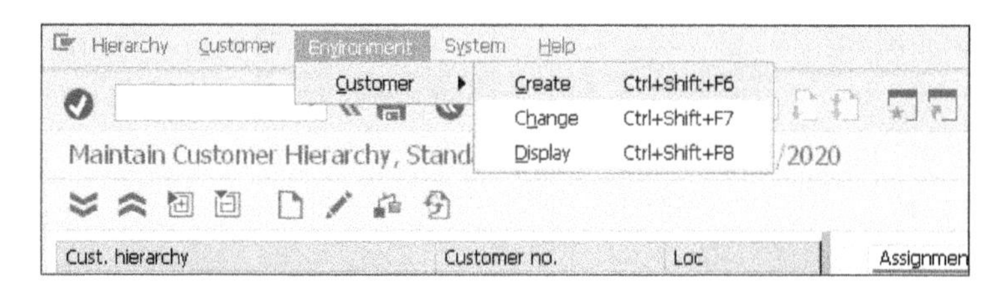

Figure 2.22 Creating Customers from within the Hierarchy

Customer hierarchies, once created, can be used in reporting and in sales pricing.

To summarize, the customer master record in SAP S/4HANA is inextricably linked to the business partner. All sales and distribution transactional data held in inquiries, quotation, sales orders, deliveries, and billing documents is closely linked and heavily reliant on the accuracy of the data held in the customer master.

2.2.2 Material Master

The material master in SAP S/4HANA interacts with all sales and distribution documents in conjunction with the customer and sales pricing to give the overall finished document. Materials within SAP S/4HANA can be viewed using Transaction MM03. You can also use the Manage Product Master app.

Note

Like many master data and transactional transactions in SAP S/4HANA, the material master is created using the *01 version of the transaction. Amendments are carried out using the *02 version, and the material is displayed using the *03 version: Transaction MM01 for create, Transaction MM02 for amend, and Transaction MM03 for display.

General Data

Depending on the setup within your system, materials can be assigned a material number manually when creating the material (called an external number range as it's assigned externally to the system), or SAP S/4HANA can assign the next available number from a predefined range (called an internal number range).

When you open an existing product in Transaction MM03, SAP S/4HANA will give you a list of views to select (see Figure 2.23).

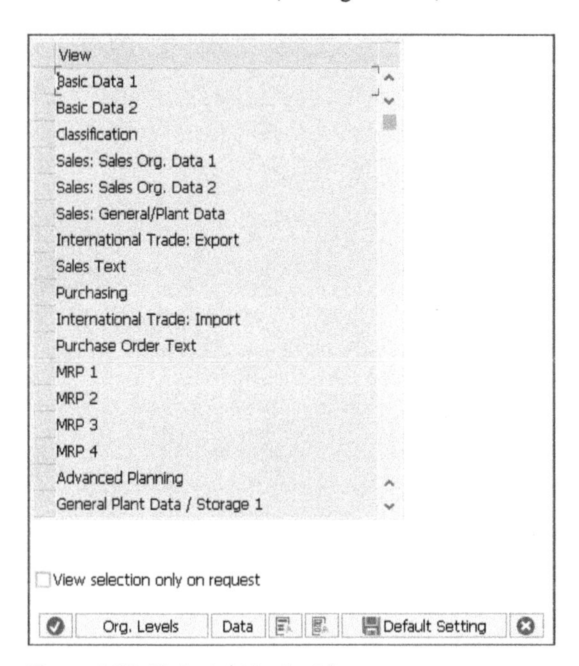

Figure 2.23 Material Master Views

Each view contains its own set of data, much like the different tabs in the customer master. You can select as many views as you want to view, and if you click the **Default Setting** button, SAP S/4HANA will remember your selection for next time.

Starting with **Basic data** views, you can see some of the basic data generalized to the material (i.e., isn't changeable depending on which organizational object is selected). This data includes such criteria as material number, description, unit of measure, and weights and dimensions (see Figure 2.24).

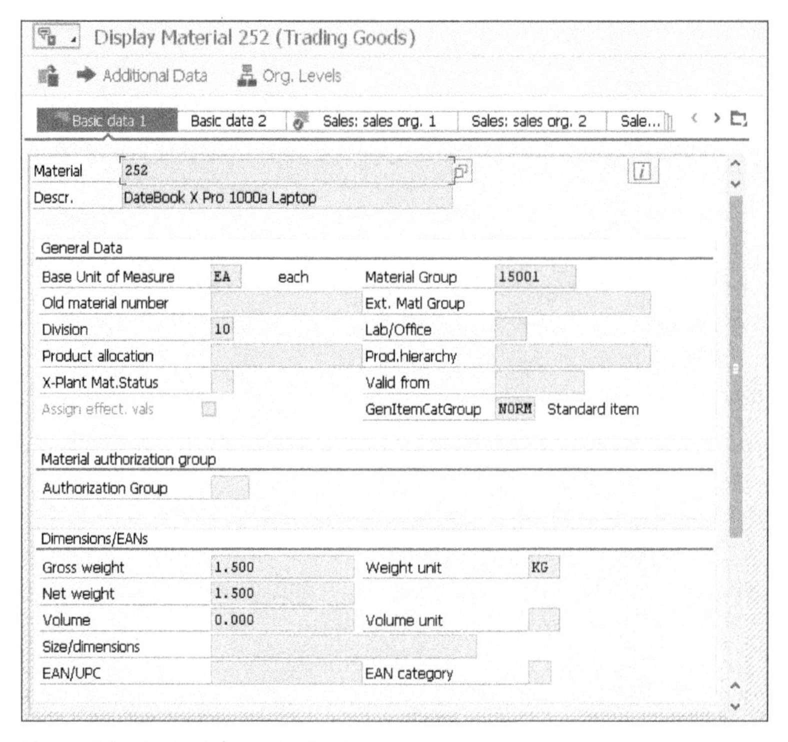

Figure 2.24 Material Master Basic Data

Sales Data

Data contained within other views may be specific to certain organizational objects. For example, the data shown in the **Sales: sales org. 1** view contains data specific to a given sales organization, distribution channel, and plant. When you select that view, you'll be asked to specify which sales organization, distribution channel, and plant you would like to see data for. Again, by clicking the **Default Setting** button, SAP will remember your selections for next time.

If you don't enter these organizational values, SAP S/4HANA will only show you the generalized data, not the data specific to these organizational objects. See Figure 2.25 for the requirement to complete the organizational levels, Figure 2.26 for the requirement to add organizational levels, Figure 2.26 for the view of the material master with the organizational levels specified, and Figure 2.27 for the view of the material master without the organizational levels specified.

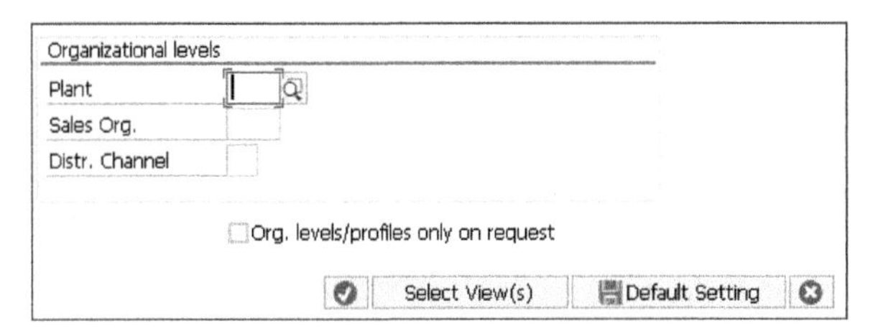

Figure 2.25 Material Master Organizational Levels

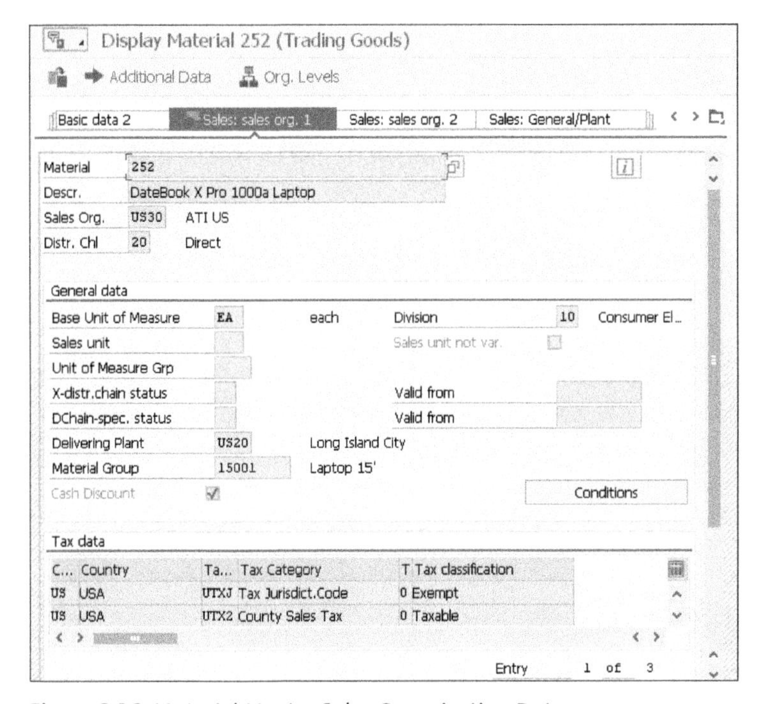

Figure 2.26 Material Master Sales Organization Data

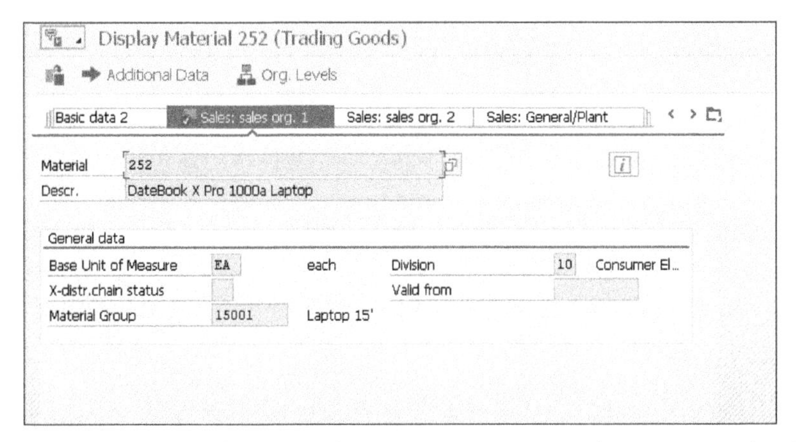

Figure 2.27 Material Master Sales Organization Data without Organizational Objects

In terms of material master data that has important direct implications on your sales documents, there are five extremely important fields in the material master that are worth exploring in a little more detail. This isn't an exhaustive list of the key fields, of course, but these are fields have the greatest impact on the sales and distribution process.

- **Delivering Plant**
  This is used to determine which plant is used in the sales order to deliver the goods to the customer (see Figure 2.28). The determination of plant in the sales order is carried out in the following order by SAP S/4HANA:
  - The plant in the customer-material info record (see later in this section for more information)
  - The plant assigned to the sold-to customer master
  - The delivering plant in the material master

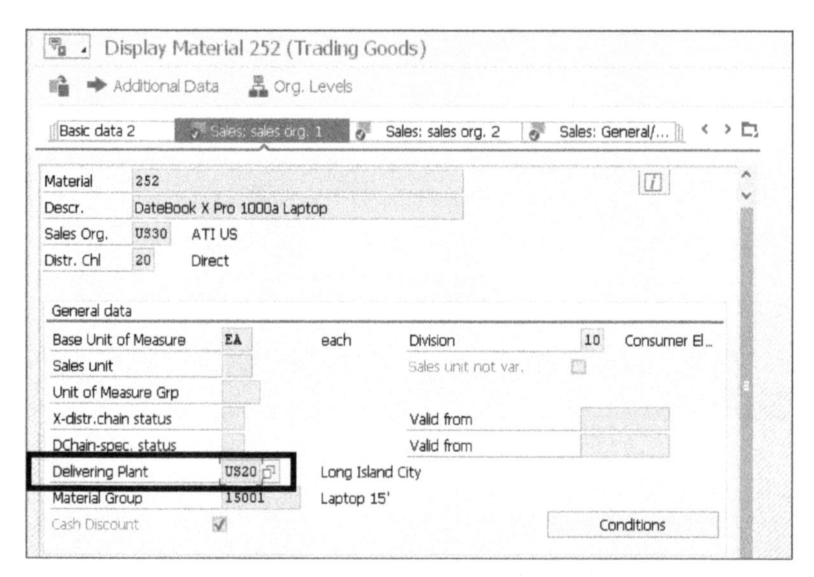

Figure 2.28 Delivering Plant

- **Item Category Group**
  This is used to determine how the material behaves in a sales document. In conjunction with other fields in the sales order, such as the sales order type, the item category group determines the item category in the sales document. The item category has a profound impact on the document, such as determining whether the item is deliverable, whether it's relevant for billing, and whether it has a bill of materials (BOM) assigned (see later in this section for more information). The item category is the most important item-level field in the sales document, so this material master field is crucial. Standard items are set as **Item Category Group NORM**, as shown in Figure 2.29.

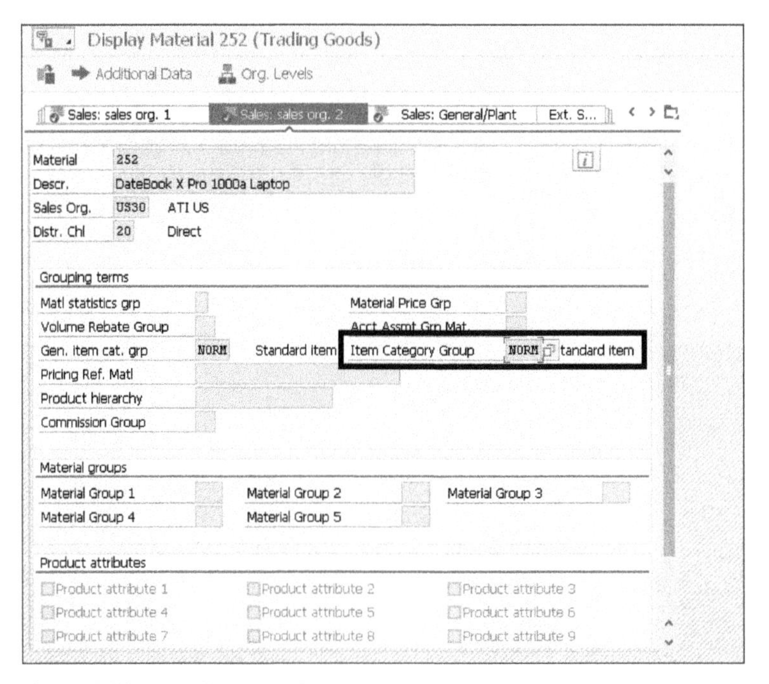

Figure 2.29 Item Category Group

- **Loading Group**
  Every material has a method by which it's loaded into a shipment, such as a crane, a forklift, or manually by hand. The loading group contains that method, and, as a result, it's important because it helps to determine the shipping point (i.e., where in the goods out area the order is sent from) in the sales order (see Figure 2.30).

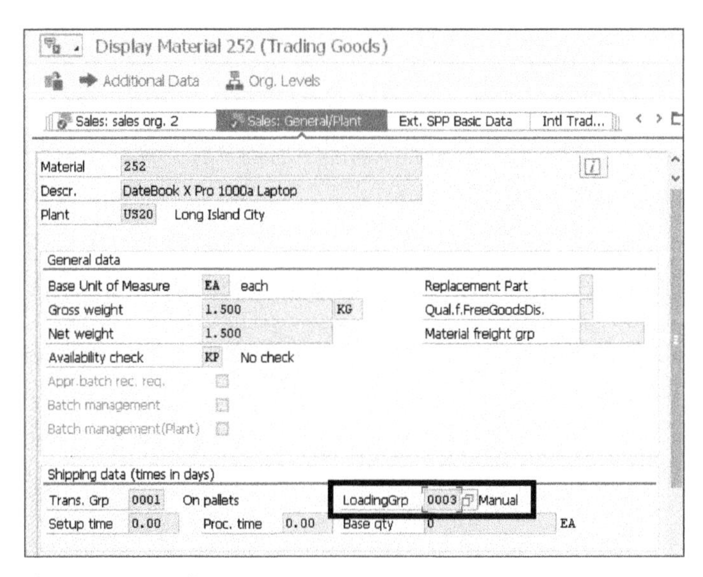

Figure 2.30 Loading Group

- **Availability Check**
  The availability check tells SAP whether to check for available stock and determine an available date (see Figure 2.31). According to the settings configured for each value, this stock check may check against open sales orders and deliveries, and it may or may not include such things as open purchase orders, inventory marked as blocked, and the like.

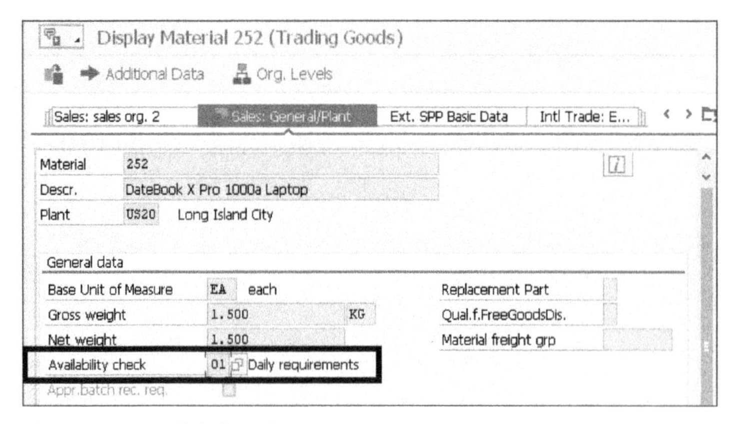

Figure 2.31 Availability Check

- **Unit of Measure**
  The unit of measure in the material master is housed in two places—the **Base Unit of Measure** and the **Sales unit** (see Figure 2.32). The **Sales unit** field is only used when the unit of measure differs for a given sales organization. Therefore, it's not uncommon to see the **Sales unit** field blank. This unit is carried through to the sales document and is used in pricing calculations as well as overall weight and dimensions calculations.

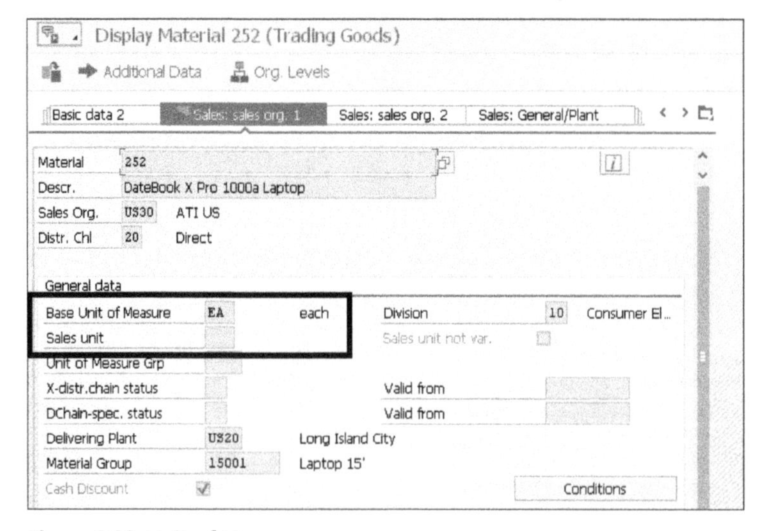

Figure 2.32 Unit of Measure

Bills of Material

Another important concept within the material master is the bill of material (BOM). BOMs in sales and distribution are packages of materials sold together and grouped under one BOM header item. For example, if you were selling a laptop starter pack, you might create a BOM with the laptop, a mouse, a separate keyboard, a power cable, and a case. All of these would be classed as components of a single BOM as follows:

- Laptop Starter Pack
  - Component 1: Laptop
  - Component 2: Mouse
  - Component 3: Keyboard
  - Component 4: Power cable
  - Component 5: Case

All the components must be set up as materials, and then they are bundled into a BOM using Transaction CS01 (again, use Transaction CS02 for change and Transaction CS03 for display). A simple BOM could look like Figure 2.33.

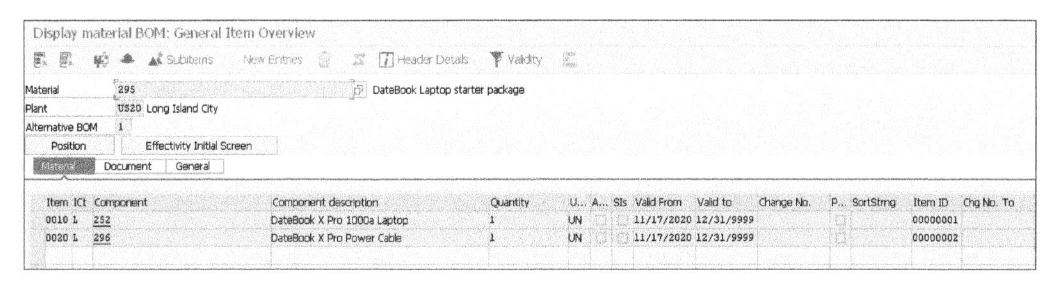

Figure 2.33 Bill of Material

In the BOM example, material 295 is the BOM header, and materials 252 and 296 are the BOM items. Creating a sales order for material 295 will automatically pull in materials 252 and 296 as components of the BOM header. BOM header materials have different item category groups from normal items—for BOM headers, use item category group LUMF.

2.2.3 Pricing

SAP S/4HANA sales pricing is one of the most powerful and flexible tools in the order-to-cash armory. Pricing in SAP covers the following:

- Material list price
- Customer-specific pricing
- Discounts
- Freight prices
- Taxation

The good news is that SAP S/4HANA sales pricing uses a standard SAP methodology called *condition technique*, which is employed in many functions in the sales and distribution area. Mastering how the condition technique works for pricing will open many other doors in sales and distribution, such as output determination, text determination, material determination, cross-selling, free goods, listings and exclusions, and batch determination. These concepts are explained in more detail in Section 2.2.4.

Condition Technique

If there is one concept that is vital to the sales and distribution experience in SAP S/4HANA, it's condition technique. So, what exactly is it? Condition technique is a methodology in SAP to retrieve master data records, and it works from five basic building blocks:

- Procedure
- Condition type
- Access sequence
- Condition table
- Condition record

As a user, the only part of this you'll see is the condition record, which is the master data (in this case, the price record).

The structure of the condition technique for pricing in sales is shown in Figure 2.34.

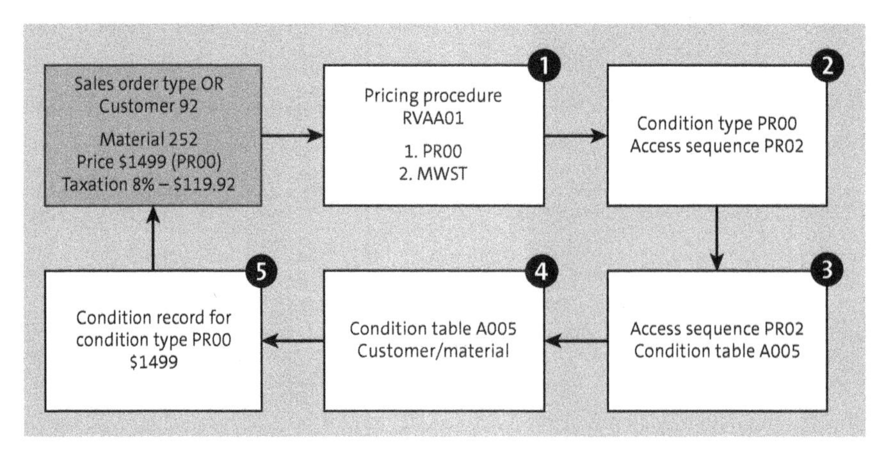

Figure 2.34 SAP S/4HANA Pricing Condition Technique

By placing a standard order for customer 92 and material 252 in the system, the condition technique immediately uses this transactional data to determine a pricing procedure for use in the sales order.

A pricing procedure gives the document a list of pricing condition types to use. The condition type is the kind of pricing required, for example, a price, discount, freight charge, taxation, and so on; each one of these has different condition types and, in many cases, several.

The condition type has an access sequence assigned to it, which is a list of tables, called condition tables, that hold the master data of the price. In this example, we have a price of $1,499 sitting in the customer/material table, which means that for customer 92 and material 252, the system has found a valid price of $1,499. This data is called a *condition record*.

This process is repeated for every condition type in the pricing procedure until all the prices, discounts, freight, and taxation are determined in the document.

Maintaining Prices

Let's move on now to the SAP S/4HANA pricing itself and explore how to create and amend a sales price. Sales pricing is created in SAP S/4HANA by using Transaction VK11 (Transaction VK12 to amend and Transaction VK13 to display). This transaction takes you to the final step in the condition technique—the condition record. A condition record for pricing contains the actual price, discount, freight amount, or taxation amount, based on criteria set out in a condition table. Figure 2.35 shows the Transaction VK11 screen, where the condition records are created.

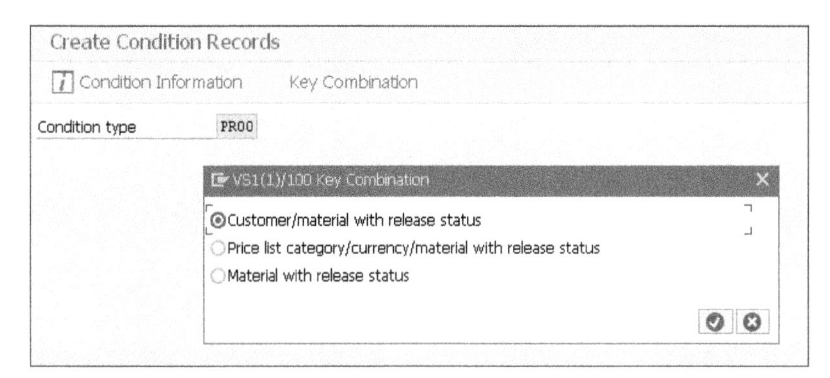

Figure 2.35 Create Condition Records

As you can see from the screen, after you enter a **Condition type** (in this case, "PR00" for a standard price), SAP S/4HANA will run through the condition technique below the condition type to show the access sequence. This is represented in the **Key Combination** popup, which is another way of describing the access sequence (see Figure 2.35).

The SAP access sequence will tell the system the order in which it should search for a pricing condition record. Listed are the condition tables that are available to house those pricing condition records; in this case, the first condition table that SAP searches for a price is the customer/material with release status table. If you select this entry and press Enter, the screen shown in Figure 2.36 appears.

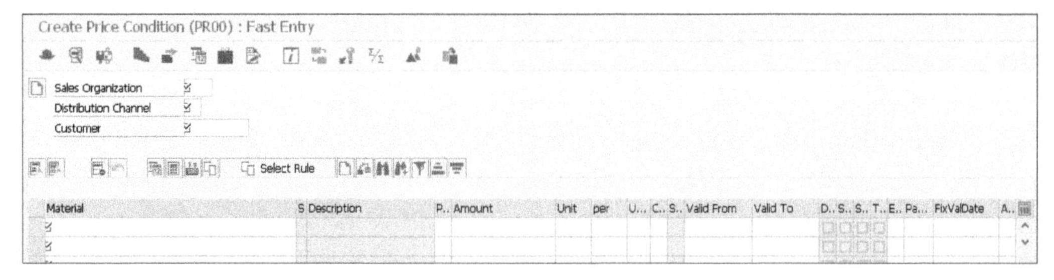

Figure 2.36 Create PROO Price

As usual with SAP screens, the mandatory fields show a small checkmark in a box—these fields must be completed before saving. From Figure 2.36, the mandatory fields for this specific condition table are as follows:

- **Sales organization**
- **Distribution Channel**
- **Customer**
- **Material**

If you enter these fields and press Enter, the data appears as shown in Figure 2.37.

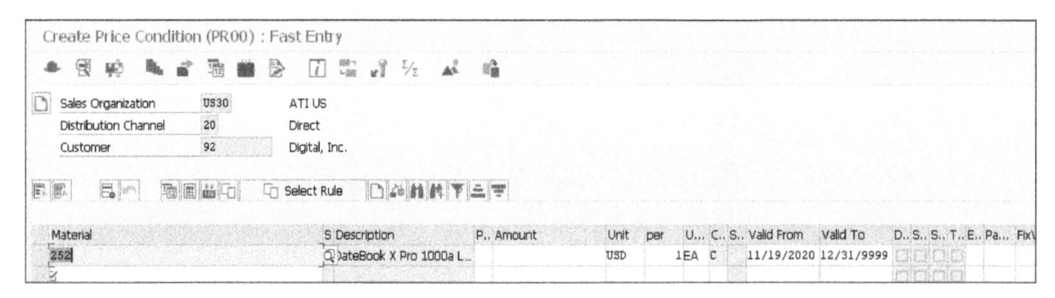

Figure 2.37 Create PROO Price Presave

The first thing to notice is that the **Amount** column is blank, denoting that the price is zero—this is because no price was entered before pressing Enter. Other data has automatically been pulled in:

- **Description**
  This is selected from the material master record. The description can't be amended manually in the condition record.
- **Unit**
  USD is selected from the sales organization default currency in Customizing. This can be amended manually in the condition record.
- **Per**
  1 is defaulted here, meaning the price refers to the price per 1 of the unit of measure. This can be amended manually in the condition record.

- **Unit of Measure**
  EA is selected from the material master record. The unit of measure can be amended manually in the condition record.
- **Calculation type**
  C is defaulted from the pricing condition type Customizing. The calculation type tells SAP how to calculate the price: Should it be calculated according to quantity (value **C**), gross or net weight, a percentage, a fixed amount, and so on? This can't be amended in the condition record.
- **Valid From/Valid To**
  The current date and 12/31/9999 are selected from the pricing condition type Customizing. These dates can be amended manually in the condition record.

At this point, you can simply add an amount and save the condition record, and it would be valid for all new sales orders created between the valid from and valid to dates. However, there are other options that should be explored in sales pricing.

Scales Pricing

One of the most useful functions is the scales function in sales pricing. This can be seen for a price by clicking the **Scales** icon, as shown in Figure 2.38.

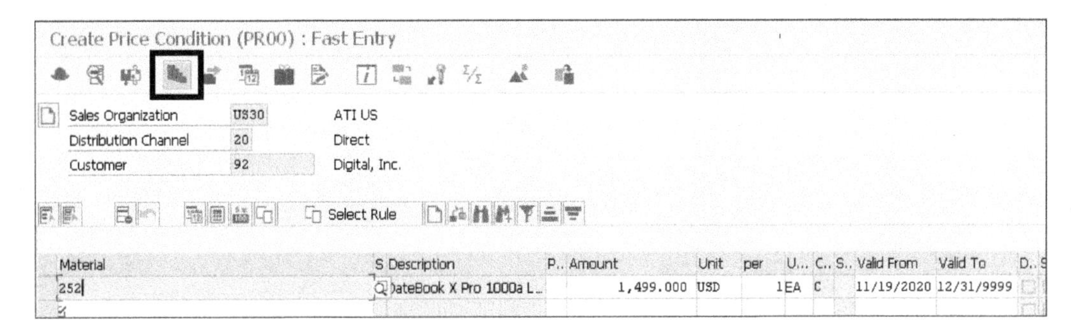

Figure 2.38 Create pricing scales

Once selected, the scales can be added into the details screen, as shown in Figure 2.39. Scales are pricing differences according to quantity or value, weight, time, or other factors, which are assigned to the condition type in Customizing.

In this example, if the customer buys 1, the price is $1,499. However, if the customer buys between 2 and 4, the unit price drops to $1,400; drops further to $1,250 if the customer buys between 5 and 9; and so on. After you've created your scales and return to the main pricing creation screen, it's possible to see that scales exist for a line because the **Scales Pricing** checkbox is populated, as shown in Figure 2.40.

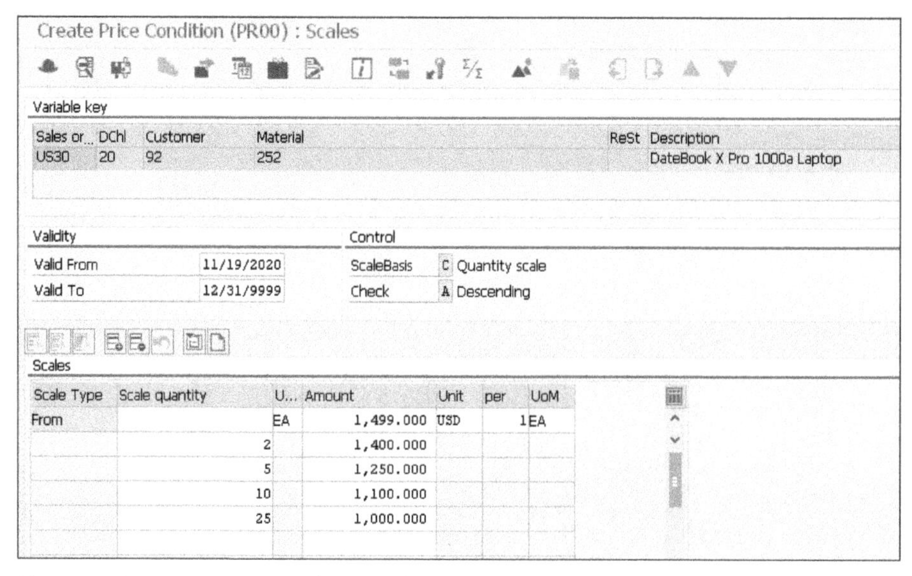

Figure 2.39 Create Pricing Scales Details

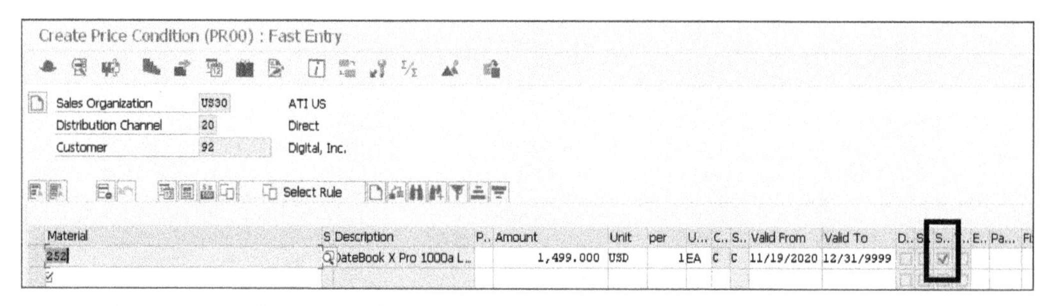

Figure 2.40 Scales Pricing Checkbox

Further functionality is available in sales pricing by selecting the **Additional Data** button, as shown in Figure 2.41.

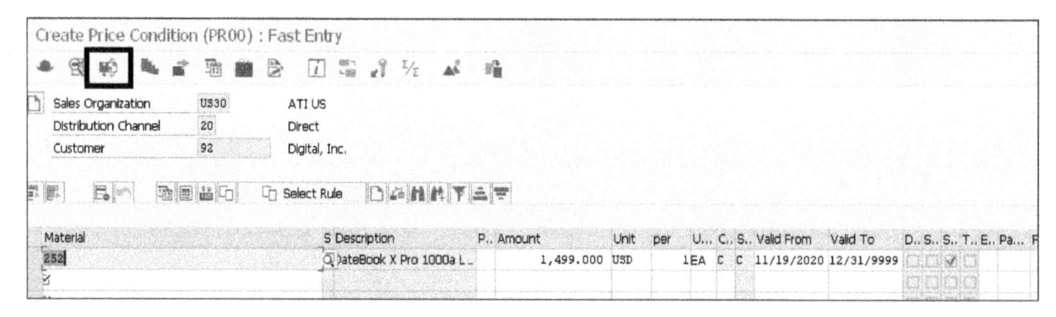

Figure 2.41 Additional Data Button

From the **Additional Sales Data** screen, as shown in Figure 2.42, you can add sales deal assignments. You can also add terms of payment, which will be used for the specific item that uses this price. This can be additionally restricted by adding a fixed value date from which the payment terms become effective.

Create Price (PR00): Additional Sales Data

Variable key

Sales or...	DChl	Customer	Material	ReSt	Description
US30	20	92	252		DateBook X Pro 1000a Laptop

Validity

Valid From 11/19/2020 Valid To 12/31/9999

Assignments

Promotion

Sales Deal

Assignments for retail promotion

Promotion

Payment

Terms of payment

Fixed Value Date Addit. Value Days

Figure 2.42 Additional Data Details

2.2.4 Other Uses for the Condition Technique

You've seen how the condition technique is used to determine sales prices in SAP S/4HANA. Now we'll explore the other master data areas that use the condition technique in sales and distribution: free goods, material determination, cross-selling, listings and exclusions, customer-material info record, and output determination.

Free Goods

The free goods functionality can be used in SAP S/4HANA to enable offers such as "buy one get one free." The master data condition records for free goods are set up using Transaction VBN1 (Transaction VBN2 for amend, Transaction VBN3 for display). The creation screen is shown in Figure 2.43.

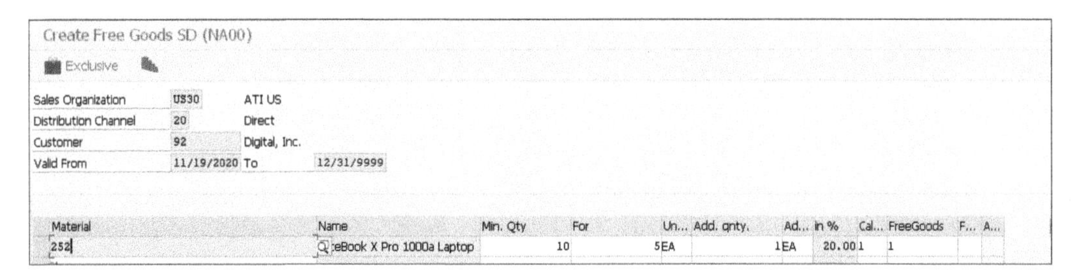

Create Free Goods SD (NA00)

Exclusive

Sales Organization US30 ATI US

Distribution Channel 20 Direct

Customer 92 Digital, Inc.

Valid From 11/19/2020 To 12/31/9999

Material	Name	Min. Qty	For	Un...	Add. qnty.	Ad...	in %	Cal...	FreeGoods	F...	A...
252	:eBook X Pro 1000a Laptop		10	5EA		1EA	20.00	1	1		

Figure 2.43 Create Free Goods

This free goods table is using **Customer** and **Material** fields, very similar to the pricing table used earlier. However, there are some additional fields to be aware of:

- **Min. Qty**
  This is the minimum quantity to be ordered before the free goods become available.
- **For**
  This is the amount ordered that triggers a free goods amount.
- **Add. qnty.**
  This is the additional number of goods supplied as free.
- **in %**
  This is the calculated percentage amount that is free.
- **Cal... Type**
  This determines how many to send if the ordered quantity isn't equal to the **For** quantity.
- **FreeGoods**
  This category is either inclusive or exclusive, so it determines whether the free goods quantity is inclusive of the total quantity ordered or in addition.
- **F...**
  This is the Free Goods Delivery Control controls whether the free goods are delivered even if the originating quantity isn't.

Let's consider an example. In Figure 2.43, we specified the following entries:

- **Material**: "252"
- **Min. qty**: "10"
- **For**: "5"
- **Add. qnty.**: "1"
- **Cal.**: "1"
- **FreeGoods**: "1"
- **F...**: [blank]

In practice, this means that no free goods will be supplied until at least a quantity of 10 of material number 252 have been ordered. If our customer orders 10, SAP S/4HANA will send an additional 1 for every 5 ordered; in this case, an additional 2 will be sent. **FreeGoods Category** is **1** (inclusive), meaning that the free goods are inclusive of the amount ordered; therefore, the customer ordered 10 and will receive 10, 2 of which will be free. The **Free Goods Delivery Control** setting is blank, so the free goods will be delivered regardless of whether the chargeable goods are delivered or not. The **Calculation Type** is used to determine how many to send in the situation where the ordered quantity isn't equal to the **For** quantity. In other words, if the **For** quantity is 5, but the customer orders 17, whether the system sends only 1 as free or 2 is controlled by the **Calculation Type**.

You may also notice an **Exclusive** button next to a gift icon in the top-left corner of the screen. This can be used to add a different material; in other words, the free goods supplied are exclusive from the original material. By selecting this button, a new field opens called **AddMat FrGd** (additional material free goods), where you specify the material number of the goods to be supplied as free, as shown in Figure 2.44.

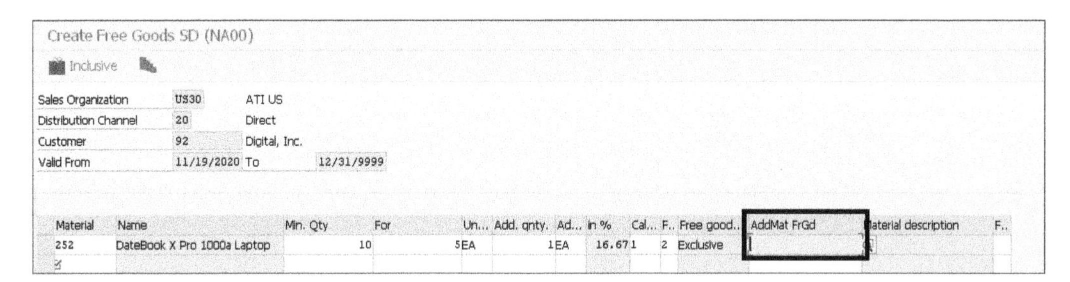

Figure 2.44 Free Goods Additional Material Field

Material Determination

SAP S/4HANA has the flexibility to offer a material replacement based on master data set up in the material determination Transaction VB11 (Transaction VB12 to amend, Transaction VB13 to display), as shown in Figure 2.45.

Create Material Entered (A001) : Fast Entry

Valid From 11/19/2020
Valid To 12/31/9999
Proposed reason

Material Entered	Name	Material	Item Description	U...	Reaso	A...
LAPTOP		252	DateBook X Pro 1000a Laptop			

Figure 2.45 Material Determination Details

In the example, we've set the system up so that if we type "LAPTOP" into the sales order creation screen in the **Material Number** field, it would automatically be replaced by material 252. This condition table only has **Material** as a field, but it's not untypical to use condition tables with customer and material fields so that the material substitution only occurs for certain customers.

Material determination also has a substitution reason code (**Proposed reason** field in the header and **Reason** field in the item data in Figure 2.45) that can be applied at the individual item level or for all material determination records in the table. This reason code controls how the system reacts when it finds a material determination condition record. Leaving the field blank means that the substitution happens automatically, but additional reason codes are available that provide a popup selection box for the new material when placing the sales order.

Cross-Selling

The cross-selling functionality is very similar to the free goods functionality except that the additional materials are chargeable. Cross-selling can be set up in Transaction VB41 (Transaction VB42 to amend, Transaction VB43 to display), as shown in Figure 2.46.

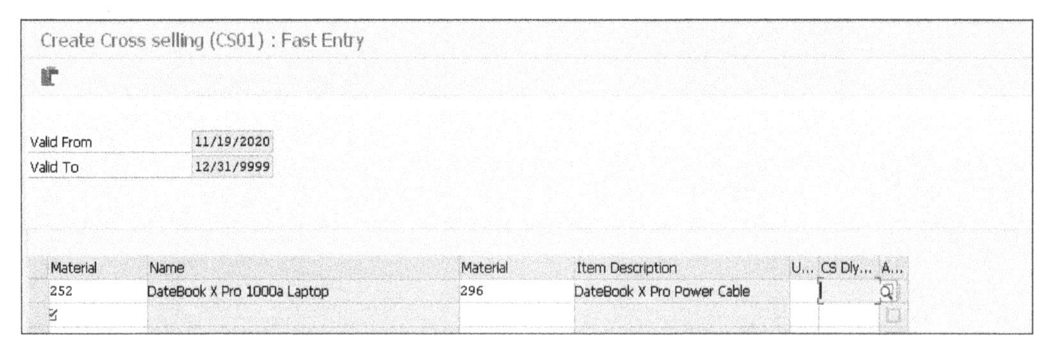

Figure 2.46 Cross-Selling Details

In the example, when a sales order for material 252 is created, the cross-selling functionality posts a dialog box to offer up an additional item—material 296—to add to the order as chargeable. The **CS Dly** (cross-selling delivery control) field controls whether the cross-sold material is supplied regardless of whether the original material is shipped or not.

Listings and Exclusions

Listings and exclusions are useful in SAP S/4HANA to restrict the sale of certain materials to certain customers. Listings and exclusions are both created via Transaction VB01 (Transaction VB02 to amend, Transaction VB03 to display). The separation of listings and exclusions is done via the condition type (**CTyp**) selected in the first screen (see Figure 2.47).

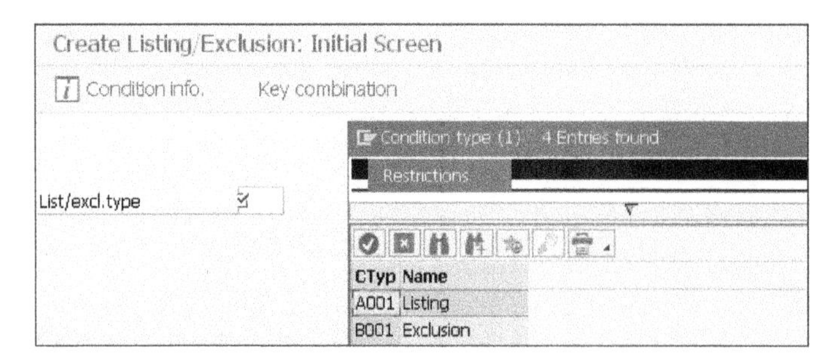

Figure 2.47 Listings and Exclusions

Listings can be used to specify a list of materials for a given customer, meaning that those specified customers are only allowed to purchase those specified materials and no others. If, during sales order creation, a record is found in the listing master data for the customer in the sales order, then the system will continue to search for the material in the listing master data for that customer. If found, the sales order will be allowed; if not found, an error message will be posted to say that the material has been excluded.

Exclusions are used to specify which materials can't be purchased by specific customers. If, during sales order creation, a record is found in the exclusion master data for the customer and material in the sales order, then the system will post an error message to say that the material has been excluded.

Note

Exclusions take priority over listings. As a result, if the combination of customer/material has been specified for listings but also specified for exclusions, then the material will be excluded.

The creation of listings and exclusions in SAP S/4HANA is extremely simple—you only need to specify the **Customer** and the **Material**, as shown in Figure 2.48.

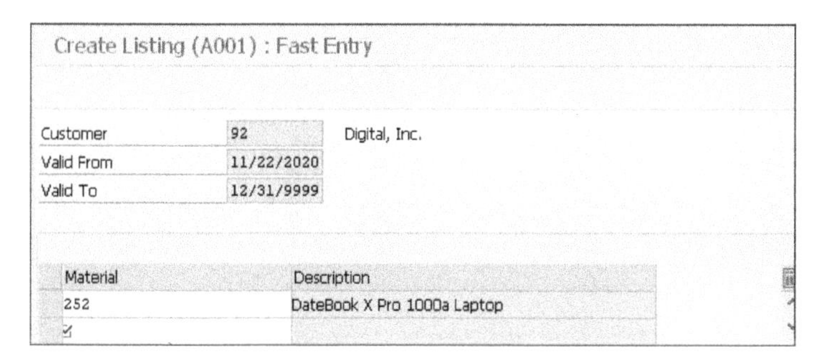

Figure 2.48 Listings and Exclusions Details

An example of an error in sales order entry when a material hasn't been listed is shown in Figure 2.49.

Figure 2.49 Listings Error Message

Customer-Material Information Record

The SAP S/4HANA customer-material info record is an important master data object where your customer's material information can be recorded, including your customer's part number, product description, and shipping information. Customer-material info records can be created using Transaction VB51 (Transaction VB52 to amend, Transaction VB53 to display).

In the example in Figure 2.50, the customer refers to material 252 as "LAPTOP-1". This means whenever we place a sales order in sales organization US30, distribution channel 20, for customer 92, we can simply type "LAPTOP-1" into the **Material No.** field, and the customer-material info record will be read and the material number automatically replaced by number 252.

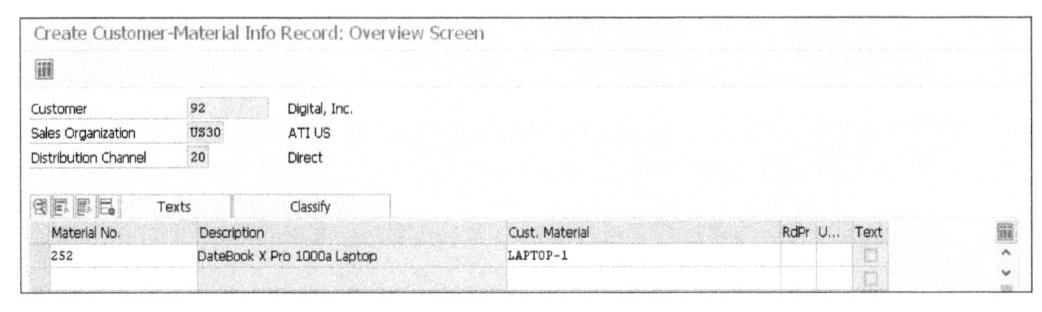

Figure 2.50 Customer-Material Info Record

Additional information can be recorded in the customer-material info record by double-clicking the line-item data, as shown in Figure 2.51.

Create Customer Material Info Record : Item Screen

Classify

Material	252		
	DateBook X Pro 1000a Laptop		
Sales Organization	US30	ATI US	
Distribution Channel	20	Direct	
Customer	92	Digital, Inc.	

Customer material

Customer Material	LAPTOP-1
Customer Description	Grey Datebook laptop
ETag	

Shipping

Plant	US20	
Delivery Priority	2	Normal item
Minimum Delivery Qty	5	EA

Partial delivery

Part.dlv./item		Underdel. Tolerance	%
Max.Part.Deliveries	3	Overdeliv. Tolerance	%
		Unlimited Tolerance	

Control data

Item usage

Units of Measure

Sales unit <-> EA

Additional Customer Materials

Customer Material Number	Customer Description of Material

Figure 2.51 Customer-Material Info Record Details

In the details screen, we can add many additional details such as the **Customer Description of Material**, the **Plant** that should always be used for shipping this product to this material, the **Delivery Priority**, the **Minimum Delivery Qty**, and whether partial deliveries are allowed and how many (**Part. dlv./item**). In this screen, we can even add an **Item usage**. This field can be used in conjunction with the material item category group of the material to determine the item category in the sales order. See Section 2.2.2 for more details on the item category group.

Output Determination

The condition technique can also be used for output determination, depending on how your SAP S/4HANA system is configured. Outputs (i.e., forms sent to customers by email, print, electronic data interchange [EDI], etc.) can use two methods of output: Business Rules Framework plus (BRFplus) or standard SAP outputs using the condition technique.

BRFplus outputs are configured using a set of freely defined rules, whereas standard SAP outputs are configured using the condition technique.

Standard SAP outputs can be set up using the following transactions:

- **Transaction VV11, Transaction VV12, Transaction VV13**
  Create, amend, and display, respectively, for sales documents (inquiries, quotation, sales orders).
- **Transaction VV21, Transaction VV22, Transaction VV23**
  Create, amend, and display, respectively, for delivery documents.
- **Transaction VV31, Transaction VV32, Transaction VV33**
  Create, amend, and display, respectively, for billing documents.

In Figure 2.52, Transaction VV11 is used to create output condition records for sales documents. Each type of sales document has a different output condition type to use.

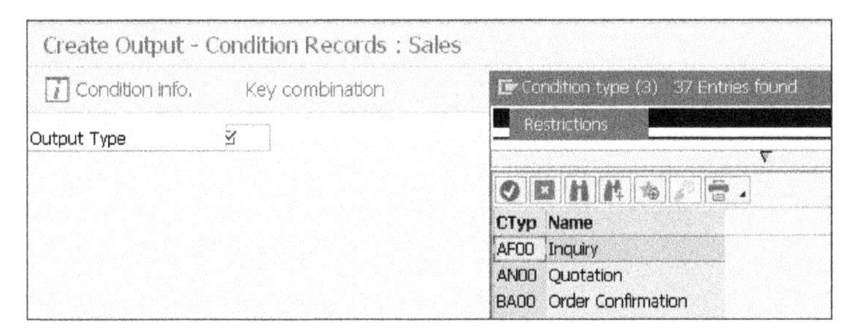

Figure 2.52 Create Output: Sales

The example in Figure 2.53 shows that for inquiries created in sales organization US30 and customer 92, the output should be sent to the sold-to party as a printed copy.

Create Condition Records (Inquiry): Fast Entry

Communication

Sales Organization US30 ATI US

Customer	Name	Funct	Partner	Medium	Date/Time	Lan...
92	Digital, Inc.	SP		1	1	

Figure 2.53 Create Output: Sales Details

The **Medium** field controls how the output is generated (in this case, printed); the **Date/Time** field determines when the output should be generated (in this case, with a periodically scheduled job, so the printout comes off with all other printouts at a given time, rather than as soon as the document is saved).

Double-clicking the line-item data or clicking the **Communication** button opens the details of the printout. The screen shown in Figure 2.54 is used to determine the number of printouts generated, where they are printed to, the name of the spool log file, and other details.

Create Condition Records (Inquiry) : Communication

Variable Key

Sales Org.	Customer	Description
US30	92	Digital, Inc.

Print Output

Output Device	LP01	Print immediately	☐
Number of messages	1	Release after output	☐
Spool request name			
Suffix 1			
Suffix 2			
SAP cover page	Do not print		
Recipient			
Department			
Cover Page Text			
Authorization			
Storage Mode	1 Print only		

Print Settings

Layout module	
Form	
SmartForm	

Figure 2.54 Create Output: Sales Communication Details

Text Determination

The condition technique can be used in sales and distribution to determine texts in the sales documents, delivery documents, and billing documents. The process for this is slightly different from the other mentioned data objects because there is no central transaction for creating texts. Instead, the texts are created from within the transactional documents.

Texts in transactional documents are available for manual entry for some text condition types or are determined from other master data objects, such as customer, material, or customer-material info records.

2.3 Service Business versus Hard Goods

Moving on from master data, we'll next explore an essential component of the sales process—the type of available sales order items. The most obvious separation of item types is between those that are deliverable, known as *delivery-related billing* in SAP S/4HANA and those that aren't deliverable, known as *order-related billing*.

> **Note**
>
> It's possible, though unusual, to have a deliverable item that is marked as being relevant for order-related billing. In this instance, the delivery document and the billing document would be generated directly from the sales order. The billing document would be generated regardless of the delivery status.

Following are examples of the two different kinds of scenarios:

- **Delivery-related billing**
  A standard sales order for goods to be delivered to a customer. The billing document is generated with reference to the goods that have been delivered, so it's logical that the delivery document should be billed.
- **Order-related billing**
  A standard sales order for services to be executed for a customer. This could be consultancy services, a contract to be billed, a subscription to a given service, or other types of orders. The important point is that normally a delivery isn't executed against the sales order. The billing document is generated against the sales order item rather than any other document.

For delivery-related billing items, the document flow will typically follow the path laid out in Figure 2.55.

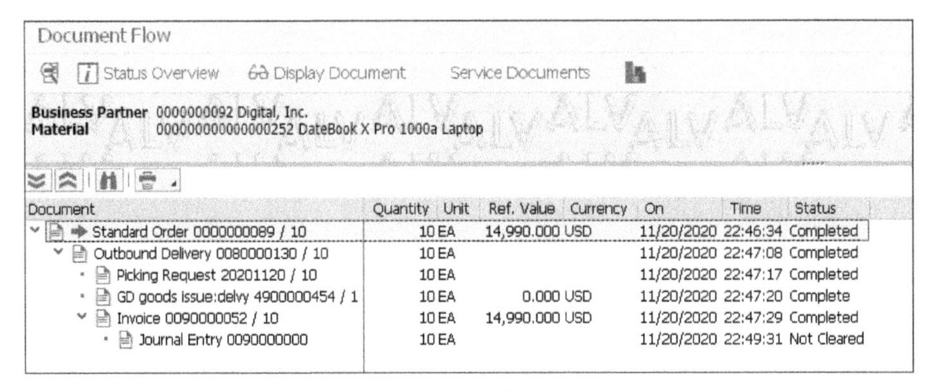

Figure 2.55 Delivery-Related Billing Document Flow

As you can see from the document flow, the invoice follows from the outbound delivery, denoting that this is a delivery-related billing item.

In contrast, Figure 2.56 shows an order-related billing document flow.

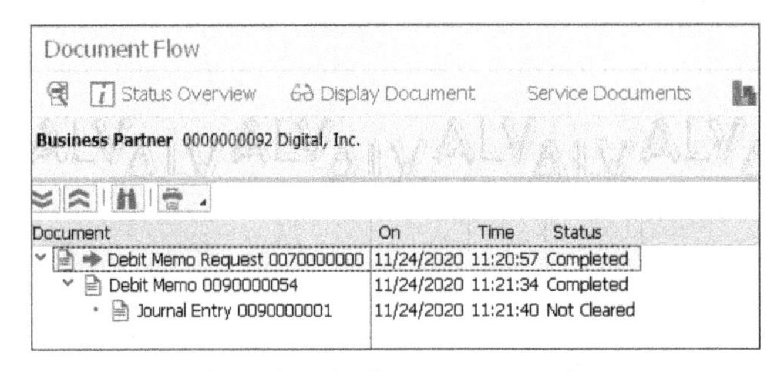

Figure 2.56 Order-Related Billing Document Flow

This example shows a debit memo request, which creates a debit memo billing document. As shown, there is no delivery document at all, and the billing document is created with reference to the sales order document (the debit memo request).

It's entirely possible for a single sales order to house both order-related billing items as well as delivery-related billing items.

2.4 Summary

Throughout this chapter, we've explored the key concepts around the setup of sales and distribution in SAP S/4HANA. From the identification of the master data building blocks, it should be clear now the vital role that master data plays in the smooth running of sales and distribution.

We've also touched on the main differences in types of sales order items that can be used in SAP S/4HANA. We'll be exploring this in much greater detail in the coming chapters.

In the next chapter, we will be investigating the details of the two available user interfaces for SAP S/4HANA – SAP GUI and SAP Fiori. This will provide you with a thorough understanding of how to set up your own SAP user interface for optimum productivity, as well as explaining some key concepts around the use of transactions of SAP Fiori apps.

Chapter 3
User Navigation

Mastering a system such as SAP S/4HANA takes time and practice. However, there are many simple tricks and tips that can help you on your way. Additionally, understanding the concepts and flows of the system can make expanding your SAP knowledge easier and more enjoyable.

In this chapter, we'll investigate how to navigate your way around the sales functions in SAP S/4HANA. This includes two user interfaces (UIs):

- **SAP GUI**
  This is the traditional graphical user interface that has been the mainstay of SAP systems in recent years.
- **SAP Fiori**
  This is the new web-based user experience (UX) introduced with SAP S/4HANA in the late part of 2015 and developed extensively ever since.

We'll also delve into the sales document itself to understand the basic structure of the document and how it's viewed in the two UIs.

3.1 Executing Transaction Codes with SAP GUI

SAP GUI is based on a menu tree with hierarchical nodes denoting the functional areas. For example, in Figure 3.1, to create a sales order, you would need to follow this menu path: **SAP Menu • Logistics • Sales and Distribution • Sales • Order • VA01 - Create.**

The VA01 code is used to start Transaction VA01 (Create Sales Order). Each transaction in SAP S/4HANA has its own transaction code in the SAP GUI. These can be reached by using the menu tree as in Figure 3.1 or by entering the transaction code in the command bar, as shown in Figure 3.2.

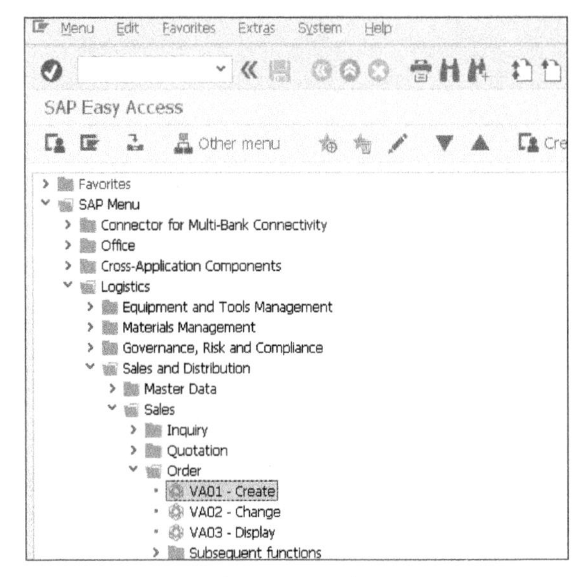

Figure 3.1 Create Sales Order in the SAP GUI Menu Tree

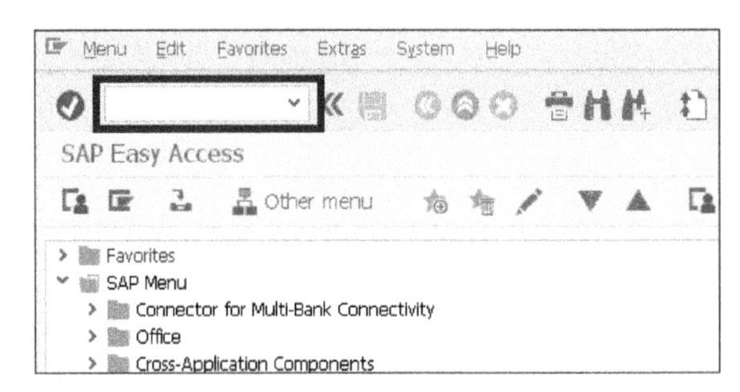

Figure 3.2 SAP GUI Command Bar

3.1.1 Updating Transaction Settings

We'll discuss more about entering transactions in the command bar later, but, first, you need to understand how to see the transaction codes. When you first log on to the SAP S/4HANA GUI, it will become clear that the transaction codes don't show in the menu tree—just the text description of the transaction is visible. To activate the display of the transaction code, choose **Extras • Settings** from the header menu, as shown in Figure 3.3.

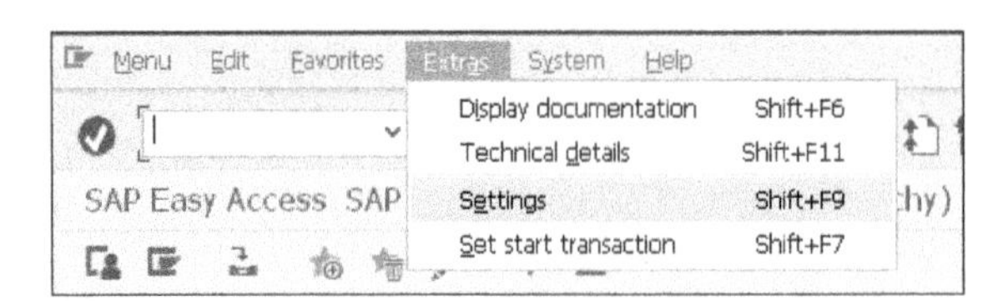

Figure 3.3 SAP GUI Menu Path for Displaying Transactions

From the popup box, select the **Display technical names** checkbox, as shown in Figure 3.4.

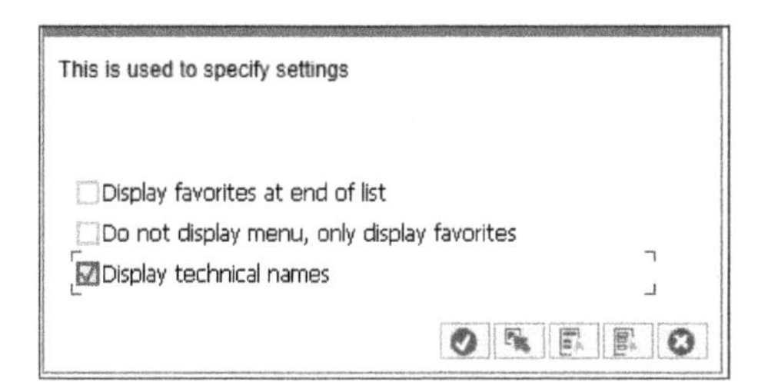

Figure 3.4 SAP GUI: Display Technical Names Setting

Once activated, your menu tree will display all the transaction codes next to each option.

Note

Transaction codes are derived from their original German terms. Take, for example, the following common transaction codes: VA01, ME21N, LT01, VL01N, and VF01.

The elements of these transaction codes can be teased out as follows:

- The "V" of VA01: This is an abbreviation of the original module that later evolved into the SD module. It stands for "Vertreib" which means *distribution*.
- The "A" stands for "Auftrag" which means *order*.
- The "L" stands for "Lieferung" which stands for *delivery*.
- The "F" stands for the fierce-looking German word "Finanzbuchhaltung," which means *financials*. (That one was easy!)
- The "M" stands for the equally concise-challenged (at least in English) term "Materialbuchhaltung" which means *material management*.
- The "E" stands for "Einkauf" which means *purchasing*.
- The "L" and "T" are the easiest ones for English speakers as they simply mean "Logistik," and "Transport," respectively.

Therefore, the inherent meaning for the above referenced transaction codes is as follows:

- VAOX: "Distribution Order"
- MEOXN: "Materials Management Purchasing"
- LTOX: "Logistics Transportation."
- VLOXN: "Distribution Delivery."
- VFOX: "Distribution Financials."

Now your German vocabulary has been enhanced as well!

3.1.2 Transactional Basics

You now have the option to follow the menu tree to open the transaction you need or to enter the transaction code into the command bar and press [Enter]. However, there are some considerations. If you're already in another transaction, you need to tell SAP S/4HANA how you would like to navigate to a different transaction: Do you want to keep the existing transaction open and start a new SAP GUI window with the new transaction, or do you want to exit the existing transaction and navigate directly to the new transaction? To follow each of these options, you need to prefix your transaction code with "/n" for exiting existing transaction and opening a new one, or "/o" for opening a new window.

For example, if you're currently in Transaction VA01 and want to open Transaction VK13, you can enter either of the following codes:

- **/nvk13**
  Exit existing Transaction VA01 without saving, and navigate directly to Transaction VK13.
- **/ovk13**
  Leave existing Transaction VA01 open, and create a new SAP GUI window with Transaction VK13 launched.

You can also use "/n" and "/o" without the transaction codes suffixed. By doing this, "/n" will return you to the main front screen menu, whereas "/o" will show you a list of your current open sessions and offer the opportunity to open a new SAP GUI window at the front screen menu.

Note
Using "/n" won't save your work, and no warning message will be issued.

Other prefixes also exist, which may be useful:

- **"/i"**
  Ends the current window.
- **"/nend"**
  Logs off all windows in the system.

While navigating around a specific transaction, you'll use the application toolbar a lot (see Figure 3.5).

Figure 3.5 SAP GUI Application Toolbar

The icons are defined in Table 3.1.

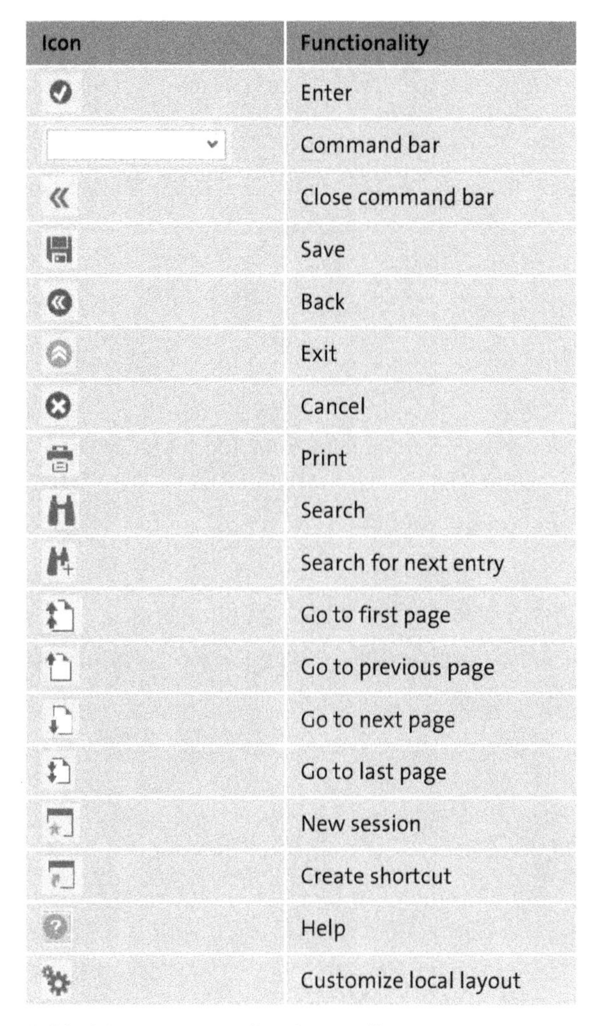

Icon	Functionality
	Enter
	Command bar
«	Close command bar
	Save
	Back
	Exit
	Cancel
	Print
	Search
	Search for next entry
	Go to first page
	Go to previous page
	Go to next page
	Go to last page
	New session
	Create shortcut
	Help
	Customize local layout

Table 3.1 SAP GUI Application Toolbar Icons

Further icons are available in the navigation area of the SAP GUI home screen, as shown in Figure 3.6.

Figure 3.6 SAP GUI Navigation Area

The icons in the navigation are defined in Table 3.2.

Icon	Functionality
	User menu
	SAP menu
	SAP business workplace
	Add to favorites
	Delete from favorites
	Change favorites
	Move favorite down
	Move favorite up

Table 3.2 Navigation Area Icons

3.1.3 Transaction Structures

Now let's look at running some specific sales transactions with a view to navigating around them. Figure 3.7 shows Transaction VA01.

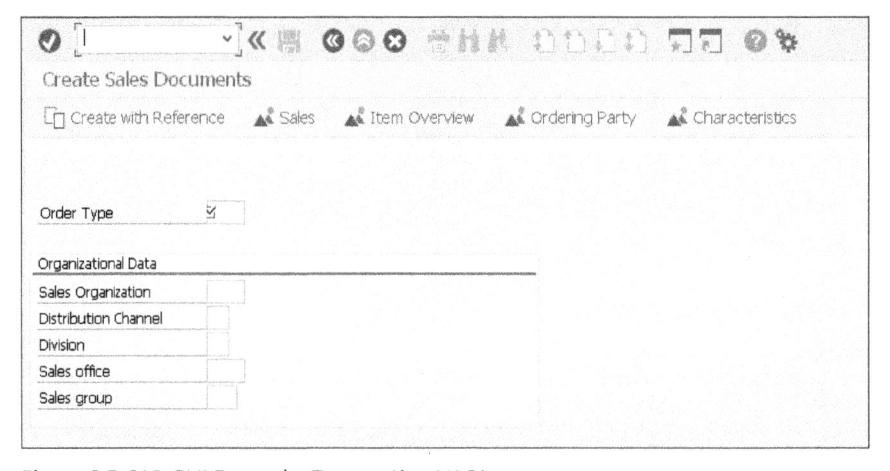

Figure 3.7 SAP GUI Example: Transaction VA01

The first thing to notice is that there is a small checkmark in a box in the **Order Type** field. This is used through SAP to denote that a value in this field is mandatory. Trying to run the transaction without entering all mandatory fields will result in an error message, as shown in Figure 3.8.

Fill out all required entry fields

Figure 3.8 SAP GUI Mandatory Fields Error Message

When you receive an error message in SAP, you can't progress any further without rectifying the error. You'll notice that error messages have a red exclamation mark next to them. There are also two other types of messages—warnings and information messages. Warning messages have a yellow exclamation mark and can be ignored by pressing Enter to move past it. Information messages have a green checkmark and are for information purposes only, so no further action is required.

3.1.4 Running Report Transactions

To progress past the Transaction VA01 screen, you enter the order type and press Enter. This is because SAP isn't being asked to carry out any action other than present the next screen to you. However, in other transactions, where SAP is required to select data based on inputs, as in a report, pressing Enter won't run the report. In these instances, you're "executing" the transaction, which demands that you select the **Clock** icon to submit the data. This can be seen by running Transaction VA05, for example, which is a report transaction, as shown in Figure 3.9.

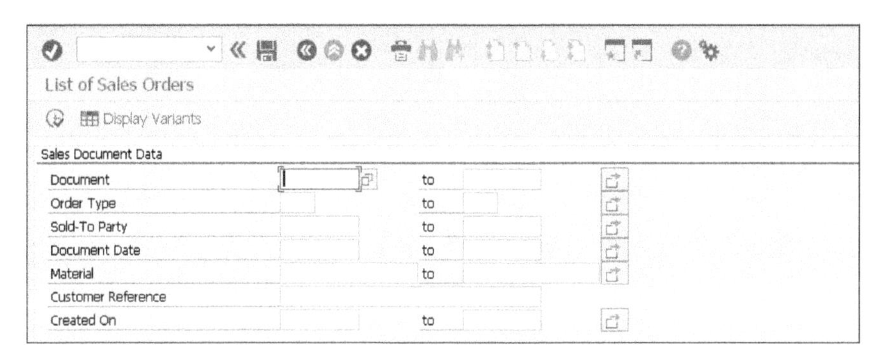

Figure 3.9 SAP GUI List Sales Orders: Transaction VA05

The **Clock** icon in the header area is used to execute the report after all your selection data is completed.

The first step in these kinds of reports is to add the selection parameters to search by. The good news here is that the techniques explored in this section apply across the board in all transactions in the SAP S/4HANA GUI, so you only need to learn these once. It's not essential to add these details, unless the field is marked as mandatory.

Note

A wildcard (* or +) can be used in your selection boxes. The * wildcard will search for everything in place of *. For example, entering "20*" in the field searches for everything beginning with 20, whereas entering "*20" searches for everything ending with 20. Entering "*20*" searches for everything containing the string "20". The + wildcard replaces a single character, so, for example, entering "20+" searches for three-character entries beginning with "20".

There are two different types of selection parameters:

- **Parameters**
  A parameter is a single field without multiple options, for example, **Customer Reference** in Figure 3.9.
- **Select-options**
  A select-option is a field where multiple selections are possible. For example, from Figure 3.9, the **Document** field has two field boxes with **to** in between and then another box to the right.

Select-option fields can be used in several ways:

1. To add a single value, type your value into the first box.
2. To add multiple single values, click on the **Multiple Selection** icon to the right of the boxes to display the multiple selection options, as shown in Figure 3.10.

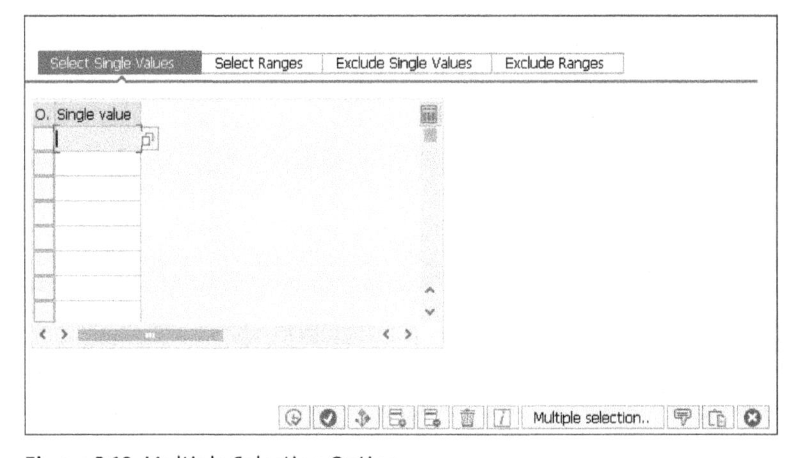

Figure 3.10 Multiple Selection Option

3. Add your multiple selections in the **Single value** field in the first tab. You can copy multiple values from your clipboard by selecting the **Clipboard** icon from the bottom right.
4. You can enter a range of values into the selection options by selecting the **Select Ranges** tab, as shown in Figure 3.11.

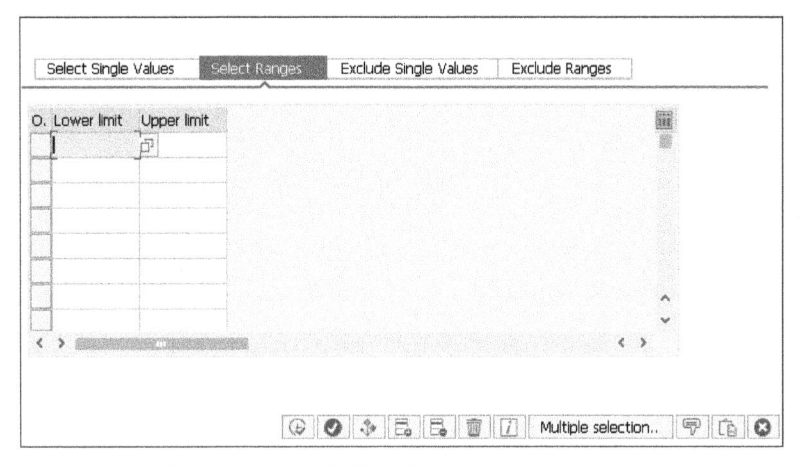

Figure 3.11 Multiple Selection Option: Select Ranges

5. Exclude single values, multiple values, or a range. The select options can be used to exclude values and ranges in the same way as including values, by selecting the **Exclude Single Values** and **Exclude Ranges** tabs.

After your select-options are completed, you can save your selections as a variant by clicking the **Save** icon. This triggers the **Variant Attributes** screen shown in Figure 3.12.

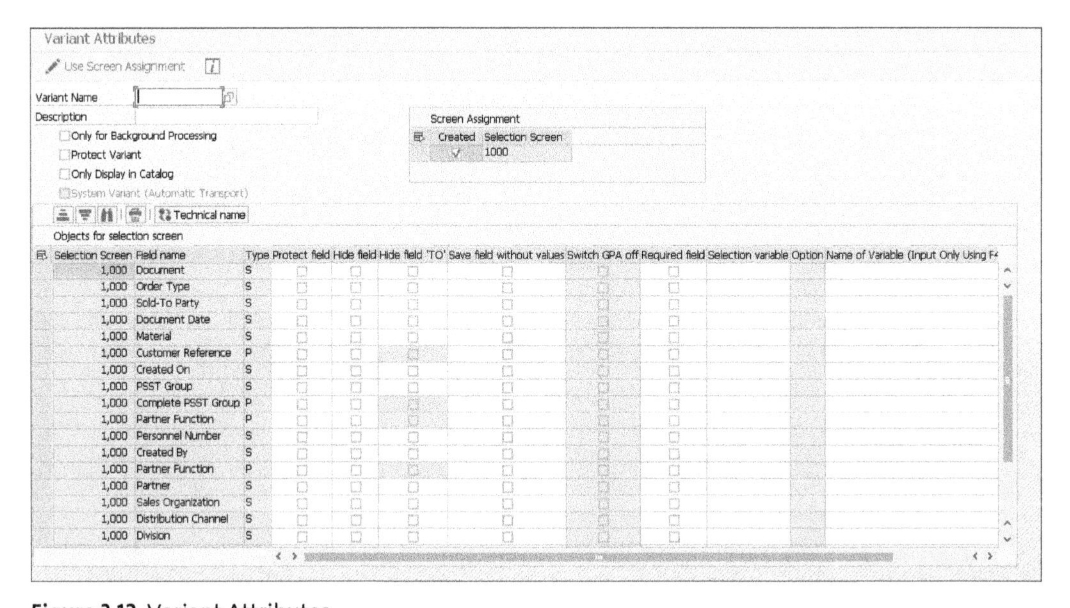

Figure 3.12 Variant Attributes

Name your variant (without spaces) in the **Variant Name** field, and add a **Description** for it. Many additional attributes can be used here, such as hiding and protecting fields when this variant is used. Additionally, you can make dynamic selections. For example, in a date field in the **Objects for selection screen** section, click in the **Selection variable** field, as shown in Figure 3.13.

Objects for selection screen

Selection Screen	Field name	Type	Protect field	Hide field	Hide field 'TO'	Save field without values	Switch GPA ...	Required field	Selection variable	Option	Name of Variable (Input Only Using F4
1,000	Document	S	☐	☐	☐	☐	☐	☐			
1,000	Order Type	S	☐	☐	☐	☐	☐	☐			
1,000	Sold-To Party	S	☐	☐	☐	☐	☐	☐			
1,000	Document Date	S	☐	☐	☐	☐	☐	☐			
1,000	Material	S	☐	☐	☐	☐	☐	☐			
1,000	Customer Reference	P	☐	☐	☐	☐	☐	☐			
1,000	Created On	S	☐	☐	☐	☐	☐	☐			

Figure 3.13 Variants: Using Selection Variables

Once in the correct field, click on the dropdown icon in the field, or press F4. This will bring up the options shown in Figure 3.14.

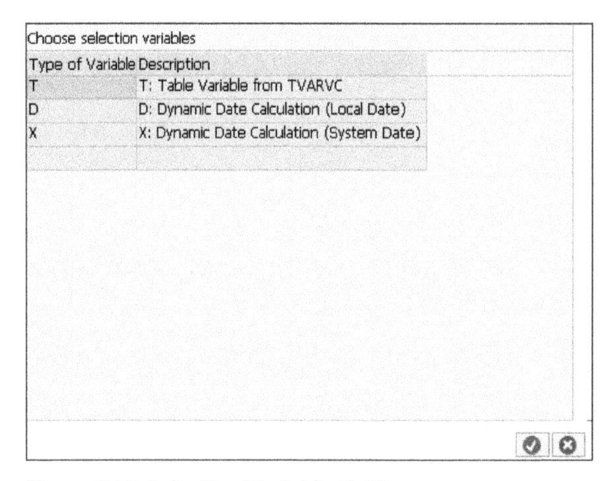

Figure 3.14 Selection Variable Options

The three options are described as follows:

- **T: Table Variable from TVARVC**
  This option is often used when running the transaction from within a program. The standard SAP table TVARVC can hold variables that can be read from these programs. This is a useful way of running these transactions without having to "hard code" values into your selections (i.e., the values can be changed in table TVARVC rather than directly in the transaction).
- **D: Dynamic Date Calculation (Local Date)**
  This selection will read the time and date assigned to your local user and calculate the values based on that.
- **X: Dynamic Date Calculation (System Date)**
  This selection will read the time and date assigned to the SAP system and calculate the values based on that.

All three options work in conjunction with the next field: **Name of Variable**. In practice, you're more likely to select **D** or **X** than **T**.

After you've chosen the selection variable, you'll need to select an appropriate entry form the **Name of Variable** field. In Figure 3.15 and Figure 3.16, a date variable (**Selection variable** "D") has been used, with the resulting options shown in the **Name of Variable** field.

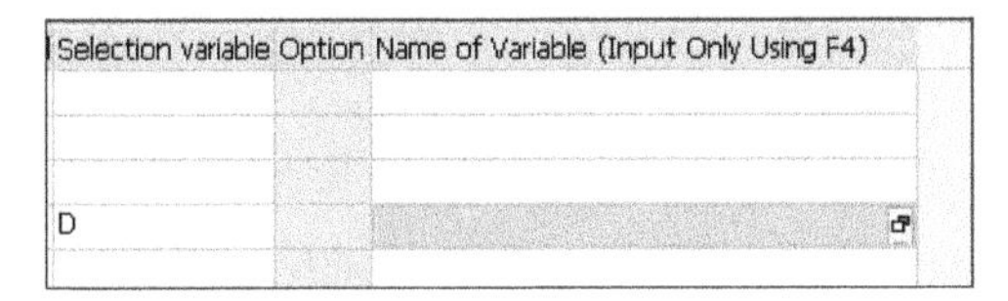

Figure 3.15 Selection Variable: Name of Variable

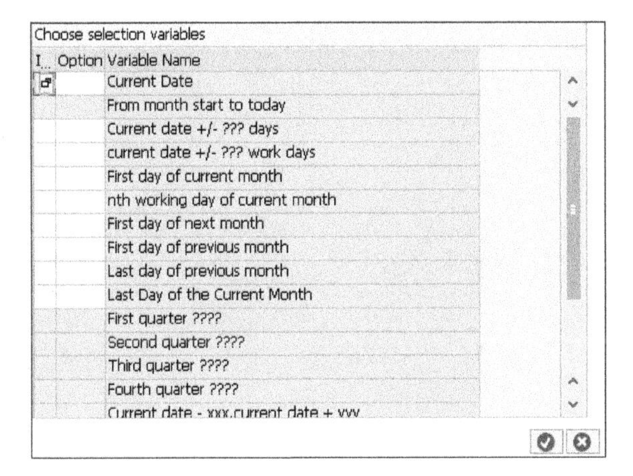

Figure 3.16 Date Selection Variable Options

From Figure 3.16, you can choose how the system calculates the date in that field when your variant has been run. For example, if you select **Current Date**, then the current date can be chosen by double-clicking the option. Additionally, by using the **Indicator** and **Option** columns, further options are available; for example, the current date can be excluded, all dates can be read except the current date, and so on.

Other options are also available here, as signified by multiple question marks. If you double-click one of these options, then further input is required. For example, selecting **Current date +/- ??? days** will open a new input box with data calculation parameters, as shown in Figure 3.17.

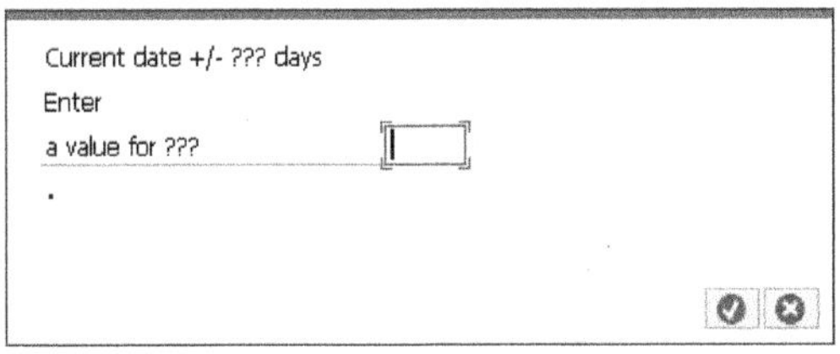

Current date +/- ??? days
Enter
a value for ???

Figure 3.17 Date Calculation Parameters

The number of days before or after the current date can be added in this selection. To select a number of days before, use the minus sign.

We mentioned earlier that select-options allow you to enter a range (e.g., from 01/01/2021 to 05/31/2021). A range can also be used in selection variables by scrolling down in the **Choose selection variables** box to see further options, as shown in Figure 3.18.

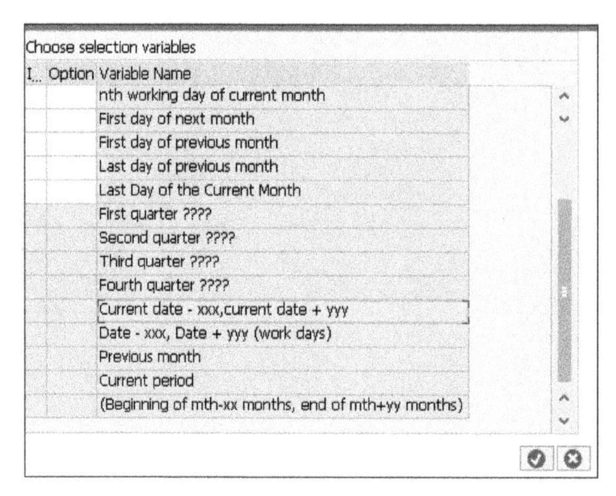

Figure 3.18 Selection Variables for Ranges

By selecting an entry such as **Current date – xxx,current date + yyy**, you get a slightly different date calculation parameter option in which you can add the number of days for the from and to options, as shown in Figure 3.19.

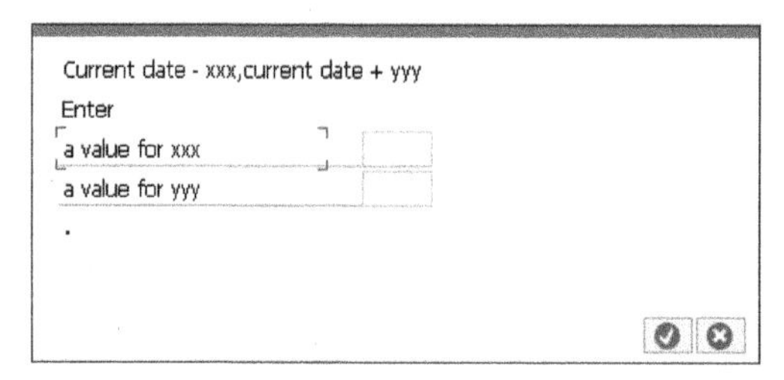

Figure 3.19 Date Calculation Parameters for Ranges

After all your variant selections are complete, save your variant; you'll be returned to the initial screen of the transaction. From now on, when using this transaction, you can always find your variant by clicking on the **Get Variants** icon. This will bring up a list of variants for you to select from, as shown in Figure 3.20.

Figure 3.20 Variant Selection

By double-clicking your variant, SAP will populate all the fields, and you're now ready to execute the report.

3.2 Running SAP Fiori Apps with the SAP Fiori Launchpad

Unlike earlier versions of SAP, SAP S/4HANA comes with a free-to-use intelligent UI called SAP Fiori. SAP Fiori runs through a web interface and offers a unique way of exploring SAP S/4HANA for sales and distribution.

If you're using SAP Fiori as your main UI with SAP S/4HANA, you're likely to be logging on through your chosen browser. However, you can also access SAP Fiori from within your SAP GUI by entering Transaction /n/UI2/FLP in the command bar. This will launch the SAP Fiori homepage, as shown in Figure 3.21.

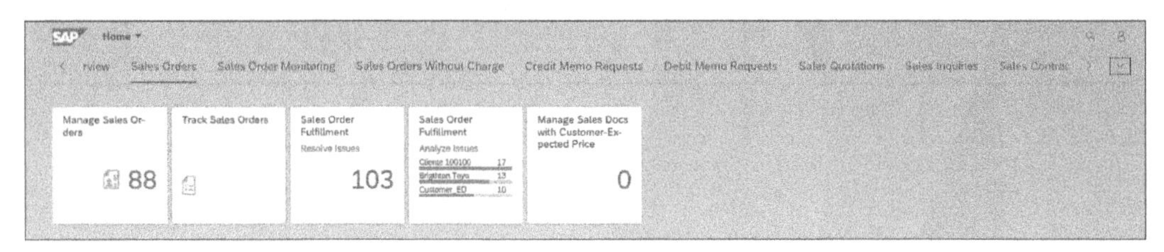

Figure 3.21 SAP Fiori Homepage

It's likely that your homepage will look different from that shown in Figure 3.21 as SAP Fiori is entirely customizable. We've already explored the architecture of SAP Fiori in Chapter 1 in detail. In this section, we'll explore the SAP Fiori apps that are available in sales and distribution and how you can make the most of using SAP Fiori as your default, but optional, UI.

3.2.1 Setting Up SAP Fiori for Maximum Productivity

SAP Fiori is a completely different way of working from the SAP GUI. The intention with SAP Fiori is to present the work to you so you don't have to search through the system to find it. Additionally, SAP Fiori is a role-based solution, so the UI will differ according to the roles assigned to you as a user. As a sales and distribution user, your visual representation of the system will be entirely different from, for example, a finance user or a manufacturing user. As already discussed in Chapter 1, this is achieved using user groups, which house SAP Fiori tiles. The tiles are used to display key information as well as to launch SAP Fiori apps. Additionally, the command bar in the SAP GUI can be activated in SAP Fiori as well, as shown in Figure 3.22.

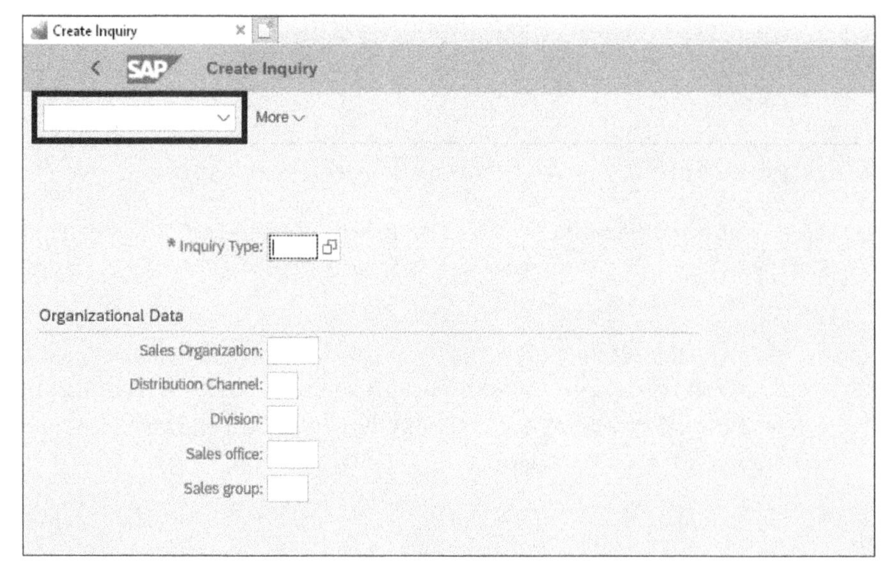

Figure 3.22 SAP Fiori Command Bar

To activate the command bar, open a transactional SAP Fiori app, such as Create Inquiry, and follow the menu path shown in Figure 3.23.

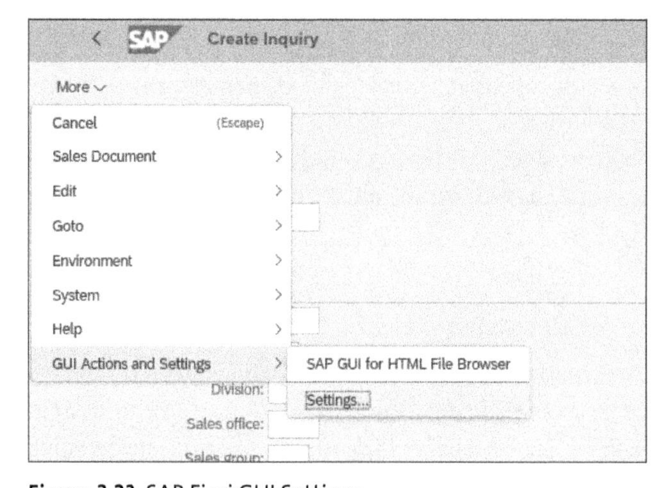

Figure 3.23 SAP Fiori GUI Settings

After the dialog box appears, select the **Show OK Code Field** option, and then click **Save**, as shown in Figure 3.24.

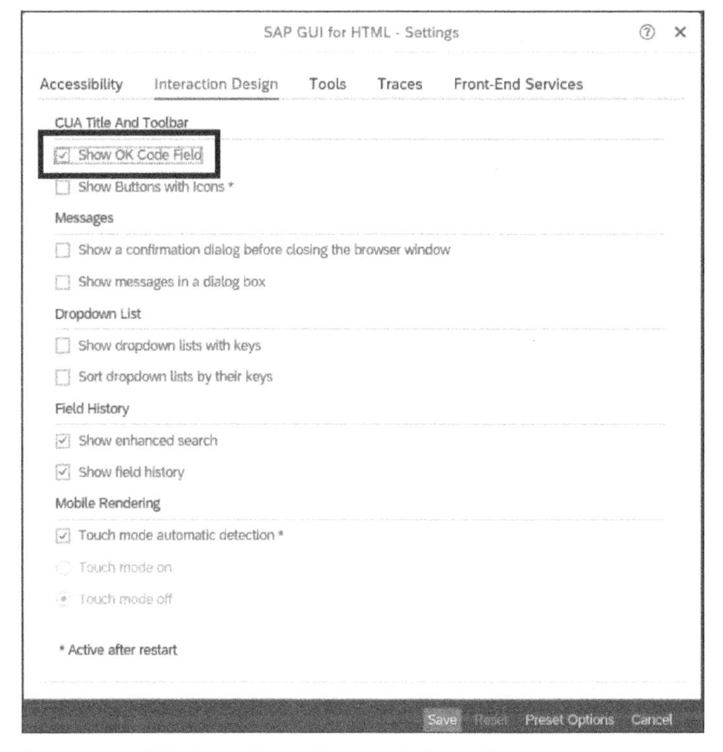

Figure 3.24 SAP Fiori: Show OK Code Field Setting

The command bar is now available for you to use in SAP Fiori in all transactional apps, in the same way as in SAP GUI.

More settings are available for you to personalize your SAP Fiori experience. By clicking on the **Person** icon in the top right of the screen, you can open the additional settings menu, as shown in Figure 3.25.

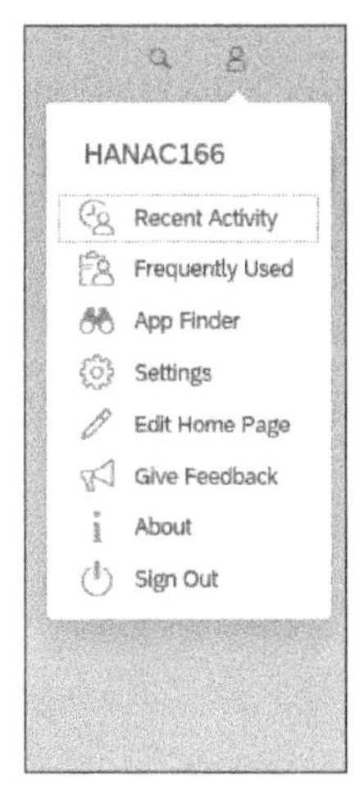

Figure 3.25 SAP Fiori User Settings

From here, you can navigate to apps you've recently used (**Recent Activity** option) and apps you frequently use (**Frequently Used** option).

By selecting **App Finder**, you can search for SAP Fiori apps from within a specific catalog, which is a list of apps available to your specific role; within a user menu; or within the SAP menu. Figure 3.26 shows the **App Finder** screen using a catalog search.

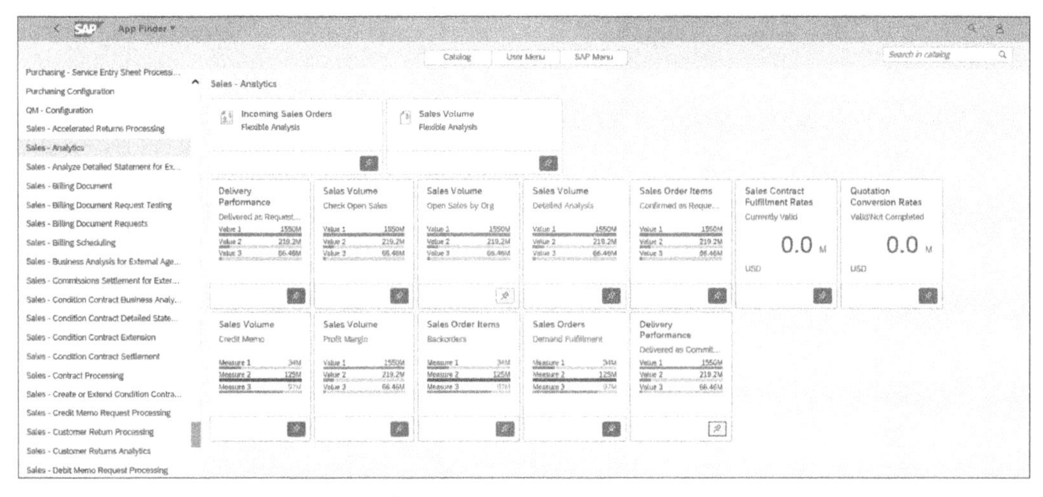

Figure 3.26 SAP Fiori App Finder: Catalog Search

All the catalogs assigned to your role are shown on the left-hand side of the screen. In this example, the **Sales - Analytics** catalog has been selected, and you can see that there are numerous tiles representing apps assigned to that catalog. The tiles showing with the blue pin in the bottom-left corner have already been assigned to a user group in your profile and therefore can already be seen. However, from Figure 3.26, you can see that there are two tiles—**Sales Volume – Detailed Analysis** and **Delivery Performance – Delivered as Committed**—which aren't assigned to any user group. From this screen, you can add these by clicking on the white background pin in the bottom left of the tile. Clicking here opens a popup box that asks which user group you would like to add the tile to, as shown in Figure 3.27.

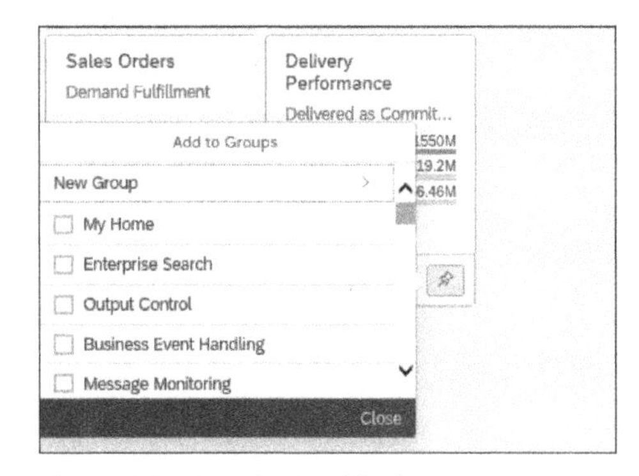

Figure 3.27 SAP Fiori: Add Tile to Group

From here, you can select the user group to add the tile to or create a new group. By selecting **New Group**, you'll be asked for the name of your new group, as shown in Figure 3.28.

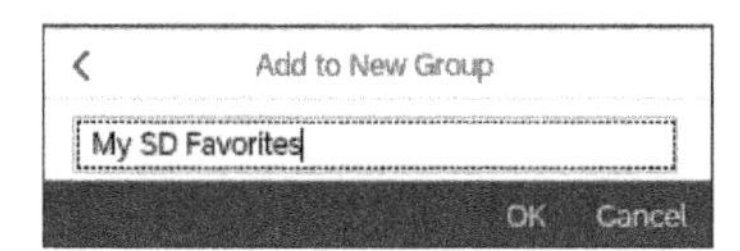

Figure 3.28 SAP Fiori: Add New Group

Once done, the new group will now be available for viewing in your user groups list, as shown in Figure 3.29.

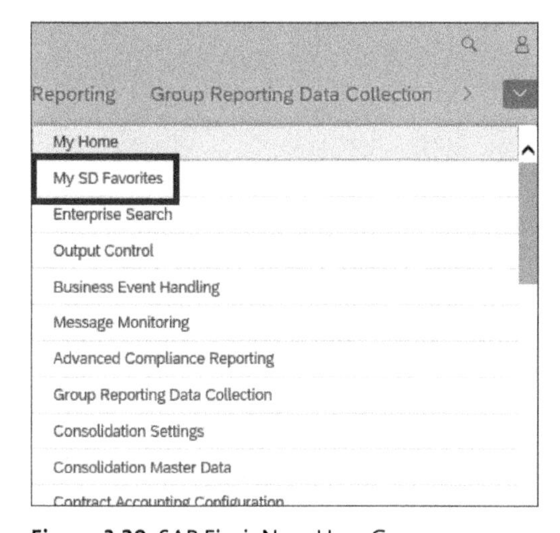

Figure 3.29 SAP Fiori: New User Group

From your additional user settings, you can also amend the settings for visual display and appearance by selecting the **Settings** option shown earlier in Figure 3.25. This opens the **Settings** menu, from where you can amend the appearance of your SAP Fiori screen and the language and regional settings. From here, you can also set some default values for populating in fields within SAP Fiori apps by using the **Default Values** option, as shown in Figure 3.30.

A further useful setting is the **Edit Home Page** function from the user settings options shown earlier in Figure 3.25. By selecting this option, you can amend the look and feel of your homepage to personalize it to your requirements, as shown in Figure 3.31.

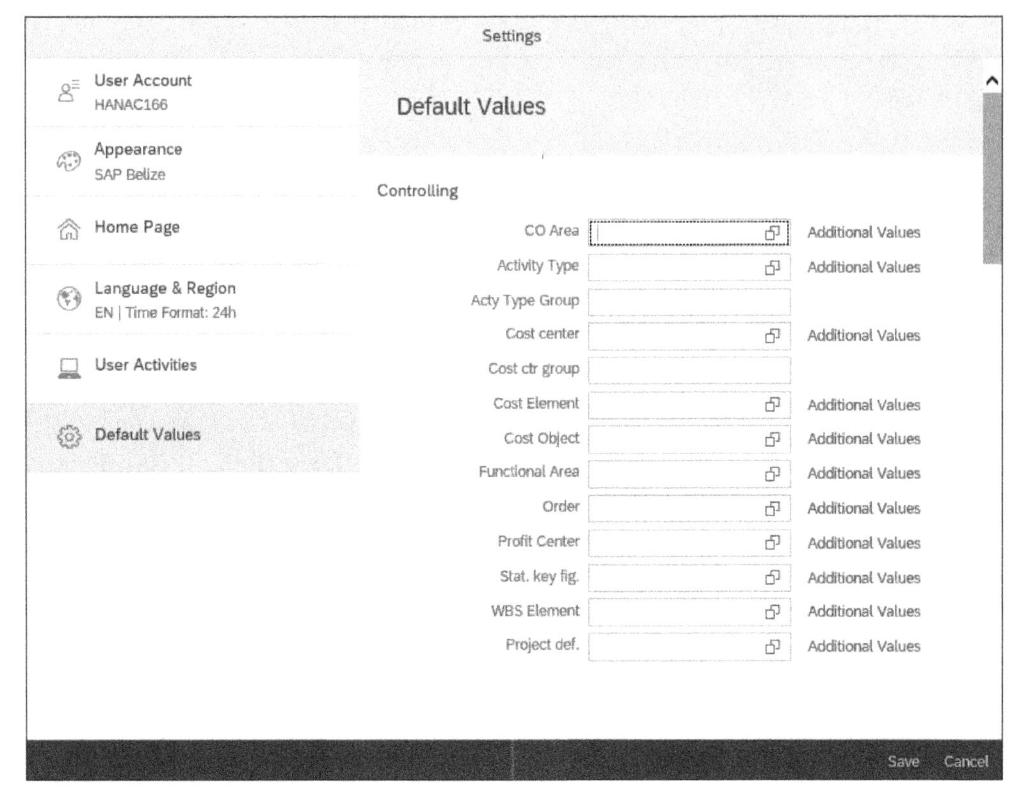

Figure 3.30 SAP Fiori: Default Values Option

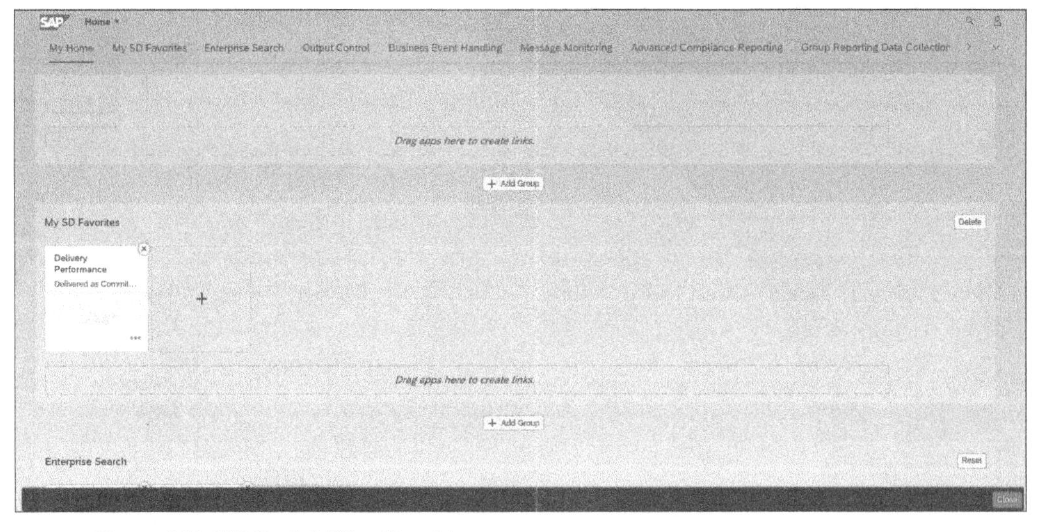

Figure 3.31 SAP Fiori: Editing Your Homepage

From within this screen, you can add or remove tiles to a specific user group, create new groups, delete user groups from your personalized view, and create links to apps instead of tiles. For example, to add the tile for the Manage Sales Inquiries app to the new user group **My SD Favorites**, which we created earlier, you click the **+** button from within that user group to open the app finder, as shown in Figure 3.26. From the app finder, you search for "Manage Sales Inquiries" and pin the tile to add it to the group, as shown in Figure 3.32.

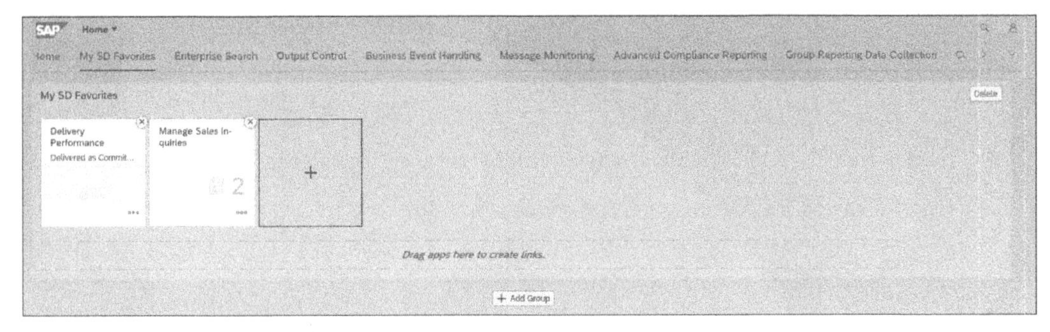

Figure 3.32 SAP Fiori: Amending the Homepage

You can then drag the new tile on to the **Drag apps here to create links.** area to represent that app as a link instead of a tile, as shown in Figure 3.33.

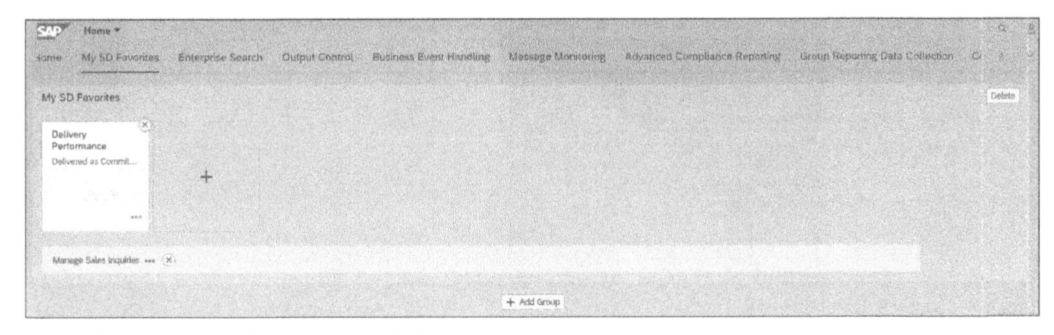

Figure 3.33 SAP Fiori: Creating Links in the Homepage

After you've completed your changes, select **Close** in the bottom right of the screen, and your new homepage will be activated, as shown in Figure 3.34.

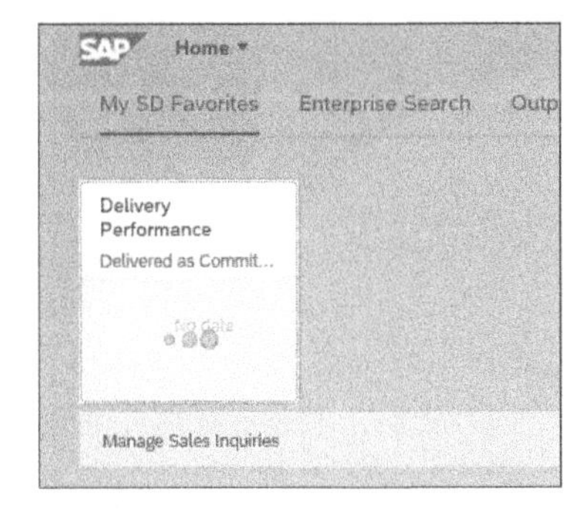

Figure 3.34 SAP Fiori: Activated New Homepage

Note

At any point in an SAP Fiori app, you can always navigate back to your previous screen by selecting the back arrow at the top left of the screen. Selecting the **SAP** button next to it will return you to your home screen.

3.2.2 SAP Fiori Apps for Sales and Distribution

Now that the homepage is fully updated and personalized to your own specific requirements, it's time to look at some useful SAP Fiori apps for sales and distribution.

First, however, let's consider some notes regarding how to navigate inside a standard SAP Fiori app. Let's work with the Manage Sales Inquiries app to explore some navigation tips. The tile has dynamic data displayed on the front of it, in this case, telling the user how many inquiries are in the system. In the example in Figure 3.35, there are two inquiries in the system.

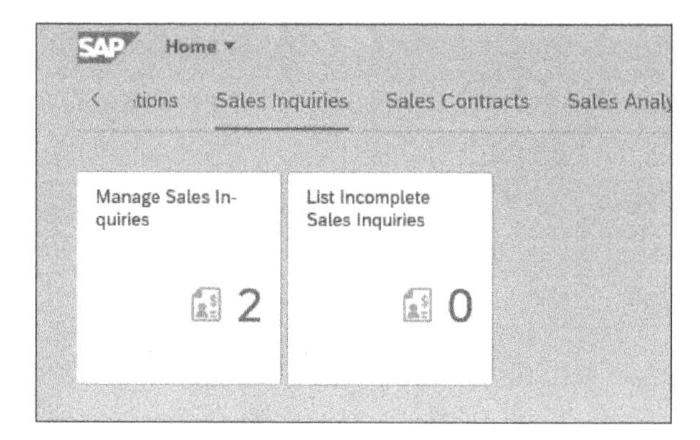

Figure 3.35 Manage Sales Inquiries Tile

This dynamic data is displayed on many analytical apps in SAP Fiori and can take the form of straightforward numbers such as we see here, or small graphs, all based on real-time analytics.

Once inside the app, you'll see that the top of the screen houses the filters bar, which is a common setting in all such SAP Fiori apps in the sales and distribution area. Here you can set your filters according to selection parameters to display the inquiries you want to see, as shown in Figure 3.36.

Additional filters are available by clicking the **Adapt Filters** option on the right-hand side of the screen. Similar to the SAP GUI, after you've set the filters you would like, you can, if needed, save the filters in the same way you would save a variant in SAP GUI—click the down arrow next to the **Standard** option to save your filters for future use, as shown in Figure 3.37.

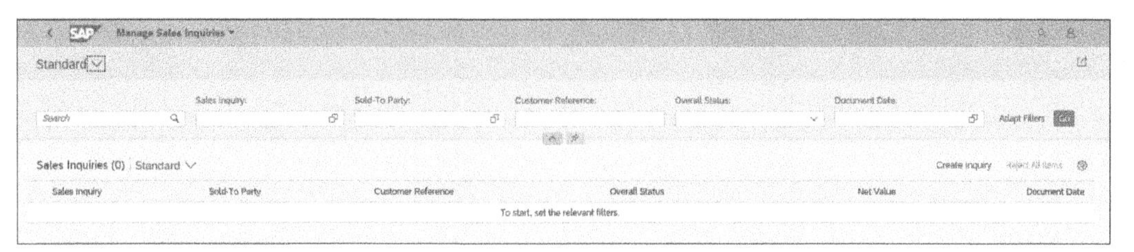

Figure 3.36 SAP Fiori Manage Sales Inquiries App: Filters

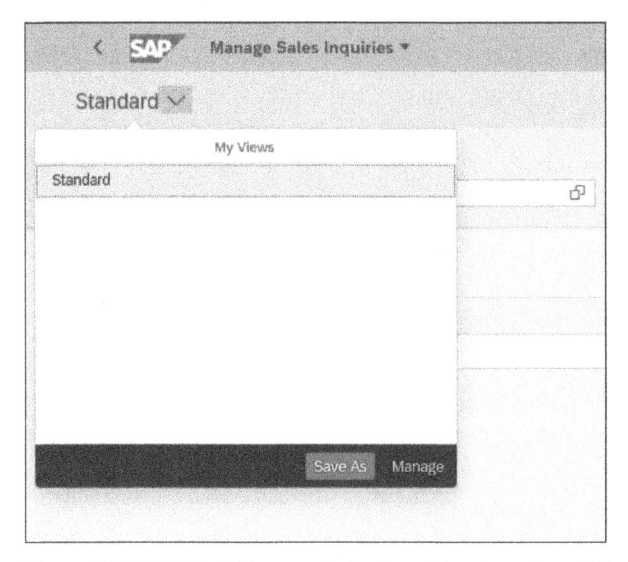

Figure 3.37 SAP Fiori Manage Sales Inquiries App: Save Filters

When you save your filters, you have the option to name your view as well as make the view the default view, public, and applied automatically on opening the app.

When you're happy with your filters, press [Enter] or click **Go** to run the report.

Another useful feature is in the top right-hand corner of the screen, where you have the **Share** option, to send the results via email or to save the view of this app as your own SAP Fiori tile, with its own name and description and entered into the user group of your choice (see Figure 3.38).

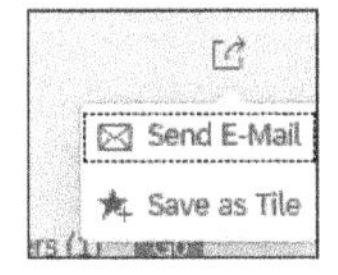

Figure 3.38 Send Email and Save as Tile Options

There are a few more options to explain in the display view of the results, as shown in Figure 3.39.

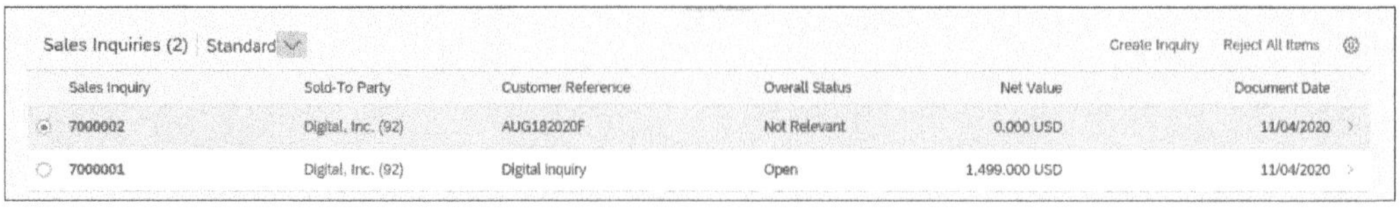

Sales Inquiries (2) Standard | Create Inquiry | Reject All Items

Sales Inquiry	Sold-To Party	Customer Reference	Overall Status	Net Value	Document Date
7000002	Digital, Inc. (92)	AUG182020F	Not Relevant	0.000 USD	11/04/2020
7000001	Digital, Inc. (92)	Digital Inquiry	Open	1,499.000 USD	11/04/2020

Figure 3.39 Display View Settings

The first thing to note is the **Settings** icon (gear) on the far-right side of the screen, from which you can amend the display by adding and removing columns and setting sort orders and filters. After you have the columns in the correct format, the display view can be saved and set as default or public in the same way as we set the filters earlier. To do this, click the down arrow next to **Standard** just above the display of the results.

By clicking on one of the lines, you'll navigate to Transaction VA13 (Display Inquiry). This drilldown functionality is common to many SAP Fiori apps. Additional options—**Create Inquiry** and **Reject All Items**—are available without having to enter Transaction VA12 (Change Inquiry), and these options are displayed above the results on the right side of the screen. When you select the radio button of one of the line items, the **Reject All Items** option becomes available, which can be used to automatically reject the inquiry without any further action. The **Create Inquiry** option is always available and will navigate you to Transaction VA11 (Create Inquiry).

This should give you a basic overview of how SAP Fiori works. Because the design elements are common across all SAP Fiori apps, you can apply the same techniques everywhere.

As discussed in Chapter 1, there are three types of apps in SAP Fiori: transactional apps, analytical apps, and factsheet apps. Transactional apps are often simply web representations of the transactions from the SAP GUI, so we should focus our attention on analytical apps and factsheet apps.

3.2.3 My Sales Overview

My Sales Overview analytical app contains a lot of information and is a useful hub for starting your SAP Fiori journey in sales and distribution (see Figure 3.40).

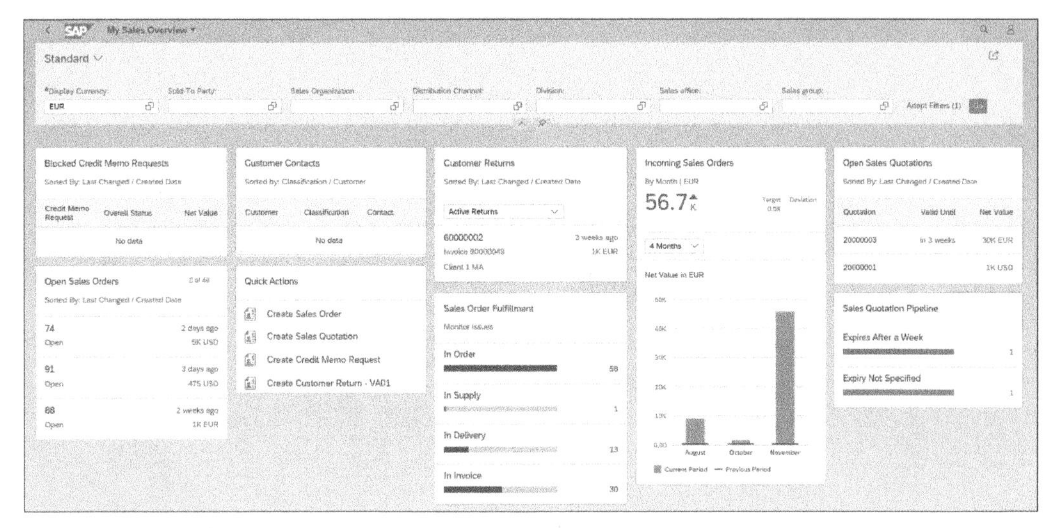

Figure 3.40 My Sales Overview App

All the data you see in the app is separated into "cards" that contain links to other transactional and factsheet apps. For example, the **Quick Actions** card has links to creating a sales order, quotation, credit memo request, or customer return. The data is all selected according to the filters you set in the filters bar; again, these can be personalized and defaulted for your user.

3.2.4 Sales Order Fulfillment Issues

From within the My Sales Overview app, it's also possible to navigate directly to other analytical apps, such as the Sales Order Fulfillment – Monitor Issues app. This is an extremely useful app as it shows errors and issues in each step of the order-to-cash process. Drilldown functionality is available here to open the issues and resolve them via quick action buttons (see Figure 3.41).

From within the app's screen, you have the ability to filter the issues by **Total Issues, In Order, In Supply, In Delivery**, and **In Invoice**, just by clicking on the relevant selection bubble at the top of the screen.

By clicking on one of the line items, you can navigate to the SAP document in question in a factsheet app. You can also take quick actions against the document from within your factsheet app, or from the **Sales Order Fulfillment Issues** screen itself. If a line is selected, SAP will recognize the actions that are available for that document and offer them as quick links (see Figure 3.42).

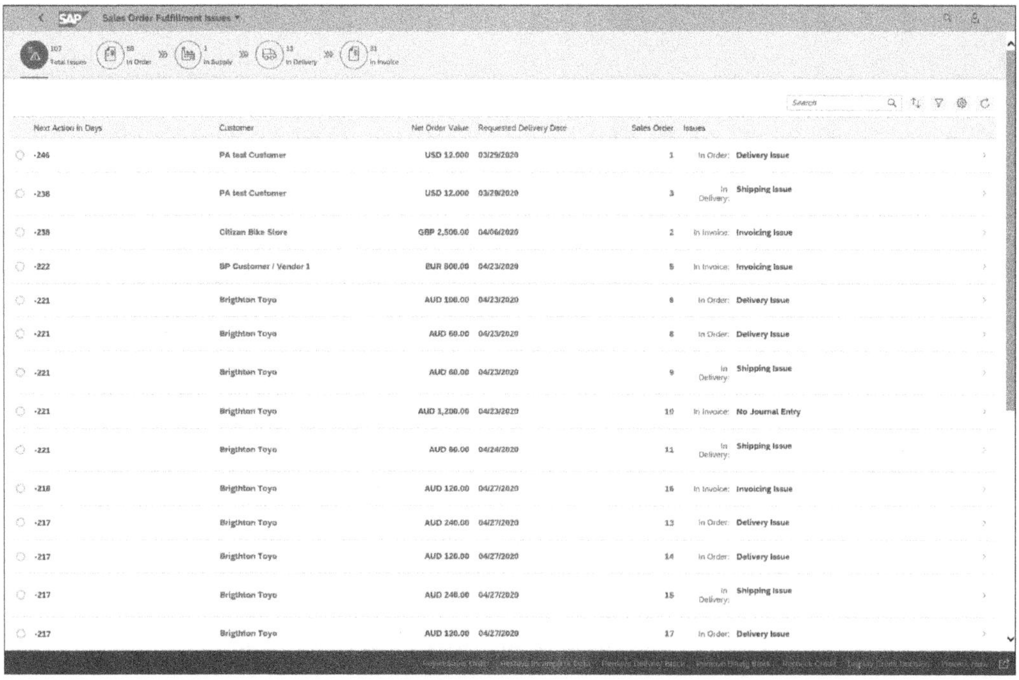

Sales Order Fulfillment Issues

107 Total Issues · 58 In Order · 1 In Supply · 13 In Delivery · 31 In Invoice

Next Action in Days	Customer	Net Order Value	Requested Delivery Date	Sales Order	Issues
-246	PA test Customer	USD 12.000	03/29/2020	1	In Order: Delivery Issue
-238	PA test Customer	USD 12.000	03/29/2020	3	In Delivery: Shipping Issue
-238	Citizen Bike Store	GBP 2,506.00	04/06/2020	2	In Invoice: Invoicing Issue
-222	BP Customer / Vendor 1	EUR 800.00	04/23/2020	5	In Invoice: Invoicing Issue
-221	Brigthton Toyo	AUD 100.00	04/23/2020	6	In Order: Delivery Issue
-221	Brigthton Toyo	AUD 60.00	04/23/2020	8	In Order: Delivery Issue
-221	Brigthton Toyo	AUD 60.00	04/23/2020	9	In Delivery: Shipping Issue
-221	Brigthton Toyo	AUD 1,200.00	04/23/2020	10	In Invoice: No Journal Entry
-221	Brigthton Toyo	AUD 60.00	04/24/2020	11	In Delivery: Shipping Issue
-218	Brigthton Toyo	AUD 120.00	04/27/2020	16	In Invoice: Invoicing Issue
-217	Brigthton Toyo	AUD 240.00	04/27/2020	13	In Order: Delivery Issue
-217	Brigthton Toyo	AUD 120.00	04/27/2020	14	In Order: Delivery Issue
-217	Brigthton Toyo	AUD 240.00	04/27/2020	15	In Delivery: Shipping Issue
-217	Brigthton Toyo	AUD 120.00	04/27/2020	17	In Order: Delivery Issue

Figure 3.41 Sales Order Fulfillment Issues App

Sales Order Fulfillment Issues

103 Total Issues · 58 In Order · 1 In Supply · 13 In Delivery · 31 In Invoice

Next Action in Days	Customer	Net Order Value	Requested Delivery Date	Sales Order	Issues
-246	PA test Customer	USD 12.000	03/29/2020	1	In Order: Delivery Issue
-221	Brigthton Toyo	AUD 100.00	04/23/2020	6	In Order: Delivery Issue
-221	Brigthton Toyo	AUD 60.00	04/23/2020	8	In Order: Delivery Issue
-217	Brigthton Toyo	AUD 240.00	04/27/2020	13	In Order: Delivery Issue
-217	Brigthton Toyo	AUD 120.00	04/27/2020	14	In Order: Delivery Issue
-217	Brigthton Toyo	AUD 120.00	04/27/2020	17	In Order: Delivery Issue
-198	Customer_ED	USD 0.000	05/17/2020	19	In Order: Incomplete, Delivery Issue, Unconfirmed Quantities
-196	TEST 2002 CUSTOMER	USD 7,425.000	05/20/2020	26	In Order: Delivery Issue
-195	Cliente 01	BRL 100.00	05/20/2020	20	In Order: Delivery Issue
-195	Cliente 01	BRL 100.00	05/20/2020	21	In Order: Delivery Issue
-195	Cliente 01	BRL 100.00	05/20/2020	22	In Order: Delivery Issue
-195	Cliente 01	BRL 200.00	05/20/2020	23	In Order: Delivery Issue
-195	Cliente 01	BRL 1,000,000,000.00	05/20/2020	24	In Order: Delivery Issue
-194	Cliente 100100	BRL 110.00	05/21/2020	28	In Order: Delivery Issue
-190	Cliente 100100	BRL 20.00	05/25/2020	34	In Order: Delivery Issue

Reject Sales Order · Resolve Incomplete Data · Remove Delivery Block · Remove Billing Block · Recheck Credit · Display Credit Decision · Process Flow

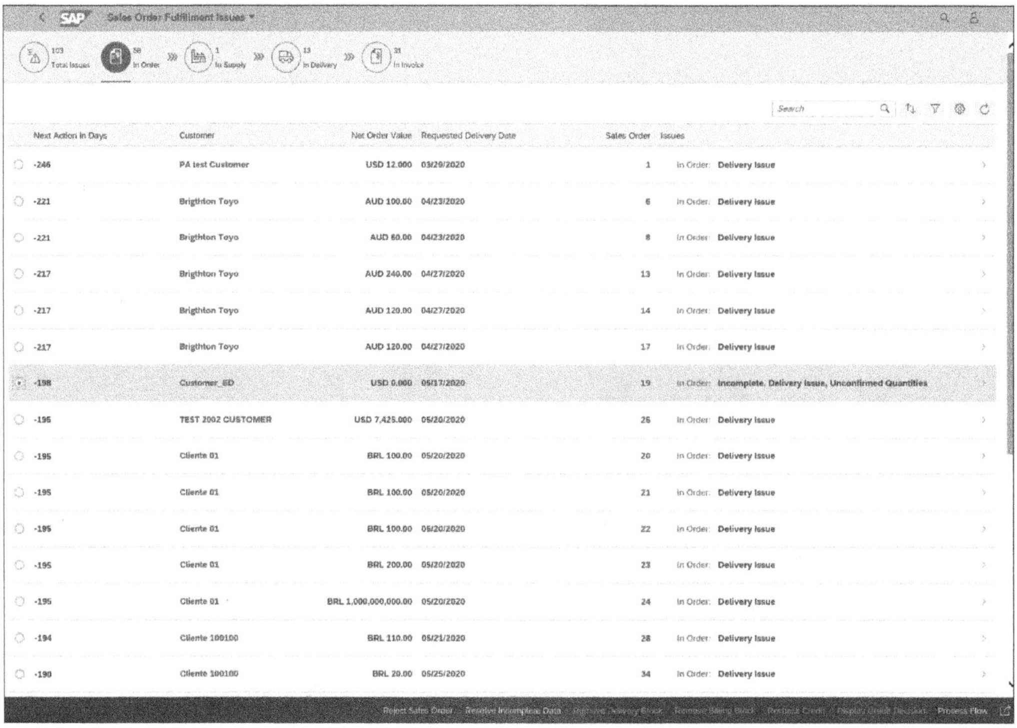

Figure 3.42 Sales Order Fulfillment Issues App: Quick Links

In Figure 3.42, sales order **19** for customer **Customer_ED** is highlighted; from that selection, the system highlights several available quick links at the bottom of the screen: **Reject Sales Order**, **Resolve Incomplete Data**, and **Process Flow**. Selecting one of these will carry out the action immediately and post a success or error message to screen. This saves you having to navigate to the document manually.

Further drilldowns are available when clicking on the customer name, as shown in Figure 3.43.

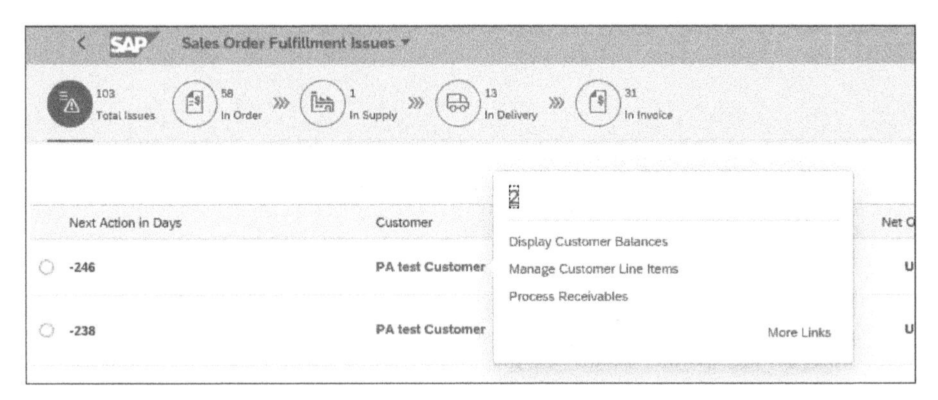

Figure 3.43 Sales Order Fulfillment Issues App: Drilldowns

In Figure 3.43, only three drilldowns are available, but you can add to this list by clicking **More Links**. This presents a whole new set of links whereby you can open transactional and factsheet apps directly, as shown in Figure 3.44.

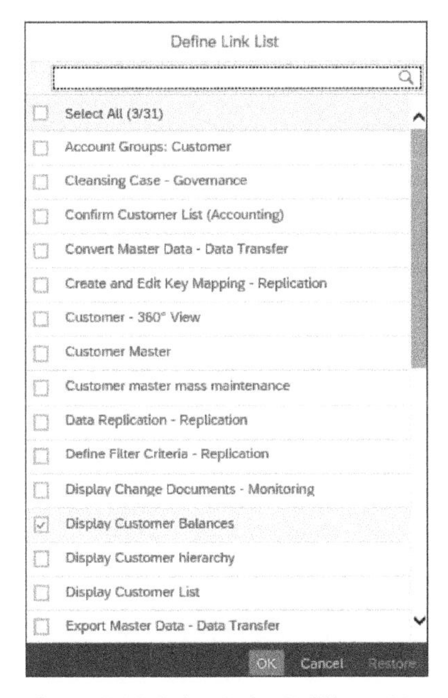

Figure 3.44 Sales Order Fulfilment Issues: Additional Links

From this list, the **Customer - 360° View** link is strongly recommended. By using this link, it's possible to get a full 360° view of the customer in the entire system: all the customer's master data and all transactional data. This is very useful for internal sales representatives and customer service users. It can be used in conjunction with the Enterprise Search functionality (discussed in Chapter 1, Section 1.2.3); if your search results show a customer number, one of the links available below the customer details is the **Customer 360° View**, as shown in Figure 3.45.

Figure 3.45 SAP Fiori: Customer 360° View

3.3 Sales and Distribution Screens

By now, you should be realizing the power of SAP S/4HANA and its uses via the SAP GUI and SAP Fiori. As a sales and distribution user, most of your time will be spent in sales screens, so it's a worthwhile exercise to give an overview of the concepts behind the structure of sales documents in SAP S/4HANA. Much more information on each type of document will be given in upcoming relevant chapters.

3.3.1 Header Information

Each sales and distribution document is separated into header and item screens and data. Header data relates to information regarding the customer and terms and conditions, whereas item data relates to information specific to the material being ordered.

Most sales and distribution documents will take you to an overview screen first, where key information at the header and the item level is displayed—in other words, a hub for the whole document. The intention is to show you information that can be changed at the overview level without having to navigate to the header or item details screen.

The separation of header and item data in sales and distribution documents makes logical sense; for example, fields such as the sales area, the customer details, the customer purchase order, and payment terms are all held at the header level as they should be applied to all items in the sales order.

Additional data at the header level includes such things as net value for the overall document and partner functions assigned. To see the header data exclusively, you'll need to select the **Header** icon, as shown in Figure 3.46.

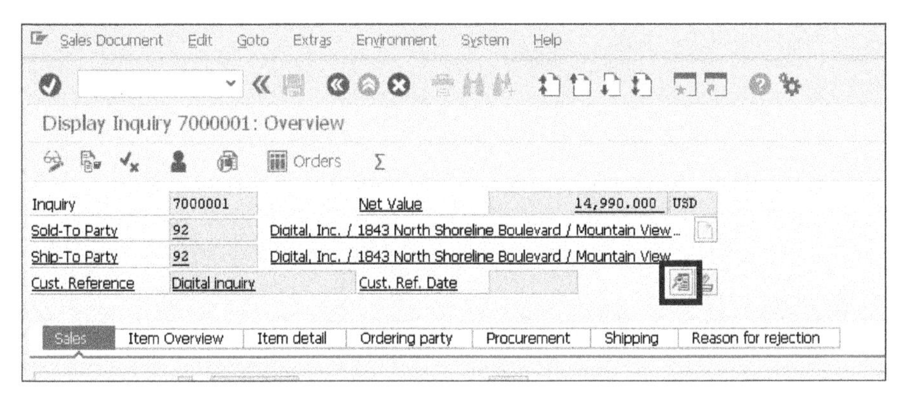

Figure 3.46 SAP GUI Sales Document Header Icon

3.3.2 Line-Item Information

Line-item information can also be viewed on the overview screen. Data such as material, quantity, delivering plant, shipping point, and price are all examples of line-item information. The line-item data can be easily navigated to by simply double-clicking the line item from the overview screen.

3.4 Summary

This chapter summarized the essential information you need in order to understand the principles behind SAP S/4HANA and how to navigate your way confidently around the sales and distribution screens. In the chapters to come, we'll delve in more detail into the individual document types to get a more comprehensive understanding of the capabilities of SAP S/4HANA sales and distribution.

Chapter 4
Presales Inquiries

This chapter introduces the initial document of the sales and distribution order-to-cash flow: the inquiry.

In this chapter, you'll get step-by-step instructions on how to create an inquiry document, with particular focus on the header and line-item sections of the screen where you'll find all critical fields for entry. We'll introduce the incompletion log and show you how to print your inquiry document as an output. After saving, we'll review the commands for changing and displaying your new document. We'll cover how to perform these functions in SAP Fiori and then close the chapter with searching for existing inquiries in SAP S/4HANA.

4.1 Process Overview

Your business is always soliciting additional orders from either brand-new customers or existing ones who buy limited ranges of products. The inquiry document process chronicles a casual nonbinding inquiry to a customer for the potential purchase of one or more of your products within a date range designed to elicit the next step—a fully legally binding quotation. Of course, your customer could also just simply accept outright the inquiry and send you their purchase order to buy the product at the indicated price.

In both cases, you'll be able to create the follow-on quotation or sales document using the inquiry document as a template to fill in fields such as **Customer**, **Material**, **Quantity**, and **Price**.

In this regard, SAP ERP also offers a very robust presales process as part of their SAP Customer Relationship Management (SAP CRM) package, which can be configured to flow into the SAP S/4HANA order-to-cash process.

As the subject in this book is limited to SAP S/4HANA, we leave the SAP CRM package by the wayside and start our sales and distribution order-to-cash process with two presales processes, which are part and parcel of SAP S/4HANA:

- **Inquiry**
  This nonbinding document is issued to a potential customer with respect to an identified interest in one of your products at a specified quantity and price.

- **Quotation**
  Potential customers who respond favorably to the inquiry may request a binding quote on the indicated product for a specific quantity and price. This quotation document will also have an expiration date regarding the promised quantity and price terms. This document may be created as a copy of the initial inquiry or as a fresh document with all the inputs made directly into all required fields.

This chapter focuses on the inquiry process, which is covered in the highlighted section of the flowchart in Figure 4.1.

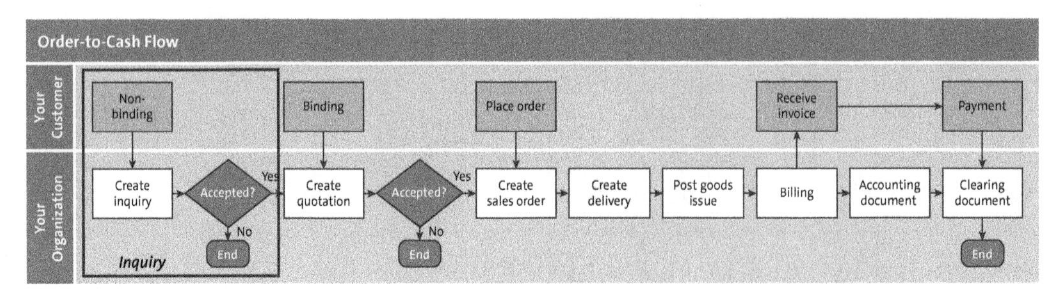

Figure 4.1 Order-to-Cash Flow: Inquiries

4.2 Document Types

The order-to-cash process is preconfigured to use the following basic document types from inquiry through billing:

- IN: Inquiry
- QT: Quotation
- OR: Standard order
- RE: Returns order
- CR: Credit memo request
- DR: Debit memo request
- LF: Outbound delivery document
- LR: Returns delivery
- F1: Sales invoice for an order
- F2: Sales invoice for a delivery
- G2: Credit memo
- L2: Debit Memo

These documents control how SAP S/4HANA will process information input by the user (or input via interface) in terms of an inquiry, quotation, sale, delivery, and so on. This means that certain documents will require specific field data and others won't. For example, inquiries, quotations, sales, and billing documents will require pricing information, but deliveries do not because they are concerned with other details related to shipping.

It's common in any SAP system to keep document templates untouched in the configuration for potential future use. For example, the default OR (normal sales) document type is typically kept clean as a reusable layout and is simply copied over repeatedly as the basis for creating new customized ZOR types, that is, order types that will be used for your business's most frequently used sales order process, incorporating whatever changes are necessary. Your company may have two or more such "standard" sales processes that use different pricing procedures. Accordingly, it's common to see multiple sales document types, such as ZOR1, ZOR2, and so on, assigned to pricing procedures ZVA001, ZVA002, and so on, respectively. SAP provides such inherent flexibility and robustness in accommodating your desired business processes.

Note that the preceding list of documents is by no means exhaustive but is provided at this point for illustrative purposes. For example, the sales and distribution process also includes many other document types such as contract documents, intercompany billings, and so on. These will be discussed in more detail in the coming chapters.

4.3 Create an Inquiry Document

In this section, we'll create an inquiry document. To do so, follow these steps:

1. Enter Transaction code VA11, as shown in Figure 4.2.

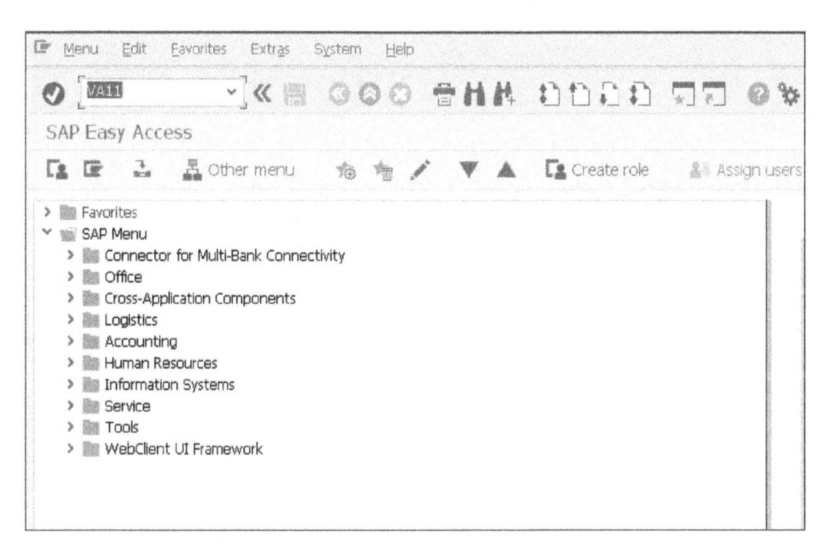

Figure 4.2 SAP Easy Access Menu: Transaction Code Field

2. In the **Inquiry Type** field, enter "IN", which is the standard document type for inquiries.

3. Now enter your organizational data (see Chapter 2, Section 2.2.1, for more details on organizational data), as shown in Figure 4.3:
   - **Sales Organization**: "US30"
   - **Distribution Channel**: "20"
   - **Division**: "10"

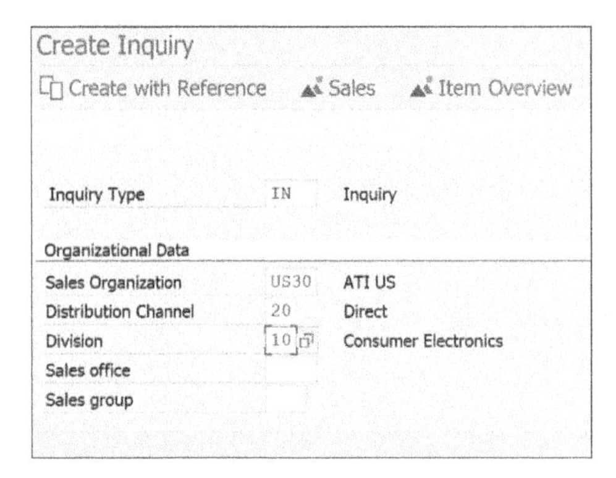

Figure 4.3 Create Inquiry Initial Screen

4. Press Enter.

You're now in the main **Create Inquiry** screen and need to enter some basic header data here to be able to proceed. Header data will apply to all items in your inquiry. For example, your inquiry document can be for one and only one customer. Multiple inquiries to multiple customers will require separate inquiry documents. Therefore, your inquiry document number is an example of header data.

4.3.1 Header Data

To get started, you'll need to specify your customer or business partner information in the form of sold-to party and ship-to party. Additional business partner functions are available as well, namely bill-to party and payer. To understand the relationships of these functions, let's explore some basic definitions (see Chapter 2, Section 2.2.1, for more comprehensive details):

- **Sold-to party**
  This is the customer entity who is requesting the inquiry from you and who receives any confirmation output from the inquiry.
- **Ship-to party**
  This is the customer entity who will receive the products if and when an order is placed. Your customer may have several locations for receiving goods; the right address for receipt is designated here.
- **Bill-to party**
  This is the customer entity who will be the recipient of the invoice after a sales order

is generated and goods issued. Again, your customer may have several entities that receive invoices.

- **Payer**
  This is the customer entity who will be responsible for paying the invoice (accounts payable from their point of view). As with the other partner functions listed here, your invoice may be paid by any number of paying entities or offices as designated by your customer. It's a good thing for your business to have such wealthy customers!

It's important to note that these partners can be, and often are, the same; SAP S/4HANA is simply giving you the flexibility to split out the functions as needed to meet the demands of our complex world. Only the sold-to party and ship-to party are available on the overview page of the **Create Inquiry** screen. Adding your customer number into either the **Sold-To Party** or the **Ship-To Party** fields, causes the system to derive all the other partner functions automatically because the sold-to party is the lead function. If more than one partner is available from the customer master data for the ship-to party, bill-to party, or payer, then the system will offer up a popup box for you to select the right one.

For simplicity's sake, all four partner functions will be the same in this manual unless otherwise noted. When you input the **Sold-To Party** and **Ship-To Party** numbers, the system automatically inputs the same numbers for the **Bill-To Party** and **Payer** in the document's **Partners** tab.

Including these customer fields, now input the following header fields (see Figure 4.4), followed by pressing [Enter]:

- **Sold-to Party**: "92"
- **Ship-to Party**: "92"
- (optional) **Cust. Reference**: "AUG182020F"
- **Valid From**: "08/18/2020"
- **Valid To**: "08/31/2020"

The **Cust. Reference** field refers to any number issued by the customer for its own tracking of the inquiry. In the sales document to follow (assuming that the inquiry and follow-on quotation documents are accepted), this field will be the customer's purchase order number. This field isn't system required. Because the field is frequently business required, however, it's included here as an optional field.

An inquiry is intended to be valid for only a specified period of time so that pricing can be correctly calculated. For example, you may have a different price in the system to use on September 1, 2020, and afterwards. If the validity dates are left blank, the system will return a price of zero, which severely limits the utility of your proposed inquiry document.

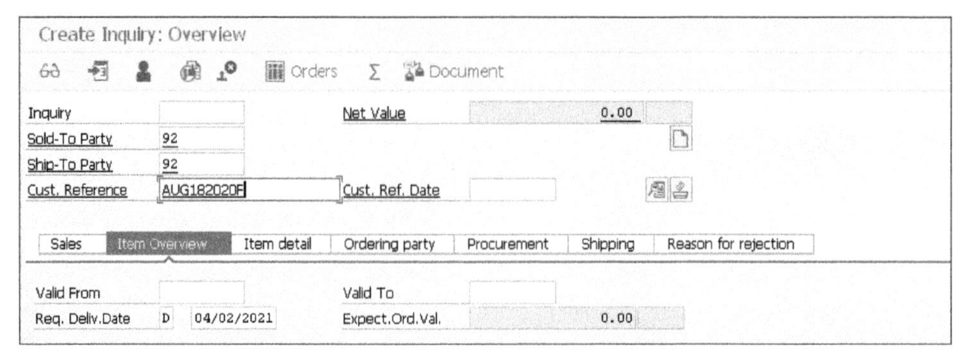

Figure 4.4 Entering Header Data in the Create Inquiry: Overview Screen

Note that the **Req. Delivery Date** field defaults to the current date (although this can be customized as needed). This is the date that the goods are to be delivered to the customer and is often changed from the current date to several days in the future to reflect a reasonable delivery time. This is a header data field and copies into the **Delivery Date** field in the **Schedule Lines** tab of the material line item where it can be changed. If changed at the line-item level, that date overrides the header date in terms of delivery planning (and the header date, interestingly, remains unchanged).

4.3.2 Line-Item Data

All required header fields have now been input. Now, input the following line-item fields:

- **Material**: "252"
- **Order Quantity**: "10"

The **Create Inquiry: Overview** screen should now look like Figure 4.5.

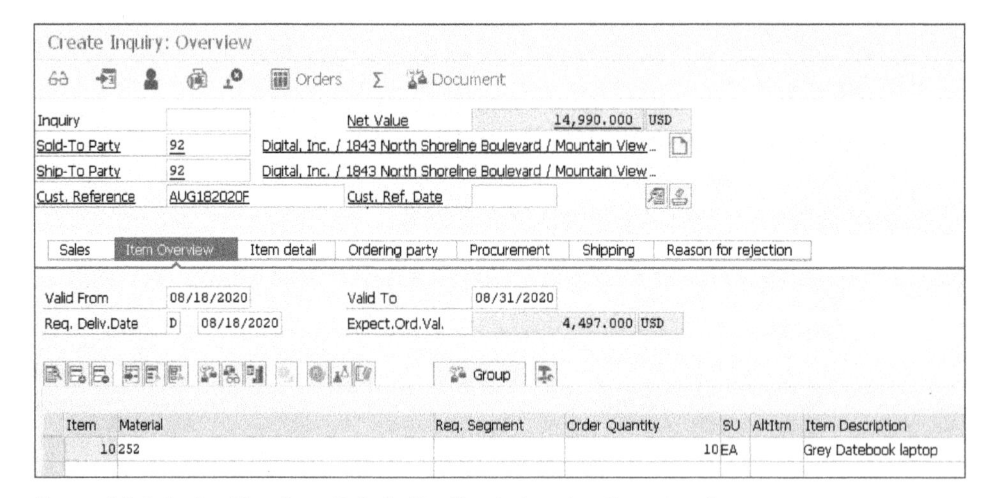

Figure 4.5 Entering Line-Item Data in the Create Inquiry: Overview Screen

At this point, your customer details, customer reference number, validity dates, material, and quantity as input and price as determined are clearly visible in both the header and line-item sections. This is all that is required to complete an inquiry.

4.3.3 Other Header and Line-Item Data

Along with the fields already mentioned in the header and line-item sections, there are some other commonly used optional or business-required fields to be aware of, as discussed in this section.

Header Data

The header data section contains many additional fields, which will potentially have repercussions on the price and availability information you provide to your customer. Remember, depending on the setup of your system, inquiry documents may generate output documents that are sent to your customer automatically, and you need to be sure that the information contained therein is accurate.

Some of these header fields are visible in the **Sales** tab of the **Create Inquiry: Overview** screen as shown in Figure 4.6:

- **Pyt Terms**
  What are the payment conditions under which your customer will be trading with you? This can be defined in the customer master data and then copied automatically into all sales and distribution documents.
- **Incoterms**
  Who will have responsibility for the shipments at which phase in the process? This can also be defined in the customer master data.
- **Doc. Currency**
  Is the currency correct? Again, this can also be set up once in the customer master data.

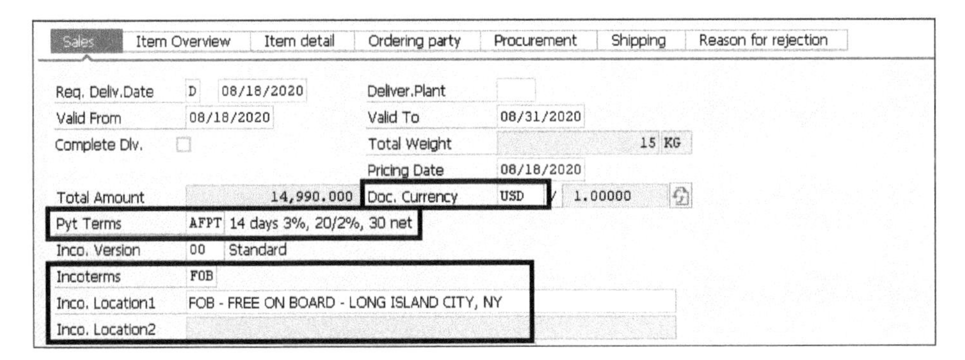

Figure 4.6 Create Inquiry: Sales Tab Fields

By clicking on the **Header** button in Figure 4.7, you can open all the header data for the inquiry.

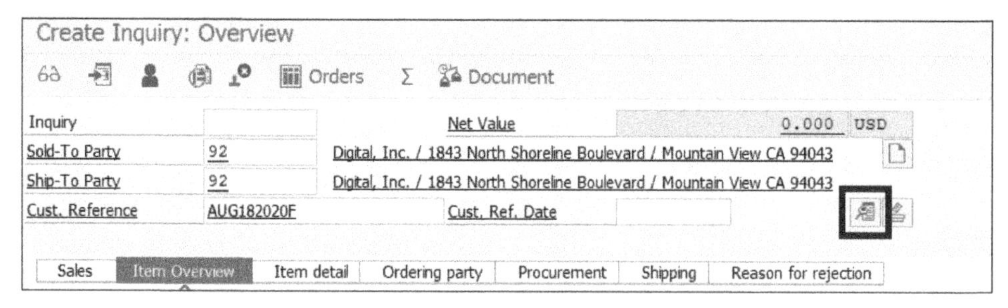

Figure 4.7 Create Inquiry: Header Button

From here, all header information is shown in various tabs, including more detailed information, such as the following:

- **Shp.Cond. (shipping condition)**
  If the customer has requested a specific shipping condition (e.g., must be delivered as a rush) or wants to pick up the products, this may have an impact on your freight price determination. This field is found on the **Shipping** tab, as shown in Figure 4.8. This can be set in the customer's master data.

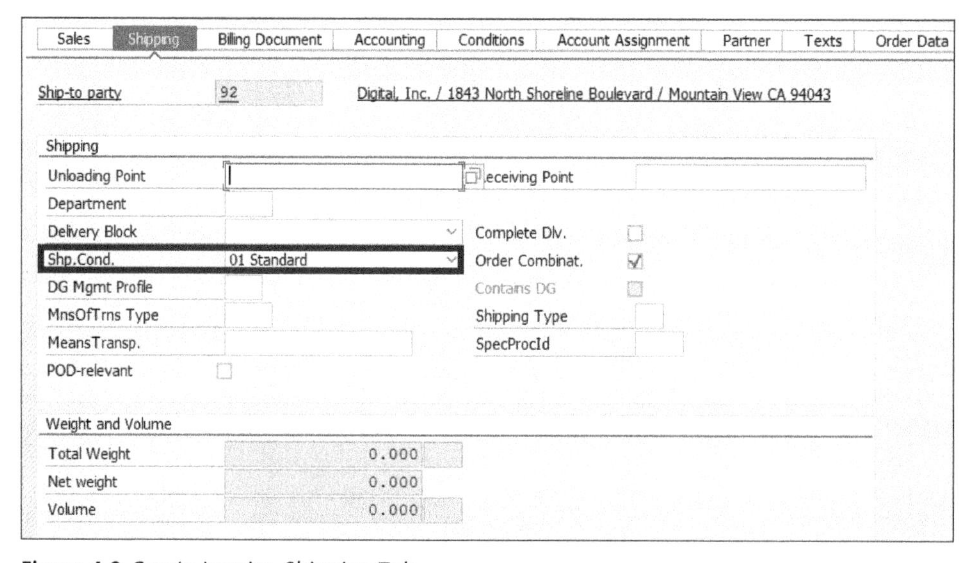

Figure 4.8 Create Inquiry: Shipping Tab

- **Partn. Funct. (partner functions)**
  If you need to change any of the partner functions, such as the bill-to party or the payer, or you want to add a new partner function for a carrier or an end customer, for example, this can be done in the **Partner** tab, as shown in Figure 4.9.

Sales | Shipping | Billing Document | Accounting | Conditions | Account Assignment | Partner | Texts | Order Data | Status

Display Range: PARALL All partners

Partn.Funct.	Partner	Name	Street	Postal C...	City	Partner Definition
AG Sold-to party	92	ital, Inc.	1843 North Shoreline Boulev...	94043	Mountain View	
RE Bill-to party	92	Digital, Inc.	1843 North Shoreline Boulev...	94043	Mountain View	
RG Payer	92	Digital, Inc.	1843 North Shoreline Boulev...	94043	Mountain View	
WE Ship-to party	92	Digital, Inc.	1843 North Shoreline Boulev...	94043	Mountain View	

Figure 4.9 Create Inquiry: Partner Tab

- **Txt ty.**
  Are there any specific header texts you want to add to the document? This means that this particular text is applicable to *all* items in the order. Depending on your setup in the system, these can be included in the output document for the customer. These texts can be added in the **Texts** tab, as shown in Figure 4.10.

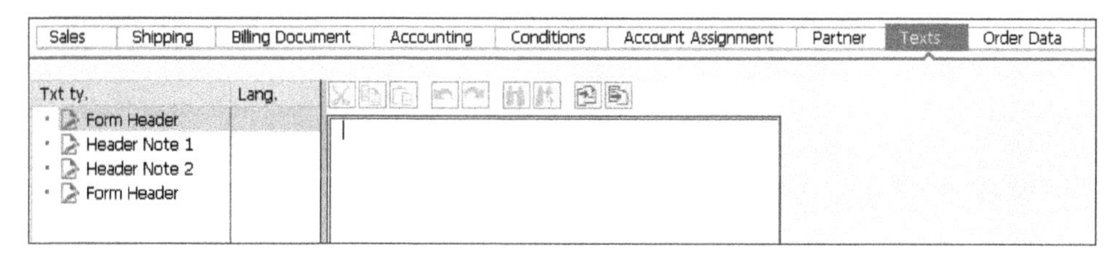

Figure 4.10 Create Inquiry: Texts Tab

Line-Item Data

By double-clicking the line items, you can open up the item data per material line in the inquiry document. Item data therefore can vary from line item to line item. The key data for an inquiry line item is the material unit price in the **Conditions** tab. (More information on pricing is available in Chapter 2, Section 2.2.3.) The following line-item fields are found in various tabs:

- **Price**
  Check that prices are correct. Do you need to add any discounts or customer-specific pricing, surcharges, or freight? All these options are available by adding new or changing existing condition types in the **Conditions** tab shown in Figure 4.11.

- **Batch**
  If the material is batch managed, has the customer requested price and availability of a specific batch? If so, this can be added in the **Sales A** tab, as shown in Figure 4.12. Note that the **Batch** field won't show if the material isn't batch managed.

Sales A | Sales B | Shipping | Billing Document | Conditions | Account Assignment | Schedule lines | Partner | Texts | Order Data

Quantity 10 EA | Net 14,990.000 USD
Tax 0.000

Condition Record | Analysis | Update

I...	CnTy	Name	Amount	Crcy	per	U...	Condition Value	Curr.	Status	Num...	ATO/MTS Component
			0.000	USD		1EA	0.000	USD		0	
	PR00	Price incl.Sales Tax	1,499.000	USD		1EA	14,990.000	USD		1	
		Gross Value	1,499.000	USD		1EA	14,990.000	USD		1	
		Discount Amount	0.000	USD		1EA	0.000	USD		1	
		Rebate Basis	1,499.000	USD		1EA	14,990.000	USD		1	
		Net Value for Item	1,499.000	USD		1EA	14,990.000	USD		1	
		Net Value 2	1,499.000	USD		1EA	14,990.000	USD		1	
		Net Value 3	1,499.000	USD		1EA	14,990.000	USD		1	
	MWST	Output Tax	0.000	%			0.000	USD		0	
		Total	1,499.000	USD		1EA	14,990.000	USD		1	
	SKTO	Cash Discount	3.000-	%			449.700-	USD		0	
	VPRS	Internal price	999.000	USD		1EA	9,990.000	USD		1	
		Profit Margin	500.000	USD		1EA	5,000.000	USD		1	

Figure 4.11 Create Inquiry: Conditions Tab

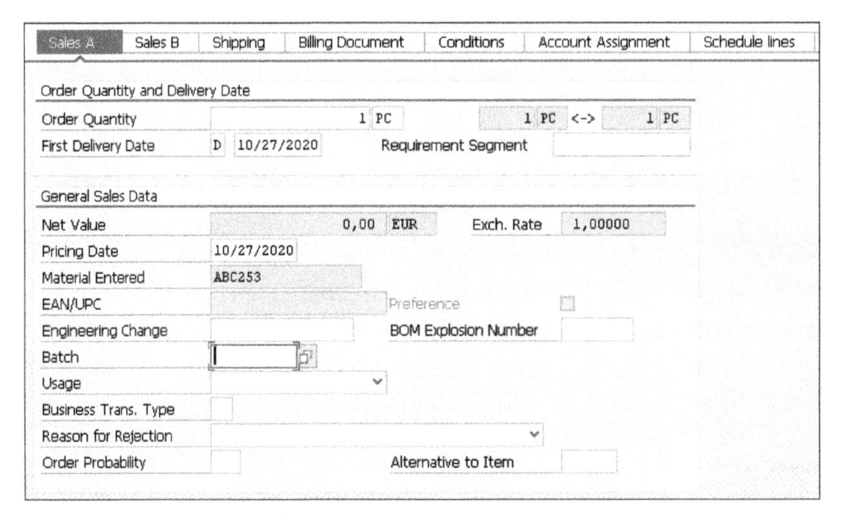

Figure 4.12 Create Inquiry: Batch Field

- **Delivery DATE**
  Has the customer requested an inquiry for delivery of products to be scheduled across multiple future dates? These dates can be changed and added in the **Schedule lines** tab, as shown in Figure 4.13. As noted previously, this line-item delivery date overrides, but doesn't change, the **Req. Delivery Date** in the header. This allows for an order of 10 pieces, for example, to be split into two (or more) schedule lines by the delivery due date. For example, 8 units can be delivered on one date and the other 2 a week later (for a total of 10).

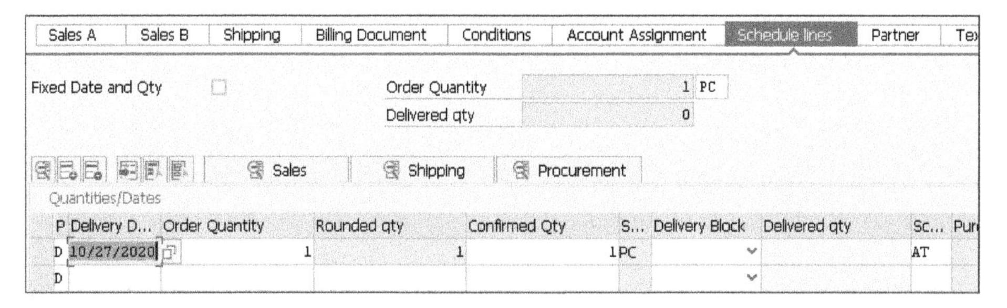

Figure 4.13 Create Inquiry: Schedule Lines Tab

- **Txt ty.**
  Are there any specific item texts you want to add to the document line item? Remember, header text applies to the entire order and all line items. Line-item text is specific only to the particular inquiry line item. For example, if one material in the inquiry needs to be kept at a special temperature, that information could be provided as text here. Depending on your setup in the system, these can be included automatically in the output document for the customer. These texts can be reviewed or added in the line-item **Texts** tab, as shown in Figure 4.14.

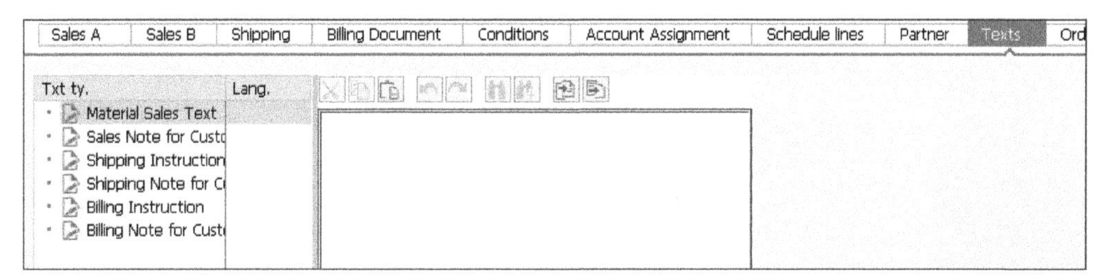

Figure 4.14 Create Inquiry: Texts Tab

4.3.4 Incompletion Log

The inquiry document is now complete for all required and many other commonly used fields. To check the incompletion status, choose **Edit • Incompletion Log**, as shown in Figure 4.15.

This launches the incompletion procedure, which checks that all system-required fields have been correctly populated in your document. If any are missing, then you'll be presented with a new screen showing which fields are missing entries. From here, you can navigate to all and fill in the missing data.

After all the required fields are completed, the following message appears on the status bar, in the lower-left corner of your screen (see Figure 4.16).

Figure 4.15 Create Inquiry: Incompletion Log

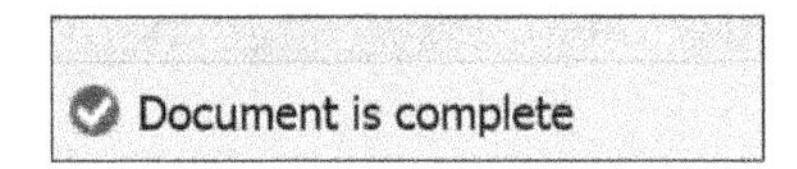

Figure 4.16 Document Complete Message

4.3.5 Printing Output

If you'll be issuing either a hard copy or soft copy output to the customer, you can look at the inquiry to be printed on the screen before completing it to ensure that everything looks correct. At this point, the inquiry is still not yet saved and therefore isn't active in the system. Accordingly, the system will generate a proposed or preview version of the document for you to review on screen. Only when you save the inquiry will a finalized version be generated with a document number and then printed/emailed to the customer.

You can also look at the output conditions to see how the specific output type was determined. Let's first look at the output itself. In the **Create Inquiry: Overview** screen, you can click the **Header Output Preview** icon, as shown in Figure 4.17. This will generate an onscreen print preview of the output.

Figure 4.17 Create Inquiry Overview: Header Output Preview Button

There is also a handy **Display Output Request** icon, as shown Figure 4.18, that will navigate you directly to the outputs screen.

Sold-To Party	92	Digital, Inc. / 1843 North Shoreline Boulevard / Mountain View...
Ship-To Party	92	Digital, Inc. / 1843 North Shoreline Boulevard / Mountain View...
Cust. Reference	AUG182020F	Cust. Ref. Date

Figure 4.18 Create Inquiry: Display Output Request Button

Next, if you want to see the technical details regarding the output type and how it was determined, there are a couple of ways to do this. You can choose **Extras • Output • Header • Edit** from the menu bar to open the output request screen to show you the **Output** type created, as shown in Figure 4.19.

Change Inquiry 10000003: Output

Communication method Processing log Further data

Inquiry 0010000003

Output

St...	Outp...	Description	Medium	Function	Partner
●○○	AF00	Inquiry	1 Print output	SP	102495

Figure 4.19 Create Inquiry: Outputs Request Screen

In the preceding example, the **AF00** standard inquiry output type has failed to print (evidenced by the red traffic light). A yellow traffic light means that it's waiting to be printed, whereas a green light means that it has printed. The term "print," of course, can mean printing a hard copy as well as creating a soft copy to be transmitted in numerous ways, including PDF via email or electronic data interchange (EDI).

All outputs store data in certain formats for review. A specific output type can be specified by following standard sales and distribution condition technique processing (see Chapter 2, Section 2.2.3, for condition technique details). If you want to see how the output has been determined, you can do this from the same output request screen. From the menu bar, choose **Goto • Determination Analysis** to access a very busy screen where you can analyze how the output has been selected, as shown in Figure 4.20.

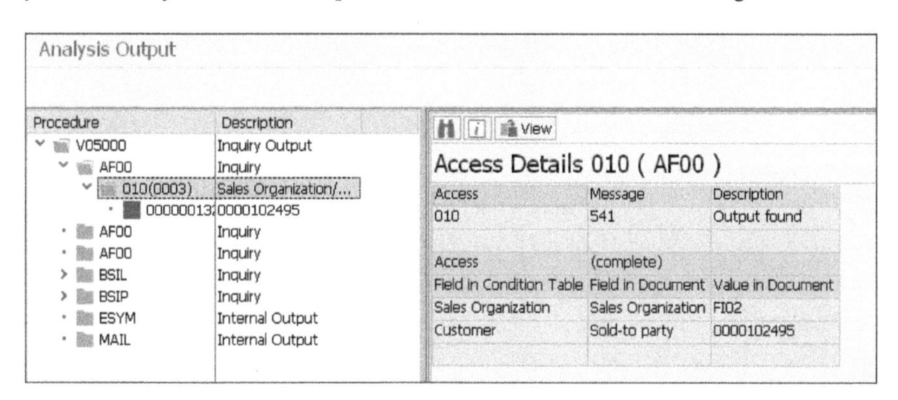

Figure 4.20 Create Inquiry: Analysis Output Screen

In this figure, on the right-hand side is given the details of how the output was determined. From here, you can see that the output type AF00 has been determined via a combination of the sales organization US30 and sold-to party 92 in the inquiry.

You're now ready to save your inquiry. Click on the **Save** icon, as shown in Figure 4.21.

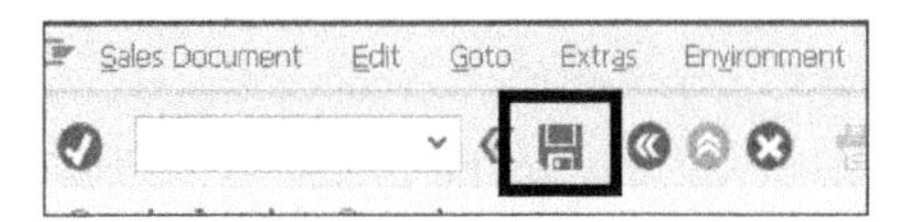

Figure 4.21 Create Inquiry: Save Icon

Your inquiry document number should appear on the status bar in the lower-left corner of your screen, as shown in Figure 4.22.

Figure 4.22 Create Inquiry: Saved Message

This inquiry document can now be used to create a quotation should the customer request an upgrade to a legally binding document. This can be done via the **Create with Reference** option.

4.3.6 Managing Sales Inquiries App

To get an overview of all inquiries in the system, it is possible to use the Manage Sales Inquiries app. To use this app, follow the steps laid out below:

1. Launch the Manage Sales Inquiries app in SAP Fiori, and click on the **Create Inquiry** link, as shown in Figure 4.23.

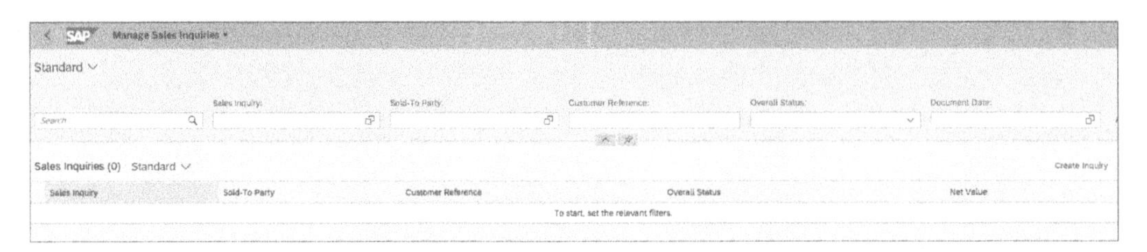

Figure 4.23 Manage Sales Inquiries App

2. In the **Create Inquiry** screen, input values for **Inquiry Type** and **Sales Organization**, **Distribution Channel** and **Division**, as you did previously in the SAP GUI screen (refer to Figure 4.3).
3. In the **Create Inquiry: Overview** screen, input the header data as shown in Figure 4.24. Press Enter.

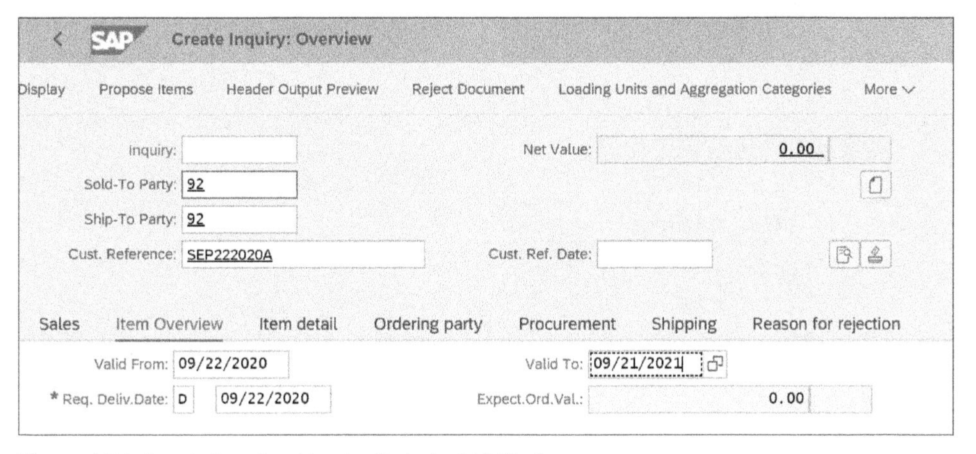

Figure 4.24 Create Inquiry: Header Data in SAP Fiori

Input the line-item information, such as **Material** number and **Order Quantity**, and then press [Enter] again.

4. To see the incompletion log, go to the menu bar, and choose **More • Edit • Incompletion Log**, as shown in Figure 4.25.

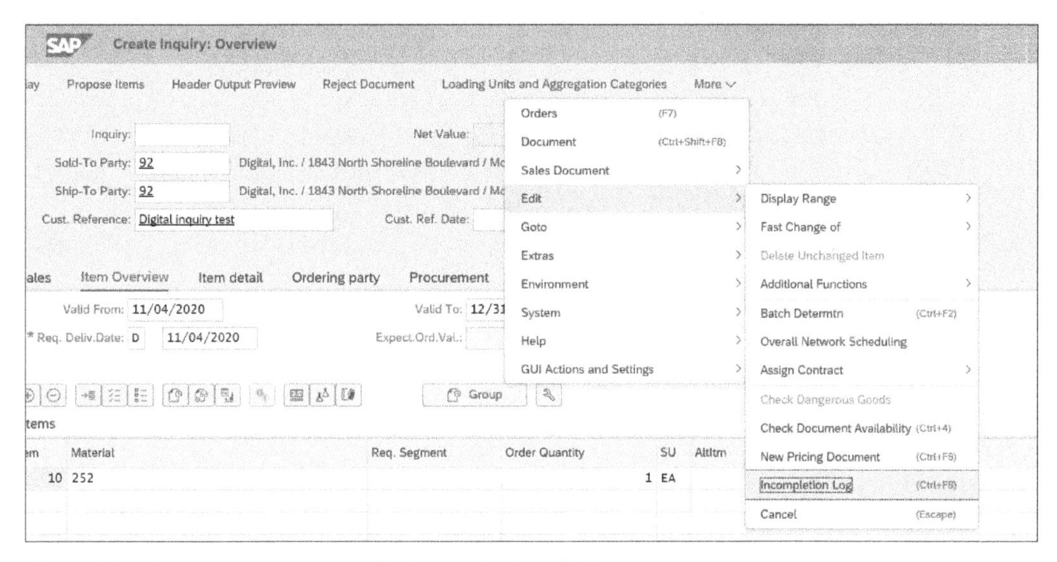

Figure 4.25 Create Inquiry: Incompletion Log in SAP Fiori

In the lower-left corner of the status bar, look for the **Document is complete** message, as shown in Figure 4.26.

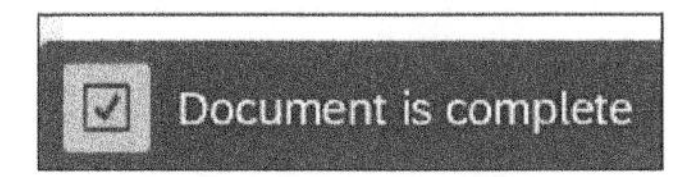

Figure 4.26 Document Complete Message

5. To save your inquiry, click on the **Save** button in the lower-right-hand corner of the SAP Fiori screen.

The message shown in Figure 4.27 should appear with your inquiry document number on the status bar in the lower-left corner of your screen.

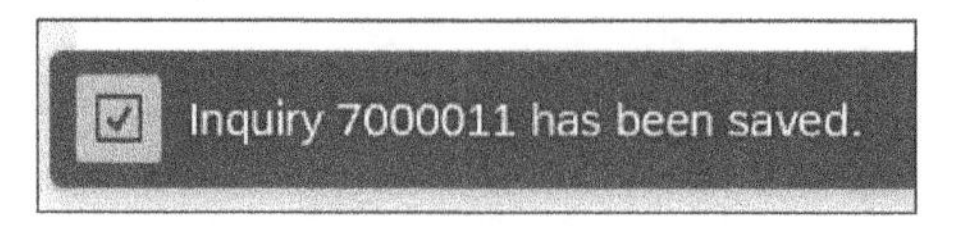

Figure 4.27 Inquiry Saved Message with Document Number

4.4 Change and Display an Inquiry Document

Once your inquiry is created, we need to visit a separate transaction in order to display or amend the Inquiry.

1. To change an inquiry, enter Transaction code VA12.
2. Likewise, to display an inquiry, enter transaction code "VA13". Remember, if you're anywhere *except* the SAP main menu, you must preface your transaction code with "/n" (without the quotation marks). For example, after saving your inquiry, you can go directly to change mode by typing "/NVA12" (without quotation marks) in the transaction code field and then pressing [Enter].
3. After creating your inquiry document in SAP per the steps in Section 4.3 and seeing the "saved" message (refer to Figure 4.27), you can also display the inquiry by clicking the **Display** icon in the same screen, as shown in Figure 4.28.

Figure 4.28 Display/Change Icon

4. This navigates directly to Transaction VA13 (Display Inquiry), where you can see the inquiry in display mode, meaning that all fields can be viewed but not amended. Switch to change mode by clicking the **Change** icon again, as shown in Figure 4.28.

Note

From Transaction VA13, pressing [Enter] will take you by default to the **Item Overview** tab in the inquiry. Alternatively, from the front screen of Transaction VA13, you can select the **Sales** tab, **Ordering Party** tab, or other tabs to navigate accordingly.

Tip

By clicking the **Change** or **Display** buttons in the toolbar, you can toggle back and forth in the document.

Identical to the **Create Inquiry** screens, the **Change** and **Display** screens are separated into three sections: overview, header, and line item. The initial screen is the **Overview** screen and shows the **Item Overview** default tab.

The main inquiry fields to be reviewed via change or display modes are as follows:

- **Inquiry**
  Found in the upper-left corner of the **Overview** screen. This field can't be changed.
- **Inquiry Type**
  For such an important field, SAP hides this in the **Sales** tab of the header section. This field can't be changed.
- **Sold-to Party/Ship-to Party**
  Found just below the **Inquiry Document Number** on the **Overview** screen. These fields can be changed if there are no subsequent documents. Please see Chapter 9, Section 9.12, for more information.
- **Sales Area**
  Like the **Inquiry Document Type**, this critical information is found in the **Sales** tab of the header section. All three component fields can't be changed.
- **Cust. Reference**
  This optional field is found just below the **Sold-to Party** and **Ship-to Party** fields on the **Overview** screen. The field can be changed.
- **Net Value**
  Found on the top right of the **Overview** screen, this field is a sum of all price conditions. If the prices are changed in the line item **Conditions** tab, then those changes will be reflected here.
- **Material Number/Description**
  Material numbers and their corresponding descriptions appear in the grid in the center of the **Overview** screen. New **Material Number** line items can be added. However, deleting them is restricted if there are follow-on documents. See Chapter 9, Section 9.12.
- **Order Quantity/Unit of Measure**
  These two fields appear together with the material numbers and descriptions in the **Overview** screen. These fields can't be changed, although there are ways to add or reduce quantities (see Chapter 9, Section 9.12.
- **Valid From/Valid To**
  These fields are found in the center of the **Overview** screen. Both the dates may be changed as necessary.

Note

For more information about which fields can and can't be changed, and how to undo or reverse documents, see Chapter 9 and the matrix therein.

By selecting the other tabs available in the **Overview** screen, you can see other key fields, as shown in Table 4.1.

Overview Tab	Field	Can Be Changed	Description
Sales	**Pyt terms**	Yes	The terms of payment allocated to the payer.
Sales	**Incoterms**	Yes	The delivery and shipping terms agreed to by the sold-to party.
Item Detail	**Item Category**	Yes, if there are no follow-on documents	A code that defines how the material behaves in the document. This is determined based on criteria set up in the configuration.
Item Detail	**Pricing Date**	Yes, if there are no follow-on documents	The date used to determine the price according to the criteria set up in the configuration.
Ordering Party	**Delivering Plant**	Yes, if there are no follow-on documents	Plant, if assigned to the customer master. This field can be found by scrolling to the right in the material grid (and can be customized to be visible without scrolling, if desired).
Reason for Rejection	**Order Reason**	Yes	Reason the inquiry was placed.
Reason for Rejection	**Reason for Rejection**	Yes, if there are no follow-on documents	Reason why the inquiry has been rejected (see Chapter 9, Section 9.12).

Table 4.1 Display Inquiry: Overview Fields

Normally the information in the **Overview** screen will be enough to give you the main points of the inquiry. However, as noted previously, more information can be found by drilling down in the header and line-item sections of the inquiry.

To access the header tabs, choose **Goto • Header** from the menu bar or select the **Header** icon, both of which are shown in Figure 4.29.

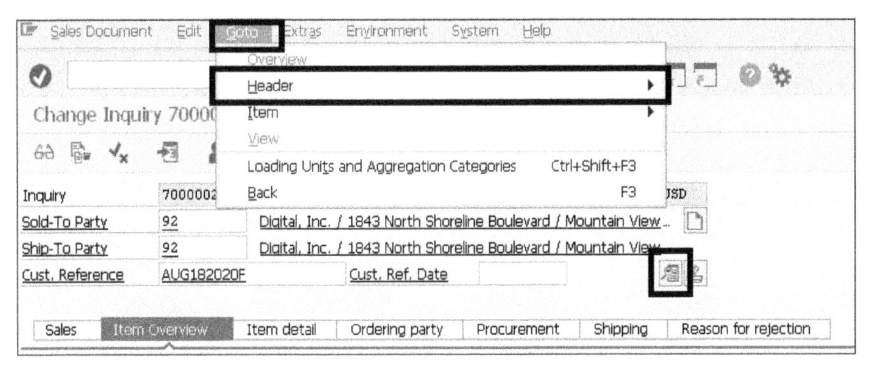

Figure 4.29 Header Options

Much of the information in the header tabs can also be found in the **Overview** screen tabs, but there are also some key bits of additional data here, the details of which can be found in Section 4.3.

To view the line-item details, choose **Goto • Item**, or click the **Item Details** icon, both of which are shown in Figure 4.30. You also can double-click on the line item itself.

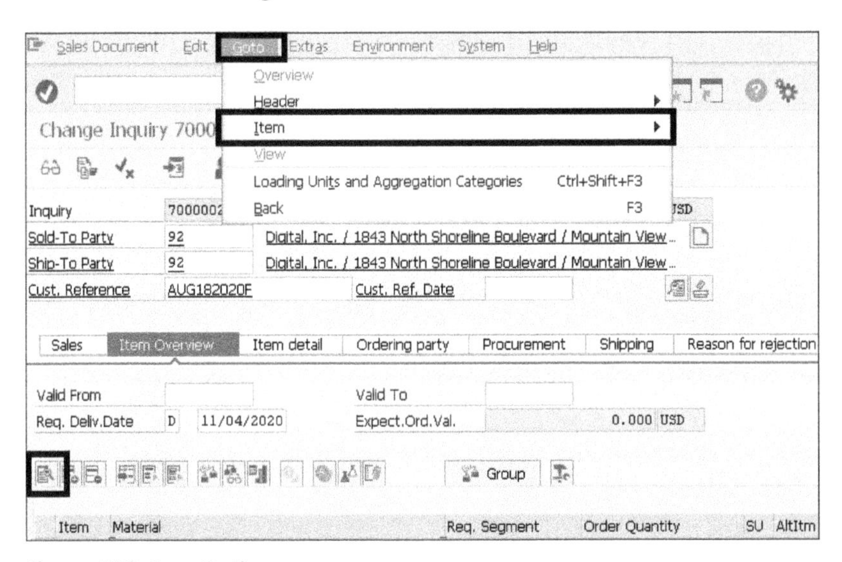

Figure 4.30 Item Options

Again, much of the information in the **Item** tabs can also be found in the **Overview** tabs. For more information, refer to the line-item fields discussed in Section 4.3.

4.4.1 Document Flow and Status Overview

Document flow is essential in understanding your transactions in terms of completeness. The **Document Flow** icon is located in the toolbar of Transaction VA12 (Change Inquiry) and Transaction VA13 (Display Inquiry), as shown in Figure 4.31.

Figure 4.31 Document Flow Icon

The document flow functionality is available in the following sales and distribution documents:

- Inquiries
- Quotations
- Sales orders
- Deliveries
- Billing documents

This icon displays all preceding and follow-on documents that have been created for the document you're currently looking at. This is critical information for determining how to complete the sales and distribution flow through billing or to reverse it, if necessary.

As an example, if your inquiry has been converted into a firm quotation, you would see that in the document flow, as shown in Figure 4.32. Furthermore, if your quotation had been converted into a sales order, that would also show, and so on all the way through to billing.

By clicking to select any one of the documents and then clicking on the **Display Document** button, you can navigate directly to that specific document in display mode.

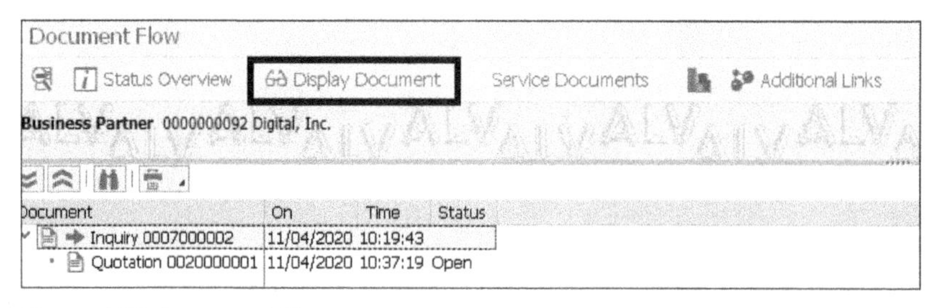

Figure 4.32 Document Flow

Another useful icon in the **Change Inquiry** and **Display Inquiry** overview screens is **Status Overview**, as shown in Figure 4.33.

Figure 4.33 Status Overview Icon

By using the **Status Overview** icon, you can get a full view of the header and item status of the inquiry as shown in Figure 4.34. Again, note that this icon is available for more than just inquiries; it's also available for these sales and distribution documents:

- Inquiries
- Quotations
- Sales orders

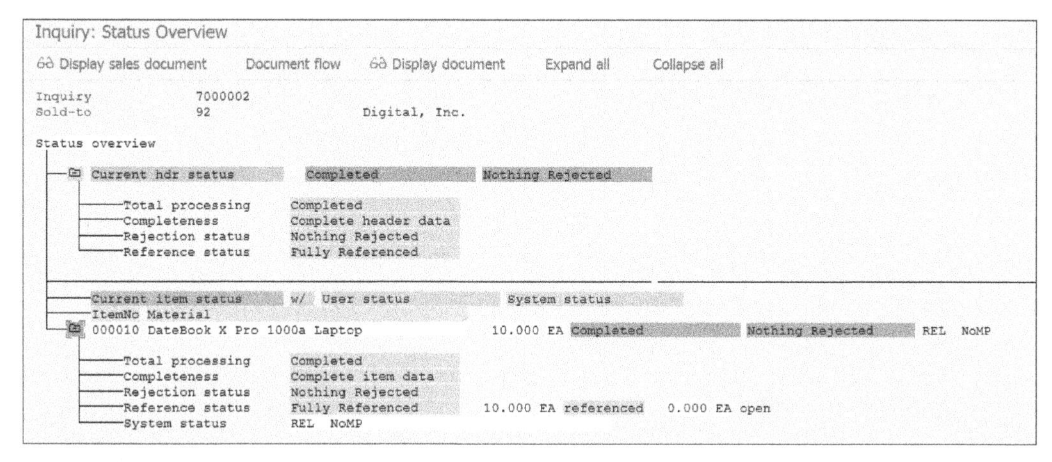

Figure 4.34 Status Overview Details

The **Inquiry: Status Overview** screen will show you the overall header and item status for the whole document, including the following item statuses:

- Complete as far as the incompletion procedure is concerned
- Referenced by a subsequent document
- Rejected

4.4.2 Create Subsequent Order

A key action from an inquiry is to create the subsequent sales order when the customer has "firmed up" its requirements into a sales order. Normally, the quotation follows the inquiry, but, in some cases, a customer will request a sales order directly from an inquiry document; in this instance, you would want to create your sales order with reference to your inquiry. To do this, choose **Sales Document • Create Subsequent Order**, as shown in Figure 4.35.

This will save any changes made to the inquiry document and immediately open the Transaction VA01 (Create Sales Order). We'll cover this in more detail in Chapter 6.

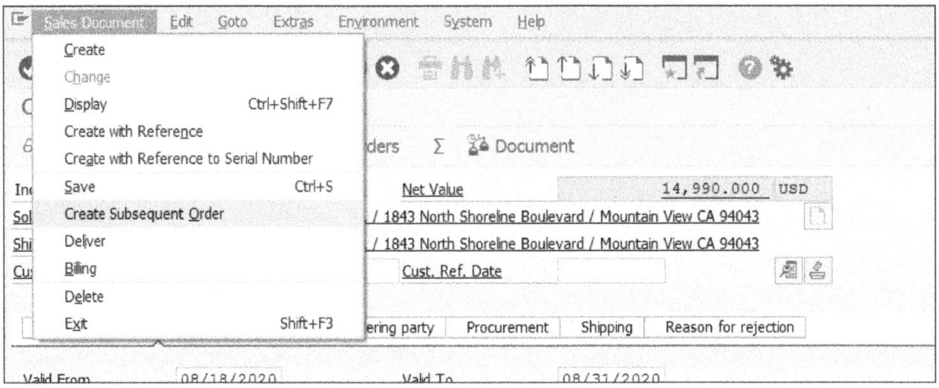

Figure 4.35 Creating a Subsequent Document

4.4.3 Create with Reference

From the same menu path, you can select **Create with Reference** to pull items from other documents into your new inquiry. Note that this can only be achieved if your system has been set up in such a way to allow copying from another document into an inquiry.

4.4.4 Mass Change

The **Edit** menu has some very useful features you can take advantage of, particularly if your inquiry has multiple items in it. Figure 4.36 shows the options for mass changing all the items in the inquiry document.

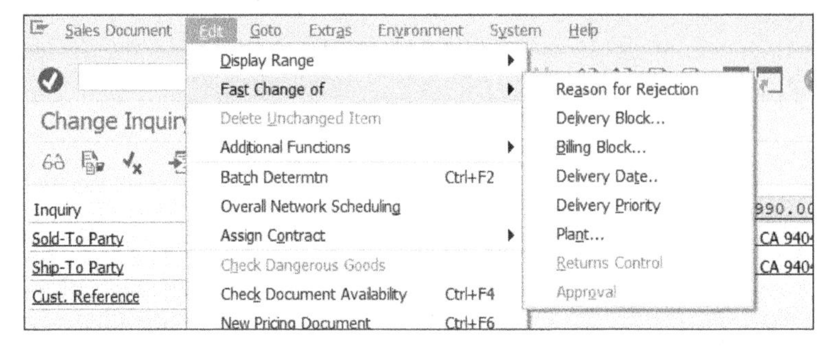

Figure 4.36 Making Mass Changes with the Fast Change Option

> **Note**
>
> The **Fast Change of** function can be used for all items or only those items that have been selected in advance.

4.4.5 Manage Sales Inquiries App

In SAP Fiori, inquiries can be accessed and amended via the "Manage Sales Inquiries" app.

1. Launch the Manage Sales Inquiries app, and input the inquiry document number to be changed or displayed in the **Sales Inquiry** field, as shown in Figure 4.37. Press Enter.

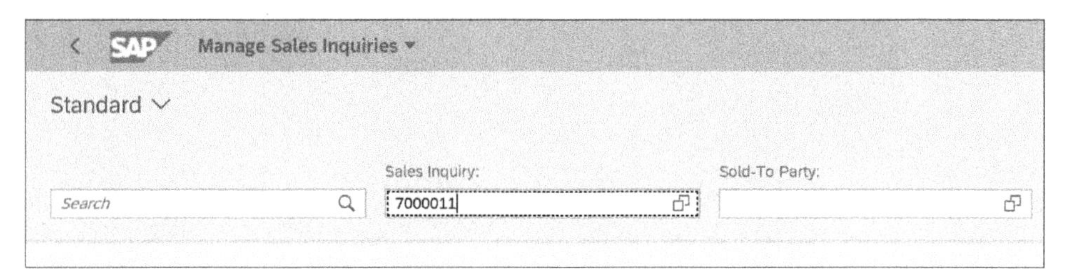

Figure 4.37 Manage Sales Inquiries App

2. Click on your document number to open the context-sensitive menu shown in Figure 4.38.

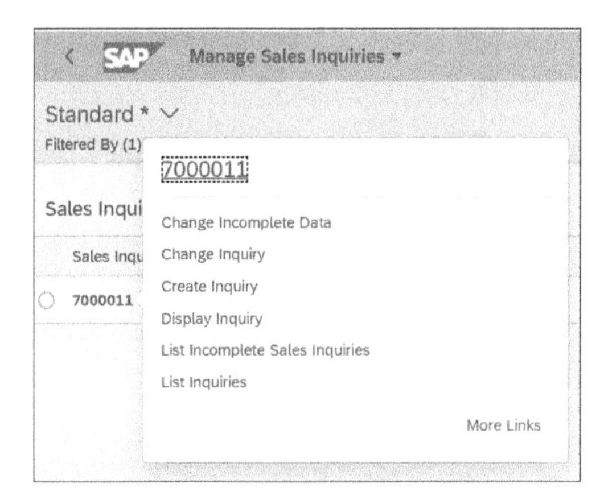

Figure 4.38 Manage Sales Inquiries: Context Menu

3. Click on the desired link in the context menu (for this example, **Change Inquiry**). The **Change Inquiry: Overview** screen appears, as shown in Figure 4.39.
4. Because there are no subsequent documents, all fields can be changed. Change the customer to "20" in both the **Sold-To Party** and **Ship-To Party** fields, and then press Enter to see the results in Figure 4.40.

Note

Refer to Section 4.4.1 for more information about which fields can be changed.

Figure 4.39 Change Inquiry: Overview Screen

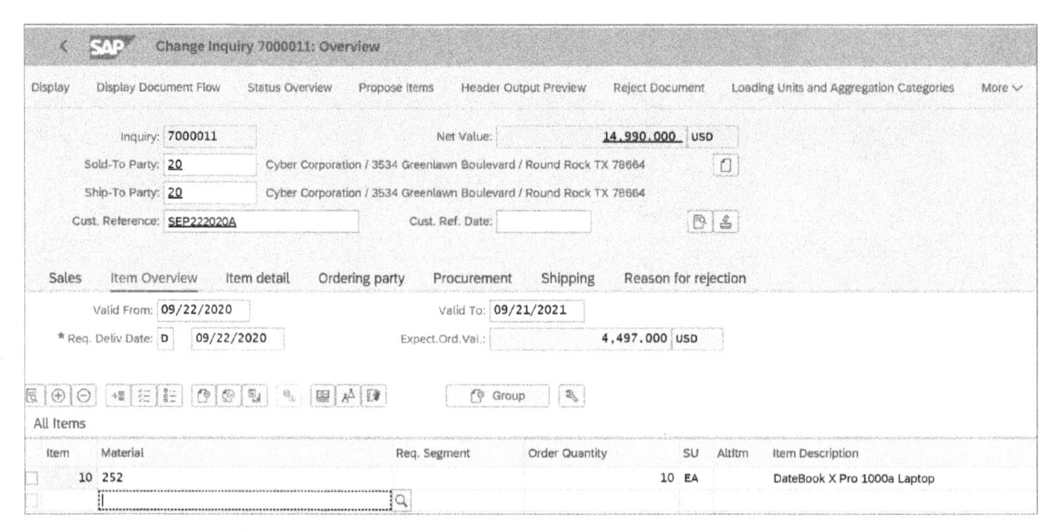

Figure 4.40 Change Inquiry Overview: Changing the Customer Number

5. To save changes to your inquiry click on the **Save** button in the lower-right corner of the SAP Fiori screen. A message should appear with your inquiry document number on the status bar in the lower-left corner of your screen, as shown in Figure 4.41.

Figure 4.41 Save Message with Document Number

4.5 List of Inquiries

You can look up inquiries based on various search criteria by using Transaction VA15 (List of Inquiries). For example, if you're unsure of the inquiry document number to be changed or displayed, you can perform a search, as shown in Figure 4.42.

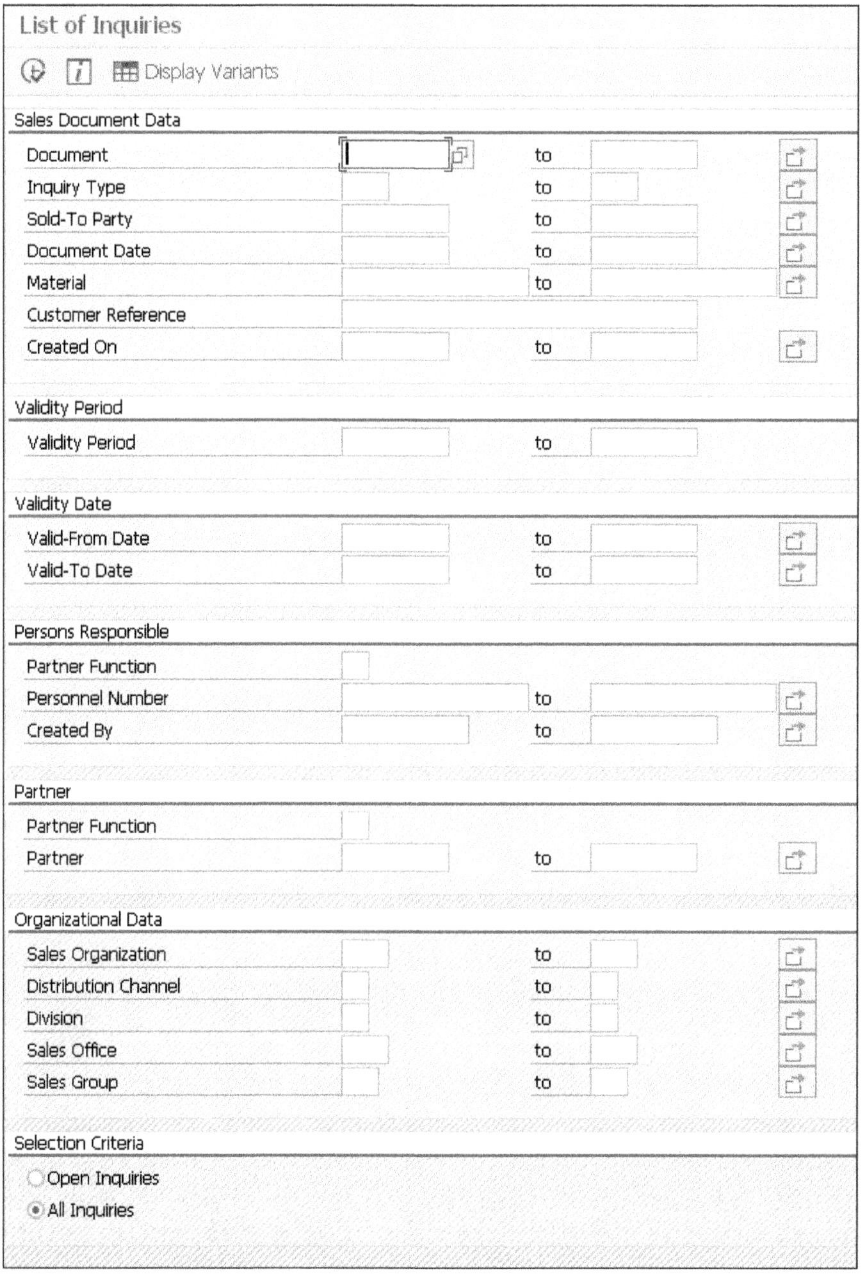

List of Inquiries

Display Variants

Sales Document Data

Document		to	
Inquiry Type		to	
Sold-To Party		to	
Document Date		to	
Material		to	
Customer Reference			
Created On		to	

Validity Period

Validity Period		to	

Validity Date

Valid-From Date		to	
Valid-To Date		to	

Persons Responsible

Partner Function			
Personnel Number		to	
Created By		to	

Partner

Partner Function			
Partner		to	

Organizational Data

Sales Organization		to	
Distribution Channel		to	
Division		to	
Sales Office		to	
Sales Group		to	

Selection Criteria

- Open Inquiries
- All Inquiries

Figure 4.42 List of Inquiries Screen

To search for an inquiry, follow these steps:

1. Scroll to the bottom of the selection screen, as shown in Figure 4.43, to see the **All Inquiries** or **Open Inquiries** (i.e., inquiries that haven't been referenced in a follow-on document, e.g., a quotation) radio buttons.

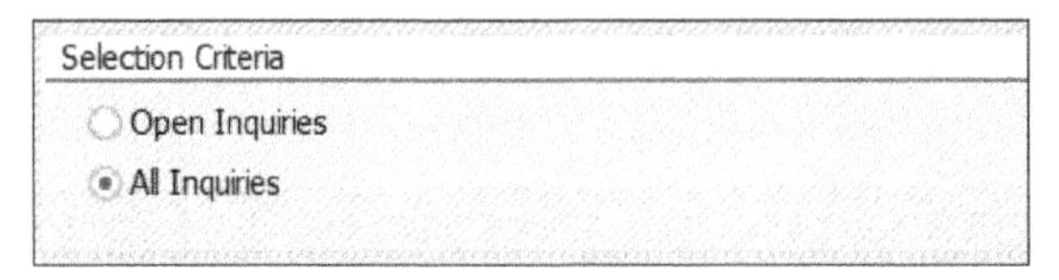

Figure 4.43 List Inquiries Selection Criteria Options

2. Input some selection parameters, such as **Sold-to Party** number and date range, into the report and execute. You have a choice of many other parameters as well, such as **Created by**, so you can easily limit the search to your own inquiries. The default columns in your output report will appear as shown in Figure 4.44, but they can be customized easily.

List of Inquiries (5 Entries)

Customer Reference	Sold-To Party	Doc. Date	Sale...	Valid from	Valid-to date	Sales Doc.	Item	Material	Order Quantity (Item)	Sal...	Net Value (Item)	Curre...
Digital inquiry	92	11/04/2020	IN	11/04/2020	12/31/2020	7000001	10	252	10	EA	14,990.000	USD
AUG182020F	92	11/04/2020	IN			7000002					0.000	USD
Inq 1	97	12/21/2020	IN			7000003	10	265	10	EA	15,000.00	EUR
	92	01/01/2021	IN	10/01/2020	12/31/2020	7000004	10	252	10	EA	14,990.000	USD
D8273464	92	03/02/2021	IN	03/02/2021	03/31/2021	7000005	10	252	1	EA	1,573.950	USD

Figure 4.44 Default Output for List Inquiries Transaction

3. To customize the columns you see in the report, you can select the **Change Layout** icon from the icon bar, as shown in Figure 4.45.

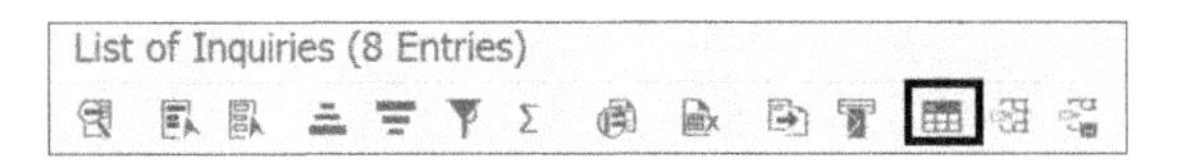

Figure 4.45 Change Layout Icon

Note

The following options are standard to all reports in SAP, so it's information you can use often.

From here, you're presented with a dialog box showing your currently selected layout (in this example, **1SAP (Inquiries – Items)**, as shown in Figure 4.46.

4. To remove displayed columns from your report, select the columns from the **Displayed Columns** list on the left, and click the right arrow to move them back to the **Column Set** list.

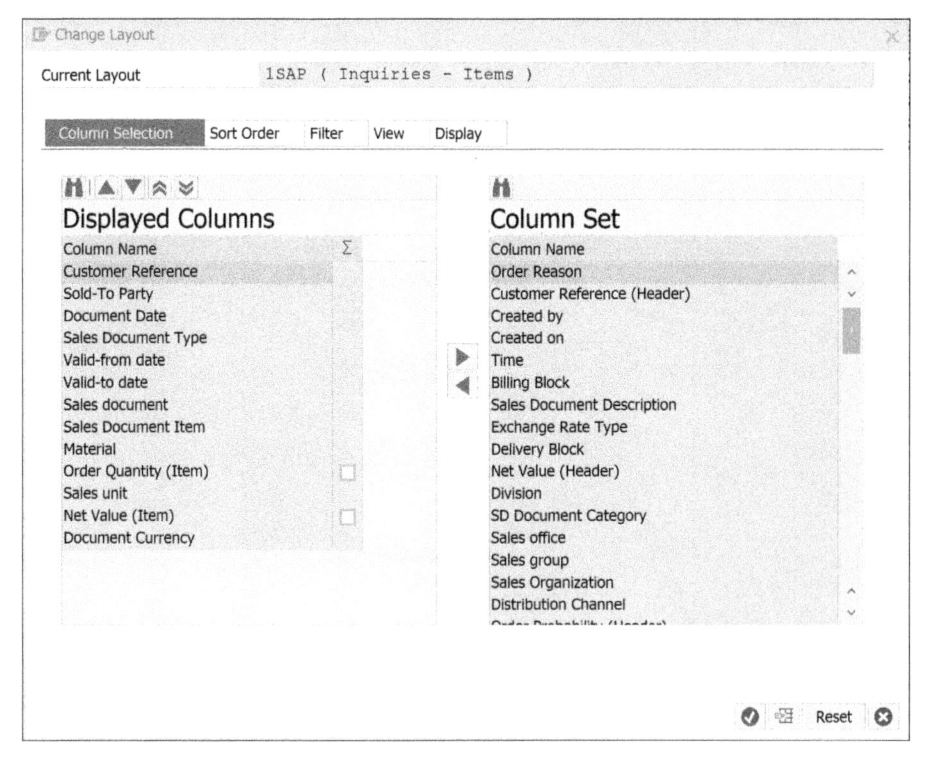

Figure 4.46 List of Inquiries: Change Layout Dialog Box

5. Similarly, to add new columns into your display, select the columns from the **Column Set** list on the right, and click the left arrow to move them to the **Displayed Columns** list.
6. Notice that some fields, such as **Order Quantity (Item)** and **Net Value (Item)**, have a checkbox available next to them in a sum column (refer to Figure 4.46). Check this box to prominently display the column total at the bottom.
7. Use the **Sort Order**, **Filter**, **View**, and **Display** tabs in this screen to change the order of the data, select filtering for certain values, and determine how the data is viewed and presented, respectively. An example of **Display** tab options is shown in Figure 4.47.

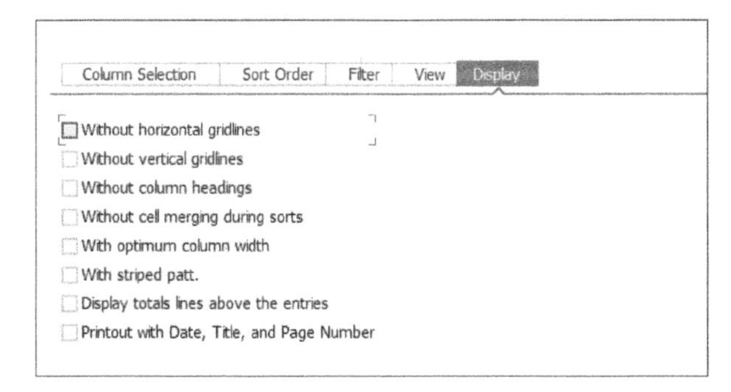

Figure 4.47 List of Inquiries: Change Layout Display Options

8. When you're happy with the layout of the **List of Inquiries** screen, save it for future use by clicking the **Save as** button, and you'll see the screen shown in Figure 4.48.

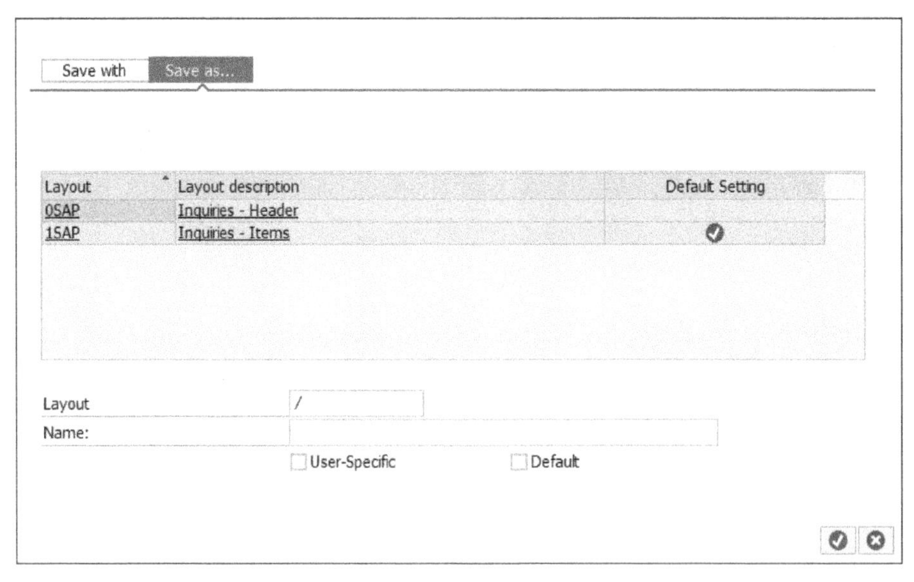

Figure 4.48 List of Inquiries: Saving the Layout

9. Create a name for your layout in the **Layout** field. Note the usage of the "/" (without quotation marks) as a possible prefix, as follows:
   - If you use "/" as a prefix for your layout name, the system will treat this as system-wide and make it visible to all users. If you are creating a system-wide layout for everyone to use by including the "/," the **User-Specific** checkbox below must NOT be clicked; otherwise, the system will throw the error "User-specific layouts must start with a letter (A-Z)."
   - If the "/" is omitted as a prefix, then the layout will be user-specific (i.e., only to be seen by you). If you are creating a user-specific layout for your own personal use by omitting the "/," you must also click the **User-Specific** checkbox; otherwise, the system will throw the error "Standard layouts must start with the character /."

   The **Default** checkbox can be clicked to select the new layout to be used automatically, whether by you as a user-specific layout or as a system-wide default by everyone.

Note

Be careful! If you leave the **User-Specific** checkbox blank, create a layout name starting with "/" so it will be system-wide, and then click the **Default** button, then any existing layout currently used by all users in the system by default will be switched to the new one. Your phone might start ringing!

After you've generated a list of inquiries, you may want to export this to Microsoft Excel. To do so, click on the **Export to Excel** icon on the toolbar, as shown in Figure 4.49. Again, this is a commonly used command in many other reports in SAP applications to facilitate various kinds of analysis.

Figure 4.49 List of Inquiries: Export to Excel Icon

This will launch Excel. Accept any warning about opening a file with a macro, and you'll be presented with your list exported into Excel, ready to be saved as an Excel file, as shown in Figure 4.50.

Document D	Sales docum	Net Value (Header)	Sold-To Part	Sales	Valid from dt	Valid to date	Customer Reference	Sales D	Material	Order Quantity (Item)	Sal	Net Value (Item)	Docume
08/18/2020	7000001	14,990.00	92	IN	08/18/2020			10	252	10	EA	14,990.00	USD
08/19/2020	7000002	14,990.00	92	IN	08/18/2020	08/31/2020	AUG182020F	10	252	10	EA	14,990.00	USD
08/20/2020	7000003	14,990.00	92	IN	08/20/2020	08/31/2020	AUG182020G	10	252	10	EA	14,990.00	USD
08/26/2020	7000004	1,499.00	92	IN	08/18/2020	08/31/2020		10	252	1	EA	1,499.00	USD
09/04/2020	7000006	1,499.00	92	IN	08/18/2020	10/31/2020	Harvey	10	252	1	EA	1,499.00	USD
09/11/2020	7000008	1,499.00	92	IN				10	252	1	EA	1,499.00	USD
09/12/2020	7000009	7,495.00	92	IN	09/12/2020	09/11/2021	SEP122020A	10	252	5	EA	7,495.00	USD
09/12/2020	7000010	7,495.00	92	IN				10	252	5	EA	7,495.00	USD

Figure 4.50 List of Inquiries: Excel View

4.5.1 Mass Change

We close our SAP GUI discussion with a little-used option in the list of inquiries: **Mass Change** (see Figure 4.51). This works similarly to the **Mass Change** feature we examined in earlier in Section 4.4.4. Note that this isn't available in the Manage Sales Inquiries app.

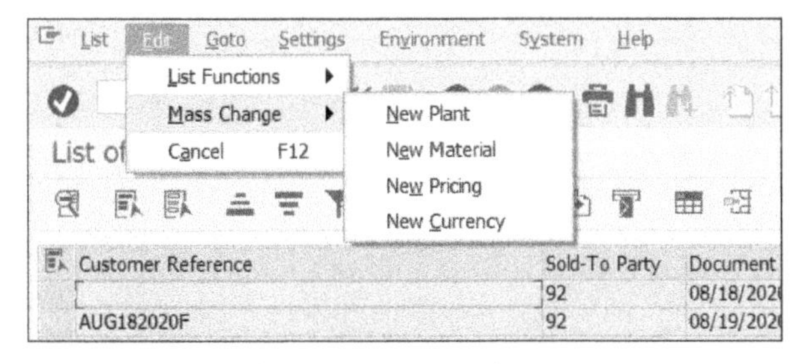

Figure 4.51 List of Inquiries: Mass Change

From here, you can select the entries you want to change and then make changes to the plant, material, pricing, or currency according to specific input parameters. For example, by selecting **New Currency** from the **Mass Change** menu options, the system will ask you which "from" and "to" currencies to use; in other words, which currencies do you want to change and to what?

The example in Figure 4.52 shows the system selecting all documents with a currency of USD and converting them to currency EUR.

Figure 4.52 New Currency Mass Change

When processing a mass change, the change is carried out by SAP in the background without any transactional foreground activity. When the mass change is completed, SAP will post a message to tell you that the inquiries in question have been changed and saved.

4.5.2 Manage Sales Inquiries

In the Manage Sales Inquiries app, there are a number of ways to search and find desired data.

First, you should be aware of the filters area, as shown in Figure 4.53, wherein you can build a set of selection parameters in the same way you do in Transaction VA15 in SAP GUI.

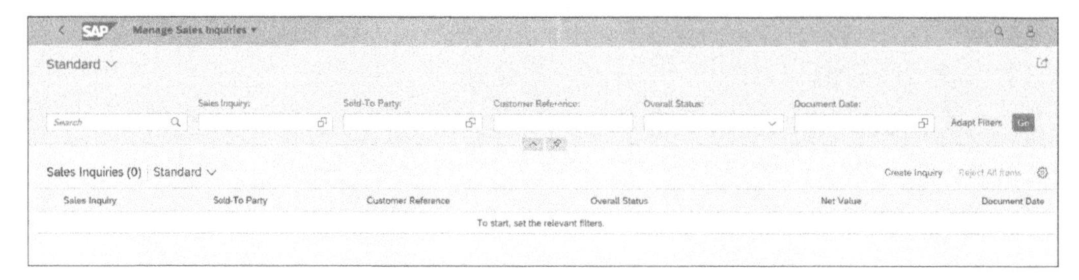

Figure 4.53 Manage Sales Inquiries: Filters

From here, you can select the **Adapt Filters** button shown in Figure 4.54, in order to amend the filters available.

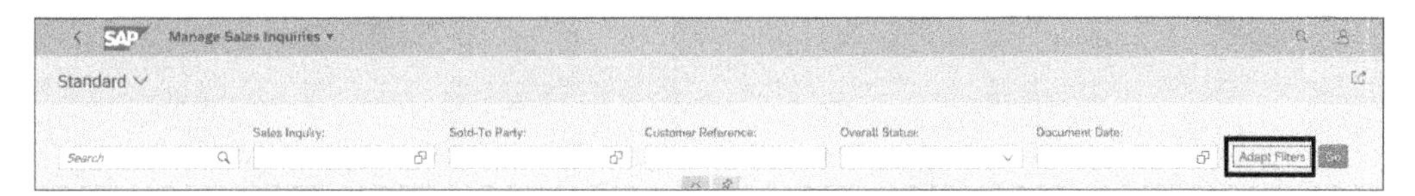

Figure 4.54 Manage Sales Inquiries: Adapt Filters

4

If you want to add sales area as a search criterion for future use, for example, follows these steps:

1. After clicking on the Adapt Filters button, click on the **More Filters** button at the bottom of the screen. This then open the **Select Filters** dialog box, as shown in Figure 4.55.

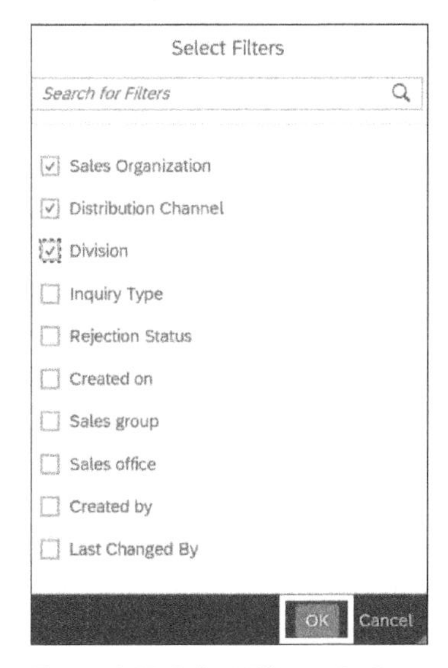

Figure 4.55 Select Filters: Options

2. Check the desired filters, which for this example are the sales area fields: **Sales Organization**, **Distribution Channel**, and **Division**. Click on the **OK** button.

   The **Adapt Filters** dialog, thus amended, then appears.

3. Click on the **Save** button. The **Save View** dialog appears.
4. For this example, enter "My Standard" into the **View** field to create a new search view.
5. Choose the **Set as Default** checkbox so the system will display this selection automatically by default. Click on **Save**.
6. The **Adapt Filters** dialog now reappears with your selected search parameters. Enter the desired sales area data to search by, and then click Go, as shown in Figure 4.56.

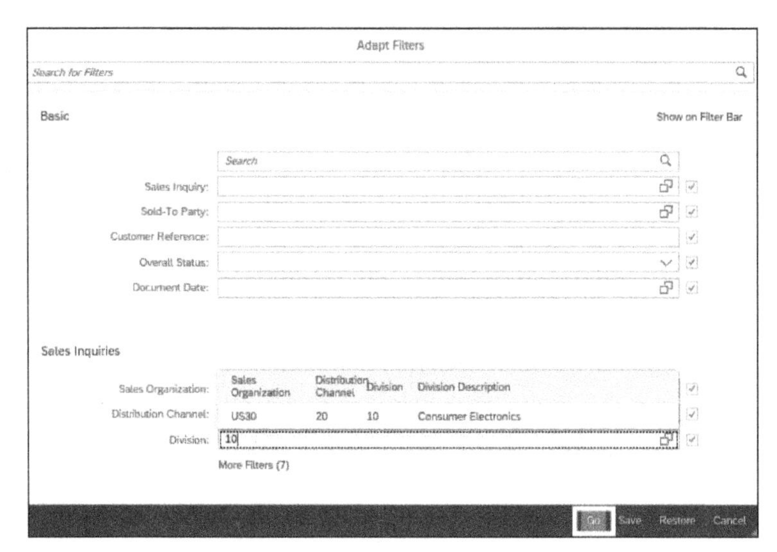

Figure 4.56 Filters Now Adapted

Your search results and new search view are output as shown in Figure 4.57.

Manage Sales Inquiries

My Standard *

Sales Inquiries (10) Standard

Sales Inquiry	Sold-To Party	Customer Reference	Overall Status	Net Value	Document Date
7000012	Cyber Corporation (20)	SEP202020B	Open	7,495.000 USD	09/22/2020
7000011	Cyber Corporation (20)	SEP222020A	Open	14,990.000 USD	09/22/2020
7000010	Digital, Inc. (92)		Open	7,495.000 USD	09/12/2020
7000009	Digital, Inc. (92)	SEP122020A	Completed	7,495.000 USD	09/12/2020
7000008	Digital, Inc. (92)		Open	1,499.000 USD	09/11/2020
7000006	Digital, Inc. (92)	Harvey	Completed	1,499.000 USD	09/04/2020
7000004	Digital, Inc. (92)		Open	1,499.000 USD	08/26/2020
7000003	Digital, Inc. (92)	AUG192020G	Open	14,990.000 USD	08/20/2020
7000002	Digital, Inc. (92)	AUG182020F	Completed	14,990.000 USD	08/19/2020
7000001	Digital, Inc. (92)		Open	14,990.000 USD	08/18/2020

Figure 4.57 Manage Sales Inquiries: Amended with Filters

Note that the search parameters are displayed on top as **My Standard**. This is to be distinguished from the **Standard** view of the search results shown in the middle of the screen.

The **Overall Status** dropdown serves to restrict output by **Completed**, **In Process**, **Not Relevant**, or **Open** inquiries (see Figure 4.58), much like the radio buttons in Transaction VA15 discussed earlier.

7. After your filters are set correctly and saved, you can do the same for your output method. Your layout settings can be amended by using the **Settings** icon, as shown Figure 4.59. The drop-down arrow next to **standard** is used to save the settings once amended.

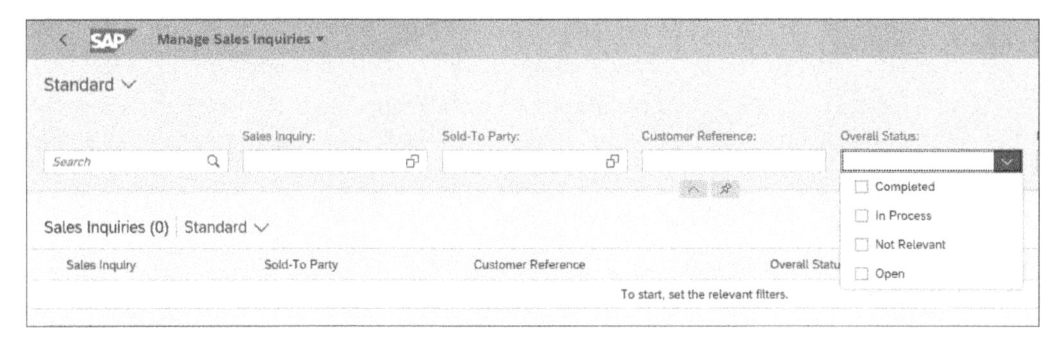

Figure 4.58 Manage Sales Inquiries: Overall Status Filter Options

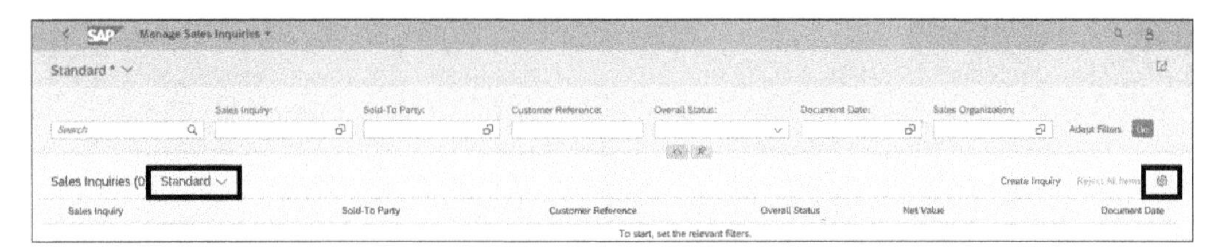

Figure 4.59 Manage Sales Inquiries: Settings and Layout Save

8. After you click the **Settings** icon, the **View Settings** dialog appears, as shown in Figure 4.60. This is where you can select and rearrange desired columns, just as in Transaction VA15.

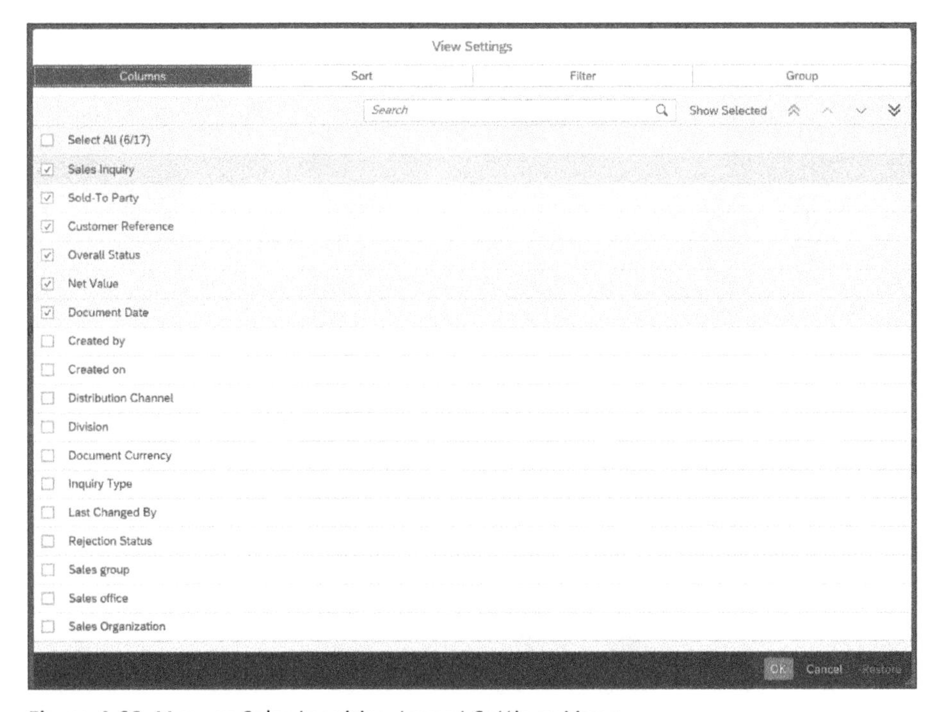

Figure 4.60 Manage Sales Inquiries: Layout Settings Menu

9. When the settings have been amended, you can save the layout by selecting the drop-down arrow next to standard, as highlighted in Figure 4.59.
10. Once back on the output results screen, explore the selected inquiry documents by clicking on the inquiry number or the customer name, and drilling down into further detailed data (see Figure 4.61).

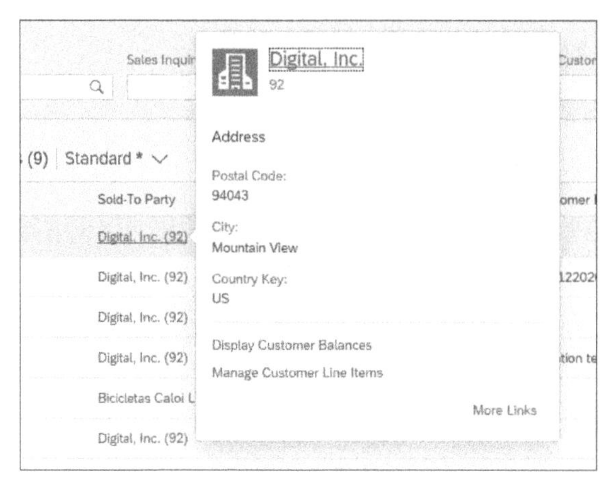

Figure 4.61 Manage Sales Inquiries: Sold-to Party Drilldown Data

11. From this option, click on the **More Links** button in the lower-right corner to add more detailed links for drilldown capabilities. Figure 4.62 shows the available drilldown options for the customer number.

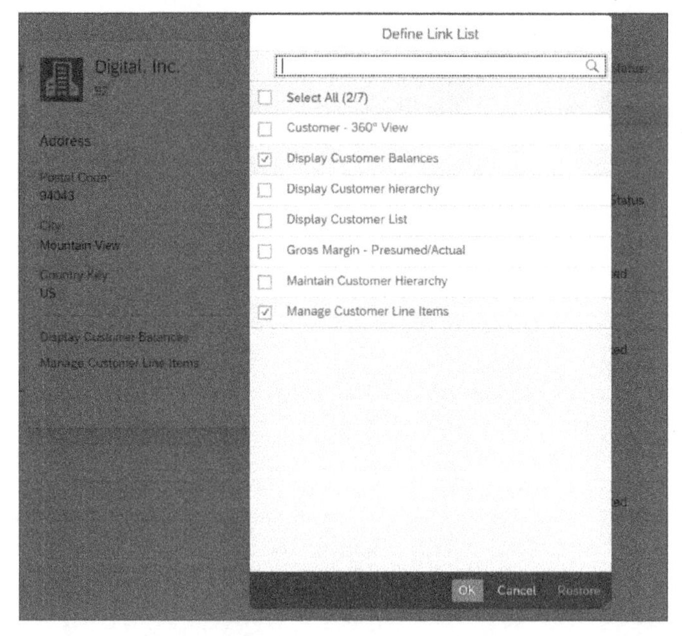

Figure 4.62 Manage Sales Inquiries: More Links

When using these drilldown options, remember that you can navigate to other apps for related data in the Manage Sales Inquiries app. You can also navigate directly to the inquiry itself by clicking anywhere on the line in the display screen.

As noted in Section 4.4.1, you can also click on the inquiry numbers directly to reveal the context-sensitive menu permitting you to open the selected inquiry in change or display modes, as shown in Figure 4.63.

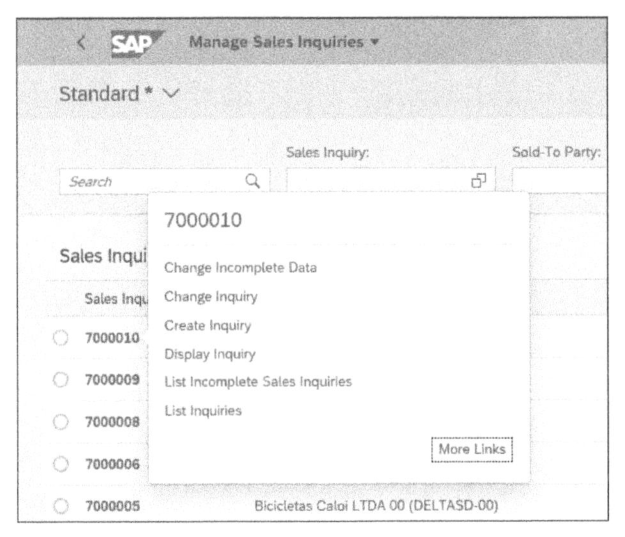

Figure 4.63 Manage Sales Inquiries: Inquiry Number Drilldown

4.6 Summary

In this chapter, we have explored the concept of the presales document, inquiries. This is traditionally the initial step in the order-to-cash process and understanding this gives you a sound knowledge of how SAP S/4HANA sales documents work for all other documents in the process: quotations, sales orders, deliveries and billing. You will find as your understanding of sales and distribution in SAP S/4HANA grows, that many of the principles that the sales and distribution module relies upon, and which have been outlined in this chapter, can be applied to all of these documents.

In the next chapter, we will build upon your new-found sales and distribution knowledge and apply it to the next document in the process: quotations.

Chapter 5
Presales Quotations

Presales starts with the nonbinding inquiry document and ends with the binding quotations document. In this chapter, we'll follow up on the inquiry created in the previous chapter and convert it into a quotation to complete the presales process (before progressing to the sales document).

This chapter is organized as follows: First, we acknowledge the previous steps in the presales processes, namely inquiries, by describing the quotation subprocess and its place in the overall order-to-cash transaction flow. Second, we'll walk through creating a quotation document with reference to the inquiry created earlier. We'll focus on all the necessary inputs from you, the user, as well as important inputs copied over from the previous document or determined by the system. As elsewhere in this book, we'll perform the walkthroughs in both SAP GUI and SAP Fiori. Third, we'll print the quotation. Fourth, we'll review changing and displaying your quotation once it's created in both SAP GUI and SAP Fiori. And, finally, we'll cover how to generate a list of all quotations in the system. This is helpful when you're searching for a quotation without knowing the document numbers but you do know the customer, date ranges, or other information).

5.1 Process Overview

After your business has sent a nonbinding inquiry to your potential customer, you may engage in further follow-on presales activities, such as phone calls, meetings, and presentations, to secure the next step in the presales process: the legally binding quotation. Of course, your customer could also just simply accept the inquiry outright, skip the quotation, and send you their purchase order to buy the product at the indicated price. In both cases, you'll be able to create either the follow-on quotation or sales document using the inquiry document as a template to fill in fields such as **Customer**, **Material**, **Quantity**, and **Price**.

In this regard, SAP also offers a very robust presales process as part of its SAP Customer Relationship Management (SAP CRM) package, which can be configured to flow into the SAP S/4HANA order-to-cash process.

As noted in Chapter 4, Section 4.1, the following presales processes are part and parcel of SAP S/4HANA:

- **Inquiry**
  This nonbinding document is issued to a potential customer with respect to an identified interest in one of your products at a specified quantity and price.
- **Quotation**
  Potential customers who respond favorably to the inquiry may request a binding quote on the indicated product for a specific quantity and price. This quotation document will also have an expiration date regarding the promised quantity and price terms. This document may be created as a copy of the initial quotation or as a fresh document with all the inputs made directly into all required fields.

This chapter focuses on the quotation process, which is covered in the brown highlighted section of the flowchart in Figure 5.1.

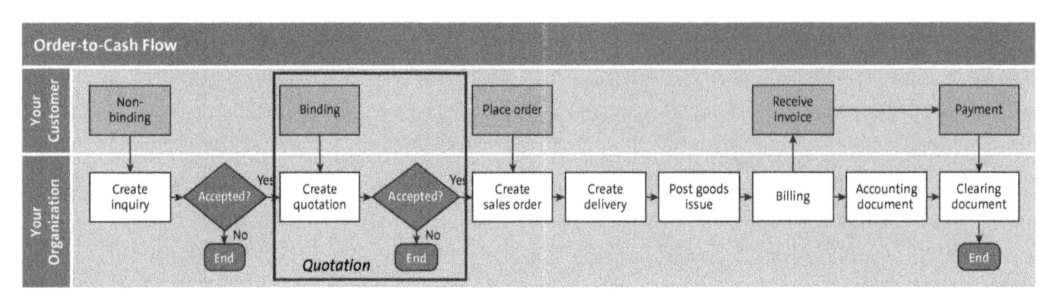

Figure 5.1 Order to Cash Flow: Quotations

5.2 Document Types

The order-to-cash process is preconfigured to use the following basic document types from quotation through billing:

- IN: Inquiry
- QT: Quotation
- OR: Standard order
- RE: Returns order
- CR: Credit memo request
- DR: Debit memo request
- LF: Outbound delivery document
- LR: Returns delivery
- F1: Sales invoice for an order
- F2: Sales Invoice for a delivery
- G2: Credit memo
- L2: Debit memo

These documents control how SAP will process information input by the user (or input via interface) in terms of an inquiry, quotation, sales, delivery, and so on. This means that certain documents will require specific field data and others won't. For example, inquiries, quotations, sales, and billing documents will require pricing information, but deliveries do not because they concern themselves with other kinds of details related to shipping.

Note

See Chapter 4, Section 4.2, for more information about document types.

5.3 Create a Quotation Document

This section will cover the creation of the quotation with reference, whereby the customer and material fields are copied over and don't need to be filled in.

Note

For both creating a quotation with and without reference to an existing inquiry, you use the same Transaction VA21. If creating the quotation without reference to an existing inquiry, complete the sales area fields as shown in Chapter 4, Section 4.3, and follow the steps in that chapter.

To create a quotation with reference to a preceding document, follow these steps:

1. Enter Transaction code VA21.
2. Enter "QT" in the **Quotation Type** field; QT is the standard SAP document type for quotations.
3. Click on the **Create with Reference** button, as shown in Figure 5.2.

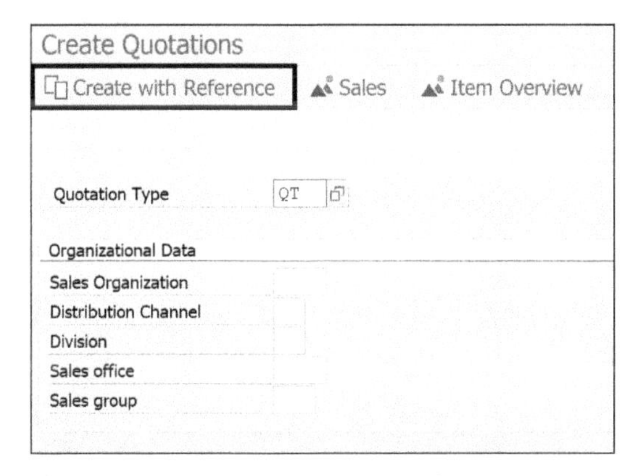

Figure 5.2 Create Quotation: Initial Screen

4. In the **Create with Reference** dialog, enter "700000001" in the **Inquiry** field. This is the document number of the inquiry created in the preceding chapter.
5. Click on the **Copy** button on the lower-right corner of the dialog, as shown in Figure 5.3.

Create with Reference

Inquiry | Quotation | Order | Contract | SchedAgree | BillDoc

Inquiry 7000001
Requested Deliv.Date

Search Criteria
Pur. Order
Sold-To Party
WBS Element

Search

Copy | Item Selection

Figure 5.3 Create with Reference Dialog

You're now in the main **Create Quotation: Overview** screen, which has been completed with some important data from your preceding document. Let's take a moment to review what has been completed on your behalf by the system.

5.3.1 Header Data

Your customer or business partner information in the form of sold-to party and ship-to party (as well as the other main functions, bill-to party and payer) have been copied over to their corresponding fields at the top of the **Create Quotation: Overview** shown in Figure 5.4. To review the relationships of these business partner functions, refer to Chapter 2, Section 2.2.1, for more comprehensive details.

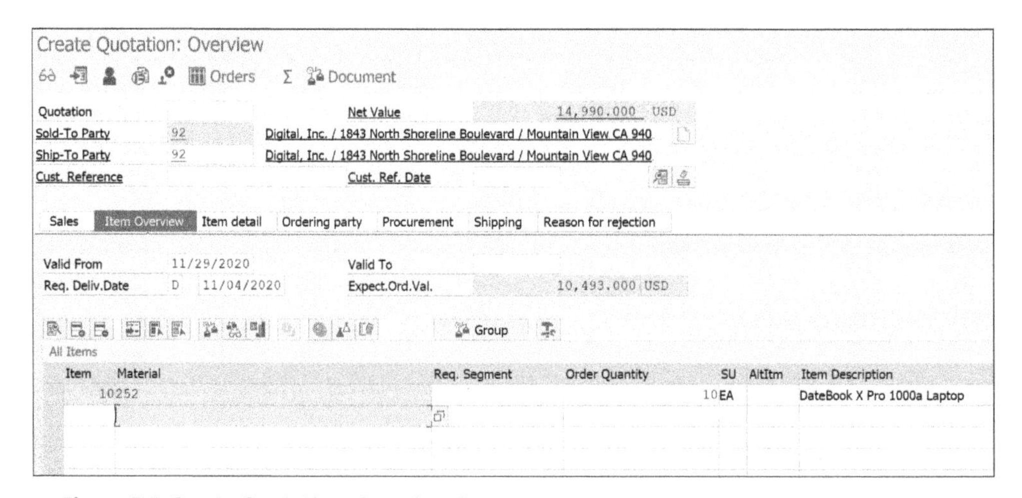

Figure 5.4 Create Quotation: Overview Screen

Review all header fields copied over from your preceding document as follows:

- **Sold-To Party: 92**
- **Ship-To Party: 92**
- (Optional) **Cust. Reference**: This field isn't copied over from the inquiry.
- **Valid From: 11/29/2020**
- **Valid To**: This field isn't copied over from the inquiry.

The **Cust. Reference** field is used for any number issued by the customer for their own tracking of the quotation. In the sales document to follow (assuming that this quotation document is accepted), this field will be the customer's purchase order number. This field isn't system required. Because the field is, frequently business required, however, it's included here as an optional field for a fresh value as received from the customer.

You'll notice that this field and the **Valid To** field aren't copied over from the inquiry. This is a signal from the system to you, the user, to input fresh values. For example, what expiration date do you want for this quotation? It's probably different from the value that was input in the preceding inquiry document.

For the purposes of this chapter, enter "NOV292020F" in the optional **Cust. Reference** field, and enter "12/31/2020" in the required **Valid To** field.

Your quotation screen should now appear as shown in Figure 5.5.

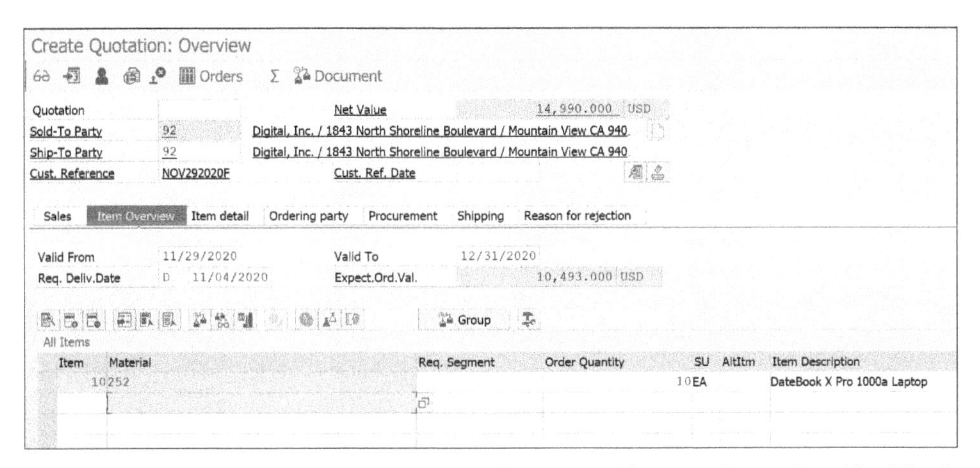

Figure 5.5 Create Quotation Overview Screen after Input of "Cust. Reference" and "Valid To" Values

Note that the **Req. Deliv.Date** field defaults to the current date (although this can be customized as needed). This is the date that the goods are to be delivered to the customer and is often changed from the current date to several days in the future to reflect a reasonable delivery time. This is a header data field and copies into the **Delivery Date** field in the **Schedule Lines** tab of the material line item where it can be changed. If changed at the line-item level, that date overrides the header date in terms of delivery planning (and the header date, interestingly, remains unchanged).

5.3.2 Line-Item Data

Review all header fields copied over from your preceding document as follows:

- **Material**: 252
- **Order Quantity**: 10

The **Create with Reference** functionality used to create your quotation does a lot of the heavy lifting on your behalf, including copying over these line-item fields. The **Material** number can't be changed, but the **Order Quantity** may be changed to suit the customer's requirements.

At this point, your customer details, customer reference number, validity dates, material, and quantity as input and price as determined are clearly visible in both the header and line-item sections. This is all that is required to complete a quotation.

5.3.3 Other Header and Line-Item Data

There are some other commonly used optional or business-required fields to be aware of. This section repeats some of the content from the Chapter 4, so feel free to skim as necessary.

Header Data

The header data section contains many additional fields that will potentially have repercussions on the price and availability information you provide to your customer. Remember, depending on the setup of your system, quotation documents may generate output documents that are sent to your customer automatically, and you need to be sure that the information contained therein is accurate.

Some of these header fields are visible in the **Sales** tab of the **Create Quotation: Overview** screen as shown in Figure 5.6:

- **Pyt Terms**
  What are the payment conditions under which your customer will be trading with you? This can be defined in the customer master data and then copied automatically into all sales and distribution documents.
- **Incoterms**
  Who will have responsibility for the shipments at which phase in the process? This can also be defined in the customer master data.
- **Doc. Currency**
  Is the currency correct? Again, this can also be set up once in the customer master data.

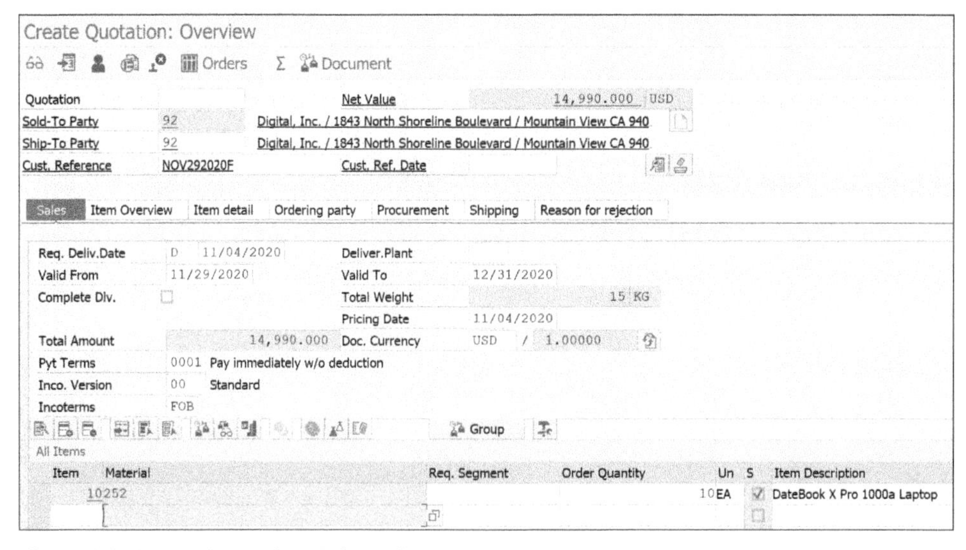

Figure 5.6 Create Quotation: Sales Tab

By clicking on the **Display Header Details** button in Figure 5.7, you can open all the header data for the quotation, as displayed in Figure 5.8.

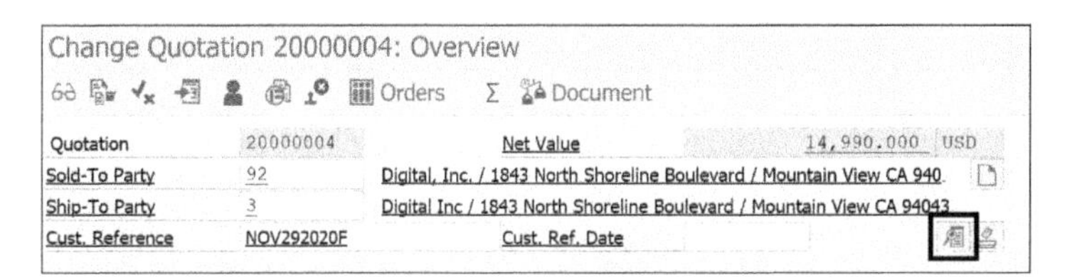

Figure 5.7 Create Quotation: Display Header Details Button

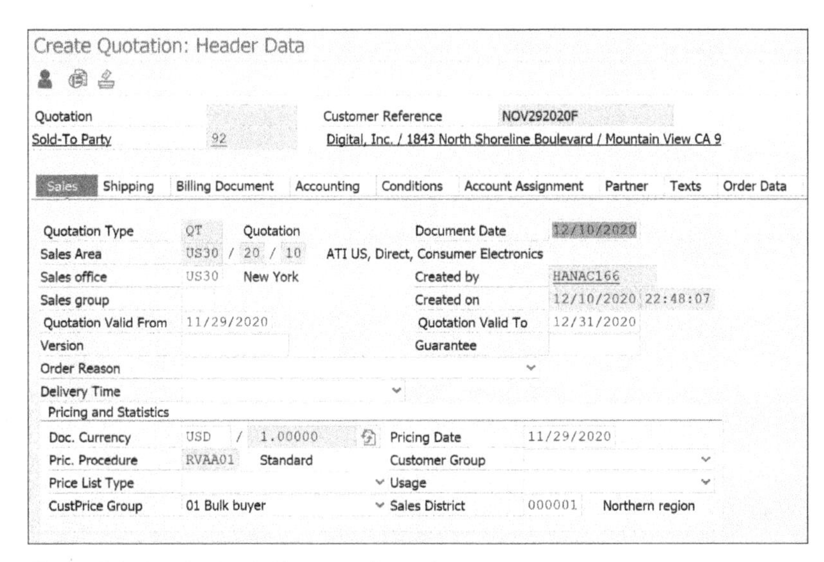

Figure 5.8 Create Quotation: Header Data

From here, all header information is shown in various tabs, including more detailed information, such as the following:

- **Shp.Cond.** (shipping condition)
  If the customer requested a specific shipping condition (e.g., must be delivered as a rush) or wants to pick up the products, this may have an impact on your freight price determination. The **Shp.Cond.** field is found on the **Shipping** tab as shown in Figure 5.9. This can be set in the customer's master data.

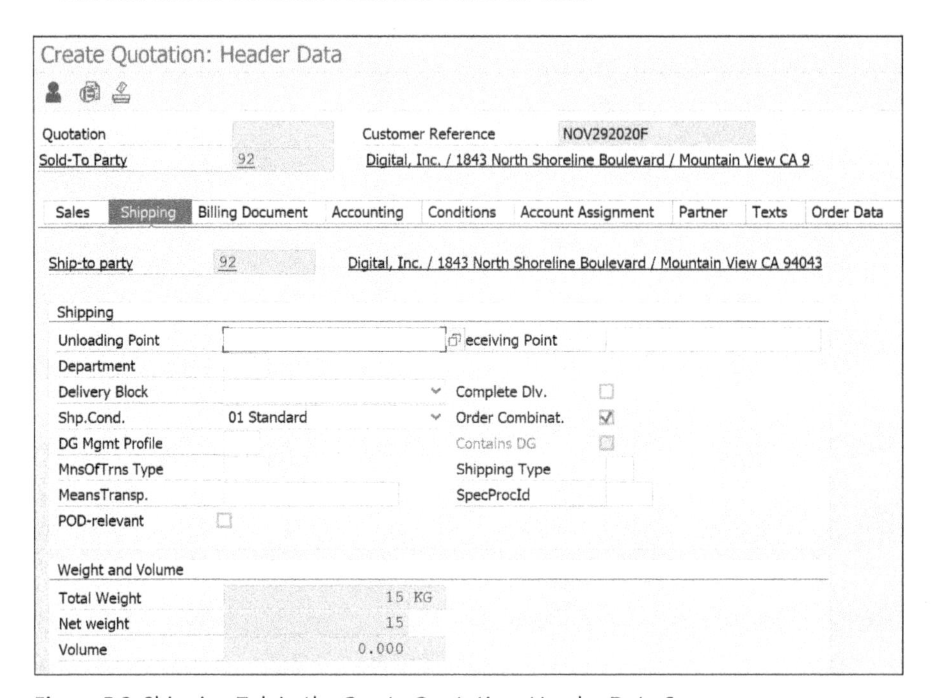

Figure 5.9 Shipping Tab in the Create Quotation: Header Data Screen

- **Partn. Funct.** (partner functions)
  If you need to change any of the partner functions, such as the bill-to party or the payer, or want to add a new partner function for a carrier or an end customer, for example, this can be done in the **Partner** tab, as shown in Figure 5.10.

- **Txt ty.**
  Are there any specific header texts you want to add to the document? This means that this particular text is applicable to *all* items in the order. Depending on your setup in the system, these can be included in the output document for the customer. These texts can be added in the **Texts** tab, as shown in Figure 5.11.

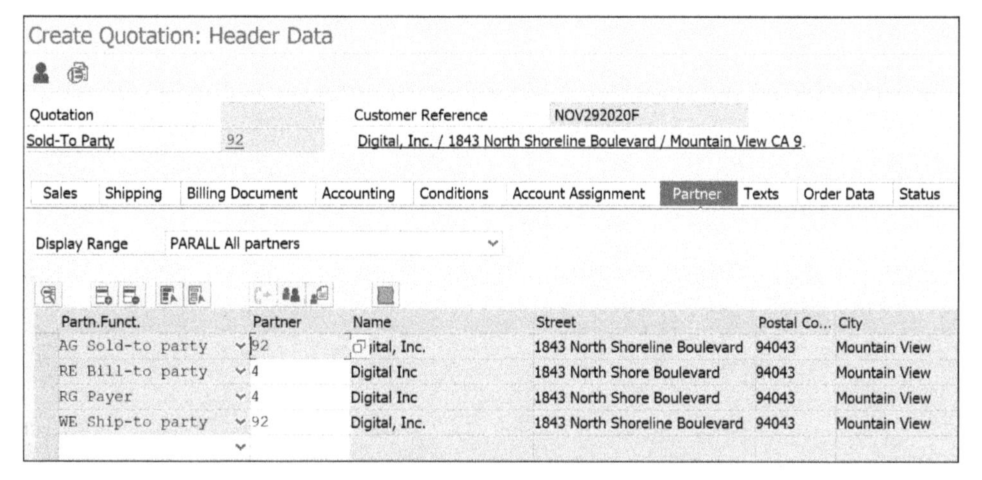

Figure 5.10 Partner Tab in the Create Quotation: Header Data Screen

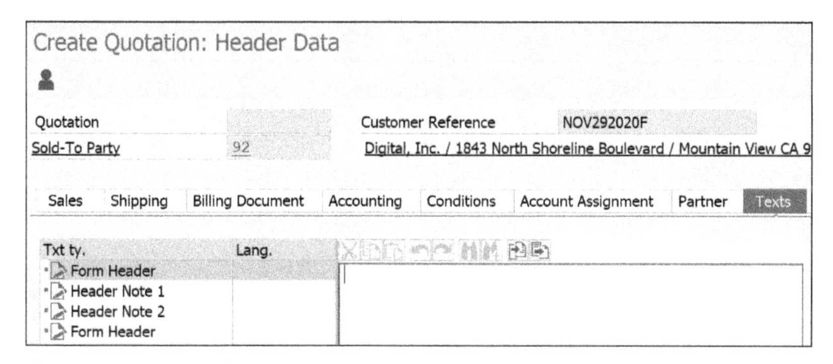

Figure 5.11 Texts Tab in the Create Quotation: Header Data Screen

Line-Item Data

By double-clicking the line items, you can open the item data per material line in the quotation document. Item data therefore can vary from line item to line item. The key data for a quotation line item is the material unit price, which is in the **Conditions** tab. (More information on pricing is available in Chapter 2.) The following line-item fields are found in various tabs:

- **Price**
  Check that prices are correct. Do you need to add any discounts or customer-specific pricing, surcharges, or freight? All these options are available by adding new or changing existing condition types into the screen shown in Figure 5.12.

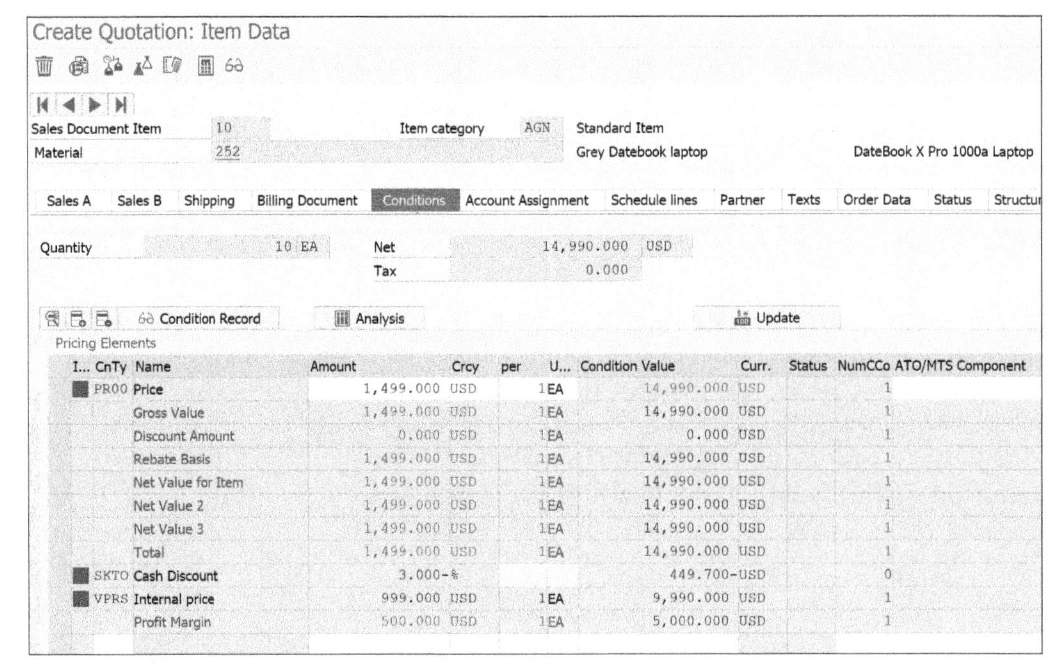

Figure 5.12 Conditions Tab in the Create Quotation: Item Data Screen

- **Batch**
  If the material is batch managed, has the customer requested price and availability of a specific batch? If so, this can be added in the **Sales A** tab, as shown in Figure 5.13. Note that the **Batch** field won't show if the material isn't batch managed.

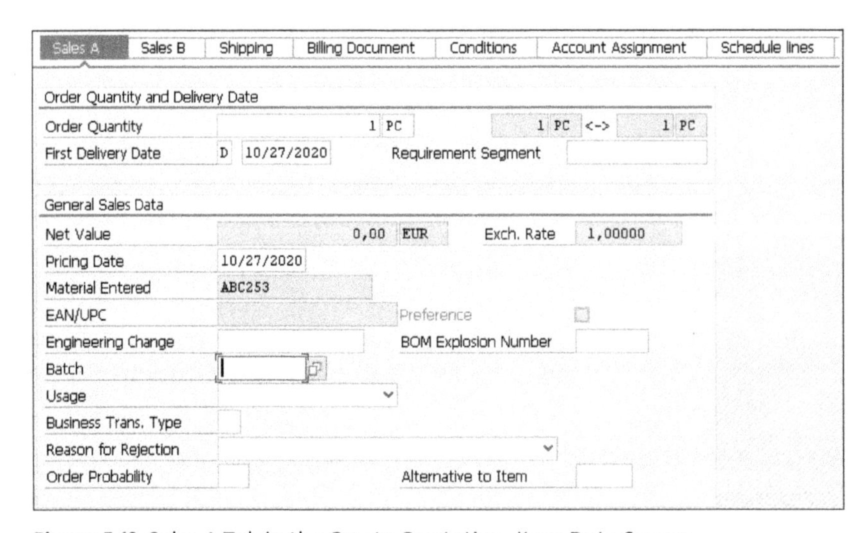

Figure 5.13 Sales A Tab in the Create Quotation: Item Data Screen

- **Delivery Date**
  Has the customer requested a quotation for delivery of products to be scheduled

across multiple future dates? These dates can be changed and added in the **Schedule lines** tab, as shown in Figure 5.14. As noted earlier, this line-item delivery date overrides but doesn't change the **Req. DelivDate** in the header. This allows for an order of, say, 10 pieces to be split into 2 (or more) schedule lines by delivery due date. For example, 8 units can be delivered on one date and the other 2 a week later (for a total of 10).

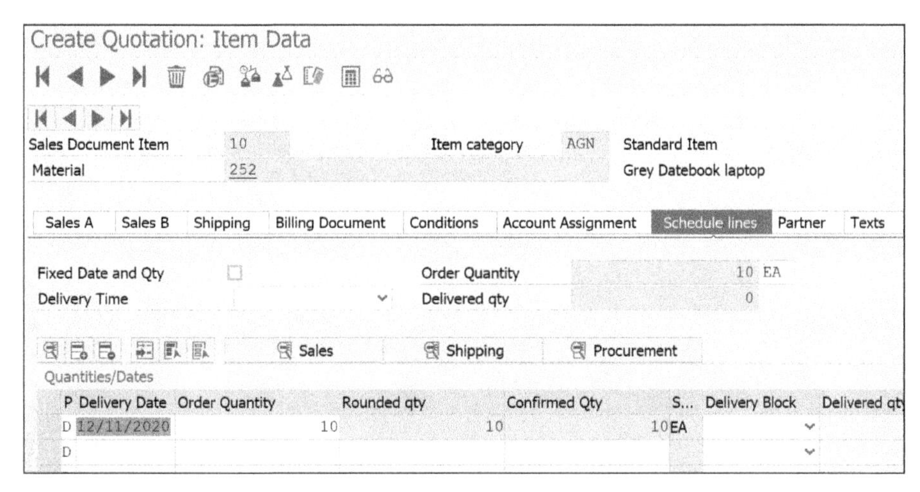

Figure 5.14 Schedule Lines Tab in the Create Quotation: Item Data Screen

- **Txt ty.**
  Are there any specific item texts you want to add to the document line item? Remember, header text applies to the entire order and all line items. Line-item text is specific only to the particular quotation line item. For example, if one material in the quotation needs to be kept at a special temperature, that information could be provided as text here. Depending on your setup in the system, these can be included automatically in the output document for the customer. These texts can be reviewed or added in the line-item **Texts** tab, as shown in Figure 5.15.

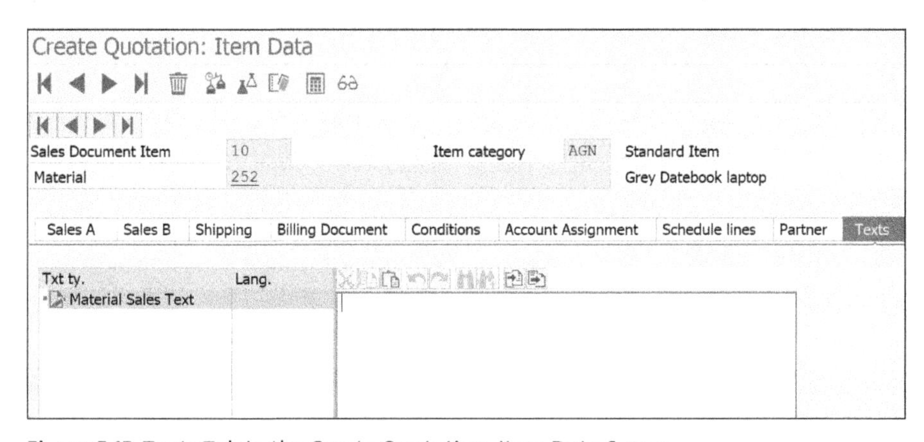

Figure 5.15 Texts Tab in the Create Quotation: Item Data Screen

Incompletion Log

The quotation document is now complete for all required and many other commonly used fields. To check incompletion status, choose **Edit • Incompletion Log** on the menu bar, as shown in Figure 5.16.

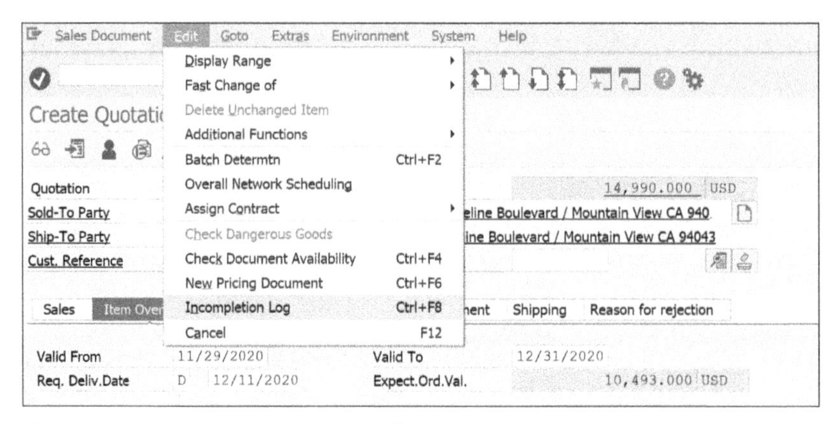

Figure 5.16 Create Quotation Incompletion Log

This launches the incompletion procedure, which checks that all system-required fields have been correctly populated in your document. If any are missing, then a new screen will appear showing which fields are missing entries. From here, you can navigate to all and fill in the missing data.

After all the required fields are completed, the following message appears on the status bar, in the lower-left corner of your screen (see Figure 5.17).

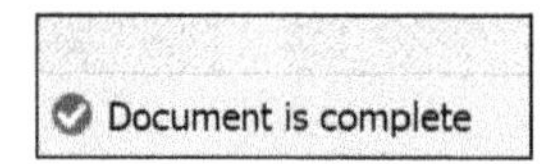

Figure 5.17 Incompletion Log Message

5.3.4 Printing Output

If you'll be issuing either a hard copy or soft copy output to the customer, you can look at the quotation to be printed on the screen before completing it to ensure that everything looks correct. At this point, the quotation is still not yet saved and therefore isn't active in the system. Accordingly, the system will generate a proposed or preview version of the document for you to review on screen. Only when you save the quotation will a finalized version be generated with a document number and then printed/ emailed to the customer.

You can also look at the output conditions to see how it was determined. Let's first look at the output itself. From within the **Create Quotation: Overview** screen, you can click the **Header Output Preview** icon, as shown in Figure 5.18. This will generate an onscreen print preview of the output.

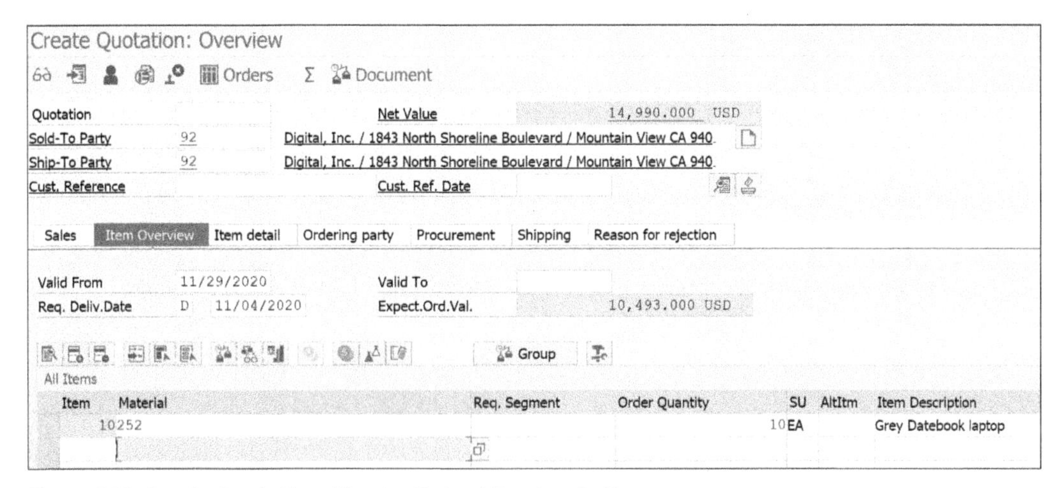

Figure 5.18 Create Quotation: Header Output Preview Button

Next, if you want to see the technical details regarding the output type and how it was determined, there are a couple of ways to do this. You can choose **Extras • Output • Header • Edit** to open the **Create Quotation: Output** screen to show you the output type created, as shown in Figure 5.19.

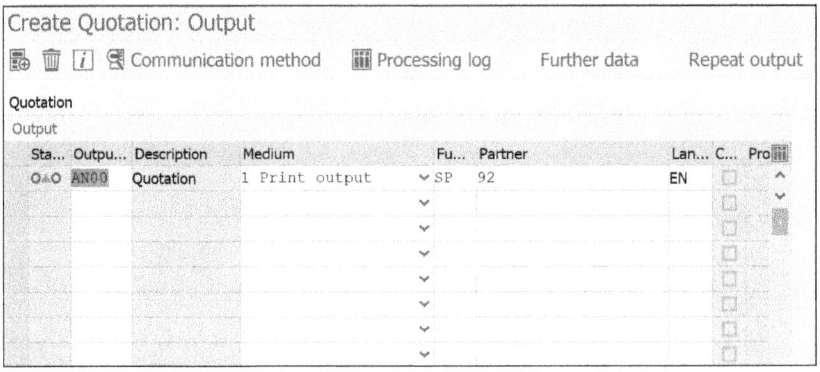

Figure 5.19 Create Quotation: Output

In the preceding example, the AN00 standard quotation output type shows a yellow traffic light, which means that it's waiting to be printed. After saving, it may show a green light to indicate that it has printed or a red traffic light to show that it has failed to print. The term "print," of course, can mean printing a hard copy as well as creating a soft copy to be transmitted in numerous ways, including PDF via email or electronic data interchange (EDI).

All outputs store data in certain formats for review. A specific output type can be specified by following standard sales and distribution condition technique processing (see Chapter 2), for condition technique details). If you want to see how the output has been determined, you can do this from the same output request screen. From the menu bar, select **Goto • Determination Analysis** to access a very busy screen where you can analyze how the output has been selected, as shown in Figure 5.20.

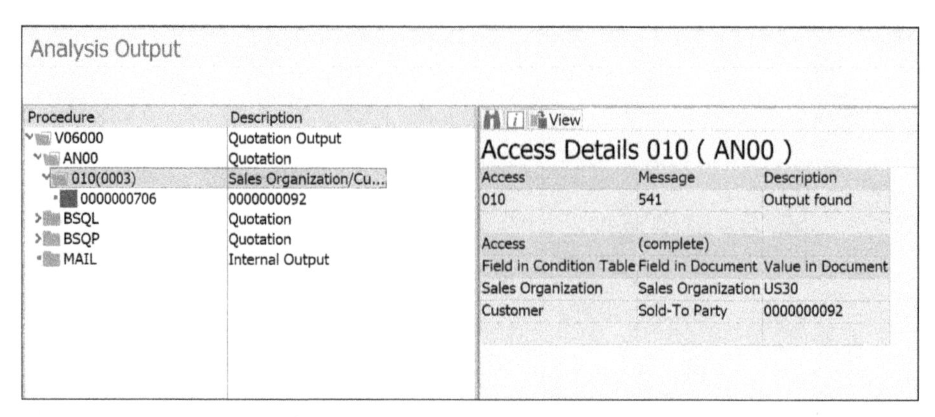

Figure 5.20 Quotation: Analysis Output

In the right side of the screen shown in the preceding figure, you can see that the output type AN00 has been determined via a combination of the sales organization US30 and customer 92 in the quotation.

You're now ready to save your quotation. Click on the **Save** icon, as shown in Figure 5.21.

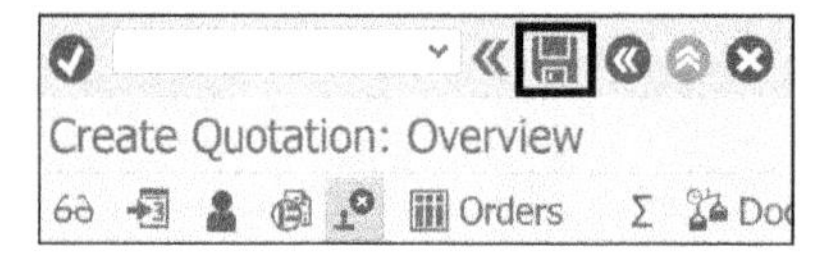

Figure 5.21 Create Quotation: Save Icon

The quotation document number should appear on the status bar in the lower-left corner of the screen shown in Figure 5.22.

Figure 5.22 Quotation: Saved Message

5.3.5 Manage Sales Quotations App FIORI

To create a quotation in SAP Fiori, proceed as follows:

1. Launch the Manage Sales Quotations app, and click on the **Create Quotation** link, as shown in Figure 5.23.

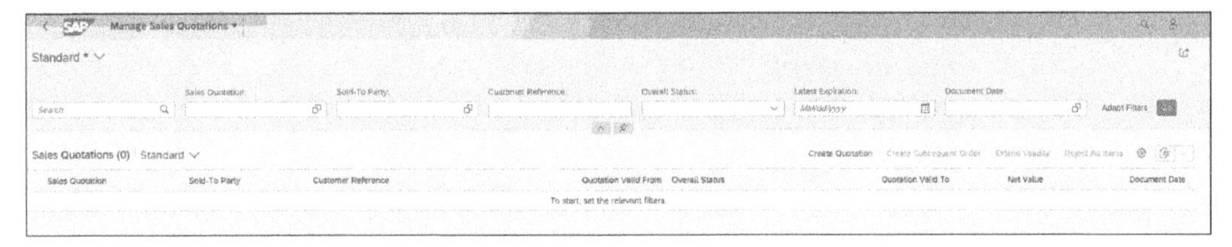

Figure 5.23 Manage Sales Quotations App

2. In the **Create Quotation: Overview** screen, input values for **Quotation Type** and **Sales Area**, as you did previously in the SAP GUI screen (refer to Figure 5.2).
3. In the **Create Quotation: Overview** screen, input all header and line-item data as shown in Figure 5.24. The screen is the same, except that now it's in a browser, which means it can be accessed via a variety of internet devices.
4. After all data is input as described in the preceding steps, press Enter, and then click **Save**.

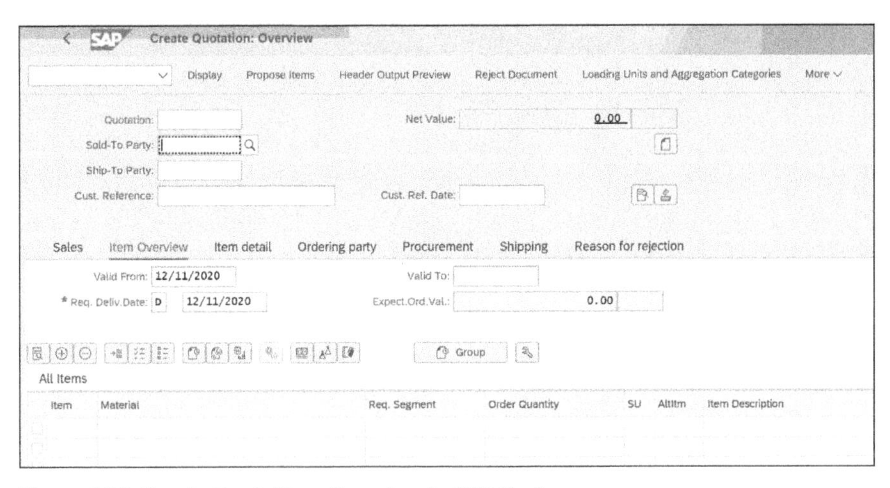

Figure 5.24 Create Quotation: Overview in SAP Fiori

5.4 Change and Display a Quotation Document (SAP GUI)

To change or display a quotation, proceed as follows:

1. To change a quotation, use Transaction VA22. Likewise, to display a quotation, use Transaction VA23. Remember that if you're anywhere *except* the SAP main menu, you must preface your transaction code with "/n," without the quotation marks or comma. For example, after saving your quotation, you can go directly to change mode by typing "/NVA12" (without quotation marks) in the transaction code field and then pressing Enter.

2. After creating your quotation document in SAP per the preceding steps in Section 4.3 and seeing the "saved" message in Figure 5.25, you can also display the quotation by clicking the **Display** icon in the same screen.

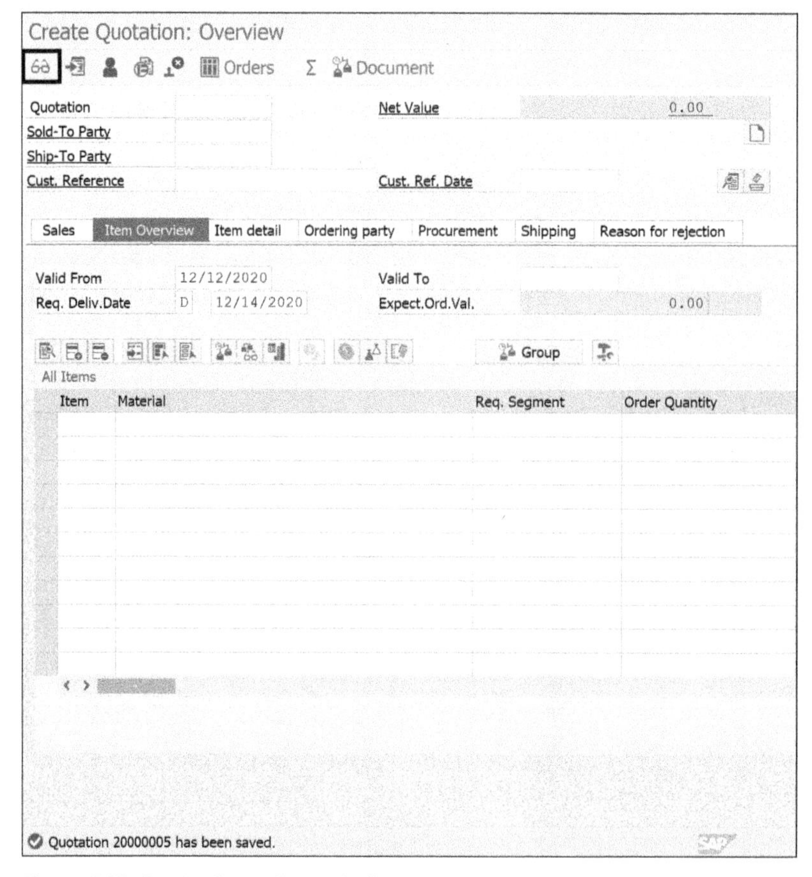

Figure 5.25 Create Quotation: Display Icon

This navigates directly to Transaction VA23 (Display Quotation), where you can see the quotation just created in display mode, meaning that all fields can be viewed but not amended.

3. Switch to change mode by the clicking the **Change** icon as displayed in Figure 5.26.

Display Quotation 20000004: Overview

Orders Σ

Quotation	20000004	Net Value	14,990.000 USD
Sold-To Party	92	Digital, Inc. / 1843 North Shoreline Boulevard / Mountain View CA 940	
Ship-To Party	3	Digital Inc / 1843 North Shoreline Boulevard / Mountain View CA 94043	
Cust. Reference	NOV292020F	Cust. Ref. Date	

Figure 5.26 Display Quotation: Change Icon

Note

By clicking the **Change** or **Display** buttons in the toolbar, you can toggle back and forth in the document.

Identical to the **Create Quotation** screens, the **Change** and **Display** screens are separated into three sections: overview, header and line item. The initial screen is the **Overview** view and shows the **Item Overview** tab.

The main quotation fields to be reviewed via change or display modes are as follows:

- **Quotation Document Number**
  Found in the upper-left corner of the **Overview** screen. This field can't be changed.
- **Quotation Document Type**
  For such an important field, SAP hides this in the **Sales** tab of the header section. This field can't be changed.
- **Sold-To Party/Ship-To Party**
  Found just below the **Quotation Document Number** on the **Overview** screen. These fields can be changed if there are no subsequent documents. Please see Chapter 9 for more information.
- **Sales Area**
  Like the **Document Type**, this critical information is found in the Sales tab of the header section. All three component fields can't be changed.
- **Cust. Reference**
  This optional field is found just below the **Sold-To Party** and **Ship-To Party** on the **Overview** screen. The field can be changed.
- **Net Value**
  Found on the top right of the **Overview** screen, this field is a sum of all price conditions. If the prices are changed in the line item **Conditions** tab, then those changes will be reflected here.
- **Material Number/Description**
  Material numbers and their corresponding descriptions appear in the grid in the center of the **Overview** screen. New **Material Number** line items can be added. However, deleting them is restricted if there are follow-on documents. See Chapter 9.
- **Order Quantity/Unit of Measure**
  These two fields appear together with the material numbers and descriptions in the **Overview** screen. These fields can't be changed, although there are ways to add or reduce quantities (see Chapter 9).
- **Valid From/Valid To**
  These fields are found in the center of the **Overview** screen. Both dates may be changed as necessary.

Note
For more information about which fields can and can't be changed, and how to undo or reverse documents, see Chapter 9 and the matrix therein.

By selecting the other tabs available in the **Overview** screen, you can see other key fields as described in Table 5.1.

Overview Tab	Field	Can Be Changed	Description
Sales	**Payment terms**	Yes	The terms of payment allocated to the payer.
Sales	**Incoterms**	Yes	The delivery and shipping terms agreed to by the sold-to party.
Item Detail	**Item Category**	No	A code that defines how the material behaves in the document. This is determined based on criteria set up in the configuration.
Item Details	**Pricing Date**	No	The date used to determine the price according to the criteria set up in the configuration.
Ordering Party	**Delivering Plant**	Yes, until the order has been delivered	Plant, if assigned to the customer master. This field can be found by scrolling to the right in the material grid (and can be customized to be visible without scrolling, if desired).
Reason for Rejection	**Order Reason**	Yes	Reason the quotation was placed.
Reason for Rejection	**Reason for Rejection**	Yes, if there are no follow-on documents	Reason the quotation has been rejected. See Chapter 9.

Table 5.1 Important Fields in Quotations

Normally, the information in the **Overview** screen will be enough to give you the main points of the quotation. However, as noted previously, more information can be found by drilling down in the header and line-item sections of the quotation:

- To access the header tabs, choose **Goto • Header**, or you can select the **Header** icon (refer to Figure 5.7).
- To view the line-item details, choose **Goto • Item**, or click the **Item Details** icon, as shown in Figure 5.27. You also can double-click on the line item itself.

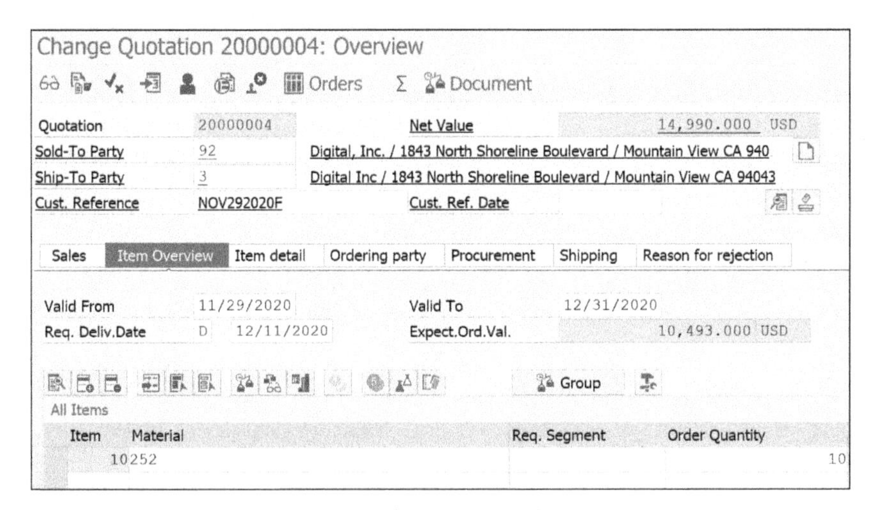

Figure 5.27 Create Quotations: Display Item Details

Again, much of the information in the **Item** tabs can also be found in the **Overview** tabs. For additional data, refer to the line-item fields discussed in Section 4.3.

5.4.1 Document Flow and Status Overview

Document flow is essential in understanding your transactions in terms of completeness. The **Document Flow** icon is located in the toolbar of the **Change Quotation** and **Display Quotation** screens (Transactions VA22 and VA23, respectively), as shown in Figure 5.28.

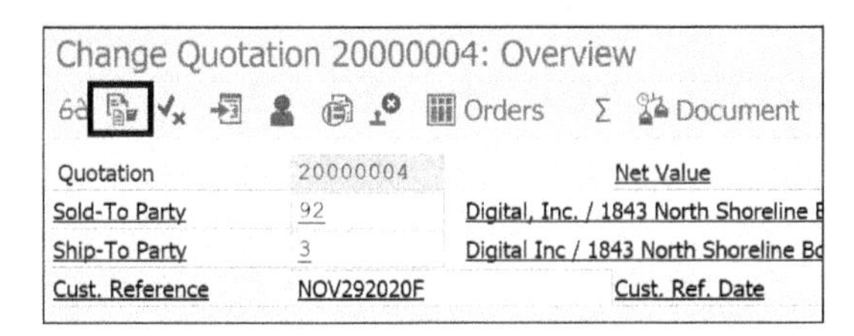

Figure 5.28 Change Quotation: Document Flow Icon

The document flow functionality is available in the following sales and distribution documents:

- Inquiries
- Quotations
- Sales orders
- Deliveries
- Billing documents

This icon displays all preceding and follow-on documents that have been created for the document you're currently looking at. This is critical information for determining how to complete the sales and distribution flow through billing or to reverse it, if necessary.

As an example, if your quotation has been converted into a sales order, you would see that in the document flow, as shown in Figure 5.29. Furthermore, if your quotation had been further processed into a delivery and billing document, these would also show.

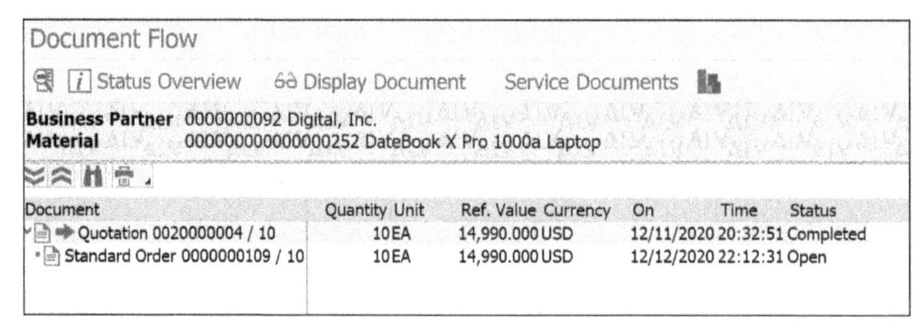

Figure 5.29 Document Flow

By clicking to select any one of the documents and then clicking on the **Display Document** button, you can navigate directly to that specific document in display mode.

Another useful icon in the **Change Quotation** and **Display Quotation** overview screens is the **Status Overview** icon, as shown in Figure 5.30.

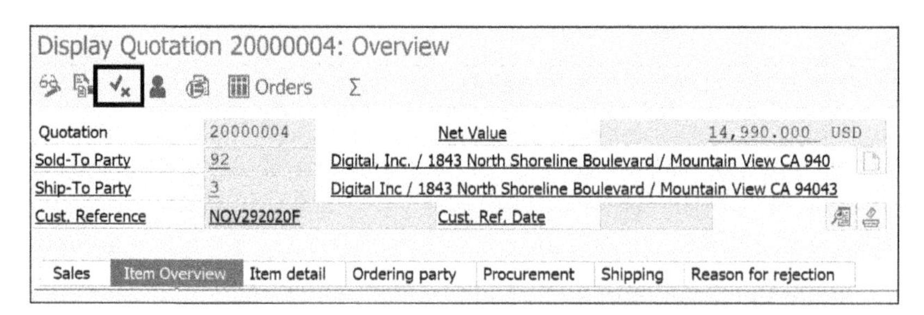

Figure 5.30 Display Quotation: Status Overview Icon

By using the **Status Overview** icon, you can get a full view of the header and item status of the quotation, as shown in Figure 5.31.

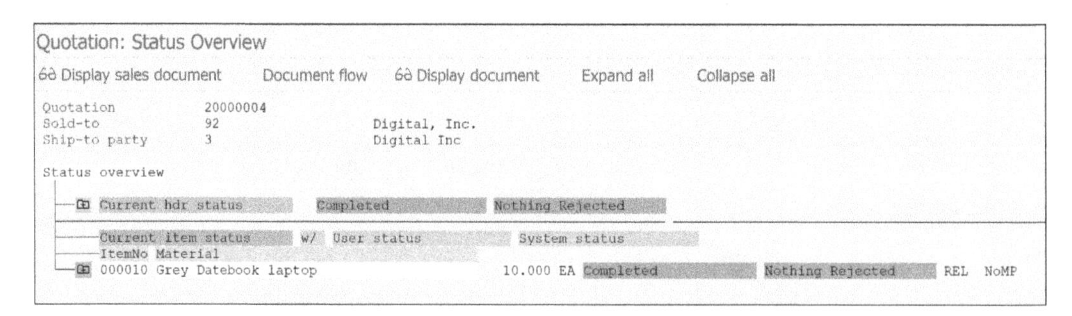

Figure 5.31 Quotation: Status Overview Screen

Again, note that this icon is available for more than just quotations; it's also available for these sales and distribution documents:

- Inquiries
- Quotations
- Sales orders

The **Quotation: Status Overview** screen will show you the overall header and item status for the whole document, including the following item statuses:

- Complete as far as the incompletion procedure is concerned
- Referenced by a subsequent document
- Rejected

5.4.2 Create Subsequent Order

A key action from a quotation is to create the subsequent sales order when the customer has "firmed up" its requirements and is ready to buy the product on the terms offered. To do this, choose **Sales Document • Create Subsequent Order**, as shown in Figure 5.32.

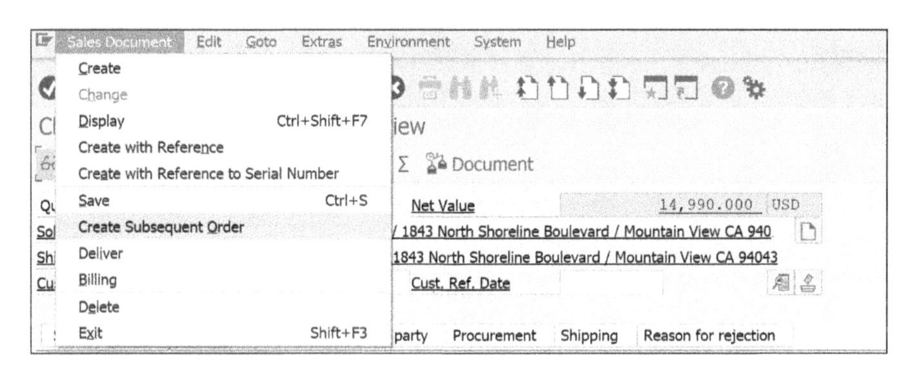

Figure 5.32 Create Subsequent Order

This will save any changes made to the quotation document and immediately open Transaction VA01 (Create Sales Order). We'll cover this in more detail in Chapter 6.

5.4.3 Create with Reference

From the same menu path, you can select **Create with Reference** to pull items from other documents into your new quotation. Note that this can only be achieved if your system has been set up in such a way to allow copying from another document into a quotation.

5.4.4 Mass Change

The **Edit** menu has some very useful features that you can take advantage of, particularly if your quotation has multiple items in it. Figure 5.33 shows the options for mass changing all the items in the quotation document.

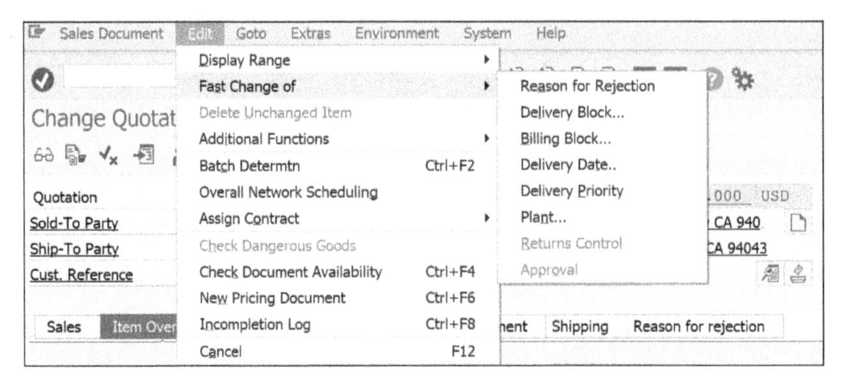

Figure 5.33 Making Mass Changes with the Fast Change Option

> **Note**
>
> The **Fast Change of** function can be used for all items or only those items that have been selected in advance.

5.4.5 Manage Sales Quotations App

To change the quotation in SAP Fiori, you use the Manage Sales Quotations app. Follow these steps to do so:

1. Launch the Manage Sales Quotations app, and input the quotation document number to be changed or displayed in the **Sales Quotation** field, as shown in Figure 5.34. Press Enter.

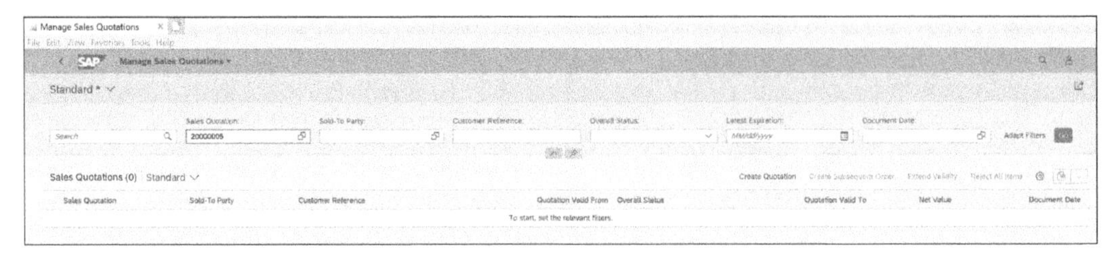

Figure 5.34 Manage Sales Quotations: Inputting Quotation Number

2. After your document has been found in the list (as shown in Figure 3.35), click (once) on your document number to open the context-sensitive menu shown in Figure 5.36.

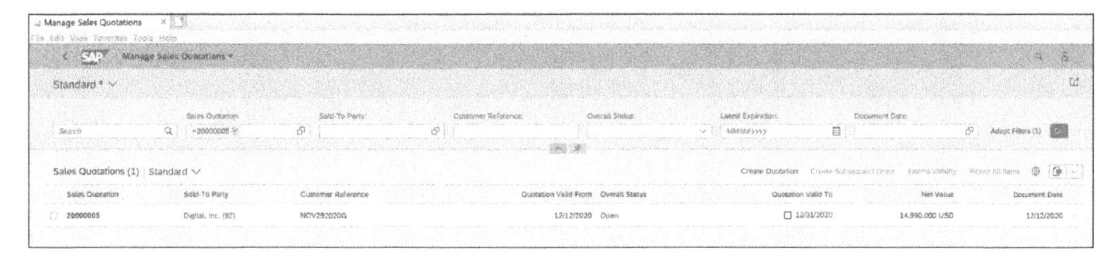

Figure 5.35 Manage Sales Quotation in SAP Fiori with Quotation number found.

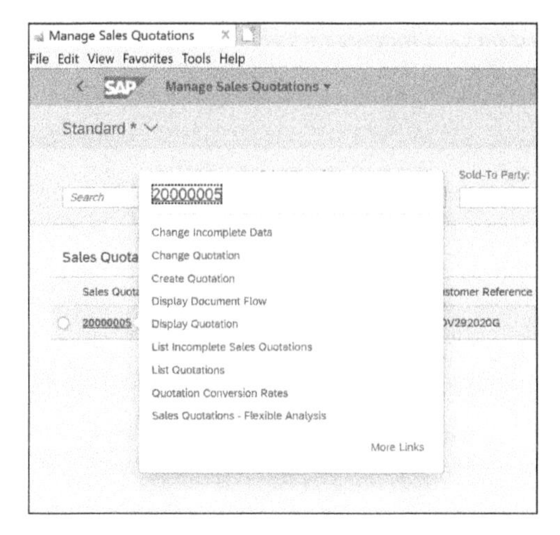

Figure 5.36 Manage Sales Quotations: Context-Sensitive Menu

3. Click on the desired link in the context menu (for this example, **Change Quotation**). The **Change Quotation: Overview** screen appears, as shown in Figure 5.37.

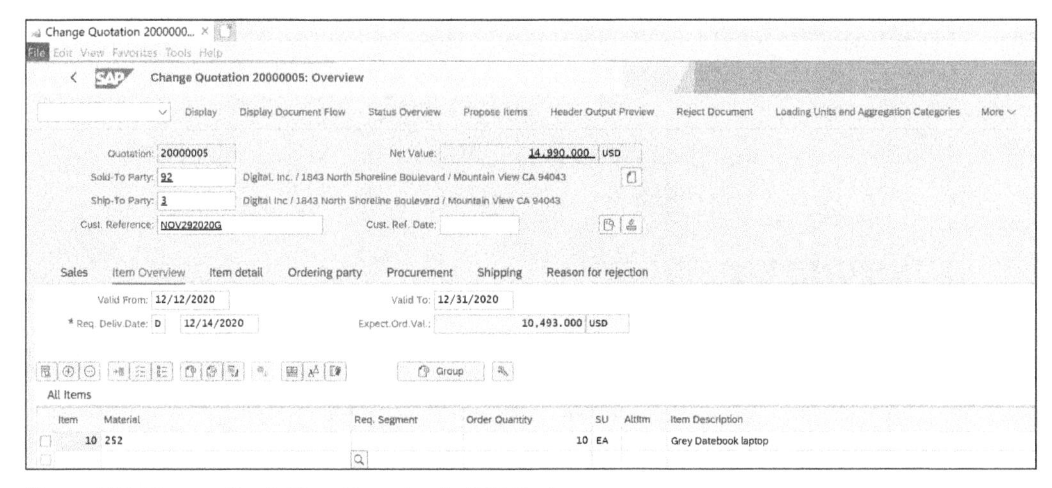

Figure 5.37 Change Quotation: Overview in SAP Fiori

4. Because there are no subsequent documents, all fields are available for change, even the customer fields. Change the customer to "12" in both the **Sold-To Party** and **Ship-To Party** fields, and then press Enter to see the results in Figure 5.38.

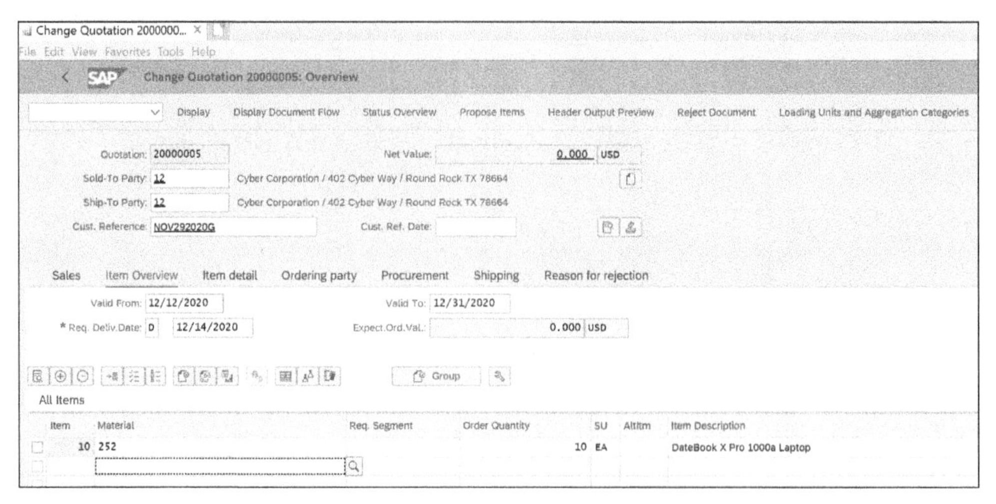

Figure 5.38 Change Quotation: Changing the Customer Number

> **Note**
> Refer to Section 5.4 for more information about which fields can be changed.

5. To save changes to your quotation, click on the **Save** button in the lower-right corner of the SAP Fiori screen (see Figure 5.39).

Figure 5.39 SAP Fiori Save Button

A message should appear with your quotation document number on the status bar in the lower-left corner of the screen, as shown in Figure 5.40.

Figure 5.40 Quotation Saved Message with Document Number

5.5 List of Quotations

If you're unsure of the quotation document number to be changed or displayed, you can search for them by using Transaction VA25 (List of Quotations), as shown in Figure 5.41.

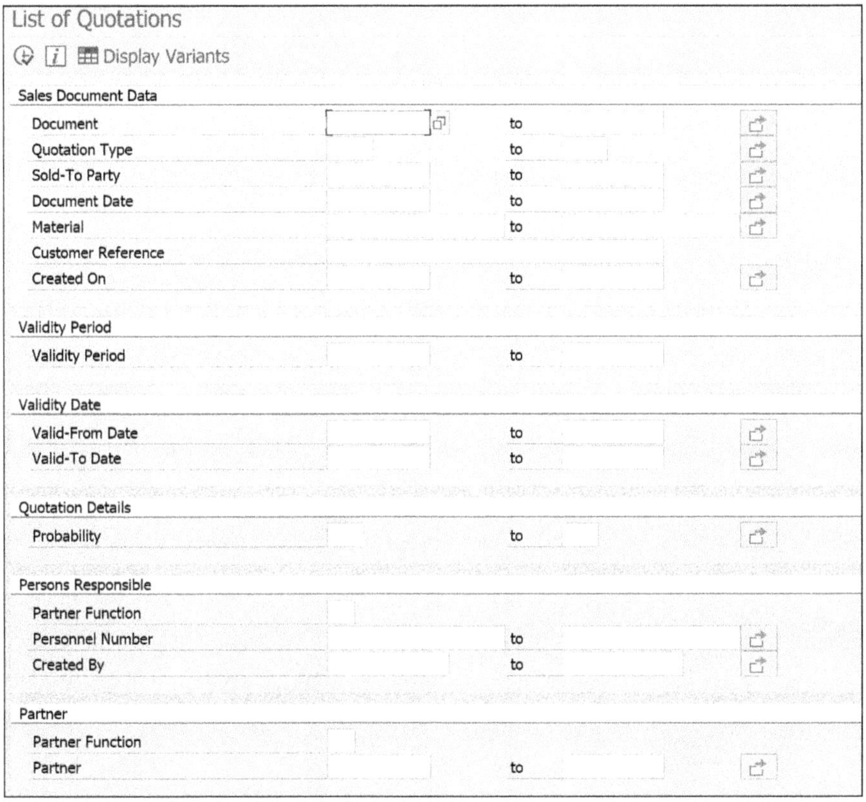

List of Quotations

Display Variants

Sales Document Data

Document		to	
Quotation Type		to	
Sold-To Party		to	
Document Date		to	
Material		to	
Customer Reference			
Created On		to	

Validity Period

Validity Period		to	

Validity Date

Valid-From Date		to	
Valid-To Date		to	

Quotation Details

Probability		to	

Persons Responsible

Partner Function			
Personnel Number		to	
Created By		to	

Partner

Partner Function			
Partner		to	

Figure 5.41 List of Quotations

To search for an inquiry, follow these steps:

1. Scroll to the bottom of the selection screen shown in Figure 5.42 to see the Selection Criteria section with options for selecting either all quotations or just open quotations (i.e., quotations that haven't been referenced in a follow-on document, e.g., a Sales Order).

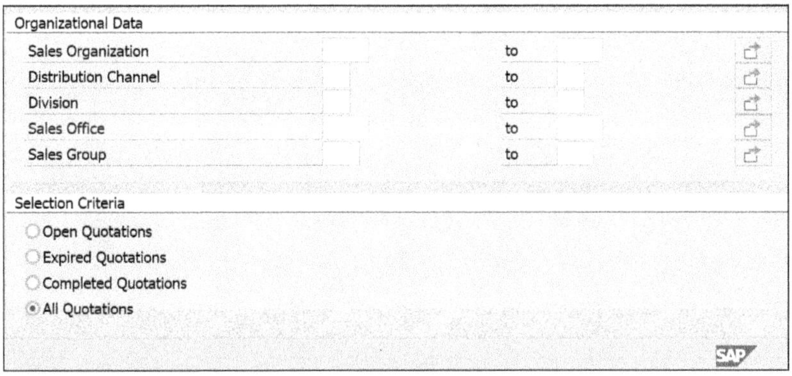

Organizational Data

Sales Organization		to	
Distribution Channel		to	
Division		to	
Sales Office		to	
Sales Group		to	

Selection Criteria

- ○ Open Quotations
- ○ Expired Quotations
- ○ Completed Quotations
- ◉ All Quotations

SAP

Figure 5.42 List of Quotation: Selection Criteria Options

2. Input some selection parameters such as the **Sold-to Party** number and date range into the report and execute. You have a choice of many other parameters as well, such as **Created by**, so you can easily limit the search to your own quotations. The default columns in your output report will appear as shown in Figure 5.43, but they can be customized easily.

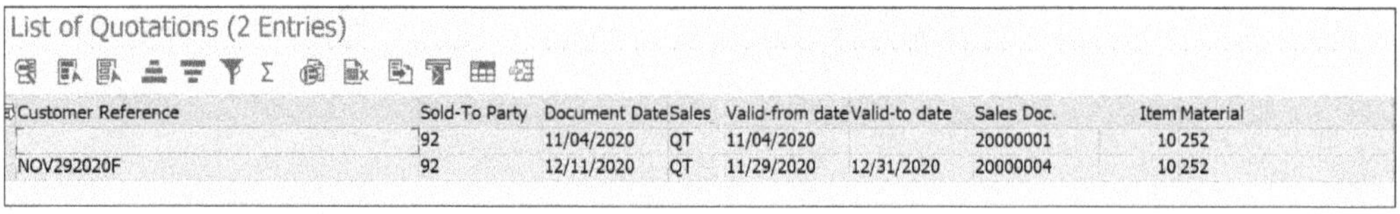

List of Quotations (2 Entries)

Customer Reference	Sold-To Party	Document Date	Sales	Valid-from date	Valid-to date	Sales Doc.	Item	Material
	92	11/04/2020	QT	11/04/2020		20000001	10	252
NOV292020F	92	12/11/2020	QT	11/29/2020	12/31/2020	20000004	10	252

Figure 5.43 List of Quotations: Search Output

Tips

Refer to Chapter 4, Section 4.5, to learn more about the following:

- After you've generated a list of quotations, you may want to export this to Microsoft Excel. Again, this is a commonly used command in many other reports in SAP applications to facilitate various of kinds of analysis.
- The mass change functionality can also be used for changing plant, material, pricing, or currency for selected line items.
- In the Manage Sales Quotations app, there are a number of ways to search and find desired data as displayed.

5.6 Summary

Congratulations on completing the last step in the presales process: the quotations document. To start, we acknowledged the previous steps in the presales processes, namely inquiries. Next, we described the quotation subprocess and its place in the overall order-to-cash transaction flow. Then we walked through creating a quotation document with reference to the inquiry created earlier.

As elsewhere in this book, this was demonstrated in both SAP GUI and SAP Fiori. After we printed the quotation, we covered changing and displaying your quotation once created in both SAP GUI and SAP Fiori. And, finally, we covered how to generate a list of all quotations in the system. This is helpful when you're searching for a quotation without knowing the document numbers but you do know the customer, date ranges, or other information).

We are ready for the main course of order-to-cash: the sales order, which is coming next.

Chapter 6
Sales Orders

It's time to introduce the sales order, the heart of sales and distribution and the order-to-cash process. Without sales, there are no invoices or revenue.

In this chapter, we'll begin by acknowledging the previous steps in the pre-sales processes, namely Chapters 4 and 5. Then, we'll build a background for understanding the different types of sales documents possible. In some cases, we've already covered such details before (we'll go deeper here).

We'll explore some of the critical functionality inherent in the sales document, most of which is automated based on the configuration of your system to your company. Many of these functionalities are described as *determinations*. This simply means the system will propose the appropriate codes on the spot based on pre-set entries in the configuration. We'll walk through of creating a sales order with a focus on all necessary inputs from you, the user, as well, as important inputs determined by the system. As elsewhere in this book, we perform the walk-throughs in both SAP GUI and SAP Fiori. Then we'll review changing and displaying your order once created in both SAP GUI and SAP Fiori. Finally, we'll cover how to generate a list of all sales orders in the system. This is of assistance when you are searching for order without knowing the document numbers.

6.1 Process Overview

After your business has sent a binding quotation to your potential customer, you may engage in further follow-on presales activities such as phone calls, meetings, and presentations to secure the next step in the end of the presales process, that is, conversion from quotation to a sales order and ringing the cash register with a bona fide sale!

In SAP S/4HANA, it must be noted that no actual general ledger accounts are affected or posted when writing a sales order, but you're well on your way. (Actually, the first account postings will be in the delivery document and process, which will be discussed in Chapter 7.) This is the step where your customer typically sends you their purchase order to buy X quantity of your product Y at price Z. Their purchase order and your sales orders are legally binding contracts to buy and sell, respectively.

As with your prior quotation document, you'll be able to create the follow-on sales document using the previous document (in this case, quotation) as a template to fill in fields such as **Customer**, **Material**, **Quantity**, and **Price**.

As noted in Chapter 4, Section 4.1, the following presales processes are part and parcel of SAP S/4HANA:

- **Inquiry**
  A nonbinding document to issue to a potential customer with respect to an identified interest in one of your products at a specified quantity and price.
- **Quotation**
  If the potential customer responds favorably to the inquiry, the customer may request a binding quote on the indicated product for a specific quantity and price. This quotation document will also have an expiration date as to the promised quantity and price terms. This document may be created as a copy of the initial inquiry or as a fresh document with all inputs made directly into all required fields.

This chapter focuses on the follow-on sales order process, which is covered in the highlighted section of Figure 6.1.

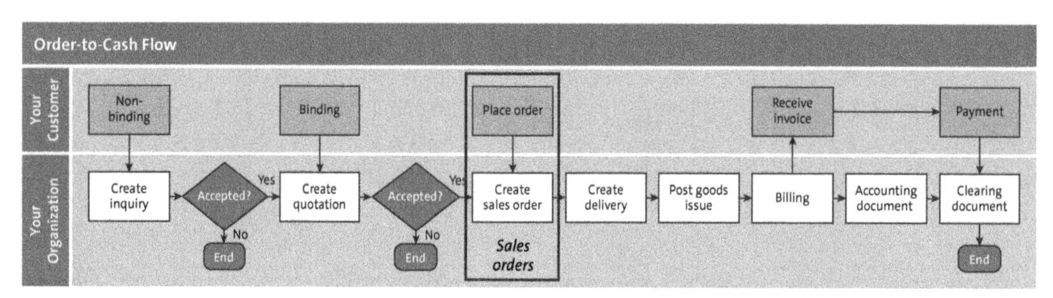

Figure 6.1 Order-to-Cash Flow: Sales Orders

6.2 Document Types

The order-to-cash process is preconfigured to use the following basic document types from inquiry through billing:

- IN: Inquiry
- QT: Quotation
- OR: Standard order
- RE: Returns order
- CR: Credit memo request
- DR: Debit memo request
- LF: Outbound delivery document
- LR: Returns delivery
- F1: Sales invoice for an order
- F2: Sales invoice for a delivery
- G2: Credit memo
- L2: Debit memo

These documents control how SAP will process information input by the user (or interface) in terms of an inquiry, quotation, sales order, delivery, and so on. This means that certain documents will require specific field data and others won't. For example, inquiries, quotations, sales orders, and billing documents require pricing information, but deliveries do not because they concern themselves with other details related to shipping.

First, let's preface our discussion by defining *sales order*, which, as introduced on Chapter 1, is the catchall label to refer to more specific document types created via Transaction VA01 (except for the last two in the upcoming list). All of these sales order types generate a printed or emailed output document or form to send to the customer, confirming all agreed trading terms. This output is normally known as an order confirmation or order acknowledgement.

In terms of sales documents, there are eight essential types as follows:

- Standard orders
- Rush orders
- Cash sales
- Consignment sales
- Third-party sales
- Returns
- Debit and credit memos
- Outline agreements

6.2.1 Standard Orders

The standard order (order type OR) is the base version of a sales document, which documents a customer's request for goods and services within a given time frame at an agreed price. Like all the documents listed previously, a standard order contains all terms and conditions relevant to the exchange of goods/services and money—such as the various business partners involved in the sale, payment terms, delivery terms, Incoterms, dates of supply, materials ordered, and sales pricing.

The standard order can be created fresh, without reference to any preceding document, or it can be created based on a presales document such as an inquiry or quotation. A third option is to create it based on an inbound purchase order received directly from the customer. Much of the rest of the remaining data in the order is automatically populated from master data held in the customer, material, and pricing master records.

The delivery document is created after the standard order and is composed of the basic logistics process of picking, packing, and goods issue (GI) posting.

The billing document type is F2, which is delivery-related billing. This means the billing document will only be created on the basis of a delivery document number where the logistics process is complete (see Figure 6.2).

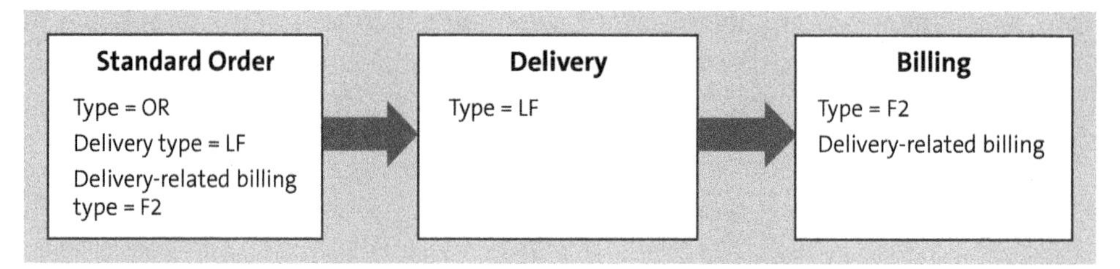

Figure 6.2 Standard Order Process

In summary:

- Sales document type is OR and is linked to delivery type LF and billing type F2.
- Standard order process is a delivery-related billing.
- Delivery is created after the sales document based on the sales document number and the shipping point.
- Billing is created from the delivery document after all logistics operations have been completed.

6.2.2 Rush Orders

In a rush order (order type SO), the customer collects the goods on the spot. The delivery is therefore created automatically in the background at the same time the rush order is saved. This is to expedite the process and allow for either a customer pickup of the goods or same-day delivery. As in a standard order, the logistics process of picking, packing, and GI posting is still normally performed. The invoice is then generated from the delivery normally, as shown in Figure 6.3.

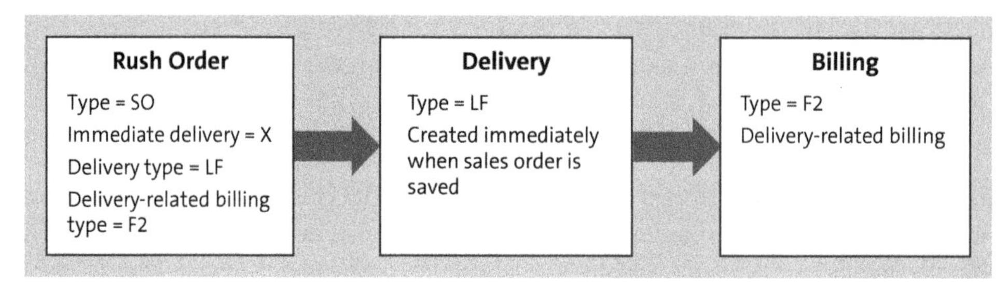

Figure 6.3 Rush Order Process

In summary:

- Sales document type is SO and is linked to delivery type LF and billing type F2.
- Rush order process is a delivery-related billing.
- Delivery is created at the same time as the sales document.
- Billing is created from the delivery document after all logistics operations have been completed.

6.2.3 Cash Sales

Like the rush order, the cash sale (order type BV) order generates a delivery as soon as the sales order is saved. Furthermore, a cash invoice can also be generated from the sales invoice. The customer typically takes possession of the goods at point of sale; otherwise, picking may be necessary depending on the scenario. After the customer has received the goods, the transaction is considered complete (see Figure 6.4).

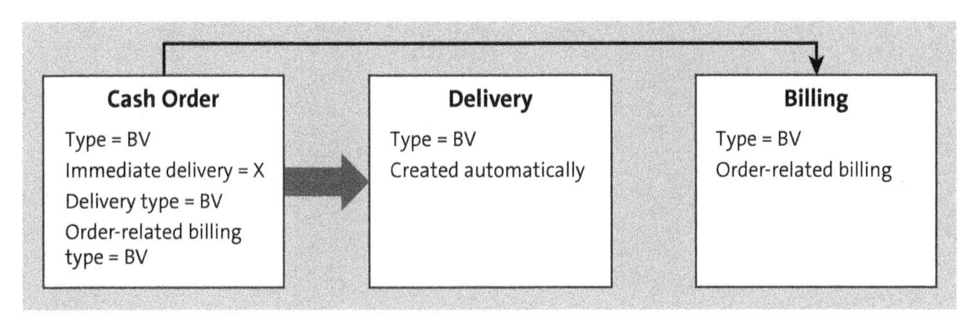

Figure 6.4 Cash Sales Process

In summary:

- Sales document type is BV and is linked to delivery type BV and billing type BV.
- Customer pays for and takes possession of the goods on the spot.
- Cash order process is an order-related billing.
- Delivery is created automatically when the sales document is created.
- Billing document (invoice) is printed immediately from the order and given to the customer as a receipt.
- Billing is created from the sales document after all logistics operations have been completed.
- No accounts receivable posting from the billing document because cash is usually received and posted directly to the cash general ledger account.

6.2.4 Consignment Sales

The consignment process is all about using your customer's warehouse as your own. Your company owns the goods, but they are physically stored at your customer's plant or warehouse.

There are four different sales document types to manage the transfer of goods from your stock to your customer's stock, where it can be consumed as well as returned to your customer's stock: consignment fill-up, consignment issue, consignment returns, and consignment pickup. Ultimately, you can pick up the stock for transfer from your customer's stock back into your own.

When your customer consumes the consignment stock, it's formally issued to them by one of the four document types mentioned, which will form the basis of an invoice to your customer.

Until consumed, consignment stock is part of your valuated stock and continues to show in your SAP S/4HANA system by way of a **Special Stock** indicator. This allows for the goods to be assigned as consignment stock to your customers. Consignment stock is always managed separately to denote special handling in terms of ownership and physical location at your customers. The advantage of this process is to reduce warehousing costs for your business.

The following four component parts of the consignment processes are shown in Figure 6.5:

- **Consignment fill-up (order type KB)**
  This is used when Your stock is transferred physically from your plant to your customer's plant where it remains under your ownership.
- **Consignment issue (order type KE)**
  This is used when your stock is consumed or sold by your customer. This provides the basis for an invoice from you to your customer.
- **Consignment returns (order type KR)**
  This is used to process a return of consignment stock from your customer to you. The stock is placed back in inventory at your customer's plant, but ownership reverts to you. Because you've issued and invoiced the goods to your customer, this document type takes the form of a credit memo and invoice.
- **Consignment pickup (order type KA)**
  This is used when your stock is physically moved back from your customer's plant to your own. The stock reverts to your normal plant stock.

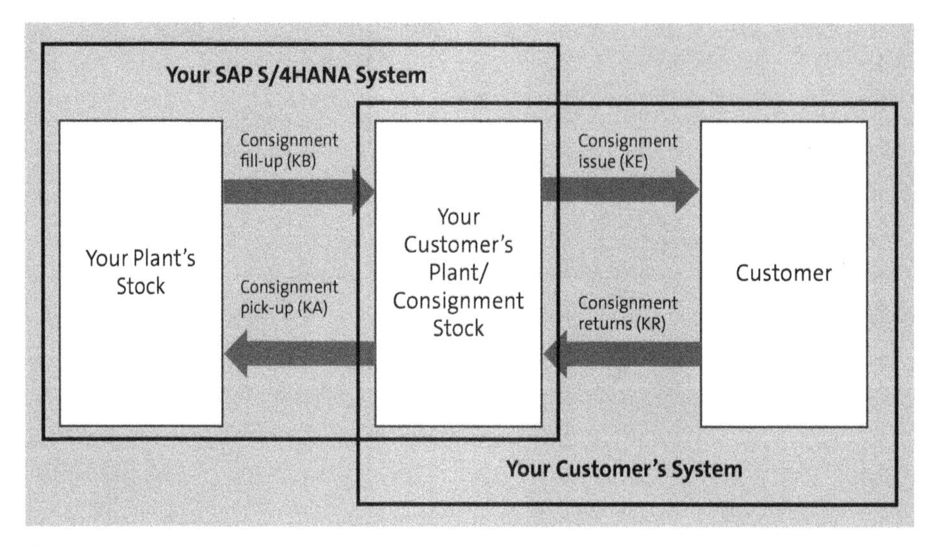

Figure 6.5 Consignment Process

6.2.5 Third-Party Sales

Third-party sales (order type OR [same as the standard order]) come in two forms: drop-ship and the cross-dock, which are discussed in the next subsections.

Drop-Ship Process

The drop-ship process uses a supplier or vendor as your warehouse because your company doesn't have the goods. You write the sales document to the customer as usual. Then you write a purchase order from your materials management module to your supplier to buy the goods and instruct them to ship directly to your customer.

As shown in Figure 6.6, the customer therefore receives the goods, and you receive the delivery notification to the same effect from your supplier (together with their invoice). The last step is to invoice your customer as normally.

The intercompany sales process is effectively a variant of this transaction where your supplier is a related company operating under a different company code (e.g., representing a subsidiary in a different country). See Chapter 8 for more information on intercompany processes.

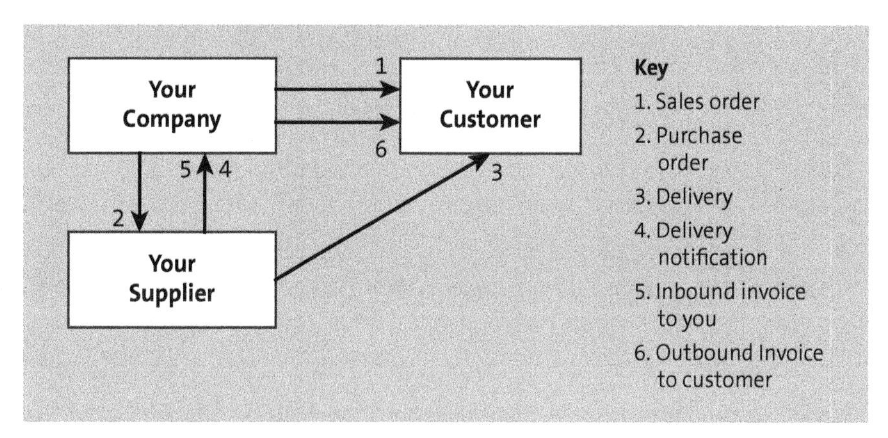

Figure 6.6 Third-Party (Drop-Ship) Sales Process

In summary:

- Sales document type is OR and is linked to billing type F1.
- Item category of goods to be is TAS.
- Drop-ship process is an order-related billing process.
- Delivery isn't managed within your company's SAP S/4HANA system because it will be between the vendor and the customer.
- Drop-ship is suitable when your company doesn't have stock on hand.

Cross-Dock Process

The cross-dock process, on the other hand, uses your vendor in the traditional way. You don't have the stock when the customer places the order, so you write a purchase order to your vendor when you write a sales order to your customer. This time, your supplier sends you the goods, whereby the newly arrived stock appears in your SAP S/4HANA system as sales order stock (E stock). This prevents it from being allocated to other orders or customers. Then you deliver and invoice your customer as normally. Figure 6.7 shows the process.

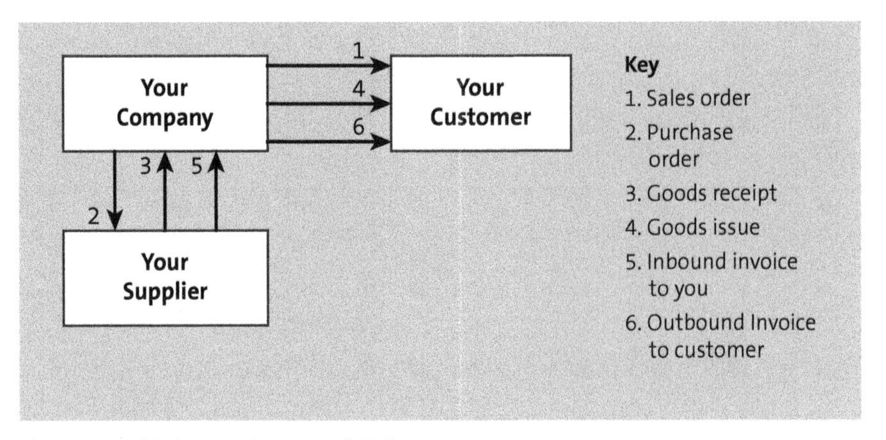

Figure 6.7 Third-Party Cross-Dock Sales Process

6.2.6 Returns

To take back goods delivered and invoiced to your customer, a returns process is available to undo the three basic steps of the order-to-cash process:

- The returns sales document is created with reference to either the original sales or billing document. A billing block is usually configured to be set automatically on creation so that a manager can review and approve any time before creation of the credit invoice. The returns order will have an **Order Reason** field (dropdown list) to categorize the nature of the return.
- The delivery document is created after the returns order and is composed of a GR posting (to undo the initial GI of the underlying order). Stock returning to inventory is typically held in **Blocked** status so it can be inspected before being put back in inventory and resold.
- The billing document type will be CR, which can be either an order-related or a delivery-related billing of the credit variety. Put another way, you can configure your SAP S/4HANA system either way to suit your business requirements. Standard SAP uses item category REN by default, which is set to order-related billing. This can be changed to delivery-related billing with a copied item category.

Note

Notice that these underlying documents are never deleted; there are general ledger account postings associated with the delivery and billing documents. These require meticulously correct counter postings to resolve all inventory and accounting positions taken with the original sale. Therefore, there will be a goods receipt (GR) posting to take the goods back into inventory, followed by a billing document of the credit variety.

Typically, a billing block is placed by default on the returns order requiring approval before creating the credit invoice to the customer. Figure 6.8 shows the returns process (see Chapter 9 for more details).

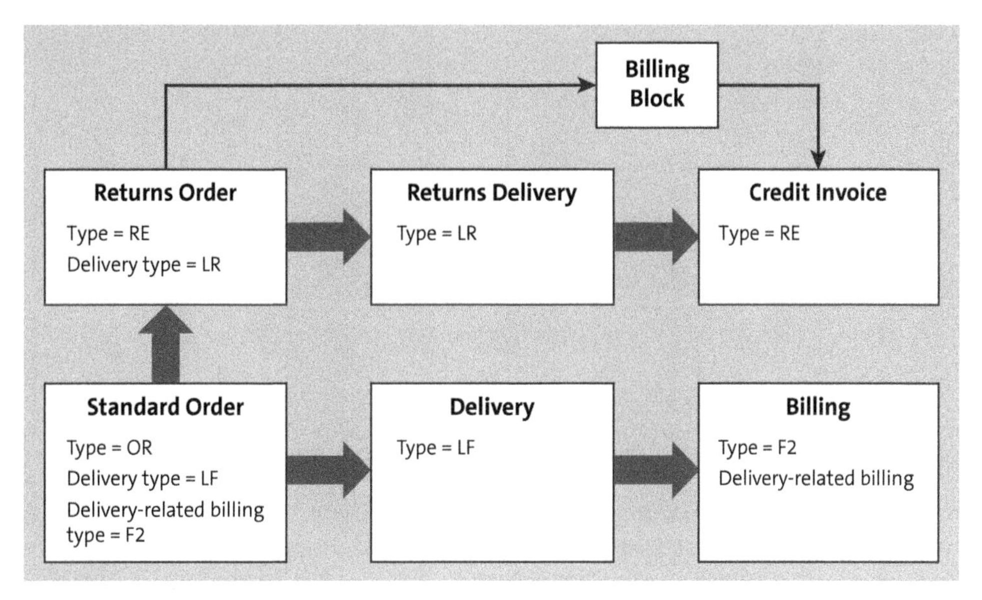

Figure 6.8 Returns Process

In summary:

- Sales document type is RE and is linked to delivery type LR and billing type CR.
- The returns process can be either an order-related or a delivery-related billing.
- Delivery is created after the sales document based on the sales document number shipping point determined for the GR.
- Billing is created from the delivery document after all logistics operations have been completed if configured as a delivery-related billing.
- Otherwise, the credit invoice billing document can be created at any time after the billing block has been removed.

6.2.7 Debit and Credit Notes

Debit and credit notes are typically created to adjust an underlying order-to-cash process that was either undercharged or overcharged, respectively. Notice there is no delivery component as no goods are issued or received. Both can be used, however, to simply bill or credit the customer for extra service fess without reference to a prior sales or billing document. Note that an order reason is usually required in the sales document, and billing blocks are usually assigned automatically, which require removal before the billing document.

To distinguish the credit memo from the returns process described in the previous section, the customer is credited without the return of any goods. Debit and credit notes form the basis of service businesses, where time and services are sold as opposed to hard goods requiring delivery (Section 6.5). Figure 6.9 shows the debit and credit memo processes.

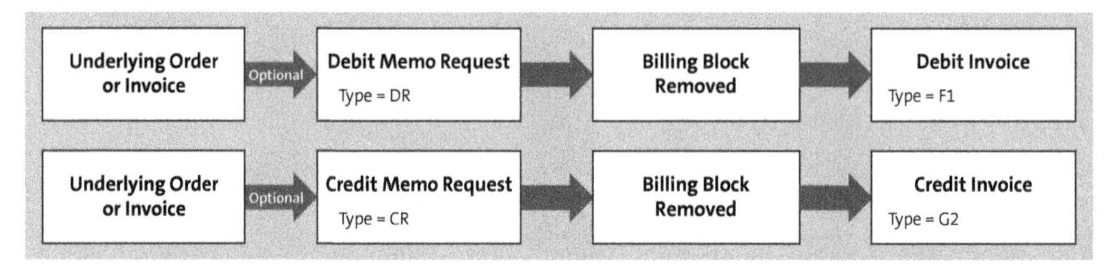

Figure 6.9 Debit and Credit Memo Processes

In summary:

- Sales document types DR Debit and CR Credit are linked to billing document type F1 (order-related billing) or G2 (credit memo).
- There is no delivery or goods movement.
- Debit and credit memos can be created both with or without reference to an underlying sales or billing document.
- The billing document can be created at any time after the billing block has been removed.

6.2.8 Outline Agreements

Many businesses engage in longer term sales arrangements whereby selected goods are sold and delivered on an ongoing schedule. These are typically limited by either a defined period of time (e.g., for six months or two years) or for a specific value (e.g., $2 million of goods). These are sometimes called blanket orders.

The two types of outline agreements are defined as follows:

- **Scheduling agreements**
  Delivery and invoicing will be periodic per a set delivery date for a specified quantity; for example, 200 pounds of products A and B are to be delivered every month for the next year. These are commonly used in automotive industries.

  It's composed of fixed dates for the delivery of specified delivery quantities in the underlying order's schedule lines. This schedule of upcoming deliveries is agreed to by the customer and forms the basis for periodic deliveries by way of delivery processing in SAP S/4HANA inclusive of all logistics processing, such as picking, packing, and GI. This process is automated to flow seamlessly into the delivery due list for daily action by the warehouse manager.

- **Contracts**
  Contracts are usually to deliver either a set value or quantity for a defined period of time. A contract is a specific type of sales document to deliver goods up to a certain quantity or dollar value. Once created, users will then create release orders with reference to an underlying contract akin to a standard order. The release order will draw down the agreed total quantity or value stipulated in the contract and form the basis for creating a delivery and the complete logistics process.

  Contracts take the following forms:

  - Master contracts (sales document type = GK): Assemble together a number of small contracts under the same terms.
  - Value contracts: Stipulate the materials or services to be ordered within a certain period of time up to a maximum value, after which the contract is fulfilled.
  - Quantity contracts: Stipulate a quantity of materials to be ordered within a certain period of time, after which the contract is fulfilled.
  - Service contracts: Stipulate services to be provided to the customer such as in consulting, rental, and maintenance businesses. These contain provisions for cancellation, pricing, and services to be provided after the contract is fulfilled within preset validity dates.

Please see Chapter 8, Section 8.5, for more information on contracts.

6.3 Item Categories

Sales documents, from inquiries to billing documents, as you've seen from Chapter 4, are split into two main parts:

- **Header section**
  This section is composed of data relevant to the entire order, such as the sold-to customer name, address, and all other relevant customer functions, including ship-to, bill-to, payer, payment terms, and terms of delivery.

- **Line item**
  In this section, each entry is for a particular material being ordered by the customer from your company. This includes information relevant to that material only, such as quantity ordered, price, and special instructions.

An item category is one such piece of line-item information. It controls how a material (or service) is priced or invoiced and whether any other special function is invoked within the sales document.

For example, a material may be available for sale on a regular-priced basis as well as being a free good in a Buy One, Get One free (BOGO) offer. A material subject to normal pricing functionality in SAP is commonly assigned to item category TAN, whereas if it's given away for free, it's assigned to item category TANN. The item category in this case is the switch in the SAP system to indicate that this material is to be priced normally or, in this case, this material is being given away free, so skip the price calculation.

Materials aren't directly assigned into item categories. As in many areas of SAP, there are one or two (or sometimes more) intermediate configuration steps that serve to both add robust functionality and, unfortunately, add complexity to the overall solution. The intermediary step in this case is to assign each material to an item category group in the material master record.

Then, in the configuration, you make a further assignment for each sales document type to the item category group, which specifically permits the combination. If not linked here, the SAP system won't allow the entry of any material belonging to that group into the specified sales document type. The general idea is that businesses like yours want to be able to control which materials belong to which kind of order. For example, let's say that your company sells both cement mixing equipment and swimming pool supplies—two very different types of products. You would typically define two different flavors of standard orders, ZOR1 for the cement mixers and ZOR2 for the swimming pool supplies. After all, you have very different types of customers and products for each business line.

How would you prevent a new employee from, say, on his first day on the job, writing a ZOR1 standard order (intended for cement mixers) and erroneously inputting a swimming pool supply chemical as one of the line items? This is an important error because you'll have very different pricing formulas for the sales of each kind of good.

You could easily create, for example, two different kinds of item category groups into which you could organize all of your products, ZCEM for cement mixing and ZPOL for the pool supplies. Then you assign sales document type ZOR1 to item category group ZCEM in the configuration. You would do the same thing by assigning sales document type ZOR2 to item category group ZPOL. Figure 6.10 provides an overview of the logic used in determining the item category.

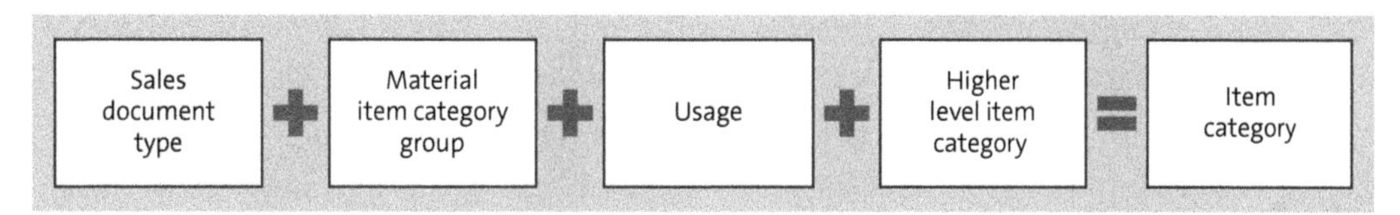

Figure 6.10 Item Category Configuration Logic

The sales document type field found in the header can be linked in the configuration to the following:

- The material item category group, which is found in the material master data.
- A usage code, which is a special field to invoke some custom functionality by ABAP code. An example could be some enhanced SAP Advanced Planning and Optimization (SAP APO) functionality.
- A higher-level item category is used in a bill of material (BOM) where the item category of the higher-level material can be taken into account.

The combination of these codes allows SAP S/4HANA to correctly propose a suitable specific item category in your sales order.

Consider this real-world example: A company was acquired, and all the acquired company's sales processes had to be rolled up into the acquiring company's SAP system. New sales document types had to be configured, and all the acquired company's products had to be created as master data in the acquiring company's SAP system. Then, consistent with the process outlined previously, the new sales document types had to be matched with the new product's item category groups. This wasn't executed very well because right after go-live, the business tried to write sales orders. Subsequently, each time they attempted to input a material, the SAP system would throw an error that the item category wasn't permitted in the sales document type. This is the kind of configuration that should really be done before go-live.

This can be a problem when rolling out a template or merging the operations of two companies. If new sales document types are to be created together with a new set of material master data to be uploaded, don't forget to make these necessary item category assignments. If not, when the business tries to add materials to new sales orders, the SAP system can throw an error that item category such and such isn't permitted in sales document type X.

It would have been easier to understand and more direct to say that material 123 wasn't permitted rather than the actual error message, which was "Item Category ZTAN isn't permitted in document type ZOR5," but this is the way the SAP system operates, and now you understand why.

So, don't be mystified by SAP's messages. If the reference isn't straightforward, the system is using an intermediary code for describing a simple situation, namely, "this material hasn't yet been designated for this kind of order."

In Figure 6.2 earlier, you saw the most basic order-to-cash process flow: the sales document starts the flow with entry of master data information such as entering the **Customer** and **Material** into a sales document. In this book, you'll recall that we actually started our explanation with some presales processes—inquiries and quotations—where the aforementioned master data is first input and then flows into the sales document. Remember, however, that not every company uses such presales processes; many start simply by the entry of sales documents.

Every company is different. Some sections of this manual will apply to you and others not. A few subjects apply to everyone, like Customer master data. There are no sales if there aren't any customers.

At this point, a distinction needs to be made between hard goods processing, as illustrated in Figure 6.2 earlier, and service processing, which was exemplified previously in Figure 6.9 (without the initial boxes for the underlying order or invoice).

6.4 Hard Goods Processing

Hard goods processing simply means the sale of physical goods that are stored in your warehouse (or in your vendor's or customer's warehouse as the case may be). Hard goods processing is distinguishable by its reliance on inventory management, warehouses, shipping, and other such logistics. Therefore, the order-to-cash flow for hard goods processing is detailed in Figure 6.2 in this sequence: Sales document > Delivery document > Billing document.

We'll be touching on inventory management in terms of its impact on the sales document level later in this chapter. And, of course, inventory management is an essential part of the next chapter, which discusses deliveries.

Before defining and examining service processing, let's look at the hard goods processing from the all-important accounting perspective.

6.4.1 Accounting Impacts

At the sales order level, while inventory levels may be reserved when material line items are input, your company's general ledger accounts remain untouched. Postings to your corporate accounts commence only at the next stage of the order-to-cash flow, which is the delivery or logistics. This is where your hard goods are processed in the warehouse for sending to the customer. The entire delivery process can be broken down into a number of possible steps:

1. The orders to be shipped on a daily basis are identified and organized together on the delivery due list, which is under the purview of the warehouse or shipping manager.
2. They may generate a pick list or a transport order so that the forklift drivers know where to go to assemble all goods scheduled for shipment that day.
3. They may need to create handling units where multiple goods are assembled together in shipping boxes and then shrink-wrapped in a conglomeration of handling units called, simply enough, a master handling unit. This is part of the packing subprocess.
4. There may be an additional shipment document.
5. Finally, the goods are marked in SAP S/4HANA as "goods post issued," which means they are out the door and on their way to the customer.

What's significant about this delivery step is that this is where your company's general ledger accounts are first impacted to cash, as shown in Figure 6.11.

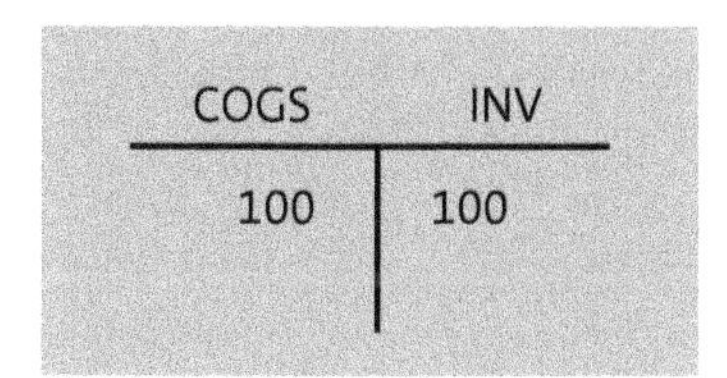

Figure 6.11 Post Goods Issue: T Account Posting

When goods are shipped out of your warehouse, your cost of goods sold (COGS) account is debited (increased) and your inventory account is credited (decreased). This example uses $100, and in typical accounting fashion, the dual entries must balance out.

These postings directly affect your company's costs and inventory levels. This is why SAP software is, in the eyes of many users, somewhat rigid with respect to the handling of important accounting data, such as postings to your company's general ledger accounts. The SAP system doesn't allow you to delete a post goods issue (PGI) document if you make a mistake. Rather, you're required to make a counter-posting to back out the entries.

Most documents in SAP, and especially all entries to the general ledger accounts, are tagged with the user ID of the person writing the document. This isn't intended as some kind of threatening gesture by management. It's simply part of working in a large modern professional organization where everyone is accountable for their actions. And the resulting audit trail is there for the reassurance and benefit of a collection of strangers working together.

The next document in the order-to-cash flow is the billing document. After the GI has been posted, SAP S/4HANA allows for generating an invoice to the customer. Figure 6.12 shows the accounting posting.

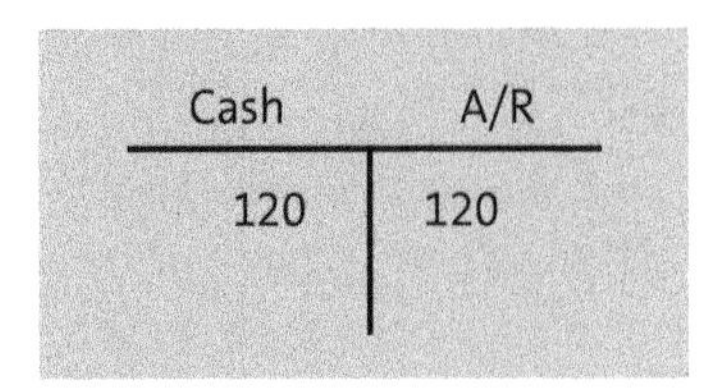

Figure 6.12 Billing Account Posting

In this T account posting, the previous COGS posting is cleared against the sales account. In this example, we're billing the customer accounts receivable account $20 more than the $100 cost, for a total of $120. The matching posting on the credit side is to the sales account.

What happens after an invoice is sent to your customer? The customer (hopefully) pays the invoice, and you settle the open receivable with a clearing document (see Chapter 12 for more on accounts receivable).

6.4.2 Schedule Lines

The **Schedule lines** tab in the sales document contains all information pertaining to the delivery of your material to the customer such as quantities to be delivered by date with a link to inventory management.

Some important fields to note in this tab are as follows:

- **Delivery Date**
  This is the date your goods are anticipated to be delivered to your customer.
- **Quantities**
  The order quantity comes directly from the amount input by you in the sales document; that is, how many units of the material does the customer want? Compare this with the **Confirmed Quantity**; that is, how many units are available at the time of order? The two quantities should match. If not, you have an inventory shortage, which can result in a partial delivery, multiple deliveries, or maybe a confirmed quantity of zero!
- **Delivery Block**
  If your delivery is blocked by the system, this dropdown list will indicate the reason.
- **Schedule Line Category**
  This field controls several critical aspects of the delivery, such as whether the material in question is suitable for delivery, the movement type to be used for the PGI, whether there is a default delivery block, whether production planning requirements apply, and if an availability check is to be performed.

As you can see, schedule line category determination as shown in Figure 6.13 is dependent on a prior piece of logic, the item category determination shown earlier in Figure 6.10. This is an example of cascading determinations. One such evaluation has an impact on the succeeding evaluation. In this way, you inform SAP S/4HANA how to handle your deliveries for groups of materials.

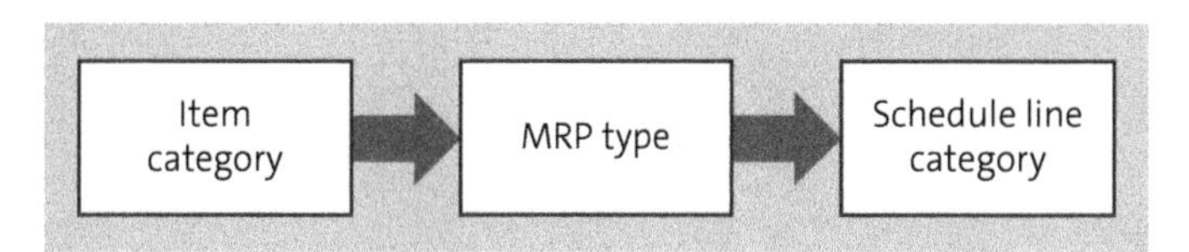

Figure 6.13 Schedule Line Category Determination

The first subject to be evaluated is the item category in the sales document (which is, as just noted, also determined). This is considered in conjunction with the material requirements planning type (**MRP Type**), which is read from the **MRP 1** view in the material master record. MRP is relevant for the make-to-order production process (as opposed to make-to-stock). You'll refer to your materials management consultant for help in setting this field up.

The result is the **Schedule Line Category** field in your sales document to be displayed in the **Schedule Line** tab. Some commonly used categories are as follows:

- CN
  No material planning. This turns off the functionality and is useful for testing functionalities other than schedule lines.
- BN
  For use in quotations. No deliveries or inventory movements are permitted.
- CP
  For use in sales documents where the material is relevant for delivery. Inventory movement type is 601.
- DN
  For use in return orders where the material is coming back in a goods return. Inventory movement type is 651.

6.4.3 Availability Check

Determining the schedule line category, as noted in the previous section, may invoke another functionality—the availability check—which is worthy of its own separate section.

SAP S/4HANA's availability check is the specific function that determines whether the material quantity in your sales document can be delivered either all together or, in the event of limited stock, spread out in several deliveries. Sometimes, availability check may determine that you don't have any stock, and your delivery may be blocked. This often causes consternation to users.

The most common check is based on available-to-promise (ATP), which is calculated as shown in Figure 6.14.

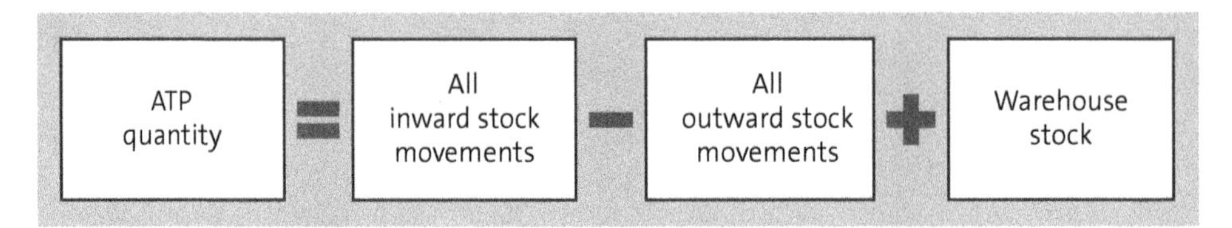

Figure 6.14 ATP Calculation

Your sales document's total quantity will be compared against the result of the ATP calculation . Essentially, this equation states that the total amount of stock available to fulfill your order is a function of three variables:

- **All inward stock movements**
  What are the scheduled inflows of stock anticipated within the delivery dates promised to the customer? For example, your company may have issued its own purchase orders to replenish stock levels, or it may have purchased raw materials scheduled to be processed in upcoming production and planned orders into finished products. All these activities serve to increase stock levels.
- **All outward stock movements.**
  While stock is scheduled to flow into your warehouse and increase levels available for future sales, stock is also flowing out due to deliveries in the near future as well as sales orders input prior to yours. This stock must be totaled and subtracted from the total amount available for your new order.
- **Warehouse stock**
  This is the physical amount of goods on hand.

Please see the discussion in sales document: line-item details in Section 6.6.2 for an example of how this is calculated.

6.4.4 Scheduling

The key date in scheduling is the material availability date, which is the date by which your goods are ready for your order and therefore to start the entire delivery/logistics process. Figure 6.15 shows an overview of all scheduling dates used in SAP S/4HANA, which is another way to examine the entire delivery/logistics process.

As you can see, these five times and dates effectively form a waterfall or cascade of one onto the other in sequential order. Each step in the process requires a certain amount of time for completion, which can be configured into your SAP S/4HANA system. All these times and dates are needed to develop a meaningful estimate as to when the goods can be expected to arrive at your customer's receiving point, otherwise known as the requested delivery date.

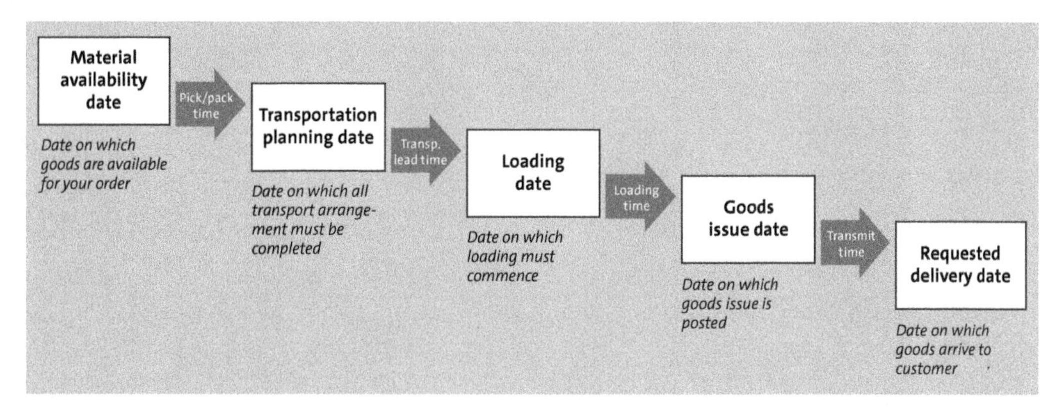

Figure 6.15 Cascade of Scheduling Dates

The first date, material availability date, is simply the date goods are available in your warehouse to be shipped in fulfillment of the customer's order. It will take picking and packing time before the goods are ready to be loaded. If transportation planning takes additional time, this must also naturally be added before the goods can be loaded into the mode of transport that has been arranged, such as the truck, train, boat, and so on.

You must account for the expected time to load the goods before the mode of transport departs your warehouse en route to your customer. GI posting typically takes place at the exact time that the truck, train, or boat leaves your premises. This corresponds to the moment when your customer takes ownership of the goods. Your customers normally will carry insurance to reimburse them in the event the goods don't arrive after leaving your premises.

Lastly, time for transportation, or the transit time, needs to be taken into account for the goods to arrive at the customer's receiving point. This should be the reasonable requested delivery date indicated in your sales order.

Backward scheduling is the calculation of this cascade of dates (and times) backwards from the arrival time at the customer's receiving point (the requested delivery date) to the material availability. All four lead times must be subtracted back accordingly, as shown in Figure 6.16.

In the example presented in Figure 6.16, the requested delivery date is February 22nd. The date on your sales order (i.e., order date) can be no later than the material available date as given, in our example, as February 13th. Here, you can see the following:

- The transit time of 4 days is subtracted back to February 18th.
- It takes a day to load the goods, so that is backed out to February 17th.

- You can see a peculiar situation in comparing the times for pick/pack to the transportation lead—the former far exceeds the latter. Why might that be true in this hypothetical example? Imagine a type of bottleneck in the warehouse where the forklift drivers are crazy busy. In fact, they are backed up a couple of days. Orders are so plentiful and the warehouse of such a size that it now takes 4 days to schedule the pick wave, print the list, add the list to the overflowing pile of lists to pick, locate the goods, pick (without error), and then pack them.

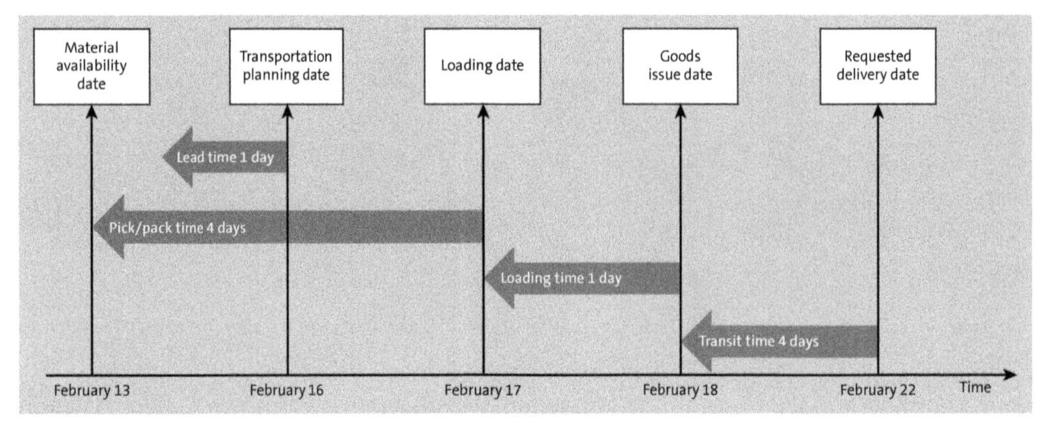

Figure 6.16 Backward Scheduling

Not everything is rosy in the real world or even in a book like this. To be perfectly honest, this kind of circumstance may not actually be all that uncommon.

Consider that, in this example, the customer is well established and has ordered the same product for years. In such a case, there may not actually be a need to plan much of anything at all; the existing route and transportation logistics are well known to our intrepid warehouse and shipping manager. Only a minimum time of 1 day is needed (if that). If a new route to a new customer is required, then the transportation planning lead time may need additional days to sort out everything.

What is significant here in terms of time is the pick/pack process, which is estimated in our example to be 4 days. This will be the driver, so to speak, of our schedule planning. Namely, the earlier of pick/pack and transportation lead planning will be the determining factor. Put another way, the longest process will have the most significant impact in pushing back the material availability date.

In this example, the material availability date is established as February 13th. As long as this is on or after the date of your sales order, this schedule plan will work for you and can be confirmed. What if the order date is after the material availability date, say February 15th? The delivery process as calculated by backward planning won't confirm a requested delivery date of February 22nd because too much time is required in the constituent steps to meet such a proposed date realistically. So, if you miss the requested delivery date accordingly, you must use forward scheduling to determine the earliest possible promise date.

Figure 6.17 should look very familiar to you, perhaps held up to a mirror. It's exactly the same style of time calculation as backward scheduling (using the same time assumptions), except in reverse.

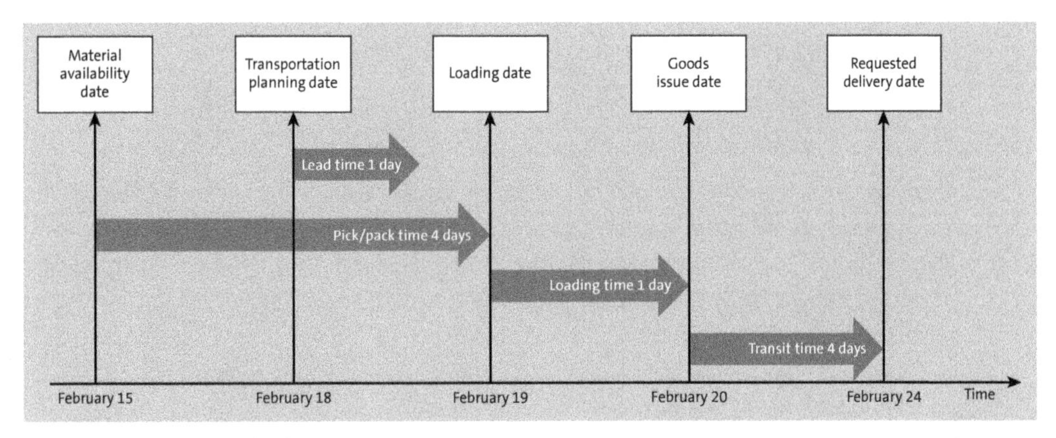

Figure 6.17 Forward Scheduling

This time, we presume that the order is placed on February 15th and that the goods are available the same day. If not, then the whole schedule must be pushed into the future by the number of days until the material is available for your order and customer. Here, you can see the following:

- You need 1 day for transportation planning time, which, as before, is of no consequence.
- What is of consequence is the backup in your warehouse, where it takes 4 days to pick/pack your goods. This is added to your material availability date of February 15th.
- Next, 1 day is needed to load the goods into the truck.
- Finally, as before, 4 days are needed to ply the highways to the receiving dock of your customer.

Accordingly, when you miss your requested delivery date, scheduling will be determined by forward scheduling as outlined here.

Your SAP S/4HANA system will first use backward scheduling to answer the following question: Are all scheduling dates, meaning the material availability date through the GI date, in the future (with respect to your order date)? If yes, then the schedule line can be confirmed. If no, meaning if any of the scheduling dates are in the past with respect to your order date, then the schedule line won't be confirmed. SAP S/4HANA will therefore calculate a new delivery date via forward scheduling. This is the confirmed quantity you see in your sales order schedule line in addition to the unconfirmed line for the original requested delivery date (confirmed quantity being equal to zero).

Backwards and forwards, your SAP S/4HANA system works hard to keep track of your materials and determine reasonable dates for delivery to your customer—after all, this is what you're paying for!

6.4.5 Plant Determination

Any time you see plant (or shipping point, route, etc.) determination in SAP S/4HANA, this is simply a set of configurable logic in the SAP system to make appropriate proposals on the spot in your transactions. For example, when you write a sales order, the materials need to be delivered from your plant, whether it be a factory, a warehouse, or both, to the customer. If you have two plants in your company, Plant A producing pool supplies and Plant B making cement, it stands to reason that you would want to ship your pool supplies from Plant A. You can easily configure SAP to do this.

As implied, the term "plant" in SAP S/4HANA can mean several things: a factory where goods are produced, a warehouse where goods are stored, or a maintenance shop where goods are reconditioned or repaired. Most factories have a place where goods are stored before they can be shipped to other warehouses or to customers.

The delivery plant is therefore the plant from which your goods are being shipped (as contrasted with the receiving plant, which is used in intercompany processes). Plants are assigned to your sales organization and distribution channel. Figure 6.18 displays the sequence of logic by which your SAP S/4HANA system proposes the correct plant for your goods in your sales document.

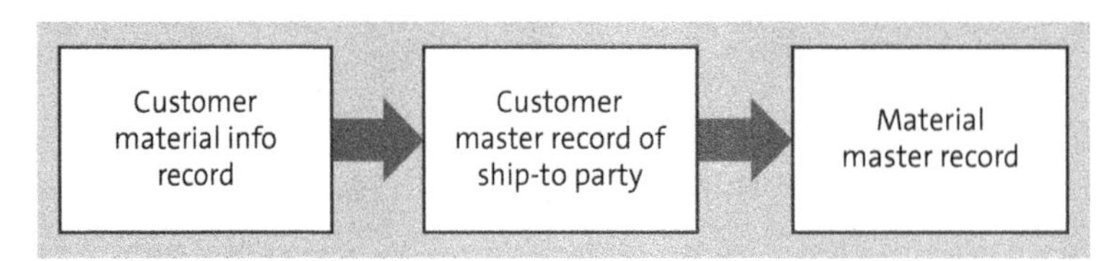

Figure 6.18 Plant Determination Logic

The first place SAP S/4HANA looks for the plant assignment is in the customer material info record, which is Transaction VD51/2/3. As you can see in Figure 6.19 in the **Shipping** section, the shipping **Plant** can be assigned on a customer-material basis.

If the **Plant** isn't assigned here, the next level in the determination logic is at the customer master record level for the ship-to function (the customer function that physically receives the goods).

Create Customer Material Info Record : Item Screen

Classify

Material	252	
	DateBook X Pro 1000a Laptop	
Sales Organization	US30	ATI US
Distribution Channel	20	Direct
Customer	92	Digital, Inc.

Customer material

Customer Material	LAPTOP-1
Customer Description	Grey Datebook laptop
ETag	

Shipping

Plant	US20	Long Island City
Delivery Priority	2	Normal item
Minimum Delivery Qty	5	EA

Partial delivery

Part.dlv./item		Underdel. Tolerance	%
Max.Part.Deliveries	3	Overdeliv. Tolerance	%
		Unlimited Tolerance	☐

Figure 6.19 Plant Assignment in the Customer Material Info Record

Lastly, if not assigned at the customer-material or customer (ship-to) levels, the shipping or delivering plant can be assigned at the material master record so that all customers receive the particular good from the plant so designated in the **Sales: Sales Org 1** view. This is a classic SAP system determination functionality, whether it be pricing or plant determination. The SAP system searches through specific criteria first, and then more generally though a logical decision tree format.

6.4.6 Shipping Point Determination

According to SAP, a "shipping point is a place or location where the goods and services are delivered to the customers." A shipping point is therefore that part of the warehouse where goods are sent out the door to a customer in a particular way. It's the organizational unit responsible for a distinctive type of shipping. A subset of a shipping point is a loading point.

By way of example, think of a giant warehouse like the one shown in Figure 6.20 with four sides to it.

Figure 6.20 Shipping Point Concept

The four sides are described as follows:

- On the east side is the ocean and a number of docks. Each dock has several giant cranes to lift packages of goods into the holds of cargo ships. This could be Shipping Point No. 1 designated for delivery to the customer over water.
- On the bottom side are railroad tracks and sidings, suitable for loading goods. The tracks align with the southern wall of the warehouse, whereas a number of loading spouts are positioned to load materials in the cars.
- On the west side is easy access to the interstate highway. This side has a number of truck bays.
- The north side faces a runway and features a number of gangways on which freight can be loaded to airplanes.

Each side therefore is a shipping point dedicated to the execution of deliveries to customers via a specific mode of transport. It can be said therefore that this warehouse has four such shipping points. Within each shipping point, on a one-to-many relationship, are loading points such as the individual truck bays, loading spouts, docks, or gangways. Commonly, a warehouse may be split into several different buildings, each with its own set of truck bays. Each set could be configured as a separate shipping point.

SAP S/4HANA can be configured to propose the correct shipping point for your customer/material combination as depicted in Figure 6.21.

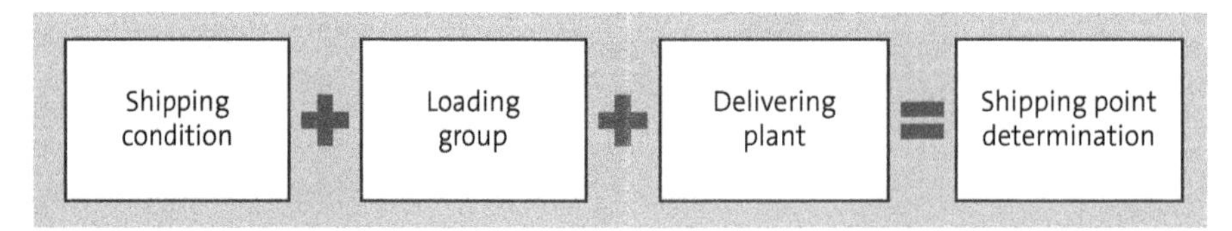

Figure 6.21 Shipping Point Determination Logic

The shipping point determination calculation includes the following:

- **Shipping condition**
  The shipping condition is set in the customer master record from where it's copied over to your sales document in the header **Shipping** tab. This is where you indicate whether the shipment is standard, rush, or customer pickup.
- **Loading group**
  The loading group identifies the team or equipment that will load the material into the transportation unit, such as cranes, loading spouts, forklifts, or hydraulic lifts. This is defined in the material master record.
- **Delivering plant**
  The delivering plant is also read from the material master record from where it's copied to your sales document in the line-item **Shipping** tab.

SAP S/4HANA will read these three fields in a special configuration table that you set up and will propose the correct shipping point based on a combination of these three fields to determine something like Ocean Dock 4 or Truck Bay Area 7, for example.

6.4.7 Route Determination

The purpose of route determination is to find the most efficient route from all those available. Once defined in the configuration, it runs in the background. The definition of both the means of transport and the individual components or legs form a rather large area of configuration all to itself.

Shipping types are still used in SAP S/4HANA, and routes can have stages assigned to them as well. They are all used in SAP S/4HANA to pass to the transportation management solution. The route in SAP S/4HANA really drives the determination of dates in the sales order and delivery. In the configuration, you set the days and time (as well as the working hours) according to the route for the following dates (available in the **Shipping** tab when you double-click the schedule line):

- Loading date (material availability date plus the loading days in configuration, which are assigned to the route)
- GI date (material availability date plus loading plus pick/pack time, which is assigned to the route)
- Delivery date (material availability date plus loading plus pick/pack transit time, which is assigned to the route)
- Transportation planning date (material availability date plus loading plus pick/pack time transit time minus transportation lead time, which is assigned to the route)

All the days set in the route are used in the ATP check in backward scheduling; that is, take the customer's requested delivery date and work backwards using all the material available in fields such as **Replenishment Lead Time** and **Goods Receipt Time**, in addition to the days in the route settings, to find the proposed material availability date.

If the proposed material availability date is in the past, then SAP uses forward scheduling to start from today and propose a material availability date in the future based on the replenishment lead time and route settings.

The route is determined and affected by the following factors in the configuration:

- **Shipping point country**
  The country code for the shipping point.
- **Destination country**
  The country of the destination.
- **Transportation group**
  This is taken from the material master.
- **Transportation zone**
  This is from the customer master of the ship-to party.
- **Shipping condition**
  This is from the customer master of the sold-to party and is available to change in the sales order.
- **Weight group**
  This is assigned in the delivery only by adding the weight of all the items together. The weight group is defined in configuration and assigned to a range of weights.
- **Dangerous goods check**
  If yes, the goods will be subject to special shipping considerations. The necessary timing impact will be added to the delivery dates mentioned previously.
- **Transportation costs**
  All related costs, such as distance-dependent, time-dependent, weight dependent, and potential penalties, are calculated for all trips and routes.
- **Trip evaluation**
  Regarding cost-effectiveness or quickest route, your company's preferences can be set up here.

As you've seen with shipping point and schedule line determinations earlier, SAP S/4HANA can be configured accordingly to propose the correct route determination for your goods, as illustrated in Figure 6.22.

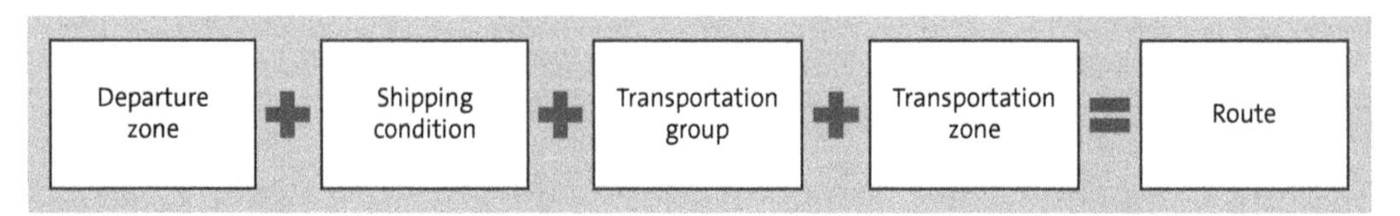

Figure 6.22 Route Determination Logic

The following are used in the calculation of the correct route determination:

- **Departure zone**
  This is the regional area where your shipping point is located. It's typically a broad geographic area of your country and may contain several shipping points.
- **Shipping condition**
  As you've seen previously, this is set in the customer master record from where it's copied over to your sales document in the header **Shipping** tab. This is where you indicate whether the shipment will be standard, rush, or customer pickup.
- **Transportation group**
  This classifies materials into groups based on similar transportation needs. For example, ice cream products need to be shipped at a certain temperature. Fragile materials will be shipped together under stringent packaging and handling requirements in padded trucks. This group is defined in the material master record.
- **Transportation zone**
  This is the location or area served by the same warehouse. It can be defined by postal code or region.

SAP S/4HANA will read these four fields in yet another special configuration table that you setup and will propose the correct route based on where these four fields point. In this way, route determination therefore selects the best result.

As you can see, there is significant interface to other modules such as SAP Global Trade Services (SAP GTS) and SAP Environment, Health, and Safety Management (SAP EHS Management). Route determination therefore tends to be a highly specialized area, and your company would be well advised to take advantage of the services of an experienced consultant to take advantage of an optimized setup.

6.5 Service Processing

As mentioned in the previous section, *service processing* resembles the debit and credit memo process described earlier. Figure 6.23 represents this process in streamlined form.

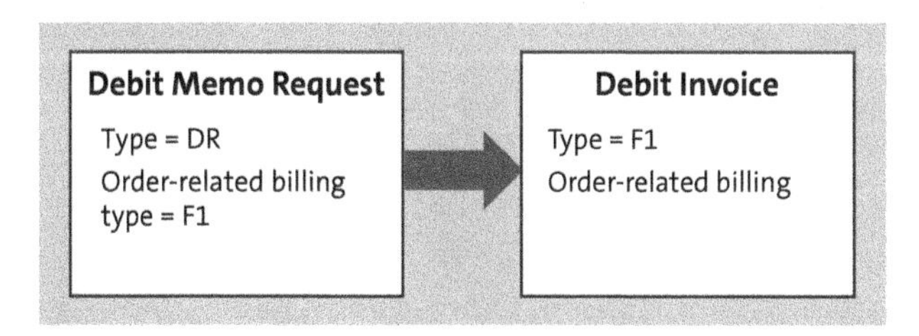

Figure 6.23 Service Processing (Debit Side Only)

Effectively, this is a subset of the hard goods processing explained previously, except that your company isn't selling physical goods that need to be carried from place to place. Billing blocks can still be used depending on your business requirements. The underlying sales or billing documents have been removed for simplification; service debit and credit notes can certainly be predicated on preceding debits and credits.

As illustrated in Figure 6.23, standard invoices are billing documents created in response to sales orders (order-related billing) as type F1 or delivery documents (delivery-related billing) as type F2. Credits are sales document type CR and billing documents G2.

Instead of hard goods, your company sells services such as consulting, engineering, surveying, consumer, and government. Accordingly, service processing in Figure 6.23 looks like hard goods processing in Figure 6.2, except that the delivery step is missing. This is true because there is no inventory management, warehouse, shipping, and other such logistics in the service industry.

If your company is in the service industry, you can skip Chapter 7, which discusses delivery. But the rest of this book applies to your company nevertheless. Also note that billing documents will never be of the type F2.

In terms of accounting impact, there is no GI posting and corresponding entries to the COGS and inventory accounts. Nevertheless, costs remain with the delivery of services rendered to the customer, such as labor and materials used in providing services. Those costs can be tracked and allocated by other methods such as work breakdown structure (WBS) elements and others outside the purview of this sales and distribution book. At billing, the general ledger account entries are the same as shown in Figure 6.12, and accounts receivable remains the same.

6.6 Create a Sales Order Document (SAP GUI)

This section provides a step-by-step walkthrough of creating a sales order document in SAP GUI, which should be very familiar to those used to SAP ERP. To create a sales order both with and without reference to an existing quotation, use Transaction VA01. If creating the sales order without reference to an existing inquiry or quotation, complete the sales area fields as illustrated in Chapter 4, Section 4.3, and follow the steps in that chapter.

Please bear in mind that common business practice is for sales orders to be written only on the receipt of a purchase order from your customer. This is a legally binding commitment to buy your product and is typically received whether you're creating your order with or without reference. This scenario will cover the creation of the sales order with reference to a quotation, whereby the **Customer** and **Material** fields are copied over and don't need to be filled in.

1. Enter "OR" in the **Order Type** field when creating the sales order with reference to a preceding document. This is the standard SAP document type for a standard order, which is a common sales document type.
2. Click on the **Create with Reference** button (see Figure 6.24).
3. In the **Create with Reference** dialog shown in Figure 6.25, enter "200000007" in the **Quot.** field. This is the document number of the quotation created in the preceding chapter.
4. Click on the **Copy** button on the lower-right corner of the dialog (Figure 6.25).

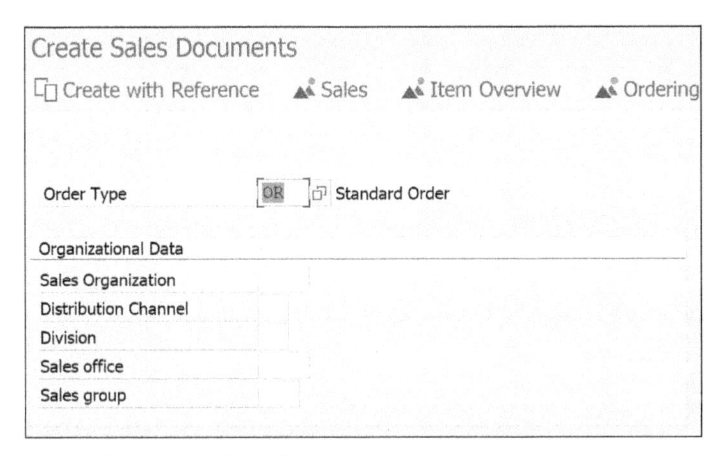

Figure 6.24 Create Sales Documents

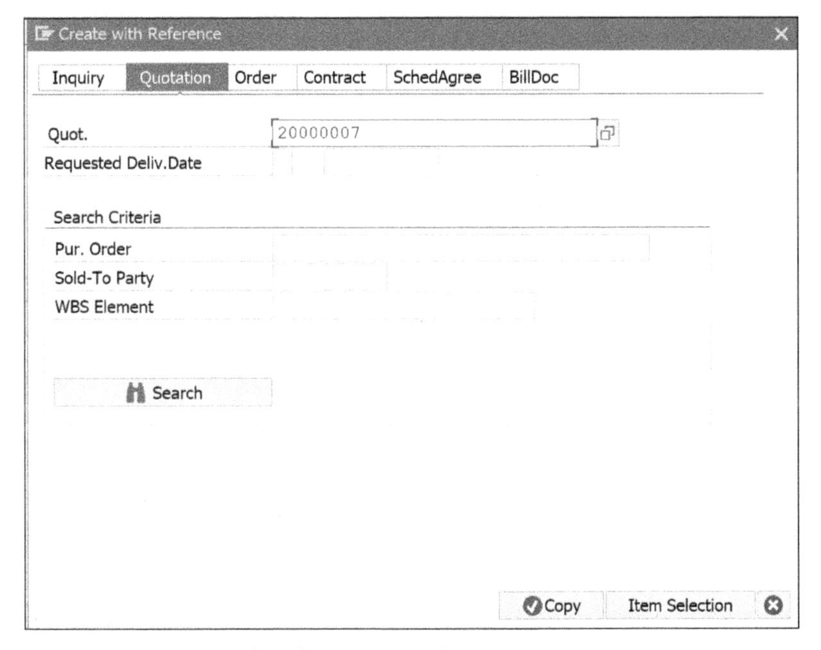

Figure 6.25 Create with Reference: Copy Button

You're now in the main **Create Standard Order** screen, which has been completed with some important data from your preceding document. Let's take a moment to review what has been completed on your behalf by the system.

6.6.1 Header Data

Your customer or business partner information in the form of **Sold-To Party and Ship-To Party** (as well as the other main functions of **Bill-To Party** and **Payer**) have been copied over. These can be seen at the top of the **Create Standard Order: Overview** screen, as shown in Figure 6.26. To review the relationships of these business partner functions, see Chapter 2 for more comprehensive details.

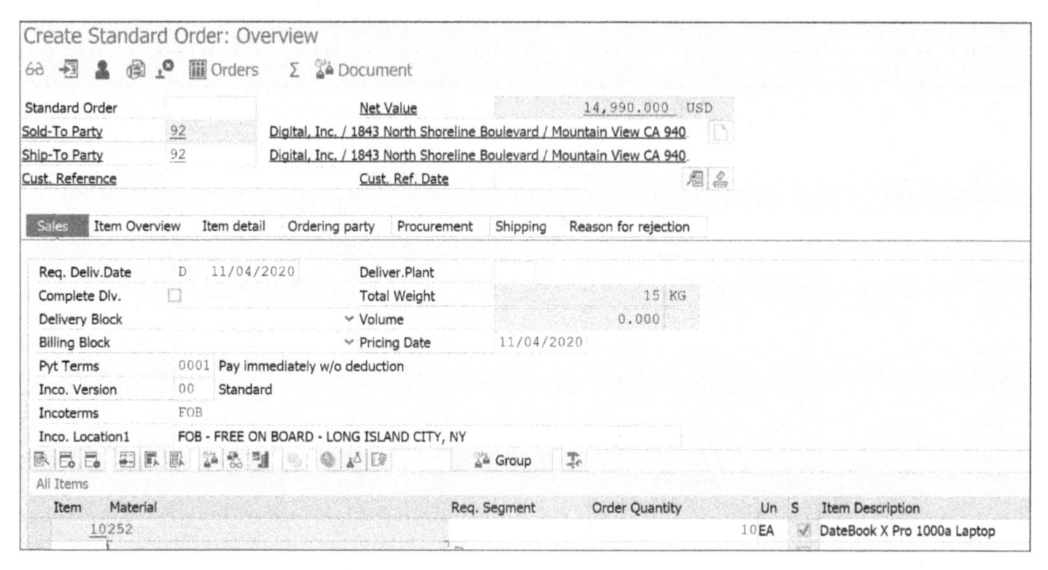

Figure 6.26 Create Standard Order

Review all header fields copied over from your preceding document as follows:

- **Sold-To Party**: 92
- **Ship-To Party**: 92
- (Optional) **Cust. Reference**: Not copied over from the quotation
- **Req. Deliv.Date**: 11/04/2020

The **Cust. Reference** field is used for any number issued by the customer for their own tracking of the order. It isn't system required. Because it's frequently business required, however, it's included here as an optional field for a fresh value as received from the customer.

You'll notice that this field isn't copied over from the underlying quotation. It's up to you, the user, to input a fresh value here; in this case, the most common entry would be your customer's purchase order number.

The **Req. Deliv.Date** field is, on the other hand, copied over from the quotation. This is the date that the goods are to be delivered to the customer and is often changed to several days in the future to reflect a reasonable delivery time. This is a header data field and copies the current date into the **Delivery Date** field in the **Schedule Lines** tab of the material line item where it can be changed. If changed at the line-item level, that date overrides the header date in terms of delivery planning (and the header date, interestingly, remains unchanged).

We'll assume that this date should be updated owing to, for example, some period of time having passed since the quotation was written. Accordingly, input the optional **Cust. Reference**, and change the **Req. Deliv.Date** as follows:

- (Optional) **Cust. Reference**: "P6525645"
- **Req. Deliv.Date**: "12/31/2020"

Press Enter after you've finished. You may receive a warning message (in yellow) and a popup message about redetermination of billing dates to which you can simply press Enter twice to clear.

Your **Create Standard Order: Overview** screen should now appear as in Figure 6.27.

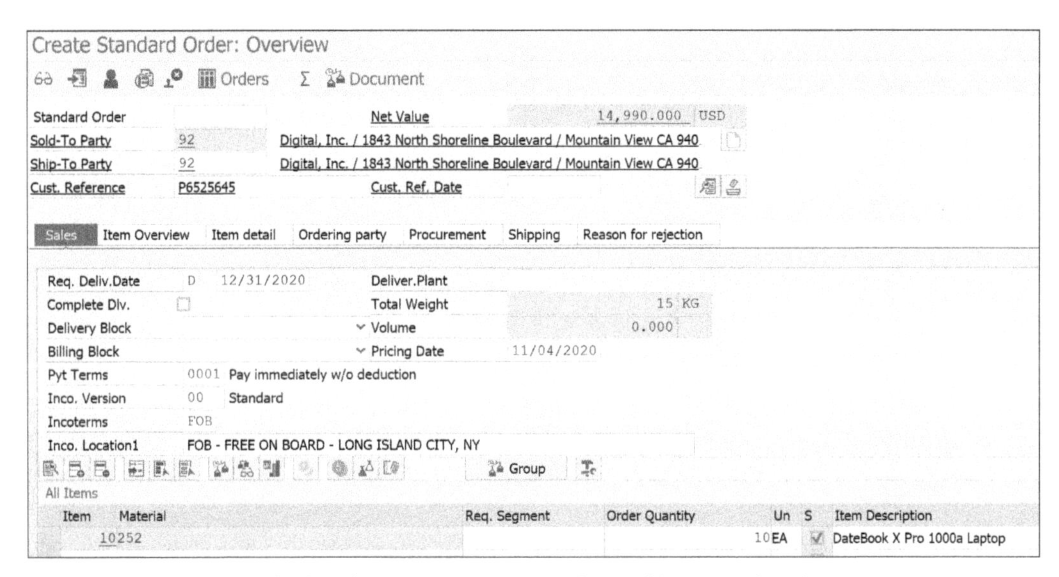

Figure 6.27 Create Standard Order: Overview Screen after Fields Are Updated

Before reviewing the line-item data, there is one important detail to check. Are the goods in stock? For example, if you've written an order for 10 units to be delivered to your customer by a certain date, does SAP S/4HANA confirm that you have stock on hand and that the stock isn't otherwise reserved for a previously written sales order? You know from the previous section that this is a very robust functionality. This can be checked right from the overview screen. First, select the line item that you want to check, and then click the **Check Item Availability** icon, as shown in Figure 6.28.

Figure 6.28 Create Standard Order: Overview Screen with Line Item Selected and Check Item Availability Icon

This will take you to the **Standard Order: Availability Control** screen shown in Figure 6.29.

Standard Order: Availability Control

One-time delivery | Complete dlv. | Delivery proposal | ATP quantities | Scope of check

Item 10 Sched.line 1
Material 252
Grey Datebook laptop
Requirement Segment
Plant US20 Long Island City
Req.deliv.date 12/29/2020 Open Quantity 10 EA
End lead time 12/30/2020
Fix Qty/Date Max.Part.Deliveries 3

One-time del. on req. del. dte
Dely/Conf.Date 12/29/2020 / 12/29/2020 Confirmed Quantity 10

Complete delivery
Dely/Conf.Date 12/29/2020 / 12/29/2020

Dely proposal
Dely/Conf.Date 12/29/2020 / 12/29/2020 Confirmed qty 10

Figure 6.29 Create Standard Order: Availability Control Screen

As you can see, SAP S/4HANA has effectively evaluated your order against available stock and has determined that all items are confirmed as available right now. If the quantity confirmed were less than your total amount input (in this example, **10**), then the reduced quantity would appear here.

Click one of the three green checkmark icons to return to the previous screen as your order is ready to be processed for delivery as soon as it's saved.

6.6.2 Line-Item Data on the Overview Screen

Review all line-item fields copied over from your preceding document as follows:

- **Material**: 252
- **Order Quantity**: 10

The **Create with Reference** functionality used to create your standard order does a lot of the heavy lifting on your behalf, including copying over these line-item fields. The **Material** number can't be changed, but the **Order Quantity** may be changed to suit the customer's requirements.

At this point, your customer details, customer reference number, requested delivery date, material, and quantity as input and price as determined, are clearly visible in both the header and line-item sections. This is all that is required to complete a standard order type of sales document.

6.6.3 Other Header and Line-Item Data

There are some other commonly used optional or business-required fields to be aware of. This section repeats some of the content from Chapter 4, which discussed inquiries, so it can be skimmed as necessary.

Header Data

The header data section contains many additional fields that will potentially have repercussions on the price and availability information you provide to your customer. Remember, depending on the setup of your system, standard order documents typically generate output documents that are sent to your customer automatically, and you need to be sure that the information contained therein is accurate.

Some of these header fields are visible in the **Sales** tab of the **Create Standard: Overview** screen, as shown in Figure 6.30.

- **Pyt Terms**
  What are the payment conditions under which your customer will be trading with you? This can be defined in customer master data and then copied automatically into all sales and distribution documents.
- **Incoterms**
  Who will have responsibility for the shipments at which phase in the process? This can also be defined in customer master data.
- **Doc. Currency**
  Is the currency correct? Again, this can also be set up once in customer master data.

By clicking on the **Display Header Details** icon shown in Figure 6.31, you can open all the header data for the quotation, as displayed in Figure 6.32.

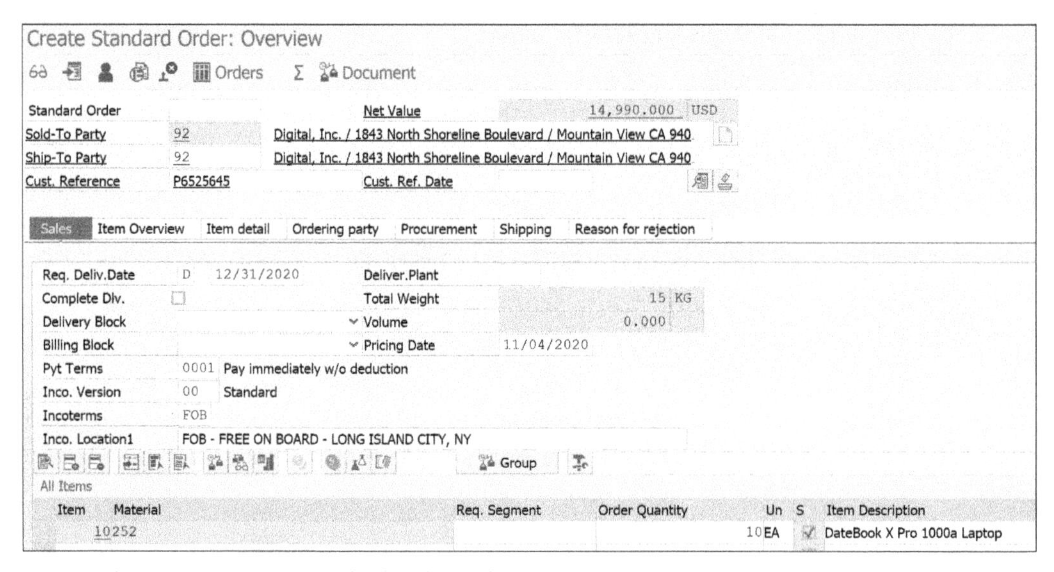

Figure 6.30 Create Standard Order: Sales Tab

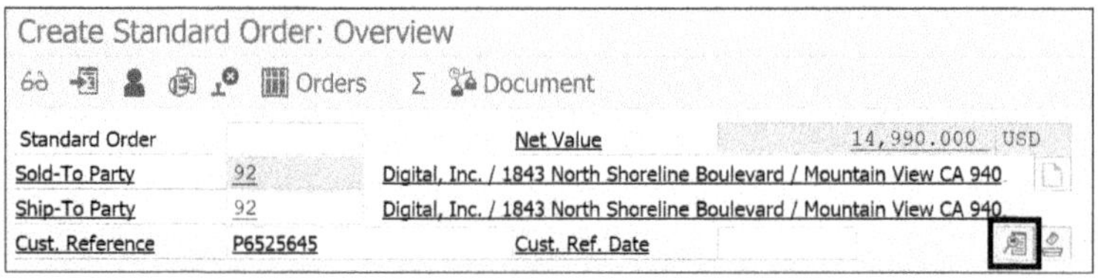

Create Standard Order: Overview
Orders
Document
Standard Order
Net Value
14,990.000 USD
Sold-To Party 92 Digital, Inc. / 1843 North Shoreline Boulevard / Mountain View CA 940
Ship-To Party 92 Digital, Inc. / 1843 North Shoreline Boulevard / Mountain View CA 940
Cust. Reference P6525645
Cust. Ref. Date

Figure 6.31 Create Standard Order: Display Header Details Icon

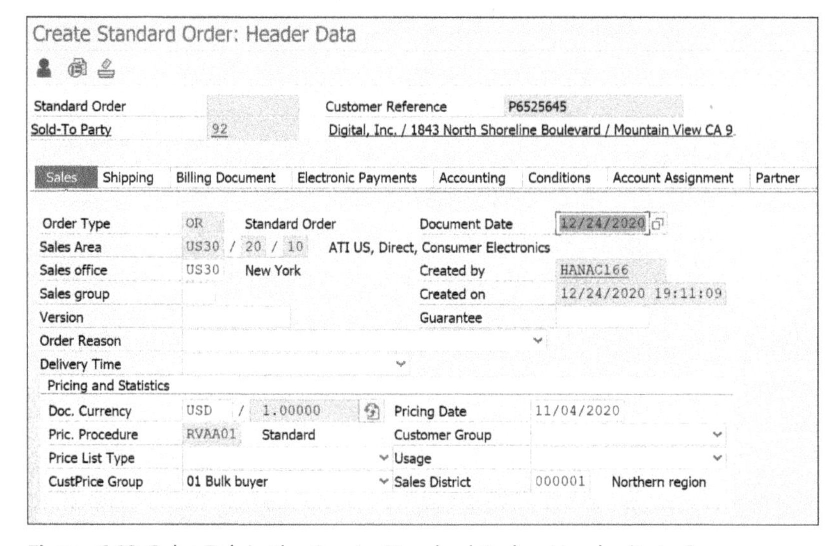

Figure 6.32 Sales Tab in the Create Standard Order: Header Data Screen

From here, all header information is shown in various tabs, including more detailed information:

- **Shp.Cond. (shipping condition)**
  If the customer has requested a specific shipping condition (e.g., must be delivered as a rush) or wants to pick up the products, this may have an impact on your freight price determination. The **Shp.Cond.** field is found on the **Shipping** tab, as shown in Figure 6.33. This can be set in the customer's master data.

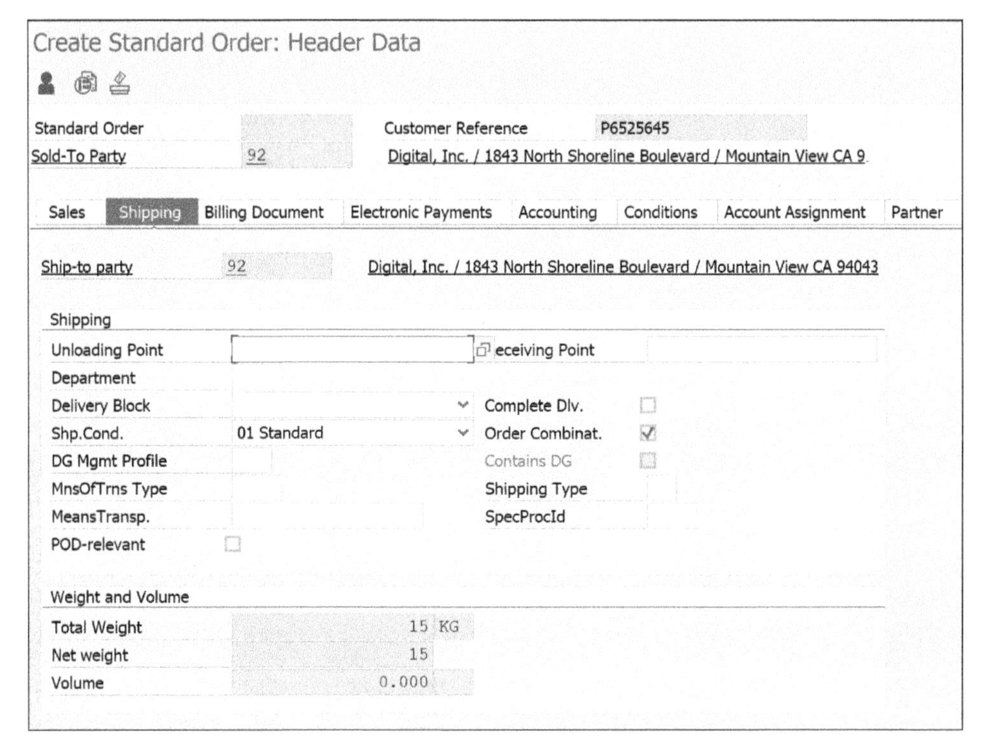

Figure 6.33 Shipping Tab in the Create Standard Order: Header Data Screen

- **Partn. Funct. (partner functions)**
  If you need to change any of the partner functions, such as the bill-to party or the payer, or you want to add a new partner function for a carrier or an end customer, this can be done in the **Partner** tab, as shown in Figure 6.34.

- **Txt ty.**
  Are there any specific header texts you want to add to the document? This means that this particular text is applicable to *all* items in the order. Depending on your setup in the system, these can be included in the output document for the customer. These texts can be added in the **Texts** tab, as shown in Figure 6.35.

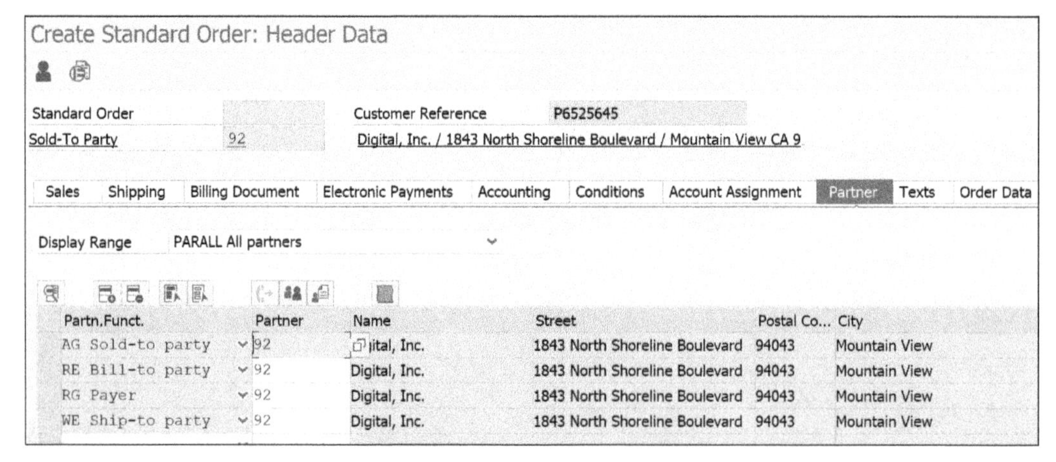

Figure 6.34 Partner Tab in the Create Standard Order: Header Data Screen

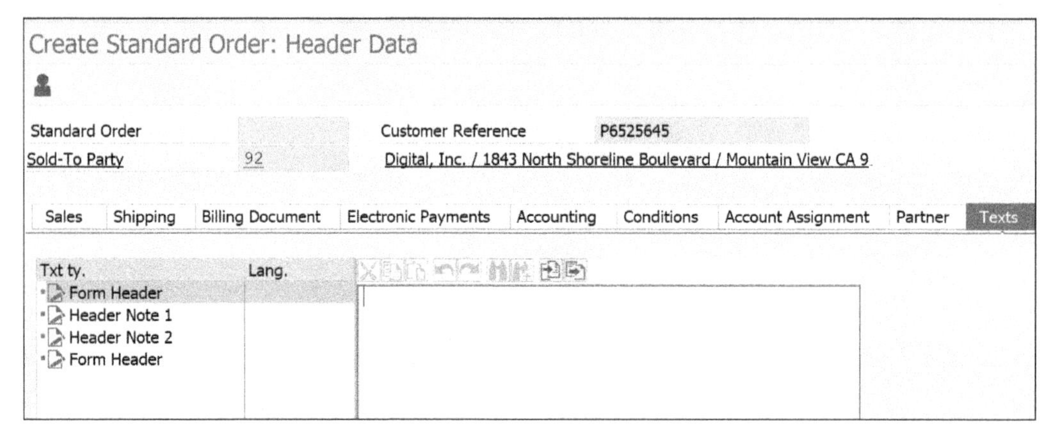

Figure 6.35 Texts Tab in the Create Standard Order: Header Data Screen

Line-Item Data

By double-clicking on the line items, you can open the item data per material line in the standard order document. Item data therefore can vary from line item to line item. The key data for a sales document line item is the material unit price, which is on the **Conditions** tab. More information on pricing is available in Chapter 2, Section 2.2. The following line-item fields are found in various tabs:

- **Price**
  Check that prices are correct. Do you need to add any discounts or customer-specific pricing, surcharges, or freight? Are all taxes calculated correctly? All these options are available by adding new condition types or changing existing condition types in the screen shown in Figure 6.36.

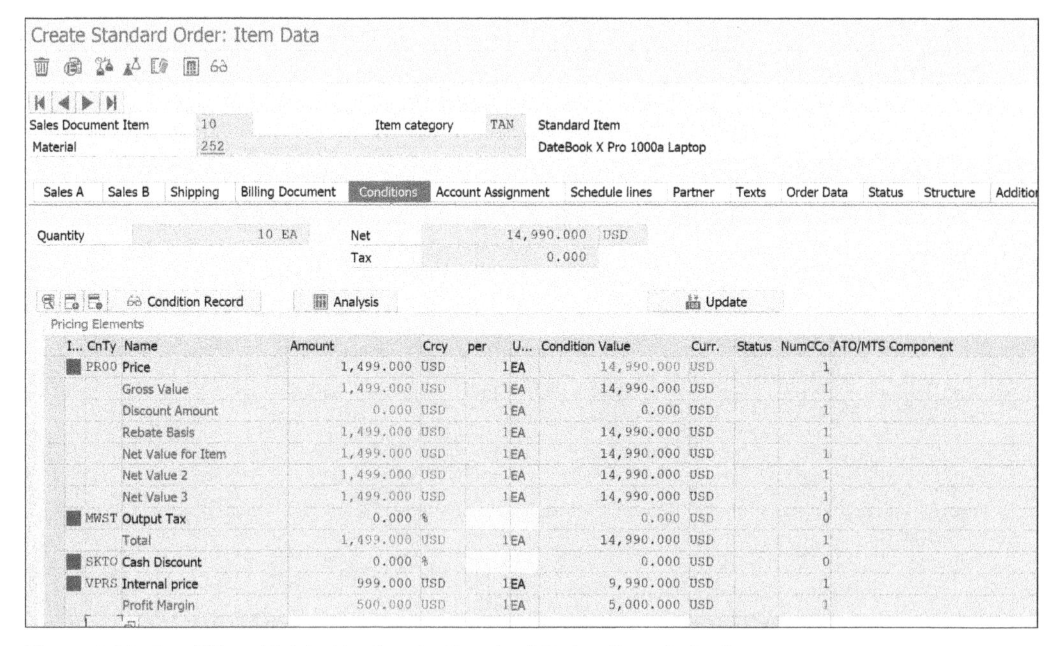

Figure 6.36 Conditions Tab in the Create Standard Order: Item Data Screen

- **Batch**
  If the material is batch managed, has the customer requested price and availability of a specific batch? If so, this can be added in the **Sales A** tab, as shown in Figure 6.37. Note that the **Batch** field won't show if the material isn't batch managed. The batch determination icon on the overview screen will run a check of the availability of the batches against predetermined rules and propose available batches.

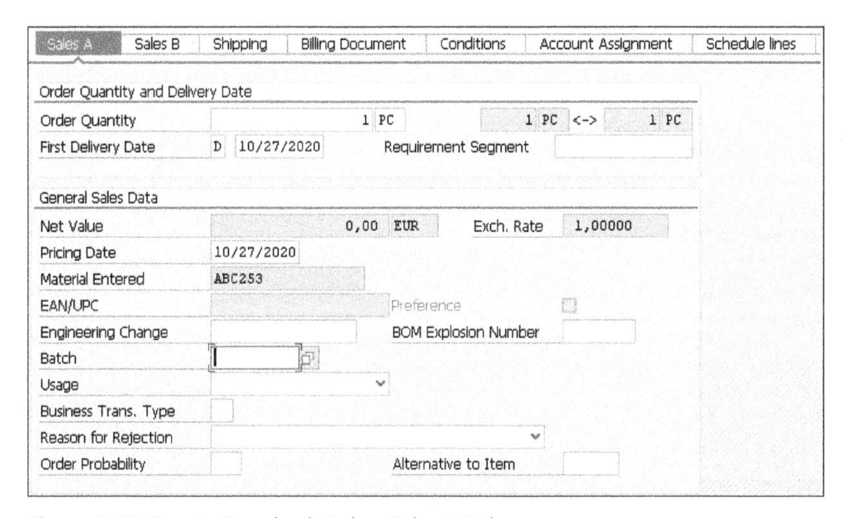

Figure 6.37 Create Standard Order: Sales A Tab

- **Delivery Date**
  As noted previously, the change in the **Req. Deliv.Date** in the header has updated the **Delivery Date** to the current date in the **Schedule lines** tab, as shown in Figure 6.38.

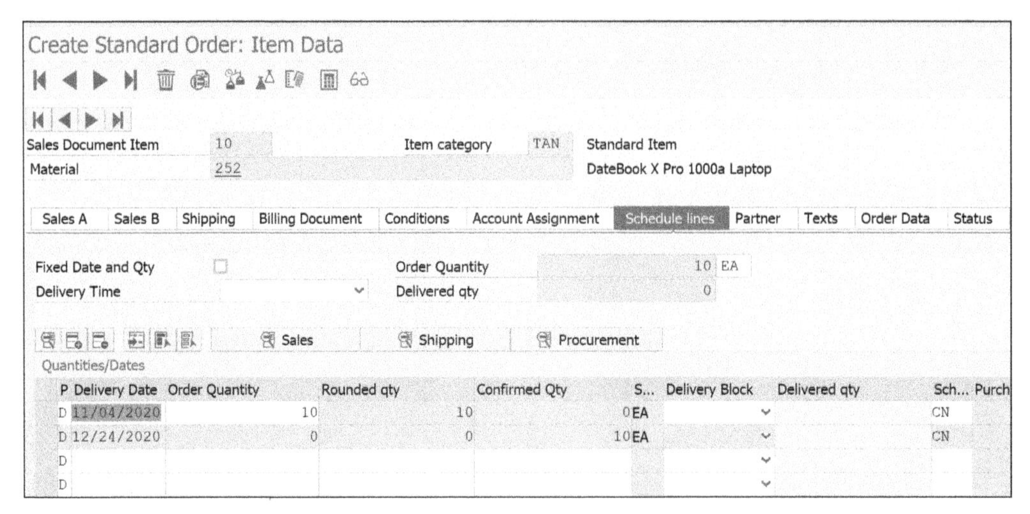

Figure 6.38 Scheduled Lines Tab in the Create Standard Order: Item Data Screen

As noted previously, the **Schedule lines** tab contains all the information pertaining to delivery of your material to the customer, such as quantities to be delivered by date with a link to inventory management.

As shown in Figure 6.38, the entries in the **Schedule lines** tab have been adjusted by the change in the header field. Specifically, the old date copied over from the quotation has been unconfirmed, that is, confirmation quantity set to zero, and the current date has been confirmed for the entire quantity.

Further changes are possible at this point. If, for example, the customer has requested delivery of products to be scheduled across multiple future dates, these dates can be changed and added in the **Schedule lines** tab shown in Figure 6.39. The two former lines were simply deleted, and two new lines have been added showing the updated requested delivery dates with the requested quantities. At this point, SAP S/4HANA takes a look ahead in the sales and distribution process and determines whether there will be enough stock available to process your order within the delivery date promised to the customer.

This is performed via SAP S/4HANA's availability check functionality (which can also be performed in the main overview screen). The most common check is based on ATP, which has already been discussed previously.

So, for example, let's say you have 10 units in your order that you would like to deliver to your customer. Based on a requested delivery date of December 31, 2020, your company has the following units in each category: 20 inward – 30 outward + 15 in stock at the warehouse

Accordingly, the system will only confirm 5 units available for delivery on December 31st. The system can further look ahead and determine that 5 more units are scheduled to be finished in production by January 5th. Thus, the system can propose two deliveries based on this order, and the **Schedule lines** tab will look like the screen shown in Figure 6.39.

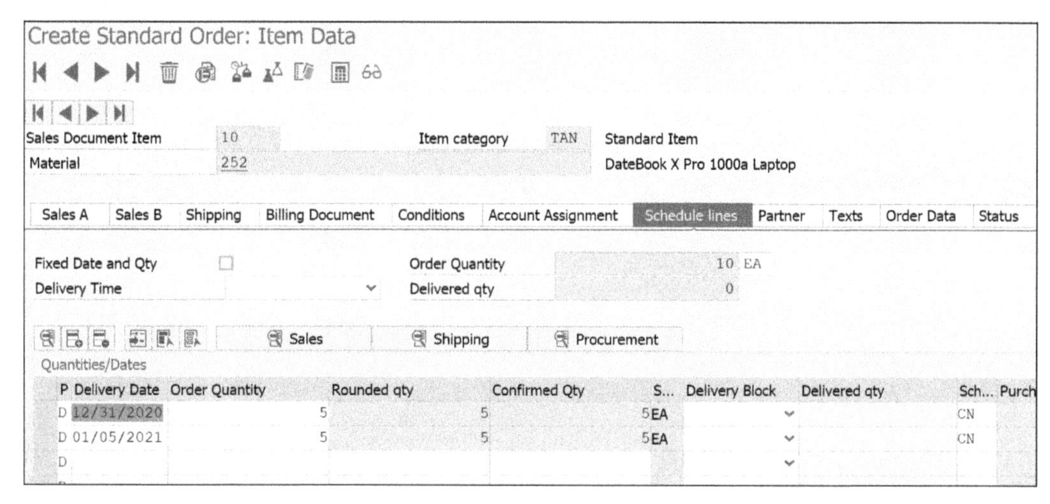

Figure 6.39 Create Standard Order: Schedule Lines after Update

If you happen to know these ATP quantities, you can input them manually, or like most SAP users, just let SAP S/4HANA calculate and confirm these stock quantities for you.

Occasionally, users are surprised when their order isn't confirmed at all, meaning deliveries aren't possible. There are many potential reasons for this. A common example is when users write sales documents and then leave them unfulfilled or open in the system; in this case, SAP will continue to reserve those quantities until all open sales orders are either delivered or closed out. Accordingly, the solution is to use Transaction VA05 to seek out all open sales order and close them (if they can't be delivered).

Note

See Chapter 7 for more details on inventory levels and stock processing.

As noted earlier, this line-item delivery date overrides but doesn't change the **Req. DelivDate** field in the header.

- **Txt ty.**
  Are there any specific item texts you want to add to the document line item? Remember, header text applies to the entire order and all line items. Line-item text is specific only to the particular quotation line item. For example, if one material in the quotation needs to be kept at a special temperature, that information could be provided as text here. Depending on your setup in the system, these texts can be

included automatically in the output document for the customer. These texts can be reviewed or added in the line-item **Texts** tab, as shown in Figure 6.40.

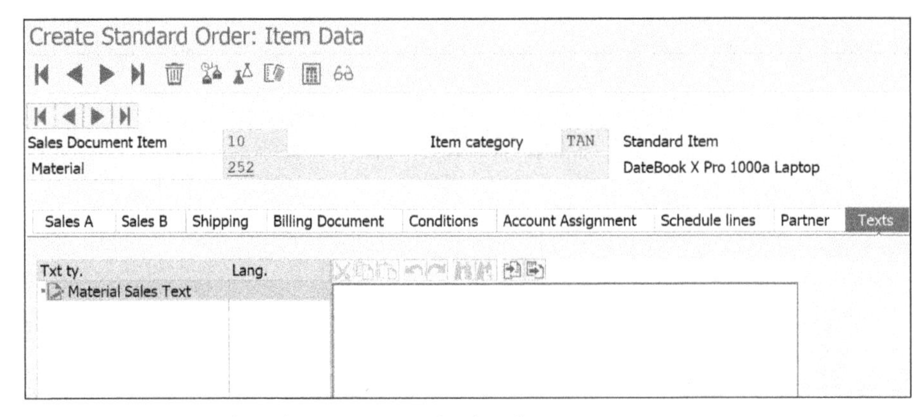

Figure 6.40 Texts Tab in the Create Standard Order: Item Data Screen

6.6.4 Incompletion Log

The standard order document is now complete for all required and many other commonly used fields. To check incompletion status, choose **Edit • Incompletion Log** from the menu bar, as shown in Figure 6.41.

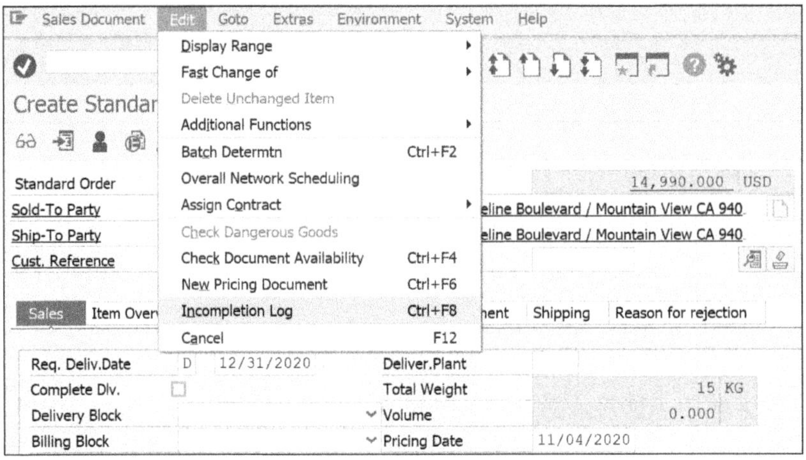

Figure 6.41 Create Standard Order Incompletion Log

This launches the SAP incompletion procedure, which checks that all system-required fields have been correctly populated in your document. If any are missing, then you'll be presented with a new screen showing which fields are missing entries. From here, you can navigate to all and fill in the missing data.

After all the required fields are completed, the following message appears on the status bar, in the lower-left corner of your screen (see Figure 6.42).

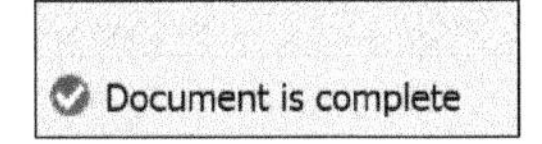

Figure 6.42 Incompletion Log Message

6.6.5 Printing Output

If you'll be issuing an output to the customer, either a hard copy or soft copy output to the customer, you can look at the standard order to be printed on the screen before completing your document to ensure that everything looks correct. At this point, your standard order is still not yet saved and therefore isn't active in the system. Accordingly, if configured, the SAP system will generate a proposed output type for your review. Only when you save the standard order will a finalized version be generated with a document number and then printed/emailed to the customer.

There are two ways to see the output processing in SAP:

- Click on the **Display Output Request** icon in the **Create Standard Order: Overview** screen, as shown in Figure 6.43.
- Choose **Extras • Output • Header • Edit** on the menu bar.

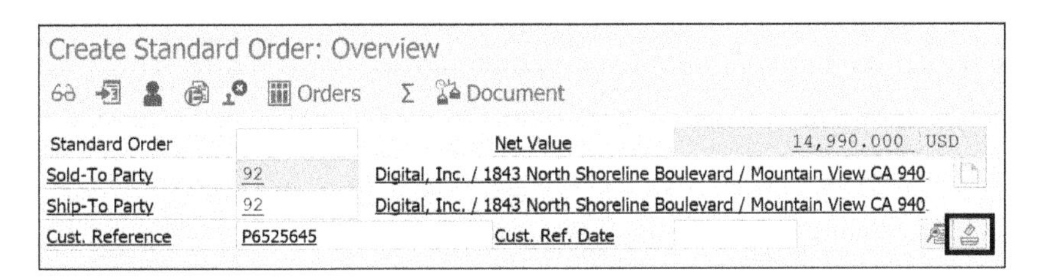

Figure 6.43 Create Standard Order: Display Output Request Icon

Either method will open the **Create Standard Order: Output** screen to show you the **Output** type created (see Figure 6.44).

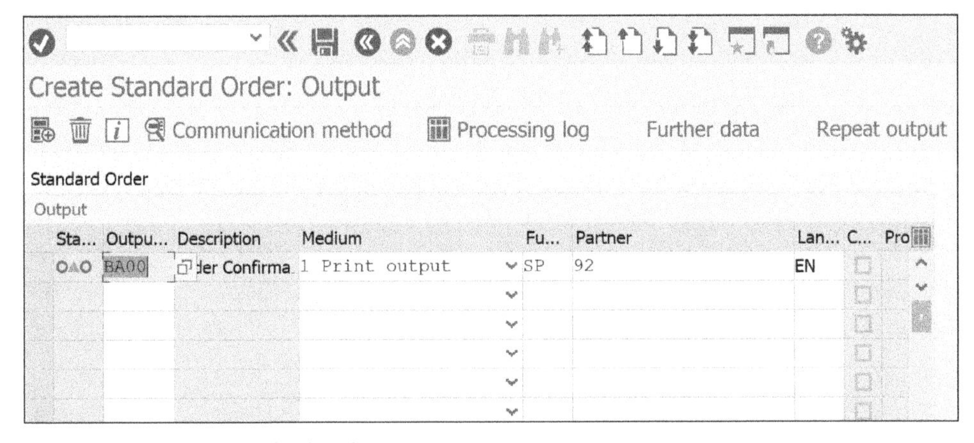

Figure 6.44 Create Standard Order: Output Screen

In this example, the **BA00** standard sales **Order Confirmation** output type shows a yellow traffic light, which means that it's waiting to be printed. After saving, it may show a green light to indicate that it has printed or a red traffic light if it fails to print. The term "print," of course, can mean printing a hard copy or creating a soft copy to be transmitted in numerous ways, including PDF via email or electronic data interchange (EDI).

All outputs store data in certain formats for review. An output type can be determined by following standard sales and distribution condition technique processing (see Chapter 2, Section 2.2, for condition technique details). If you want to see how the output has been determined, you can do this from the same output request screen. From the menu bar, choose **Goto • Determination Analysis** to show you a very busy screen where you can analyze how the output has been selected (see Figure 6.45).

Analysis Output

Procedure	Description
V10000	Order Output
BA00	Order Confirmation
010(0003)	Sales Organization/Cu...
0000000726	0000000092
BA00	Order Confirmation
BA00	Order Confirmation
BAV0	Order confirm. VMI
BSOL	Order Confirmation
BSOP	Order Confirmation
BSTL	Order Confirmation
BSTP	Order Confirmation
ESYM	Internal Output
JRMS	DRM Claim Request
KRML	Credit Processing
MAIL	Internal Output
MAND	SEPA Mandate

View

Access Details 010 (BA00)

Access	Message	Description
010	541	Output found

Access	(complete)	
Field in Condition Table	Field in Document	Value in Document
Sales Organization	Sales Organization	US30
Customer	Sold-To Party	0000000092

Figure 6.45 Create Standard Order Analysis Output

In this example, you can see that the output type **BA00** has been determined via a combination of the **Sales Organization US30** and **Customer 92** in the sales order.

You're now ready to save your sales order. Click on the **Save** icon, as shown in Figure 6.46.

Figure 6.46 Create Standard Order

The standard order document number should appear on the status bar in the lower-left corner of the screen shown in Figure 6.47.

Figure 6.47 Standard Order Saved Message

This standard order document can now be used to create a delivery document to proceed in the next step of the order-to-cash process. Keep in mind that up to now, no general ledger accounts have been impacted. This means that neither inquiry, quotation, nor sales order documents have any impact on profit/loss accounting in your company. Stock levels have been impacted or reserved by the availability check functionality.

If your sales document was for a service rather than for a physical good or you wrote a sales order for several hours of consulting time already delivered, you've written an order-based billing document, as opposed to the delivery-based billing that you've just completed here. If so, you'll skip the delivery process and go straight to billing to create your invoice based on your sales document because you won't be completing the delivery portion of the order-to-cash process.

6.7 Managing Sales Orders App

In this section, we introduce the new SAP Fiori apps in SAP S/4HANA and provide the same kind of walkthrough as we did in Section 6.6 covering SAP GUI previously. Users experienced in SAP ERP should recognize many similarities in the basic screens, such as Transaction VA01. However, navigating to those basic screens and using the search functions in SAP Fiori is a little different. These will be highlighted in this SAP Fiori section.

Now let's create a sales order in SAP Fiori by following these steps:

1. Launch the Manage Sales Orders app, and click on the **Create Sales Order - VA01** link, as shown in Figure 6.48.

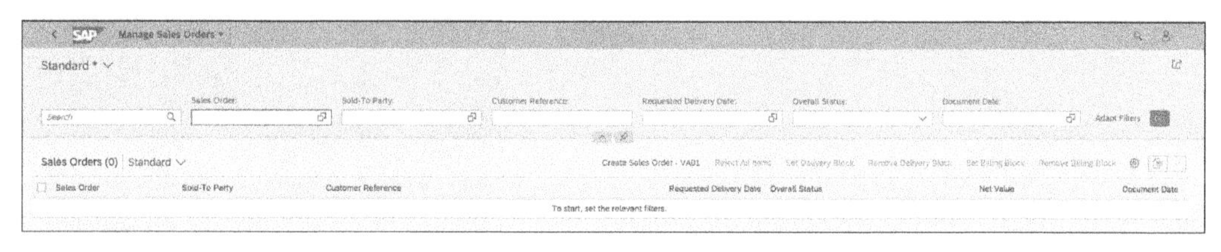

Figure 6.48 Manage Sales Orders App

2. In the **Create Sales Order** screen, enter "OR" for the **Order Type** and **Sales Area**, as you did previously in the SAP GUI screen shown in Figure 6.24.

3. Choose **More • Sales Document • Create with Reference**, as shown in Figure 6.49.

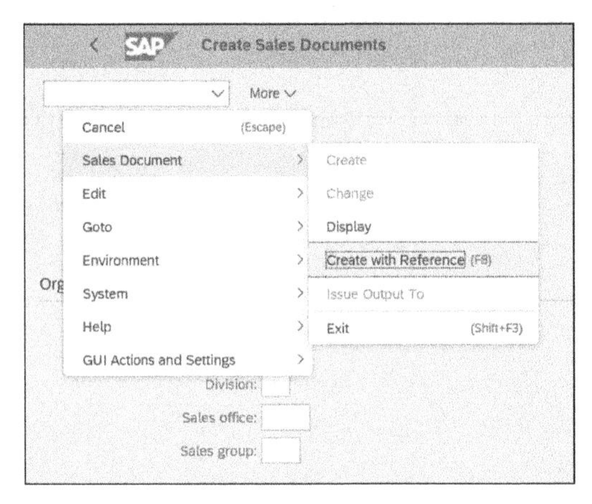

Figure 6.49 Create Sales Documents with Reference in SAP Fiori

4. In the **Create with Reference** dialog which follows, enter the quotation document number into the **Quot.** field, as shown in Figure 6.50. SAP S/4HANA will validate your entry by displaying further details of your quotation document.
5. Click on the **Copy** button in the lower-right corner.

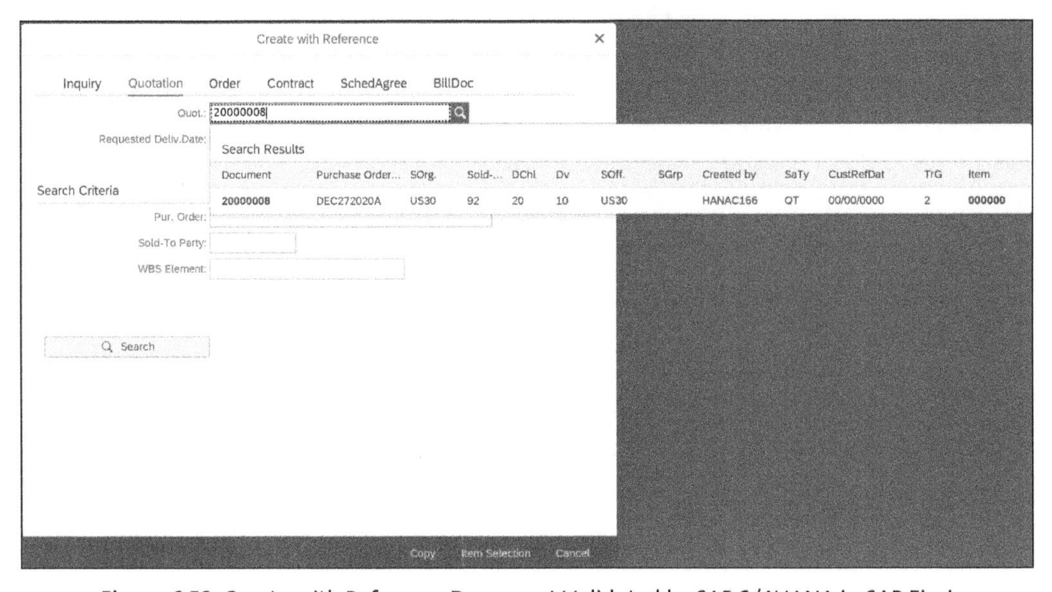

Figure 6.50 Create with Reference Document Validated by SAP S/4HANA in SAP Fiori

After input of the **Cust. Reference** field, your screen looks like Figure 6.51.

6. After all data is input as described in the SAP GUI steps previously, click on the **Save** button in the lower-right corner, as shown in Figure 6.52.

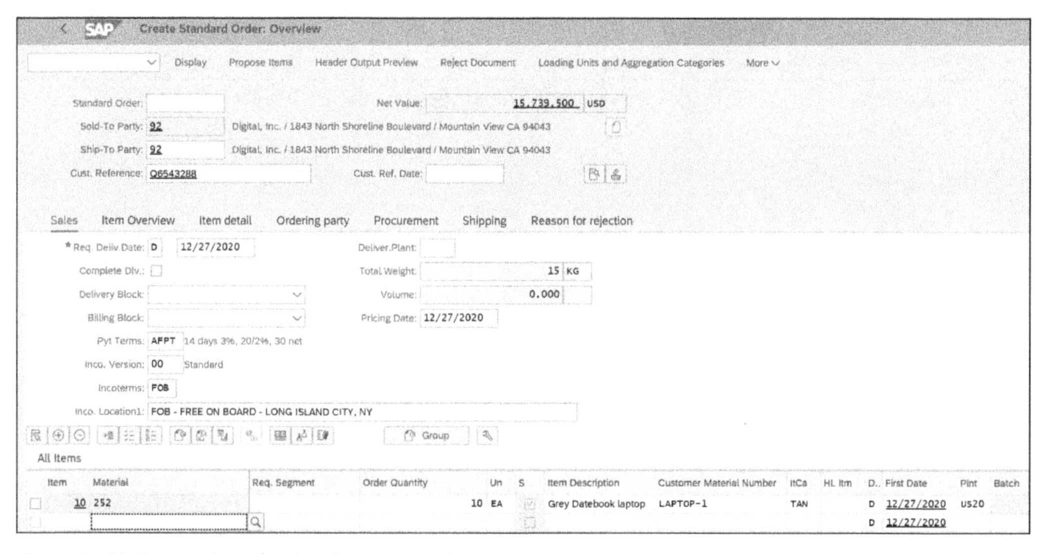

Figure 6.51 Create Standard Order in SAP Fiori

Figure 6.52 Save Button in SAP Fiori

After saving, look for the confirmation message that your standard order has been saved, as shown in Figure 6.53.

Figure 6.53 Standard Order Saved Message in SAP Fiori

6.8 Change and Display a Sales Order Document (SAP GUI)

We'll first look at changing and displaying your sales documents in SAP GUI, which again will be very familiar to SAP ERP users.

To change a Standard Order, use Transaction VA02. Likewise, to display a standard order, use Transaction VA03.

> **Note**
>
> Remember that if you're anywhere *except* the SAP main menu, you must preface your transaction code with "/n," without the quotation marks or comma. For example, after saving your standard order, you can go directly to change mode by typing "/NVA02" (without quotation marks) in the transaction code field and then pressing [Enter].

After creating your sales document in SAP per the steps in Section 6.6, and seeing your "saved" message as shown previously in Figure 6.47, you can also display the sales order by clicking on the **Display** icon in the same screen, as shown in Figure 6.54.

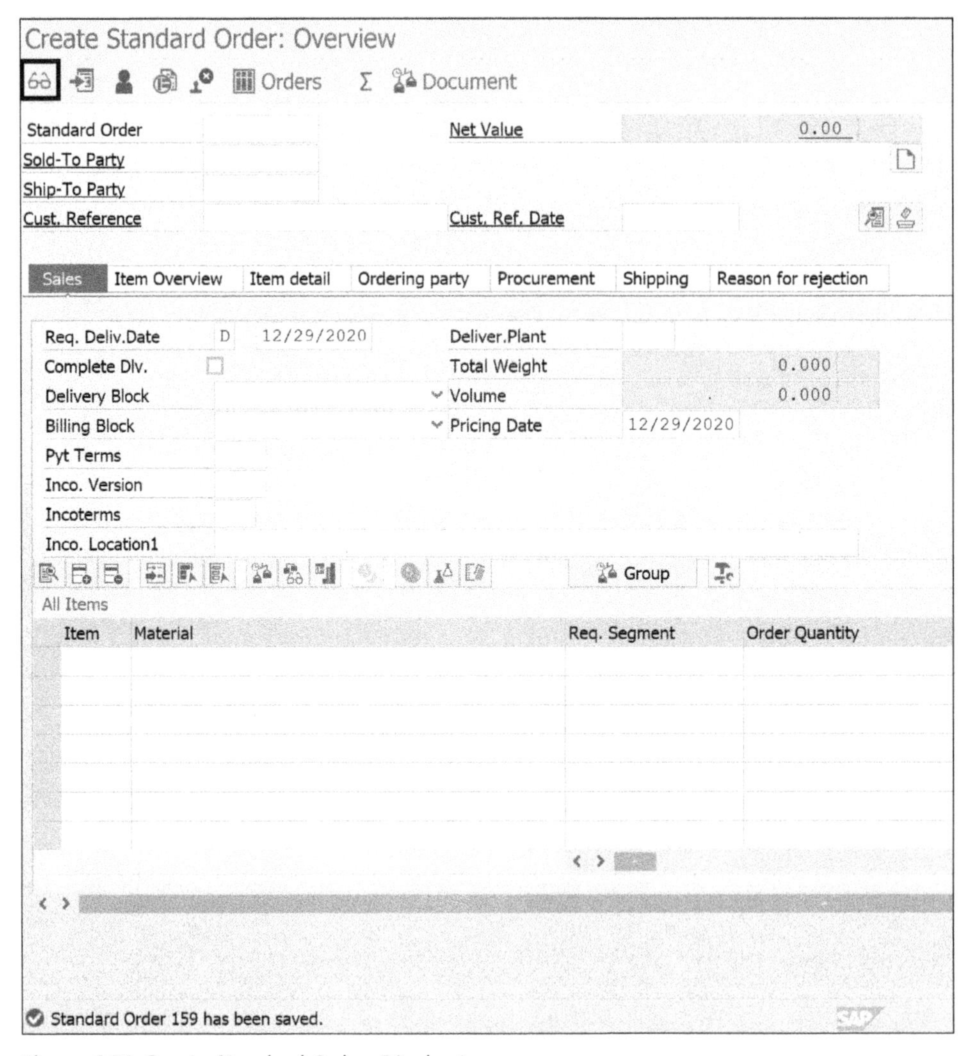

Figure 6.54 Create Standard Order: Display Icon

This navigates directly to Transaction VA03 (Display Standard Order), where you can see the standard order just created in display mode, meaning that all fields can be viewed but not amended.

Here, you can switch to change mode by the clicking the **Change** icon, as displayed in Figure 6.55.

By clicking the **Change** or **Display** icons in the toolbar, you can toggle back and forth in the document.

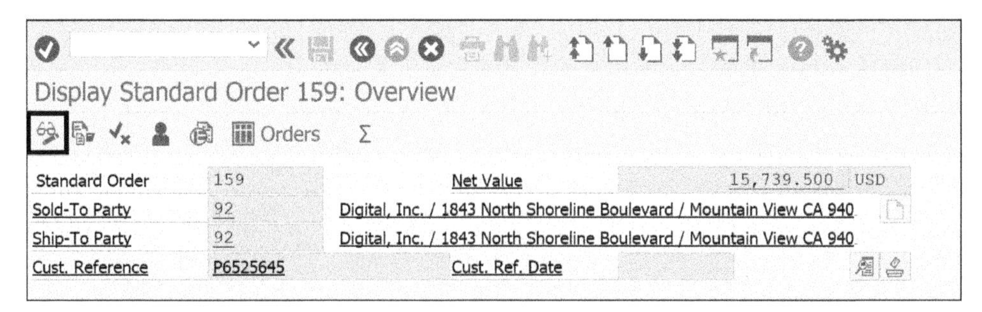

Figure 6.55 Display Standard Order: Change Icon

Identical to the **Create Inquiry** and **Create Quotation** screens, the **Change** and **Display** screens are separated into three sections: overview, header, and line item. The initial screen is the **Overview** view and shows the **Item Overview** tab.

The main standard order fields to be reviewed via change or display modes are as follows:

- **Standard Order Document Number**
  Found in the upper-left corner of the **Overview** screen. This field can't be changed.
- **Standard Order Document Type**
  For such an important field, SAP hides this in the **Sales** tab of the header area. This field can't be changed.
- **Sold-To Party/Ship-To Party**
  Found just below the standard order **Document Number** on the **Overview** screen. These fields can be changed if there are no subsequent documents. Please see Chapter 9 for more information.
- **Sales Area**
  Like the **Document Type**, this critical information is found in the **Sales** tab of the header area. All three component fields can't be changed.
- **Cust. Reference**
  This optional field is found just below the **Sold-To Party** and **Ship-To Party** fields on the **Overview** screen. The field can be changed.
- **Net Value**
  Found on the top right of the **Overview** screen, this field is a sum of all price conditions. If the prices are changed in the line item **Conditions** tab, then those changes will be reflected here.
- **Material Number/Description**
  Material numbers and their corresponding descriptions appear in the grid in the center of the **Overview** screen. New **Material Number** line items can be added. However, deleting them is restricted if there are follow-on documents (see Chapter 9).
- **Order Quantity/Unit of Measure**
  These two fields appear together with the material numbers and descriptions in the

Overview screen. These fields can't be changed, although there are ways to add or reduce quantities (see Chapter 9).

- **Valid From/Valid To**
  These fields are found in the center of the **Overview** screen. Both dates may be changed as necessary.

Note

For more information about which fields can and can't be changed, and how to undo or reverse documents, see Chapter 9 and the matrix therein.

6.8.1 Overview Tabs

By selecting the other tabs available in the **Overview** screen, you can see other key fields as described in Table 6.1.

Overview Tab	Field	Can Be Changed	Description
Sales	**Payment terms**	Yes	The terms of payment allocated to the payer.
Sales	**Incoterms**	Yes	The delivery and shipping terms agreed by the sold-to party.
Item Detail	**Item Category**	No	A code that defines how the material behaves in the document. This is determined based on criteria set up in the configuration.
Item Details	**Pricing Date**	Yes, until the order is invoiced	The date used to determine the price according to the criteria set up in the configuration.
Ordering Party	**Delivering Plant**	Yes, until order is delivered	Plant, if assigned to the customer master. This field can be found by scrolling to the right in the material grid (and can be customized to be visible without scrolling, if desired).
Reason for Rejection	**Order Reason**	Yes	Reason the quotation was placed.
Reason for Rejection	**Reason for Rejection**	Yes, if there are no follow-on documents	Reason why the quotation has been rejected. See Chapter 9.

Table 6.1 Modifying Overview Fields, by Tab

6.8.2 Header and Line-Item Tabs

Normally, the information found in the **Overview** screen will be enough to give you all the basic details of the order. However, as noted earlier, more information can be found by drilling down in the header and line-item sections of the quotation.

To access the header tabs, you can choose **Goto • Header**, as shown in Figure 6.56, or by using the header icon, as shown in Figure 6.57.

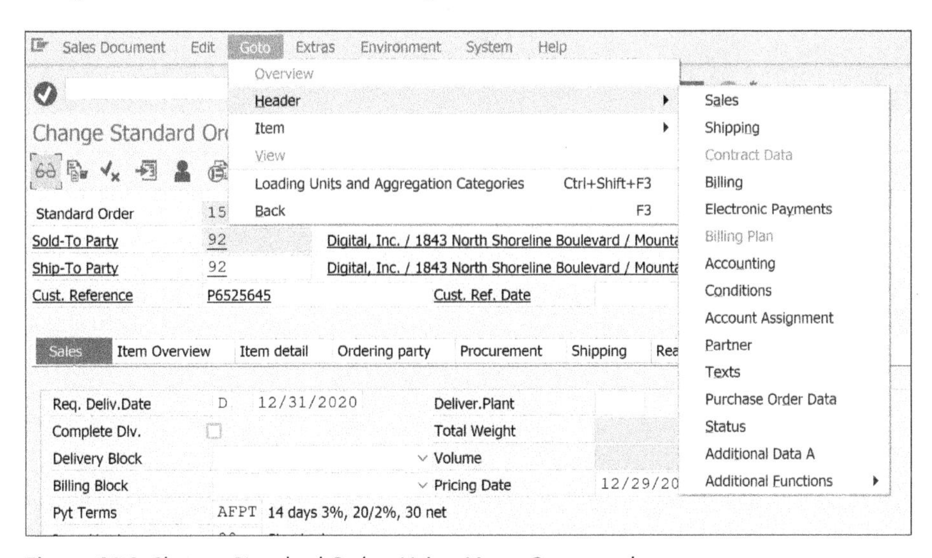

Figure 6.56 Change Standard Order: Using Menu Commands

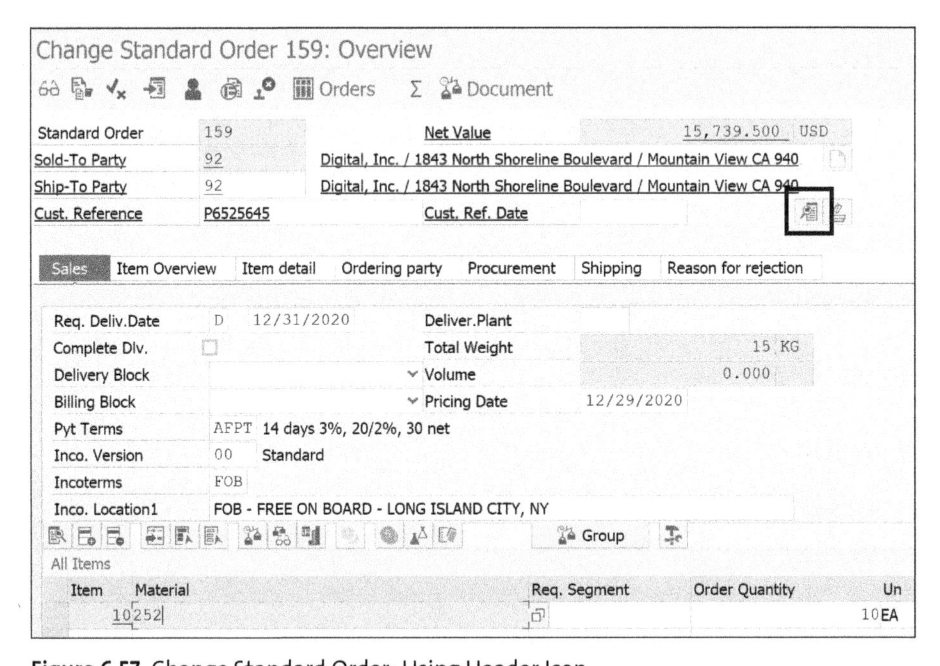

Figure 6.57 Change Standard Order: Using Header Icon

To view the line-item details, you can choose **Goto • Item**, or click the **Item Details** icon, both of which are shown in Figure 6.58. You also can double-click on the line item itself.

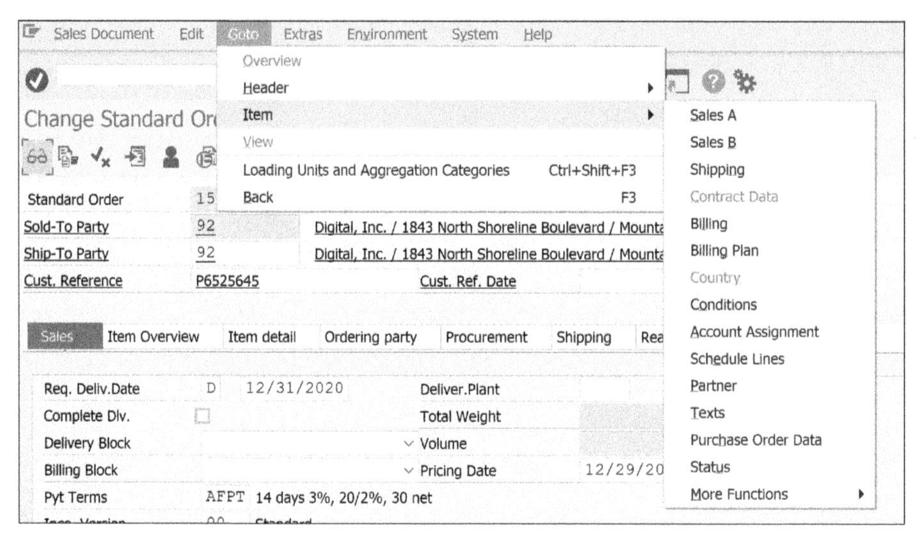

Figure 6.58 Change Standard Order: Using the Menu Command or Item Details Icon

Again, much of the information in the **Item** tabs can also be found in the **Overview** tabs, shown in Figure 6.59. For additional data, refer to the line-item fields discussed earlier.

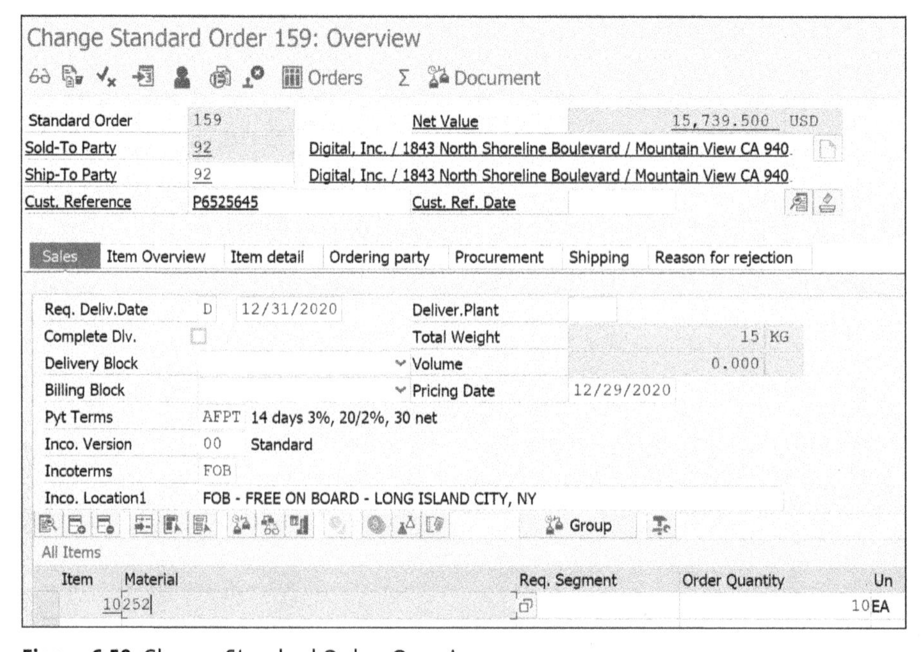

Figure 6.59 Change Standard Order: Overview

6.8.3 Document Flow and Status Overview

Document flow is essential in understanding your transactions in terms of completeness. For example, as you'll see in Chapter 9, it's critical to understand the level of completeness in order to know the correct procedure for undoing an incorrect data entry.

The **Document Flow** icon is located in the toolbar of the **Change Standard Order** screen (Transaction VA02), as shown in Figure 6.60.

Figure 6.60 Change Standard Order: Document Flow Icon

Document flow is available in the following sales and distribution documents:

- Inquiries
- Sales orders
- Deliveries
- Billing documents

The **Document Flow** icon displays all preceding and follow-on documents that have been created for the document you're currently looking at. This is critical information for determining how to complete the sales and distribution flow through billing or to reverse it, if necessary.

As an example, if your standard order had been converted from an underlying inquiry or quotation, you can see this in the document flow, as shown in Figure 6.61. Furthermore, if your underlying document (whether it be an inquiry or quotation) had been further processed into a delivery and billing document, these would also show.

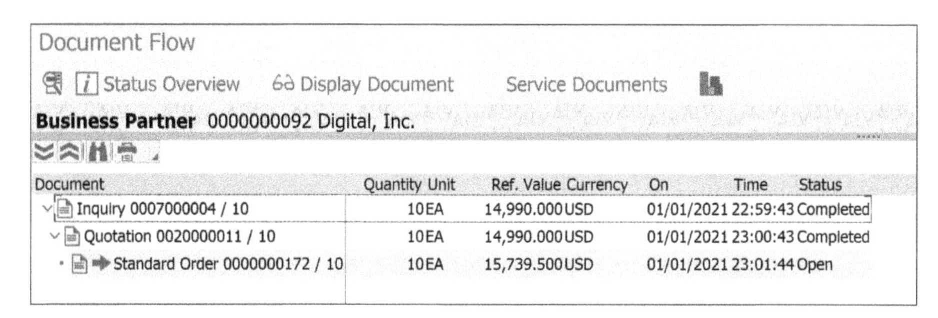

Figure 6.61 Change Standard Order: Document Flow

Note

We'll show the subsequent documents in Chapter 7 when we discuss delivery and in Chapter 8 when we discuss billing.

By clicking to select any one of the documents and then clicking on the **Display Document** button, you can navigate directly to that specific document in display mode.

Another useful button in the **Change Standard Order/Display Standard Order** overview screens is the **Status Overview** icon, shown in Figure 6.62.

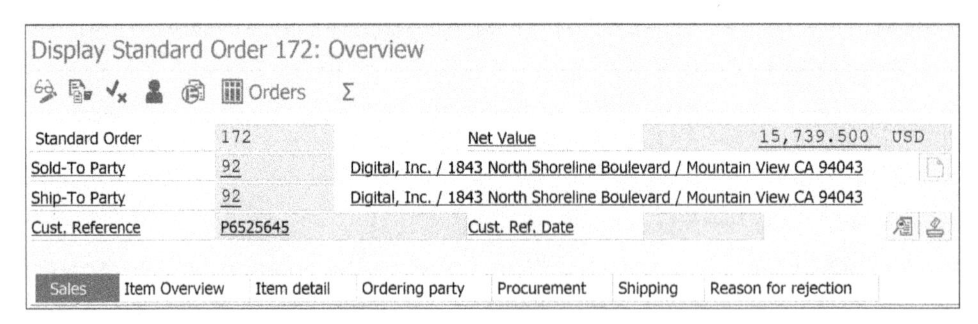

Figure 6.62 Display Standard Order: Status Overview Icon

By using the **Status Overview** icon, you can get a full view of the header and item status of the sales order, as shown in Figure 6.63.

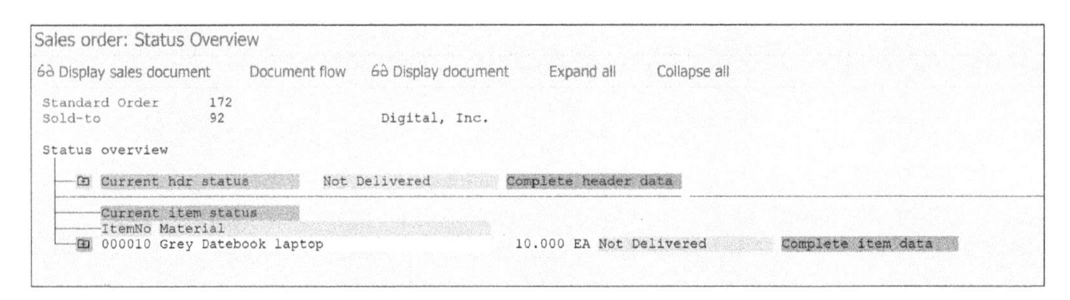

Figure 6.63 Sales Order: Status Overview Display

Again, note that this icon is available for more than just sales orders—it's also available for all sales and distribution documents listed here:

- Inquiry
- Quotation
- Billing

The **Status Overview** screen will show you the overall header and item status for the whole document, including the following item statuses:

- Complete as far as the incompletion procedure is concerned
- Referenced by a subsequent document
- Rejected

As you can see in Figure 6.63, our sales order has yet to be delivered.

6.8.4 Create Subsequent Document

A key action from a sales order is to create the subsequent order-to-cash document, which is the **Delivery** command to deliver the goods to the customer. (This should not be confused with the other command available **Create Subsequent Order**). To do this, choose **Sales Document • Deliver**, as shown in Figure 6.64.

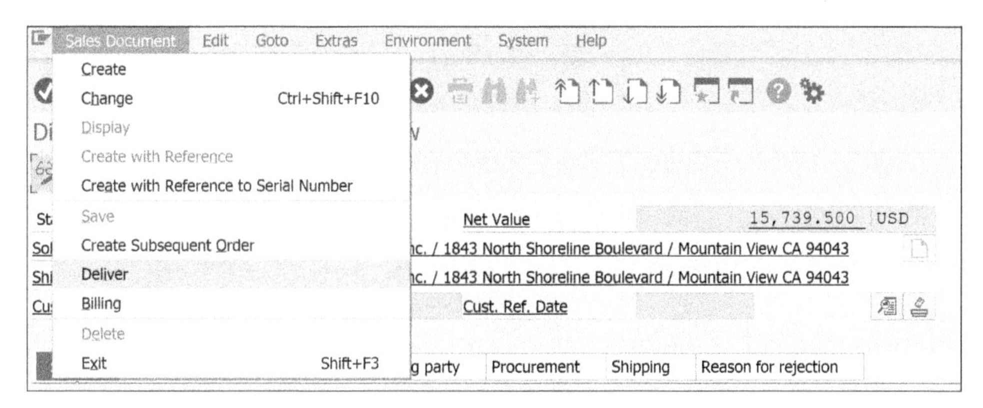

Figure 6.64 Display Standard Order: Deliver Command

This will save any changes made to the sales document and immediately open Transaction VL01N (Create Delivery). See Chapter 7 for more on that topic.

6.8.5 Create with Reference

From the same menu, you can select **Create with Reference** to pull items from other documents into your new sales order. Note that this can only be achieved if your system has been set up in such a way to allow copying from another document into a sales order.

6.8.6 Mass Change

The **Edit** menu path has some very useful features that you can take advantage of, particularly if your standard order has multiple items in it. Figure 6.65 shows the options for mass changing all the items in the quotation document.

Note

The **Fast Change of** function can be used for all items or only those items that have been selected in advance.

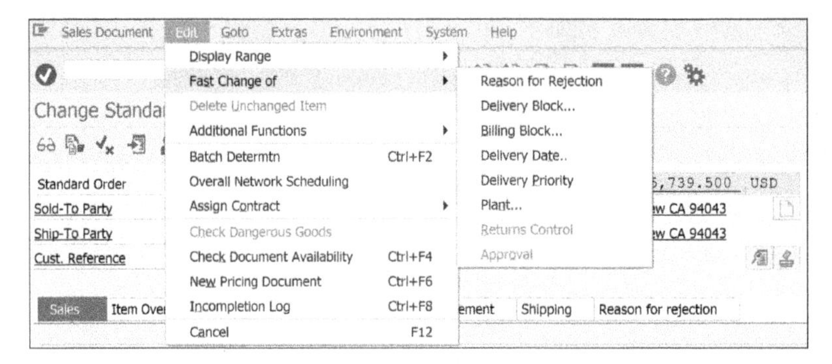

Figure 6.65 Change Standard Order: Fast Change Options

6.9 Change and Display a Sales Order Document (SAP Fiori)

As you've seen, apps are used to create or access sales documents in SAP Fiori. The following steps walk through how to use SAP Fiori apps for these purposes:

1. Launch the Manage Sales Orders app, and enter the sales document number to be changed or displayed in the **Sales Order** field, as shown in Figure 6.66. Press [Enter], as shown in Figure 6.67.

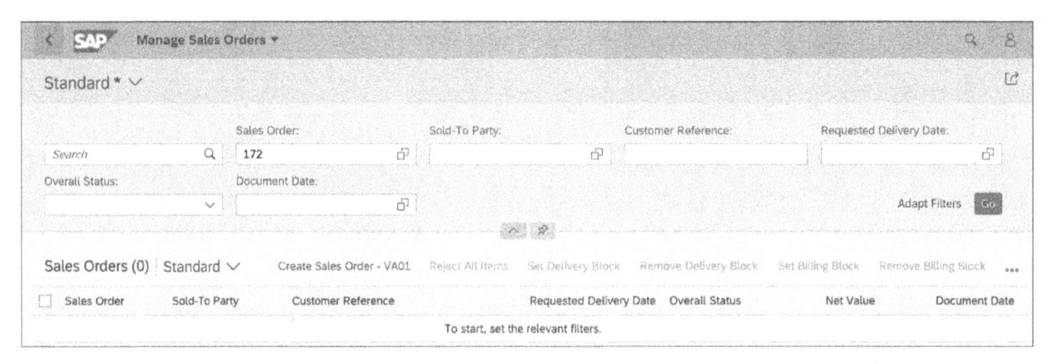

Figure 6.66 Manage Sales Orders: Sales Order Number Input

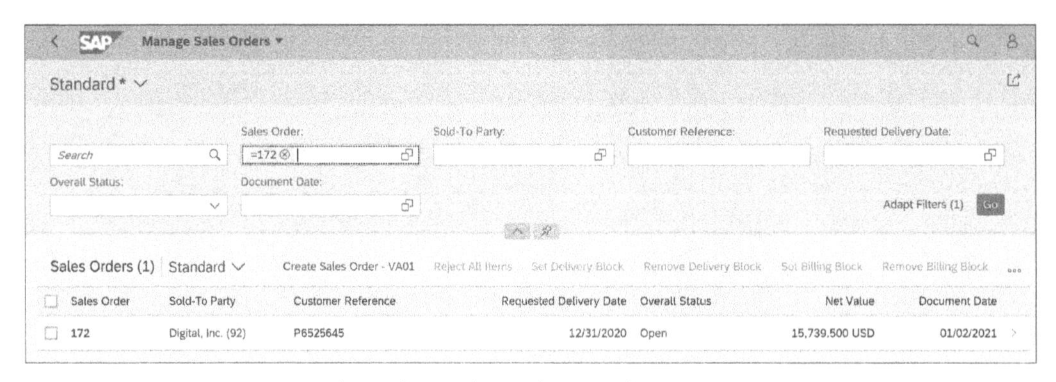

Figure 6.67 Manage Sales Orders: Sales Order Found

2. After your document has been found in the list, click (once) on your document number to open the context-sensitive menu as shown in Figure 6.68.

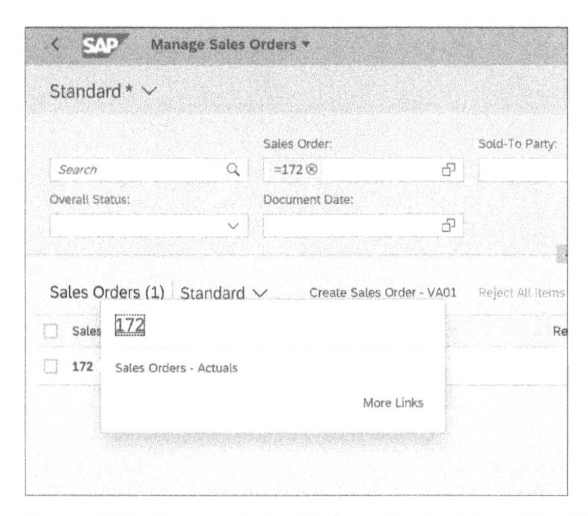

Figure 6.68 Manage Sales Orders: Context-Sensitive Menu

3. Click on the **Sales Orders – Actuals** link to open the sales order in display mode.
4. The **Display Standard Order: Overview** screen appears, as shown in Figure 6.69.

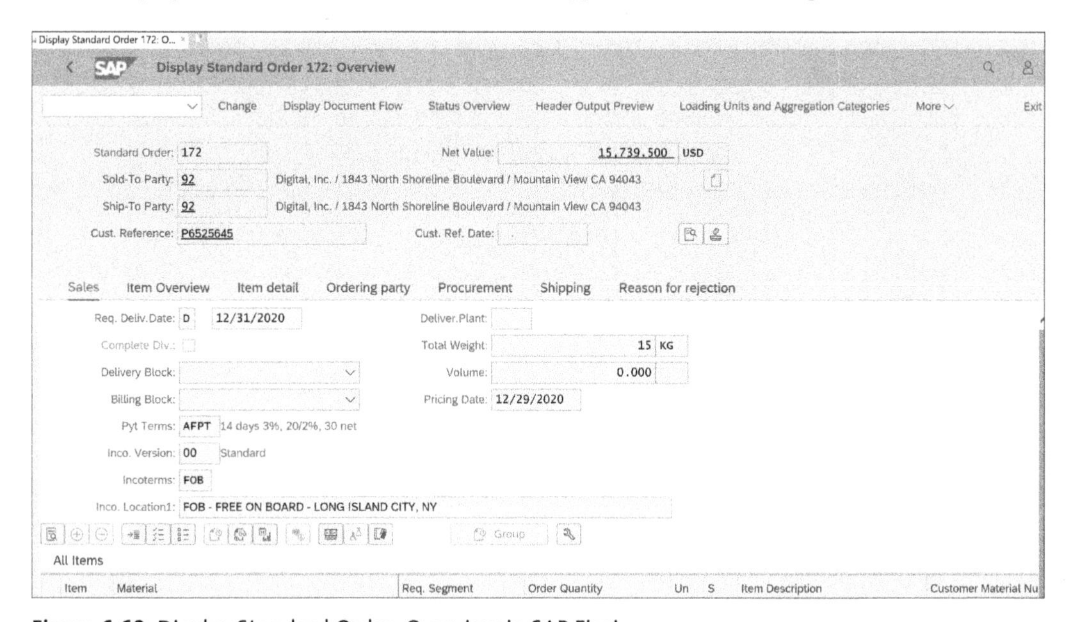

Figure 6.69 Display Standard Order: Overview in SAP Fiori

5. Click on the **Change** icon on the toolbar, as shown in Figure 6.70, to toggle from display mode to change mode.

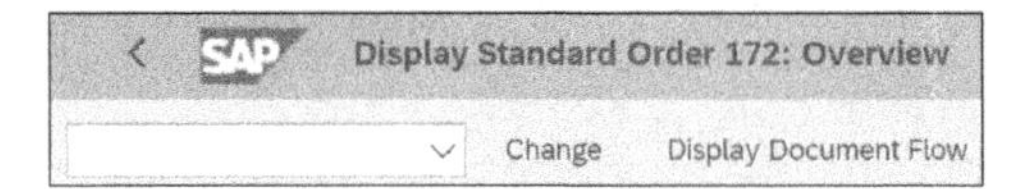

Figure 6.70 Display Standard Order 172: Overview in Change Mode (Display Icon Appears)

As there are no subsequent documents, all fields except the customer fields are available for change. In this case, because the sales order is created with reference to preceding documents (e.g., an inquiry and quotation), the **Sold-To Party** is locked to the original. However, the **Ship-To Party** field can be changed.

Change the **Ship-To Party** from **92** to **3**, and then press `Enter` to see the results in Figure 6.71.

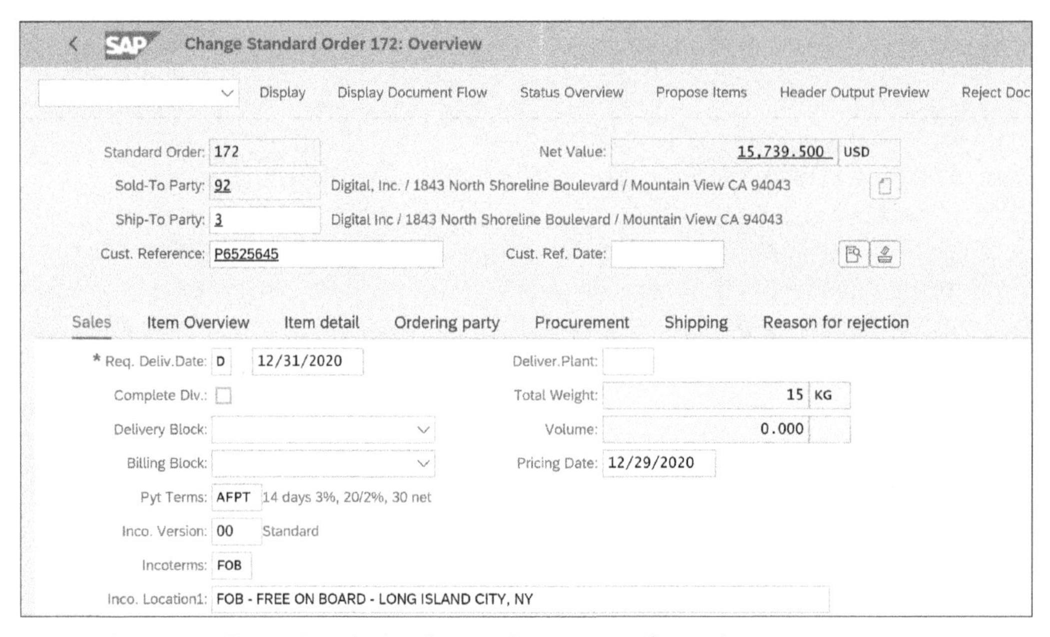

Figure 6.71 Change Standard Order 172: Ship-to Party Changed

Refer to Table 6.1 for more information about which fields can be changed.

To save changes to your sales document, click on the **Save** button in the lower-right corner of the SAP Fiori screen, as shown in Figure 6.72.

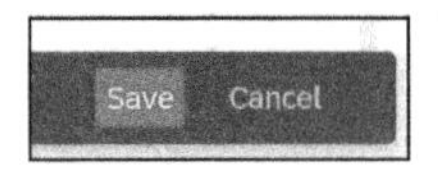

Figure 6.72 SAP Fiori: Save Button

A message should appear with your sales document number on the status bar in the lower-left corner of the screen, as shown in Figure 6.73.

Figure 6.73 Standard Order: Saved Message

6.10 List of Sales Orders (SAP GUI)

If you're unsure of the sales document number to be changed or displayed, you can search them by using Transaction VA05 (List of Sales Orders), as shown in Figure 6.74.

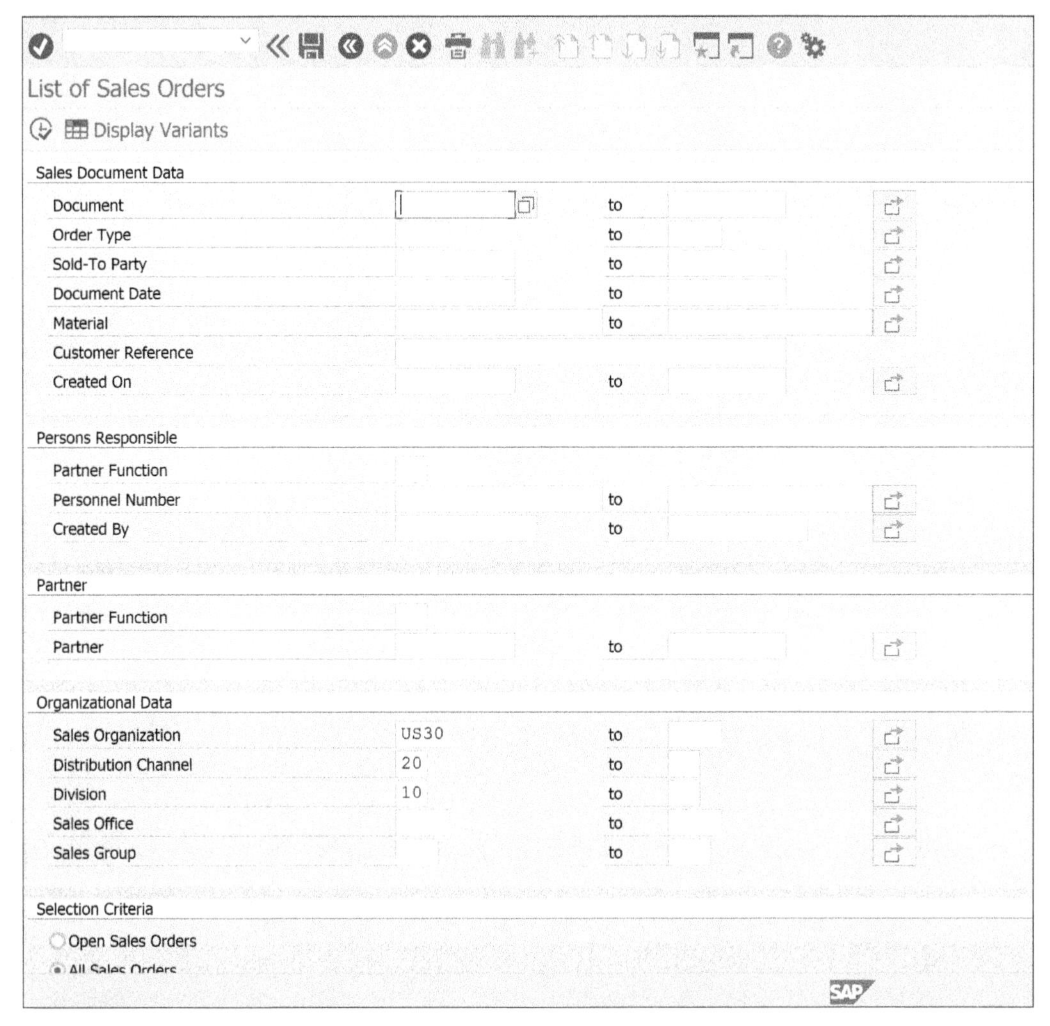

Figure 6.74 List of Sales Orders

Scroll to the bottom of the selection screen, as shown in Figure 6.74, to see radio button options for selecting either all sales orders or just open sales orders (i.e., those sales orders that haven't been referenced in a follow-on document, e.g., a delivery or billing document).

Input some selection parameters, such as **Sales Area**, **Sold-to Party** number, and a date range into the report, and execute. You have a choice of many other parameters as well, such as **Created by**. Thus, you can easily limit the search to your own sales orders. The default columns in your output report will appear as shown in Figure 6.75, but they can be customized easily.

You can double-click a sales document to quickly access the order in change mode.

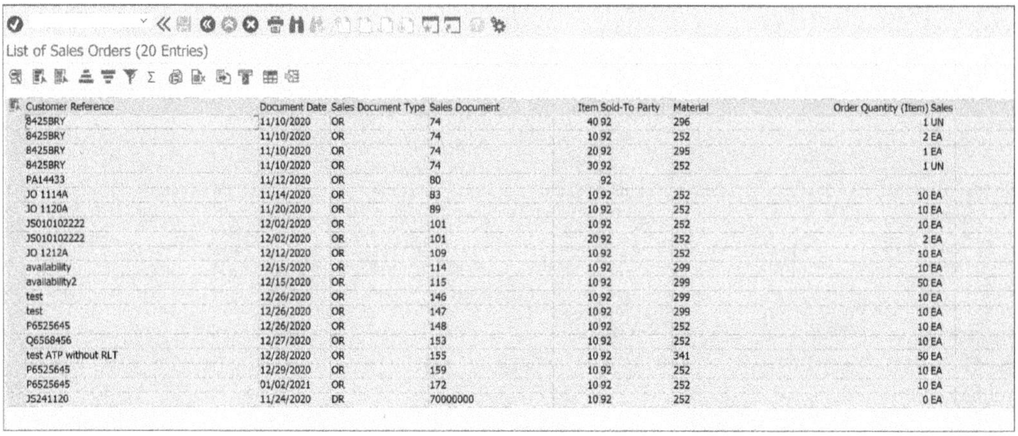

List of Sales Orders (20 Entries)

Customer Reference	Document Date	Sales Document Type	Sales Document	Item	Sold-To Party	Material	Order Quantity (Item)	Sales
8425BRY	11/10/2020	OR	74	40	92	296	1	UN
8425BRY	11/10/2020	OR	74	10	92	252	2	EA
8425BRY	11/10/2020	OR	74	20	92	295	1	EA
8425BRY	11/10/2020	OR	74	30	92	252	1	UN
PA14433	11/12/2020	OR	80		92			
JO 1114A	11/14/2020	OR	83	10	92	252	10	EA
JO 1120A	11/20/2020	OR	89	10	92	252	10	EA
JS010102222	12/02/2020	OR	101	10	92	252	10	EA
JS010102222	12/02/2020	OR	101	20	92	252	2	EA
JO 1212A	12/12/2020	OR	109	10	92	252	10	EA
availability	12/15/2020	OR	114	10	92	299	10	EA
availability2	12/15/2020	OR	115	10	92	299	50	EA
test	12/26/2020	OR	146	10	92	299	10	EA
test	12/26/2020	OR	147	10	92	299	10	EA
P6525645	12/26/2020	OR	148	10	92	252	10	EA
Q6568456	12/27/2020	OR	153	10	92	252	10	EA
test ATP without RLT	12/28/2020	OR	155	10	92	341	50	EA
P6525645	12/29/2020	OR	159	10	92	252	10	EA
P6525645	01/02/2021	OR	172	10	92	252	10	EA
JS241120	11/24/2020	DR	70000000	10	92	252	0	EA

Figure 6.75 List of Sales Orders: Output Display

To customize the columns you see in the report, see Chapter 4, Section 4.5.

After you've generated a list of sales orders, you may want to export this list to Microsoft Excel. Again, this is a commonly used command in many other reports in SAP applications to facilitate various kinds of analysis. To do so, please refer to Chapter 4, Section 4.5.

Mass Change

The mass change functionality can also be used as explained in Chapter 4, Section 4.5, for changing plant, material, pricing, or currency for selected line items.

List of Sales Orders (SAP Fiori)

In the Manage Sales Orders app, there are a number of ways to search and find desired data, as explained in Chapter 4, Section 4.5.

6.11 Summary

In this chapter, we walked through the essence of sales and distribution—the creation, editing, and displaying of a sales document. We examined the different kinds of sales documents, together with exploring the details of the core functionalities and components.

You should now be able to create, change, and view sales documents in both SAP GUI and SAP Fiori.

Now that your sales order is complete, it's time to deliver it, which is the subject of the next chapter.

Chapter 7
Delivery

This chapter introduces details regarding the first step in the logistics process of sales and distribution: delivery.

Throughout the chapter, we'll focus on key definitions in the delivery process within SAP S/4HANA, how to create a delivery document, and where it sits in the overall sales and distribution document flow. This will include such key elements as batch determination, delivery splits, picking, packing, shipments, and the goods issue (GI) concept.

7.1 Process Overview

After the sales process is complete, the order-to-cash flow moves into the distribution phase, with the creation of delivery documents. These are often also called outbound deliveries within SAP S/4HANA, to differentiate from inbound deliveries, which can be used by the purchase order process. As shown from the order-to-cash flow in Figure 7.1, the delivery document is created with reference to a sales order or more than one sales order.

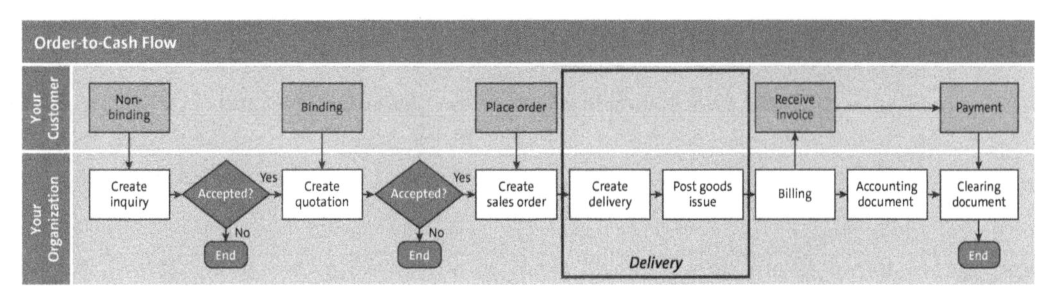

Figure 7.1 Order-to-Cash Flow: Delivery

7.2 Document Types

As with sales orders, deliveries in SAP S/4HANA are preconfigured to use several document types, examples are shown in Figure 7.2.

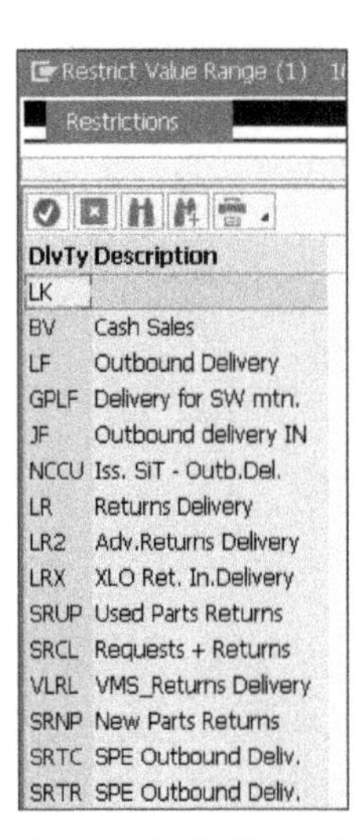

Figure 7.2 Outbound Delivery Document Types

Delivery document types are used to control the behavior of the delivery in the SAP system, for example, determining which number range should be used for delivery documents and which partners and outputs are relevant.

As with sales documents, it's very common to keep document templates untouched in the configuration for potential future use, so you may find in your SAP system a copied version of a standard delivery type, such as LF, copied to ZLF, thus allowing the flexibility to customize a business-specific scenario within the ZLF delivery type.

7.3 Create a Delivery Document

In this section, we'll create a delivery document. Deliveries are different from the sales documents we've explored so far, such as inquiries, quotations, and sales orders, in that it's normal to create a delivery with reference to a sales order. Depending on how your system is set up, deliveries can be created without reference to a source sales order, but that is an unusual process and not a part of the standard order-to-cash flow.

Several prerequisites are essential before you can create a delivery document from a sales order:

- The sales order must contain deliverable items, as defined by the item category.
- The sales order type must be configured to allow deliveries to be created.
- The sales order can't be blocked with a delivery block, at the header or item levels.
- The sales order can't have other blocks—that is, credit blocks, export license blocks, and embargo blocks—in place that don't allow progression to delivery.
- The sales order can't be incomplete for a field that must be complete before a delivery is allowed.

- There must be sufficient unrestricted stock of the material in the plant and storage location to meet the required amount (partial deliveries may be allowed depending on the partial delivery settings in the sales order).

The good news is that when attempting to create a delivery for one of the preceding scenarios, the SAP system will offer an error message with text explaining the reason, as shown in Figure 7.3.

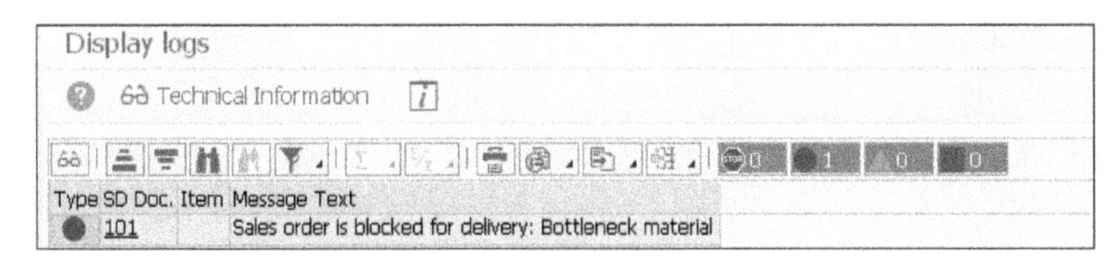

Figure 7.3 Outbound Delivery Error Message

There are several ways to create an outbound delivery with reference to a sales order in SAP S/4HANA. Each different way corresponds to a specific scenario. The SAP menu tree for the outbound delivery process is shown in Figure 7.4.

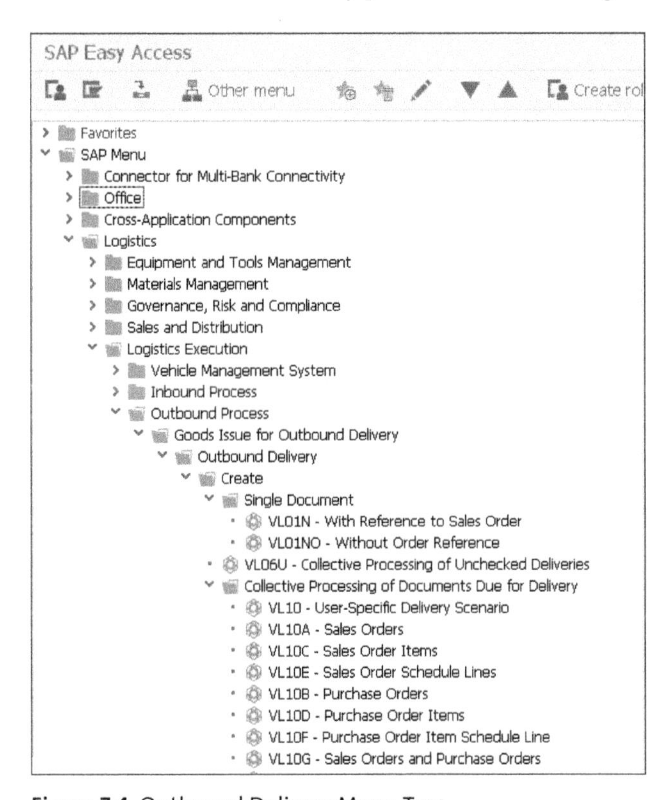

Figure 7.4 Outbound Delivery Menu Tree

As shown from the menu tree, there are many transactions relating to outbound deliveries, as follows.

- Transaction VL01N: Create delivery with reference to sales order
- Transaction VL01NO: Create delivery without reference (from within **Display/ Change Sales Order**, select **Sales Document • Deliver**)
- Transaction VL10* (suite of transactions): Collective delivery processing

There are also SAP Fiori apps for use with outbound deliveries:

- Create Outbound Deliveries – From Sales Orders
- Create Delivery with Reference to Sales Order
- Create Outbound Deliveries
- Manage Sales Orders

Let's deal with these in turn.

7.3.1 Creation of a Single Delivery Using Transaction VL01N

This is the classic way to create an outbound delivery in SAP S/4HANA with reference to a single sales order, as shown in Figure 7.5. As this is a common use case, we'll explore all the elements that make up the delivery in this section.

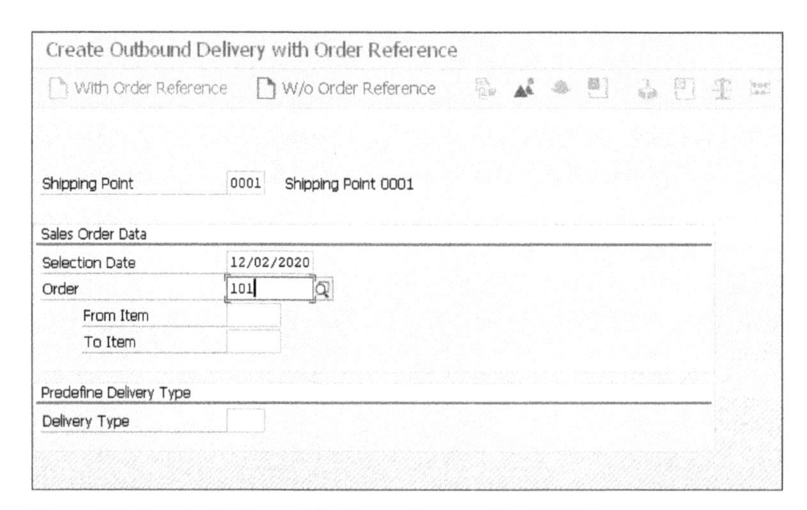

Figure 7.5 Create Outbound Delivery: Transaction VL01N

Creation of the Delivery

In the main screen of Transaction VL01N, you define the shipping point you want to use for the delivery (**Shipping Point** is a mandatory field). Additionally, you can specify a given date, so that SAP will only create deliveries for items up to and including that date. This date refers to the material availability date in the sales order schedule line, which is the date by which the material becomes available for picking and is therefore the date at which the delivery should be created. As we're creating the delivery for a single sales order, the sales order number is a mandatory field (**Order** field) in the selection screen for Transaction VL01N. The selection can also be narrowed down by **Item Number** for the sales order number. Finally, the **Delivery Type** can be specified, although this isn't required usually as the **Delivery Type** will be defaulted in from the configuration settings from the sales order.

Note

A single delivery can be created with reference to multiple sales orders if the delivery split criteria doesn't mandate a split. More details of the delivery split criteria will follow in Section 7.3.6.

After you press [Enter], if there are items on the sales order specified for the shipping point specified that have a material availability date equal to or before the date specified, then the delivery screen will show the details in an overview screen, as shown in Figure 7.6.

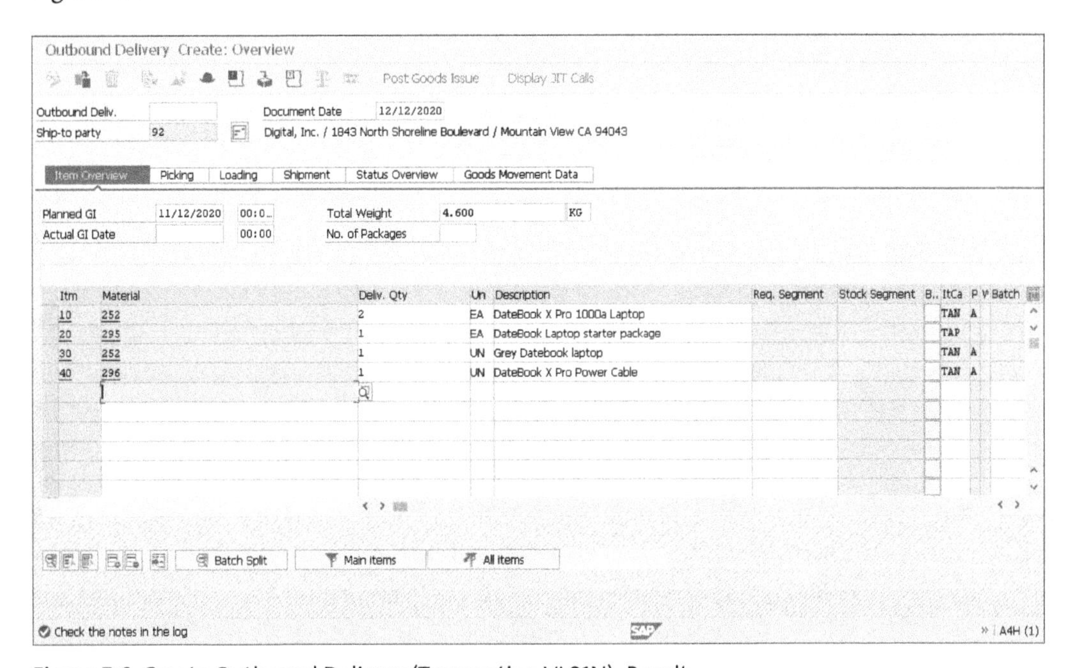

Figure 7.6 Create Outbound Delivery (Transaction VL01N): Result

At this point, the delivery can be saved, which will allocate a delivery document number, but there are areas to explore before saving.

The Delivery Log

There is a "log" in the screen that will contain useful information. At the bottom of the screen shown earlier in Figure 7.6, there is an information message: **Check the notes in the log**. To do that, click the log icon at the top of the screen.

Once selected, the log will display all messages that SAP has posted in relation to its attempt to create the delivery for all items in the sales order. An example for this order is shown in Figure 7.7.

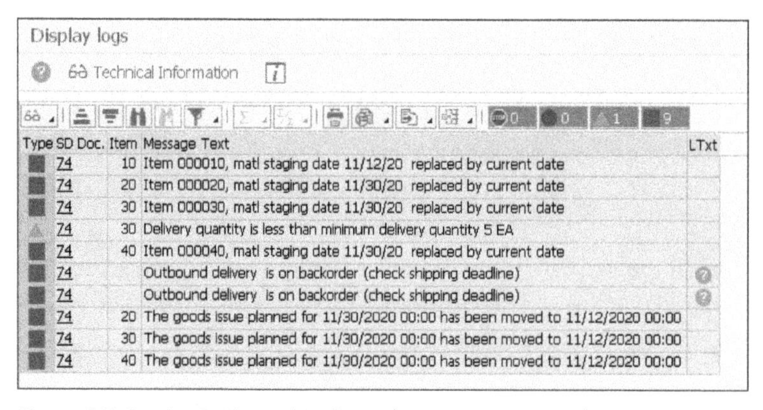

Figure 7.7 Create Outbound Delivery (Transaction VL01N): Log

You can see immediately from the log that the information is broken down by sales order document (document number **74**), item number, and message. There is also a traffic light system here to alert you to important messages where necessary. This example has nine green traffic light messages, which should be viewed as informational messages, and one yellow traffic light message, which should be viewed as a warning message.

The initial messages for these items refer to a replacement of the material staging date. The material staging date is the date on which the materials need to be "pulled" from their storage location into the picking area. This date is determined in the sales order according to the lead time, required delivery date, and route determination rules assigned to the schedule line (see Chapter 6 for more information). In our example, the sales order had an original material staging date in the past, and this therefore has been replaced by the current date. Remember that the example has been run on a nonproduction system, so the rescheduling job isn't active. Normal practice in SAP clients would be to run an overnight rescheduling job to redetermine all these dates in sales orders accordingly.

There is a further set of messages referring to goods issue (GI) dates. The GI is the date on which the goods leave the warehouse and ownership is officially transferred to the customer (depending on the Incoterms applied to the sales order). GI is an official step in the SAP S/4HANA order-to-cash document flow and has its own document number. We'll talk more about GI processing later in Section 7.4.3. The logic behind the GI date is the same as the logic behind the material staging date: the GI date is determined in the sales order according to rules set in the schedule line category.

Another message is also posted here: **Outbound delivery is on backorder (check shipping deadline)**. This is simply a message to state that the delivery has been created from a backorder, meaning that the planned GI date in the sales order can't be met by the delivery.

From the delivery overview screen, shown earlier in Figure 7.6, you can see that the material, quantity, planned GI date, and batch number (if the material is batch managed) have all been determined automatically. All this data has been pulled in from the sales order, except for the batch number, which has been determined according to a set of rules in the batch selection master data. If a batch has been entered into the sales order, then this is used, and the batch selection master data isn't used for batch determination. In this example, the batch field is grayed out, meaning that the materials aren't batch managed.

Picking in the Delivery

Moving to the **Picking** tab, the delivery presents you with the **Pick Date/Time** and the **Picked Qty** fields, as shown in Figure 7.8.

Figure 7.8 Create Outbound Delivery (Transaction VL01N): Picking

There are several things to note at this point. You can see that the storage location (**SLoc** column) has been determined for each of the items. This is automatically determined by configuration in the background according to a combination of the **Shipping Point**, **Plant**, and **Storage Conditions** fields in the material master. The **Storage Conditions** field in the material master tells the system how to store the product. Typical values are **Cold storage**, **In pallets**, and so on.

You can also see from Figure 7.8 that the **Pick Qty** is available for selection. This can be manually updated after the physical picking is complete. Bear in mind that this field is only available for updating if the delivery isn't relevant for warehouse management

(WM). We'll discuss WM and extended warehouse management (EWM) later in this chapter in Section 7.4.1. In our example, the delivery document isn't relevant for WM, as shown by the **OverallWMStatus** field. The **OvrllPickStatus** (overall picking status) field is also displayed here to show whether the delivery has been picked or not. As with all SAP status fields, there are four values:

- **[blank]**
  The document isn't relevant for this activity.
- **A**
  The document hasn't yet been processed.
- **B**
  The document has been partially processed.
- **C**
  The document has been completely processed.

These fields are shown in Figure 7.9.

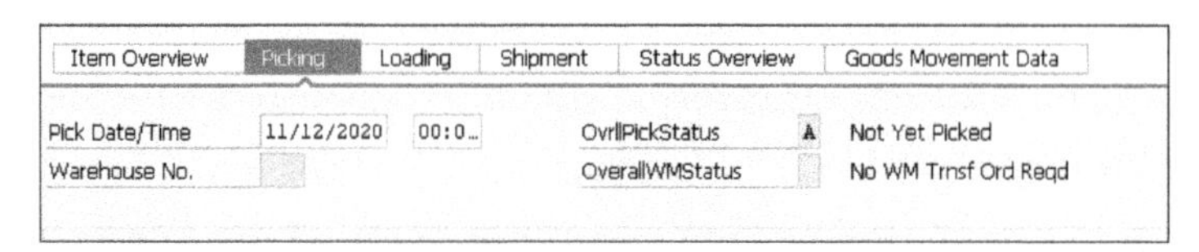

Figure 7.9 Create Outbound Delivery: Status Fields

In addition, notice that the **Pick Quantity** for one of the items—item 20—is grayed out. This is because item 20 isn't a pickable item, as it's the bill of materials (BOM) header. Only the components are pickable.

Figure 7.8, shown earlier, also shows the **Stag. Date** (staging date) and time for the material. This is determined by the material availability date and time, discussed earlier in this chapter.

Delivery Loading

Selecting the **Loading** tab from the overview screen to access more data related to how the delivery is loaded after picking and packing are completed (see Figure 7.10).

Item Overview | Picking | Loading | Shipment | Status Overview | Goods Movement Data

Loading Date 11/12/2020 00:00 Loading Point
Door for Whse Staging Area

Itm	Material	Deliv. Qty	Un	Gross Weight	Un	Volume	V...	Batch	B..	Plnt	SLoc	Description
10	252	2	EA	3	KG					US20	1000	DateBook X Pro 10
20	295	1	EA		KG					US20	1000	DateBook Laptop s
30	252	1	UN	1.500	KG					US20	1000	Grey Datebook lapt
40	296	1	UN	0.100	KG					US20	1000	DateBook X Pro Po

Figure 7.10 Create Outbound Delivery: Loading

Loading activity happens immediately before the goods leave your site, and the **Loading Date** is determined by the shipping point, the route, and the loading group of the material master. Additionally, a **Loading Point** can be added, which denotes the physical location where loading of the delivery takes place, typically a loading bay. Volumes and weights can be manually amended at this point.

Delivery shipment

The **Shipment** tab, as shown in Figure 7.11, shows you details of the transportation planning of the delivery. In complex scenarios, it's possible to group multiple deliveries together into one shipment for transportation planning purposes. You can also use the transportation management functions in SAP S/4HANA to determine route stages for the specific delivery method. This screen shows the **Route** determined for this delivery as well as any specific **Route Schedule** that can be used to set a given date for shipment.

Item Overview | Picking | Loading | Shipment | Status Overview | Goods Movement Data

TranspptnPlanng 11/12/2020 00:00 Route 000012 North-south Route
Trns.Plan.Stat. A Open Transp.Planning Route Schedule

Itm	Material	Gross Weight	Un	Volume	V...	Deliv. Qty	Un	Description
10	252	3	KG			2	EA	DateBook X Pro 1000a Laptop
20	295		KG			1	EA	DateBook Laptop starter package
30	252	1.500	KG			1	UN	Grey Datebook laptop
40	296	0.100	KG			1	UN	DateBook X Pro Power Cable

Figure 7.11 Create Outbound Delivery: Shipment

Status Overview

The **Status Overview**, as shown in Figure 7.12, shows the status of each process connected with the delivery, using the blank, **A**, **B**, and **C** values discussed earlier.

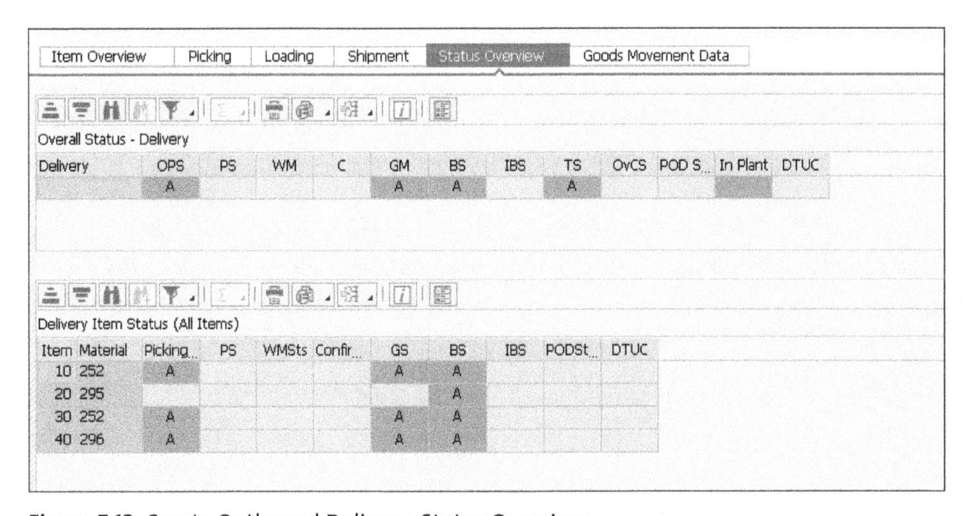

Figure 7.12 Create Outbound Delivery: Status Overview

The processes connected to the delivery are as follows:

- Picking status
- Packing status
- Warehouse management status
- Picking confirmation status
- Goods movement status
- Billing status
- Intercompany billing status
- Transportation planning status
- Credit status
- Proof of delivery status

The statuses for these processes can be viewed at the header (applying to the whole delivery) or item (applying to the individual items on the delivery) levels.

Goods Movement Data

The next tab, **Goods Movement Data**, as shown in Figure 7.13, shows the planned goods movement date (**Pl. Gds Mvmt** field) and actual goods movement date (**Act. Gds Mvmt** field). The actual goods movement date is populated automatically when the delivery is goods issued, which is when the goods leave your premises and become the property of the customer.

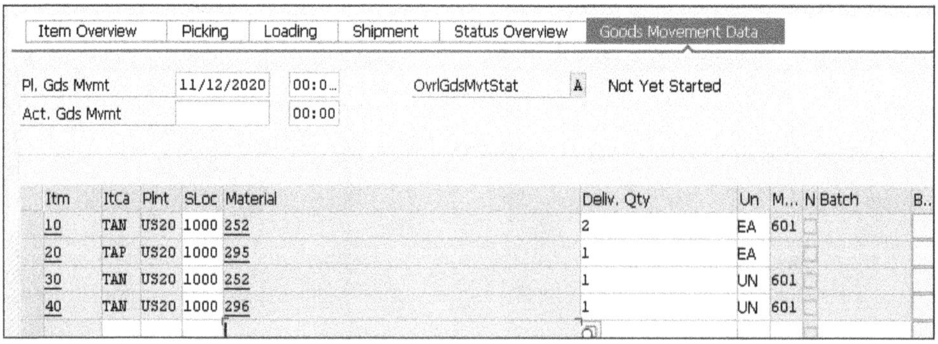

Item Overview | Picking | Loading | Shipment | Status Overview | Goods Movement Data

Pl. Gds Mvmt 11/12/2020 00:0... OvrlGdsMvtStat A Not Yet Started
Act. Gds Mvmt 00:00

Itm	ItCa	Plnt	SLoc	Material	Deliv. Qty	Un	M...	N	Batch	B..
10	TAN	US20	1000	252	2	EA	601			
20	TAP	US20	1000	295	1	EA				
30	TAN	US20	1000	252	1	UN	601			
40	TAN	US20	1000	296	1	UN	601			

Figure 7.13 Create Outbound Delivery: Goods Movement Data

You can also see that there is a "movement type" field here, with **601** populated. We'll explore more about movement types when we discuss GIs in Section 7.4.3.

Saving the Delivery

At this point, you should save the delivery to generate the delivery document number. One the document is saved, you can navigate to the display menu from Transaction

VL01N by choose **Outbound Delivery • Display**, as shown in Figure 7.14, or by using Transaction VL03N.

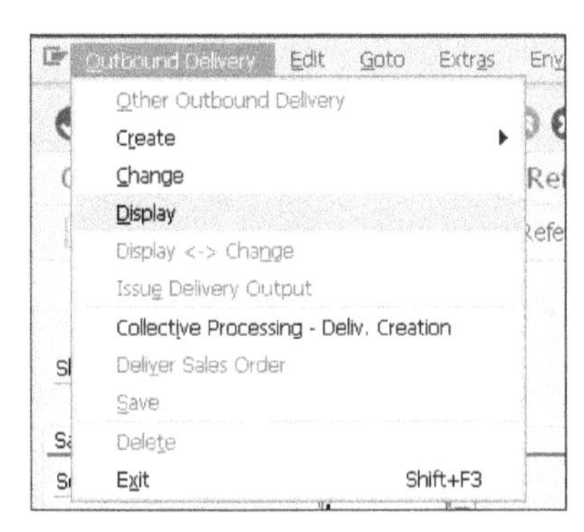

Figure 7.14 Create Outbound Delivery: Display Document

From within the display screen for the delivery, you can view the document flow in the same way as any other document flow in other sales and distribution documents, that is, by selecting the **Document Flow** icon or by pressing F7. This will show you the delivery number below the sales order number that the delivery has been created with reference to, as shown in Figure 7.15.

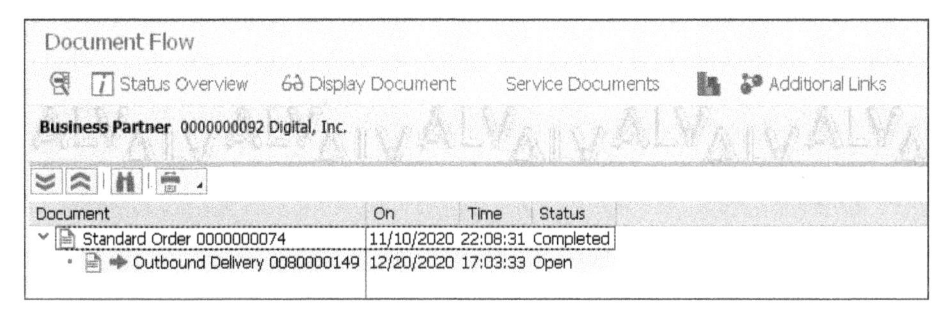

Figure 7.15 Display Outbound Delivery: Document Flow

After the delivery document is created and saved, this is the trigger for the distribution portion of the order-to-cash flow to get underway. There are three ways in which the distribution is handled in SAP S/4HANA:

- Inventory-managed logistics (inventory management)
- Warehouse-managed logistics (WM)
- Extended warehouse-managed logistics (EWM)

SAP S/4HANA recommends that only inventory-managed and extended warehouse-managed logistics methods are used, as WM is due to be phased out in future releases of SAP S/4HANA.

Sales and distribution processes around outbound deliveries, which use WM or EWM methods, hand over the process flow to the overall supply chain area for logistical processes. This is deeply engrained with the material requirement planning (MRP) cycles, procurement, and production activities, so we'll restrict our discussions to the sales and distribution process around the outbound delivery and simply give an overview of the process followed by WM and EWM in SAP S/4HANA.

Inventory Managed Logistics

In SAP S/4HANA inventory-managed logistics, the supply chain activities of picking and packing are all carried out within the outbound delivery document. The delivery document itself is used for triggering the warehouse tasks of picking, packing, loading, transportation, and GI. The process flow for this option is shown in Figure 7.16. This is the simplest way for the order-to-cash flow to complete the distribution process.

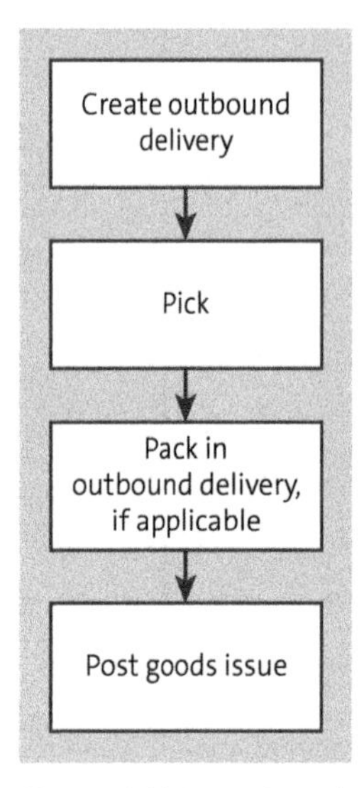

Figure 7.16 Inventory-Managed Logistics: Process Flow

Warehouse-Managed Logistics

In SAP S/4HANA warehouse-managed logistics, the supply chain activities for the warehouse are separated from the outbound delivery by creation of a transfer order. This transfer order is a separate SAP document with its own number range and activities assigned to it. The transfer order houses information such as storage sections and storage bins for greater granularity of warehouse inventory management.

In Figure 7.17, you can see the WM portion of the process flow in the green boxes.

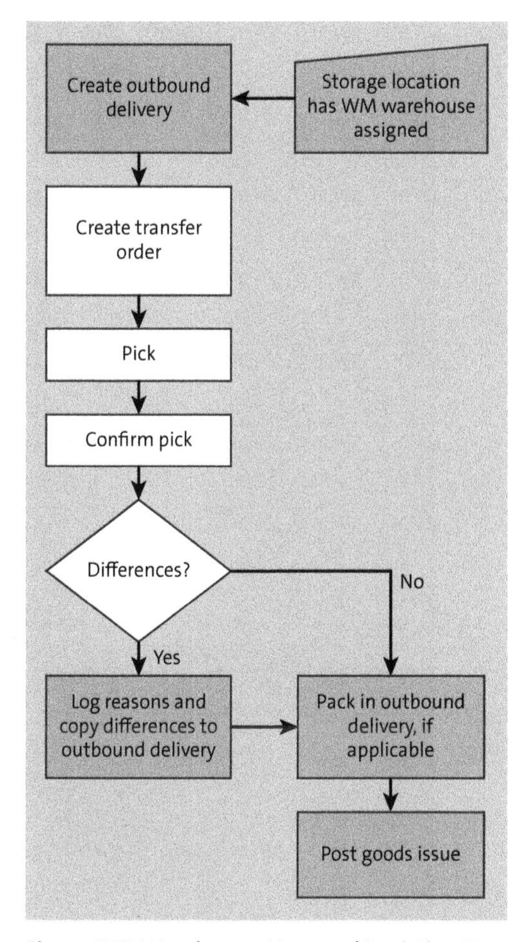

Figure 7.17 Warehouse-Managed Logistics: Process Flow

Extended Warehouse Managed Logistics

In SAP S/4HANA extended warehouse-managed logistics, all the supply chain activities are carried out in EWM. For use with SAP S/4HANA, SAP EWM can be a decentralized component of the SAP landscape, or it can be entirely integrated within your SAP S/4HANA environment (embedded extended warehouse management [EWM]). The embedded option is the recommended approach.

EWM is a much more comprehensive way of managing inventory in your SAP S/4HANA system, allowing for options such as serial numbers, batch numbers, minimum shelf life, vendor-managed inventory, yard management, and value-added services. It's more suited to medium- and large-sized warehouses with flexible and automated processes that demand high-performance, high-volume operations.

The process flow for EWM logistics is shown in Figure 7.18. The orange boxes show the EWM processes that sit outside the standard outbound delivery processes.

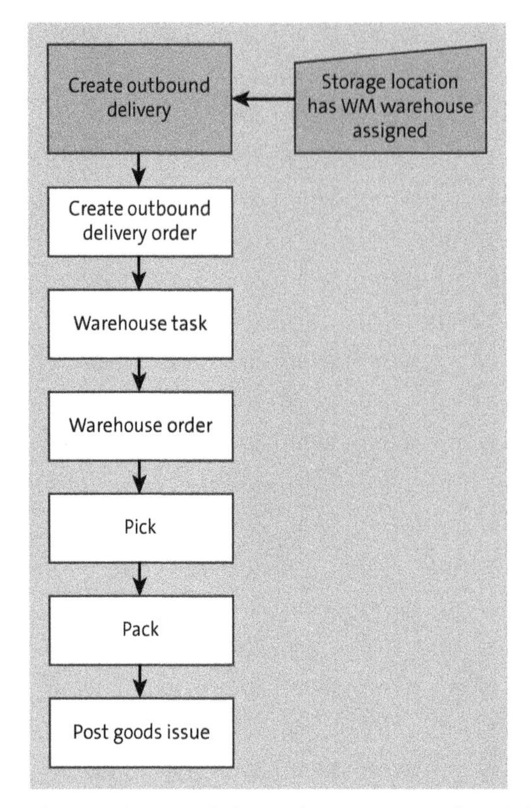

Figure 7.18 Extended Warehouse Managed Logistics: Process Flow

7.3.2 Creation of a Single Delivery without Reference Using Transaction VL01NO

This transaction is used to generate a delivery *without* reference to a sales order. The applicable scenarios aren't common but can include the following:

- Creation of a delivery directly from the project systems functionality
- Creation of a delivery when the sales order processing has come from another linked system via electronic data interchange (EDI)

The functionality of Transaction VL01NO is almost identical to Transaction VL01N, with the exception that there is no sales order entry field in the initial screen, as shown in Figure 7.19.

As shown, there are mandatory fields to be completed, which are normally automatically determined when creating with reference to a sales order, as they are pulled in directly from the source document.

The **Delivery Type** is normally different in this scenario, as the configuration behind the **Delivery Type** must allow creation without reference to a sales order. In the example in Figure 7.20, the **Delivery Type** is **LO** (**Delivery w/o Ref.**).

Create Outbound Delivery Without Order Reference

With Order Reference W/o Order Reference Post Goods Issue

Shipping Point
Delivery Type

Sales Area
Sales Organization
Distribution Channel
Division

Figure 7.19 Create Delivery without reference: Transaction VL01NO

Create Outbound Delivery Without Order Reference

With Order Reference W/o Order Reference Post Goods Issue

Shipping Point 0001 Shipping Point 0001
Delivery Type LO Delivery w/o Ref.

Sales Area
Sales Organization US30 ATI US
Distribution Channel 20 Direct
Division 10 Consumer Electronics

Figure 7.20 Create Delivery without Reference: Initial Screen Entry

Fields in the delivery that must be populated are as follows (see Figure 7.21):

- **Ship-to party**
- **Planned GI**
- **Material**
- **Deliv. Qty**

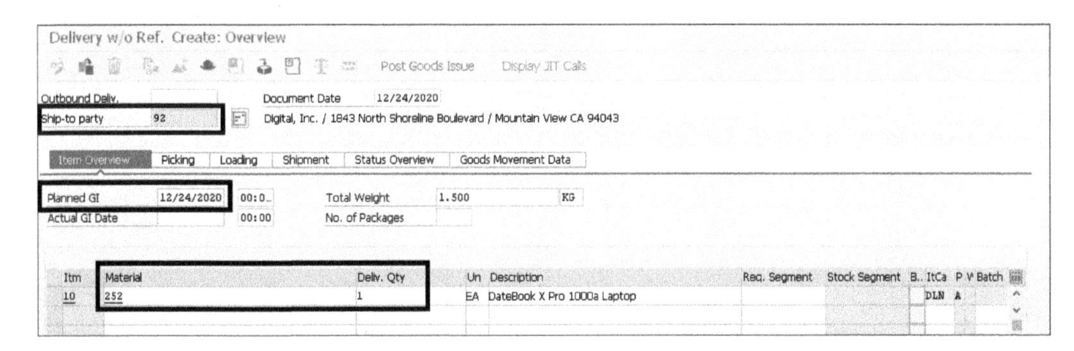

Figure 7.21 Create Delivery without Reference: Mandatory Fields

If the material is batch managed, then the **Batch** number must also be maintained. After these mandatory fields have been completed as a minimum, the delivery can be saved as normal. By returning to the display transaction and viewing the document flow, you can see that the delivery has no other assigned document so far (see Figure 7.22).

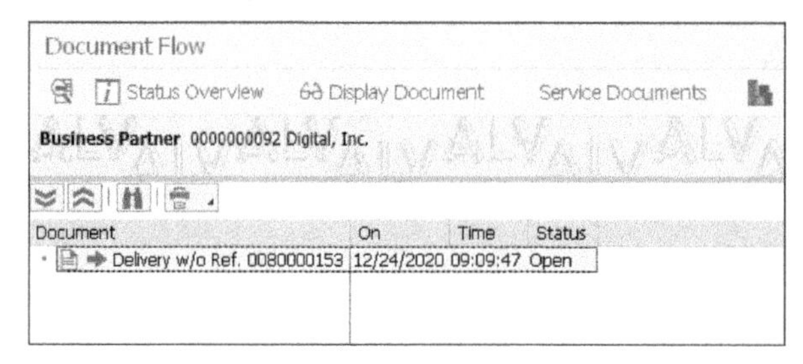

Figure 7.22 Delivery without Reference: Document Flow

From this point forward, the delivery behaves in the same way as a delivery with reference behaves, and it can be passed forward for subsequent functions such as picking, packing, and GI as normal.

7.3.3 Creating a Delivery from within a Sales Order

Often, when creating or displaying a sales order, you want to push it through to delivery immediately, and this can be achieved by a menu function from within the sales order. In the example in Figure 7.23, Transaction VA03 is used to display the sales order; from here you choose **Sales Document • Deliver**.

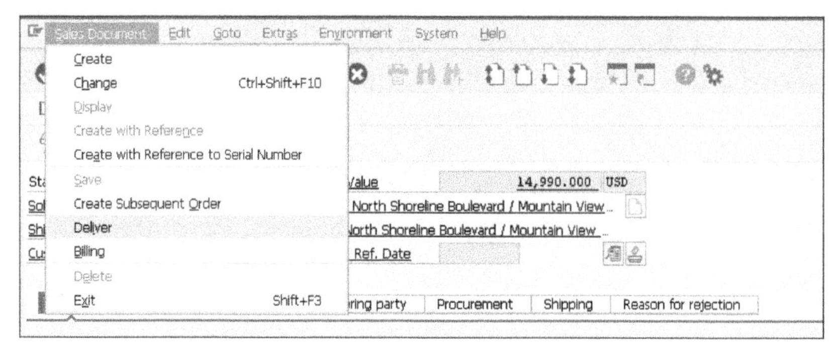

Figure 7.23 Create Delivery from Sales Order

By following this menu path, the SAP system skips the initial screen of Transaction VL01N by using all the details from the sales order:

- Shipping point
- Selection date = current date
- Sales order number

The selection date used is the current date, meaning that if any items aren't deliverable up to today, the delivery won't be created.

Once in the delivery creation screen from this menu path, everything operates in the same way as through Transaction VL01N.

7.3.4 Collective Delivery Processing

Until now, we've been processing deliveries one at a time through single document processing options such as Transaction VL01N. In this section, we'll explore the options for collective delivery processing—creation of multiple deliveries for multiple sales orders—via the Transaction VL10* suite of transactions.

Figure 7.24 shows the SAP menu tree for these options.

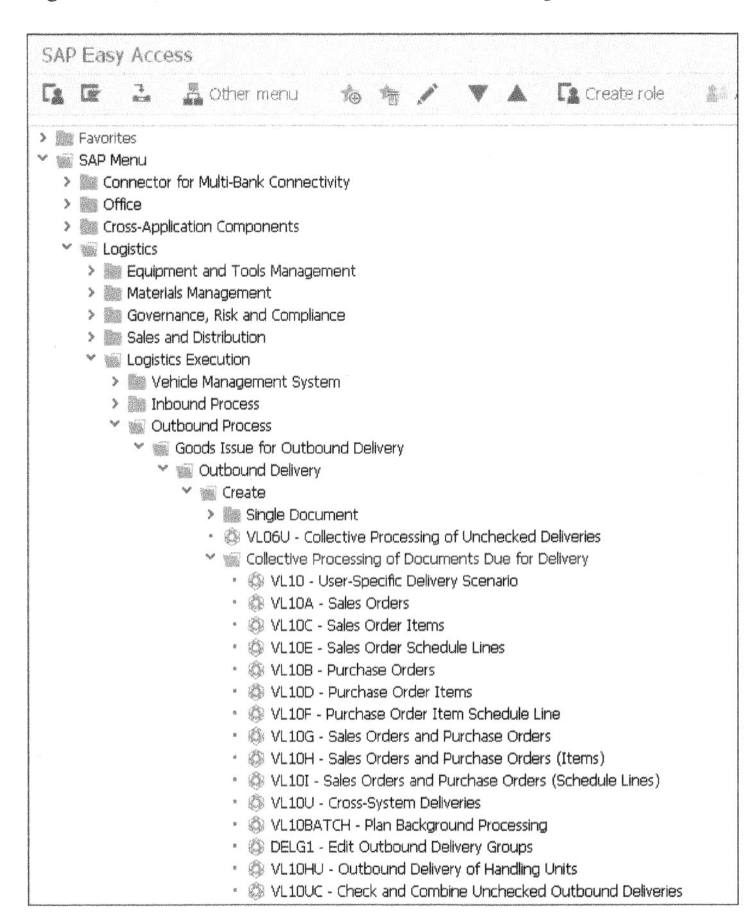

Figure 7.24 Collective Delivery Processing: Menu Tree

In collective delivery processing, you can run multiple sales orders through to delivery using a single transaction. Additionally, the transactions available can be scheduled to create a delivery due list run, which normally runs periodically for given plants to create deliveries at key times of the logistics cycle.

We'll begin our analysis of collective delivery processing with Transaction VL10, which will give you an insight into how all the other variants of this transaction operate.

The descriptive name of Transaction VL10 is User-Specific Delivery Scenario, meaning that settings for the user who runs the transaction control how the transaction is executed. These settings are contained within your SAP user definition and can be viewed by accessing Transaction SU3 or from anywhere in the SAP GUI by following the menu path shown in Figure 7.25.

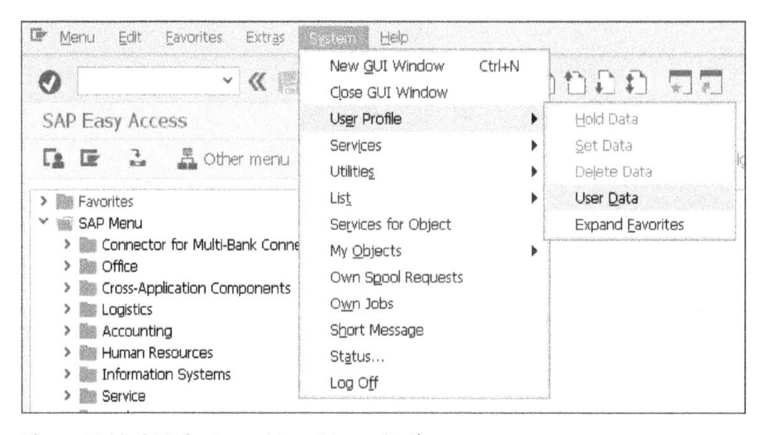

Figure 7.25 SAP System: User Menu Path

This menu path, or Transaction SU3, will take you to the user screen, where you can select the **Parameters** tab to default in certain values in certain fields in SAP standard screens, as shown in Figure 7.26. The parameters are set according to parameter IDs (PIDs), which are used by specific programs in the system.

Transaction VL10 uses a parameter from your user record to default a specific role into the transaction. The parameter used to set the role in the transaction is LE_VL10_SZENARIO.

The role determines how the transaction is run, that is, whether you want to create deliveries for sales orders, sales order items, sales order schedule lines, purchase orders, and so on. You can view Transaction VL10 as a default cockpit for all, with the default set according to the user's PID.

Let's look at an example. If the PIDs are left as they are, with no setting for the LE_VL10_SZENARIO PID, then the Transaction VL10 screen looks like Figure 7.27.

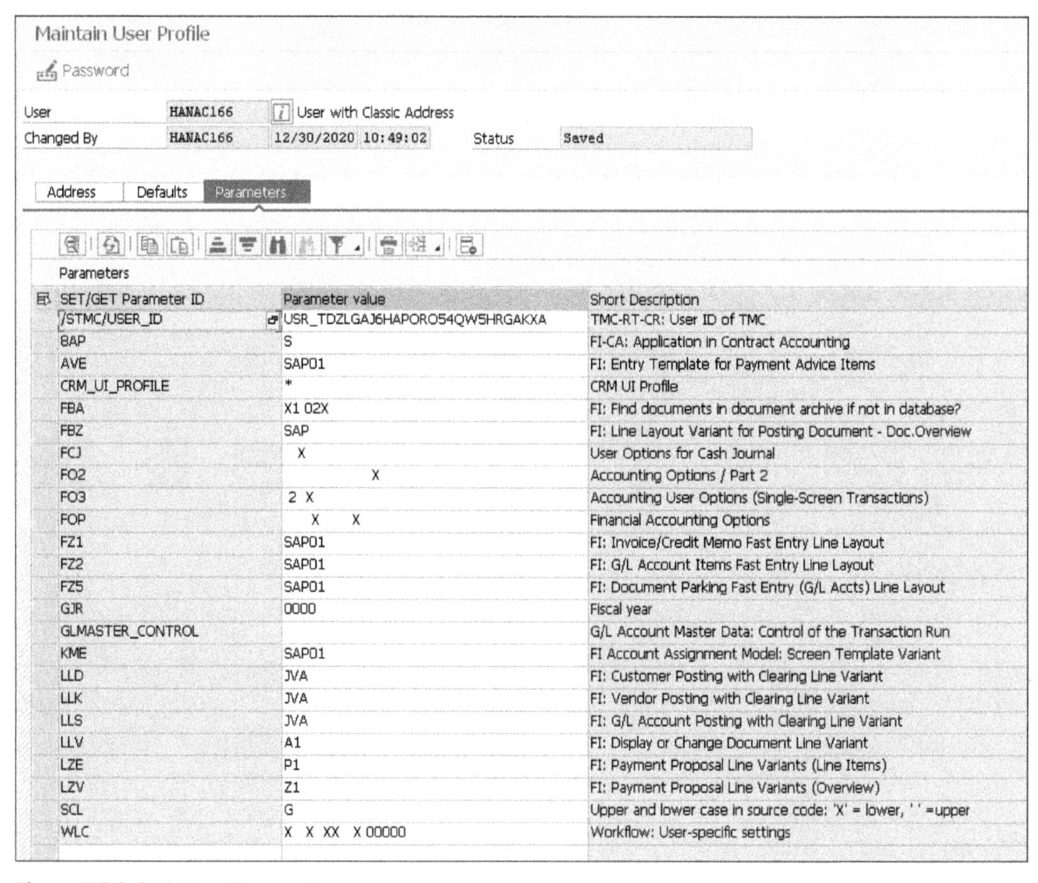

Figure 7.26 SAP User Parameters

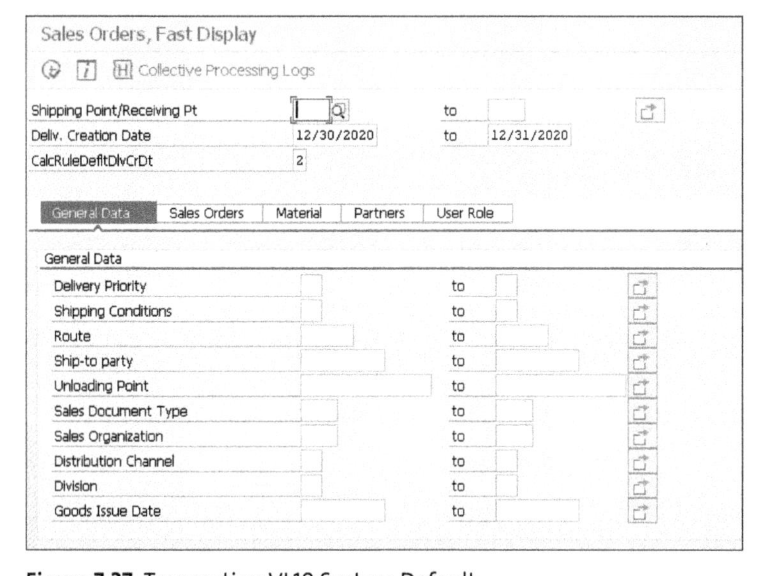

Figure 7.27 Transaction VL10 System Default

By selecting the **User Role** tab, you can see that the default **Role** used is **0001**, which defaults in various selection options for the transaction, such as data selection with sales orders only (see Figure 7.28).

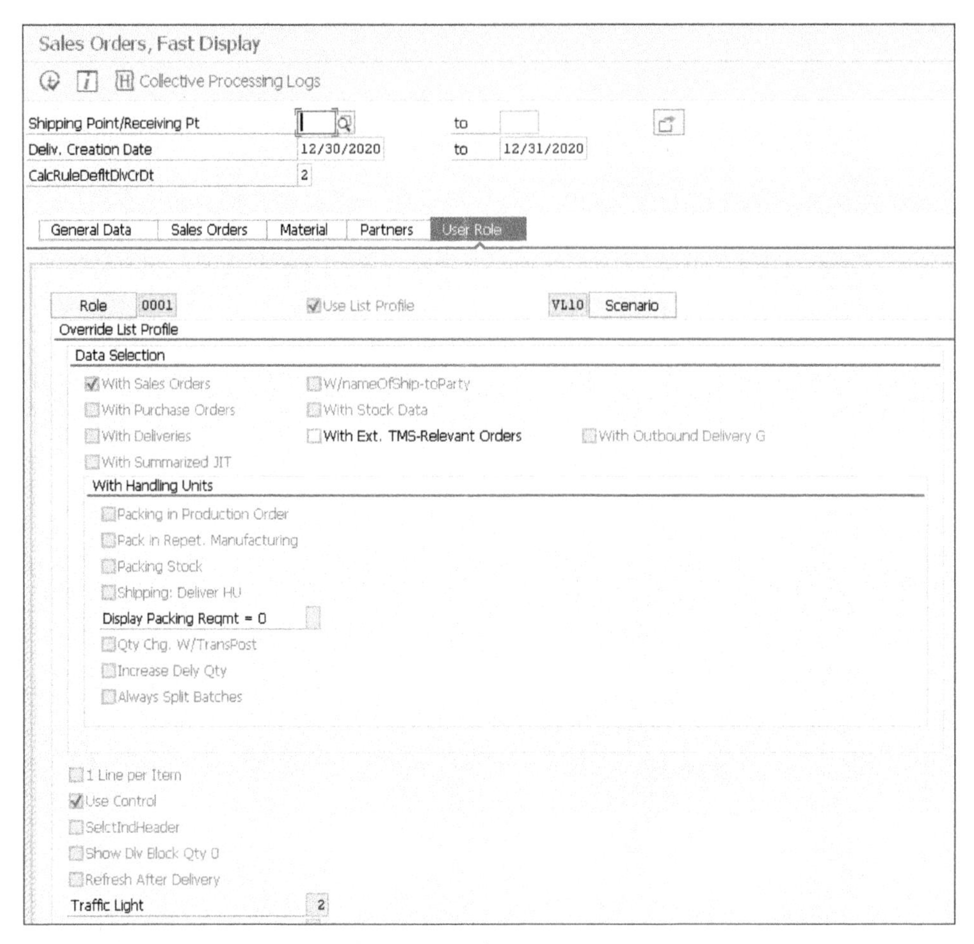

Figure 7.28 Transaction VL10: Default User Role

Now, if you amend the user PID to default in **Role 0002** (purchase orders), as shown in Figure 7.29, you get a very different result when you open Transaction VL10, as shown in Figure 7.30.

Parameters

SET/GET Parameter ID	Parameter value	Short Description
/STMC/USER_ID	USR_TDZLGAJ6HAPORO54QW5HRGAKXA	TMC-RT-CR: User ID of TMC
8AP	S	FI-CA: Application in Contract Accounting
AVE	SAP01	FI: Entry Template for Payment Advice Items
CRM_UI_PROFILE	*	CRM UI Profile
FBA	X1 02X	FI: Find documents in document archive if not in database?
FBZ	SAP	FI: Line Layout Variant for Posting Document - Doc.Overview
FCJ	X	User Options for Cash Journal
FO2	X	Accounting Options / Part 2
FO3	2 X	Accounting User Options (Single-Screen Transactions)
FOP	X X	Financial Accounting Options
FZ1	SAP01	FI: Invoice/Credit Memo Fast Entry Line Layout
FZ2	SAP01	FI: G/L Account Items Fast Entry Line Layout
FZ5	SAP01	FI: Document Parking Fast Entry (G/L Accts) Line Layout
GJR	0000	Fiscal year
GLMASTER_CONTROL		G/L Account Master Data: Control of the Transaction Run
KME	SAP01	FI Account Assignment Model: Screen Template Variant
LLD	JVA	FI: Customer Posting with Clearing Line Variant
LLK	JVA	FI: Vendor Posting with Clearing Line Variant
LLS	JVA	FI: G/L Account Posting with Clearing Line Variant
LLV	A1	FI: Display or Change Document Line Variant
LZE	P1	FI: Payment Proposal Line Variants (Line Items)
LZV	Z1	FI: Payment Proposal Line Variants (Overview)
SCL	G	Upper and lower case in source code: 'X' = lower, ' ' =upper
WLC	X X XX X 00000	Workflow: User-specific settings
LE_VL10_SZENARIO	0002	Default Scenario for Creating Deliveries (TA VL10)

Figure 7.29 Transaction VL10: Parameter ID Change

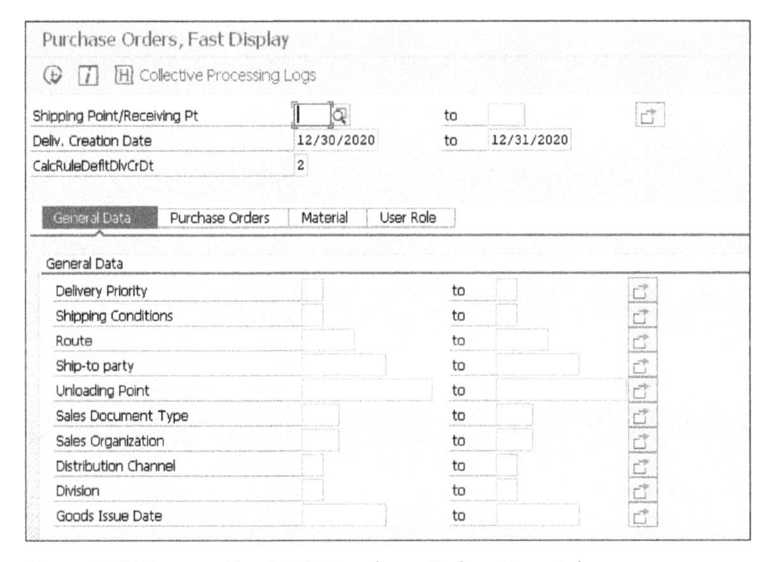

Figure 7.30 Transaction VL10: Purchase Orders User Role

As shown in Figure 7.30, the default here is to create deliveries from purchase orders, rather than sales orders. All these different variations of Transaction VL10 can be found in the Transaction VL10 suite:

- **Transaction VL10A**
  Creates deliveries for sales orders.

- **Transaction VL10B**
  Creates deliveries for purchase orders
- **Transaction VL10C**
  Creates deliveries for sales order items
- **Transaction VL10D**
  Creates deliveries for purchase order items
- **Transaction VL10E**
  Creates deliveries for sales order schedule lines
- **Transaction VL10F**
  Creates deliveries for purchase order schedule lines
- **Transaction VL10G**
  Creates deliveries for sales orders and purchase orders
- **Transaction VL10H**
  Creates deliveries for sales orders and purchase orders (items)
- **Transaction VL10I**
  Creates deliveries for sales orders and purchase orders (schedule lines)

Each variation can be represented by a specific user **Role** found in the **User Role** tab of Transaction VL10. By using one of the preceding transactions, you're simply defaulting in the user **Role** for that scenario.

> **Note**
>
> There are key differences between Transaction VL10A, Transaction VL10C, and Transaction VL10E, even though they all relate to sales orders. Transaction VL10A will show only one line in the delivery due list for the whole sales order, whereas Transaction VL10C will show a line for each sales order item, and Transaction VL10E will show a line for each sales order schedule line. This is useful if you want to create deliveries selectively within individual sales orders.

Creating Deliveries with Transaction VL10*

Let's now look at how you use the Transaction VL10* suite of transactions to create deliveries. The first thing to note when entering Transaction VL10 is the header fields in the selection:

- **Shipping Point**
  The area in the warehouse where the goods are shipped from.
- **Delivery Creation Date**
  This is a selection range of dates for which deliveries should be created. The delivery creation date is taken from the earliest of the material availability date or the transportation planning date from the sales order.

- **Calculation Rule for default Delivery Creation Date**
  A dropdown menu for this field shows the numerous entries that are used to default in the delivery creation date. this is useful for when you're running your delivery due lists as a background job.

There are additional fields in the **General Data, Sales Orders, Material,** and **Partners** tabs in the transaction, which can be used to restrict the selection of sales orders to create deliveries. A prime example of this is the **Delivery Priority** field; typically, a delivery due list run is scheduled for high-priority sales orders more frequently, with lower-priority delivery due list runs scheduled for overnight only, for example.

In this example, the delivery due list has been run with blank date ranges, so that all dates are picked up. It's likely that your SAP system is set up only to allow a certain number of days in the future (by default, 30 days), in which case, SAP will post a message to advise that the delivery creation "to" date will be set to the current date plus 30 days. After the transaction runs, the **Activities Due** screen appears, as shown in Figure 7.31.

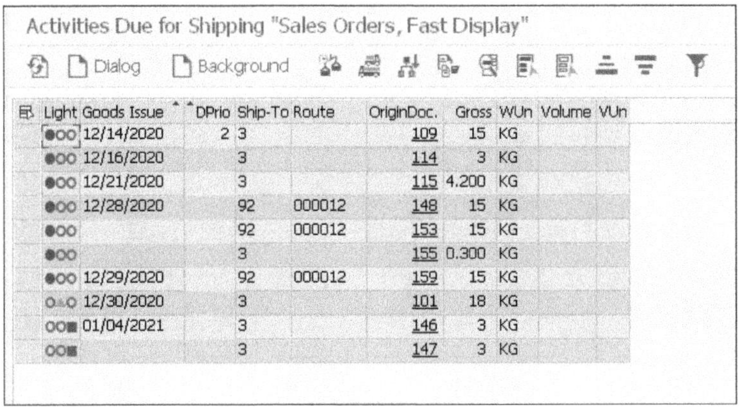

Activities Due for Shipping "Sales Orders, Fast Display"

Dialog Background

Light	Goods Issue	DPrio	Ship-To	Route	OriginDoc.	Gross	WUn	Volume	VUn
●OO	12/14/2020	2	3		109	15	KG		
●OO	12/16/2020		3		114	3	KG		
●OO	12/21/2020		3		115	4.200	KG		
●OO	12/28/2020		92	000012	148	15	KG		
●OO			92	000012	153	15	KG		
●OO			3		155	0.300	KG		
●OO	12/29/2020		92	000012	159	15	KG		
O●O	12/30/2020		3		101	18	KG		
OO●	01/04/2021		3		146	3	KG		
OO●			3		147	3	KG		

Figure 7.31 Transaction VL10: Activities Due Screen

The **Activities Due** screen details all the sales orders due for delivery between the date ranges selected in the selection screen. Remember, we're using Transaction VL10 with the default user **Role**, so only one line per sales order will be shown; if we had used Transaction VL10C or Transaction VL10E, we would see one line per item or one line per schedule line, respectively. As usual with SAP reports, it's possible to amend the layout of the report in the normal way using the **Change Layout** icon.

One of the first things to notice in Figure 7.31 is the use of traffic lights in the report. Each sales order has a red, yellow, or green traffic light, which denote the following:

- **Red**
  The delivery is overdue, and the planned GI date (as shown in the second column) is in the past. It's probable that the customer won't receive the delivery on time.

- **Yellow**
  The delivery should be created immediately as the planned GI date is today or tomorrow.
- **Green**
  The delivery isn't due for immediate processing as the planned GI date is two days or more in the future.

The **OriginDoc.** (originating document) column houses the sales order number and is hyperlinked, so you can click on it to navigate directly to the sales order.

To create the deliveries, you have two options: **Dialog** creation (creates the deliveries directly in Transaction VL01N in the foreground) or **Background** (creates the deliveries in the background). Select the line items you want to create the deliveries for, and then select the option relevant for you. For this example, the delivery will be created in background for originating sales order 101, as shown in Figure 7.32. Bear in mind that although this example is for one document only, multiple documents can be processed in exactly the same way.

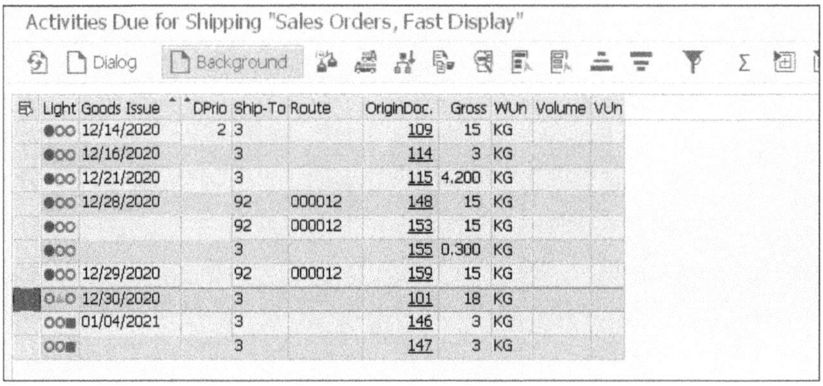

Activities Due for Shipping "Sales Orders, Fast Display"

Dialog Background

Light	Goods Issue	DPrio	Ship-To	Route	OriginDoc.	Gross	WUn	Volume	VUn
	12/14/2020	2	3		109	15	KG		
	12/16/2020		3		114	3	KG		
	12/21/2020		3		115	4.200	KG		
	12/28/2020		92	000012	148	15	KG		
			92	000012	153	15	KG		
			3		155	0.300	KG		
	12/29/2020		92	000012	159	15	KG		
	12/30/2020		3		101	18	KG		
	01/04/2021		3		146	3	KG		
			3		147	3	KG		

Figure 7.32 Transaction VL10: Create Delivery in Background

After selecting the **Background** button, the display changes to show the item selected in green at the top of the display. A message also appears: **See log for information about creating deliveries.** To see the delivery number created, click on the **Show/Hide Delivery** icon . This then shows the delivery number in the report, as shown in Figure 7.33.

The delivery number is hyperlinked for easy navigation to display the document.

From the selection screen of the Transaction VL10* suite, you can navigate to the processing logs to display the deliveries created. The selection screen shows the **Collective Processing Logs** button at the top of the screen (see Figure 7.34).

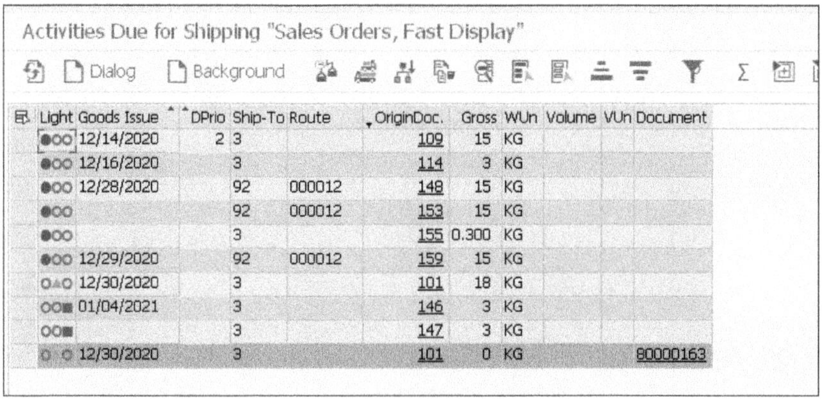

Figure 7.33 Transaction VL10: Showing the Delivery Number

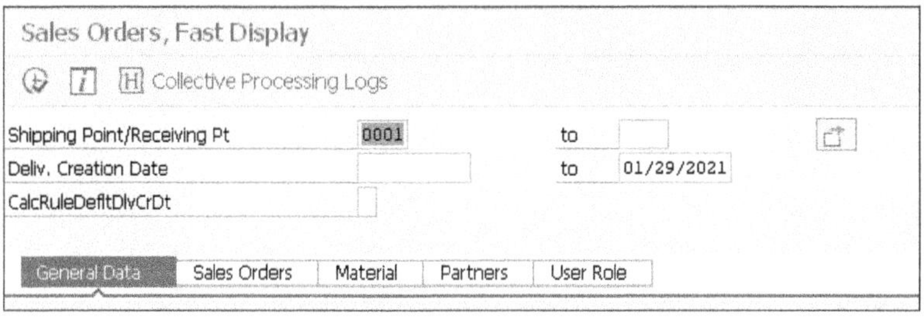

Figure 7.34 Transaction VL10: Collective Processing Logs Button

By clicking the button, you're taken to a selection screen, as shown in Figure 7.35, to report the deliveries created. Each delivery due list run that results in delivery creation is allocated a collective run number.

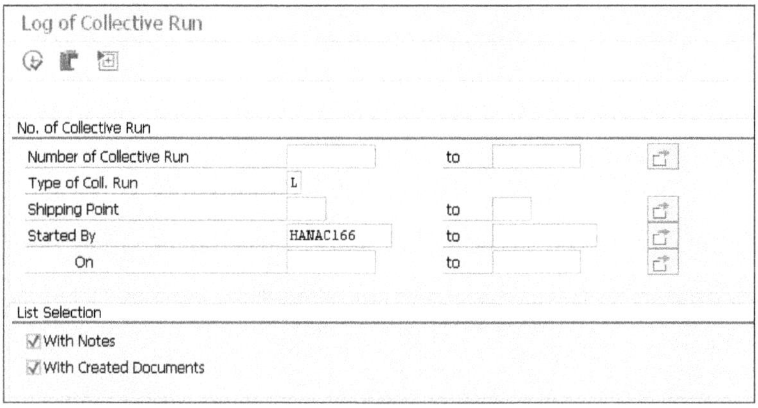

Figure 7.35 Collective Processing: Log of Collective Run

Executing the report shows the group run number and details (see Figure 7.36).

Log of Collective Run

Choose Save Documents

Group	Created by	Created on	No.	Err.	ShPt	Gross	WUn	Volume	VUn	MaxTim	Time
151	HANAC166	12/30/2020	1		0001	18	KG			0.00	15:26:26

Figure 7.36 Transaction VL10: Collective Processing Run Details

From here, you can navigate to the log, if any notes exist with error or warning messages, using the **Log** icon. You can also navigate to the delivery documents themselves by using the **Documents** button. This opens another screen to show the list of documents for that collective run, as shown in Figure 7.37.

Log of Collective Run

Choose Save Disp. doc. Document flow

Group	Document	Sort
151	80000163	

Figure 7.37 Transaction VL10: Collective Processing Run Documents

Further drilldown functionality is available here to display the delivery or display the document flow for the delivery.

The functionality represented by the Transaction VL10* suite is often used in business operations for scheduling a delivery due list to run in the background automatically on a regular basis. This can be done by selecting your parameters and saving the set as a variant, and then scheduling as any normal job in Transaction SM36 (normally done by your IT team under instruction from the business). The batch job can be run from the Transaction VL10 screen by selecting **Program • Execute in Background**, as shown in Figure 7.38.

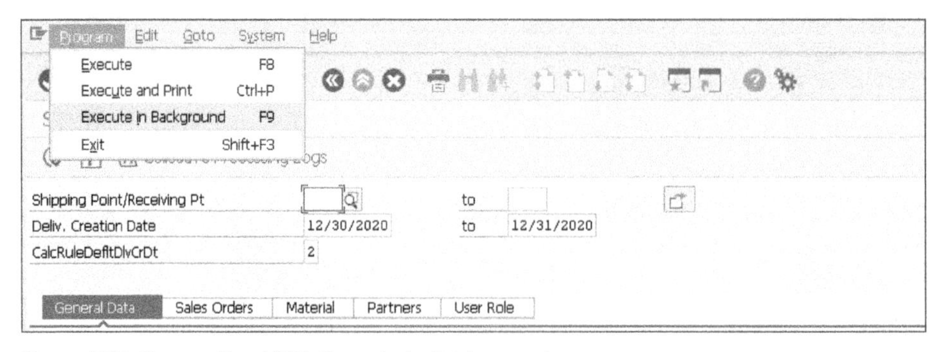

Figure 7.38 Transaction VL10: Execute in Background

Alternatively, a background job can be created by using Transaction VL10BATCH. Opening Transaction VL10BATCH will show you all available variants for the delivery due list program (including any you've saved directly in any of the Transaction VL10* suite), as shown in Figure 7.39.

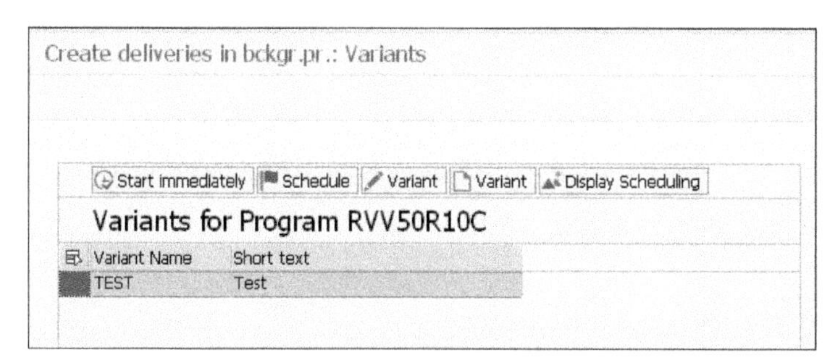

Figure 7.39 Transaction VL10BATCH: Initial Screen

From here you can perform the following:

- Start a delivery due list run by selecting the variant and clicking the **Start immediately** button.
- Schedule a delivery due list run by selecting the variant and clicking the **Schedule** button.
- Amend an existing variant by selecting the variant and clicking the **Variant** button with a pencil on it.
- Create a new variant by clicking on the **Variant** button with a blank page on it.
- Display all scheduled delivery due list runs by clicking the **Display Scheduling** button.

Each option walks you through the steps required to complete the task.

7.3.5 SAP Fiori Apps

Various SAP Fiori apps are available within SAP S/4HANA to create deliveries, as follows:

- **Create Outbound Deliveries – From Sales Orders**
  This app is reflective of the SAP GUI Transaction VL10, as shown in Figure 7.40. The selection parameters from Transaction VL10 are available via the standard SAP Fiori filters bar. Note that no traffic light system is available in this SAP Fiori app. Navigation to the sales order factsheet app is supported by clicking the line, and deliveries can be created or scheduled by selecting the **Create Deliveries** button or the **Schedule Delivery Creation** button.

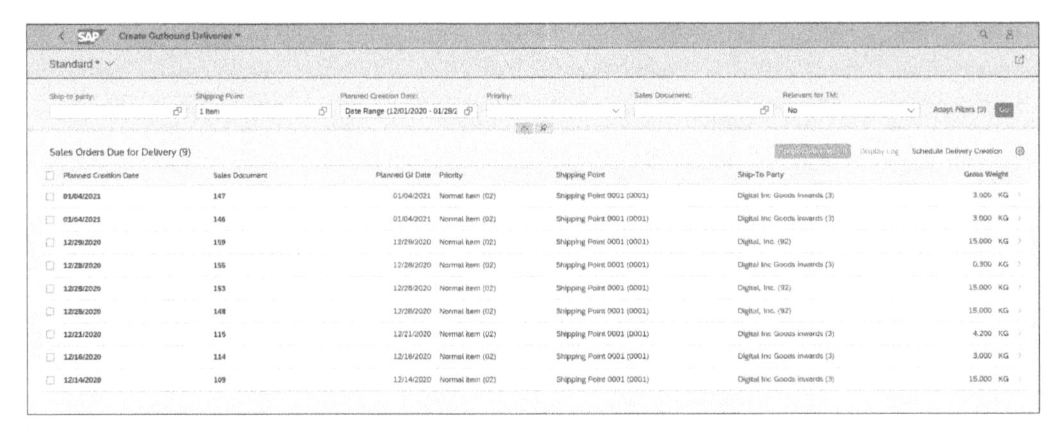

Figure 7.40 Create Outbound Deliveries from Sales Orders App

- **Schedule Delivery Creation**
  This app is used in the same way as Transaction VL10BATCH in SAP GUI. Once opened, the app displays all existing scheduled jobs according to the criteria set in the filter bar. To add a new job, simply click the plus sign in the app, as shown in Figure 7.41. The SAP Fiori app will then walk you through the steps required to schedule the delivery due list run.

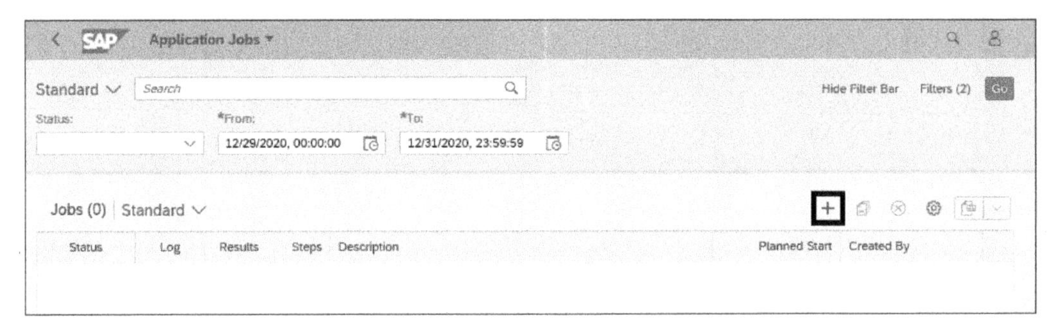

Figure 7.41 Schedule Delivery Creation App

- **Create Outbound Delivery without Order Reference**
  This app is an exact replication of the SAP GUI Transaction VL01NO.
- **Create Delivery with Order Reference**
  This app is an exact replication of the SAP GUI Transaction VL01N.
- **My Documents Due for Delivery; My Items Due for Delivery; My Schedule Lines Due for Delivery**
  These three apps replicate SAP GUI Transactions VL10G, VL10H, and VL10I, respectively.

7.3.6 Delivery Splits

When creating deliveries, it's important to understand that SAP provides standard code for how the deliveries are split. SAP will always try to reduce the number of deliveries to a minimum to keep operational costs low. In this way, you'll encounter the following scenarios:

- **Single sales order delivered on one delivery document**
  This is the standard, simple scenario.
- **Single sales order split into multiple delivery documents**
  This is a very common scenario and is usually split due to differing material availability dates or transportation planning dates, although splits for other reasons are also common.
- **Multiple sales orders delivered on one delivery document**
  This scenario is also very common and occurs frequently when a customer who regularly orders from you has multiple sales documents for which the delivery split criteria all match.
- **Multiple sales orders delivered on multiple delivery documents**
  Again, this is very common and often is a mixture of the previous two scenarios.

To get a feel for how the system splits deliveries, a list follows with some typical fields that the SAP system will treat as criteria for splitting into multiple deliveries if they aren't the same in the source sales orders. These criteria can be found in the header area of the delivery document and therefore must be identical in the source document to be merged into one delivery document. The fields are as follows:

- Ship-to Party
- Shipping Point
- Plant
- Sales Organization
- Delivery Priority
- Transportation Planning Date
- Loading Date
- Planned GI Date
- Route
- Incoterms
- Storage Location

Additional item-level fields can also be added to the delivery split criteria in configuration settings.

7.4 Changing a Delivery Document

After a delivery document is created and saved, the outbound logistics process is kicked off. As already discussed in Section 4.3, this outbound process can take the form of inventory-managed logistics, warehouse-managed logistics, or extended warehouse-managed logistics.

7.4.1 Picking

Picking is the process by which the warehouse picks the products from the storage locations according to the pick lists provided. These pick lists are normally generated as an output against the delivery document (for inventory management logistics), the transfer order (for WM logistics), or the warehouse order (for EWM logistics).

Again, the WM and EWM processes are deeply embedded in the supply chain process, and because we're more concerned with the sales and distribution processes, we'll restrict our discussions to the inventory management logistics process.

In the delivery document, there is a **Picking** tab at the overview level, as shown in Transaction VL02N (Change Delivery) in Figure 7.42.

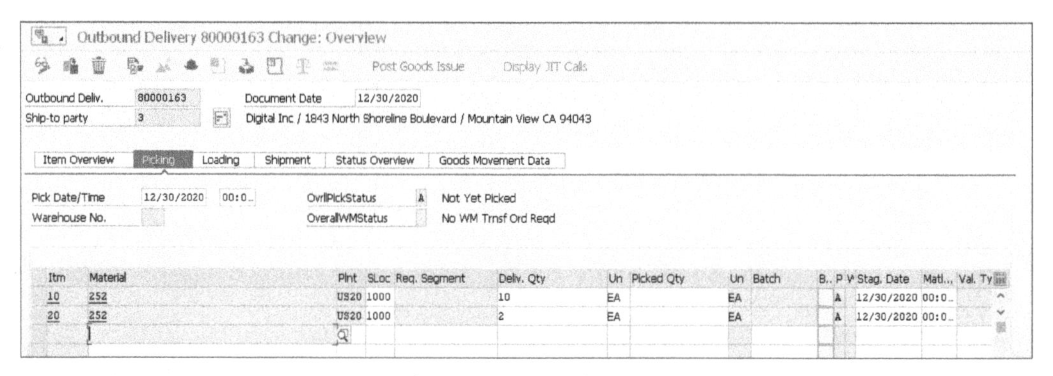

Figure 7.42 Transaction VL02N (Change Delivery): Picking

The first thing to notice here is that a storage location (**SLoc**) of **1000** is defined. This is automatically determined according to set rules in configuration and is based on the following:

- Shipping point of the delivery
- Plant of the delivery
- **Storage Conditions** field in the material master

The storage location is the location from which the goods are picked and isn't normally automatically determined in the sales order, so this is usually the first place you'll see it. However, it's possible manually to add a storage location to the sales order, and when this happens, the value is respected in the delivery, regardless of the configuration settings. After a delivery item becomes fully picked, the storage location becomes grayed out in the document and can't be changed.

The second thing to notice is that the overall pick status (**OvrlPickStatus**) is set to **A** (**Not Yet Picked**), meaning that the picking hasn't yet been carried out (statuses are discussed in Section 7.3.1). This is further evidenced by the missing **Picked Qty** value.

To update this, simply add your picked quantity into the **Picked Qty** field, and save the delivery. If your picked quantity is less than your delivery quantity, then only the picked amount will go forward to further processing, such as GI; the remaining quantity remains as ready to pick, and the pick status (**OvrllPickStatus**) is updated to **B** (**Partially Picked**).

Notice also that the **Deliv. Qty** field is available for updating so that you can reduce the delivery quantity in the event of inventory shortfalls. After the delivery quantity is reduced, then the status for the sales order item will become open again, and the remaining quantity will become available for creation of further deliveries, if the inventory situation allows.

Figure 7.43 shows the effect of amending the **Pick Qty** for one of the items: the **OvrllPickStatus** shows as **B** (**Partially Picked**), whereas the item pick status (four columns to the right of the **Picked Qty** field) show as **C** (**Completely Picked**) for the picked item and **A** (**Not Yet Picked**) for the other.

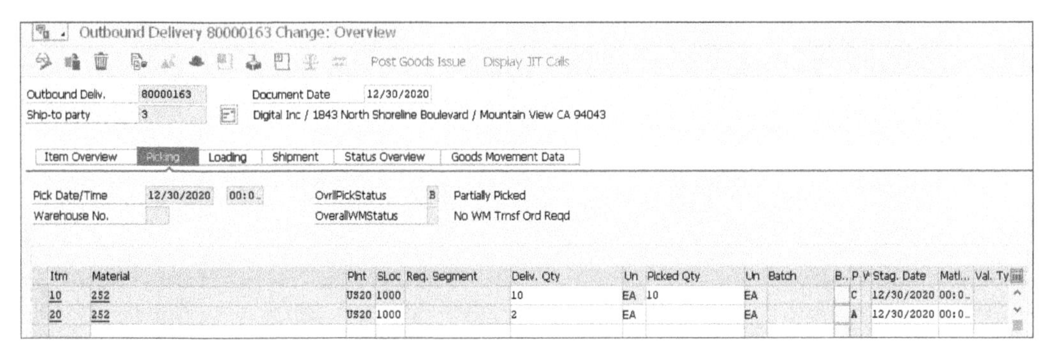

Figure 7.43 Delivery Picking Status Change

After the delivery is picked and saved, the document flow is updated, as shown in Figure 7.44.

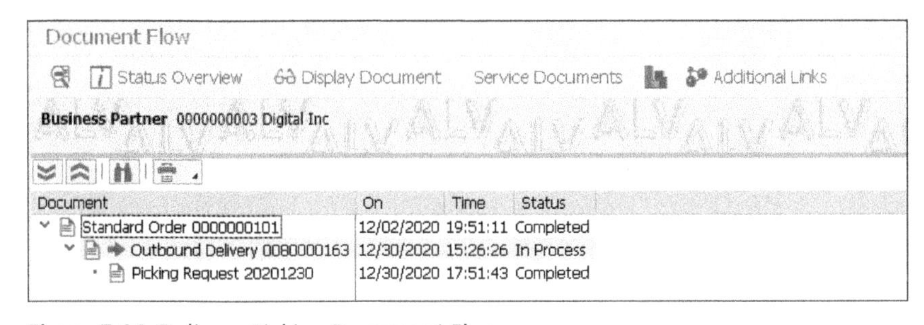

Figure 7.44 Delivery Picking Document Flow

7.4.2 Packing

Packing is a further step in the outbound logistics process and is controlled, as so many other things are in SAP S/4HANA sales and distribution, by the item category of the material. The item category determines whether the material must be packed or whether packing is optional.

Further packing functionality is available to automate packing based on a packing proposal. These can be created using Transaction POP1 to create, Transaction POP2 to amend, and Transaction POP3 to display. However, this is relatively advanced packing functionality, and, for the purposes of this exercise, we'll explain how simple packing works in the system to get a good overview of the principle.

The material master in SAP S/4HANA has a material group packaging materials (**Matl Grp Pack.Matls**) field in the **Basic data 1** screen of the material master, as shown in Transaction MM03 (Display Material) in Figure 7.45.

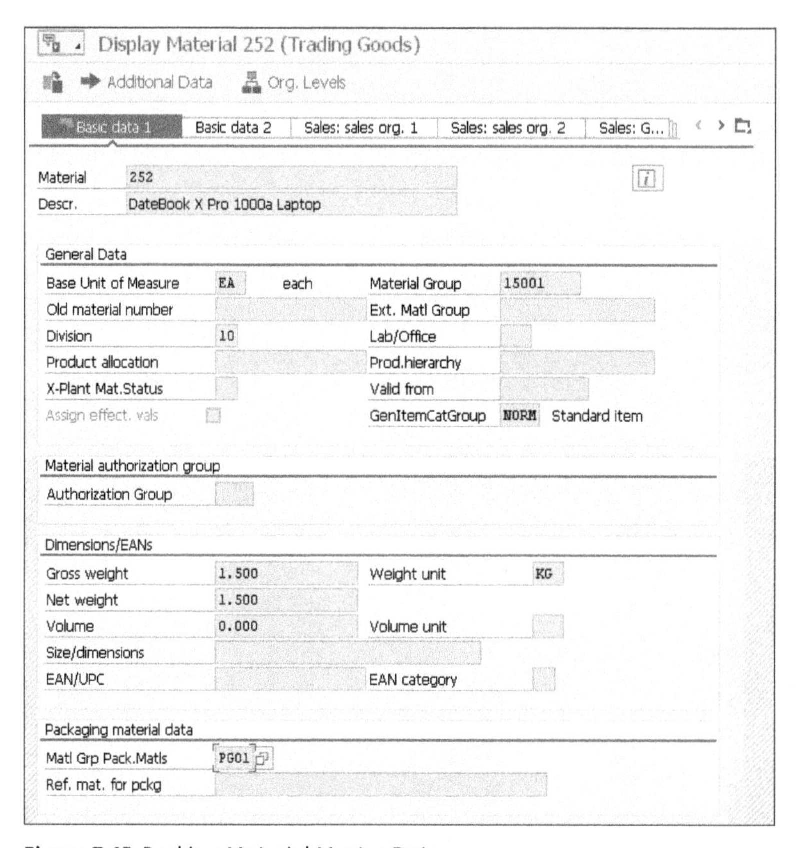

Figure 7.45 Packing Material Master Data

Note

The **Ref. mat. for pckg** field (reference material for packaging) under the **Matl Grp Pack.Matls** field can be used in automatic packing determination to group together multiple materials to use the same automatic packing determination.

The **Matl Grp Pack.Matls** field is used to group together materials for the purposes of identifying suitable packaging materials. For example, materials such as bottles would need packing separately from other materials, so the suggested packing materials would be different. This field is used to distinguish between the different types of packing materials.

The packing materials themselves are also set up as material master records, although the settings are very different. One of the key fields in the packing material master record is the **Packaging Mat. Type** (note that this is a different field from the **Matl Grp Pack.Matls** field). Figure 7.46 highlights the new field.

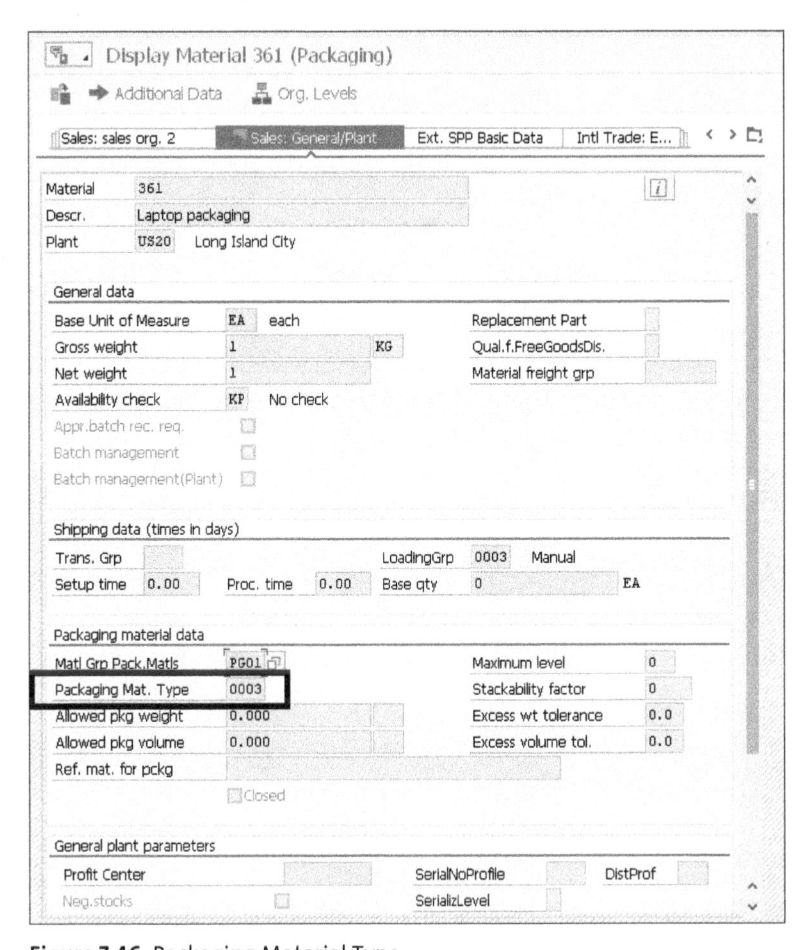

Figure 7.46 Packaging Material Type

This field is linked to the originating material setting in the following way: In a delivery, you may have a material number 252 – Laptop, which you want to pack using packaging material number 361 – Laptop Packaging. Material 252 has the **Matl Grp Pack.Matls** set as **PG01**. In SAP configuration settings, a mapping table shows that for PG01, there are multiple “allowed” packing material types (see Figure 7.47 for the configuration table controlling this). As shown in Figure 7.46, packaging material **361** has a **Packaging Mat. Type** of **0003**. Per the configuration shown in Figure 7.47, the **Mat.Grp PM PG01** allows any packaging material with a **PkgMtlType** of **0001**, **0002**, **0003**, **T001**, **T002**, or **ZPAL**. Using this method, packaging material 361 will be allowed for material 252.

Display View "Allowed Pack.Material Types per Material Group Pack. Mat

Mat.Grp PM	Description	PkgMtlType	Description
PG01	Packaging Mat	0001	Pallet
PG01	Packaging Mat	0002	Carton
PG01	Packaging Mat	0003	Box
PG01	Packaging Mat	T001	Palette
PG01	Packaging Mat	T002	PackMat2 Pallet
PG01	Packaging Mat	ZPAL	Pallet
PG02	Aux material	0004	Lid/Cover
PG02	Aux material	0005	Wrap
PG03	Meant Of Trans (MOT)	0005	Wrap

Figure 7.47 Allowed Combinations of Packing Materials

In practice, this works within a delivery by selecting the **Packing** icon. This option is available on the initial screen of Transaction VL02N (Change Delivery) or within the transaction. Once selected, the **Processing of Handling Units for Outbound Delivery** screen will be displayed, as shown in Figure 7.48.

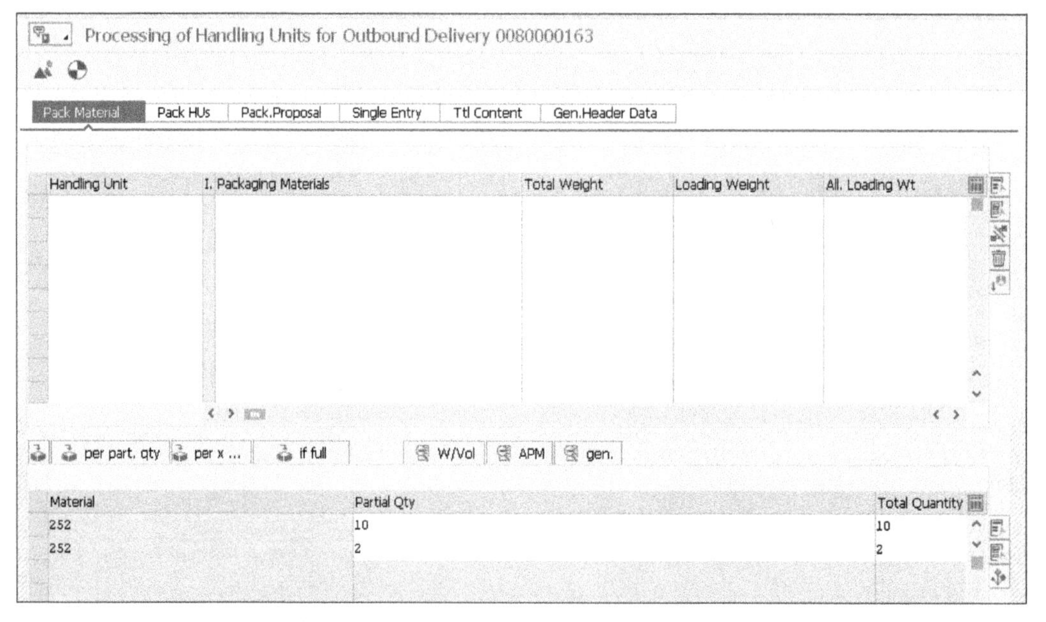

Figure 7.48 Processing of Handling Units

Note

A handling unit is an SAP transactional data object, with its own number range and is defined as a physical unit consisting of both packing materials and the goods contained within them. As with other SAP S/4HANA transactional data objects, it has header- and item-level details. The handling unit can be used to generate a packing list.

This is the screen where packing takes place. To pack each item, select the items you want to pack, and click on the **Packing** icon again, as shown in Figure 7.49.

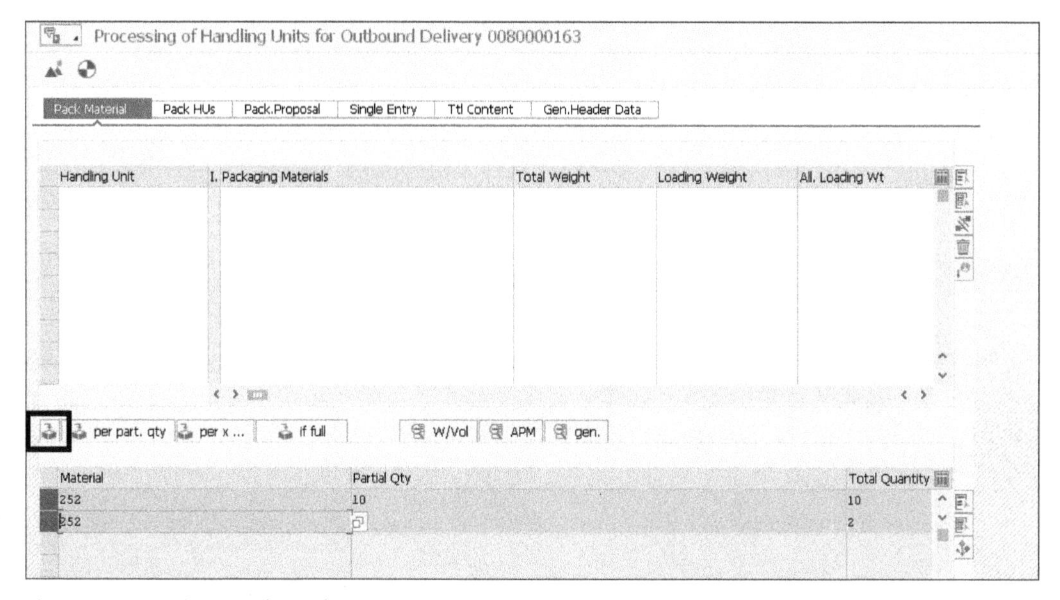

Figure 7.49 Packing in the Delivery

After you click the **Packing** icon, a popup message asks whether you want the system to search for allowed packaging materials. By selecting **Yes**, the system will find all packaging materials allowed for the packaging material group setting of the materials selected. For example, in Figure 7.50, there are 10 allowed packing materials.

The packing material used in this example is one of the materials selected, so by double-clicking that material number, the materials and packaging are packed into a handling unit. This will then move the materials from the bottom of the screen into a single handling unit at the top of the screen. All the weights of the materials are summed, including the weight of the packing material, to give a **Total Weight** for the handling unit (see Figure 7.51).

0000000000000000252 (1) 10 Entries found

Restrictions

Material	Material description	PkMtT	GrPMt	BUn
361	Laptop packaging	0003	PG01	EA
CARTON	Carton	T001		EA
CARTON_RF	Carton RF	T001	PG01	EA
PAL00	Wooden Pallet	0001	PG01	PC
PALLET	PALLET	0001	PG01	EA
PALLET_RF	PALLET_RF	T002	PG01	EA
PBO-EWMS4-PAL00	Palette EUROPE 1200 X 800	0002	PG01	PC
PBO-EWMS4-PAL01	Palette américaine 1200 X 1000	0002	PG01	PC
PBO-PK415	PALLET	0001	PG01	PC
PK-415	PALLET	0001	PG01	PC

Figure 7.50 Allowed Packing Materials

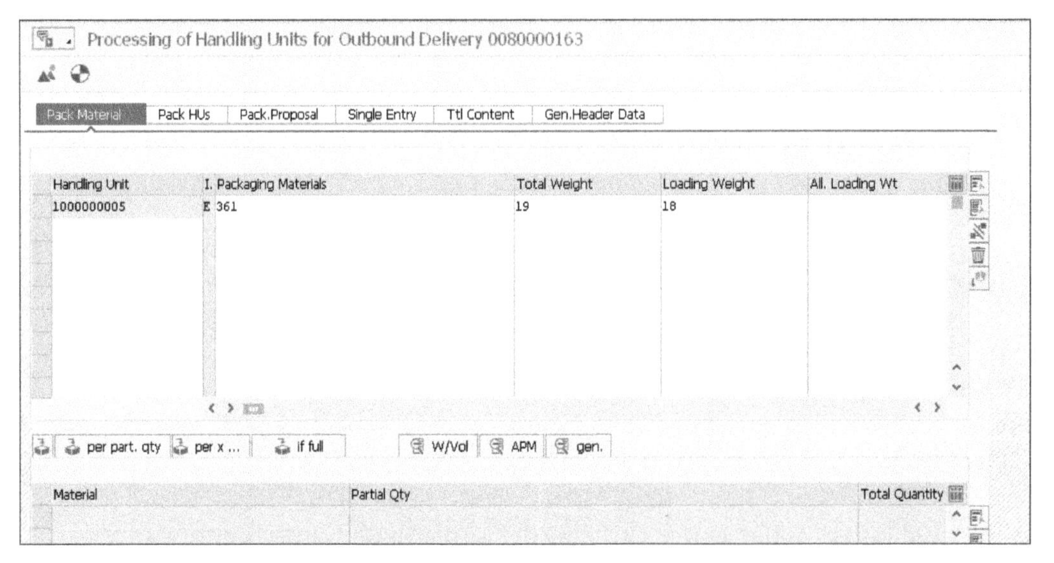

Figure 7.51 Handling Unit Creation

Note

If the dimensions of the materials don't fit into the dimensions of the packing material, then an error message will be posted.

Now the delivery has been saved, fully picked, and packed, the overall delivery status reveals that only goods movement and billing is outstanding, as shown in Figure 7.52.

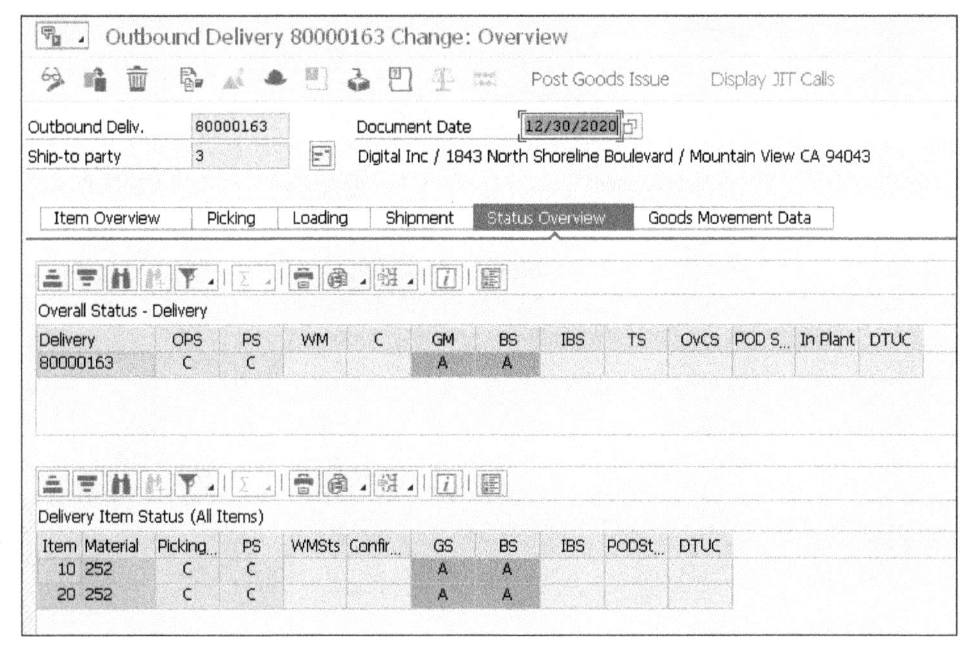

Figure 7.52 Delivery Status

The document flow of the delivery shows the picking and packing (**Handling Unit**), as shown in Figure 7.53.

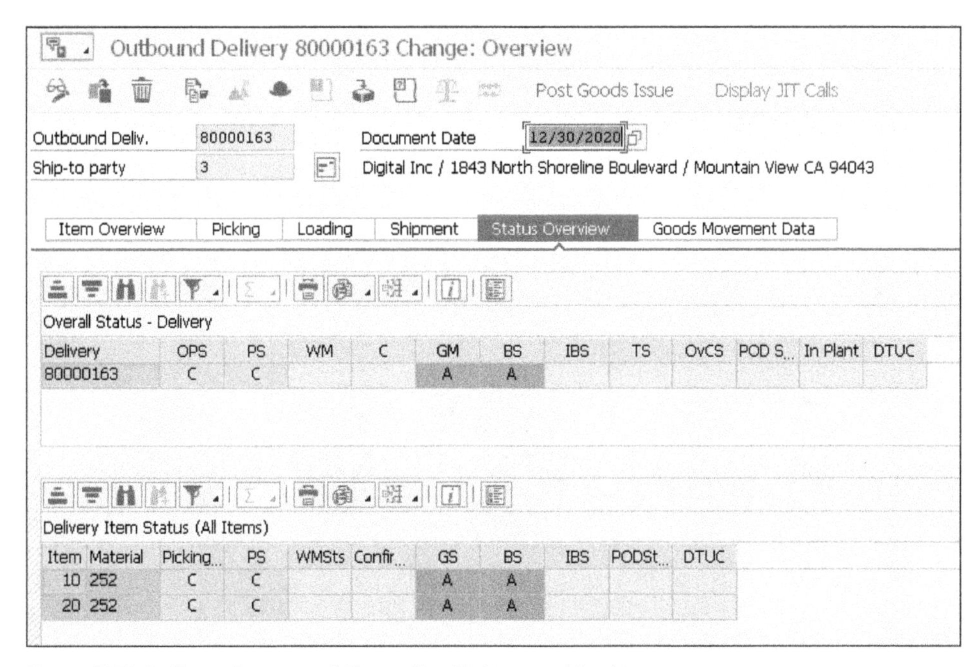

Figure 7.53 Delivery Document Flow after Picking and Packing

7.4.3 Post Goods Issue

The goods movement for a delivery is the inventory movement steps that represent the final step in the outbound delivery logistics before billing. The goods movement is carried out by the post goods issue (PGI) step. After PGI is carried out, depending on the Incoterms of the delivery, ownership of the goods may pass to the customer or the carrier—the goods aren't held anywhere as stock in the SAP S/4HANA system.

Carrying out the PGI for the delivery is extremely simple. After picking is completed (and packing if it's marked as mandatory), then PGI can be carried out by clicking on the **Post Goods Issue** button on the front screen of Transaction VL02N or within the transaction.

The GI uses a movement type to create its own document number in the system and adds it to the document flow. There are material movements and accounting entries associated with the goods movement document, which can be seen when navigating to the goods movement document from the document flow.

7.4.4 Printing Delivery Outputs

Outputs for deliveries are generated in the same way as for other sales and distribution documents. These can be seen by following the menu path in Figure 7.54.

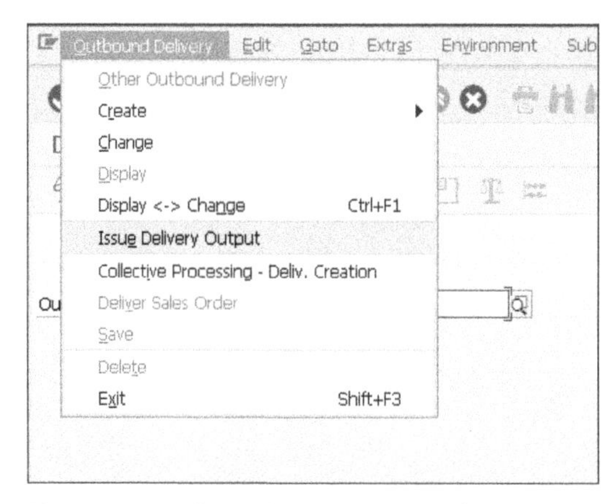

Figure 7.54 Delivery Output Menu Path

From the popup box that appears, select the output line, and click on the **Print Preview** icon to display the output. The output condition records determine whether the output is printed, emailed, or sent via EDI to the customer. These condition records are master data entered through Transaction VV21 for deliveries. If the Business Rules

Framework plus (BRFplus) approach to outputs is taken in your SAP system, then the output condition records are entered via Transaction OPD, which opens a web interface for maintenance of the business rules for outputs.

7.4.5 Delivery Monitor

SAP S/4HANA gives you a centralized cockpit to carry out any tasks required for deliveries. This is accessed in the SAP GUI by using Transaction VL06O, or in SAP Fiori via the My Outbound Delivery Monitor app.

The SAP GUI version of the **Outbound Delivery Monitor** screen is shown in Figure 7.55.

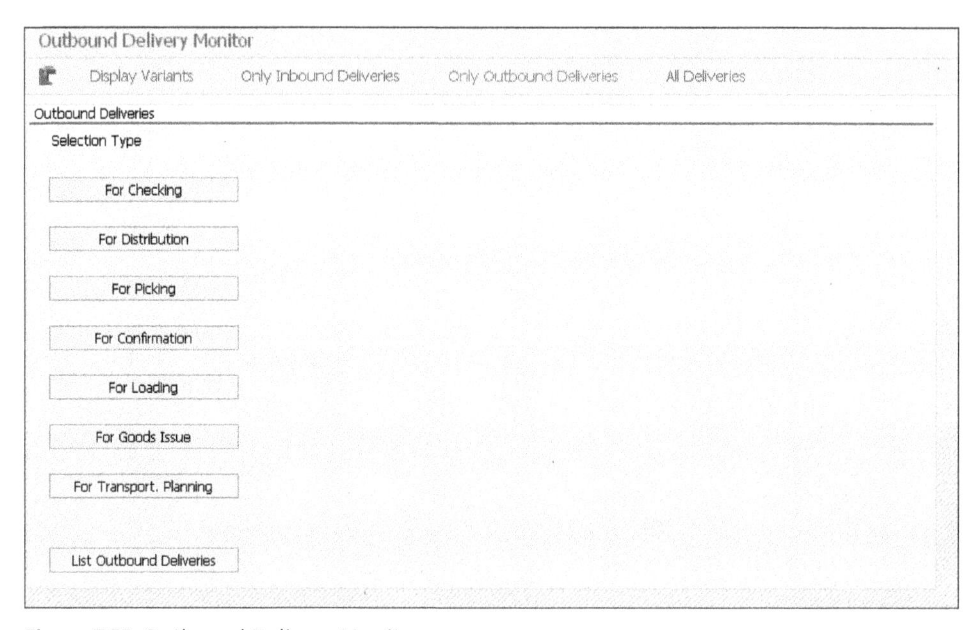

Figure 7.55 Outbound Delivery Monitor

The **Outbound Delivery Monitor** screen offers a selection of reports based on the status of the delivery, with the ability to navigate to the delivery to update accordingly. For example, if you need to see all deliveries that have yet to be picked, select the **For Picking** option. Bear in mind that with some of these options, there are buttons available that are related to WM logistics, such as **Create TO in Background**, which will create a transfer order. This is only relevant for WM logistics processes.

Each option will take you into a report-type transaction where you can specify certain selection criteria to restrict your results. The example in Figure 7.56 shows the **List Outbound Deliveries** option.

General Delivery List - Outbound Deliveries

Output in Background

Organizat. Data

Sales Organization		to	
Distribution Channel		to	
Division		to	
Shipping Point/Receiving Pt		to	

Document Editing

Created by		to	
Created on		to	

Time Data

Picking Date		to	
Loading Date		to	
Transptn Plang Date		to	
Pland Gds Mvmnt Date	12/31/2020	to	01/08/2021
Act. Gds Mvmnt Date		to	
Delivery Date		to	

Picking Data

Warehouse Number		to	

Check at Header Level
Check at Item Level
Exclude Existing WM Groups

Storage location		to	
Door for Whse No.		to	

Doc. Data

Delivery		to	
Delivery Type		to	
Group		to	

Figure 7.56 List Outbound Deliveries

7.5 Further Delivery Processing

It's worth briefly touching on additional functionality in the outbound logistics area related to deliveries.

7.5.1 Shipments

A useful optional function in the process flow is the shipment, which is a collection of deliveries with the same route. A single delivery has a route assigned to it that may contain several stages. Potentially, you may have multiple deliveries, which are goods issued on the same day and have the same route applied. In this instance, it may be useful to create a shipment.

A good example of this would be a grocery delivery truck. Each customer will have their own delivery created in the system, but an overall shipment document will group them all together where they are on the same route.

In SAP S/4HANA, shipments are created in Transaction VT01N. When creating a shipment, you must assign a transportation planning point to group together shipments for administrative purposes. Additionally, in the same way that deliveries have delivery types, shipments also have shipment types.

When using Transaction VT01N, deliveries can be added by using the **Deliveries** button, as shown in Figure 7.57.

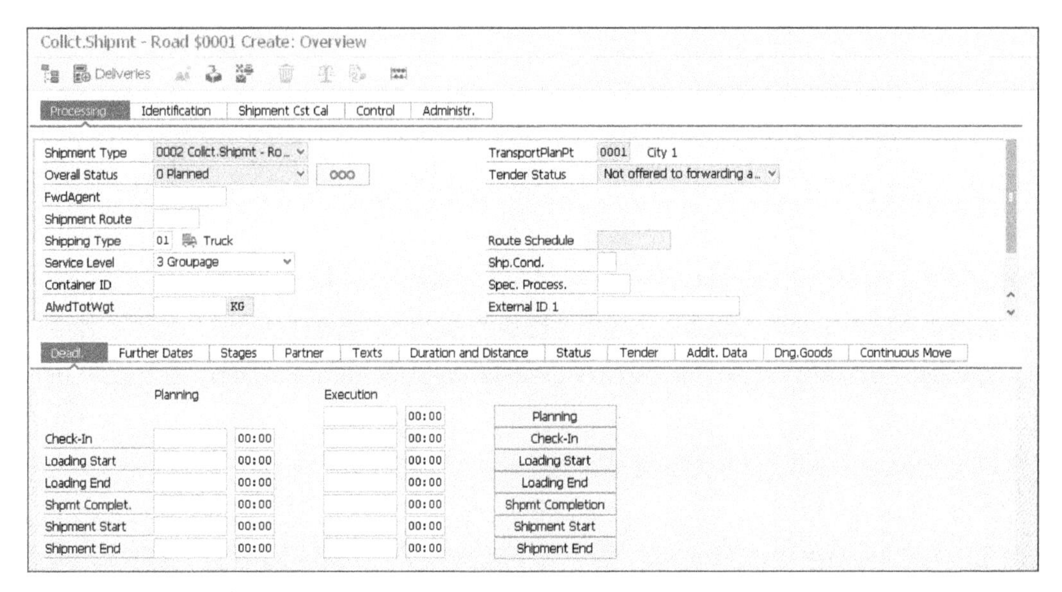

Figure 7.57 Create Shipment

7.5.2 Proof of Delivery

In some business scenarios, it should not be possible to bill the customer until you've had confirmation that the goods have been delivered. This is possible in SAP using the proof of delivery (POD) functionality. This functionality stops billing documents being generated until the POD status is marked as **Complete**. Furthermore, where there are quantity differences, the billing document will copy through the POD quantity rather than the delivery quantity.

Again, this functionality is activated by item category in the delivery document. However, to have the flexibility that this functionality can be assigned to some customers and not others, the **POD-Relevant** flag must be maintained in the customer master too, as shown in Figure 7.58.

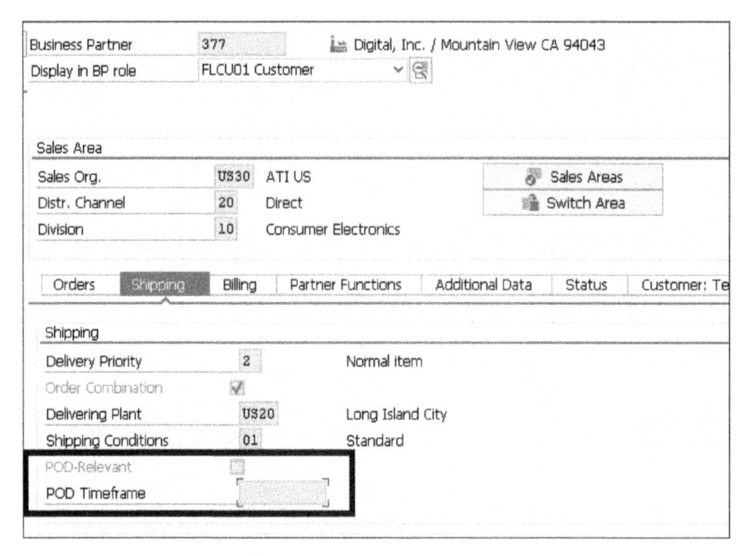

Figure 7.58 Proof of Delivery in the Customer Master

The **POD Timeframe** field in the customer master is used to specify how many days should elapse before the POD is automatically confirmed.

The POD confirmation step can be carried out in Transaction VLPOD, where quantity differences can be recorded. Additionally, Transaction VLPODQ can be used to confirm entire quantities without differences more efficiently. Often the POD process is automated via interfaces from external carriers.

7.6 Summary

You should now be fully aware of the role that the sales and distribution delivery document plays in the overall order-to-cash flow. Once completed, the delivery status will still be marked as **In Progress** because there is a key step outstanding in the process: billing.

In the next chapter, we'll explore all facets of billing, including how the SAP system billing documents affect the delivery documents.

Chapter 8
Billing

This chapter will introduce details around the final step in the logistics process of sales and distribution: billing.

Billing is the process whereby you can send invoice documents to your customers, and information about the process is available in each of the previous steps in the order-to-cash cycle. It's useful to view the billing process not only as the step to get an invoice to your customer but also as a way to interact between sales and distribution and the finance functions.

As a part of the explanation of the process, we'll explore key areas of billing in SAP S/4HANA such as standard customer invoicing, intercompany billing, billing plans, and different types of billing (e.g., debits and credits). We'll also investigate the difference between billing for certain types of transactions, such as goods (delivery-related billing) and services (order-related billing). Finally, we'll look into the architecture of billing as well as how the details from the billing document are passed on to the finance area through the accounting document.

8.1 Process Overview

After the outbound logistics are completed by the delivery process, the order-to-cash flow moves into its final phase: billing. The billing phase is represented in the order-to-cash flow in Figure 8.1.

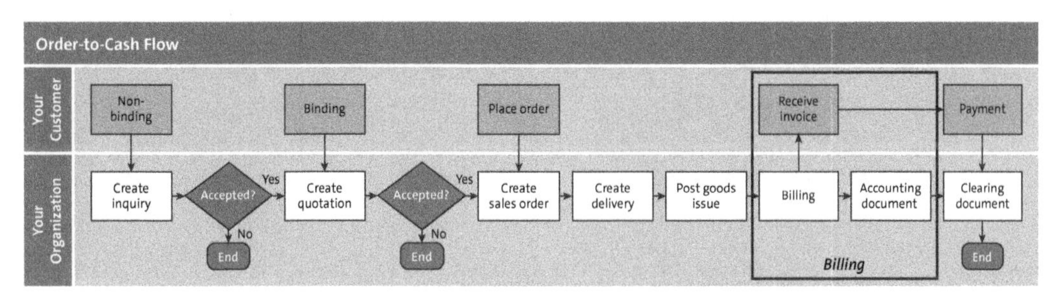

Figure 8.1 Order-to-Cash Flow: Billing

In this flow, the billing document is created with reference to a delivery document, but as you'll see, a billing document can be created with reference to a sales order as well, depending on the setup of the material being billed.

8.2 Document Types

As with all such documents in SAP sales and distribution, billing documents have their own document types, examples of which are shown in Figure 8.2.

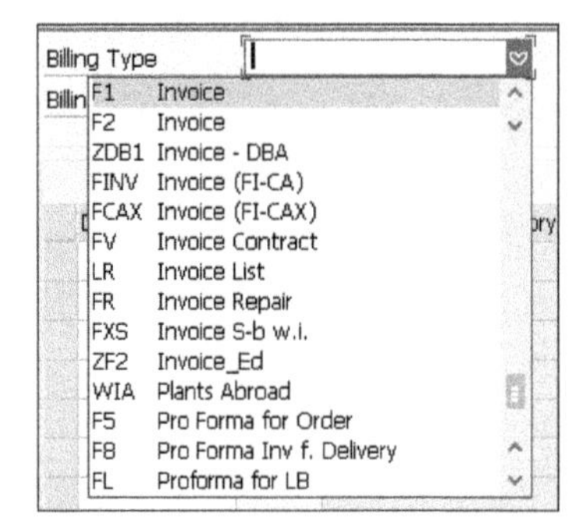

Figure 8.2 Example Billing Types

Each billing type has configuration assigned to it that determines how the document behaves, including settings such as these:

- Number range assignment
- Transfer to accounting rules
- Partner determination
- Text determination

Additionally, billing types are set up within the configuration of sales order types, so the system knows which billing type to use by default when processing a sales order or a delivery through to billing.

For billing types, the copy control rules are key settings as they determine whether a specific preceding document type (i.e., sales order or delivery) can be billed with the specified billing type. We'll explore more detail around copy control rules in the coming sections.

8.3 Standard Invoices

Standard invoices are billing documents created in response to sales orders (order-related billing) or delivery documents (delivery-related billing). The determination of whether an item in a sales order should be order-related or delivery-related billing is done via the configuration of the item category for the sales order item. Each item category has a field called **Billing Relevance** in the Customizing area of the SAP system, as shown in Figure 8.3.

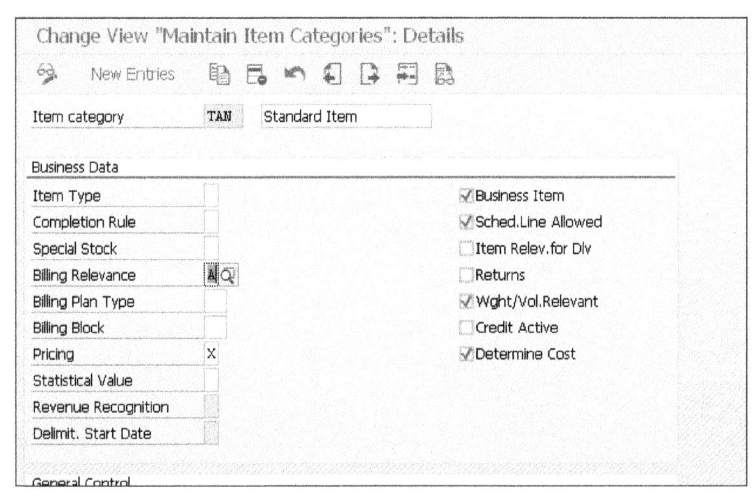

Figure 8.3 Billing Relevance in Item Category Configuration

The setting contained in this field determines whether the item is relevant for delivery-related billing or order-related billing.

After the billing relevance is established, the billing type is determined from the sales order type configuration settings, as shown in Figure 8.4.

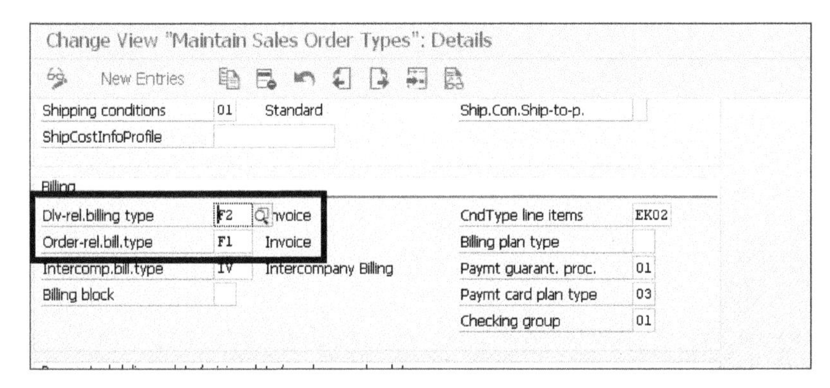

Figure 8.4 Assignment of Billing Type to Sales Order Type

As you can see, the standard delivery-related billing type is F2, and the standard order-related billing type is F1.

As with other sales and distribution documents, the structure of the billing document is separated into two levels: header and item. Additionally, as with other documents, there is an overview available that provides much of the pertinent information for the billing document. For billing, the overview screen is minimal, as shown in Figure 8.5.

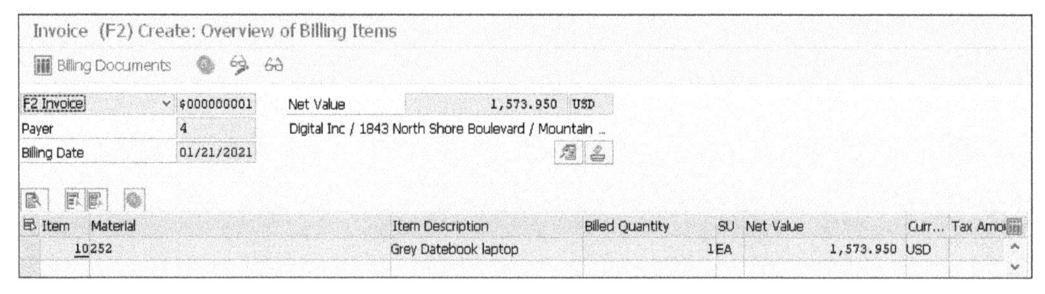

Figure 8.5 Billing Document: Overview

The overview shows the header data at the top and the items data at the bottom.

8.3.1 Header Data

To explore the header data, select the **Header** icon, or choose **Goto • Header • Header Detail**. This takes you into the main header area of the document, as shown in Figure 8.6.

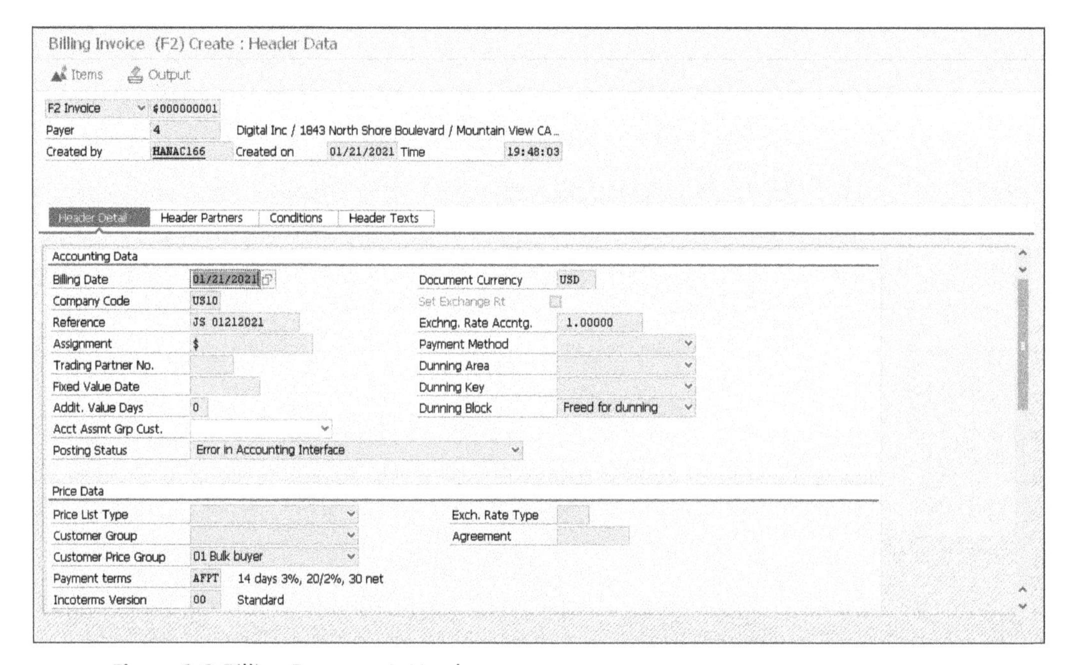

Figure 8.6 Billing Document: Header

Note

The key partner function used in the billing document is the payer. The payer partner function is where the credit limit is housed and where the debit on the accounting ledger entry is posted.

The first tab, **Header Detail**, separates the billing document data into four areas:

- **Accounting Data**
- **Price Data**
- **Taxes**
- **General Information**

Accounting Data

The most important field in the header **Accounting Data** section is the **Billing Date**, which is the date in which the invoice is processed and the date used to pass on to accounting. This date and, therefore, by definition, the date on which the billing document is created, can be derived in several ways:

- **Invoicing dates from customer**
  The **Invoicing Dates** field in the customer master record can be used to specify dates on which the customer can be billed (see Figure 8.7). For example, some customers require that they are only billed at the end or the beginning of each month.

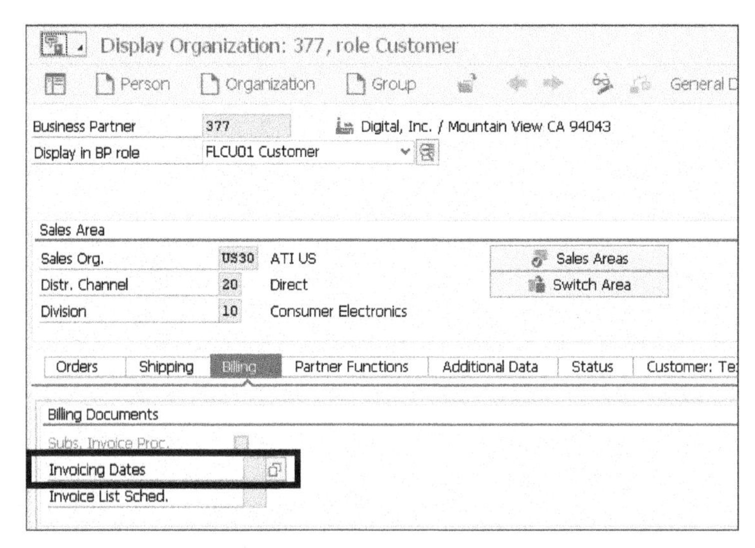

Figure 8.7 Invoicing Dates in the Customer Master

The field reads a factory calendar, which can be set up so that it only counts specific days and can exclude public holidays or weekend days, according to the definition of the calendar. In this way, for instance, a calendar can be selected that only allows billing on the last day of the month.

It's worth noting that the **Invoicing Dates** field can also be applied in the sales order manually, in the **Billing Document** tab, as shown in Figure 8.8. This field is automatically populated from the payer's customer master.

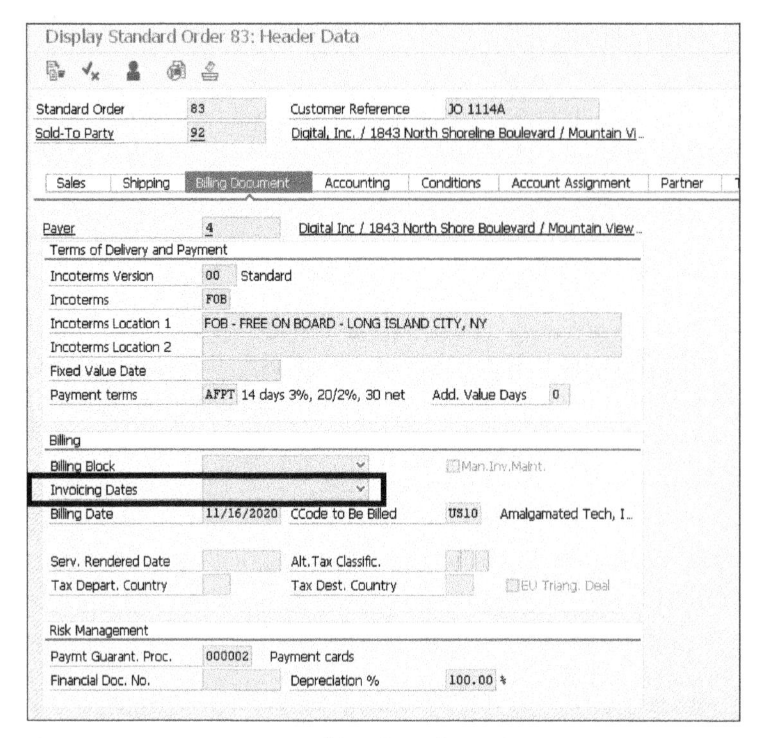

Figure 8.8 Invoicing Dates Field in the Sales Order

- **Actual goods issue (GI) date**
  If no **Invoicing Dates** field is specified, and the sales order is delivery-related billing, then the **Actual GI date** from the delivery is taken as the billing date. This can be seen in the delivery in Figure 8.9.

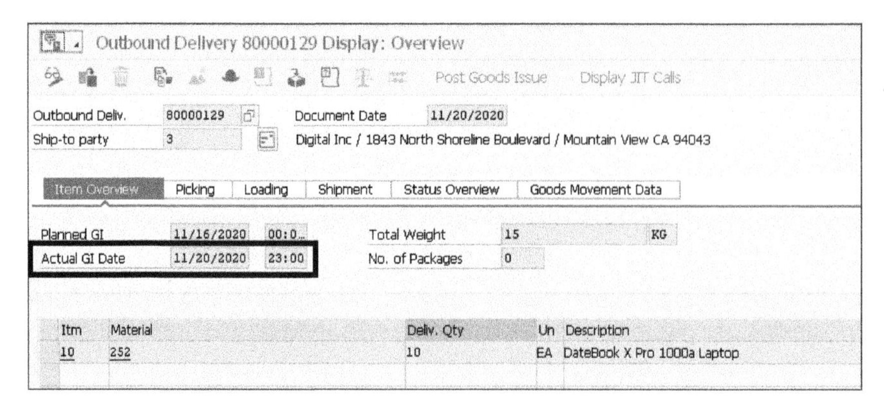

Figure 8.9 Actual GI Date in the Delivery Document

- **Billing date from the sales order**
  For order-related billing items, the **Billing Date** from the **Billing Document** tab in the sales order is used, as shown in Figure 8.10.

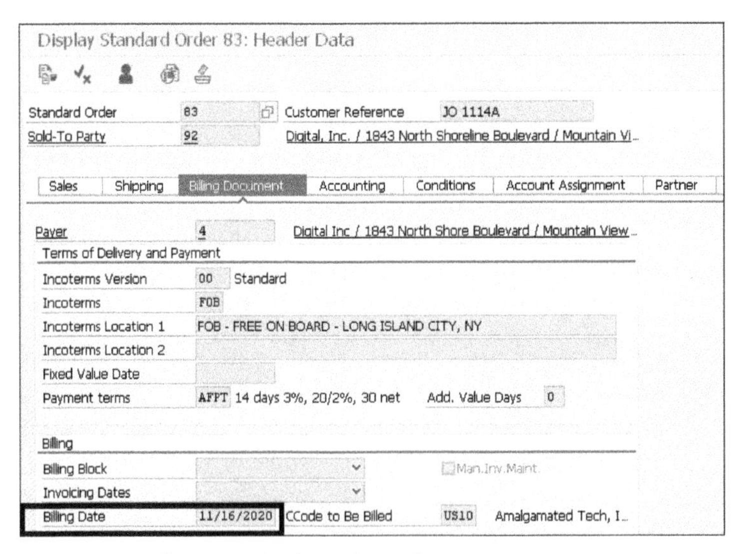

Figure 8.10 Billing Date in the Sales Order

- **Billing date from billing plan**
  Contracts for services and maintenance have a billing plan assigned to them (more details on this later in Section 8.5). The billing plan has billing dates assigned that are used to bill the item, as shown in the **Billing Date** field on the **Billing Plan** tab at the item level of the sales contract, as shown in Figure 8.11.

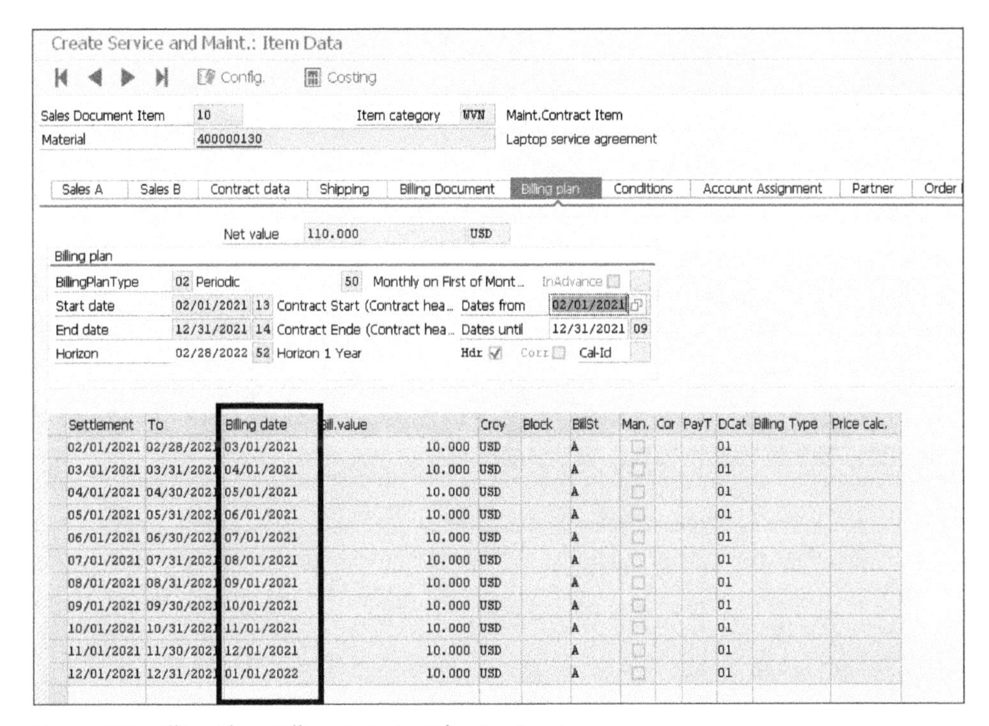

Figure 8.11 Billing Plan: Billing Date in Sales Contract

Additional accounting data items available in the billing document, as shown in Figure 8.6, include the following:

- **Assignment**
  This shows additional information for the accounting document in finance (also known as the journal entry).
- **Posting Status**
  This is the status of the transfer to accounting.

Price Data

Like the **Accounting Data** fields, many of the fields in the **Price Data** area of the billing document **Header Detail** tab are passed from the preceding document (either a sales order or a delivery document). These fields are shown in Figure 8.12.

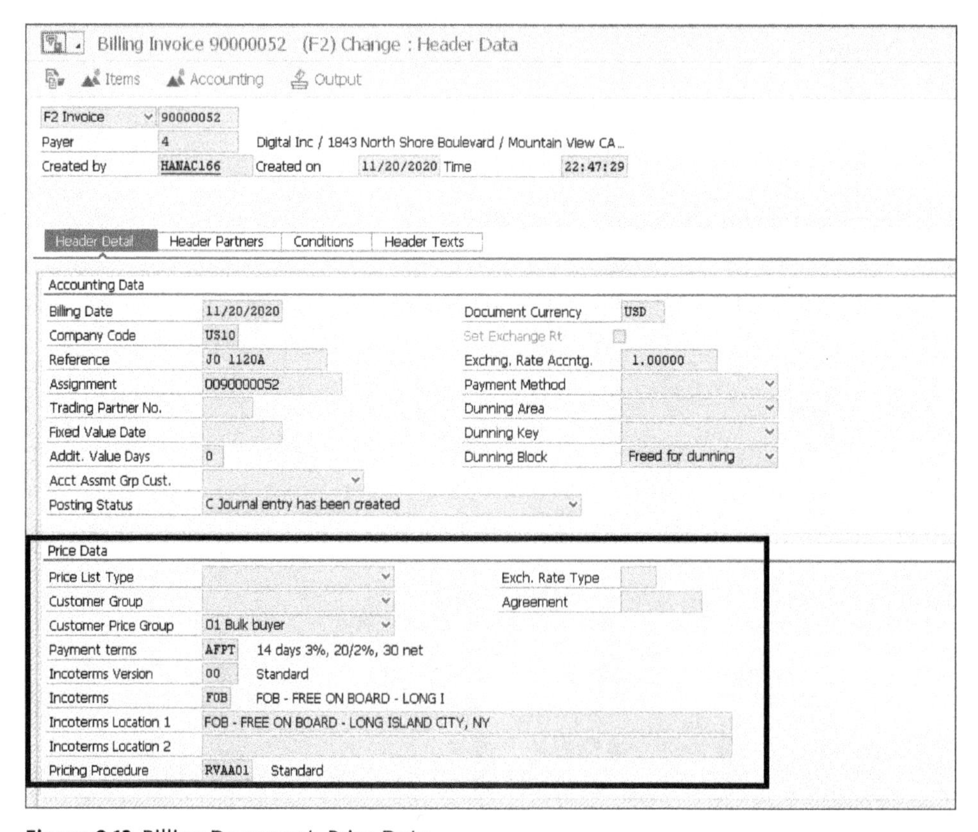

Figure 8.12 Billing Document: Price Data

Taxes

The data relevant for taxes is available in the **Taxes** section of the billing document **Header Detail** tab, as shown in Figure 8.13.

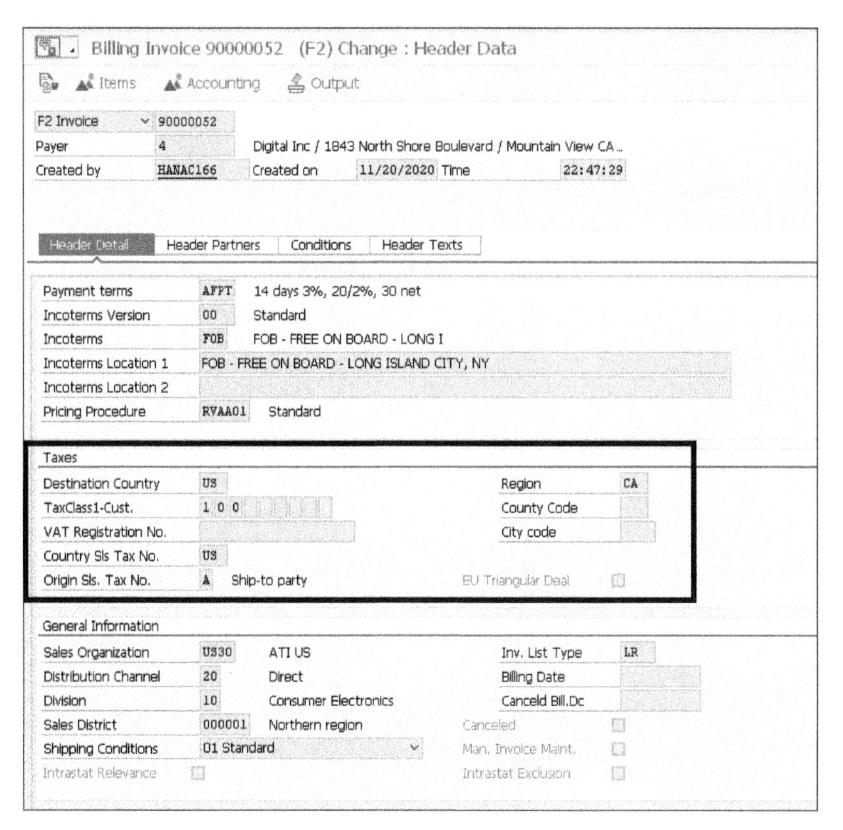

Figure 8.13 Billing Document: Taxes Data

The **Destination Country** and **Region** are taken from the ship-to party. The **County Code** and **City code** are specific to the United States for tax purposes, where county and city taxation rules can apply.

Much of the tax data in this section is determined according to a configuration setting that determines from where tax information should be retrieved. In Figure 8.13, the **Origin Sls. Tax No.** field shows **A Ship-to party** as the origin of the taxation fields. This determination follows a standard rule in configuration assigned to the sales organization. As mentioned, our example has determined the ship-to party as the source for tax determination, so the **TaxClass1-Cust.**, the **VAT Registration No.**, and the **Country Sls Tax No.** are all derived from the ship-to party.

The **EU Triangular Deal** checkbox is available in the sales order too. This is a manual setting and is used when trading within the European community. Under EU triangulation rules, trading where the sales organization, the ship-to party, and the plant are all in different EU countries must be registered in the EC Sales Listing as an EU triangulation deal. This flag controls this setting.

General Information

The **General Information** area shows additional information relevant for the header of the billing document, as shown in Figure 8.14.

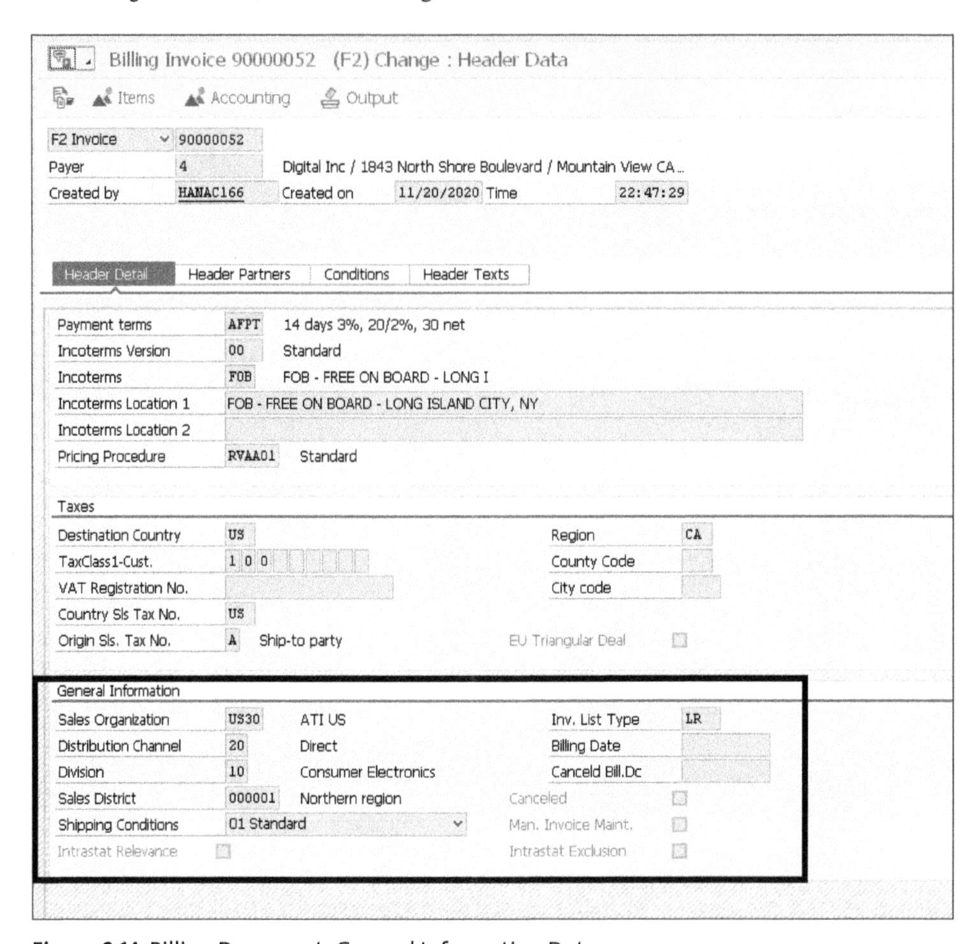

Figure 8.14 Billing Document: General Information Data

Each field in the Header Detail tab can be summarized as follows.

- **Sales Organization, Distribution Channel, Division, Sales District**, and **Shipping Conditions**
  These fields are all pulled in from the sales order.
- **Inv. List Type**
  This field is assigned to the billing type in configuration (invoice lists are discussed later in Section 8.8). The **Billing Date** field below **Inv. List Type** refers to the billing date for the invoice list.
- **Canceled**
  This checkbox indicates whether the billing document has been canceled with an invoice reversal document. An invoice reversal generates another SAP document on

the ledger, which is a reversal of the original invoice. The **Canceld Bill.Dc** field shows the number of the invoice reversal. More details on invoice cancellations can be found in Chapter 9, Section 9.12.

- **Man. Invoice Maint.**
  If checked, this will hold the invoice from being released to accounting. The setting can be maintained in the customer master and is pulled through to the sales order, where it can be manually overridden if required.
- **Intrastat Relevance**
  This is checked when the departure country and destination country are both in the European Union.
- **Intrastat Exclusion**
  This is checked to exclude the invoice from inclusion in the EU Intrastat report.

Billing Header Partners

The **Header Partners** tab in the billing document header shows the partners that are relevant for billing documents. Within the standard SAP system, this is the sold-to party, the bill-to party, and the payer, as shown in Figure 8.15.

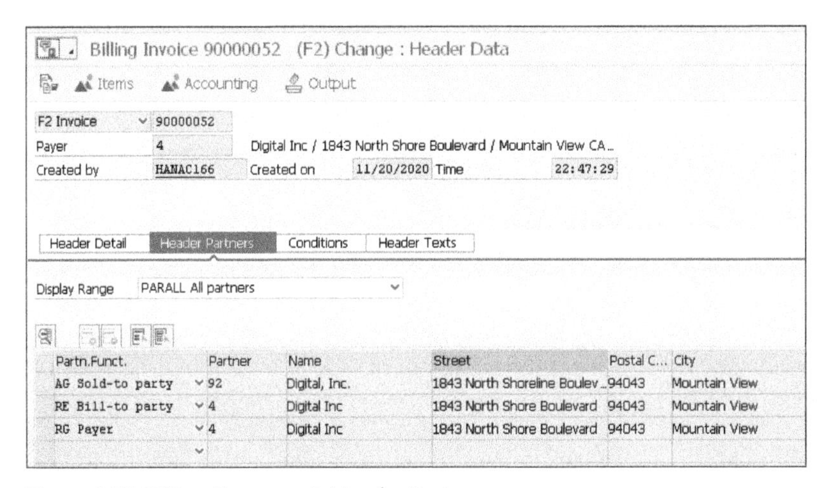

Figure 8.15 Billing Document: Header Partners

Billing Conditions

Prices in the preceding documents are pulled into the header **Conditions** tab. The prices of all the items are rolled up into the header **Conditions** tab to give a full grand total of each pricing condition, as shown in Figure 8.16.

> **Note**
>
> Pricing in the billing document is usually, but not always, copied from the preceding document. In some cases, the pricing may need to be redetermined, and this is set in

the configuration of the copy control from the preceding document to the billing document.

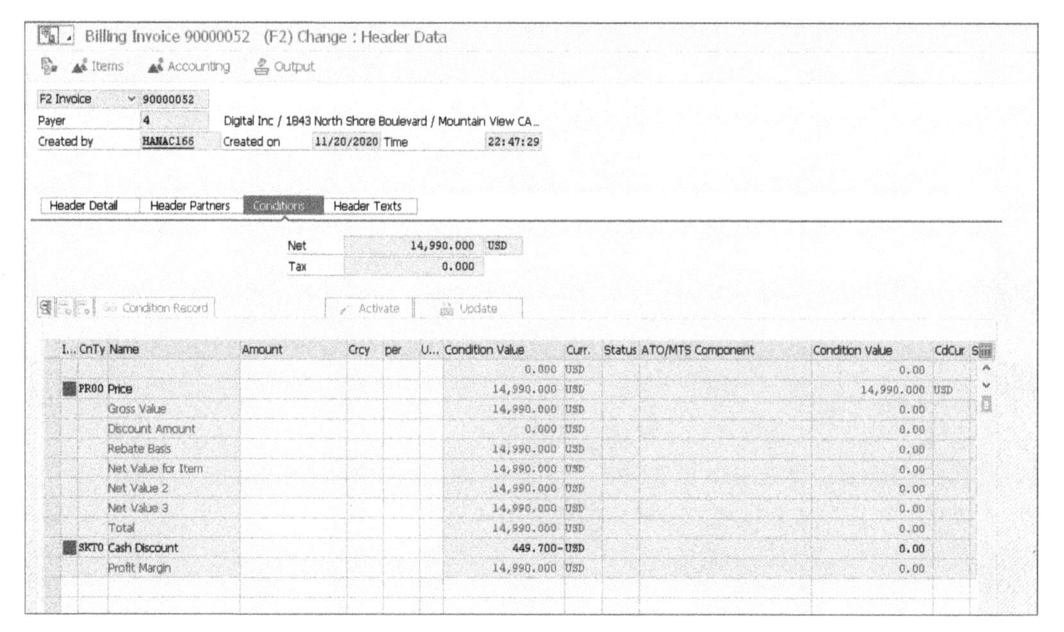

Figure 8.16 Billing Document: Header Conditions

Billing Header Texts

Texts in the billing document can be determined from master data (e.g., the customer master) or can be pulled in from source documents (e.g., the delivery or sales order). This is controlled by the text type (**Txt ty.**), shown in Figure 8.17.

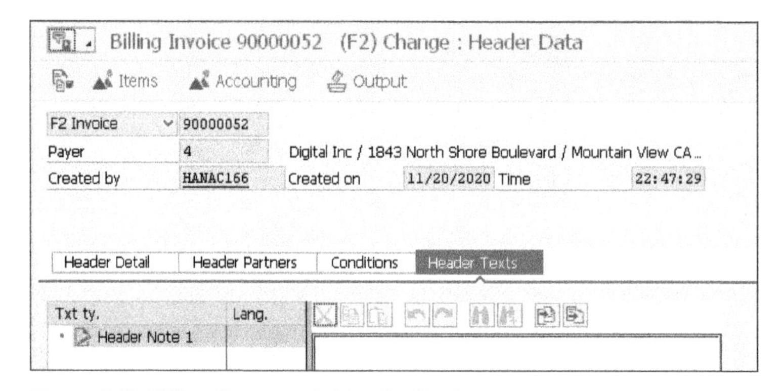

Figure 8.17 Billing Document: Header Texts

In this example, there is only one text type, **Header Note 1**, which has no text applied. Text can be manually added here on creation of the billing document too.

8.3.2 Billing Item Data

You can access the billing item data by double-clicking one of the line items from the overview screen, or by highlighting the line, and selecting **Goto • Item • Choose** from the menu bar. This takes you to the **Item Detail** tab of the item data, as shown in Figure 8.18.

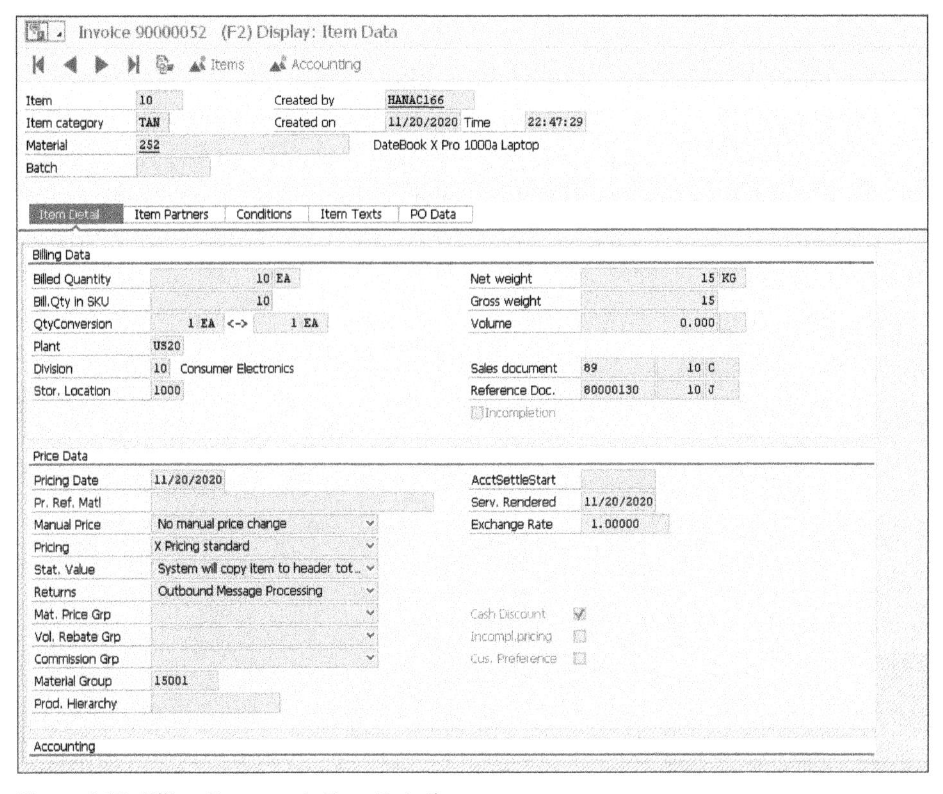

Figure 8.18 Billing Document: Item Detail

The **Item Detail** tab is separated into five areas: **Billing Data**, **Price Data**, **Accounting**, **Account Assignment**, and **Sales Order Data**.

Billing Data

The billing data is composed entirely of data pulled in from the sales order and the delivery, as shown in Figure 8.19.

Each field in the **Item Detail** tab can be summarized as follows.

- **Billed Quantity**
  This field is populated by the quantity from the delivery that was goods issued. If the billing document is an order-related billing document, then this quantity is determined by the order quantity or the billing plan in the case of contracts.

- **Bill.Qty in SKU**
  This field refers to the quantity that was delivered and goods issued in the unit of measure used in the stock-keeping unit (SKU). It's not unusual for a delivery to be created in a unit of measure such as casks, while the selling unit of measure is different, perhaps in bottles.
- **QtyConversion**
  This field converts the delivered quantity into the billed quantity via a unit of measure conversion factor, which is specified in the material master record.

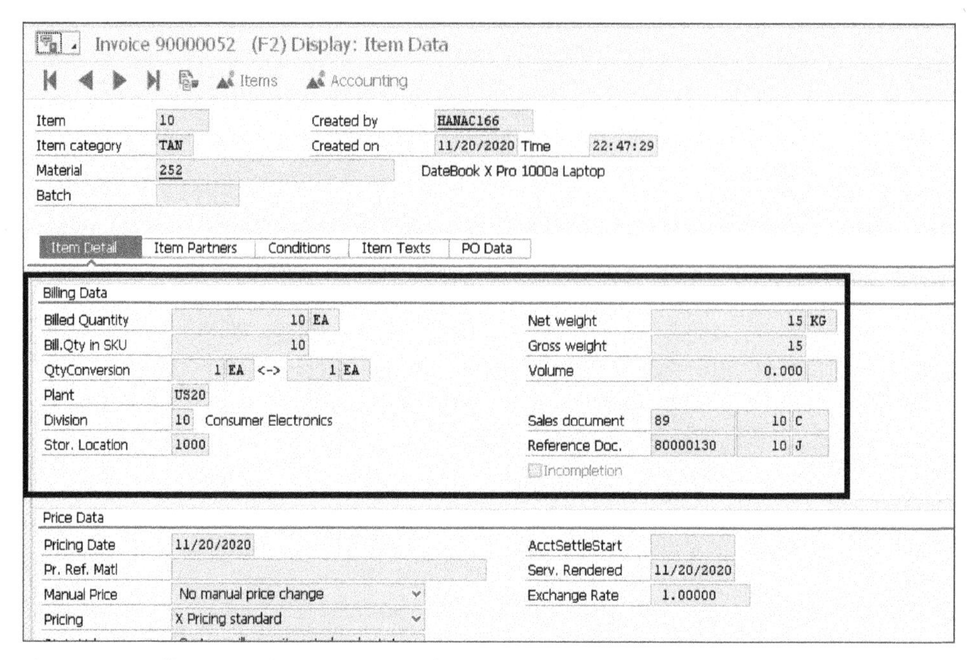

Figure 8.19 Billing Document: Item Detail

Price Data

The **Price Data** area in the billing document shows all the transactional and master data fields that have been pulled into the billing document from other documents or master data objects for use in deriving a price (see Figure 8.20).

Each field in the **Price Data** section can be summarized as follows:

- **Pricing Date**
  This is the date the system uses to determine the price in the billing document; it's proposed from the **Billing Date**.
- **Pr. Ref. Matl**
  This is the material used as a reference to determine the pricing. This field is pulled in from the same field in the sales order.

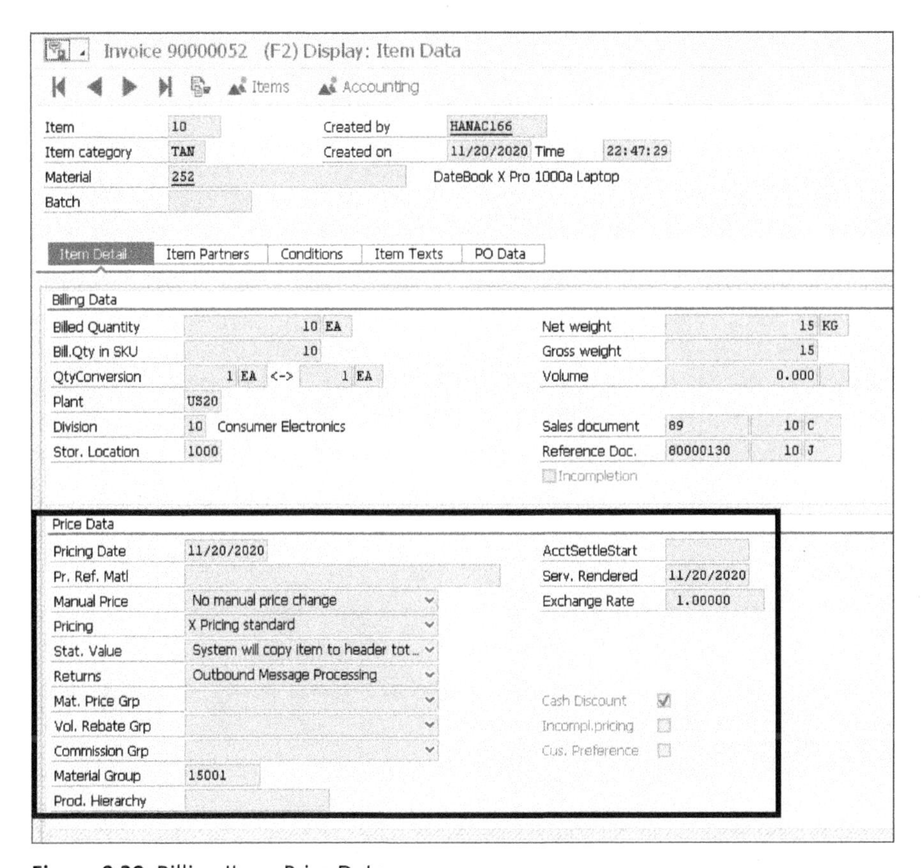

Figure 8.20 Billing Item: Price Data

- **Manual Price**
  This field shows the status of the pricing as to whether there has been any manual intervention for the item price.
- **Pricing**
  This field shows the setting behind the configuration of the pricing in your system. Most standard items will use **Pricing Standard.** However, some items, such as returnable packaging, will have the setting **Pricing for Empties** here. Where the item is billed as a result of a free goods determination, the setting will be **Pricing for Free Goods (100% Discount).**
- **Stat. Value**
  This is determined by the configuration of the item and indicates whether the system will take the value of the item into account when calculating the total document value.

- **Returns**
  This field is an indicator to determine whether the document item refers to an outbound movement of goods or services or a return. This is usually [blank] for **Outbound Processing,** such as standard invoices and debits, and set to **X** for **Returns** for returns and credits.
- **Mat. Price Grp, Vol. Rebate Grp, Commission Grp, Material Group, Prod. Hierarchy**
  These fields are all taken from the preceding sales order and are master data assigned to the material.
- **Serv. Rendered**
  This is the date that the system will use to calculate taxes. For delivery-related items, this refers to the GI date. For order-related items where a service is being billed and you want to bill for hours, for example, then it's possible to enter this date manually.

Accounting

The **Accounting** section in the **Item Detail** tab shows all the fields that are used in the calculation of the correct accounting information for the purposes of account determination in finance. The billing item accounting data is shown in Figure 8.21.

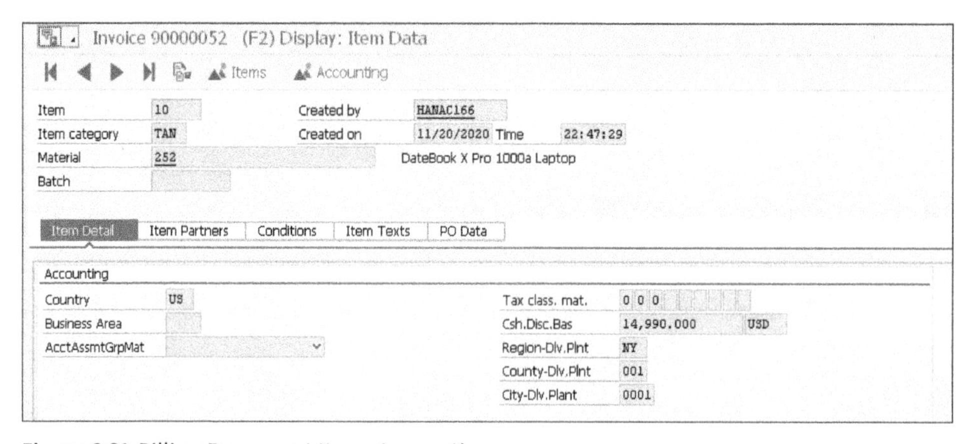

Figure 8.21 Billing Document Item: Accounting

The **Country** field in this section specifies the departure country of the goods (the country of the plant) and is used for calculation of taxes. The **Region-Dlv.Plnt**, **County-Dlv.Plnt**, and **City-Dlv.Plnt** are also derived from the plant.

Account Assignment

The **Account Assignment** section, shown in Figure 8.22, contains financial information related to the allocation of cost and profit. From a sales and distribution process perspective, this information isn't a concern.

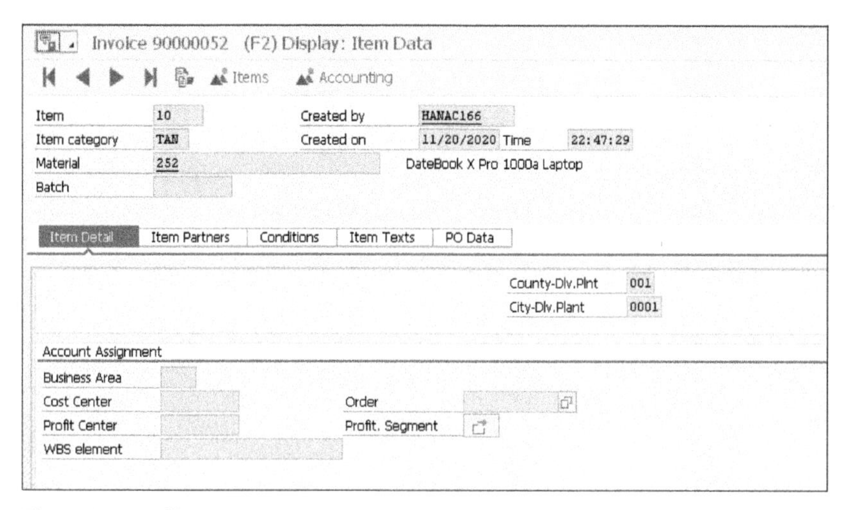

Figure 8.22 Billing Document Item: Account Assignment

Sales Order Data

The **Sales Order Data** section of the **Item Detail** tab shows the details that have been pulled in from the sales order for the item in question, as shown in Figure 8.23.

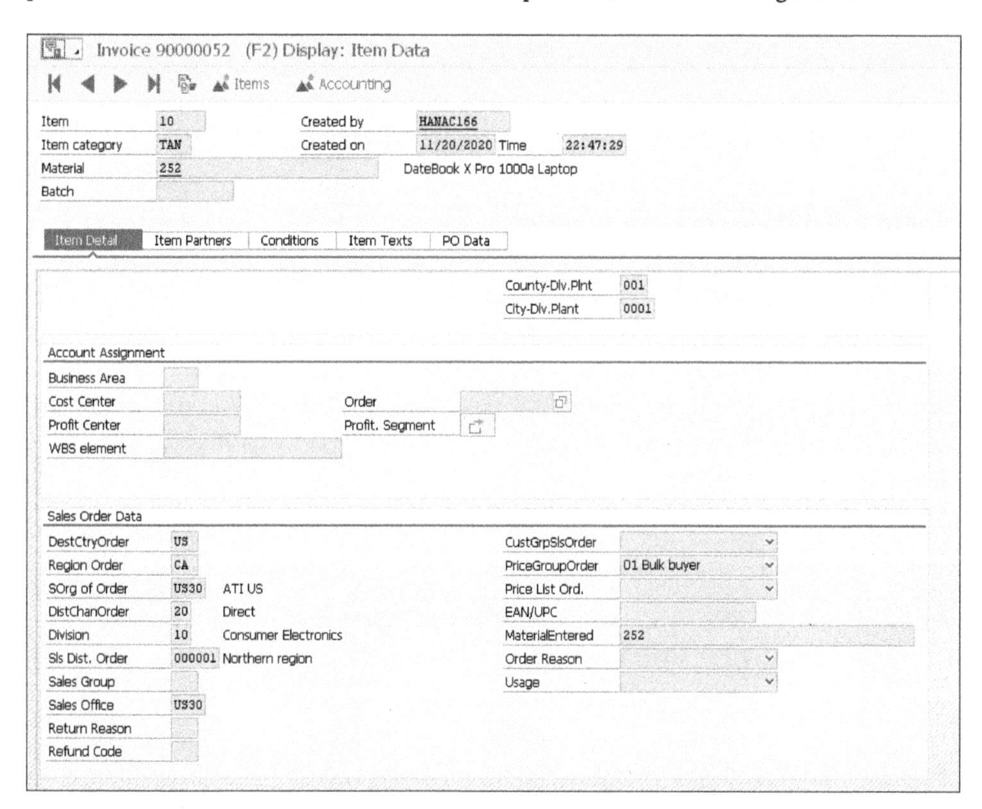

Figure 8.23 Billing Document Item: Sales Order Data

The data held here is all pulled from the sales order item.

8.3.3 Item Partners

The **Item Partners** tab holds all the partners that are relevant for billing items. These partners are copied down from the header partners in many cases, such as for sold-to, bill-to, and payer functions. However, additional partners are relevant for items; in the standard SAP system, this includes the ship-to party. This means items within a single billing document can have a different ship-to party, as shown in Figure 8.24.

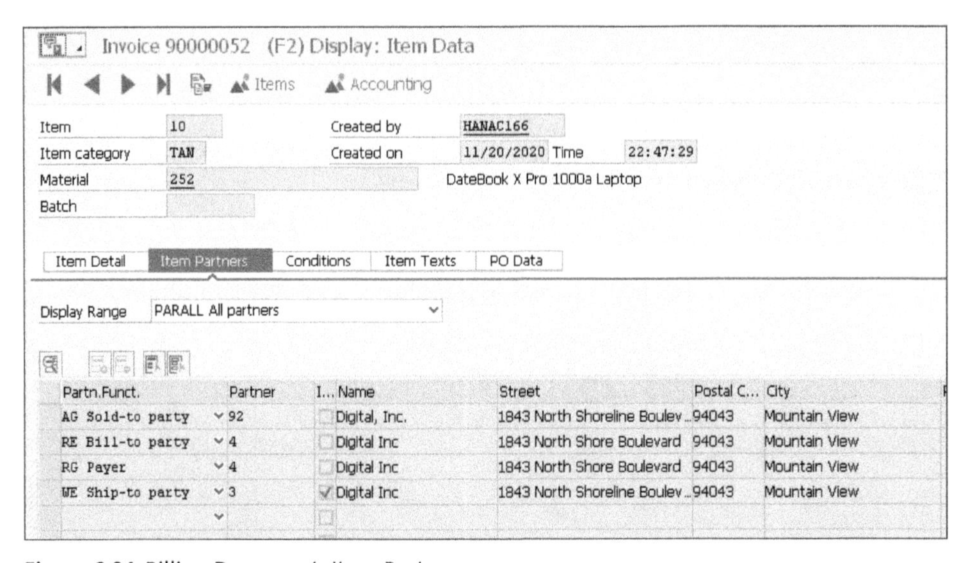

Figure 8.24 Billing Document: Item Partners

The billing **Item Partners** tab shows the business partners that are used for the billing document. You'll notice that the **Sold-to party**, the **Bill-to party**, and the **Payer** are all also included in the billing document header **Partners** tab. This is because these functions are cascaded down to the items. The exception here is the **Ship-to party**, which has a tick in the box in the **Item Partners** column. This shows that the ship-to party is actually an item-level partner function and can differ for each item.

8.3.4 Conditions

The **Conditions** tab is where all the pricing is housed in the billing document (see Figure 8.25), in the same way as it's housed in the **Conditions** tab of the sales order.

The billing document item **Conditions** tab shows the prices, discounts, surcharges, and taxes relevant for that specific item in the billing document. This detail is normally copied from the sales order unchanged, although it's typical to redetermine taxes in the billing document. All these copy control settings are carried out in configuration of the SAP S/4HANA system.

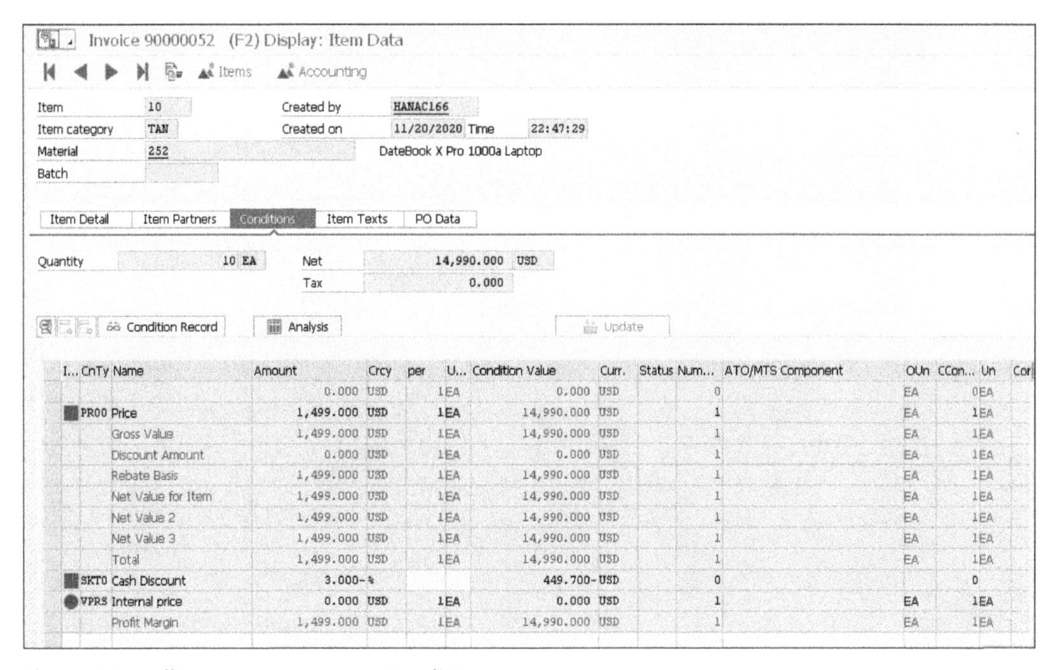

Figure 8.25 Billing Document Item: Conditions

8.3.5 Item Texts

Item texts are determined for billing documents in the same way they are for header texts, except they refer to item-level fields such as materials. Depending on the text types, they can be copied from preceding documents or be manually entered (see Figure 8.26).

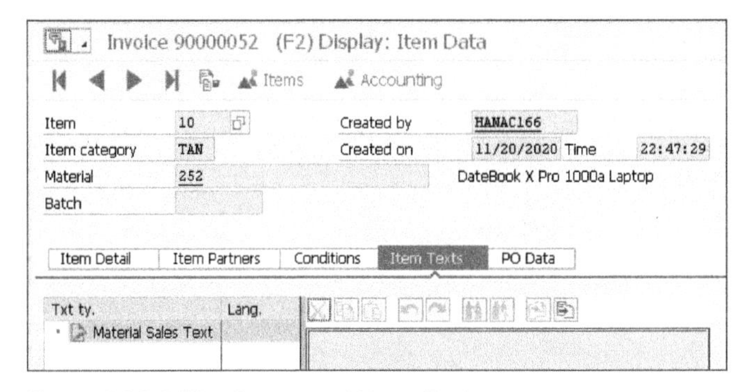

Figure 8.26 Billing Document Item: Texts

8.3.6 PO Data

The **PO Data** tab houses all the data relating to the customer's purchase order, which was used to create the original sales order (see Figure 8.27). All the information in this tab is pulled directly from the sales order item.

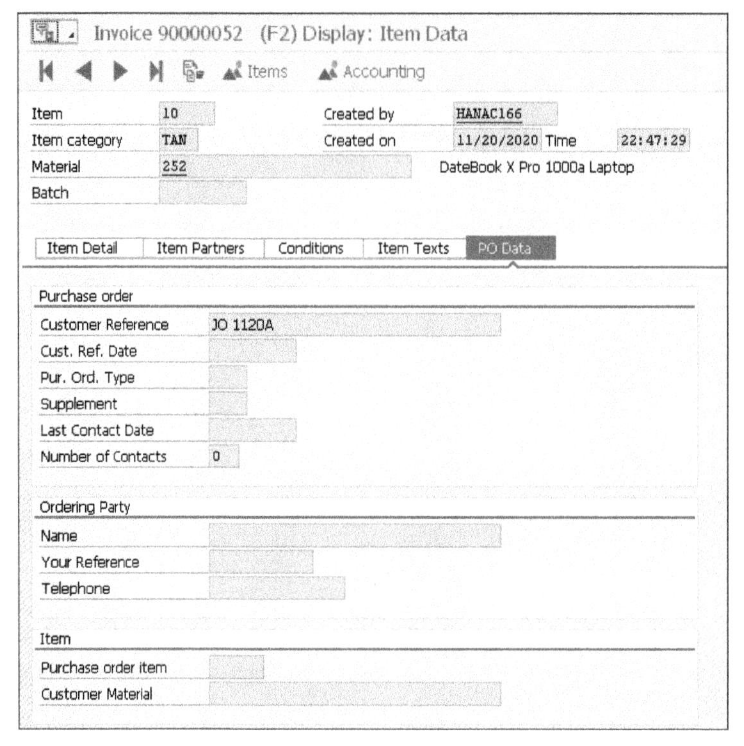

Figure 8.27 Billing Document Item: PO Data

After the billing document is saved, an entry is placed in the document flow in the same way as for the other sales documents we've explored so far (see Figure 8.28).

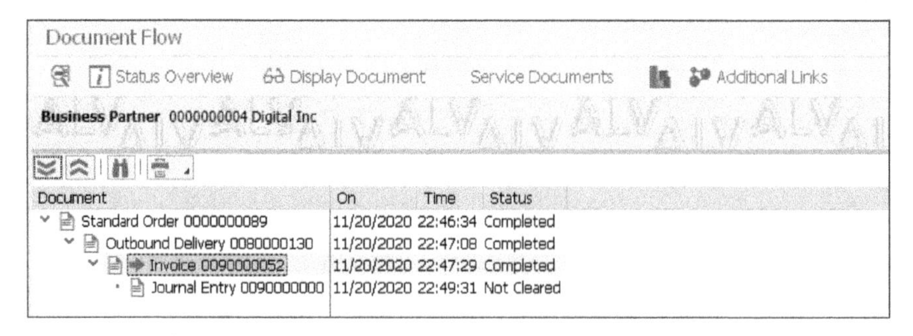

Figure 8.28 Billing Document Flow

You can see that the billing document, once saved, has an entry entitled **Journal Entry**. We'll cover this further when we discuss the transfer to accounting in Section 8.8.3.

Note

As with other documents, when launching the document flow, you'll only see documents that relate to the specific document you're viewing. Therefore, when viewing the document flow for a billing document, you won't see, for example, picking or packing documents, as they are assigned to the delivery and have no bearing on the billing document.

8.4 Debit Memos and Credit Memos

Now that we've explored the basic structure around an SAP S/4HANA billing document, let's review some other types of billing documents aside from standard invoices.

Debit memos and credit memos are types of billing documents created in response to a customer complaint. Their overall effect on financial receivables is as follows:

- **Credit memo**
  Reduces financial receivables, as a credit is posted to the customer's account.
- **Debit memo**
  Increases financial receivables, as a debit is posted to the customer's account.

Credit memos and debit memos are typically created due to incorrect pricing or defective goods. Credit memos and debit memos are created with reference to credit memo requests and debit memo requests, which are sales order types (see Chapter 6, Section 6.2.7).

Credit memos and debit memos are created as order-related billing, so they don't have delivery documents allocated to them; the billing document is created directly with reference to the credit/debit memo request sales order. The standard SAP S/4HANA billing type for credit memos is G2 and for debit memos is L2. It's not uncommon for these documents, especially for credit memo billing documents, to have their own number range. Aside from the billing type and the description, the SAP billing document for credit and debit memos looks the same as a standard invoice when viewed in Transaction VF03, as shown in Figure 8.29.

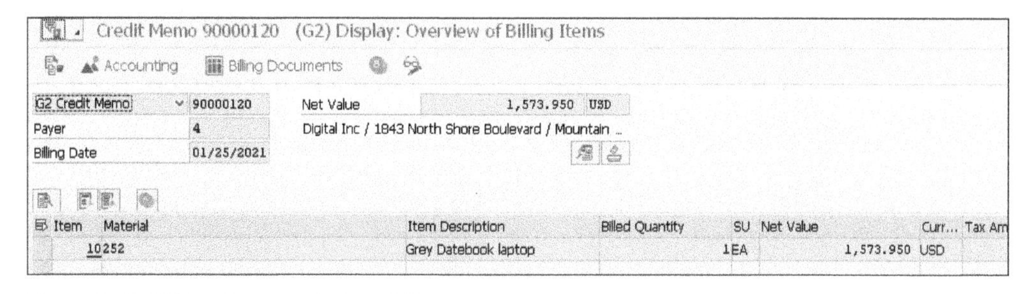

Figure 8.29 Billing Document: Credit Memo

A few changes can be seen in the item details for credit memos and debit memos. The reference sales order has a document category assigned to it, which is different from standard sales orders. Credit memo request sales orders have a document category of

K, which can be seen in Figure 8.30, whereas debit memo request sales order have a document category of L and standard sales orders C. Additionally, the **Returns** field in the credit memo **Item Detail** tab has the value **X Returns** to denote that the item isn't an outbound processed item such as a standard sale or debit.

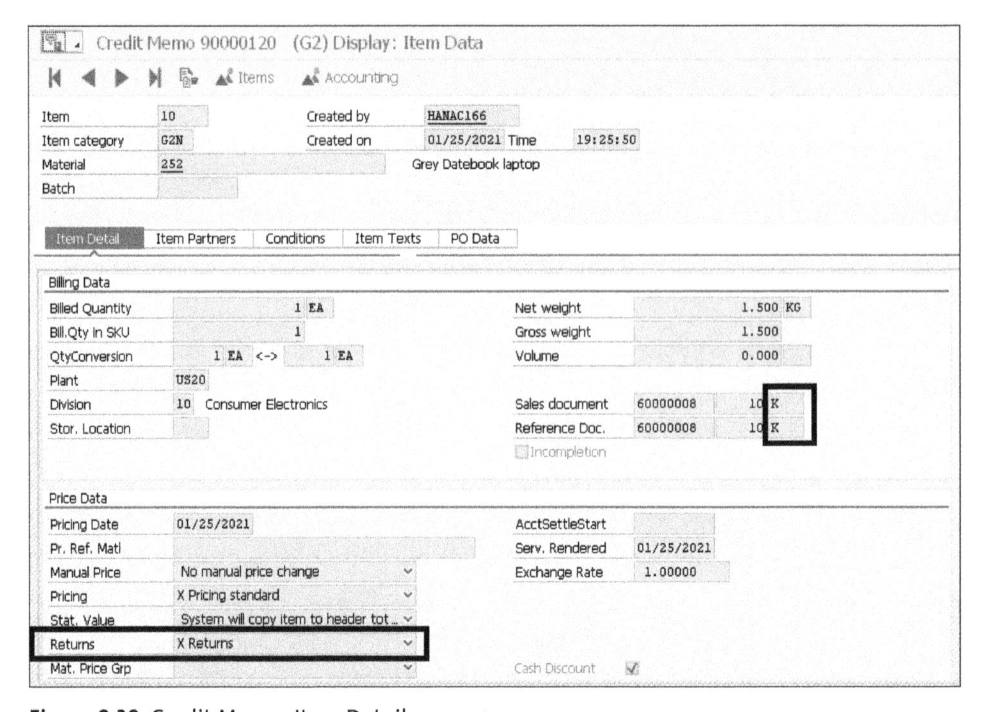

Figure 8.30 Credit Memo: Item Detail

8.5 Billing Plans

SAP S/4HANA billing plans are simply a schedule of dates for which billing should take place for a given item. Normally, a billing plan is assigned to an item in a contract, so that billing for the item can be scheduled out into the future. However, it's possible, though unusual, to create billing plans for sales orders.

> **Note**
>
> Billing plans can be defined at the header level in contract documents. When defined at the header level, all the items follow the same billing schedule.

The definition of whether an item is relevant for a billing plan is determined according to the item category. The billing relevance of the item category tells SAP S/4HANA whether to create a billing plan. If the billing relevance determines a billing plan, an additional **Item** tab will become available in the sales document to show the billing plan. It's normal practice in contracts for all items to have billing plans, as shown in Figure 8.31.

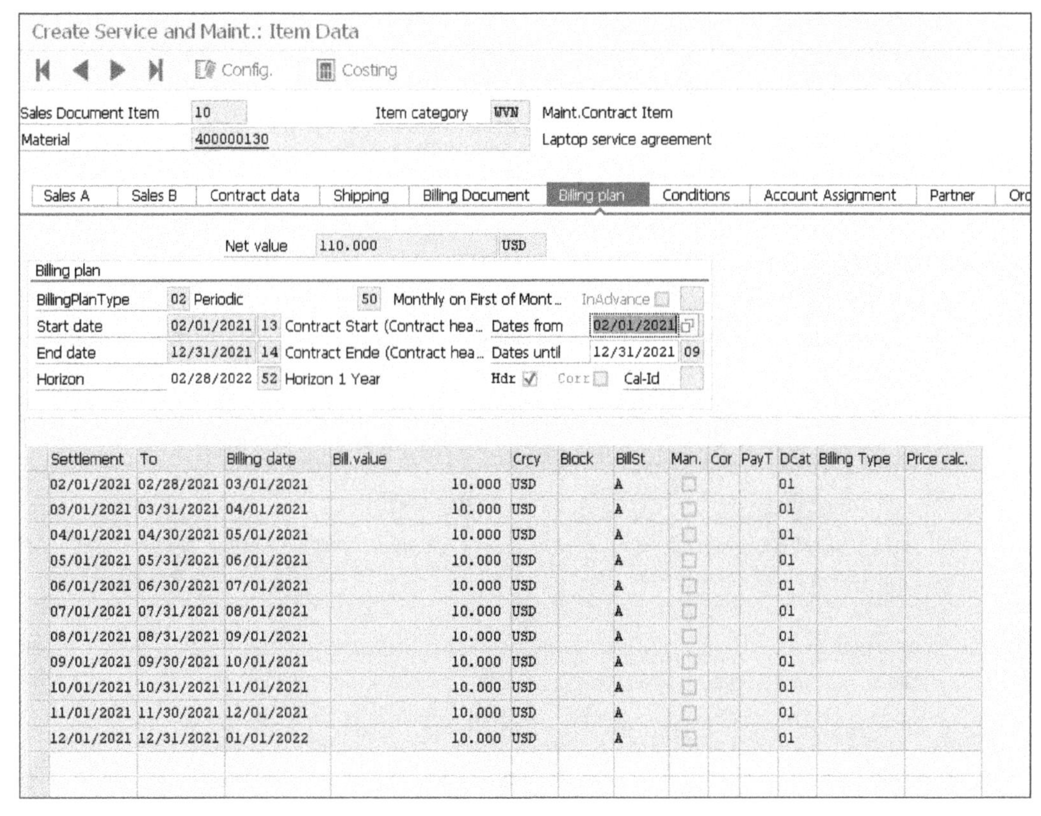

Figure 8.31 Billing Plan in Contract

SAP S/4HANA has two types of billing plans available:

- **Periodic billing**
  Denoted by **BillingPlanType 02**. The total amount of the item is billed for each billing date in the billing plan. The start and end date of the billing plan are taken directly from the contract start and end date. The number of billing lines are determined according to the field "the rule for the origin of next billing/invoice date", which in Figure 8.31, has a value of 50. In configuration, this value is set to **Monthly on the first of the month**. As a result, there are 11 billing plan lines, determined by virtue of the fact that the start date is January 2nd, and the end date is December 31st, and within those from and to dates are 11 "first of the months."

- **Milestone billing**
  Denoted by **BillingPlanType 01**. The total amount of the item is shared between specific dates allocated to milestones. These milestones are created within the project systems functional area of SAP S/4HANA. Typically, you would use this approach

when you need to bill your customer a percentage of the overall amount when certain milestones are reached (e.g., milestone billing is commonly used in the construction industry).

For both types of billing plan, when creating a billing document, the billing date is always taken from the billing plan.

8.6 Intercompany Billing

Within large organizations, the concept of intercompany billing is very common. When a plant ships products direct to a customer, but the plant belongs to a different company code from the selling organization of the sales order, intercompany billing is triggered.

Let's look at a standard example, which isn't relevant for intercompany billing, and compare it with a scenario that is relevant:

- Customer: 92
- Sales organization: US30
- Material: 252
- Quantity: 10
- Plant: US20

To determine whether a scenario is relevant for intercompany billing, you need to look at the organizational units in the document:

- Sales organization: US30
- Plant: US20

In this example, sales organization US30 belongs to company code US10 in the underlying configuration of SAP S/4HANA, as shown in Figure 8.32.

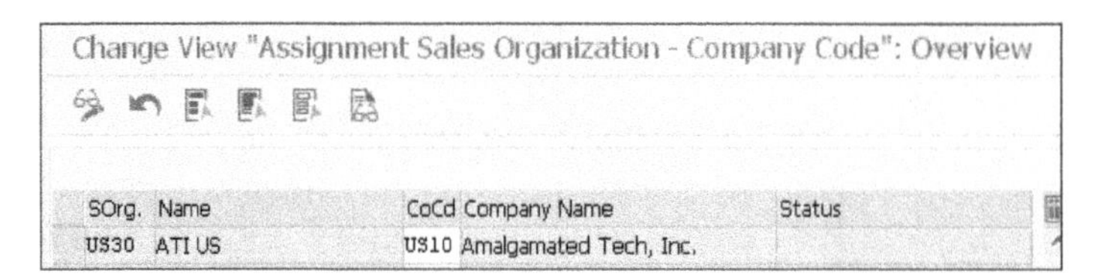

Figure 8.32 Assignment of Sales Organization to Company Code in Configuration

Now let's look at the assignment of the plant to the company code.

As shown in Figure 8.32 and Figure 8.33, the plant and the sales organization are both assigned to the same company code. This means that the selling organization and the shipping organization are owned by the same entity, so no intercompany billing is required.

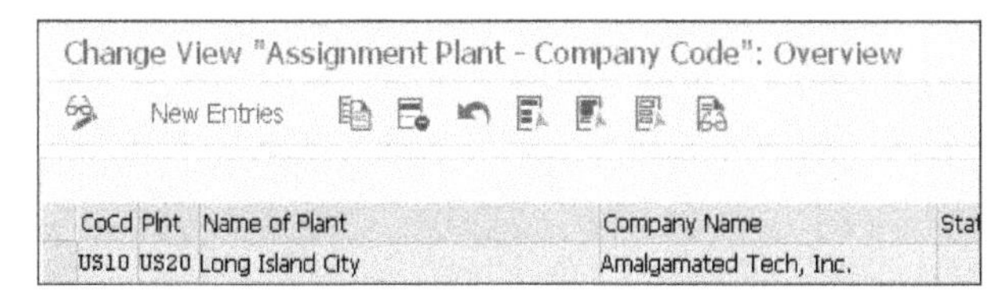

Figure 8.33 Assignment of Plant to Company Code

Let's compare this with another scenario:

- Customer: 92
- Sales organization: US30
- Material: 252
- Quantity: 10
- Plant: MX10

To determine whether a scenario is relevant for intercompany billing, you again need to look at the organizational units in the document:

- Sales organization: US30
- Plant: MX20

We've already established that sales organization US30 is owned by company code US10. However, plant MX20 is owned by company code MX10. Therefore, this is an intercompany billing scenario.

So, how does intercompany billing work? SAP S/4HANA automatically recognizes that it's dealing with two separate company codes and therefore understands that it needs to generate two billing documents from the delivery. The first billing document will be the standard billing document to the customer, billing type F2, for delivery-related billing. The second document will be the intercompany billing document, billing type IV.

In the example shown in Figure 8.34, you can see the **Status Overview** tab in the delivery document. At the item level, there is an intercompany billing status. For standard deliveries not relevant for intercompany billing, this would be blank.

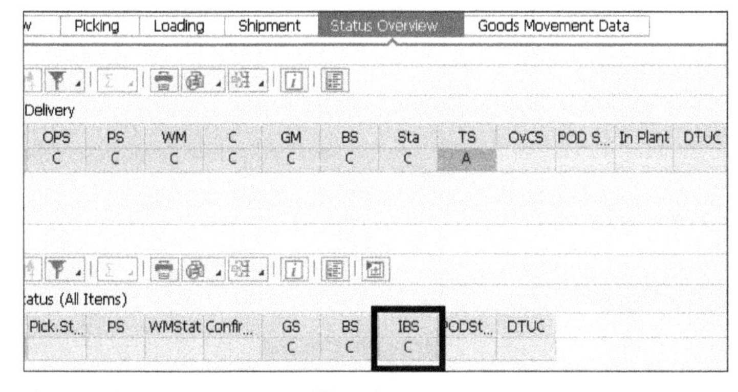

Figure 8.34 Intercompany Billing Status

Both the standard billing document and the intercompany billing document will both appear in the document flow for the delivery.

8.7 Creating a Billing Document

As already mentioned, billing documents can be created from a delivery, where delivery-related billing is relevant, or from a sales order, where order-related billing is relevant. Both of these options use the same methods:

- Transaction VF01 to create a single billing document
- Transaction VF04 for multiple billing documents
- Create Billing Documents app in SAP Fiori
- Create Billing Documents – Billing Due List Items app in SAP Fiori

8.7.1 Creating a Billing Document Using Transaction VF01

Billing documents are normally created collectively using an overnight batch run, but it's possible, and not unusual, to create a billing document manually. For this approach, you use SAP GUI Transaction VF01. Both order-related and delivery-related billing can be carried out in Transaction VF01. In this section, we'll explore how to create a single billing document with reference to the source: either a sales order, as in order-related billing, or a delivery, as in delivery-related billing.

8.7.2 Delivery-Related Billing

In this example, sales order number 223 has a delivery-related item that has been delivered and goods issued under delivery 80000179 and is therefore ready to be billed. Follow these steps:

1. Enter Transaction "VF01", or choose **Logistics • Sales and Distribution • Billing • Billing Document • Create.**
2. Add the delivery document number "80000179" into the **Document** field. There are other fields available at this point, but none are required when billing an entire delivery document. However, the options are there to default additional data into the ensuing billing document, such as the **Billing Type**, **Billing Date**, **Serv. Rendered**, **Pricing Date**, or **Item**, as shown in Figure 8.35.
3. Press Enter to enter into the billing document details. From here you can navigate around the header and item sections of the billing document, as discussed earlier in this chapter. It's not necessary to enter any further details at this point; your billing document is ready to be saved.

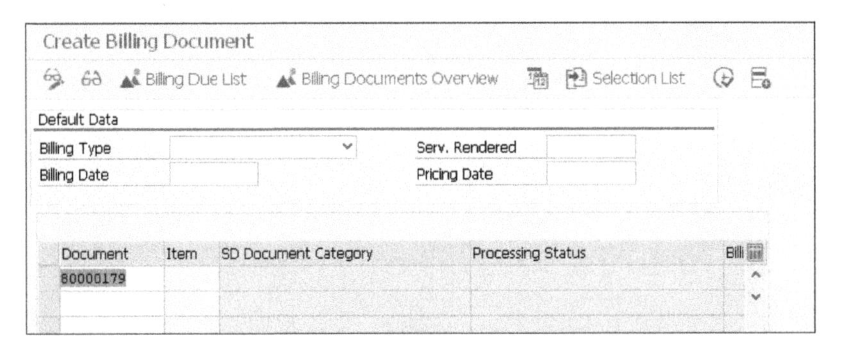

Figure 8.35 Creation of Billing Document in Transaction VF01

Once saved, the document flow for your billing document will look like Figure 8.36.

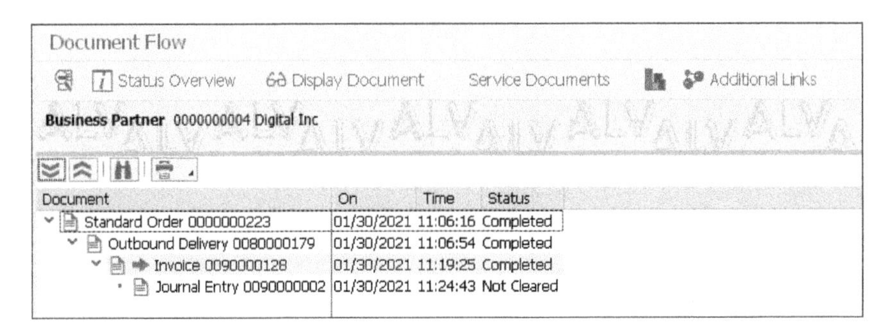

Figure 8.36 Billing Document Flow

Remember that the document flow always starts from the document you entered. Looking at the billing document, the document flow only shows the documents that are directly related to the billing document. This is why you can't see the documents such as picking and GI because these are related to the delivery only and have no bearing on the billing document.

Another document you can see in the document flow is the **Journal Entry**. This document is posted to the financial ledger in SAP S/4HANA and is often also referred to as an accounting document. We'll discuss the transfer to accounting later in Section 8.8.3.

Note

Several requirements must be met before a billing document can be created. These requirements can be customized in the copy control area of SAP S/4HANA configuration. However, standard copy control rules won't allow a billing document to be created if the source document or sales order has a billing block assigned to it, or the customer has a billing block on their master data. Additional checks include that for third-party sales, the invoice receipt must have been posted for the assigned purchase order.

8.7.3 Order-Related Billing

In this example, contract number 40000009 is set to order-related billing via the settings for the item category.

> **Note**
>
> You can create a billing document for order-related billing items directly from the sales order or contract in Transactions VA03/VA43 or Transactions VA02/VA42 by selecting **Sales Order • Billing** from the menu bar.

You can bill the contract in the same way you bill the delivery-related sales order. Remember, the contract has a billing plan with separate billing dates, as shown in Figure 8.37. This is important when you come to order-related billing through Transaction VF01, as you'll see.

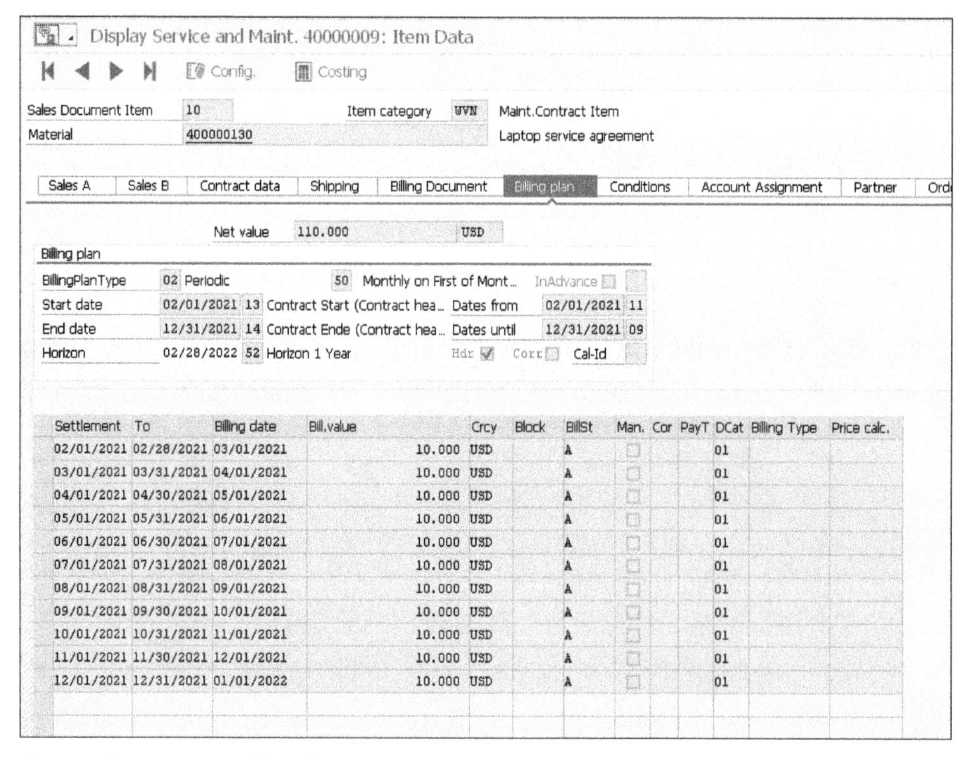

Figure 8.37 Contract Billing Plan

To bill the contract, follow these steps:

1. Enter Transaction "VF01" or choose **Logistics • Sales and Distribution • Billing • Billing Document • Create**.
2. Enter contract number "40000009" into the **Document** field.

Press [Enter], and you're taken to a billing document overview screen, as shown in Figure 8.38. This overview shows you that for this document, there are 11 lines that require billing. As you can see from the billing plan in Figure 8.37, each of these lines has a different billing date. It's important, therefore, to understand that Transaction VF01 is a crude tool for billing contracts as all the billing dates will be billed at once. In this example, 11 different billing documents are created because the billing date is a part of the billing split criteria (invoice splits are discussed further in Section 8.8.1).

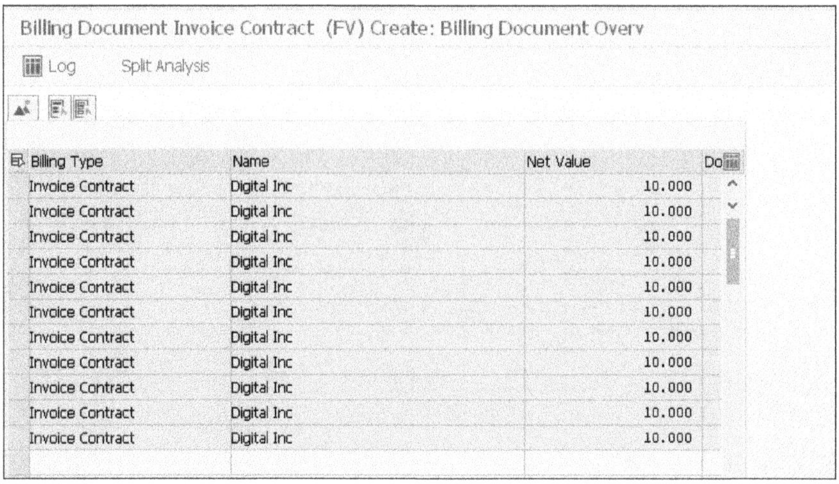

Billing Document Invoice Contract (FV) Create: Billing Document Overv

Log Split Analysis

Billing Type	Name	Net Value	Do
Invoice Contract	Digital Inc	10.000	
Invoice Contract	Digital Inc	10.000	
Invoice Contract	Digital Inc	10.000	
Invoice Contract	Digital Inc	10.000	
Invoice Contract	Digital Inc	10.000	
Invoice Contract	Digital Inc	10.000	
Invoice Contract	Digital Inc	10.000	
Invoice Contract	Digital Inc	10.000	
Invoice Contract	Digital Inc	10.000	
Invoice Contract	Digital Inc	10.000	
Invoice Contract	Digital Inc	10.000	

Figure 8.38 Contract Billing Overview

Once saved, the billing document appears in the document flow as normal.

8.7.4 Creating a Billing Document Using Transaction VF04

Using Transaction VF04 is a much more flexible way of generating billing documents. A selection screen is provided for selecting the correct sales orders and deliveries to be billed. Furthermore, you can restrict your selection by many more criteria, meaning you don't have to specify the document number to be billed. In this way, Transaction VF04 is the generally accepted method for running overnight billing for all relevant documents. The selection screen is shown in Figure 8.39.

Let's run this transaction with the following settings:

- **Billing Date From = [blank]; To = "03/01/2021"**
  This means that all documents with a billing date up to and including 03/01/2021 will be selected for billing.
- **Sales Organization = "US30"**
  Only documents in US30 will be selected.

- **Order-Related**
  Select this checkbox so that all documents relevant for order-related billing will be selected.
- **Delivery-Related**
  Select this checkbox so that all documents relevant for delivery-related billing will be selected.

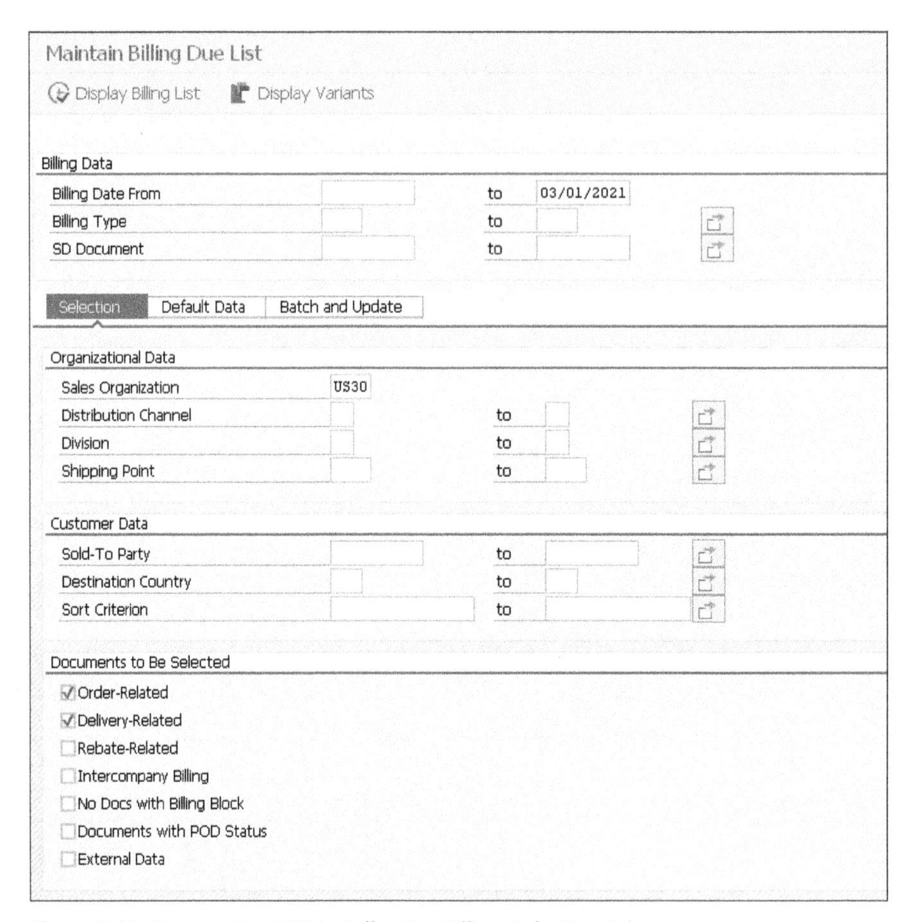

Figure 8.39 Transaction VF04: Collective Billing Selection Screen

After running this selection, click on the **Display Billing List** button to see one line, as shown in Figure 8.40.

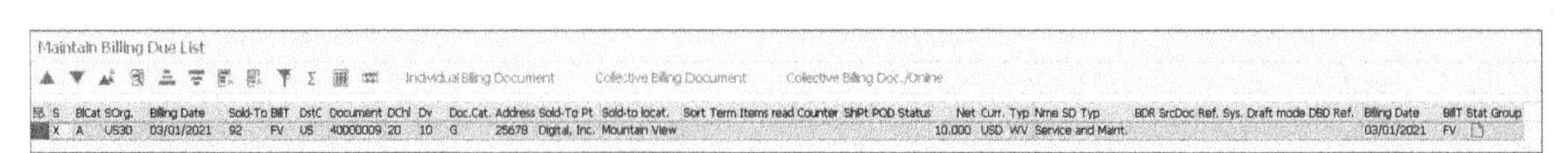

Figure 8.40 Transaction VF04 Results

This contrasts with the same result for the document with Transaction VF01, where there were 11 results. This is because the selection was restricted by billing date, so only the first billing date from the billing plan on the contract was relevant.

At this point, there are three options for billing:

- **Individual Billing Document**
  This creates a single billing document in the foreground for each of the lines selected.
- **Collective Billing Document**
  This attempts to create in the background a single billing document for all lines selected, dependent on the invoice split criteria.
- **Collective Billing Doc./Online**
  This carries out the same as the **Collective Billing Document**, but in the foreground so you can see the results.

After the billing document is saved, you'll see the confirmation message posted, as shown in Figure 8.41.

Figure 8.41 Billing Document Saved Message

8.7.5 Creation of Billing Documents in SAP Fiori

The Create Billing Documents app is an SAP Fiori representation of Transaction VF01, so we don't need to discuss this app further. However, the Create Billing Documents – Billing Due List Items app is a replacement for Transaction VF04, and while it has the same functionality, the look and feel is different. The tile has the number of sales documents that appear as "ready to bill" (i.e., on the billing due list) on the front, as shown in Figure 8.42. Figure 8.43 shows the app itself.

The normal filter bars are available in the SAP Fiori app, but there are additional useful settings, as shown in Figure 8.44, that are available by clicking the **Settings** icon at the bottom right of the screen.

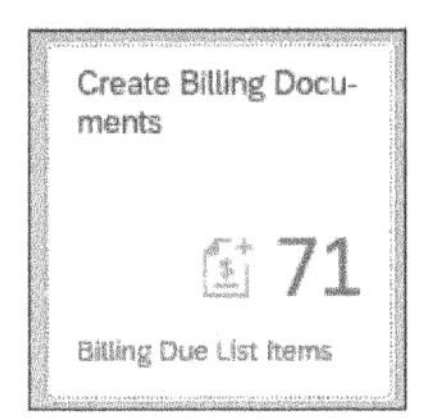

Figure 8.42 Create Billing Documents – Billing Due List Items App Tile

Create Billing Documents

Standard

Search

Hide Filter Bar Filters (1)

Sales document: SD Document Category: Sold-To Party: Billing Date To: 01/30/2021

Billing Due List Items (48)

Sales document	SD Document Category	Sold-To Party	Billing Date	Net Value
40000008	Contract	Client 1 MA (97)	01/01/2021	0.00 EUR
40000006	Contract	Client 1 MA (97)	01/01/2021	200.00 EUR
40000007	Contract	Client 1 MA (97)	12/31/2020	1,000.00 EUR
80000151	Delivery	Client 1 MA (97)	12/23/2020	-70.00 EUR
70000004	Debit Memo Request	Client 1 MA (97)	12/19/2020	1,980.00 EUR
80000142	Delivery	PBO Client 01 (PBO-CL01)	12/15/2020	20.000 USD
80000140	Delivery	Client 1 MA (97)	12/13/2020	1,100.00 EUR
40000006	Contract	Client 1 MA (97)	12/01/2020	200.00 EUR
60000002	Returns	Client 1 MA (97)	11/13/2020	1,100.00 EUR
80000110	Delivery	Z200 as cust in Z100 (Z200)	08/07/2020	0.00
80000109	Delivery	Z200 as cust in Z100 (Z200)	08/06/2020	0.00
80000108	Delivery	Z200 as cust in Z100 (Z200)	08/05/2020	0.00
80000107	Delivery	Z200 as cust in Z100 (Z200)	08/05/2020	0.00
80000106	Delivery	Z200 as cust in Z100 (Z200)	08/05/2020	0.00
80000105	Delivery	Z200 as cust in Z100 (Z200)	08/05/2020	0.00
80000101	Delivery	Z200 as cust in Z100 (Z200)	08/05/2020	0.00
80000100	Delivery	Z200 as cust in Z100 (Z200)	08/05/2020	0.00
80000099	Delivery	Z200 as cust in Z100 (Z200)	08/05/2020	0.00
80000096	Delivery	Z200 as cust in Z100 (Z200)	08/04/2020	0.00
80000095	Delivery	Z200 as cust in Z100 (Z200)	08/04/2020	0.00

More

[20 / 48]

Figure 8.43 Create Billing Documents – Billing Due List Items App

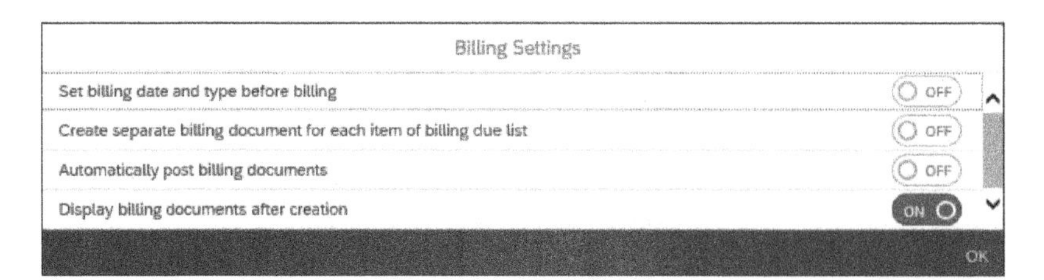

Figure 8.44 Create Billing Documents – Billing Due List Items App: Settings

After you select one of the sales documents to be billed, the **Create** button at the bottom right becomes available. Choosing this button creates and saves the billing document.

8.7.6 Changing Billing Documents

After they are saved, billing documents can be changed in a very limited way. This is because after the document has been generated and passed to accounting, it's not recommended to change much of the data therein as all amounts, values, and settings have been locked in place in the accounting document. The options for changing are as follows:

- Transaction VF02
- Manage Billing Documents app

All the header and item fields are grayed out, denoting that they can't be amended. Texts at the header and item levels are the only data items that can be amended.

8.7.7 Printing Outputs

In the same way that outputs can be printed for sales documents and delivery documents, they can also be printed for billing documents. The menu path for displaying the types of output generated is shown in Figure 8.45.

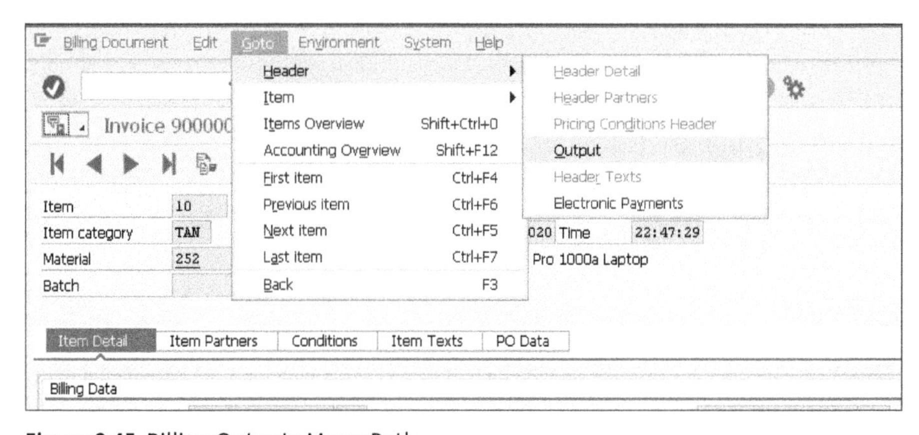

Figure 8.45 Billing Outputs Menu Path

Once in the screen, you can see that standard output type **RD00** has been defined but not yet sent, as shown by the yellow triangle **Status** in the output in Figure 8.46.

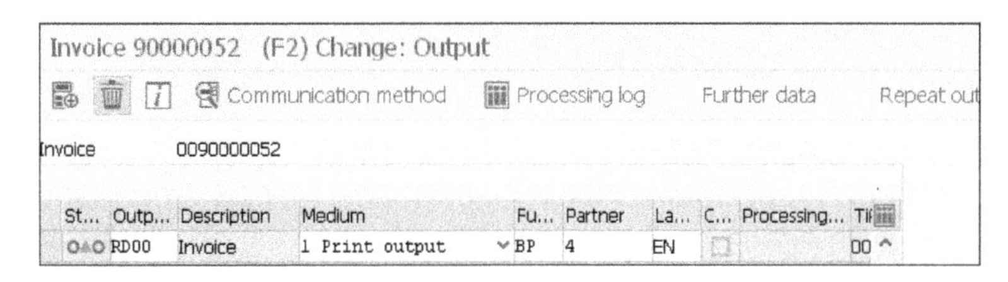

Figure 8.46 Billing Output Status

To display a print preview or to print the output, return to the initial screen of Transaction VF02 or Transaction VF03, and choose **Billing Document • Issue Output To**. This then presents you with the screen shown in Figure 8.47, from where you can preview the printout or print to a specified device.

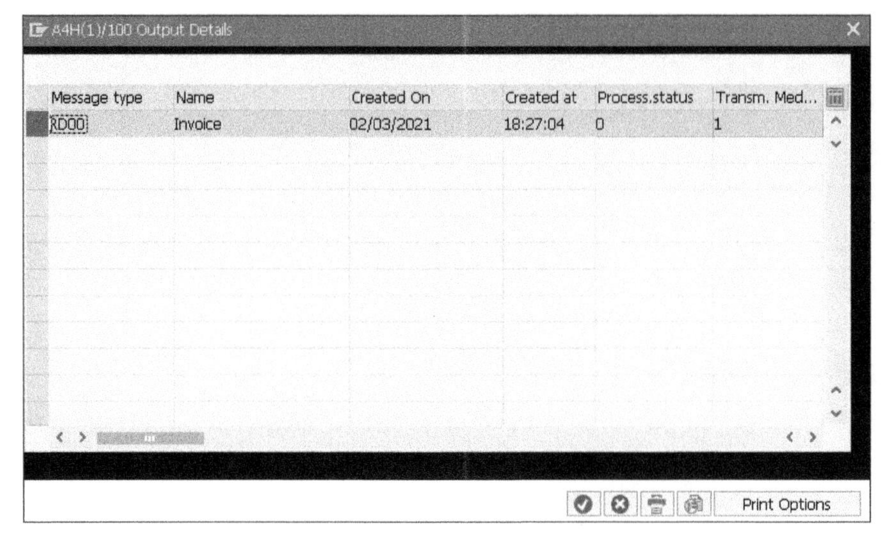

Figure 8.47 Billing Output Printing and Previewing Options

8.8 Other Billing Functionality

In this short section, we'll preview the available additional billing functionality, such as invoice splits and invoice lists, before giving a brief overview of the transfer to accounting step in the process.

8.8.1 Invoice Splits

Billing documents are, as you've seen, created with reference to sales orders in order-related billing, or reference to deliveries in delivery-related billing. However, there is functionality in SAP S/4HANA to determine whether billing documents are created with reference to a single preceding document or multiple preceding documents.

As an example, let's say our customer, Digital Inc., wants separate billing documents for certain product lines. This is an example of a customized invoice split, which can be achieved using the SAP invoice split functionality.

The invoice split functionality is contained within the copy control rules in SAP S/4HANA, which determine how the system sets the rules for copying data from the delivery or sales order to the billing document. These rules are set within the configuration by your SAP S/4HANA consultants and usually rely very heavily on master data from the customer or the material.

There are standard fields in SAP S/4HANA that are used to split invoices, such as sales organization, payer, billing type, and so on. SAP S/4HANA has a handy option to check why invoices have split from each other. The menu path is shown in Figure 8.48.

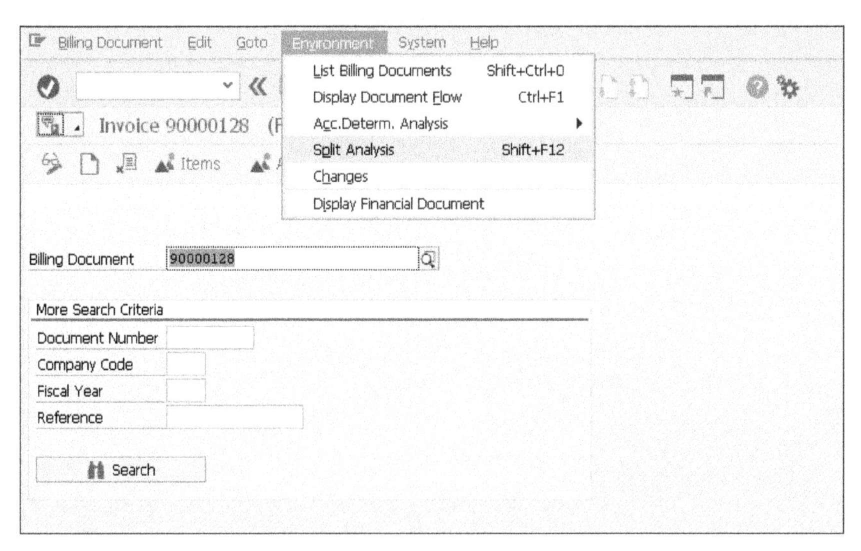

Figure 8.48 Invoice Split Menu Path

By opening this option and then adding the other billing document number you want to analyze, you'll be shown the relevant fields that are different in the header of each billing document, which has enforced the split, as shown in Figure 8.49.

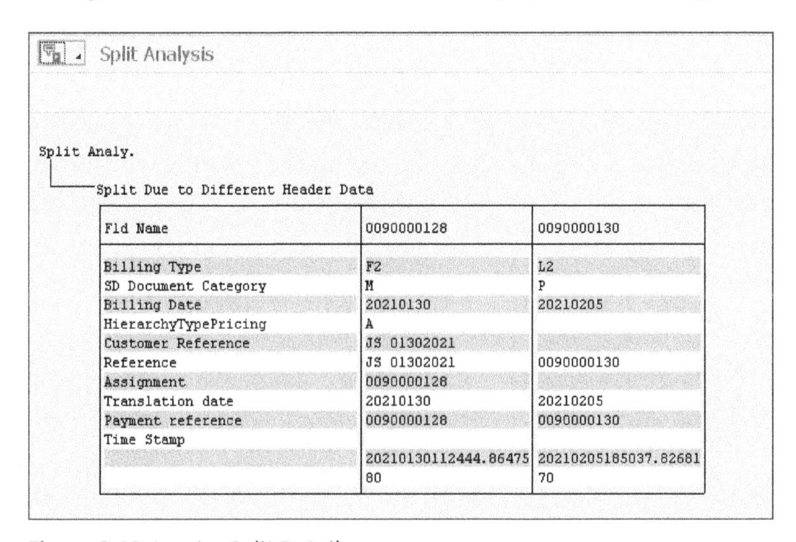

Fld Name	0090000128	0090000130
Billing Type	F2	L2
SD Document Category	M	P
Billing Date	20210130	20210205
HierarchyTypePricing	A	
Customer Reference	JS 01302021	
Reference	JS 01302021	0090000130
Assignment	0090000128	
Translation date	20210130	20210205
Payment reference	0090000128	0090000130
Time Stamp	20210130112444.8647580	20210205185037.8268170

Figure 8.49 Invoice Split Details

Fields in addition to the standard splits are populated within a database table field in the header of the billing document. The example of separating billing documents by product line can be handled here by adding item-specific details into this header field, thus enforcing an invoice split due to differing header data.

The field itself can't be viewed in the billing document display transactions, but rather is a background field. The database table for the billing header document is table VBRK, and the field populated is **Combination Criteria** (technical name ZUKRI, thus VBRK-ZUKRI). This field is just a string of data, made up of master and transactional fields from the source document, which must be the same in the two potential billing documents for the invoice to be merged into one. For example, if you want to split invoices for the Digital Inc. customer based on product line, you might do the following:

1. Set a value for the customer master for Digital Inc. in a specific field, such as **Customer Group**. Let's say the value is **001**, which denotes **Relevant for invoice split based on product line.**
2. Set a value for the material master in a specific field, such as **Material Group**. Let's say the values are **A01** and **A02**, which denotes **Product line 1** and **Product line 2**.
3. Set some code in the copy control rule in Customizing from the delivery type to the billing type for a specific item category that does the following:
   - Reads the customer master **Customer Group**, and if the value is **001**, adds the **Material Group** into the **VBRK-ZUKRI** field.
   - If the customer master **Customer Group** isn't **001**, then don't add the **Material Group** into the **VBRK-ZUKRI** field.

The preceding steps will lead to a situation where billing documents for Digital Inc. will be split for different product lines; that is, materials with a **Material Group** of **A01** will appear on different invoices from those materials with a **Material Group** of **A02**.

8.8.2 Invoice Lists

An invoice list is just that: a list of invoices. Typically, this is used to generate a list of all invoices in a given month to be sent to a payer. The invoice list can only be generated if the **Invoice List Sched.** field in the payer's customer master is populated with a factory calendar relating to the dates you want the invoice list to be created for. This field has the calendar **US** in Figure 8.50.

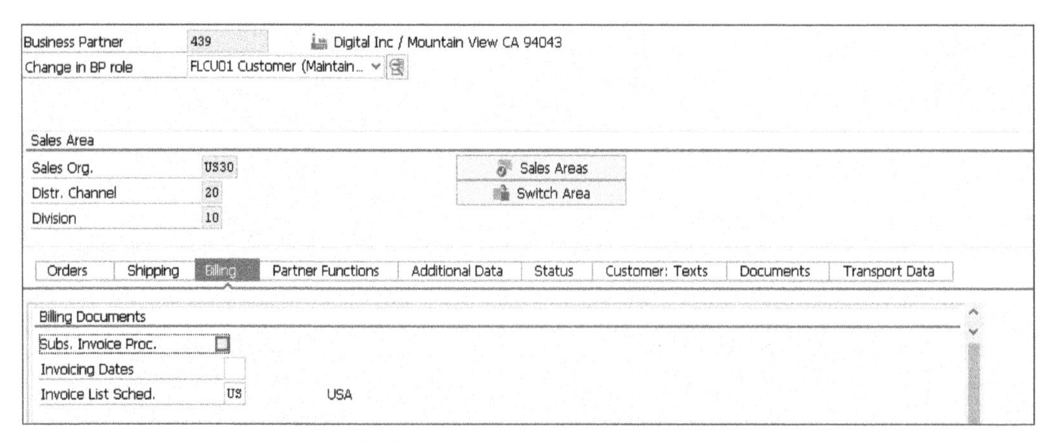

Figure 8.50 Invoice List Schedule in Customer Master

After this requirement is met, the invoice list can be created with reference to the billing document numbers in Transaction VF21. Figure 8.51 shows the creation screen, which follows the format of the billing document screen, with an overview, a header, and items. The difference here is that the items are the billing documents that make up the invoice list. Navigating to the items by highlighting the line and selecting **Item • Details** from the menu bar will take you directly to the billing document in Transaction VF03.

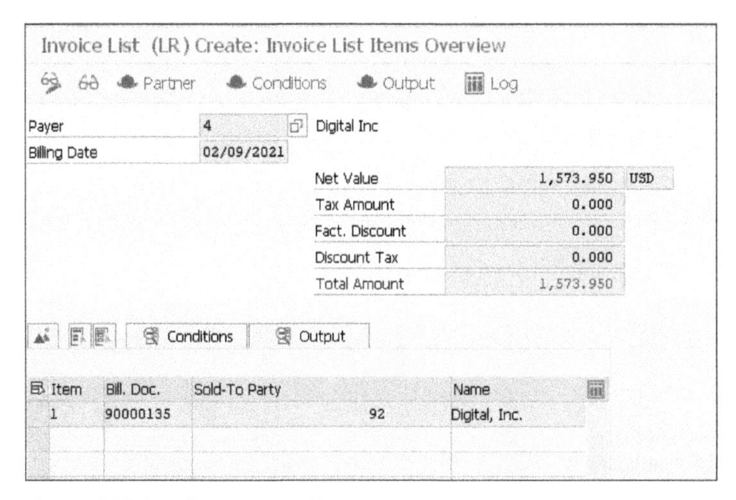

Figure 8.51 Invoice List Creation

As with other sales documents, it's possible to create an output against the invoice list that can be mailed, emailed, or sent via EDI to the payer.

Although you can't navigate to the document flow from the Transaction VF23 (Display Invoice List), the invoice list appears in the document flow against the billing document, as shown in Figure 8.52.

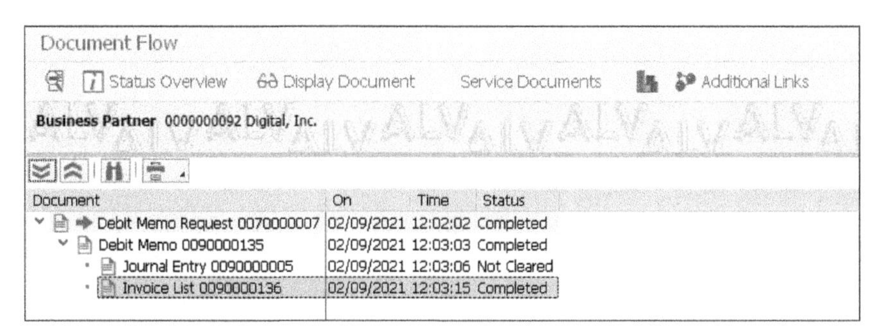

Figure 8.52 Invoice List Document Flow

8.8.3 Transfer to Accounting

We've already seen that billing documents are transferred to accounting by way of the journal entry, which is shown in the document flow in Figure 8.52. The accounting document, or journal entry, is the connection between sales and distribution and finance in SAP system. The document itself is a financial document and captures all the details from the relevant billing document in a specific manner, allocating moneys to the correct company, country, and currency according to different rules based on customer, pricing conditions, and type of transaction. As a sales and distribution user, it's not necessary to go into details here other than to point out some key processes.

Viewing Transfer to Accounting Errors

Typically, SAP S/4HANA systems are set up to release the billing document to accounting as soon as it's saved. If there are errors in the transfer, these can be viewed in Transaction VFX3, as shown in Figure 8.53.

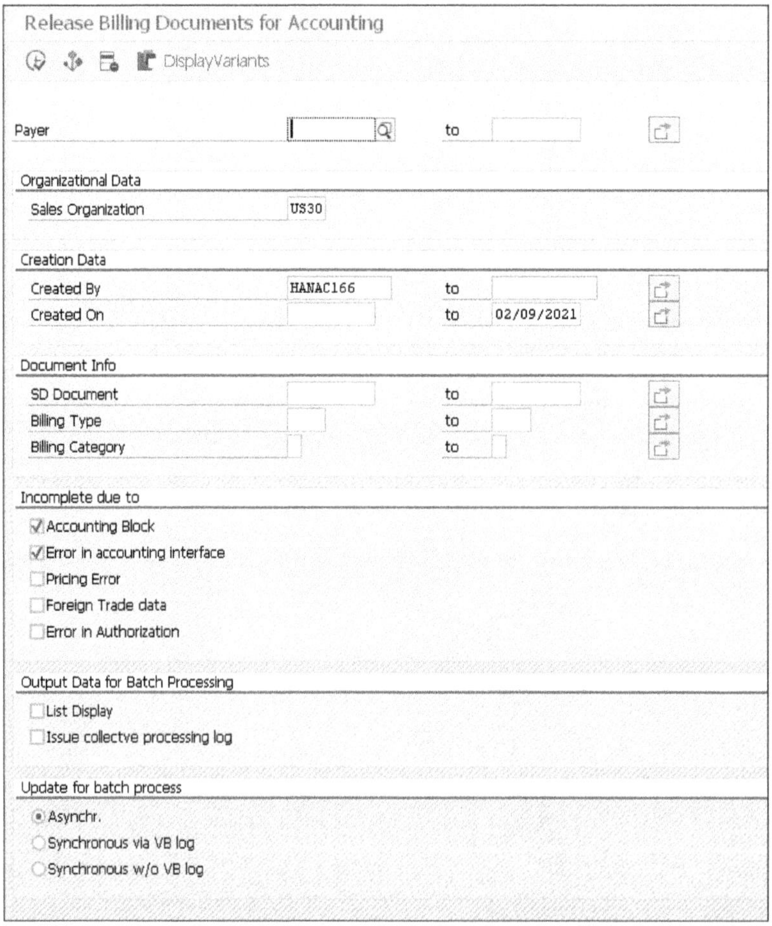

Release Billing Documents for Accounting
DisplayVariants
Payer to
Organizational Data
Sales Organization US30
Creation Data
Created By HANAC166 to
Created On to 02/09/2021
Document Info
SD Document to
Billing Type to
Billing Category to
Incomplete due to
Accounting Block
Error in accounting interface
Pricing Error
Foreign Trade data
Error in Authorization
Output Data for Batch Processing
List Display
Issue collectve processing log
Update for batch process
Asynchr.
Synchronous via VB log
Synchronous w/o VB log

Figure 8.53 Releasing Billing Documents to Accounting in Transaction VFX3

From here, you can see the error in the **Incomplete due to** column of the report, as shown in Figure 8.54. From here, you can navigate directly to the billing document as well as attempt to post to accounting again by highlighting the line and using the Release to Accounting icon (green flag). This icon also exists on the initial screen of Transaction VF02 (Change Billing Document).

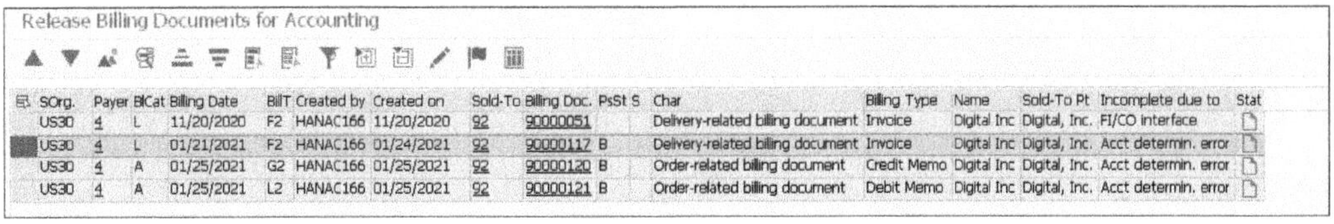

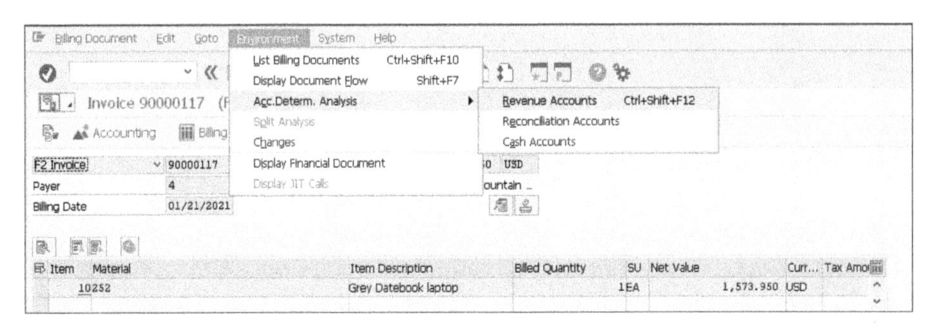

Figure 8.54 Transaction VFX3 results

Errors such as **Acct determin. error** (account determination error) are likely to be master data errors and can normally be identified from within the billing document itself by analyzing the account determination via the menu path shown in Figure 8.55.

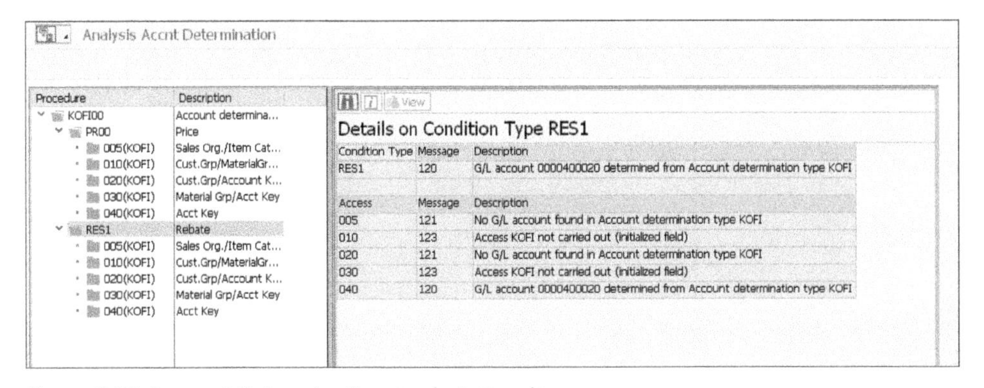

Figure 8.55 Account Determination Analysis

This menu reruns the account determination in simulation to see where the error is. Figure 8.56 shows the pricing condition types used in the billing document and whether a general ledger account has been determined for the data in each table. If no general ledger account is found, then the document can't be passed to accounting.

Figure 8.56 Account Determination Analysis Results

8.9 Summary

With the completion of the billing process, we've finalized the order-to-cash process. In the remaining chapters, we'll explore more niche scenarios in the sales and distribution area, such as reversals, settlement management, and warranty and repairs.

Chapter 9

Reversals

Data entry errors come in all shapes and sizes. Some errors have no accounting impact, which means they can be corrected simply long after the goods have been delivered and invoiced. Other errors, such as incorrect customer or material impacts, have left accounting postings by the wayside that must be offset by new, corrective documents.

This chapter provides the guidance and the Rosetta Stone for deciphering exactly what to do in case you made a data entry mistake, depending on the level of completion of your transaction. Accordingly, we'll cover the step-by-step entry of a complete reversal for demonstration purposes. At each step in the process, the level of completion will be verified to serve as a referential checkpoint in the reversal process.

This chapter is divided into two sections. The first considers a completed order-to-cash transaction where a serious basic error has been made, say the entry of an incorrect customer number or sales document type was used. We'll walk through backing out of the three levels of completed documents: sales order, delivery, and billing.

The second section is the reversal matrix, intended as a useful reference going forward. The matrix defines numerous combinations of common mistakes and relates them to different levels of completion. The exact steps necessary to correct the error are succinctly indicated.

No work on sales and distribution in SAP S/4HANA would be complete without a review of reversing an order-to-cash transaction flow.

We hope that this is just one more reason to keep this business user guide on your office bookshelf, at least for the next few years!

9.1 Process Overview

After your order-to-cash process has been completed through the billing document, you may find that you may have made some mistakes that require correction. Mistakes in some fields are easier to fix than others.

Also of critical importance is the level of completion of your order-to-cash process. If you discover your mistake early on, for example, after creating only the sales document, you're in luck. You can pretty much just go back into your document in change mode and correct any field. After you create the next document in sequence, in this case, the delivery document, some fields get tied down due to subsequent documents.

Bear in mind that SAP S/4HANA is a rigorous system that has its origins in accounting. After you create documents that impact your company's general ledger accounts, audit and control standards require you to correct errors not by deleting documents, but by creating new offsetting documents. For this reason, many users feel that SAP S/4HANA in general can be somewhat unwieldy. This is an unfortunate misnomer.

This complete reversal process overview is illustrated in Figure 9.1. You may recognize certain features of this process flow from Figure 6.8 and Figure 6.9 in Chapter 6. That is entirely intended as this reversal process is essentially an amalgam of the returns and debit/credit memo processes.

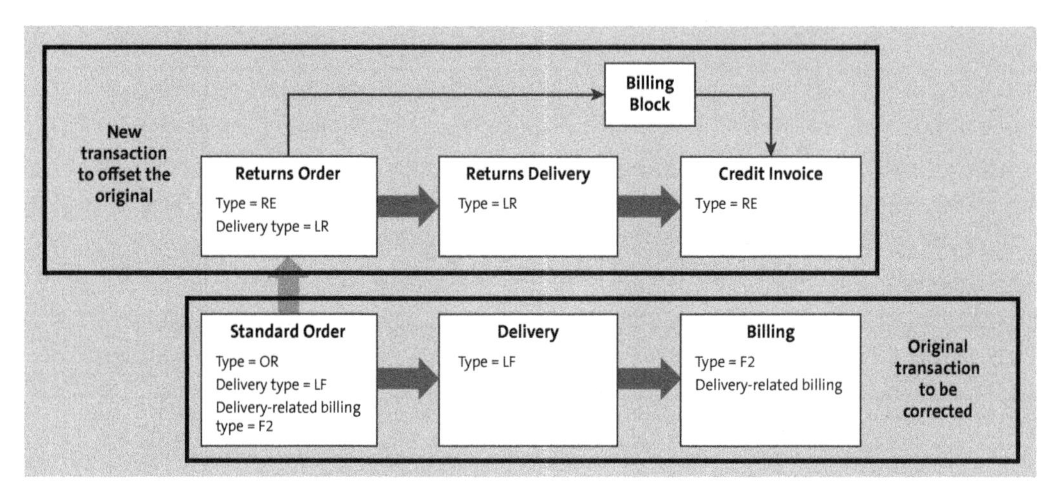

Figure 9.1 Reversal Process Overview

The completed order-to-cash flow is depicted in the bottom half where you have completed order, delivery, and billing documents that form the basis for the corrective return order, return delivery, and credit invoice. The returns order is created with reference to the original order so that once created, the subsequent documents simply copy the incorrect information and create the required offsets in a simple and automatic way.

The key to the whole process is the interface, the link between the original transaction and the new returns process, which is the copy function underlying the **Create with Reference** command. This is represented by the green arrow in Figure 9.1.

9.2 Document Types

The original order-to-cash transaction that is to be corrected consists of the following standard document types (as shown previously in the bottom set of documents in Figure 9.1).

- OR: Standard order
- LF: Outbound delivery document
- F2: Sales invoice for a delivery

The subsequent series of offsetting transactions consists of the following standard document types (also shown earlier in Figure 9.1 as the top set of documents):

- RE: Returns order
- LR: Returns delivery
- CR: Credit memo request

Refer to Chapter 6 for further information on these document types.

9.3 Create a Returns Order Document (SAP GUI)

The example presented here assumes that you have a completed (but incorrect) order-to-cash transaction from sales document through billing and associated accounting document. The accounting document must have an **Uncleared** status. If the accounting document has been cleared, then you must consult with accounting before engaging in any steps here.

The nature of the error is a fundamental one as described in the reversal matrix at the end of this chapter. Two examples of this type of error are (1) an incorrect customer number that is embedded through the document flow, and (2) the wrong sales document type that points to an incorrect business process, as described in Chapter 6, Section 6.3. Perhaps you chose a sales document type for cement mixing and included pool supplies, and due to incorrect item category assignments, managed to follow through to billing before the error was realized. A veritable cascade of errors would cause extra work to correct the item category assignments.

We aren't going to go that far. The reversal process itself is fairly automatic, and the nature of the original error, in terms of the following discussion isn't critical. We simply want to show you what the complete backing out process looks like.

We also assume that the transaction to be reversed is of a hard goods type. If it was from a service processing scenario, the process is simpler in that the returns delivery, complete with the post goods returns, is omitted. Of course, this process could also be used to simply reverse a completely correct order where the customer wants to return the goods and receive full credit.

Note that because the two presales documents covered in this book have no impact on your company's general ledger accounts, they don't require a new offsetting document. The inquiry is nonbinding, so it can be effectively ignored.

The quotation, on the other hand, is a legally binding document, and it can't be deleted after subsequent documents are created. If you have a quotation left over after a full order-to-cash reversal, you can change the **Valid To** date to yesterday and save, which will effectively terminate the legal effect.

Let's get started.

9.3.1 Level of Completion: Document Flow

The first thing to do is to confirm the completeness of the original transaction to be reversed. Go to Transaction VA03 (Display Sales Order) and input the sales document number to be reversed. Click on the **Document Flow** icon shown in Figure 9.2.

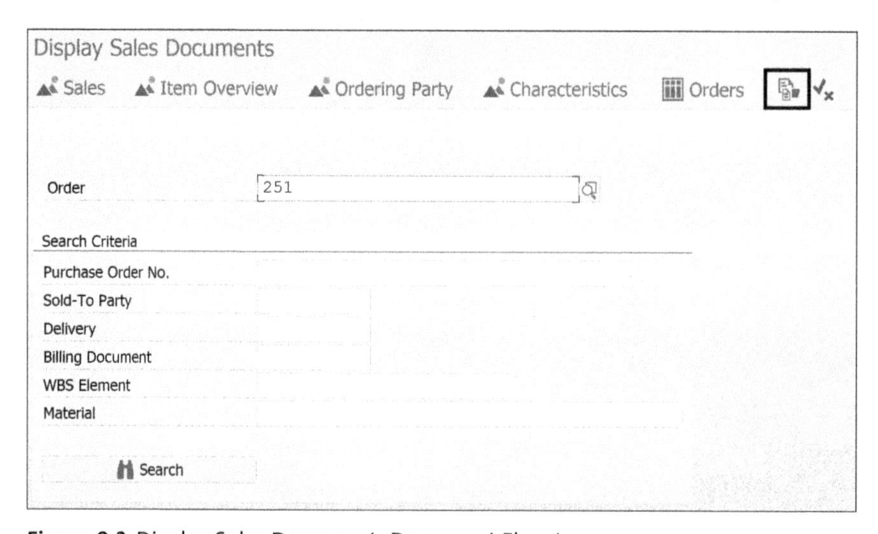

Figure 9.2 Display Sales Document: Document Flow Icon

This displays the following example of a completed order-to-cash transaction, as shown in Figure 9.3.

Document Flow

Status Overview | Display Document | Service Documents

Business Partner 0000000092 Digital, Inc.

Document	On	Time	Status
Standard Order 0000000251	02/28/2021	21:39:44	Completed
Outbound Delivery 0080000193	02/28/2021	21:40:33	Completed
Picking Request 20210228	02/28/2021	21:40:44	Completed
GD goods issue:delvy 4900001066	02/28/2021	21:40:47	Complete
Invoice 0090000140	02/28/2021	21:41:02	Completed
Journal Entry 0090000007	02/28/2021	21:41:06	Not Cleared

Figure 9.3 Document Flow from Display Sales Documents

All key documents are shown here. Note that the delivery document breaks down into two subdocuments: the picking request and the post goods issue (PGI). From this screen, you can open any one of these documents by clicking once to select it and then clicking on the **Display Document** button.

The key here is to note the level of completion, as follows:

- Is it complete through the customer invoice? If there is no invoice and only complete through the delivery document (with no picking or goods issue [GI] yet done), there will be much less work to do to reverse this. The matrix in Section 9.12 will give the exact steps.
- Is there an accounting document, and has it been cleared? If so, you need to stop—this doesn't apply to you, and you'll need to consult with accounting.
- If there is only a sales document and no follow-on delivery, you're in luck! You can simply change the sales document for most errors.

9.3.2 Creating the Returns Order

Now that we've confirmed a completed flow, let's reverse it to review all the steps involved:

1. As you did with the original transaction, go to Transaction VA01, and enter "RE" in the **Order Type** field in preparation to create with reference to a preceding document. (RE is the standard SAP system document type for a returns order). The **Create Sales Documents** initial screen shows the inputs (see Figure 9.4).

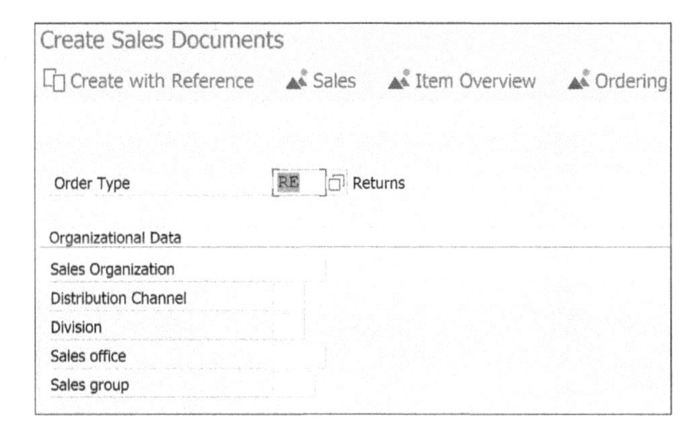

Figure 9.4 Create Sales Documents

2. Click on the **Create with Reference** button.
3. In the **Create with Reference** dialog shown in Figure 9.5, enter "251" in the **Order** field. This is the sales document number of the order-to-cash transaction to be reversed.
4. Click on the **Copy** button in the lower-right corner of the dialog.

You're now in the main **Create Returns Order** screen, which has been completed with some important data from your preceding document. Let's take a moment to review what has been completed on your behalf by the system.

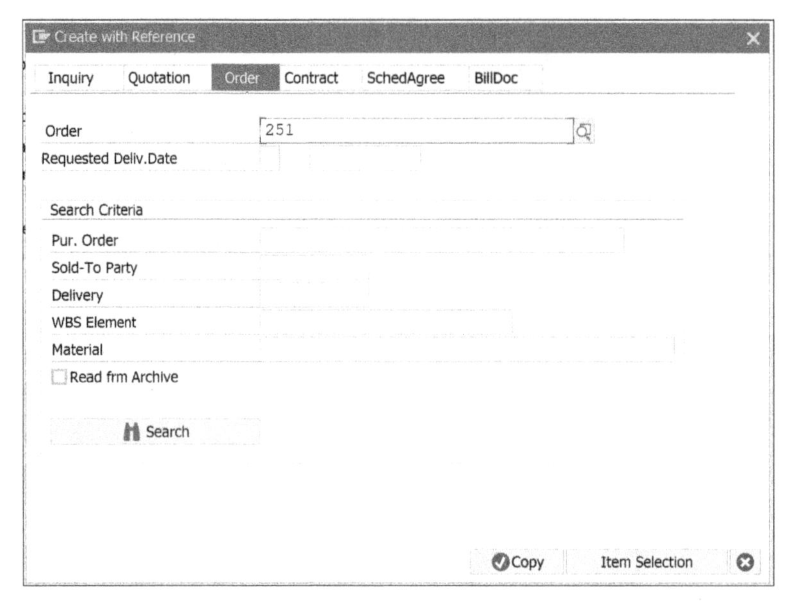

Figure 9.5 Create with Reference

9.3.3 Header Data

Your customer or business partner information in the form of sold-to party and ship-to party (as well as the other main functions, bill-to party and payer) have been copied over. These can be seen at the top of the **Create Standard Order: Overview** screen, as shown in Figure 9.6. To review the relationships of these business partner functions, refer to Chapter 2 for more comprehensive details.

Figure 9.6 Create Returns Order

Review all the header fields copied over from your preceding document as follows:

- **Sold-To Party: 92**
- **Ship-To Party: 3**
- (Optional) **Cust. Reference**: Not copied over from the underlying sales document
- **Req. Deliv.Date: 03/01/2021**

As previously explained, the **Cust. Reference** field is used for any number issued by the customer for their own tracking of the order. It's not normally system required. For reversal purposes, you can input any valid reference from the customer or use one meaningful for your company as this field isn't validated.

The **Req. Deliv.Date** field is also not copied over from the quotation. This is the date that the goods are to be received back from the customer. For our purposes, we'll simply use the current date. If, in your case, some physical movement of goods is involved, you may want to coordinate with your warehouse manager to input a different date. As in the underlying sales document, this header data field is copied into the **Delivery Date** field in the **Schedule lines** tab of the material line item, where it can be changed.

Accordingly, enter "Q876" in the optional **Cust. Reference** field, and press Enter. Your **Create Returns: Overview** screen should now appear, as shown in Figure 9.7.

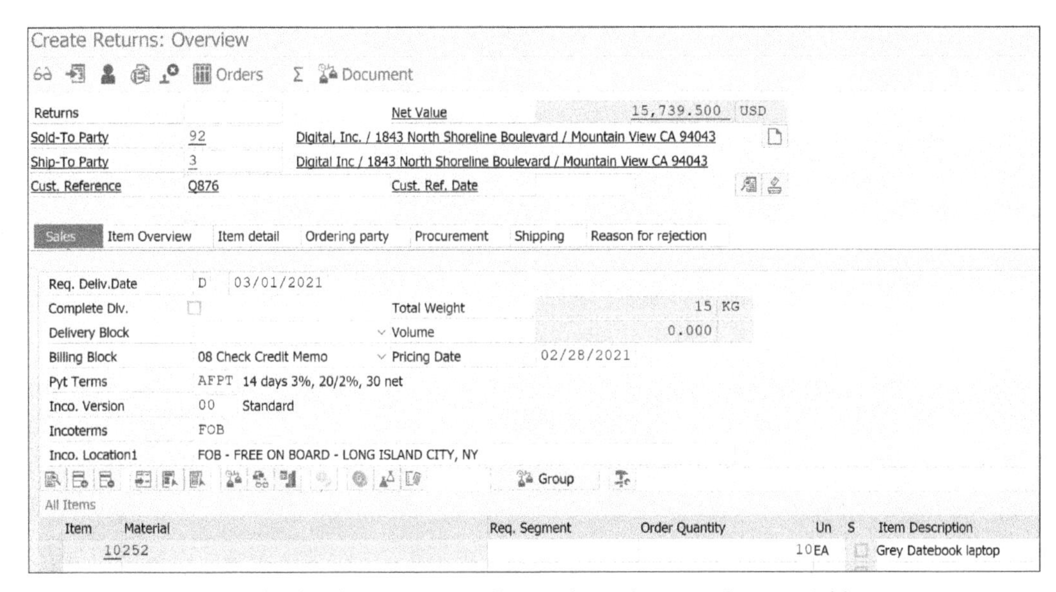

Figure 9.7 Create Standard Order: Overview after Update of Cust. Reference Field

Before reviewing the line-item data, there is one other header field to input in the **Sales** tab: the **Order Reason** field, which is required for a returns order.

Choose **Goto • Header • Sales** in the menu bar, as shown in Figure 9.8.

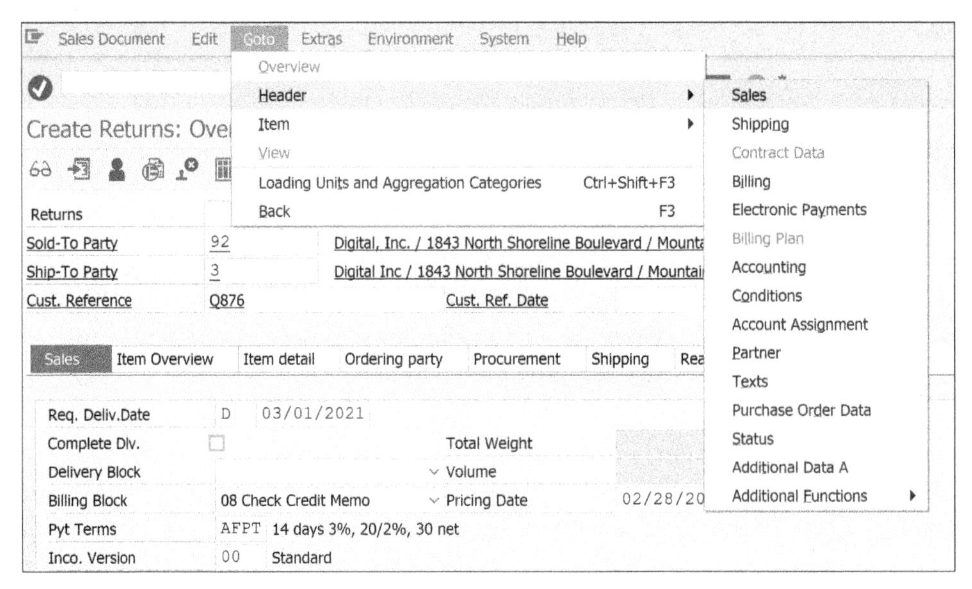

Figure 9.8 Choosing Sales in the Menu Path

Once in the **Sales** tab of the header, enter "101" (**Poor Quality**) in the **Order Reason** field. These order reasons are easy to add by configuration. You may use a different one that is more suitable in your company. **Poor Quality** is used here strictly for illustrative reasons.

Press [Enter] to accept the entry, and then click on the green **Go Back** icon.

Let's briefly review the line-item data before saving. Generally, everything important has been copied over from the underlying sales document, and nothing further needs to be input.

9.3.4 Line-Item Data on the Overview Screen

Back in the **Create Returns: Overview** screen, you can review all line-item fields copied over from your preceding document as follows:

- **Material: 252**
- **Order Quantity: 10**

The **Create with Reference** functionality is used to create your standard order and does a lot of heavy lifting on your behalf, including copying over these line-item fields. The **Material** number can't be change, but the **Order Quantity** may be changed to suit the customer's requirements (e.g., if you want to take back only half the order, you could reduce the **Order Quantity** to **5**).

At this point, your customer details, customer reference number, material, order reason, and quantity as input and price as determined are clearly visible in both the header and line-item sections. This is all that is required to complete a returns order type of sales document.

9.4 Incompletion Log

As a final check that everything is complete and ready to go, let's go to the incompletion log. As previously shown in Chapter 6, choose **Edit • Incompletion Log**, as shown in Figure 9.9.

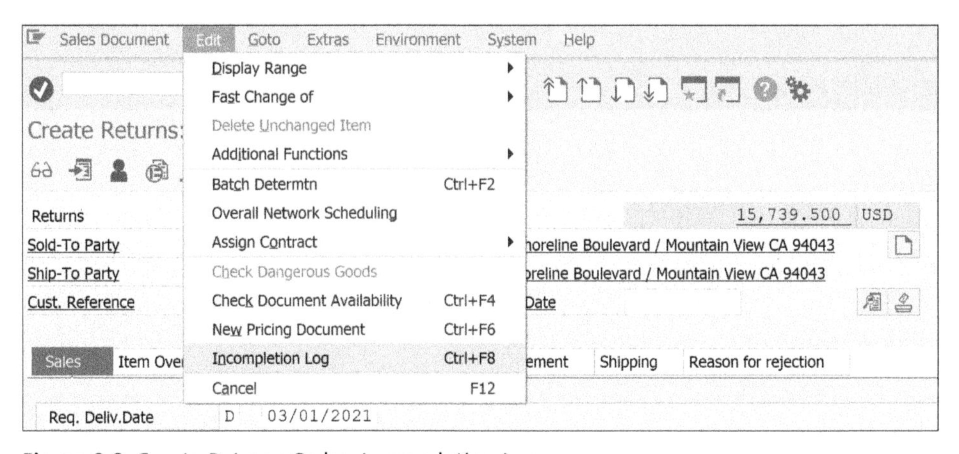

Figure 9.9 Create Returns Order: Incompletion Log

The following message appears on the status bar, in the lower-left corner of your screen, as shown in Figure 9.10.

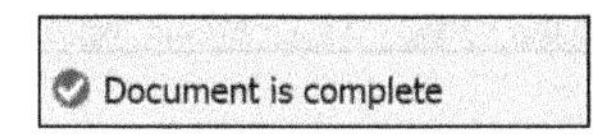

Figure 9.10 Incompletion Log Message

You're now ready to save your returns order. Click on the **Save** icon, as shown in Figure 9.11.

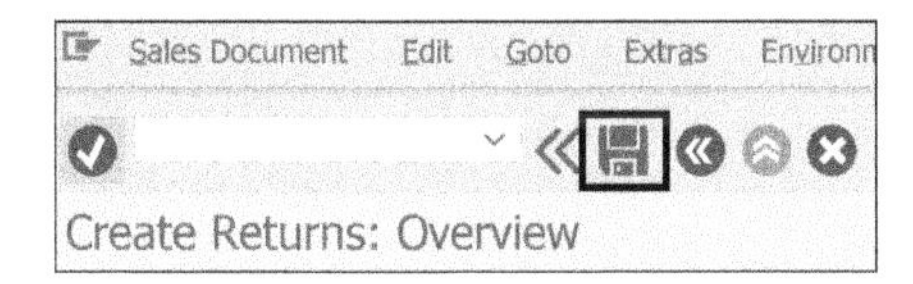

Figure 9.11 Create Returns Order: Save Icon

A message should appear with your returns order document number on the status bar in the lower-left corner of your screen, as shown in Figure 9.12.

Figure 9.12 Returns Saved Message

This returns order document can now be used to create a returns delivery document to proceed in the next step of the order-to-cash process.

At each step in this reversals process, for training (and self-audit) reasons, we'll look at the document flow to ensure that the system made changes correctly. We'll also do this strictly from the point of view of the underlying Sales Order 251 each time to see the complete picture.

Go to Transaction VA03, input **Order** number "251", and click on the **Document Flow** icon as you did previously. The following flow appears, as shown in Figure 9.13.

Document Flow

Status Overview   Display Document   Service Documents

Business Partner 0000000092 Digital, Inc.

Document	On	Time	Status
Standard Order 0000000251	02/28/2021	21:39:44	Completed
Outbound Delivery 0080000193	02/28/2021	21:40:33	Completed
Picking Request 20210228	02/28/2021	21:40:44	Completed
GD goods issue:delvy 4900001066	02/28/2021	21:40:47	Complete
Invoice 0090000140	02/28/2021	21:41:02	Completed
Journal Entry 0090000007	02/28/2021	21:41:06	Not Cleared
Returns 0060000009	03/01/2021	16:28:45	Open

Figure 9.13 Document Flow after Creation of Returns Order

Notice the new document at the bottom, the **Returns** order. As we successively process the reversal, the follow-on documents will appear below the **Returns** order to mirror the original transaction, which is composed of six documents. In addition, note that the status of the returns document is **Open**.

As with your original standard order, was your sales document for a service rather than for a physical good? If so, your reversal process will similarly skip the delivery level and go straight to billing to create your credit invoice.

9.5 Create a Returns Delivery Document

However, for the rest of us, we'll proceed to undo the delivery level, inclusive of all relevant subprocesses with the following steps:

1. Go to Transaction VL01N, and enter the following, as shown in Figure 9.14:
   - **Shipping Point**: "0001"

- **Order**: "60000009" (this is the returns order number created in the preceding section)

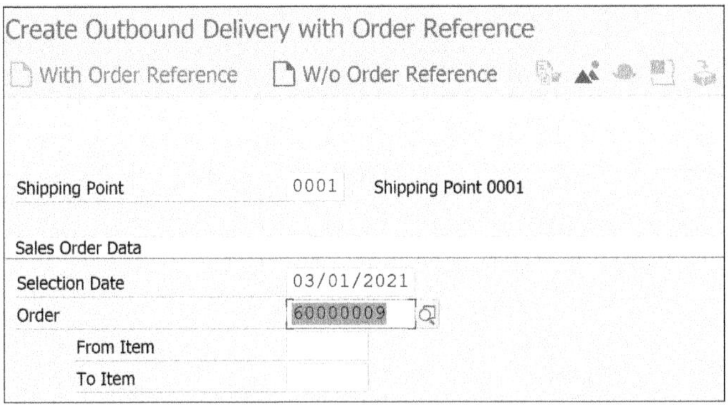

Create Outbound Delivery with Order Reference
With Order Reference W/o Order Reference
Shipping Point 0001 Shipping Point 0001
Sales Order Data
Selection Date 03/01/2021
Order 60000009
From Item
To Item

Figure 9.14 Create Outbound Delivery with Order Reference

The shipping point can be retrieved from the returns (or any sales) document in the line item **Shipping** tab for the material being processed for delivery.

Note

While the **Shipping Point** field is line-item data at the sales order level, it's header level here in the delivery. In addition, ignore that the transaction is called Create Outbound Delivery. Because a returns order is input, the system will automatically convert to a Create Inbound Delivery.

2. Press Enter to progress to the **Returns Delivery Create: Overview** screen, as shown in Figure 9.15.

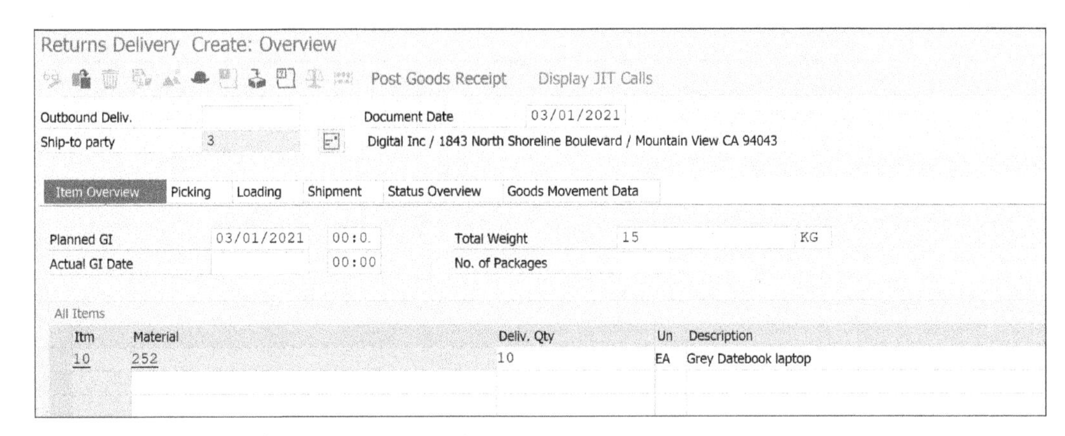

Figure 9.15 Returns Delivery Create: Overview

3. Click on the **Picking** tab to progress to the screen in Figure 9.16.

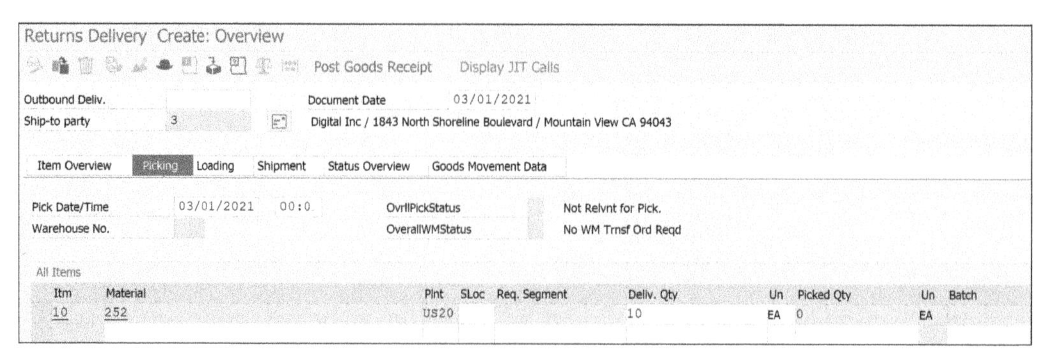

Figure 9.16 Returns Delivery Create: Picking Tab

4. In the **Picking**, enter "1000" in the **SLoc** (storage location) field.
5. Click on the **Post Goods Receipt** button shown in Figure 9.16. This will designate the exact section of the warehouse to which the goods will be replaced (permitting them to be picked again in the future).

A message should appear with your returns delivery document number on the status bar in the lower-left corner of your screen, as shown in Figure 9.17.

Figure 9.17 Returns Delivery Saved Message

This returns delivery document can now be used to create a credit invoice document to proceed in the next step of the order-to-cash process.

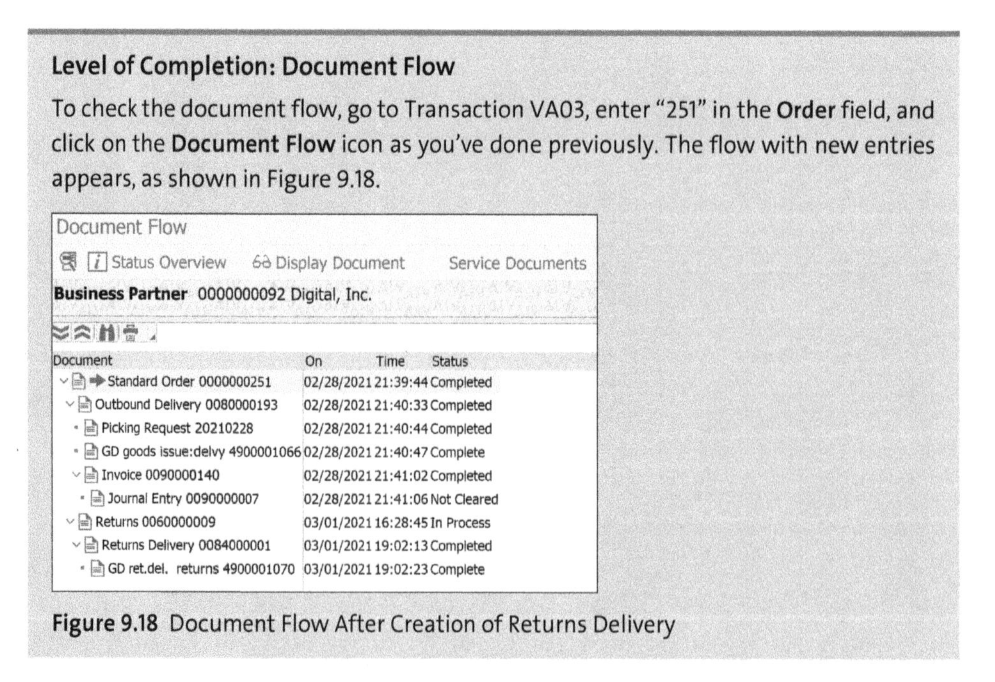

Level of Completion: Document Flow

To check the document flow, go to Transaction VA03, enter "251" in the **Order** field, and click on the **Document Flow** icon as you've done previously. The flow with new entries appears, as shown in Figure 9.18.

Figure 9.18 Document Flow After Creation of Returns Delivery

Notice the new documents at the bottom, the **Returns Delivery**, together with the subdocument for the post goods return. The **Picking Request** isn't reversed as it's not relevant for the returns (there is no such thing as "picking" goods for return to stock). As previously noted, new reversal documents appear successively as we process the new offsetting documents.

Note the status for all documents is **Open** with the following exceptions:

- **Journal Entry 90000007** is **Not Cleared**. This is correct as accounting is responsible for clearing this document.
- **Returns 60000009** remains **In Process** because it's not yet invoiced.

We're almost done. The last step will be to create the credit invoice.

But first, we'll cover another way to reverse the GI as an optional step and then remove the billing block from the returns order.

9.6 Optional Goods Issue Reversal

This step is listed as optional because the previous step, create returns delivery, included the GI reversal, namely the post goods receipt. However, in certain cases listed in the matrix in Section 9.12, where the level of completion is the PGI (i.e., billing hasn't yet been performed), it's preferable to simply reverse the PGI as a potential corrective step. This prevents the needless creation of a billing document when reversal has already been indicated.

Accordingly, for the purposes of the matrix, let's do a review of this transaction just for reference by following these steps:

1. Go to Transaction VL09 (Reverse Goods Movement), as shown in Figure 9.19.

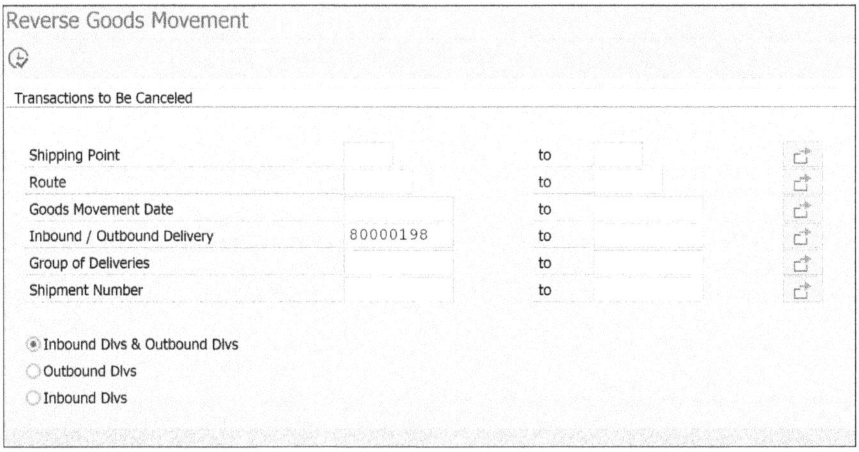

Reverse Goods Movement

Transactions to Be Canceled

Shipping Point		to	
Route		to	
Goods Movement Date		to	
Inbound / Outbound Delivery	80000198	to	
Group of Deliveries		to	
Shipment Number		to	

(•) Inbound Dlvs & Outbound Dlvs
( ) Outbound Dlvs
( ) Inbound Dlvs

Figure 9.19 Reverse Goods Movement

2. Enter "80000198" in the **Inbound/Outbound Delivery** field, as shown in Figure 9.19.

   The document number to input is the umbrella delivery document number and not the specific GI.

3. Click on the **Execute** icon to progress to the screen shown in Figure 9.20.

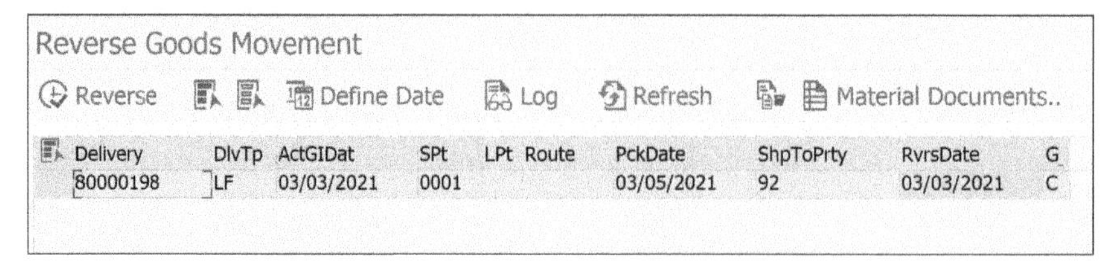

Figure 9.20 Reverse Goods Movement with Line Item Found

4. Click the box at the left-hand side of the line that is bracketed in Figure 9.20 to select the line item. The selected line item should be highlighted, as shown in Figure 9.21.

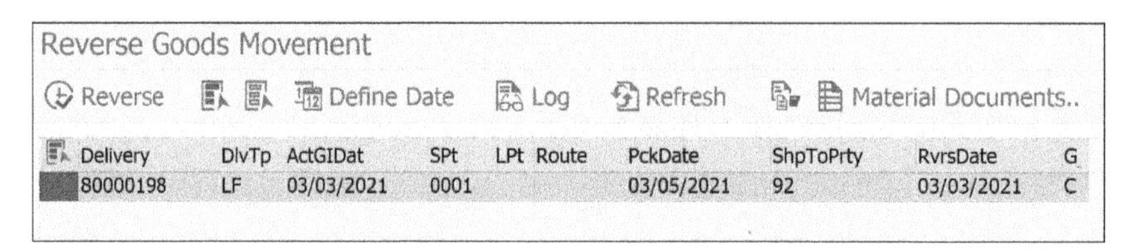

Figure 9.21 Reverse Goods Movement with Line Item Selected

5. Click the **Reverse** button in Figure 9.21 to progress to the dialog, as shown in Figure 9.22.

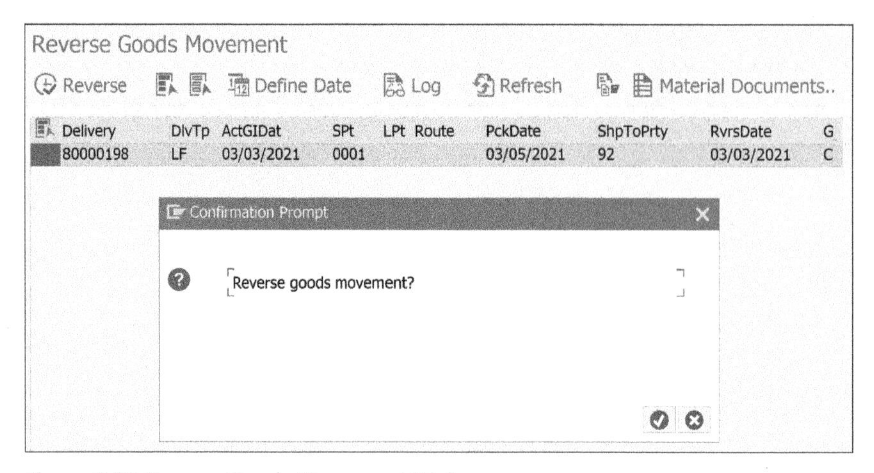

Figure 9.22 Reverse Goods Movement Dialog

6. Click **Execute** (green checkmark) to process the reversal of your PGI. Review the success message, as shown in Figure 9.23.

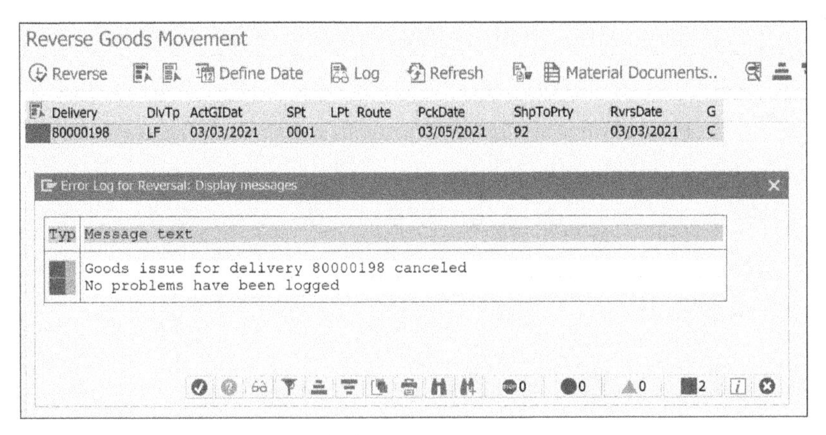

Figure 9.23 Goods Issue Canceled Message

7. Click on **Execute** (green checkmark) to close the message. Click **Exit** to leave the transaction. Don't forget to check the document flow to validate that the desired GI to be canceled is now accompanied by a corresponding reversal document.

There's just one more thing to do before we offset the billing document in our demonstration of a complete reversal: remove the billing block.

9.7 Remove Billing Block

In all honesty, you can remove the billing block from the returns order at the same time you created it two steps ago. We made it a separate activity here because it's likely that approvals may be needed or someone with a different user role may need to log in and remove it. This is how it's done:

1. Go to Transaction VA02 (Change Sales Documents), and enter "60000009" in the **Document** field, as shown in Figure 9.24.

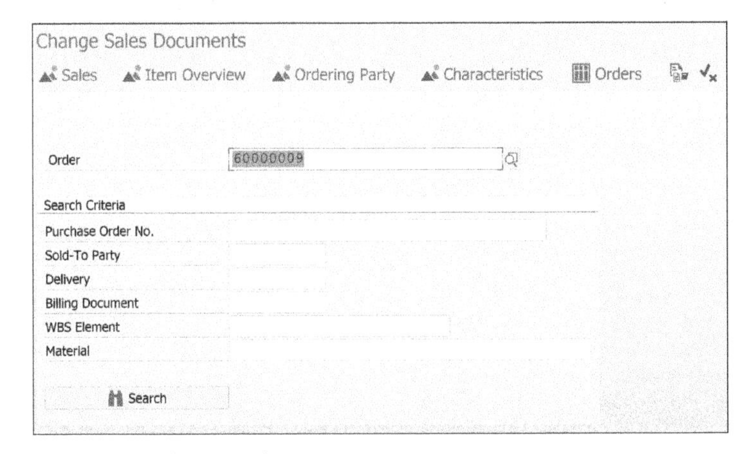

Figure 9.24 Change Sales Documents

2. Press Enter to progress to the **Change Returns: Overview** screen shown in Figure 9.25.

Change Returns 60000009: Overview
Orders Σ Document
Returns 60000009 Net Value 15,739.500 USD
Sold-To Party 92 Digital, Inc. / 1843 North Shoreline Boulevard / Mountain View CA 94043
Ship-To Party 3 Digital Inc / 1843 North Shoreline Boulevard / Mountain View CA 94043
Cust. Reference Q876 Cust. Ref. Date
Sales Item Overview Item detail Ordering party Procurement Shipping Reason for rejection
Req. Deliv.Date D 03/01/2021
Complete Dlv. Total Weight 15 KG
Delivery Block Volume 0.000
Billing Block 08 Check Credit Memo Pricing Date 02/28/2021

Figure 9.25 Change Returns: Overview Screen

3. Click on the **Billing Block** dropdown list, as shown in Figure 9.26, and be sure to choose the last possible row, which is blank.

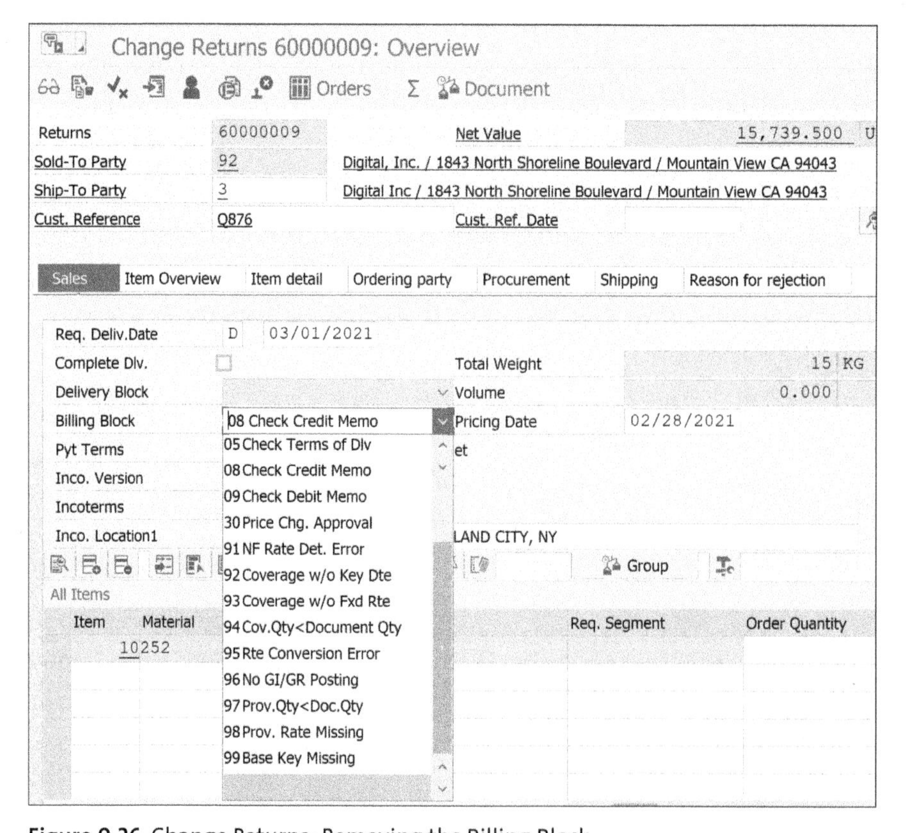

Figure 9.26 Change Returns: Removing the Billing Block

After selecting the last blank row and pressing Enter, your **Change Returns: Overview** screen will appear, as shown in Figure 9.27.

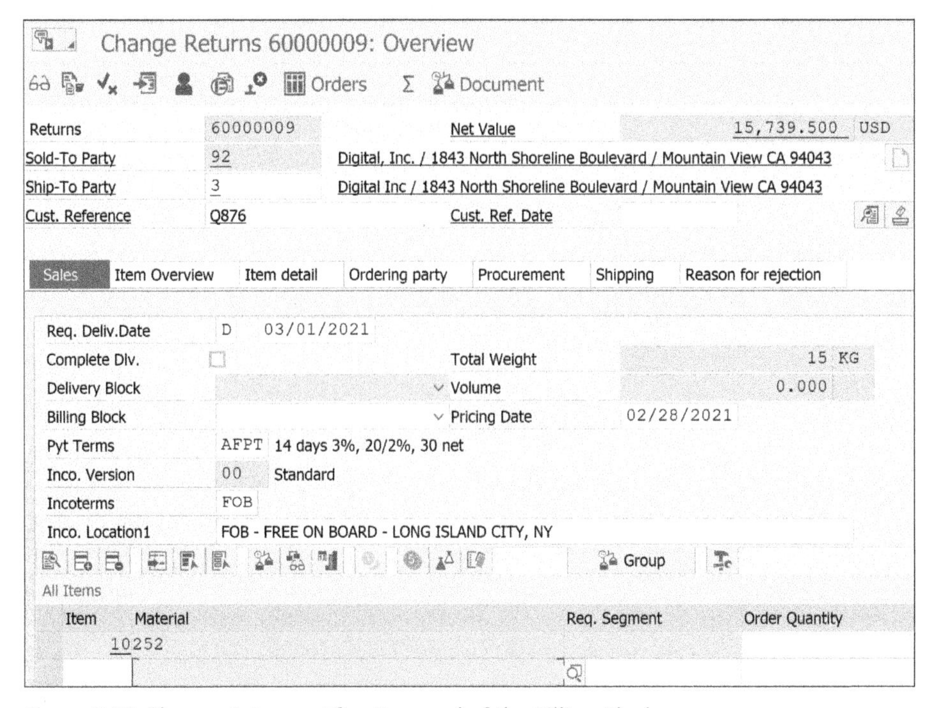

Figure 9.27 Change Returns: After Removal of the Billing Block

4. Click on the **Save** button to receive the returns saved message in the lower-left corner of the screen, as shown in Figure 9.28.

Figure 9.28 Returns Order Saved Message

> **Note**
> As there haven't been any new documents created in this step, we'll skip the document flow. You're invited of course to run it again just for practice.

9.8 Create a Credit Invoice

Now we're ready for the credit invoice. Follow these steps to create one:

1. Go to Transaction VF01 (Create Billing Document), and enter "60000009" in the **Document** field, as shown in Figure 9.29.

The document number must be the returns order and not the returns delivery. The CR billing document type to be created in this step is order-based. As a matter of fact, you can create the CR billing document with reference to the RE sales document before completing the returns delivery (unless your system is configured otherwise). This gives you extra flexibility to credit the customer first and deal with your own goods movements/inventory levels later.

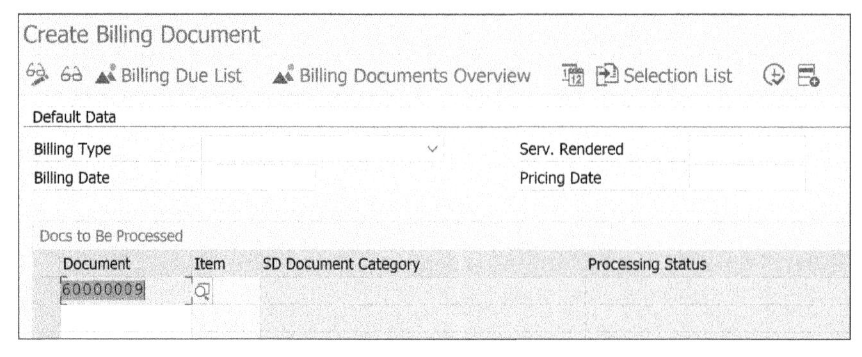

Figure 9.29 Create Billing Document

2. Click on the **Execute** button or press [Enter] to go to the screen shown in Figure 9.30.

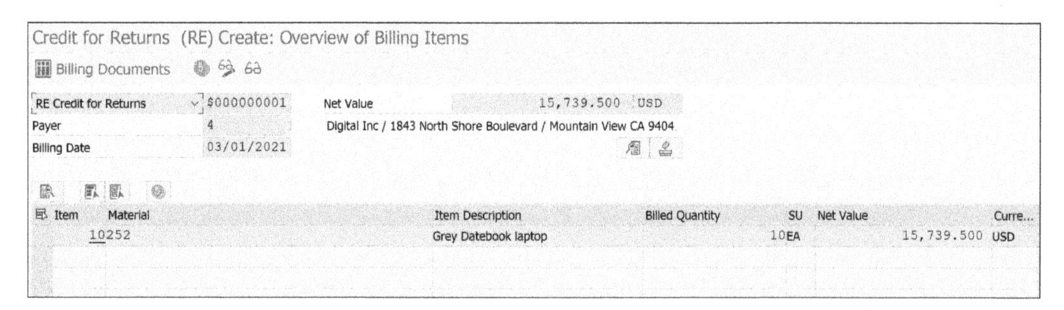

Figure 9.30 Credit for Returns RE Create: Overview of Billing Items Screen

> **Note**
>
> All fields are shaded. Only the **Billing Date** field in the header **Detail** tab is available for changing as required by your business circumstance.

3. Click on the **Save** icon (Figure 9.31), and look for the message that the document has been saved (Figure 9.32).

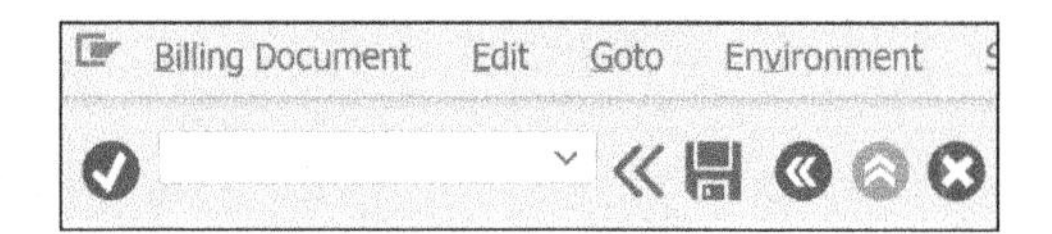

Figure 9.31 Billing Document: Save Icon

Figure 9.32 Billing Document: Saved Message

Level of Completion: Document Flow

To check the document flow, go to Transaction VA03 (Display Sales Documents), enter "251" in the **Order** number field, and click on the **Document Flow** button as you've done previously. The completed flow with all entries appears, as shown in Figure 9.33.

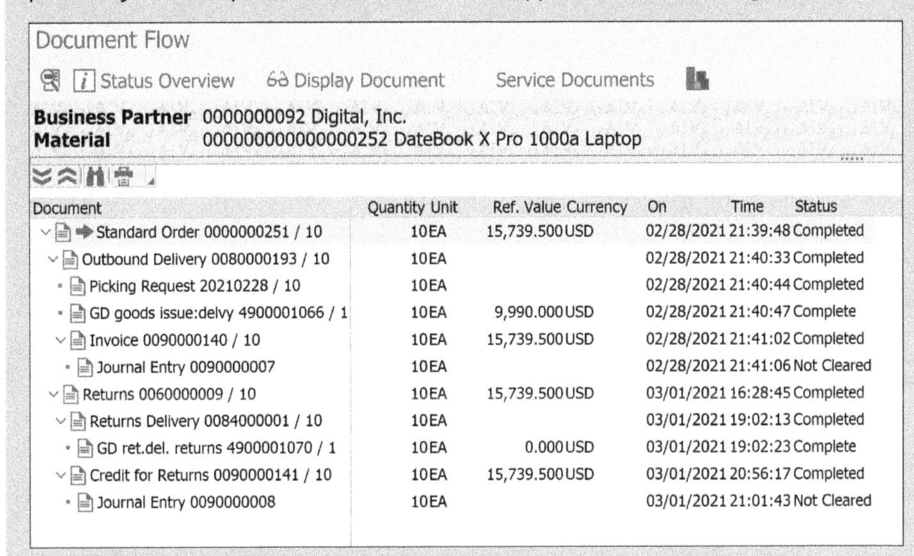

Document	Quantity	Unit	Ref. Value	Currency	On	Time	Status
Standard Order 0000000251 / 10	10	EA	15,739.500	USD	02/28/2021	21:39:48	Completed
Outbound Delivery 0080000193 / 10	10	EA			02/28/2021	21:40:33	Completed
Picking Request 20210228 / 10	10	EA			02/28/2021	21:40:44	Completed
GD goods issue:delvy 4900001066 / 1	10	EA	9,990.000	USD	02/28/2021	21:40:47	Complete
Invoice 0090000140 / 10	10	EA	15,739.500	USD	02/28/2021	21:41:02	Completed
Journal Entry 0090000007	10	EA			02/28/2021	21:41:06	Not Cleared
Returns 0060000009 / 10	10	EA	15,739.500	USD	03/01/2021	16:28:45	Completed
Returns Delivery 0084000001 / 10	10	EA			03/01/2021	19:02:13	Completed
GD ret.del. returns 4900001070 / 1	10	EA	0.000	USD	03/01/2021	19:02:23	Complete
Credit for Returns 0090000141 / 10	10	EA	15,739.500	USD	03/01/2021	20:56:17	Completed
Journal Entry 0090000008	10	EA			03/01/2021	21:01:43	Not Cleared

Figure 9.33 Completed Reversal Document Flow

Notice the new documents at the bottom, the **Credit for Returns**, together with the associated accounting document, **Journal Entry**.

The five reversal documents back out the six original documents as follows:

- **Order level**
  Original standard order 251 reversed by returns order 60000009.
- **Delivery level**
  Original outbound delivery 80000193 reversed by returns delivery 84000001. GI 4900001066 reversed by goods returns 4900001070. The original picking request 20210228 doesn't require a reversal document.
- **Billing level**
  Original invoice 90000140 reversed by credit for returns 90000141. Original journal entry 90000007 reversed by journal entry 90000008.

Note

The status for all documents is now **Completed** (or **Complete**), except for the two journal entries (or accounting documents), which are listed as **Not Cleared**. That is the job of the accounts receivable department. Your job in the sales and distribution order-to-cash role is now completed. See Chapter 12 for some insights as to what happens after your job is done.

9.9 Create Returns Order (SAP Fiori)

The reversal process in SAP Fiori is very similar. The key difference is that it's initiated by way of a SAP Fiori tile or app. Luckily, these tiles can be looked up via Transaction SAPGUI. To do so, follow these steps:

1. Launch the VA01 Create Sales Orders app, and, as you did in the SAP GUI in Section 9.3, enter "RE" in the **Order Type** field in preparation to create with reference a preceding document. RE is the standard SAP document type for a returns order.

   This SAP Fiori screen looks almost identical to the SAP GUI screen, except for the next step.

2. Choose **More • Sales Document • Create with Reference**, as shown in Figure 9.34.

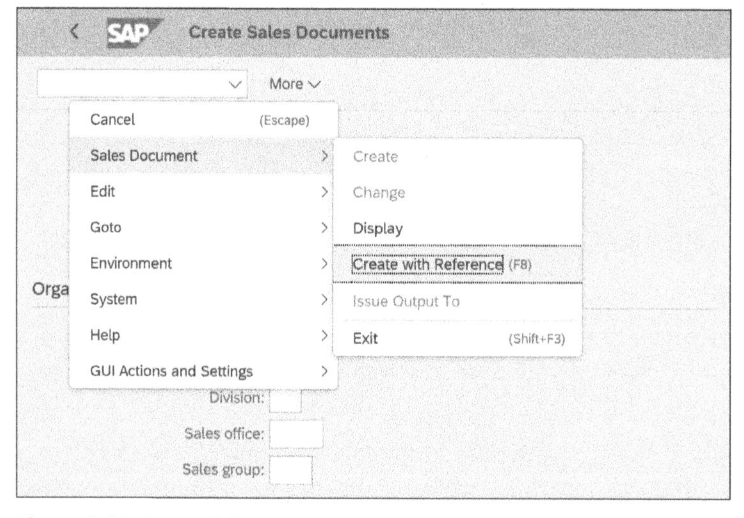

Figure 9.34 Create Sales Documents in SAP Fiori Menu

Note

The **RE** entry in the **Order Type** field is obscured by the cascading menus.

3. In the **Create with Reference** dialog, as shown in Figure 9.35, enter "253" in the **Order** field. This is the sales document number of the order-to-cash transaction to be reversed.

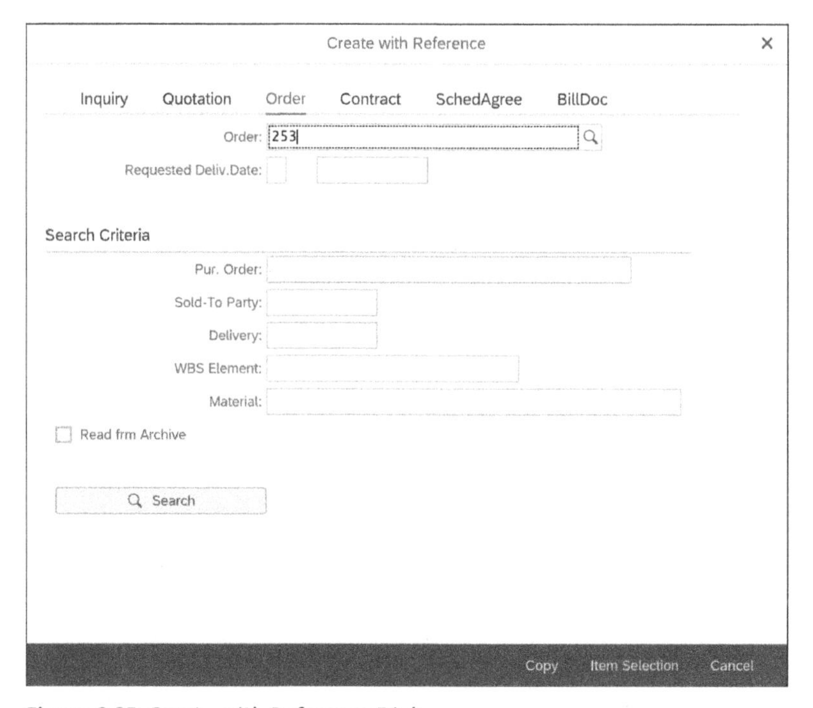

Figure 9.35 Create with Reference Dialog

4. Click on the **Copy** button in the lower-right corner of the dialog.
5. You're now in the main **Create Returns: Overview** screen, which, like with the SAP GUI screen, has been completed with the customer and material information.
6. After (a nonvalidated) input of the **Cust. Reference** field, your screen looks like Figure 9.36. Click on the **Header Output Preview** button.

Note

Note the system automatically opens the header **Sales** tab and highlights **Order Reason** as missing data.

7. Select **Poor Quality** as the **Order Reason**, and press Enter.

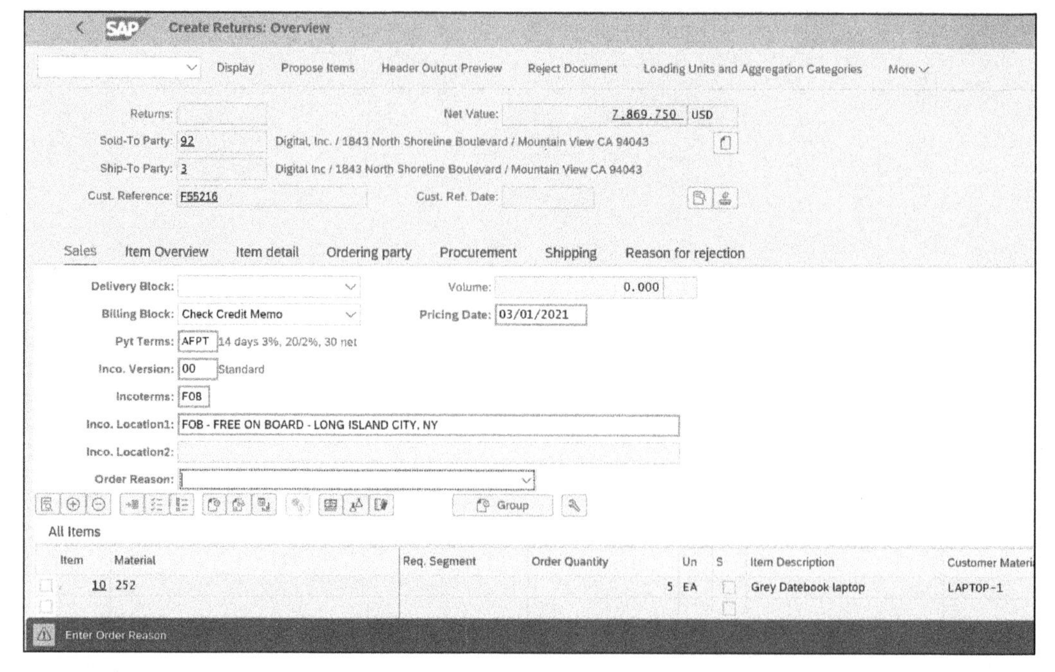

Figure 9.36 Create Returns: Sales Tab in Header

9.9.1 Remove Billing Block

Now let's remove the billing block (as opposed to coming back to it as we did in SAP GUI) and then save the sales document:

1. Click the Go Back arrow as circled in red in Figure 9.37.

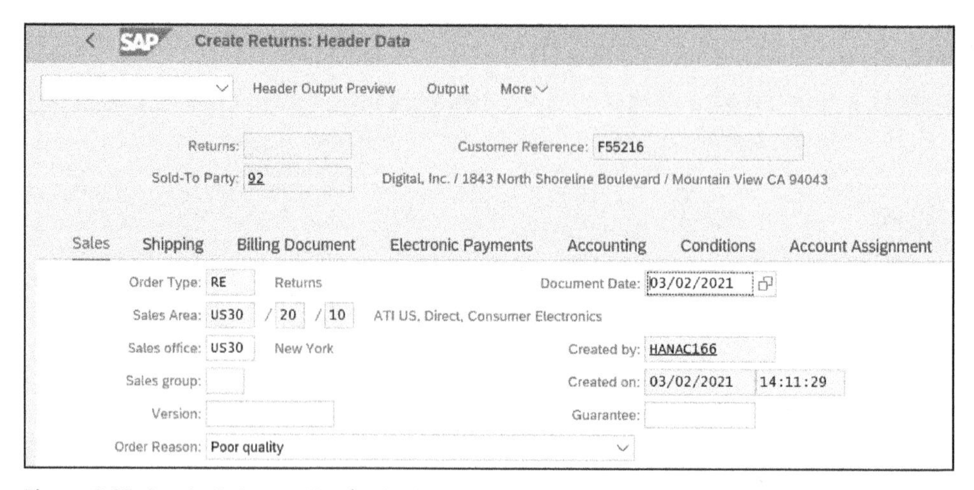

Figure 9.37 Create Returns: Header Data

2. Click the **Billing Block** dropdown, and scroll to the bottom. Select the last entry, the empty row, as shown in Figure 9.38.

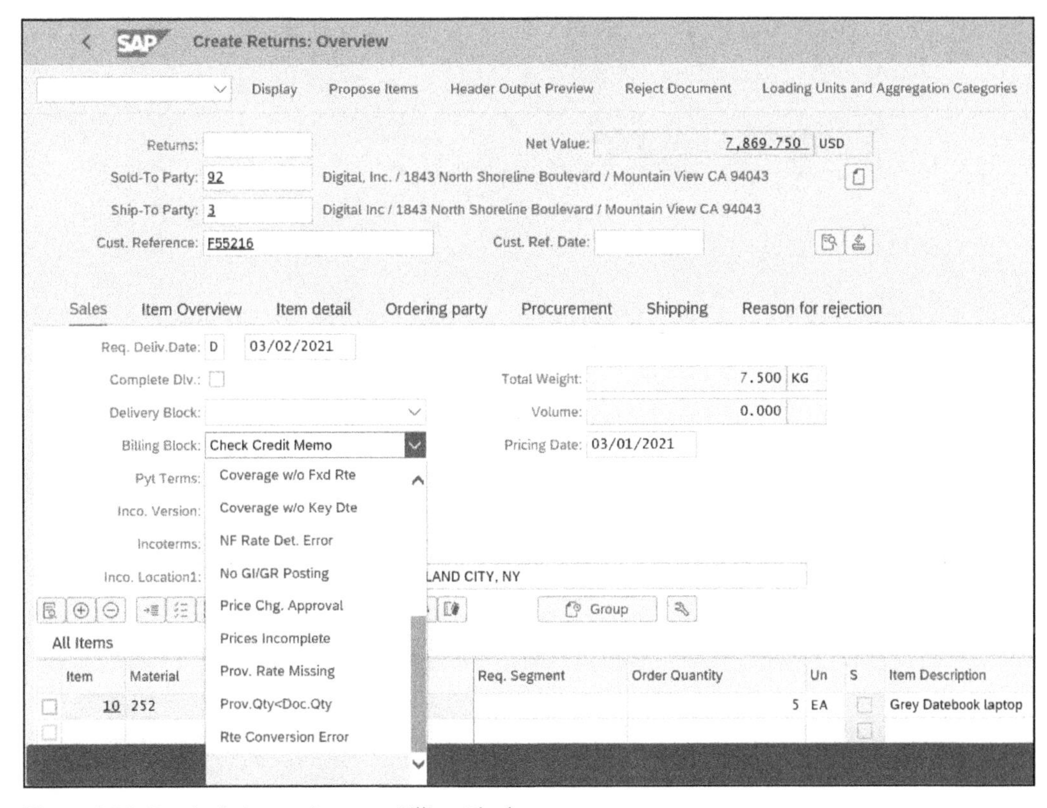

Figure 9.38 Create Returns: Remove Billing Block

3. The document is now complete. Click on the **Save** button in the lower-right corner, as shown in Figure 9.39.

Figure 9.39 Save button in SAP Fiori

4. After saving, look for the confirmation message that your standard order has been saved, as shown in Figure 9.40.

Figure 9.40 Returns Saved Message

This returns order document can now be used to create a returns delivery document to proceed in the next step of the order-to-cash process.

9.9.2 Level of Completion: Document Flow

To check the document flow, follow these steps:

1. In the **Create Returns: Overview** screen showing the saved message, click on **Display** in the menu bar, as shown in Figure 9.41.

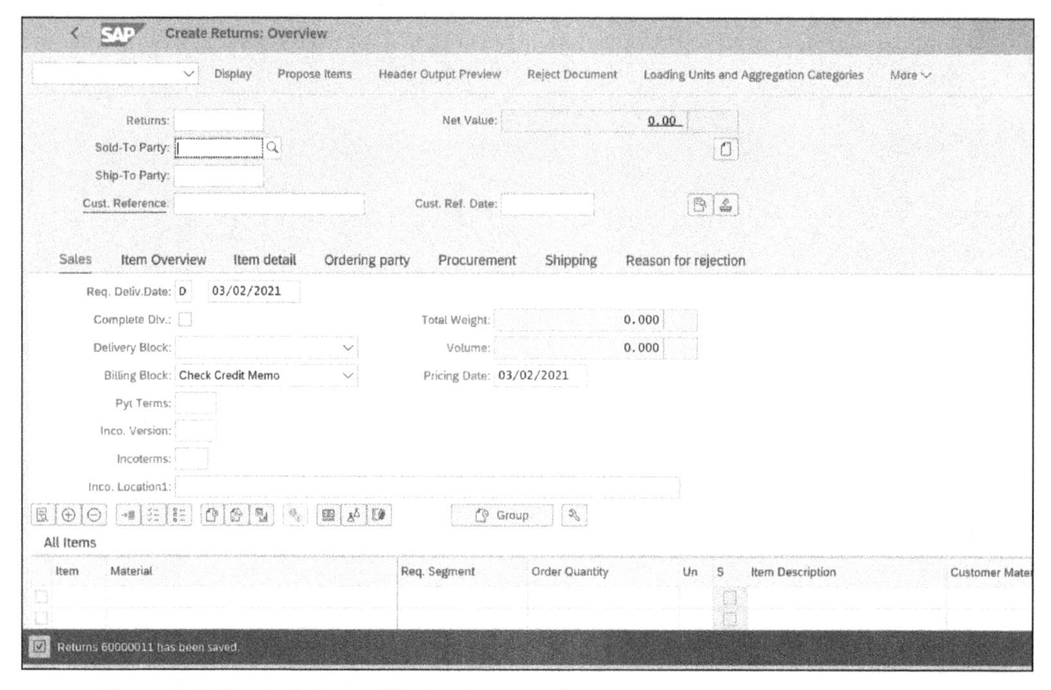

Figure 9.41 Create Returns: Display Command

2. Click on the **Go Back** arrow in the **Create Returns: Overview** screen to change the order number, as shown in Figure 9.42.

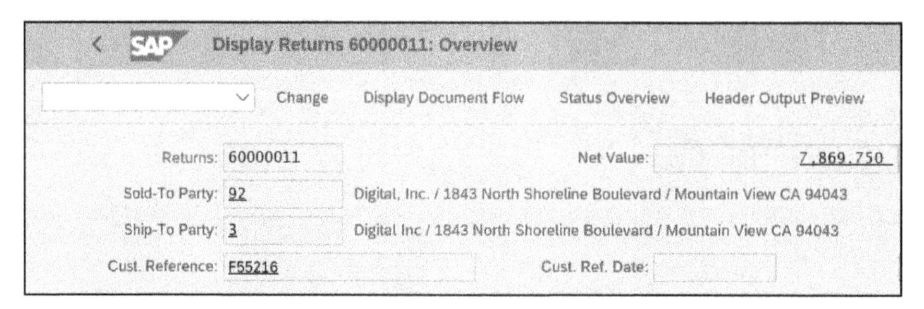

Figure 9.42 Display Returns: Overview

3. Change the **Order** number to the underlying sales document of the transaction to be reversed, in this case, "253" (as opposed to the new sales document just created).
4. Click on the **Display Document Flow** button, as shown in Figure 9.43.

This brings up the document flow in SAP Fiori, which is very similar to the SAP GUI screen, as shown in Figure 9.44.

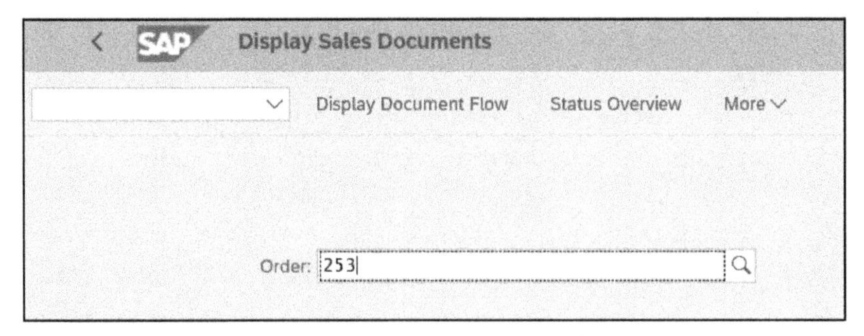

Figure 9.43 Display Sales Documents

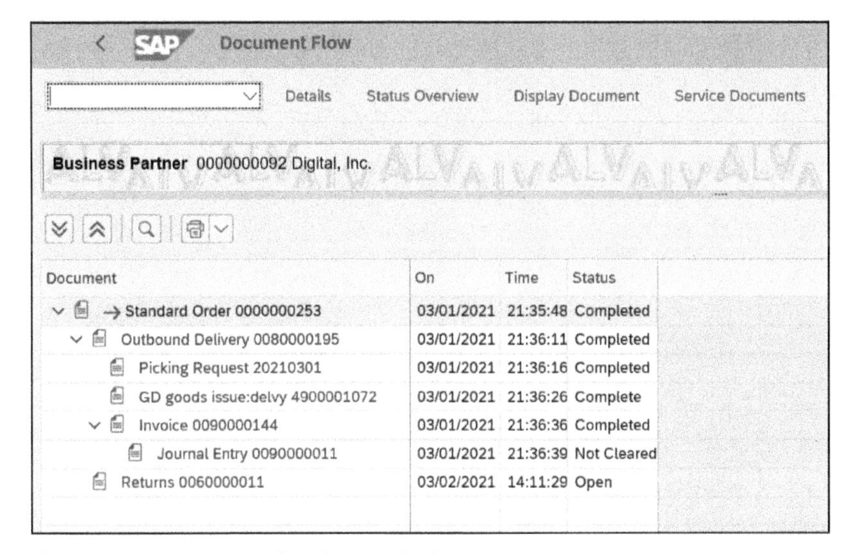

Figure 9.44 Document Flow in SAP Fiori

Note

Notice the new document at the bottom, the **Returns** order. As we successively process the reversal, the follow-on documents will appear below the returns order to mirror the original transaction, composed of six documents.

Note

Note that the status of the returns document is **Open**.

9.10 Create a Returns Delivery Document

Now let's undo the delivery level, inclusive of all relevant subprocesses, and then create the credit invoice immediately thereafter. The document flow at each step in SAP Fiori is omitted in this section, but as a good practice, you should check it at every step, especially if this is your first time doing a reversal in SAP Fiori.

1. Launch the VL01N Create Outbound Delivery with Order Reference app in SAP Fiori, and, as you did in Section 9.3 earlier, input the following fields. To get to this app, you can use the same transaction code as in SAP GUI, taking care to precede the code with the prefix "/n" (without quotation marks) because you aren't in the main menu.
   - **Shipping Point**: "0001"
   - **Order**: "60000011" (returns order number created in the previous section)
2. Click on the **Continue** button in the lower-right corner to progress to the **Returns Delivery Create: Overview** screen, as shown in Figure 9.45.

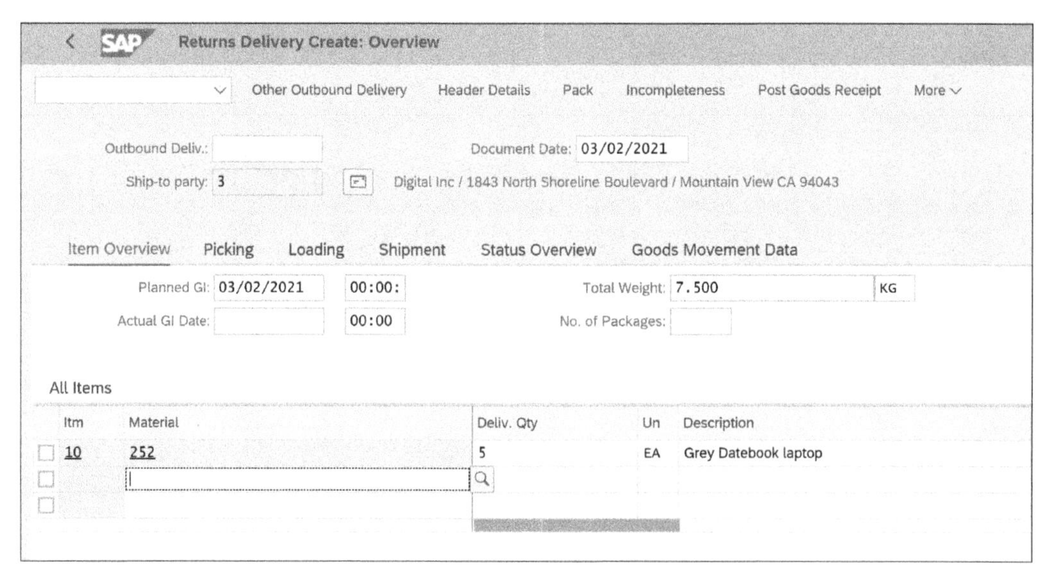

Figure 9.45 Returns Delivery Create: Overview Screen in SAP Fiori

3. Click on the **Picking** tab to progress to the screen in Figure 9.46.
4. Enter "1000" in the **SLoc** (storage location) field. This will designate the exact section of the warehouse to which the goods will be replaced (permitting them to be picked again in the future).
5. Click on the **Post Goods Receipt** button in Figure 9.46.

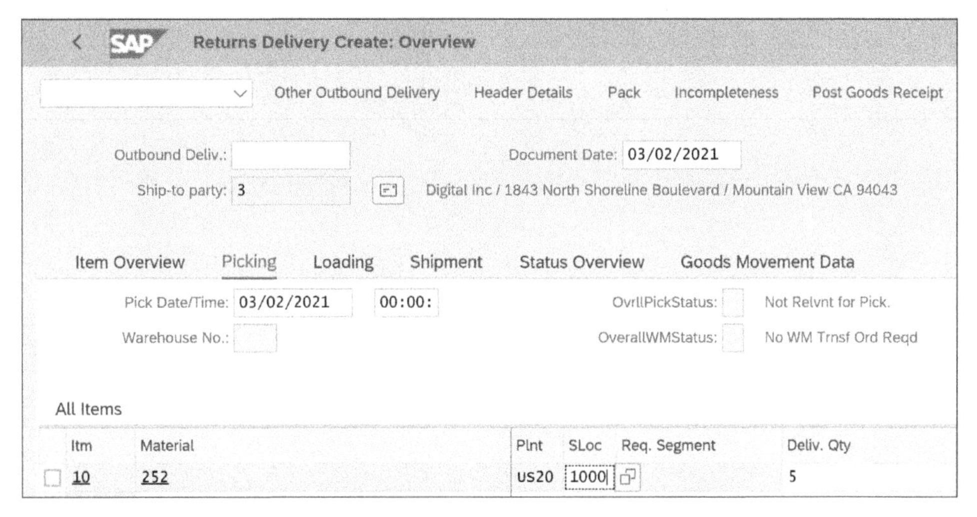

Figure 9.46 Returns Delivery Create: Picking Tab

A message should appear with your returns delivery document number on the status bar in the lower-left corner of your screen, as shown in Figure 9.47.

Figure 9.47 Returns Delivery Saved Message

This returns delivery document can now be used to create a credit invoice document to proceed in the next step of the order-to-cash process.

9.11 Create a Credit Invoice (SAP Fiori)

The last step is to create the credit invoice. Remember, this time, we've already removed the billing block from the returns document. Follow these steps:

1. Launch the VF01 Create Billing Document app in SAP Fiori, and enter "60000011" in the **Document** field, as shown in Figure 9.48.

   This entry may not be necessary if you launched the Create Billing Document app immediate after generating the returns delivery because SAP S/4HANA will load the correct reference number for you at no extra charge.

   As previously noted, the document number must be the returns order and not the returns delivery.

2. Click on the **Execute** button in the lower-right corner.

   Note that all fields are shaded. Only the **Billing Date** field in the header **Detail** tab is available for changing as required by your business circumstance (see Figure 9.49).

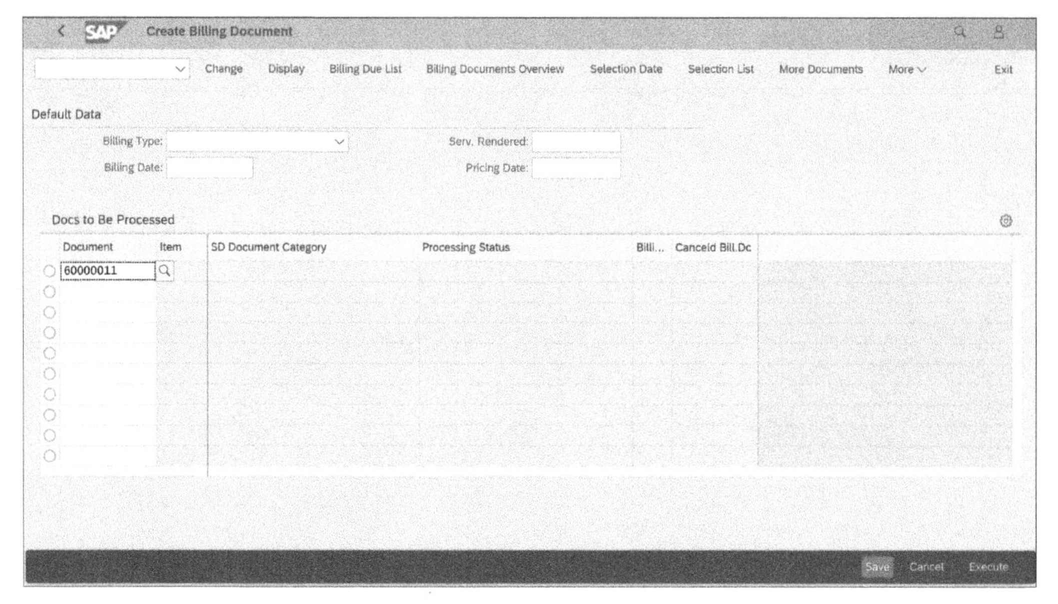

Figure 9.48 Create Billing Document App

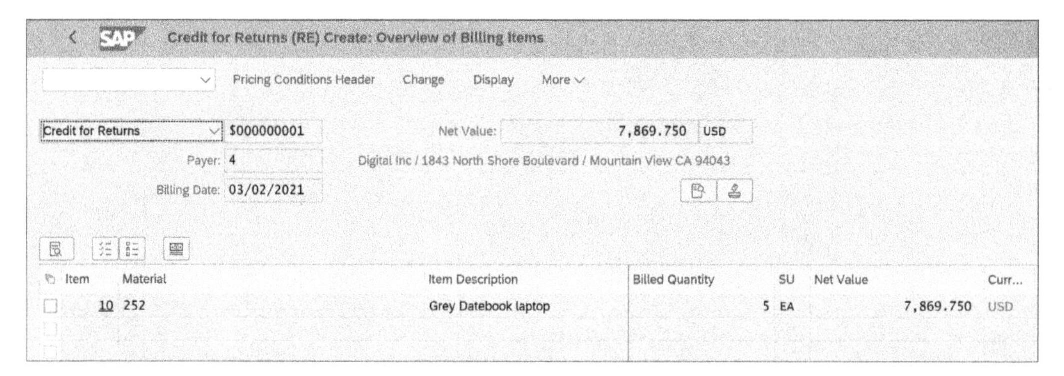

Figure 9.49 Credit for Returns (RE) Create: Overview of Billing Items Screen in SAP Fiori

3. Click on the **Save** button in the lower-right corner, and the saved message appears, as displayed in Figure 9.50.

Figure 9.50 Billing Document Saved Message

Level of Completion: Document Flow

To check the document flow in SAP Fiori, launch the VA03 Display Sales Documents app, input **Order** number "253", and click on the **Display Document Flow** button as you've done previously. The completed flow with all entries appears, as shown in Figure 9.51.

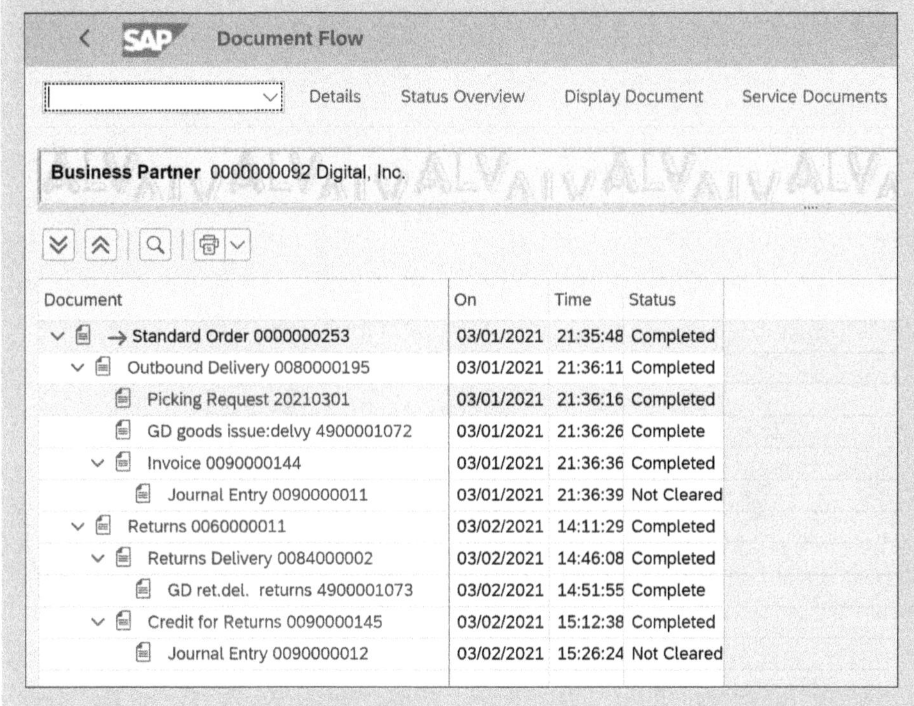

Figure 9.51 Completed Reversal Document Flow in SAP Fiori

This display is virtually identical to what you saw in the SAP GUI before. Notice the new documents at the bottom: the **Credit for Returns** and the associated accounting document (labeled as the **Journal Entry**).

The five reversal documents back out the six original documents as follows:

- **Order level**
  Original standard order 253 reversed by returns order 60000011.
- **Delivery level**
  Original outbound delivery 80000195 reversed by returns delivery 84000002. GI 4900001072 reversed by goods returns 4900001073. The original picking request 20210301 doesn't require a reversal document.
- **Billing level**
  Original invoice 90000144 reversed by credit for returns 90000145. Original journal entry 90000011 reversed by journal entry 90000012.

Note the status for all documents is now **Completed** (or **Complete**), except for the two journal entries (or accounting documents), which are listed as **Not Cleared**. Accounting will take care of these.

Your job in reversing the erroneous original sales and distribution order-to-cash role is now completed. See Chapter 12 for some insights as to what happens after your job is done.

9.12 Reversal Matrix

The matrix shown in Table 9.1 will serve as your reference aid in determining the exact steps necessary for correcting errors in your sales, delivery, and billing documents based on the following three factors:

- Field that needs to be changed
- Document of the erroneous field
- Level of completion in your order-to-cash transaction

As you've seen countless times in this book, after a field is input in a certain document (typically the sales document), it can be copied over into subsequent documents. This is both a blessing and a curse in that the copy function saves you work—as long as you don't make a mistake, that is. Unfortunately, if you're like the rest of us, wrong entries will be made from time to time, even to the best of us—hence, the raison d'être of this chapter.

Use this matrix as soon as an error is discovered in your order-to-cash transaction. The questions to ask are as follows:

- Which field is wrong?
- In which document?
- How far along are you in the order-to-cash transaction?

The main diagnostic tool is the document flow, as you've seen more than a few times in this chapter, from the underlying sales document. This will answer the question posed by the third column of the matrix: "And your level of completion is?"

Level of completion means that the document has been saved and/or posted.

Note that the matrix includes the PGI subdocument as a potential level, as this is distinct from the umbrella delivery document. The PGI document actually hits your company's general ledger accounts and locks down many fields after those postings are made. Accordingly, it generally needs to be reversed to fix many wrong data entries. This can be done by either creating a returns delivery (inclusive of the post goods receipt) or by reversing the GI.

Note

This matrix isn't exhaustive. It's possible to make some changes directly on subsequent documents that will unfortunately not be reflected on previous documents. In such cases, your documents can get out of sync one to the other. This isn't recommended.

Accordingly, this matrix is conservatively biased to maintain 100% synchronization between all documents. This is why you'll see a lot of "delete document B, change document A, re-create document B" guidance.

If your company uses the embedded extended warehouse management (EWM) or warehouse management (WM) functionalities, some of the delivery steps may be more complicated, and you'll need to consult the teams in question for further guidance.

If your company has defined pricing on the basis of fields listed in the matrix, such as order reason, plant, etc., you'll need to check pricing at the sales document level (and possibly billing document level if prices are redetermined there) also after making these changes.

As noted previously, it makes sense in certain places to use Transaction VL09 (Reverse Goods Movement). Remember that if you do create a returns delivery, there is no need to separately reverse the PGI because the returns delivery is inclusive of this step.

Your warehouse manager is able to make some delivery date changes on his side. You may want to consult with him first. In the absence of that specific guidance, the matrix guides you safely and conservatively to simply reverse the transaction and start over with correct dates. For the purposes of a general book like this, this is prudent advice (even if perhaps too cautious by creating an extra document). But the point about offsetting documents remains of the essence.

If this field needs to be changed	In this Document	And your level of completion is	Then follow these steps
Order Type	Sales document	Sales document	Go to Menu Path: **Sales Document • Delete** to delete the order and start over. Exception: Change to allowed "**Alternative Order Types.**" This is fairly rare.
Create with Reference document number	Sales document	Sales document	Go to Menu Path: **Sales Document • Delete** to delete the order and start over.
Sold-to Party	Sales document	Sales document	Change **Sold-to** in **Sales Document Overview**
Ship-to Party	Sales document	Sales document	Change **Ship-to** in **Sales Document Overview**

Table 9.1 Correction Matrix

If this field needs to be changed	In this Document	And your level of completion is	Then follow these steps
Bill-to Party	Sales document	Sales document	Change **Bill-to** in **Sales Document Header • Partner**
Payer	Sales document	Sales document	Change **Payer** in **Sales Document Header • Partner**
Cust. Reference	Sales document	Sales document	Change **Cust. Reference** in **Sales Document Overview**
Cust Ref. Date	Sales document	Sales document	Change **Cust. Ref. Date** in **Sales Document Overview**
Req. Deliv. Date	Sales document	Sales document	Change the **Delivery Date** in the **Sales Document Line Item • Schedule Line tab.**
Pricing Date	Sales document	Sales document	Change **Pricing Date** in **Sales Document Overview**
Order Reason	Sales document	Sales document	Change **Order Reason** in **Sales Document Header • Sales**
Material	Sales document	Sales document	Change **Material** in **Sales Document Overview**. Materials can be deleted or added.
Order Quantity	Sales document	Sales document	Change **Quantity** in **Sales Document Overview**
Plant	Sales document	Sales document	Change **Plant** in **Sales Document Line Item • Shipping** tab
Payment Terms	Sales document	Sales document	Change Payment Terms in **Sales Document Header • Billing** tab
Incoterms	Sales document	Sales document	Change **Incoterms** in **Sales Document Header • Billing** tab
Document Currency	Sales document	Sales document	Change **Document Currency** in **Header • Sales** tab
Shipping Condition	Sales document	Sales document	Change **Shipping Condition** in **Header • Shipping** tab
Texts	Sales document	Sales document	Change **Text** in either **Sales document Header** or **Line Item Text**

Table 9.1 Correction Matrix (Cont.)

If this field needs to be changed	In this Document	And your level of completion is	Then follow these steps
Price Conditions	Sales document	Sales document	Change **Price Condition** in sales document either manually or via VK11 or VK12 and update pricing in **Line Item • Conditions**
Batch	Sales document	Sales document	Change **Batch** in **Line Item • Sales** tab
Order Type	Sales document	Delivery document	1. Go to menu path in **Delivery Document: Outbound Delivery • Delete** to delete the **Delivery Document** 2. Go to menu path: **Sales Document • Delete** to delete the order and start over.
Create with Reference document number	Sales document	Delivery document	1. Go to menu path in **Delivery Document: Outbound Delivery •** Delete to delete the **Delivery Document** 2. Go to menu path: **Sales Document • Delete** to delete the order and start over.
Sold-to Party	Sales document	Delivery document	1. Go to menu path in **Delivery Document: Outbound Delivery • Delete** to delete the **Delivery Document** 2. Go to menu path: **Sales Document • Delete** to delete the order and start over.
Ship-to Party	Sales document	Delivery document	Change **Ship-to** in **Sales Document Overview**
Bill-to Party	Sales document	Delivery document	Change **Bill-to** in **Sales Document Header • Partner**
Payer	Sales document	Delivery document	Change **Payer** in **Sales Document Header • Partner**
Cust. Reference	Sales document	Delivery document	Change **Cust. Reference** in **Sales Document Overview**
Cust Ref. Date	Sales document	Delivery document	Change **Cust. Ref. Date** in **Sales Document Overview**

Table 9.1 Correction Matrix (Cont.)

If this field needs to be changed	In this Document	And your level of completion is	Then follow these steps
Req. Deliv. Date	Sales document	Delivery document	1. Go to menu path in **Delivery Document: Outbound Delivery • Delete** to delete the Delivery Document 2. Delete the Schedule line with the wrong **Delivery Date** in **Sales Document Line Item • Schedule Line** tab. 3. Add a new schedule line with the correct delivery date and save the sales order. 4. Create a new delivery document and validate the new date.
Pricing Date	Sales document	Delivery document	Change **Header Pricing Date** in **Sales Document Overview**. Validate that the date is correct for each line item in **Line Item Sales A** tab.
Order Reason	Sales document	Delivery document	Change **Order Reason** in **Sales Document Header • Sales**
Material	Sales document	Delivery document	1. Go to menu path in **Delivery Document: Outbound Delivery • Delete** to delete the **Delivery Document** 2. Change **Material** in **Sales Document Overview** and save the sales order. 3. Create a new delivery document.
Order Quantity	Sales document	Delivery document	1. Go to menu path in **Delivery Document: Outbound Delivery • Delete** to delete the **Delivery Document** 2. Change **Material Quantity** in **Sales Document Overview** and save the sales order. 3. Create a new delivery document.

Table 9.1 Correction Matrix (Cont.)

If this field needs to be changed	In this Document	And your level of completion is	Then follow these steps
Plant	Sales document	Delivery document	1. Go to menu path in **Delivery Document: Outbound Delivery • Delete** to delete the delivery document 2. Change **Plant** in **Sales Document Line Item • Shipping** tab 3. Create a new delivery document.
Payment Terms	Sales document	Delivery document	Change **Payment Terms** in **Sales Document Header • Billing** tab
Incoterms	Sales document	Delivery document	1. Go to menu path in **Delivery Document: Outbound Delivery • Delete** to delete the delivery document 2. Change **Incoterms** in **Sales Document Header • Billing** tab. 3. Create a new delivery document.
Document Currency	Sales document	Delivery document	Change **Document Currency** in **Header • Sales** tab
Shipping Condition	Sales document	Delivery document	1. Go to menu path in **Delivery Document: Outbound Delivery • Delete** to delete the delivery document 2. Change **Change Shipping Condition** in **Header • Shipping** tab and save the sales order. 3. Create a new delivery document, taking care to note the new shipping point from the sales order
Texts	Sales document	Delivery document	Change text in either sales document header or line item text
Price Conditions	Sales document	Delivery document	Change price condition in sales document line items either manually or via VK11 or VK12 and update pricing in **Line Item • Conditions**

Table 9.1 Correction Matrix (Cont.)

If this field needs to be changed	In this Document	And your level of completion is	Then follow these steps
Batch	Sales document	Delivery document	Change batch in **Delivery Document Overview**. Exception: The customer may require a specific batch as stipulated in the Sales document and making a change in the delivery may be problematic. If so, reverse everything and restart with a new sales document.
Order Type	Sales document	Post goods issue	1. Create returns order with reference to the underlying sales document 2. Create returns delivery and post goods receipt 3. Create a new sales document with correct document type 4. Create new delivery and post goods issue
Create with Reference document number	Sales document	Post goods issue	1. Create returns order with reference to the underlying sales document 2. Create returns delivery and post goods receipt 3. Create a new sales document with correct reference document number 4. Create new delivery and post goods issue
Sold-to Party	Sales document	Post goods issue	1. Create returns order with reference to the underlying sales document 2. Create returns delivery and post goods receipt 3. Create a new sales document with correct sold-to party 4. Create new delivery and post goods issue

Table 9.1 Correction Matrix (Cont.)

If this field needs to be changed	In this Document	And your level of completion is	Then follow these steps
Ship-to Party	Sales document	Post goods issue	1. Create returns order with reference to the underlying sales document 2. Create returns delivery and post goods receipt 3. Create a new sales document with correct ship-to party 4. Create new delivery and post goods issue
Bill-to Party	Sales document	Post goods issue	Change **Bill-to** in **Sales Document Header • Partner**
Payer	Sales document	Post goods issue	Change **Payer** in **Sales Document Header • Partner**
Cust. Reference	Sales document	Post goods issue	Change **Cust. Reference** in **Sales Document Overview**
Cust Ref. Date	Sales document	Post goods issue	Change **Cust. Ref. Date** in **Sales Document Overview**
Req. Deliv. Date	Sales document	Post goods issue	1. Create returns order with reference to the underlying sales document 2. Create returns delivery and post goods receipt 3. Create a new sales document with correct required delivery date 4. Create new delivery and post goods issue
Pricing Date	Sales document	Post goods issue	Change **Header Pricing Date** in **Sales Document Overview**. Validate that the date is correct for each line item in **Line Item Sales A** tab.
Order Reason	Sales document	Post goods issue	Change **Order Reason** in **Sales Document Header • Sales**

Table 9.1 Correction Matrix (Cont.)

If this field needs to be changed	In this Document	And your level of completion is	Then follow these steps
Material	Sales document	Post goods issue	1. Reverse goods issue 2. Go to menu path in **Delivery Document: Outbound Delivery • Delete** to delete the delivery document 3. Change material in sales document line item 4. Create new delivery and post goods issue
Order Quantity	Sales document	Post goods issue	1. Reverse goods issue 2. Go to menu path in **Delivery Document: Outbound Delivery • Delete** to delete the delivery document 3. Change material in sales document line item (alternatively, if you need to deliver more material, you could add another line item in your existing sales document and create a new delivery). 4. Create new delivery and post goods issue
Plant	Sales document	Sales document	1. Reverse goods issue 2. Go to menu path in **Delivery Document: Outbound Delivery • Delete** to delete the delivery document 3. Change **Plant** in **Sales Document Line Item • Shipping** tab 4. Create new delivery and post goods issue
Payment Terms	Sales document	Post goods issue	Change **Payment Terms** in **Sales Document Header • Billing** tab

Table 9.1 Correction Matrix (Cont.)

If this field needs to be changed	In this Document	And your level of completion is	Then follow these steps
Incoterms	Sales document	Post goods issue	1. Reverse goods issue 2. Go to menu path in **Delivery Document: Outbound Delivery • Delete** to delete the delivery document 3. Change **Incoterms** in **Sales Document Header • Billing** tab. 4. Create new delivery and post goods issue
Document Currency	Sales document	Post goods issue	Change **Document Currency** in **Header • Sales** tab
Shipping Condition	Sales document	Post goods issue	1. Reverse goods Issue 2. Go to menu path in **Delivery Document: Outbound Delivery • Delete** to delete the delivery document 3. Change **Change Shipping Condition** in **Header • Shipping** tab and save the sales order. 4. Create a new delivery document, taking care to note the new shipping point from the sales order, and post goods issue
Texts	Sales document	Post goods issue	Change text in either sales document header or line item text
Price Conditions	Sales document	Post goods issue	Change price condition in sales document line items either manually or via VK11 or VK12 and update pricing in **Line Item • Conditions**. Exception: Delivery costs in delivery document will require deletion of delivery document.

Table 9.1 Correction Matrix (Cont.)

If this field needs to be changed	In this Document	And your level of completion is	Then follow these steps
Batch	Delivery document	Post goods issue	1. Reverse goods issue 2. Undo the material pick quantity in the delivery document overview 3. Change the batch number in the delivery document overview Exception: The customer may require a specific batch as stipulated in the sales document and making a change in the delivery may be problematic. If so, reverse everything and restart with a new sales document.
Order Type	Sales document	Billing document	1. Create returns order with reference to the underlying sales document 2. Create returns delivery and post goods receipt 3. Create credit invoice to finish reversal 4. Create a new sales document with correct document type 5. Create new delivery and post goods issue 6. Create new billing document
Create with Reference document number	Sales document	Billing document	1. Create returns order with reference to the underlying sales document 2. Create returns delivery and post goods receipt 3. Create credit invoice to finish reversal 4. Create a new sales document with correct document reference number 5. Create new delivery and post goods issue 6. Create new billing document

Table 9.1 Correction Matrix (Cont.)

If this field needs to be changed	In this Document	And your level of completion is	Then follow these steps
Sold-to Party	Sales document	Billing document	1. Create returns order with reference to the underlying sales document 2. Create returns delivery and post goods receipt 3. Create credit invoice to finish reversal 4. Create a new sales document with correct sold-to party 5. Create new delivery and post goods issue 6. Create new billing document
Ship-to Party	Sales document	Billing document	1. Create returns order with reference to the underlying sales document 2. Create returns delivery and post goods receipt 3. Create credit invoice to finish reversal 4. Create a new sales document with correct ship-to party 5. Create new delivery and post goods issue 6. Create new billing document
Bill-to Party	Sales document	Billing document	1. Cancel billing document 2. Change bill-to party in sales document header partner tab 3. Create new billing document
Payer	Sales document	Billing document	1. Cancel billing document 2. Change payer party in sales document header partner tab 3. Create new billing document
Cust. Reference	Sales document	Billing document	1. Cancel billing document 2. Change customer reference in sales document overview 3. Create new billing document

Table 9.1 Correction Matrix (Cont.)

If this field needs to be changed	In this Document	And your level of completion is	Then follow these steps
Cust Ref. Date	Sales document	Billing document	1. Cancel billing document 2. Change customer reference date in sales document overview 3. Create new billing document
Req. Deliv. Date	Sales document	Billing document	1. Create returns order with reference to the underlying sales document 2. Create returns delivery and post goods receipt 3. Create credit invoice to finish reversal 4. Create a new sales document with correct ship-to party 5. Create new delivery and post goods issue 6. Create new billing document
Pricing Date	Sales document	Billing document	Depends if pricing is done at sales or billing level. If at sales level: 1. Cancel Billing Document 2. Change Pricing Date in Sales document line item Sales A tab 3. Create new Billing document 4. If at Billing level: 5. Cancel Billing Document 6. Create new Billing document 7. Change Pricing Date in Billing Header Detail tab 8. Update Pricing in Billing Header Conditions tab 9. Save new Billing document
Order Reason	Sales document	Billing document	Change order reason in **Sales Document Header • Sales**

Table 9.1 Correction Matrix (Cont.)

If this field needs to be changed	In this Document	And your level of completion is	Then follow these steps
Material	Sales document	Billing document	1. Create returns order with reference to the underlying sales document 2. Create returns delivery and post goods receipt 3. Create credit invoice to finish reversal 4. Create a new sales document with correct material 5. Create new delivery and post goods issue 6. Create new billing document
Order Quantity	Sales document	Billing document	If you need to ship more of the same material, create a new sales order for the additional quantity. If you need to reduce the quantity processed in your transaction: 1. Create returns order with reference to the underlying sales document for the excess quantity only 2. Create returns delivery and post goods receipt to take back the excess quantity 3. Create credit invoice to credit customer for the excess quantity 4. If there are other reasons why the order quantity needs to be reset to the correct amount, effect a complete reversal: 5. Create returns order with reference to the underlying sales document 6. Create returns delivery and post goods receipt 7. Create credit invoice to finish reversal 8. Create a new sales document with correct quantity 9. Create new delivery and post goods issue 10. Create new billing document

Table 9.1 Correction Matrix (Cont.)

If this field needs to be changed	In this Document	And your level of completion is	Then follow these steps
Plant	Sales document	Sales document	1. Create returns order with reference to the underlying sales document 2. Create returns delivery and post goods receipt 3. Create credit invoice to finish reversal 4. Create a new sales document with correct plant in **Sales Document Line Item • Shipping** tab 5. Create new delivery and post goods issue 6. Create new billing document
Payment Terms	Sales document	Billing document	1. Cancel billing document 2. Change payment terms in **Sales Document Header • Billing** tab 3. Create new billing document
Incoterms	Sales document	Billing document	1. Cancel billing document 2. Reverse goods issue 3. Go to menu path in **Delivery Document: Outbound Delivery • Delete** to delete the delivery document 4. Change **Incoterms** in **Sales Document Header • Billing** tab. 5. Create new delivery and post goods issue 6. Create new billing document
Document Currency	Sales document	Billing document	1. Cancel billing document 2. Change currency in **Sales Document Header • Sales** tab 3. Create new billing document

Table 9.1 Correction Matrix (Cont.)

If this field needs to be changed	In this Document	And your level of completion is	Then follow these steps
Shipping Condition	Sales document	Billing document	1. Cancel billing document 2. Reverse goods issue 3. Go to menu path in **Delivery Document: Outbound Delivery • Delete** to delete the delivery document 4. Change **Change Shipping Condition** in **Header • Shipping** tab and save the sales order. 5. Create a new delivery document, taking care to note the new shipping point from the sales order, and post goods issue 6. Create new billing document
Texts	Sales document	Billing document	Change text in either sales or billing document header or line item text
Price Conditions	Sales document	Billing document	1. Cancel billing document 2. Change price condition in sales document line items either manually or via VK11 or VK12 and update pricing in **Line Item • Conditions** 3. Create new billing document
Batch	Delivery document	Billing document	1. Cancel billing document 2. Reverse goods issue 3. Undo the material pick quantity in the delivery document overview 4. Change the batch number in the delivery document overview 5. Post goods issue 6. Create new billing document
Any other field	Delivery document	Billing document	1. Cancel billing document 2. Reverse goods issue 3. Change field in delivery document 4. Post goods issue 5. Create new billing document

Table 9.1 Correction Matrix (Cont.)

If this field needs to be changed	In this Document	And your level of completion is	Then follow these steps
Custom Fields	Sales document	Billing document	Check with your SAP team for any special functionality or impact

Table 9.1 Correction Matrix (Cont.)

9.13 Summary

In this chapter, we have examined the inevitable question of erroneous data entries. Correcting these in SAP S/4HANA requires diligent analysis as to the type of error and the level of completion. Accordingly, we covered the step-by-step process of a complete reversal for demonstration purposes. At each step in the process, the level of completion will be verified to serve as a referential checkpoint in the reversal process. Firstly, we considered a completed order-to-cash transaction where a serious basic error has been made, say a bad entry of an incorrect customer number or sales document type. We walked through backing out of the three levels of completed documents: sales order, delivery, and billing. The second section of the chapter is your reversal matrix, intended as a useful reference going forward. The matrix defines numerous combinations of common mistakes and relates them to different levels of completion. The exact steps necessary to correct the error are succinctly indicated.

No work on sales and distribution in SAP S/4HANA would be complete without a review of reversing an order-to-cash transaction flow. You should refer to this section throughout your adventures in SAP S/4HANA.

Chapter 10
Rebates and Settlement Management

This chapter give you step-by-step instructions for how to create condition contracts, as well as how to use the various functionality of the condition contract.

Rebate management is a critical part of any company. By implementing an effective rebate strategy and practices, many companies not only achieve sales targets but also boost revenue and increase profitability.

In this digital era, SAP has provided a revolutionary offering in rebate processing. Faced with challenges in SAP ERP in terms of process mapping, retro functionality, and performance, SAP responded with the rebate and settlement management functionality in SAP S/4HANA, which offers much innovation and many process improvements. There is flexibility to define condition contracts (rebate agreements), pricing, effective accrual management, and efficient settlement processing.

Compared to SAP ERP, there are a lot of distinguishing factors in SAP S/4HANA that make the entire process smooth and flawless. Business users can create rebate agreements by using single transactions for both customers and vendors. Due to SAP Fiori, the frontend is also improved. Gains have been made in performance as well, especially in retro processing, which was a main issue in SAP ERP. By introducing an in-memory database and improvements in technical architecture, performance is improved drastically.

10.1 Process Overview

Rebate processing comprises the following processes:

- **Creation of condition contract (rebate agreement)**
  The condition contract is a master document that contains details about rebate agreements with customers. This document has influence on all subsequent processes. It includes details about customer, pricing condition, status (status functionality is a critical part of the condition contract and governs the various controls for releasing, locking, and settlement functionalities), and the settlement functionality.
- **Sales order processing**
  After creation of the rebate agreement, a sales order is created for booking sales. The

rebate condition is determined in the sales order based on the condition record maintained in the condition contract. For example, if the sales order is created for 1000USD for material X, and a 2% rebate condition record is maintained in the condition contract, a 20USD rebate will be applied in the sales order.

- **Invoice processing**
  A sales invoice is booked after a material is dispatched and the customer is to be billed. Business volume is determined at the sales invoice level.
- **Accrual processing**
  Accrual processing is required to calculate the estimated payment to the customer. Organizations want to keep an eye on estimated payments for in-process condition contracts. Accrual calculation and reversal of the accrual process takes place during the execution of the condition contract and settlement process. Based on the settlement type, accruals are accumulated per the set frequency. During the settlement, accumulated accruals are reversed.
- **Settlement processing**
  The rebate and settlement functionality offers the following types of settlement based on business requirements, which are defined at the condition contract level:
  - Delta accrual settlement
  - Delta settlement
  - Partial settlement
  - Final settlement

10.2 Condition Contract Management

The condition contract functionality offers various types of contracts in the settlement management area. Condition contracts are used to enter all the details of a rebate agreement with the customer. Thus, this is also called a master document, which is a source document for settlement. Condition contracts capture all the details related to customer, rebates and accruals conditions, status management, organizational data (related to sales area), settlement calendar, and provision of applicable settlement type. The following SAP Fiori apps are available for condition contracts:

- Manage Customer Condition Contract
- Manage Workflow for Condition Contract
- Extend Condition Contract

Transaction WCOCO is used for creating condition contracts for customers (sales process) and vendors (purchase process). To access the transaction, follow the menu path, **Logistics • Settlement Management • Condition Contract Management • Master Data • WCOCO • Edit/Display**.

The condition contract functionality offers different types of condition contracts, as listed in Table 10.1.

Contract type	Description
0S01	Sales Rebate
0S02	Sales Rebate - Multiple Customers
0S03	Sales Rebate - 2Step
0S04	Sales Rebate - Mult. Customers - 2Step
0SG1	Sales Rebate Goods Related
0SG2	Sales Rebate Goods Rel. - Mult. Customers
0SG3	Sales Rebate Goods Related - 2Step
0SG4	Sales Rebate Goods Related - 2Step
0ST1	Sales Rebate TPM
0ST2	Sales Rebate TPM - Multiple Customers
0ST3	Sales Rebate TPM with Claims
0ST4	Sales Rebate TPM with Claims - Mult Cust
SBBI	Sales Bonus Based on Billing Documents

Table 10.1 Condition Contract Types

10.2.1 Types of Condition Contracts

Types of condition contracts include the following:

- **Condition contract for a single customer**
  When a condition contract is customer specific, this type of condition contract is used. All the details, such as validity, pricing, and settlement, entered in the condition contract will be applicable to that specific customer.
- **Condition contract for multiple customers**
  For these types of condition contracts, maintenance of the customer isn't needed at the condition contract level; instead, it's determined at subsequent applicable documents, which is mainly driven by business volume selection criteria maintained at the condition contract level. However, settlement would be carried out per individual customer.
- **One-step condition contract and two-step condition contract**
  One step and two-step condition contracts are defined based on how the settlement document is released to accounting. There is no change in condition contract

creation and processing. In one-step condition contract settlement, documents are released to accounting directly, where in two-step condition contracts, it follows park and post functionality, which means settlement documents aren't directly released to accounting and instead follow the park and post rule.

- **Goods-related condition contract**
  For condition contracts eligible for goods-related transactions during settlement processing, there is a configuration option available to determine taxes during settlement.
- **Royalty settlement scenarios and sales bonus–based settlement**
  Royalty settlement scenarios and sales bonus–based settlement belong to purchase-based rebates processing; however, business volume data is determined from sales invoice processing. Although principally this scenario belongs to purchase rebates, due to integrated business process configuration, it's required in the sales rebate scenario.
- **Trade promotion management (TPM) condition contract**
  Condition contract types are also defined for TPM.

The screen layout for condition contracts will differ based on the backend configuration; for example, sales data–relevant attributes will be shown in the sales contract, whereas purchasing-relevant attributes will be shown in the purchase condition contract. However, for royalties and commission condition contracts, both sales and purchasing organizational data is needed.

The condition contract screen has the following tabs (as seen in Figure 10.1):

- **Basic Data**
  This tab includes fields such as **Contract Type**, Condition Contract Validity, **Contract Category**, **Payment terms**, **Contract currency**, **Payment Method**, **VAT Reg. No.**, and **Tax Country**. The **Contract Category** field controls the relevancy of the condition contract with the following options:
  - **Sales Rebate**
  - **Purchase Rebate**
  - **Commission Settlement**
  - **Royalties Settlement**
- **Conditions**
  This tab appears below the **Basic Data** tab. The condition record for rebates or accrual condition can be maintained. This functionality is the same as the pricing condition record. There is no separate transaction code in SAP Easy Access to maintain the condition record; instead, this can be maintained in the condition contract only. Pricing determination is the same as the condition technique in sales pricing.

  Condition type configuration is similar to the configuration of pricing in classic rebate management. However, an important point to note is that condition contracts will have a separate pricing procedure from the sales document pricing procedure. The conditions relevant for condition contracts are assigned to a condition type group. The condition type group is assigned to the condition contract type.

Figure 10.1 Sales Rebate Overview Screen

- **Sales**
  In this tab (as seen in Figure 10.2), details related to the sales organization/distribution channel and division are entered. **Sales office** and **Sales group** fields can be entered based on business requirements. The condition contract sales area and sales order–related sales area must match or the condition contract won't get determined in the sales order. The condition contract is defined at the sales area level.

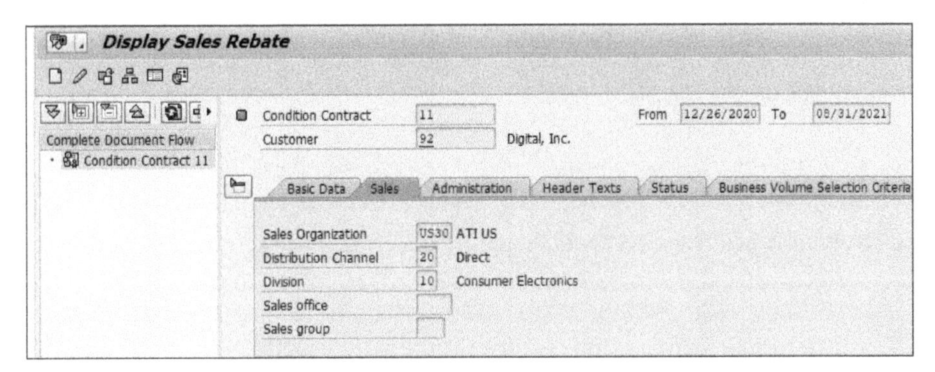

Figure 10.2 Display Sales Rebate: Sales Tab

- **Administration**
  This tab controls details such as when the condition contract was created or changes with the date and time. This information is required for tracking, compliance, and audit purposes.

- **Header Texts**
  Text fields are used for storing or communicating important information related to customer or interdepartmental communication.
- **Status**
  As shown in Figure 10.3, the status functionality in condition contracts controls subsequent processing of documents. Followings are condition contract statuses:
  - **New**
  - **Released**
  - **Locked**

  By default, the status of new contracts is always **New**. Condition contracts need to be released for determining in the sales order. Workflow functionality can be enabled based on the condition contract status. After settlement is done, the condition contract status changes to **Locked** so that no posting can be done in the condition contract.

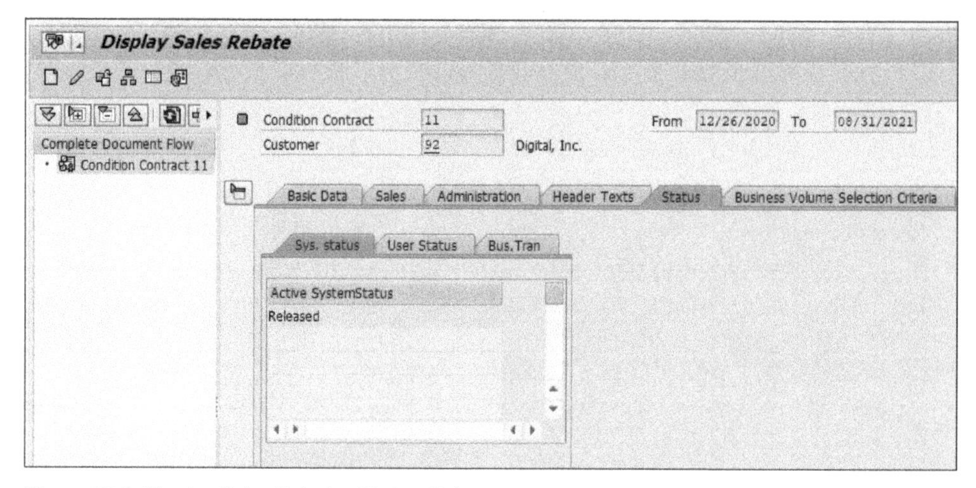

Figure 10.3 Display Sales Rebate: Status Tab

- **Business Volume Selection Criteria**
  Business volume functionality (Figure 10.4) is one of the most important parts of the end-to-end process. There is a lot of flexibility in defining and selecting business volume. Based on business volume selection criteria maintained in the condition contract, the system will determine the condition contract in the sales order. For example, if the selection criteria are maintained based on the customer and sales organization, the system will check this combination in the sales order to determine the condition contract. The following fields can be selected for business volume determination:
  - **Customer**
  - **Sales Org**
  - **Customer Hierarchy**
  - **Product Hierarchy**

- **Material Group**
- **Material**
- **Material Group 1**
- **Material Group 2**
- **Material Group 3**
- **Material Group 4**
- **Material Group 5**
- **Material Group Hierarchy**
- **Sales Order Reason**

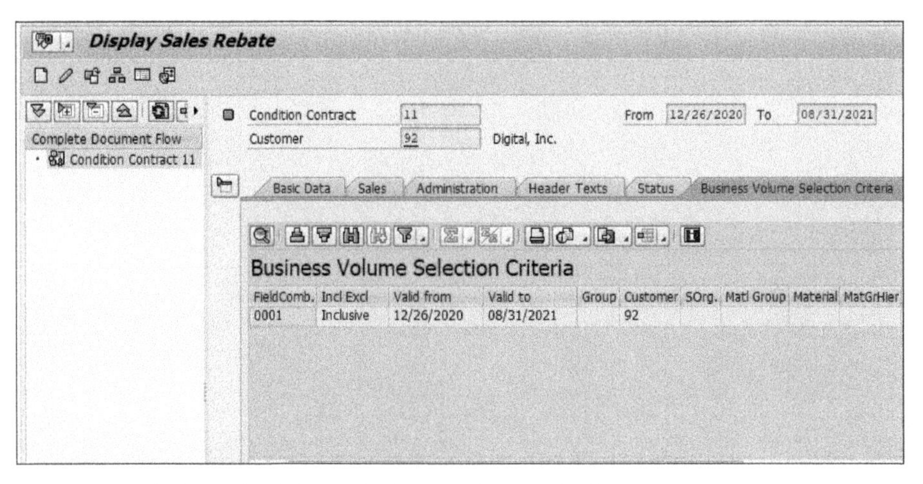

Figure 10.4 Display Sales Rebate: Business Volume Selection Screen

- **Settlement Data**
  Settlement-related information is entered at the condition contract level (as seen in Figure 10.5). The end-to-end settlement process governs based on details entered at this level. The following details related to settlement can be entered at the condition contract level:
  - **Settlement Material**
  - **Settlement Type Customer**
  - **Contract Extension Calendar**
  - **Amount Fields Group**
  - **Settlement Unit of Measure**

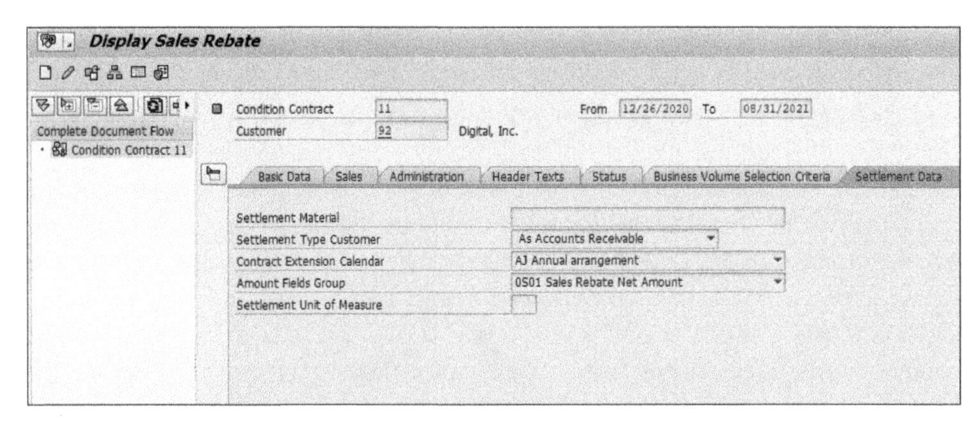

Figure 10.5 Display Sales Rebate: Settlement Data Tab

- **Settlement Calendar**
  The settlement calendar is used for settlement dates generation (as seen in Figure 10.6). The settlement type has to be defined to carry out the settlement process for the condition contract. Following are the settlement types that can be defined:
  - **Final Settlement**
  - **Partial Settlement**
  - **Delta Settlement**
  - **Delta Accruals**

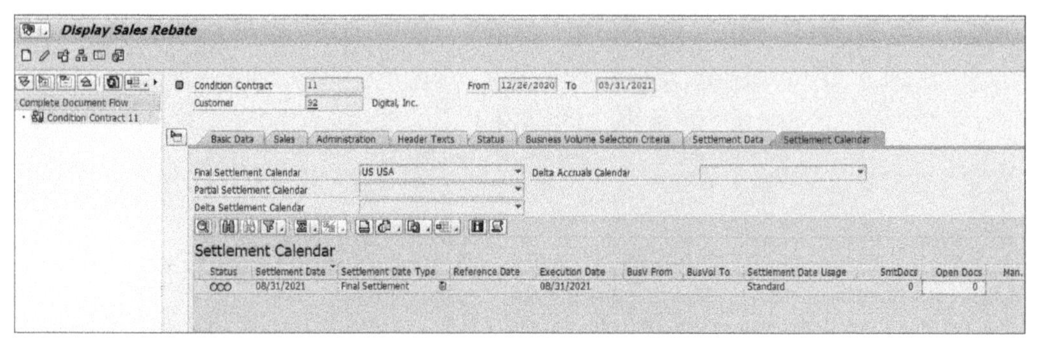

Figure 10.6 Display Sales Rebate: Settlement Calendar Tab

After settlement execution, the following details are updated related to the settlement document:

- Number of settlement documents
- Number of open settlement documents
- Number of manual settlement documents
- Number of open manual settlement documents

By default, the contract validity will be the settlement date. Maximum years for settlement calendar generation can be defined in condition contract processing. If no value is defined, the system considers five years as the default for settlement calendar generation.

During settlement processing, the condition contract picks the "from" settlement date from the settlement calendar maintained in the condition contract, as the system doesn't take into consideration any date that is manually entered. For partial settlement, the system adjusts all the previous accruals by reversing them. Scheduling partial settlements in the settlement calendar depends on the requirements of the organization. For final settlement, which is processed at the end of the contract validity date, the rebate is calculated on the total business volume for the entire validity of the condition contract and all previous accruals, and settlements are adjusted accordingly. Again, the final settlement is a mandatory procedure.

10.2.2 Condition Contract Search

When a sales document is created, the system determines the related condition contract based on the following sequence:

1. The system checks if the pricing procedure defined at the sales document level is related to the condition contract, as well as whether the condition types defined in the condition contract are maintained in the sales document pricing procedure.
2. If condition types are defined in the sales document pricing procedure per the condition contract pricing procedure, then the condition type groups are determined.
3. After the system determines the condition type groups, the related condition contract is determined.
4. Based on these condition contract types (determined in step 3), the system looks for the condition contract numbers related to the customer used in the sales document.
5. Business volume data is also checked if the selection criteria defined in the sales document attributes is per the business volume selection criteria. For example, if the business volume selection criteria are defined for the customer or material, then the system checks for the valid customer or material defined in the sales order.
6. If all determination factors match as mentioned, then the condition contract number will be triggered in the sales order pricing.

Figure 10.7 shows rebate condition **RES1** determined at the sales order level.

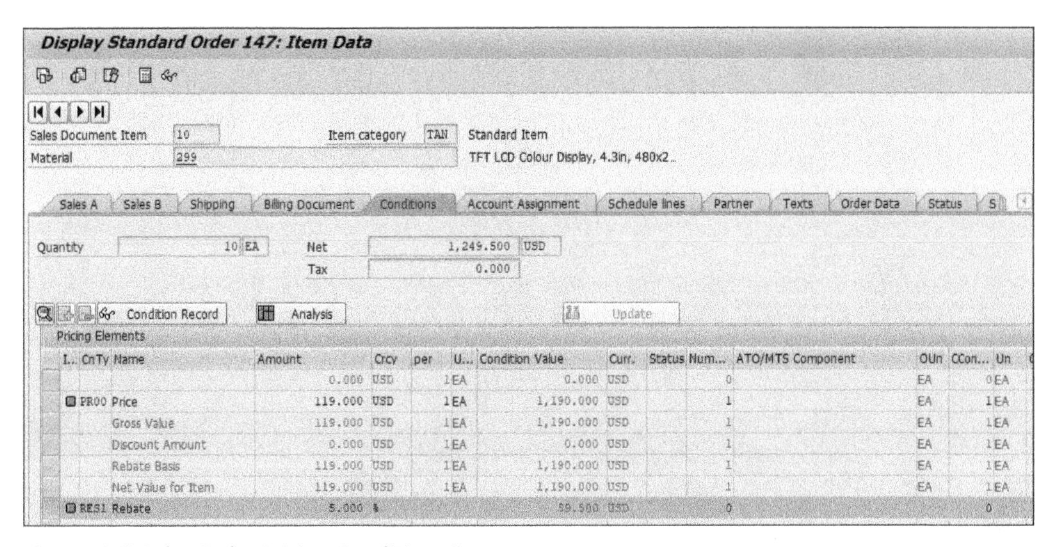

Figure 10.7 Sales Order Pricing Condition View

Figure 10.8 shows the condition contract determination in the **Analysis Pricing** screen.

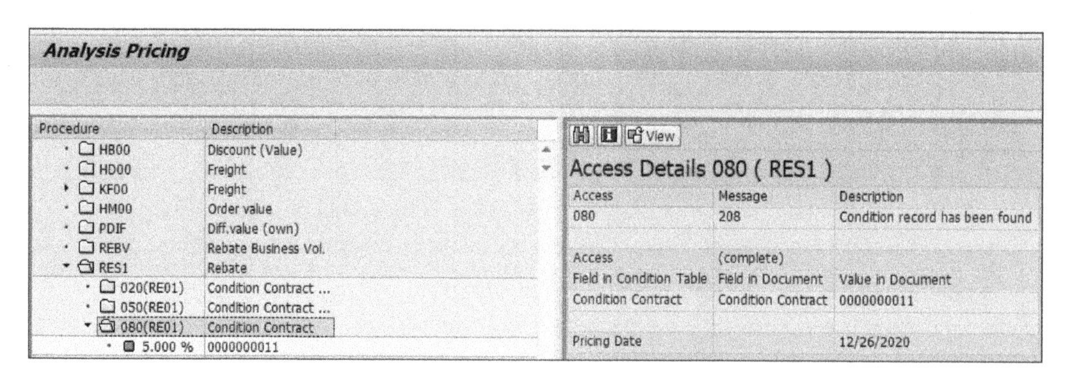

Figure 10.8 Sales Order Pricing Analysis

10.2.3 Mass Processing

This feature enables execution of various functionalities of the condition contract at the mass level. For example, using this process validity of multiple condition contracts can be extended in one go. By using the mass processing feature, business users not only save time but also reduce data errors.

The condition contract functionality offers the following process for mass processing:

- **Condition contract validity**
  Condition contracts that are due for validity extension can be extended using Transaction WCB_VALIDITY_CHANGE (as shown in Figure 10.9). The contract validity can be extended for multiple condition contracts, and the system also can extend the settlement date of these condition contracts accordingly. For example, 20 condition contracts are due for extension on June 30, 2021, and these condition contracts need to be extended to December 31, 2021. Upon extension, the settlement date is also extended to December 31, 2021.

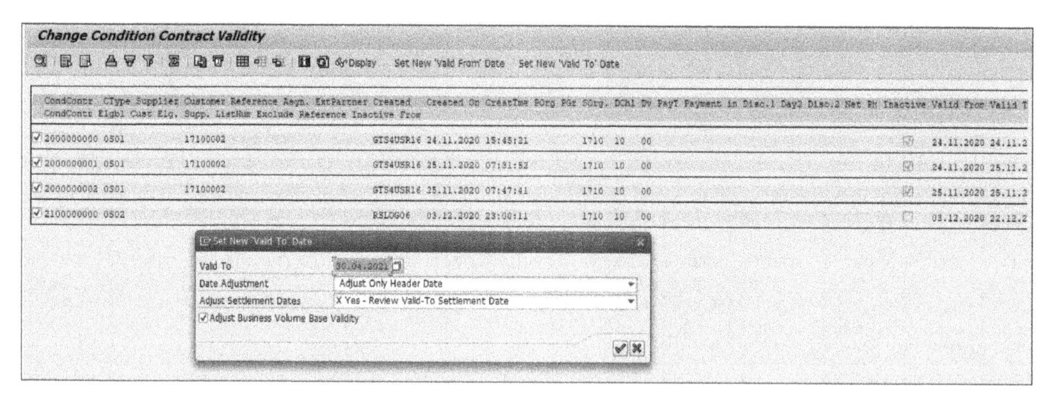

Figure 10.9 Condition Contract Validity Extension

Condition contract extension can be done using Transaction WB2R_EXTENSION as well. These transaction codes can be run in simulation mode to check if the selected condition contract can be extended or not. All applicable condition contracts can be extended. Upon execution of this transaction in simulation mode, it displays the following log shown in Figure 10.10.

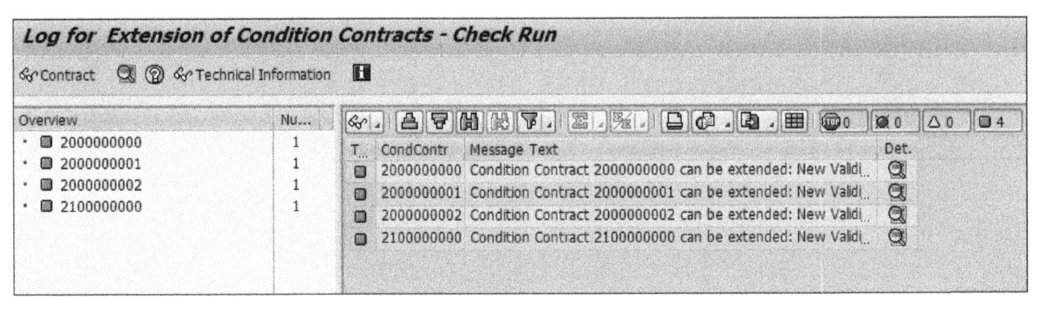

Figure 10.10 Condition Contract Extension Run in Simulation Mode

- **Perform business transactions from condition contracts**
  There is a need to perform various business transactions using mass-processing features. The following business transactions can be performed using report WCOCO_ACTION.
  - Release
  - Lock
  - Delete logically
  - Prepare for archiving
  - Request for approval
  - Reject approval
  - Lock settlement
  - Request settlement approval
  - Reject settlement approval
  - Set user status
  - New user status

  Releasing the condition contract is mandatory for any condition contract to perform any business transaction such as creation of subsequent documents. Such business transactions can be executed using report WCOCO_ACTION.

  Figure 10.11 shows how to perform business transactions from condition contracts.

Perform Business Transaction for Condition Contracts

Document Data

Condition Contract Type		to	
Condition Contract Category		to	
Condition Contract		to	
Contract Process Variant		to	
Reference		to	
Assignment		to	
Created By		to	
Created On		to	

Contract Partner

Supplier		to	
Customer		to	

Document Status

Status		to	

Organizational Data for Contract Partner

Purchasing

Purchasing Organization		to	
Company Code		to	

Sales

Sales Organization		to	

Figure 10.11 Perform Business Transactions for Condition Contracts

10.3 Accrual Processing

This section defines accrual processing and different calculation types. The accruals are posted as provisional entries in the books of account upon posting billing documents. Accrual posting provides visibility to management for estimated rebate payouts in advance. For any provisional entry, an accounting document is also generated as an accrual that gets cleared after the actual rebate payment is done.

10.4 Account Determination for Accruals

Like rebate condition types, accrual condition types are also defined and determined at the following document levels in settlement processing:

- Condition contract
- Sales order
- Invoice
- Settlement document

The condition type should be defined as an accrual condition. If these conditions aren't defined as accrual conditions, they can be defined as references of an accrual condition. Accrual condition types need to be defined in both pricing procedures, that is, settlement pricing procedure and sales document pricing procedure.

- Accrual condition types values are posted in the books of account as provisional entries. The determination criteria is the same as revenue account determination during invoice posting. Following are the determination criteria:
- Sales organization
- Chart of accounts
- Account assignment group of customers
- Account assignment group of material
- Account keys
- Accrual condition can be maintained in the condition screen of the condition contract. There is no separate condition master (e.g., Transaction VK11 for sales pricing conditions) for accrual conditions. The system determines the accrual condition type validity the same as it does for condition contract validity. The calculation type can be maintained as follows:
- Percentage
- Fixed amount
- Quantity
- Gross weight
- Net weight
- Volume
- Formula
- Percentage (in hundreds)
- Per mile (in thousand points)
- Condition can be maintained scale-wise if scale-wise maintenance is allowed at the condition type configuration level. The scale basis could be as follows:
- Value scale
- Quantity scale
- Gross weight scale
- Net weight scale
- Volume scale
- Scale based on formula
- Point scale

- Condition change history can be accessed from the **Condition** tab in the condition contract, as shown in Figure 10.12.

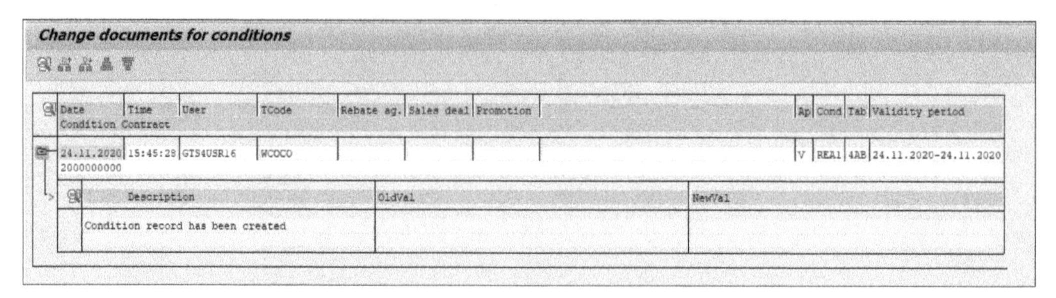

Figure 10.12 Change Documents for Conditions

- Condition type–related data can be exported into a local file as well from the **Condition** tab in the condition contract. Figure 10.13 shows rebate accrual condition (**REA1**) determined at the condition contract level.

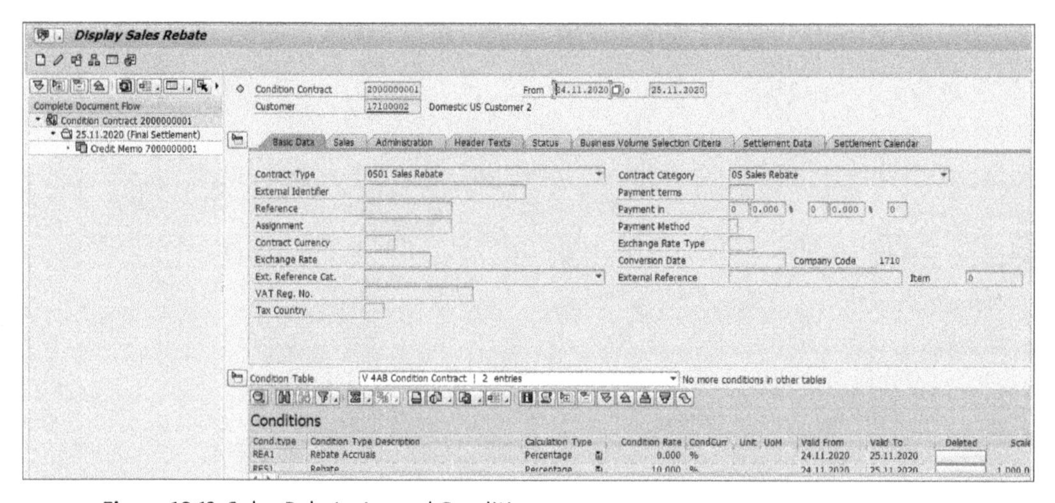

Figure 10.13 Sales Rebate Accrual Condition

- Settlement calendar for delta accruals can be maintained in the condition contract (as seen in Figure 10.14). Accruals will get accumulated and reversed based on the schedule maintained in the condition contract. Accrual calculation can also be automated based on the schedule.

- Accrual conditions are determined at the sales order and invoice level (as seen in Figure 10.15). When an invoice accounting document is posted, it creates provisional entries. Based on the settlement type, these accruals get accumulated and then reversed.

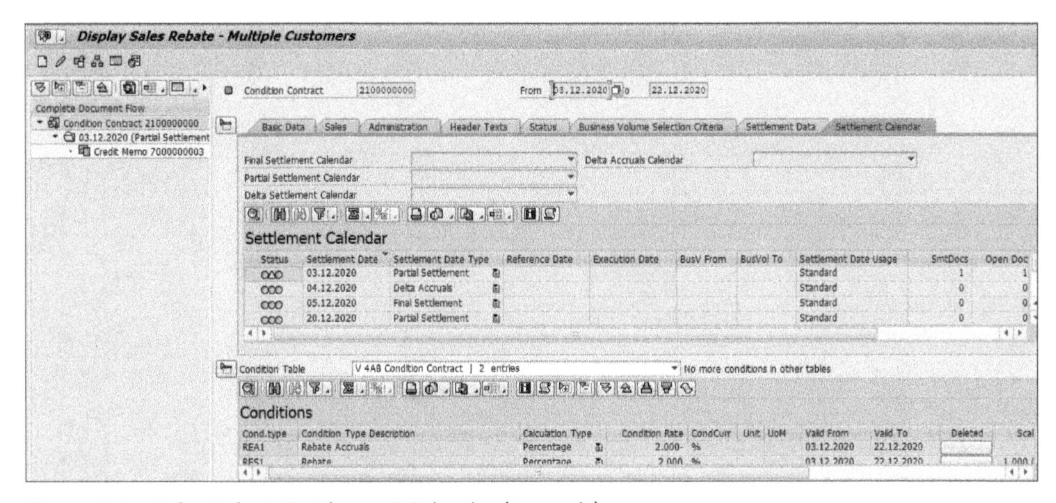

Figure 10.14 Sales Rebate Settlement Calendar (Accruals)

Customer Settlement: Accruals Reversal for Obsolet Condition Contracts

Partner

Customer		to	

Contract Selection

Condition Contract	2000000000	to	
Contract Process Variant		to	
Condition Contract Type		to	
Condition Contract Category		to	
Company Code		to	
Purch. organization		to	
Purchasing Group		to	
Sales Organization		to	
Distribution Channel		to	
Division		to	
Status	ICC04	to	

Default Data

Posting Date	20.03.2021
Document Date	20.03.2021
Activity Reason	

Program Run Control

☑ Check Run Only

List Range	Message Log
Save Application Log	Only in Productive Run

Figure 10.15 Accrual Reversal for Condition Contracts

During the settlement process, the following scenarios may occur:

- Reversal of accruals
- Correction of accruals
- Update of accruals

Reversal of accruals can be done using Transaction WB2R_SAC.

To correct the accruals, use Transaction WB2R_SC_CORR (as seen in Figure 10.16).

Correction Customer Settlement Condition Contract

Settlement Control
Settlement Date 01012020 to 01032021
Settlement Date Type to
Customer to
Settlement Execution Date to

Contract Selection
Condition Contract to
Condition Contract Type to
Condition Contract Category to
Company Code to
Purch. organization to
Purchasing Group to
Sales Organization to
Distribution Channel to
Division to

Default Data
Posting Date 20.03.2021
Document Date 20.03.2021
Settlement Type
Activity Reason

Filter Criteria

Figure 10.16 Correction of Accruals

Figure 10.17 shows the log for the correction of accruals.

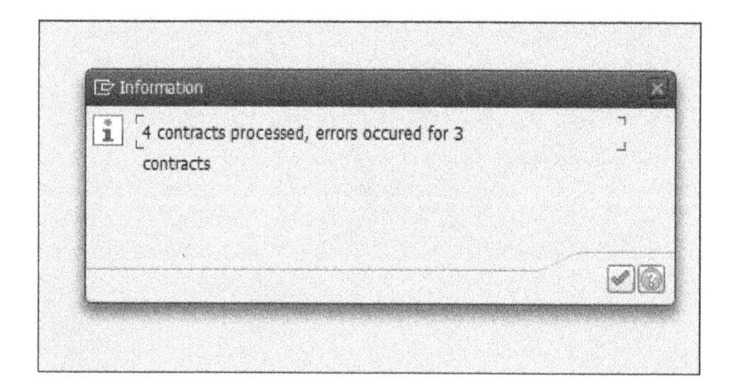

Figure 10.17 Correction of Accruals Log

To update the accruals, you use Transaction WB2R_UAC (as seen in Figure 10.18).

Accruals aren't mandatory in the settlement process. You don't have to run an accrual update before settlement execution.

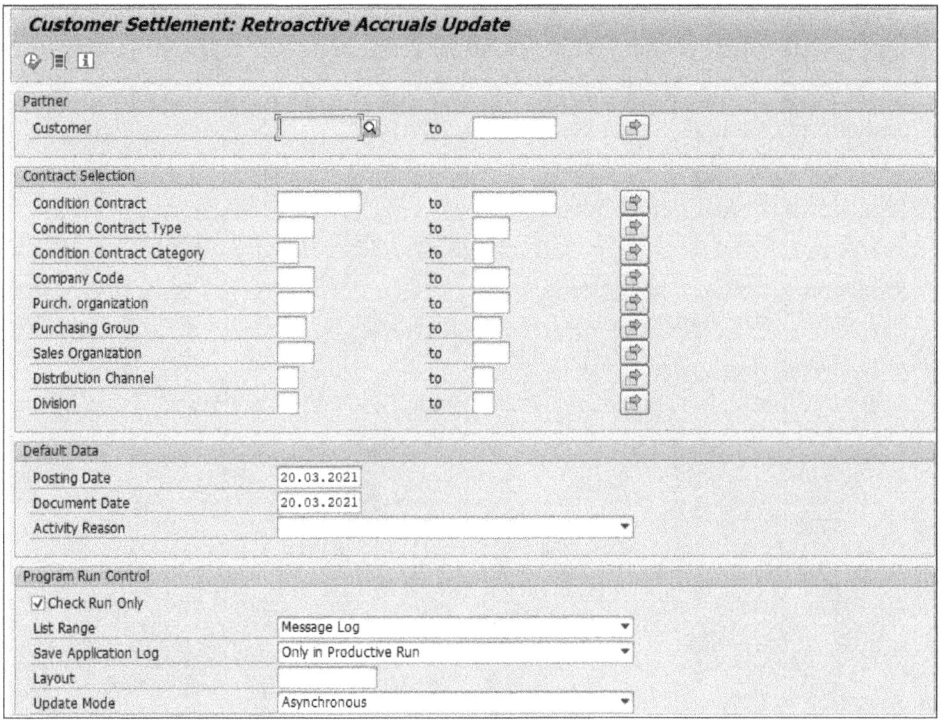

Figure 10.18 Accruals Updates

10.5 Processing Settlements

This section defines the settlement management process with step-by-step execution and reporting functionalities.

10.5.1 Settlement Calculation Processing

The condition contract settlement comprises the following subprocesses (as seen in Figure 10.19):

- **Business volume determination**
  The business volume process is one of the most distinguished process in the settlement management. Multiple selection criteria are available in this functionality, which is the basis for determining the rebate value. Based on the busine volume criteria, the selected system also determines the condition contract in the sales order. For example, if customer XYZ1 is selected as a business volume selection criterion in the condition contract, and the rebate rate is 2%, only those sales orders will be accounted for in the rebate calculations that have customer XYZ1 and are created within the validity of condition contract. There is a lot of flexibility offered in this

functionality. Selection could be based on single or multiple customers and materials. Provision can be made to exclude some of the materials that aren't necessarily relevant for rebate calculations.

- **Settlement calendar**
  The settlement calendar is maintained in the condition contract.
- **Creation of the settlement documents**
  Settlement document is created upon execution of settlement process
- **Pricing in settlement documents**
  Calculation of the rebate amount, taxes, and so on.
- **Accruals posting and reversal**
  Accrual accumulated and posted which gets reversed upon reversal.

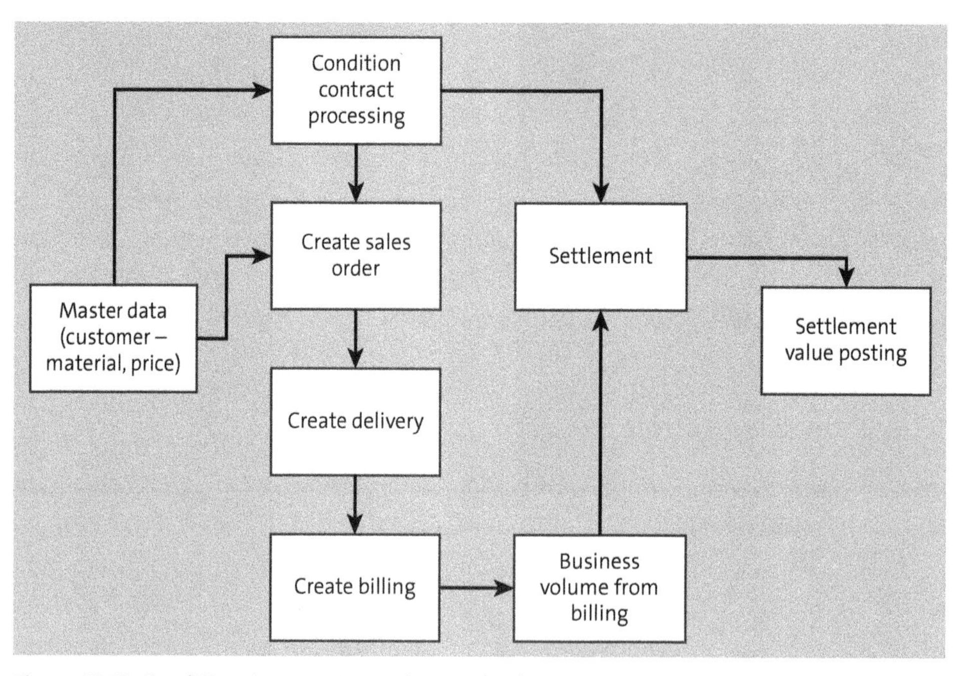

Figure 10.19 Condition Contract to Settlement High-Level Flow

10.5.2 Settlement Types in Condition Contracts

Settlement types include the following:

- **Partial settlement**
  Condition contracts can be settled partially if required. This is applicable where a condition contract is created for a longer duration, that is, one year or more than one year contract. Partial settlement has to be done before final settlement. In partial

settlement, the amount gets credited partially. There could be multiple partial settlements for a single condition contract. During final settlement, the partially settled amount gets settled cumulatively.

- **Final settlement**
  Final settlement is the last step of settlement processing; the customer will get all the dues of the eligible rebate. A credit memo is generated for the final settlement. If there are any delta accruals or partial settlements for the condition contract, during the final settlement process, all the delta accruals and partial settlements are reversed, and the final amount is credited to the customer in the form of a credit memo. After the final settlement is done, the status of the condition contract is set to **Locked** so that no further processing will be allowed.
- **Delta settlement**
  Delta accrual settlements can be scheduled periodically in the settlement processing. The purpose of delta accrual settlement is to get estimated payables for the scheduled period. Upon delta accrual settlement, a journal entry is posted.

Like the sales document flow, settlement documents can be navigated to from the condition contract document flow, if the condition contract is settled. A settlement document is created as a credit memo. This document has the following tabs (as seen in Figure 10.20):

- **Basic Data**
  This tab contains the accounting data of the settlement document. When the settlement document is posted, the status of the settlement document, condition contract reference, and credit note amount breakdown (gross amount, net amount, and difference, if any) is displayed in this screen along with the material details.
- **Item Overview**
  This tab contains net and gross amount of credit note with the material details.
- **Additional Data**
  This tab contains the information of additional details like if material is eligible of cash discount or price determination of the item is incomplete.
- **Activity Reasons**
  This tab contains the information of activity reason like if it is due to condition contract reversal, condition contract settlement correction, condition contract settlement correction due to wrong condition rate or due to wrong business volume.
- **Flexible Overview**
  This tab contains the information of flexible overview of settlement document. This includes details like Material, quantity, material group, pricing date, quantity, net price etc.

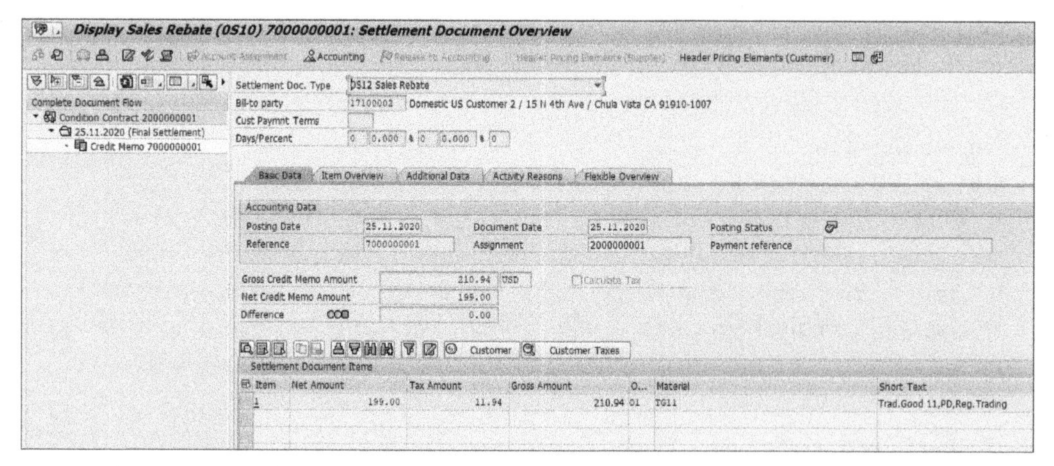

Figure 10.20 Settlement Document Overview

For each settlement document, accounting and controlling documents are posted. Entries posted in these documents can be navigated to from the **Accounting** tab of the credit memo. Figure 10.21 shows an accounting document posted that has the credit memo document number in the **Reference** field.

Display Document: Data Entry View

Taxes | Display Currency | General Ledger View

Data Entry View

Document Number	1600000001	Company Code	1710	Fiscal Year	2020
Document Date	25.11.2020	Posting Date	25.11.2020	Period	11
Reference	7000000001	Cross-Comp.No.			
Currency	USD	Texts Exist		Ledger Group	

C...	Itm	PK	S	Account	Description	Amount	Curr.	Tx	BusA	Cost Center	Profit Center	Segment	TTy	Trs
17...	1	11		17100002	Domestic US Customer 2	210.94-	USD	O						
	2	40		22001000	Sales Tax Accrued	11.94	USD	O						M...
	3	40		44001000	Sales Rebates	199.00	USD	O						0S1

Figure 10.21 Settlement Document Accounting Entries

Figure 10.22 shows the controlling document (actual cost document) entry, which has the credit note reference.

Display Actual Cost Documents

Document | Master Record

Layout	1SAP	Primary cost posting
COarea currency	USD	USD
Valuation View/Group	0	Legal Valuation

DocumentNo	Doc. Date	Document Header Text	RT	RefDocNo	User Name	Rev	RvE
A00001NT00	25.11.2020	Sales Rebate	R	7000000001	GTS4USR16		

PRw	OTy	Object	CO Object Name	Cost Elem.	Cost element name	Val/COArea Crcy	Total quantity	PUM	O	OffsetAcct
1	PSG	1622		44001000	Sales Rebates	199.00			D	17100002

Figure 10.22 Settlement Actual Cost Document

The **Flexible Overview** tab (as seen in Figure 10.23) has the credit note item information, including **Material**, **Matl Group**, **UoM** (unit of measure), and so on.

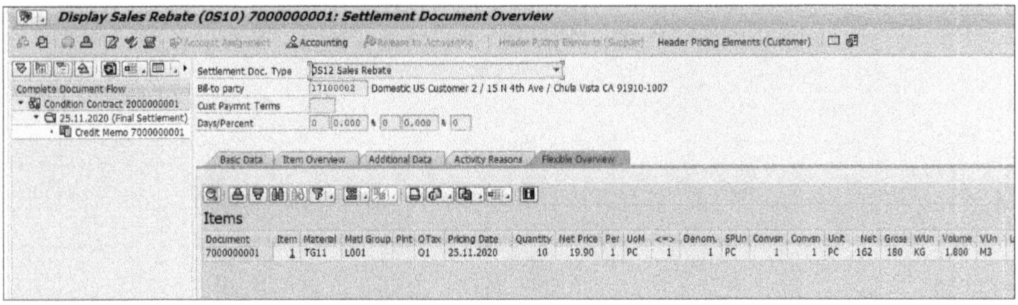

Figure 10.23 Flexible Overview of Settlement Document

The settlement document can be reversed if needed. Reversal entry can be executed using Transaction WB2R_CANCEL_DOCS (as seen in Figure 10.24).

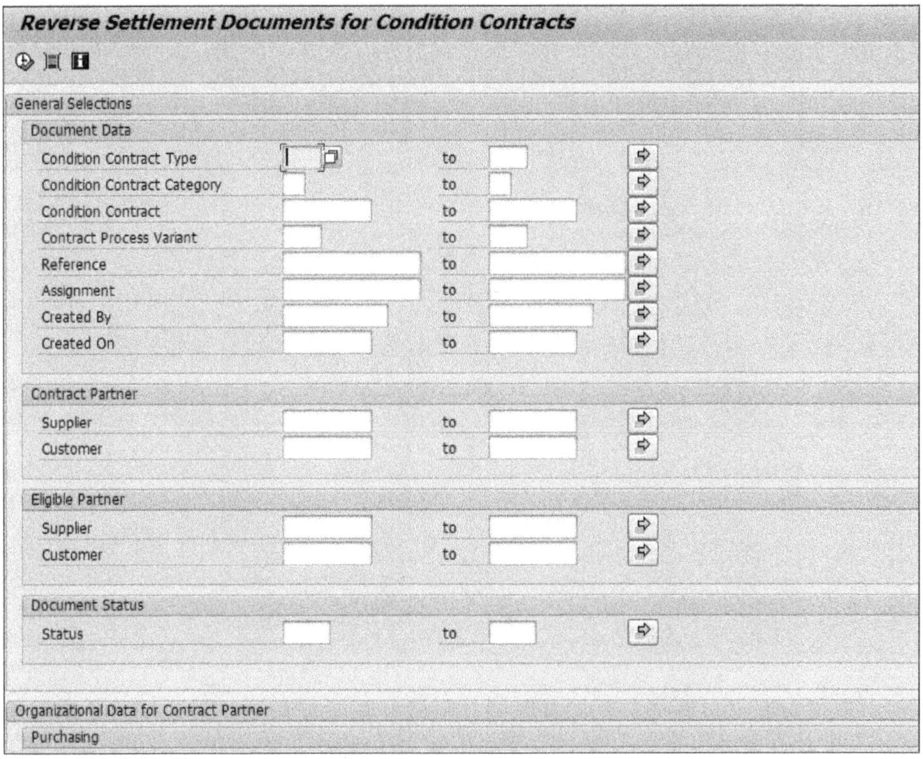

Figure 10.24 Reverse Settlement Document for Condition Contracts

The transaction can be run in simulation mode before the live run to check if the reversal can be done for a particular settlement document (as seen in Figure 10.25).

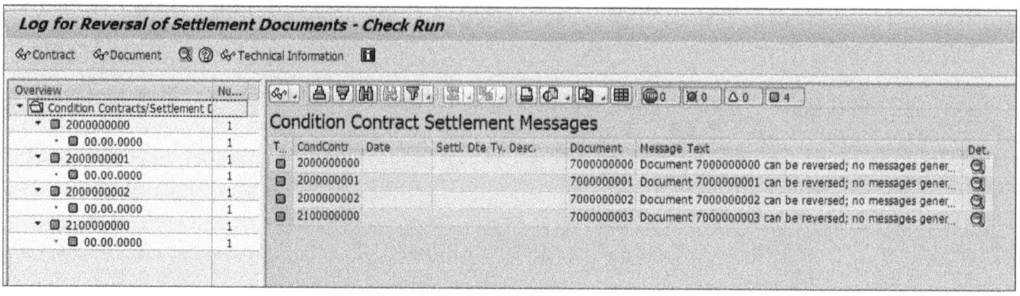

Figure 10.25 Log for Reversal of Settlement Documents

Business volume is defined at the condition contract level, determined at the invoice level, and posted at the settlement document level. Business volume is calculated in condition type REBV at the invoice level. As a prerequisite for this calculation, the condition type has to be defined in the pricing procedure. Reports are also available to check the determined business volume. Transaction code to execute this report is WB2R_BUSVOL (as seen in Figure 10.26).

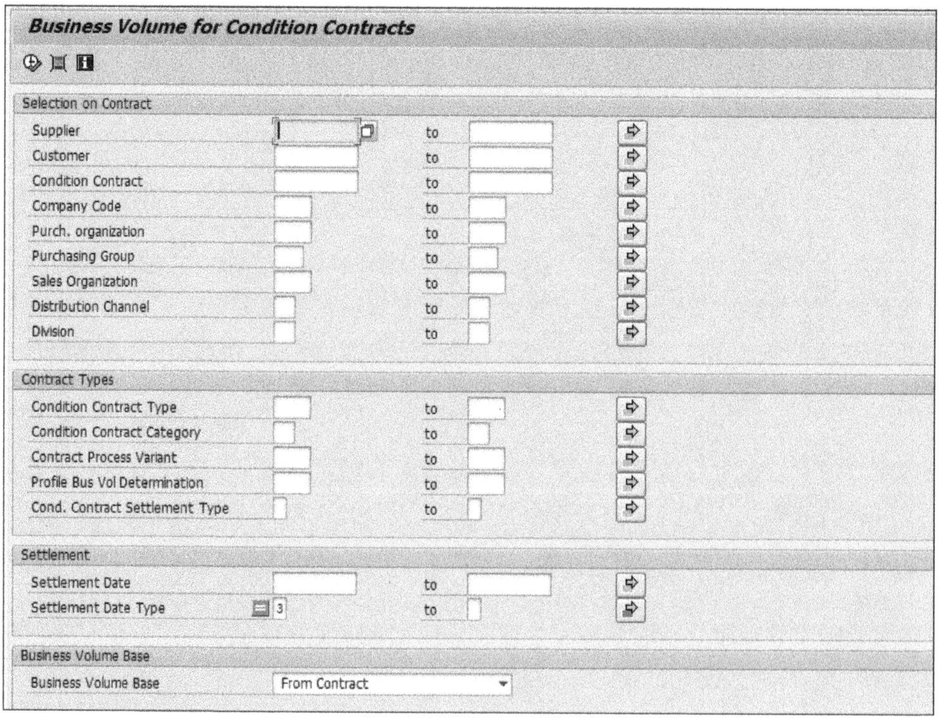

Figure 10.26 Business Volume for Condition Contracts

This report fetches details about condition contracts, customers, quantities, and business volume (as seen in Figure 10.27). There is also an option to navigate the condition contract.

Business Volume for Condition Contracts

Display

CondContr	Date	SettDateTy	Customer	Quantity	Unit	Currency	REBV
2000000000	24.11.2020	Final Settlement	17100002	20	PC	USD	4,090.00
2000000001	25.11.2020	Final Settlement	17100002	30	PC	USD	6,190.00
2000000002	25.11.2020	Final Settlement	17100002	10	PC	USD	2,100.00

Figure 10.27 Business Volume for Condition Contracts Report Output

Another report (WB2R_BVDETAIL) is available to check the business volume in detail. Figure 10.28 shows the selection criteria to check business volume in detail.

Detailed Statement for Condition Contract Settlement

Document Category
Document Category: B Settlement Document

Program Run Control
Maximum Number of Hits

Document Selection
Document Number to
Contract to
Settlement Date to
Posting Status R to
Document is Reversed to
Item to
Material to

Business Volume Selection
Date for Settlement to
Document Type Business Volume to
Maximum No. of Output Lines 1000000

Figure 10.28 Detailed Statement for Condition Contract Selection Criteria

Figure 10.29 shows the information condition contract-wise: settlement document, invoice number, and business volume posted.

Detailed Statement for Contract Settlement

Contract | Business Volume Document | Settlement Document

Detailed Statement

CondContr	Document	Item	Doc. Type	Doc. ID	Doc. ID 2	Doc. ID 3	Doc. Item	Date	Quantity	UoM	Crcy	Net	Gross	WUn	Volume	VUn	Points	Unit	SettlDocTy	BusVol 1	BusVol 2	BusVol 3
2000000000	7000000000	1	SD Billing Document	0090000028			000010	24.11.2020	10	PC	USD									1,990.00	0.00	0.00
2000000001	7000000001	1	SD Billing Document	0090000028			000010	24.11.2020	10	PC	USD									1,990.00	0.00	0.00
2000000002	7000000002	1	SD Billing Document	0090000030			000010	25.11.2020	10	PC	USD									2,100.00	0.00	0.00

Figure 10.29 Detailed Statement for Condition Contract Report Output

In this example, **Invoice** number **90000028** is navigated to from the report output itself (as seen in Figure 10.30).

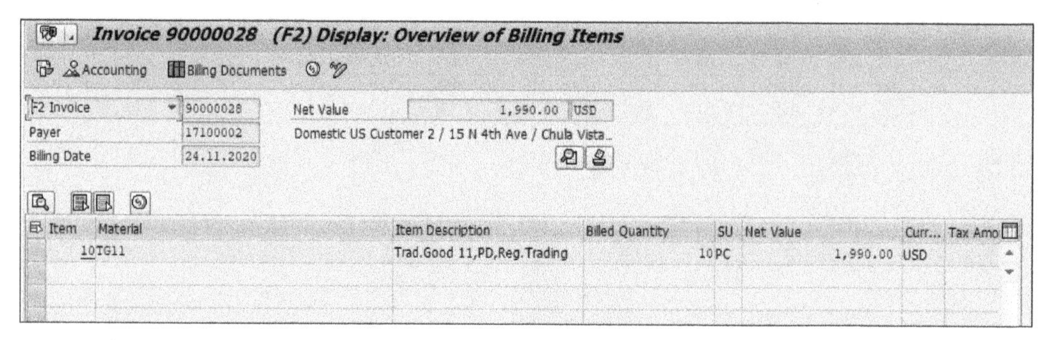

Figure 10.30 Navigation to Invoice

To check detailed statements of the settlement document report, use Transaction WB2R_BVDETAIL_IDA (as seen in Figure 10.31).

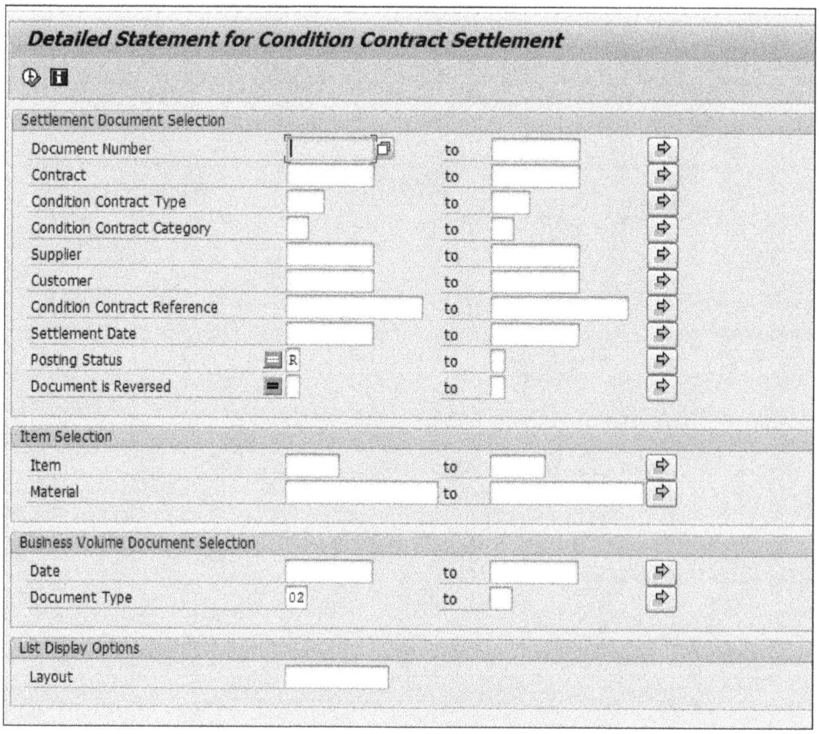

Figure 10.31 Detailed Statement for the Condition Contract

The report output shows the detailed statement of the settlement document, which can be drilled down at various levels in the settlement processing (as seen in Figure 10.32).

Detailed Statement for Contract Settlement

Condition Contract | Business Volume Document | Settlement Document

Detailed Statement for Contract Settlement (#3)

Condition Contract	CC Type Desc.	Month	Quantity	UoM	BusVol 1	BV Doc. C.	Customer	Customer Descr.	Settl. Crcy	Settlement Date	Material Desc.
			30	PC	6,080	USD					
– 2000000000 (1) [Condition Contract]			10	PC	1,990.00	USD					
– 24.11.2020 (1) [Settlement Date]			10	PC	1,990.00	USD					
– 7000000000 (1) [Settlement Document]			10	PC	1,990.00	USD					
– 0090000028 (1) [Document ID Business Volum...			10	PC	1,990.00	USD					
2000000000	Sales Rebate	11.2020	10	PC	1,990.00	USD	17100002	Domestic US Customer ...	USD	24.11.2020	Trad.Good 11,PD

Figure 10.32 Report Output Drilldown

Report WB2R_SETTL_VAL_IDA shows the detailed information of the settled condition contract (as seen in Figure 10.33). Date-wise, all the settlements carried out for each condition contract can be checked in this report.

Settlement Amounts for Contract Settlement

Condition Contract

Settlement Amounts for Contract Settlement (#4)

CondContr	SttlmtDate	SetDate...	Curren...	Customer	Contract Partner Customer Description	SmtMon...	SettDate...	SmtDtTyDes	SmtD...	SmtNetA...	SmtGr.A...	SmtCsDsc...	SmtEffV...	Smt
2000000000	24.11.2020	8	USD	17100002	Domestic US Customer 2 91910-1007 Chula Vista USA	11.2020		Final Settlement	1	199.00	210.94	0.00	210.94	
2000000001	25.11.2020	8	USD	17100002	Domestic US Customer 2 91910-1007 Chula Vista USA	11.2020		Final Settlement	1	199.00	210.94	0.00	210.94	
2000000002	25.11.2020	8	USD	17100002	Domestic US Customer 2 91910-1007 Chula Vista USA	11.2020		Final Settlement	1	231.00	244.86	0.00	244.86	
2100000000	03.12.2020	2	USD			12.2020	1	Partial Settlement	1	0.00	0.00	0.00	0.00	

Figure 10.33 Settlement Amount Report

Upon completion of settlement processing, the settlement status gets updated in the condition contract (**Settlement Calendar** tab as seen in Figure 10.34).

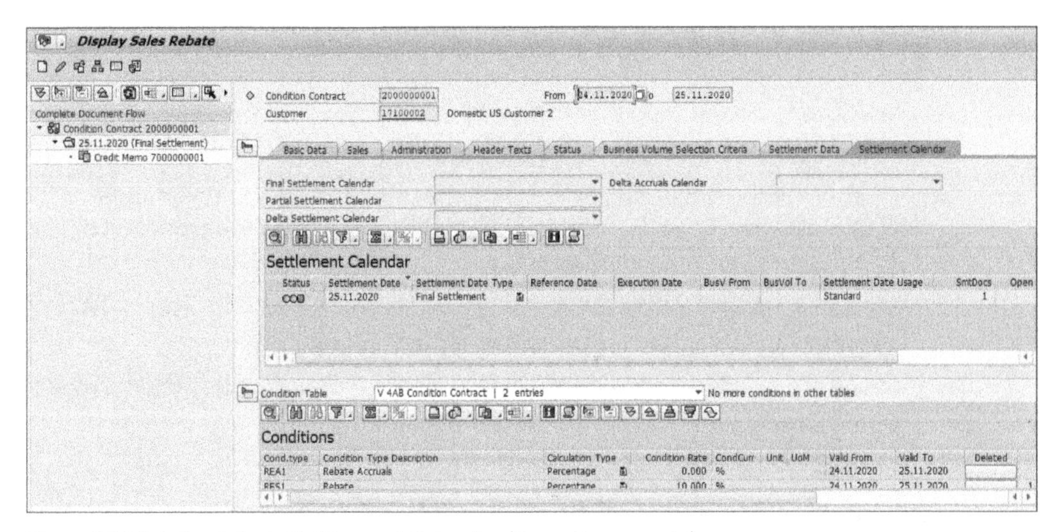

Figure 10.34 Sales Rebate Settlement Calendar (Open Documents)

Settlement document types are configured based on the type of settlement. The following settlement document types can be used in different scenarios:

- Customer settlement
- Pro forma settlement
- Manual settlement
- Delta accrual settlement
- Accrual reversal

Various controls related to settlement document types, such as change log, cancellation, taxation, accounting, and so on, are activated based on relevance.

10.6 Summary

The settlement management process provides an end-to-end solution for rebate management. In the SAP ERP Rebate Management solution, there were a lot of gaps related to process and system performance. The settlement management offering in SAP S/4HANA has many advantages:

- **Improved performance**
  There were a lot of issues in SAP ERP related to performance, especially regarding retroactive rebate calculation. Due to a revamped architecture, in-memory SAP HANA database, and integrated business processes, there are no such performance-related issues in the SAP S/4HANA solution.
- **Flexible and improved reporting**
  Many reports are available for each process and subprocess in settlement management processing. For example, reports are not only available for the condition contract, accruals, and settlement management areas but also for the subprocesses, such as business volume determination, and so on.
- **SAP Fiori apps for transactions and analytics**
  Settlement management offers SAP Fiori apps in different processes. Along with transactional apps, analytics apps help to perform analysis at different levels. Following are a few SAP Fiori apps: available
  - Analyze Detailed Statement Purchasing Rebates - Design Studio/Analyze Detailed Statement Purchasing Rebates Flexible Analysis (Design Studio)
  - Analyze Detailed Statement Sales Rebates - Design Studio/Analyze Detailed Statement Sales Rebates Flexible Analysis (Design Studio)
  - Manage Customer Condition Contract
  - Manage Settlement Documents
  - Manage Workflow Condition Contract
- **Automation of processes**
  Settlement management offers automation of processes from the condition contract to settlement; that is, some of the processes are automated using batch job scheduling. Due to automation monitoring, these processes become easier.

- **Mass execution of transactions**
  Some of the critical transactions, such as Condition Contract Validity Extension, are available to execute on a mass level.
- **Status management**
  All the processes are governed by the effective use of user status and system status. Unless the condition contract is released, no posting and no subsequent processes can be made in the condition contract. After settlement is done, the condition contract status is set to **Locked** so that no posting can be made.
- **Workflow enables processes**
  The workflow can be configured for the condition contract release process.
- **Execution of processes in simulation mode**
  Reports related to condition contract, accruals update, reversal, settlement, and settlement reversal can be executed in simulation mode before live execution.
- **Traceability and compliance**
  Any process is important from a traceability and compliance point of view. Settlement management processes, such as workflow management, status management, batch processing, and end-to-end process integration, make the entire process comprehensive from a compliance point of view.

Chapter 11
Warranty and Repairs

This chapter introduces the concept of warranty and repairs. This process details how a customer complaint can be tracked through the system via SAP notifications, and how service orders are created for repairs.

Strictly speaking, this functionality is not part of the standard sales and distribution suite but is covered in the customer service function. As a result, we'll provide an overview only, rather than go into depth in this area.

11.1 Process Overview

The process for repairs in SAP S/4HANA is shown in Figure 11.1.

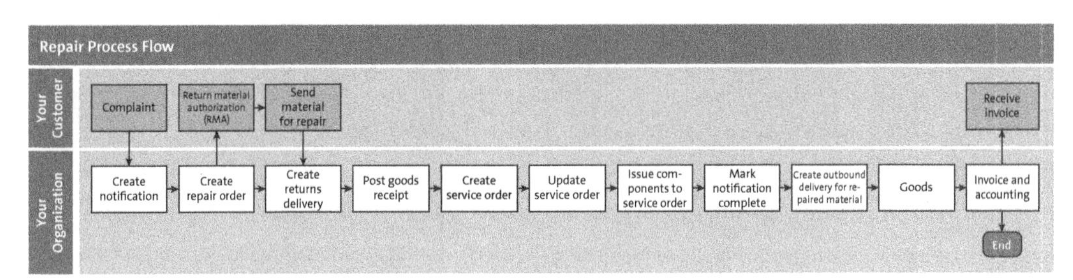

Figure 11.1 SAP S/4HANA Repair Process Flow

The process flow covers the entire customer service function, about which an entire book could be written. For the purposes of this book, let's concentrate on some of the touchpoints that affect the sales and distribution area.

11.2 Documents in the Repair Process

The full repair process is described in the following list:

1. Create the complaint, which results in the repair process. This is carried out in the SAP Notifications area, which isn't covered by the sales and distribution process. Notifications for repairs are created in Transaction IW51 in SAP S/4HANA, as shown in Figure 11.2.

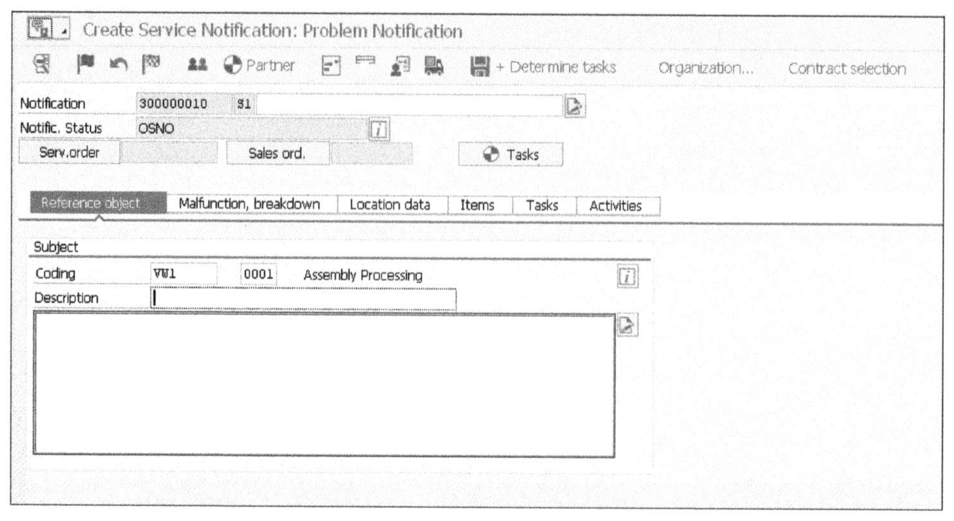

Figure 11.2 Create Service Notification

The service notification holds all the details of the complaint: what is wrong with the product, what needs repairing, who the customer is, and what activities need to be carried out.

2. Create the repair order. After the complaint is defined, there is an **Action box** section on the far-right side of the notification that holds the next steps for the process, as shown in Figure 11.3.

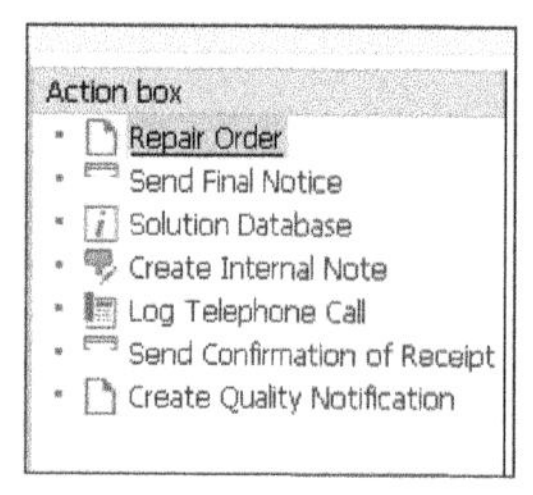

Figure 11.3 Service Notification: Action Box

3. One of the available actions here is to **Repair Order**. Selecting this will open a popup box to select the repair order type, sales area, customer, and a few other options. The process will take you through to creation of the repair order as a sales document type in Transaction VA01. Furthermore, as shown in Figure 11.4, you have an option either to create the sales order in the background and save the notification in one step (**Save notification and order**), or save the notification and edit the sales order in foreground (**Save notification and edit order**).

Figure 11.4 Service Notification Repair Order Options

4. Generate the return material authorization (RMA). After the repair order is created, normally the RMA output can be sent to the customer. This is used by the customer to send back the materials for repair.
5. After the goods are received, you temporarily revert to the sales and distribution area, albeit with some unfamiliar screens. Here you create the returns delivery via Transaction VRRE, as shown in Figure 11.5. Then, you post goods receipt in Transaction VL02N as normal.

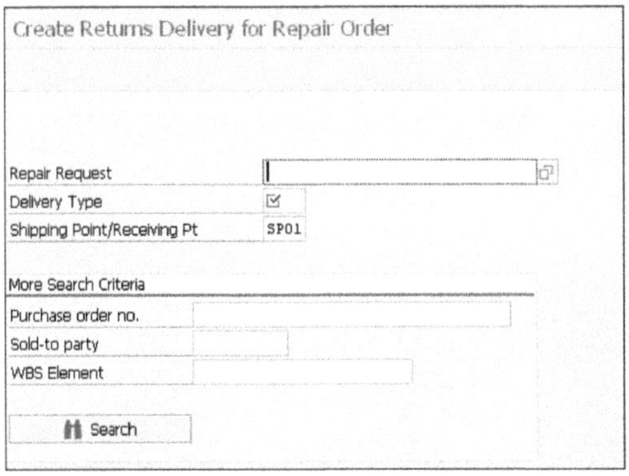

Figure 11.5 Create Returns Delivery for the Repair Order

6. Create the service order. After the goods are receipted, you're back in the customer service area. The service order needs to be created from within the repair order itself, taking you to Transaction IW31.
7. Update the service order. After the service order is created, this must be updated to add some key information in Transaction IW32:
   - Operations required in the repair
   - Components needed for the repair
   - Settlement rule of the cost center
8. Issue components to the repair order. After the service order is created and the key data added, components for the repair must be issued in Transaction IW42, after which the notification is also marked as **Complete**.
9. Create the outbound delivery. You're now at the point at which the repair has been carried out. This means that the repaired materials must be shipped back to the customer by creating an outbound delivery with reference to the original repair order in the now-familiar Transaction VL01N. The outbound logistics process then kicks in as usual the order-to-cash process flow, with goods issue as normal.
10. Create the billing document. If the repair has been carried out for a customer out of warranty, then a billing document must be created as usual.

All the documents in the full warranty and repair process sit together within the document flow.

11.3 Summary

This chapter has shown you an extremely high-level overview of the warranty and repairs process. As you've seen, there are several overlaps between the customer service module and sales and distribution, but there are many areas of difference too. This chapter has simply scratched the surface of this function. More information is, of course, available by researching the customer service functionality within SAP S/4HANA.

Chapter 12
Accounts Receivable

While not part of sales and distribution, the processing of invoice documents continues by way of receipt of cash and generating a clearing document.

So far, we've created a sales order, delivered it to the customer, and then generated an invoice to the customer. This chapter explains passing the billing information to accounting, and gives an overview of their processes for the benefit of sales and distribution personnel.

12.1 Process Overview

What happens after you send your invoice to your customer? Well, technically speaking, that's the end of the sales and distribution process flow. Yes, there is a process that takes the baton further, but as it's not part of sales and distribution, it's actually outside the scope of this manual. However, it's such a critical part of the business process of selling goods and sending invoices that we include this chapter as an extra bonus.

The epilogue to the invoice process is itself a compelling story and we're happy to reveal such details to you. Accordingly, this chapter focuses on the accounts receivable process, which is covered in the final highlighted section of the flowchart in Figure 12.1.

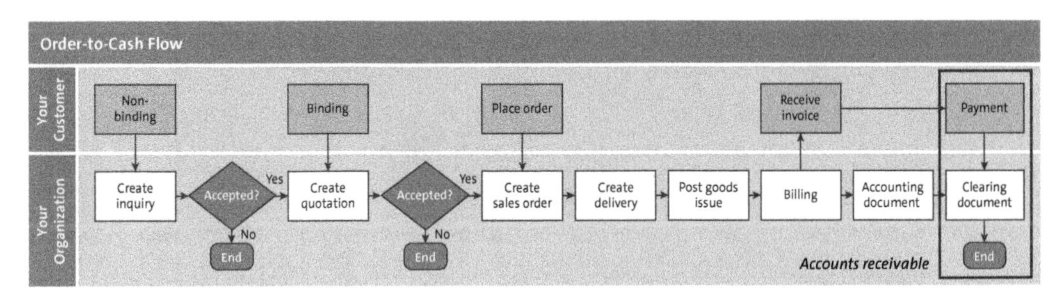

Figure 12.1 Order-to-Cash Flow: Accounts Receivable

12.2 Document Types

The accounts receivable process is preconfigured to use the following basic document types:

- AB: Accounting document
- CO: Posting
- DA: Customer document
- DG: Customer credit memo
- DR: Customer invoice
- DZ: Customer payment
- KG: Vendor credit memo
- KN: Net vendors
- KR: Vendor invoice
- KZ: Vendor payment
- RV: Billing document transfer
- SA: General ledger accounts

This nonexhaustive list of accounting document types controls how SAP will process customer receivables and vendor payables.

For the purposes of this chapter, we'll focus primarily on types AB, RV, and DZ to discuss what happens when your customer pays your invoice and other adjustments are made.

12.3 Overview of Accounts Receivable for Sales and Distribution People

You've seen in Chapter 8 that an invoice is finally created, along with an accounting document. Both the sales and distribution process and the chapter ended there. But that's not the end of the process chain from the point of view of your company. We don't want to leave this as a mystery, so this chapter on accounts receivable is to give you an overview of what happens to your invoice. Hopefully, it's paid as a result of accounts receivable process. (If not, then it starts a new legal process outside the scope of this book.) This, therefore, is the epilogue to our sales and distribution story.

We won't attempt a step-by-step explanation of how to process your company's accounts receivables in SAP S/4HANA. That is properly the subject of a different manual covering the financial accounting functionality. But it's useful for the sales and distribution user and consultant to have an idea of what happens after you create your billing document.

12.3.1 Accounting Impact

Let's start with the T account presented in Figure 6.12 of Chapter 6, Section 6.4.1. This is the accounting associated with the billing document posting. The customer accounts receivable account is debited and the sales revenue account is credited for the same amounts.

The essential point of this accounts receivable chapter is that your customer sends funds to your collections department in response to your invoice.

Figure 12.2 shows the new T account postings when cash is received. The inbound customer payment is handled as a debit to the cash account together with a corresponding credit to the customer accounts receivable account. This credit consequently clears the open customer accounts receivable (on the debit side) from Figure 6.12 in Chapter 6.

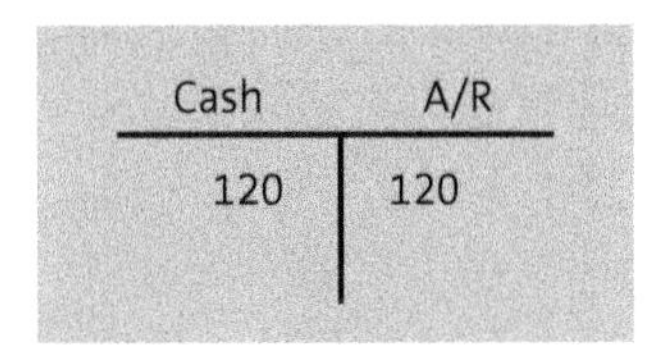

Figure 12.2 Clearing Account Posting

At a very high level, this is the happy ending to our order-to-cash story. The customer wanted a product that you sell. You sent the customer a general nonbinding price for the material. The customer responded by requesting a specific price for a specific quantity. After receipt of your quotation, your customer placed the order, and you wrote a sales order. The order was delivered and invoiced. Finally, the customer settles the invoice with payment. This is the essence of all commerce in an SAP S/4HANA format.

12.3.2 Clearing a Receivable in SAP S/4HANA

With respect to SAP S/4HANA, let's give a cursory review of how your accounts receivable department will process this posting. There are many potential complexities in this process, but a simple explanation should allow you to become familiar with the basic idea.

As noted previously in Chapter 8, your sales and distribution billing document, whether type F1 (order-based) or F2 (delivery-based), on completion will create an associated accounting document of type RV. This is what is specifically passed to your friends in accounts receivable.

For the sake of simplicity, your customer can pay with specific reference to an invoice or pay on account, meaning they can send a single large payment to settle numerous open invoices.

Technically speaking, the accounts receivable team monitors all funds receipt on a daily basis. All money received must be allocated to open receivables or customer accounts. If funds received from a customer can't be so specifically linked, the funds are placed in a suspense account and you may hear from your accounting person who may need to know why funds were received from your customer, but no corresponding accounting document could be found. If your company uses a billing purpose only process where real-looking invoices are purposefully generated *without* accounting documents, you may find that, occasionally, a customer might actually pay one. Such invoices are typically generated for customs purposes or down payments, for example.

Assuming that there are no such issues, your accounting person may process the inbound payment via Transaction F-28 where input of the general ledger account is required. This is used for an actual receipt of cash to clear an open item. Alternatively, they may use Transaction F-32 to clear an open item without an actual receipt of cash. This adjustment is used to clear an open item. Posting either transaction creates a clearing document that results in the account postings shown earlier in Figure 12.2.

From the sales and distribution point of view, you'll definitely benefit from periodically reviewing your customer's accounts receivable position. For example, are they paying their invoices? Are there any that remain open? You can do this by running the Customer Line Item Display report.

12.3.3 Customer Line Item Display

Open and settled, or cleared, accounting documents may be looked up in a way similar to the list of inquiries, quotations, sales orders, and other documents covered previously. Transaction FBL5N opens the selection parameter screen, as shown in Figure 12.3.

This list display is oriented toward customers, specifically the payer function (because they are the precise business party that will be submitting payments). You can input a single customer number or multiple values, including ranges. You can also search all accounting documents by the entire company code. Be careful with this, however, because in a large company, this will output the mother lode.

There are radio buttons to select **Open items** (i.e., unpaid or unsettled), **Cleared items** (i.e., paid or settled), or **All items** (both). In the following example, one customer is chosen and **All items** is selected to show both open and cleared items. Click the **Execute** button, and you'll see the display in Figure 12.4.

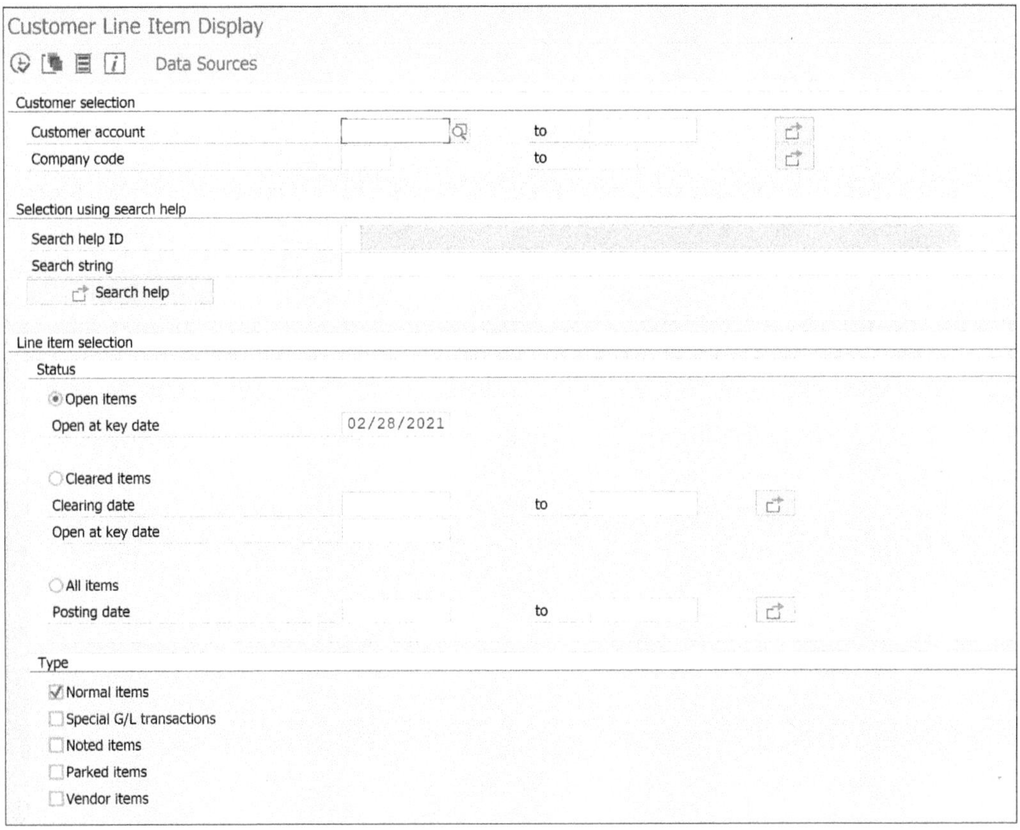

Customer Line Item Display

Data Sources

Customer selection

Customer account ______ to ______

Company code ______ to ______

Selection using search help

Search help ID

Search string

Search help

Line item selection

Status

(•) Open items

Open at key date 02/28/2021

( ) Cleared items

Clearing date ______ to ______

Open at key date

( ) All items

Posting date ______ to ______

Type

[x] Normal items

[ ] Special G/L transactions

[ ] Noted items

[ ] Parked items

[ ] Vendor items

Figure 12.3 Customer Line Item Display Screen

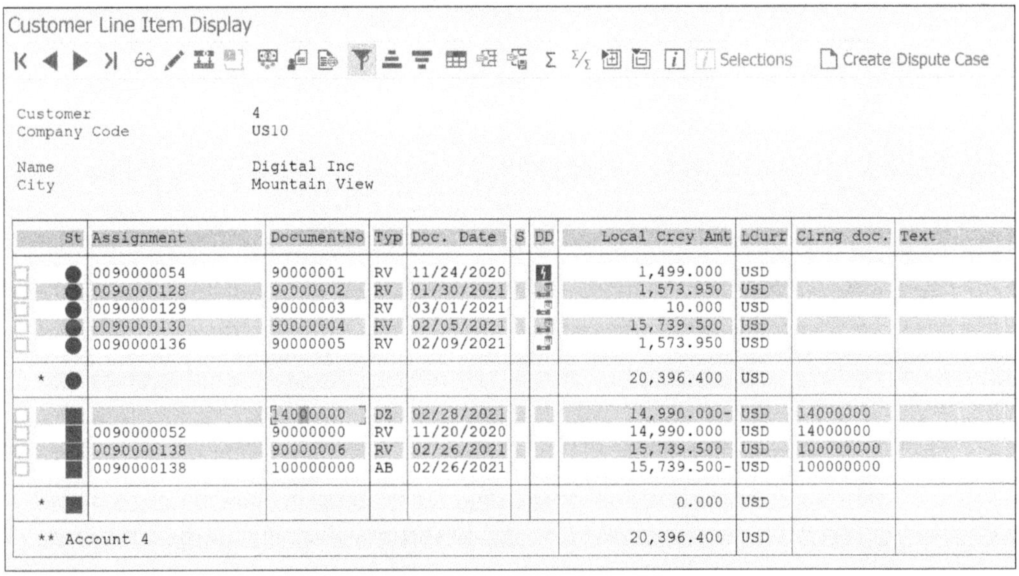

Customer Line Item Display

Selections Create Dispute Case

Customer 4
Company Code US10

Name Digital Inc
City Mountain View

	St	Assignment	DocumentNo	Typ	Doc. Date	S	DD	Local Crcy Amt	LCurr	Clrng doc.	Text
	●	0090000054	90000001	RV	11/24/2020			1,499.000	USD		
	●	0090000128	90000002	RV	01/30/2021			1,573.950	USD		
	●	0090000129	90000003	RV	03/01/2021			10.000	USD		
	●	0090000130	90000004	RV	02/05/2021			15,739.500	USD		
	●	0090000136	90000005	RV	02/09/2021			1,573.950	USD		
*	●							20,396.400	USD		
	■		1400000000	DZ	02/28/2021			14,990.000-	USD	14000000	
	■	0090000052	90000000	RV	11/20/2020			14,990.000	USD	14000000	
	■	0090000138	90000006	RV	02/26/2021			15,739.500	USD	100000000	
	■	0090000138	100000000	AB	02/26/2021			15,739.500-	USD	100000000	
*	■							0.000	USD		
** Account 4								20,396.400	USD		

Figure 12.4 Customer Line Item Display for One Customer (Payer)

There may be some differences from your particular company's display of this information, depending on how your system is configured, so treat this simplistic review with some flexibility.

The display is broken down into two sections:

- The first section with the red circles displays all **Open** items; for our simplistic purposes this will mean unpaid invoices.
- The second section with the green squares displays all **Cleared** items, which again, for our purposes, means paid or otherwise closed due to some adjustment.

At the far left is the cleared/open items status symbol (**St** column). The red circles on the right indicate that the line items are **Open**. Green squares indicate **Cleared** status.

The **Assignment** column displays the sales and distribution billing document number, which will be easily recognizable to sales and distribution people. Technically, the accounting documents in the **DocumentNo** field are assigned to sales and distribution billing documents.

The middle columns display accounting document numbers in the aforementioned **DocumentNo** column, along with its type, document date, and status icon (labeled as the **Net Due Date Symbol**). Here we see three different types of accounting documents.

- **RV: Billing Document Transfer**
  In SAP S/4HANA, this accounting document is labelled as a Journal Entry and is linked to a sales and distribution billing document type F1 or F2 (or other derivatives).
- **DZ: Customer Payment**
  This is the customer payment.
- **AB: Accounting Document**
  This is used for clearings other than customer payment.

The next columns to the right are the invoice amounts (**Local Crcy Amt**), local currency (**LCurr**), and clearing document (**Clrng doc.**).

As you can see in this display, the top five line items of type RV are all unpaid invoices, some of them several months old. All have red circles in the left column, and the first invoice number 0090000054 has a red lightning icon indicating a further due date status of **Overdue**. All the amounts are positive values, which, for accounting purposes, represents debits (increases) to the customer accounts receivable account.

12.3.4 Cleared Documents

Let's examine the cleared documents section. First, cleared documents are organized in sets of two. You'll see four lines in this cleared section, which is to be interpreted as two sets of cleared documents. The first set is extracted into Figure 12.5.

St	Assignment	DocumentNo	Typ	Doc. Date	S	DD	Local Crcy Amt	LCurr	Clrng doc.
■		14000000	DZ	02/28/2021			14,990.000-	USD	14000000
■	0090000052	90000000	RV	11/20/2020			14,990.000	USD	14000000

Figure 12.5 Cleared Invoice Example

The billing document to the customer was number 0090000052, as shown in the **Assignment** column for the second line item, and was issued on November 20, 2020. On the far right of the same line item, you can see the corresponding document used to clear this formerly open receivable, namely clearing document number 14000000, which was created on February 28, 2021.

The clearing document also appears as the top line item, and you can see it's number again in the **DocumentNo** field together with type **DZ** (customer payment). Consistent with dual-entry accounting principles, you can see that the clearing document's negative amount debits the cash account. To be clear, it's not the sales and distribution billing document that is cleared, but rather the associated accounting document number 90000000. In summary, considered together, they net out to zero and close out those accounts.

The next two line items in the cleared section display a case where accounting document number 90000006 (related to sales and distribution billing document number 0090000138) is offset by a credit invoice accounting document type AB under number 100000000. This was an adjustment due to a reversal and not an inbound customer payment. See Chapter 9 for more details on reversals.

With only one invoice paid, you might be well advised to discuss the situation with your customer and your credit management team.

12.3.5 Other Reporting

A principal interest for all business managers is to generate profit and loss (P&L) reports by customer, material or service, sales office or region, sales area, division, company, or the entire enterprise. This is well out of scope of order-to-cash processing, but that doesn't mean you, as a business manager, shouldn't have an interest. Unfortunately, as this is a subject of much complexity and personalization, there is no out-of-the-box profitability report in SAP S/4HANA.

A major dependency for good P&L reporting is the successful implementation of cost accounting so that cost of goods or services sold can be properly linked with sales, together with all other sales, general, and administrative (SGA) expenses (otherwise known as overhead) not linked to any particular product, but nevertheless allocated to your group.

There are, of course, many robust tools in SAP S/4HANA to employ to create meaningful reports. Core data services (CDS) views are new in SAP S/4HANA. These are temporary structures comprising data from various tables that can be used programmatically to fulfill business requirements. They are intended to replace Sales Information Systems in SAP ERP, which is expected to be sunsetted.

Probably the most useful tool is SAP BusinessObjects. This robust tool works as a sort of spreadsheet on steroids, capable of pulling data from various modules in real time and permits very complex modeling. This is our recommendation as to the best tool to use for P&L and all other types of reporting.

Consult your company's SAP Team as to which tool and report has been developed for your business area.

12.3.6 Closing Periods

The first week of every month is normally an intense period of time at every company. The same can be said for the first week every 4 months and every 12 months. These periods are known as the monthly closing, quarterly closing, and annual closing. These periods are distinctive for the reason that the previous accounting period—month, quarter, or year—remains open. This means that you have a few days in which you can invoice your customer either in the new or current accounting period or in the previous period.

It frequently happens that your accounting liaison may ask you to reverse a billing document posted on March 3, when for accounting or business reasons it should be closed on February 26 in the previous month when the delivery took place. This will keep your order-to-cash transactions from being split across accounting periods, which can skew periodic reporting.

This is easy to do after your billing document has been reversed. When recreating your billing document, take care to go to the billing document header, as shown in Figure 12.6, and change the **Billing Date** to the desired period.

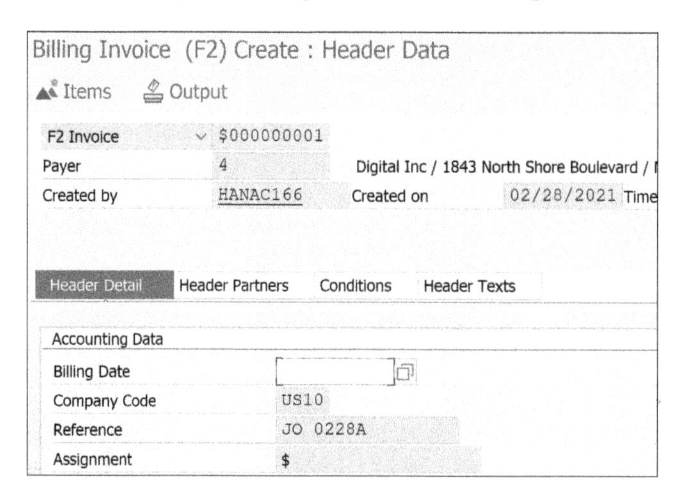

Figure 12.6 Change Billing Date in the Billing Document Header

12.3.7 Summary

This chapter described how an accounts receivable department processes a billing document generated to a customer. We covered the accounting postings, gave an overview of the clearing process in SAP S/4HANA, and showed how a customer's account may be reviewed. Finally, we discussed other reporting methodologies, as well as a briefly covered the closing period.

Appendices

Appendix A
Key Transaction Codes

Selected transaction codes (Table A.1), function key shortcuts (Table A.2), and tables (Table A.3) are provided here for your reference. These lists are by no means exhaustive, but they should serve as an excellent start point. Note that many transaction codes follow the logic "YY0X" where "YY" is a functional prefix, such as VA for Sales Order, and the "X" means 1 for create, 2 for change, and 3 for display. The entire series of each transaction suite isn't included in the reference table here, but you should feel free to extrapolate liberally. We've also included some transaction codes from other modules as they are frequently used in sales and distribution.

Transaction Code	Transaction
AL11	SAP Directories for Exported Files
BD12	ALE Customer Master Push
BD20	ALE Customer Master Push
BD87	Re-execute EDI
BP	Maintain Business Partner
BUP1	Create Business Partner
BUP2	Change Business Partner
BUP3	Display Business Partner
CNR3	Work Centers
CO06	Backorder Reprocessing
CS03	Display Sales BOM
CUTABLEINFO	Variant Configuration by Sales Order
DB02	Database Information
DP91	Resource-Related Billing Request
FBL3	G/L Account Line-Item Display
FBL5	Display Customer Line Items

Table A.1 Selected Transaction Codes

Transaction Code	Transaction
FBL5N	Display Customer Line Items
FD33	Credit Line Review
FSP0	Edit G/L Account Chart of Accounts Data
GR55	Report Painter
HU02	Pack Materials in to HUs
IQ03	Display Material Serial Number
LS24	Stock per Material
LT03	Create Transfer Order
LT10	Stock Transfer
MB56	Batch Where-Used List
MB5B	Stock for Posting Date
MB5C	Pick-Up List
MB5S	List of GR/IR Balances
MIGO	Goods Receipt
MM03	Display Material Master
MMBE	Stock Overview
MMPV	Close Accounting period
MSC3N	Display Batches
NACE	Conditions for Output Control
OPD	Output Control in BRFplus
POF1	Packing Determination
POP1	Create Packing Instruction
RPC0	Set Currency
SCAL	Display Calendar
SCMP	Table Compare
SDMO	Search Transaction Codes
SE01	Transport Organizer

Table A.1 Selected Transaction Codes (Cont.)

Transaction Code	Transaction
SE10	Transport Overview
SE16	Table Browser
SE16N	Table Browser
SM30	Table Maintenance
SPAD	Printer IP Addresses
SQVI	QuickViewer
SU01	Maintain Users
SU3	Display Own User
UKM_CASE	Credit Release
V.02	Incomplete Orders
V.15	Backorders
V.21	Log of Collective Run
V/76	Product Hierarchy
V/LD	Price Report
V_UC	Incomplete Outbound Deliveries
V_V2	Rescheduling of Sales Orders
V23	Sales Documents Blocked for Billing
VA03	Display S/O
VA05	List of Sales Orders
VA14L	Sales Documents Blocked for Delivery
VA35	List of Scheduling Agreements
VA35N	List of Scheduling Agreements
VA43	Display Sales Contracts
VA45	List of Contracts
VB01	Create Material Exclusion/Listing
VB13	Display Material Determination
VB43	Display Cross Selling

Table A.1 Selected Transaction Codes (Cont.)

Transaction Code	Transaction
VCH3	Display Batch Search Strategy
VD52	Customer Material Records
VD53	Display Customer Info Record
VDH1N	Maintain Customer Hierarchy
VF01	Create Single Billing Document
VF04	Billing Due List
VF11	Reverse Billing Document
VF31	Mass Bill Document Print
VK11	Create Condition Records
VL01N	Create Deliveries
VL02N	Change Delivery
VL06C	View Deliveries Ready for Confirmation
VL06G	View Deliveries Ready for PGI
VL06O	List of Deliveries
VL09	Reverse PGI
VL10A	Delivery Due List
VL10B	Create Deliveries for STOs
VL10E	Create Outbound Deliveries for SSAs
VT01N	Create Shipment document
VT03N	List of Shipments
VV13	Display Output – Sales
VV23	Display Output – Deliveries
VV33	Display Output – Billing
WCOCO	Maintain Condition Contract (Settlement Management)
WE09	IDoc List
WE19	Test Tool for IDoc Processing
WE42	Incoming EDI

Table A.1 Selected Transaction Codes (Cont.)

These function keys will work in Transactions VA01/02/03 to help you hop to master data, navigate, or display help.

Function Key	Shortcut
F1	Application help
F2	Display header/item conditions
F3	Back to previous screen
F4	Possible entries
F5	Display document flow
F6	Display customer master
F7	Display list of sales orders
F8	Display material master
F9	Select item row
F10	Go to menu bar
F11	Incompletion log
F12	Cancel and close the document

Table A.2 Function Key Shortcuts

Table	Description
ACDOCA	Universal Journal Entry Line Items (new for SAP S/4HANA)
BUT000	Business Partner General Data
BUT020	Business Partner Addresses
BUT0ID	Business Partner ID Numbers
BUT100	Business Partner Roles
E071K	Transport Requests
EKPV	Sales Area for PO
KNB1	Customer to Company Code
KNVV	Customer Sales Area
KONP	Master Data Pricing

Table A.3 Selected Tables

Table	Description
LFB1	Vendor to Company Code
LIKP	Delivery Header
LIPS	Delivery Item
LMF1	Vendor to Purchase Organization
LMF2	Vendor to Receiving Plant
PRCD_ELEMENTS	Historical or Transactional Pricing Records (new for SAP S/4HANA)
T683S	Assignment of Pricing Conditions to Pricing Procedures
T683V	Assignment of Sales Area, Document Pricing Procedure, Customer Pricing Procedure
TBTCP	Active Jobs/Background Job Step Overview
TRDIRT	Programs
TSTC	Link between Programs and Transaction Codes
TVAK	Sales Order Type and Document Pricing Procedure
TVCPF	Sales Doc to Billing Document Copy Control
TVKO	Sales Organization to Company Code
TVKOL	Picking Location Determination
TVKWZ	Plant to Sales Organization
TVSTZ	Shipping Point Determination
TVSWZ	Shipping Point to Plant Assignment
VBAK	Sales Order Header
VBAP	Sales Order Item
VBEP	Sales Order Schedule Lines
VBRK	Billing Header
VBRP	Billing Item

Table A.3 Selected Tables (Cont.)

Appendix B
SAP Fiori Apps

In Chapter 1, we discussed the use of SAP Fiori in the order-to-cash world. In this appendix, you'll find useful apps for the day-to-day processing of sales and distribution documents via analytics, easy-to-use factsheets, and the beauty and synchronized nature of transactional apps.

This section isn't designed to give you full functionality in a how-to-use guide, but rather give you a taste of the kind of SAP Fiori apps that are available so you can experiment and discuss with your SAP analyst.

A useful way of seeing all the available SAP Fiori apps for your instance is to access the SAP Fiori apps reference library website at *https://fioriappslibrary.hana.ondemand.com/sap/fix/externalViewer/*.

The SAP Fiori apps reference library allows you to search through all available apps in the SAP Fiori landscape and get details and documentation for each of them. Note, however, that there are literally thousands of SAP Fiori apps (11,230 at the last count, for SAP S/4HANA version 2020) and not all of them will be activated in your version of SAP S/4HANA. That particular task was undertaken when the system was first built as part of the implementation project.

The first thing to note is that the normal SAP GUI transactions are also available in SAP Fiori. Simply type the transaction code into the search box to bring up the SAP Fiori app, and away you go!

Cast your mind back to Chapter 1, where we discussed the various types of SAP Fiori apps, and you'll remember that there are three types:

- Transactional apps
- Factsheet apps
- Analytical apps

In this appendix, we'll focus on each type separately.

B.1 Transactional Apps

Aside from the usual transactions available in sales and distribution in the SAP GUI, there are some key SAP Fiori apps that are very useful. These apps are prefixed with the word “Manage” and allow you to navigate around sales and distribution documents with ease, including shortcut menu options to carry out quick changes. Figure B.1 shows the tile of the Manage Sales Order app, showing the total number of sales orders in the system (238) as dynamic data on the front.

Figure B.1 Manage Sales Order Tile

Once inside the app, the normal filters and variants can be applied, and shortcut actions are listed above the results, as shown in Figure B.2.

Manage Sales Orders

Standard *

Sales Order: Sold-To Party: Customer Reference: Requested Delivery Date: Overall Status: Document Date:

Search

Adapt Filters Go

Sales Orders (238) Standard

Create Sales Order - VA01 Reject All Items Set Delivery Block Remove Delivery Block Set Billing Block Remove Billing Block

Sales Order	Sold-To Party	Customer Reference	Requested Delivery Date	Overall Status	Net Value	Document Date
247	Aj10 customer (99040)	456	02/18/2021	Open	100,000.000 USD	02/18/2021
246	Aj10 customer (99040)	abc	02/18/2021	Open	0.000 USD	02/18/2021
245	Aj10 customer (99040)	123	02/18/2021	Open	0.000 USD	02/18/2021
244	Aj10 customer (99040)	123	02/17/2021	Open	1,000.000 USD	02/17/2021
243	Digital, Inc. (92)	JO 0216A	02/17/2021	In Process	17,313.450 USD	02/16/2021
242	Aj10 customer (99040)	123	02/16/2021	Open	0.000 USD	02/16/2021
241	Digital, Inc. (92)	Sales BOM	02/16/2021	Open	1,102.500 USD	02/16/2021
240	j1 customer (99037)	JJL	02/11/2021	Open	1,000,000.000 USD	02/11/2021
239	j1 customer (99037)	XYZ	02/10/2021	In Process	100,000.000 USD	02/10/2021
238	Ysing ltd (99029)	CD01 test2	02/10/2021	Open	450.000 USD	02/10/2021

Figure B.2 Manage Sales Orders App

Many useful “Manage” apps are available as listed here (the same format is used in every app):

- Manage Sales Orders (referenced in Chapter 6)
- Manage Sales Inquiries
- Manage Sales Quotations
- Manage Credit Memo Requests

- Manage Sales Contracts
- Manage Customer Returns
- Manage Sales Scheduling Agreements
- Manage Outbound Deliveries
- Manage Billing Documents
- Manage Credit/Debit Memos
- Manage Invoice Lists

A very similar style of transactional app is Track Sales Orders. Slightly more information and options are available here by clicking on the customer; this brings up additional links (with options to add more links), as shown in Figure B.3.

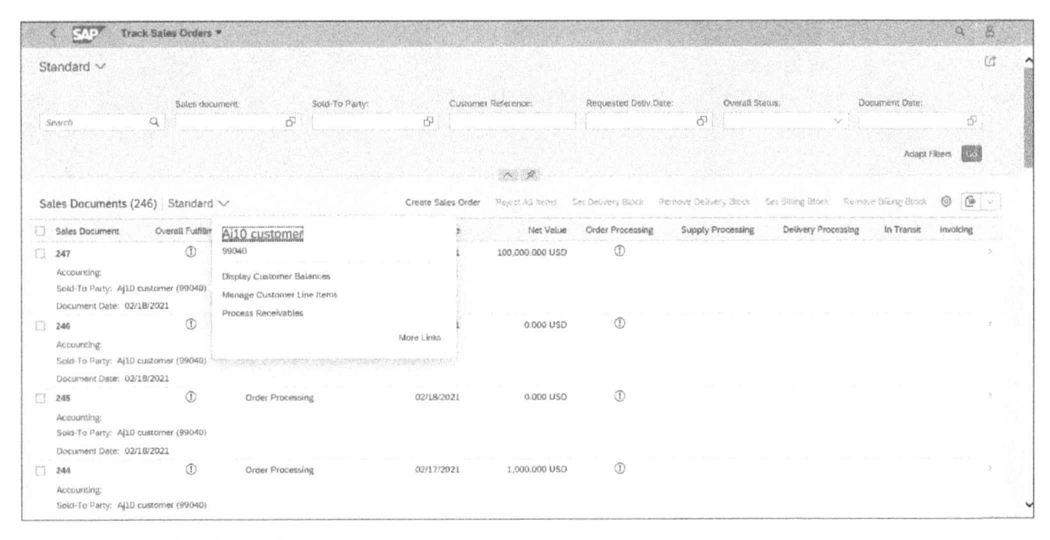

Figure B.3 Track Sales Orders App

B.2 Factsheet Apps

Factsheet apps are normally navigated to from other apps. For example, from within the Track Sales Orders app, you can click on the **Sold-To Party** name, then the **More Links** option to add the Customer – 360° View app to your selection, which is a good example of a factsheet app.

This is a useful SAP Fiori app as it lists all the details for your customer, as shown in Figure B.4.

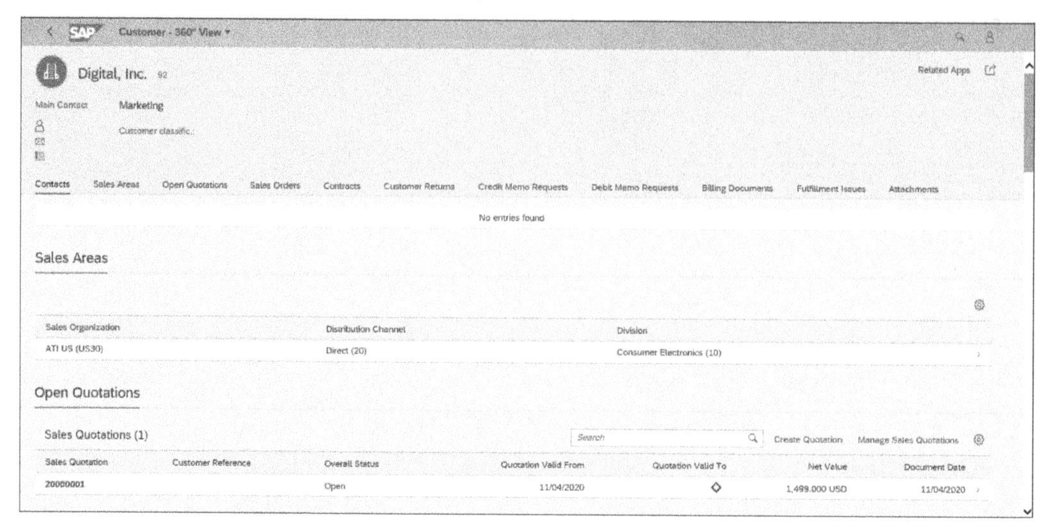

Figure B.4 Customer: 360° View App

B.3 Analytical Apps

There are several useful SAP Fiori analytical apps:

- **Sales Management Overview**
  Provides a graphical overview of many sales data cards (see Figure B.5).

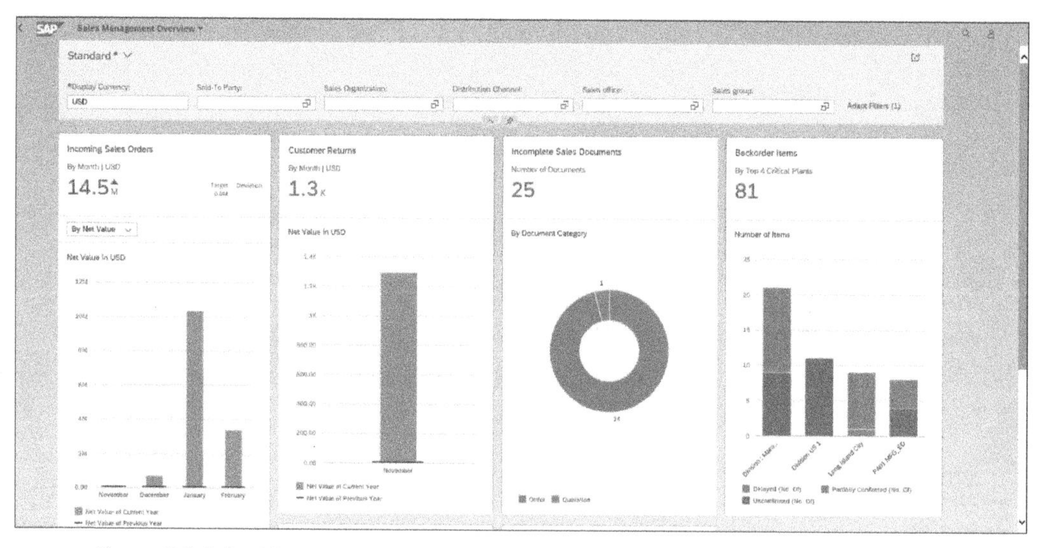

Figure B.5 Sales Management Overview App

- **My Sales Overview**
  An overview that can be seen as a landing page for all things sales related, with functions to create and display key sales data, as shown in Figure B.6.

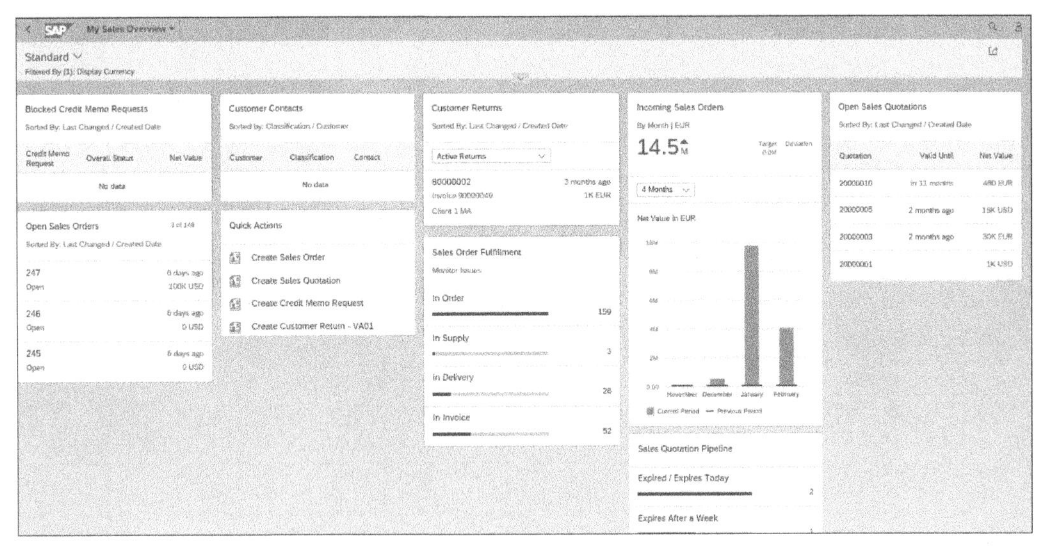

Figure B.6 My Sales Overview App

- **Sales Order Fulfillment Issues**
  Discussed briefly in Chapter 1, this is a very useful app that allows you to resolve issues in the supply chain (see Figure B.7). Note that this app can be accessed from the My Sales Overview app.

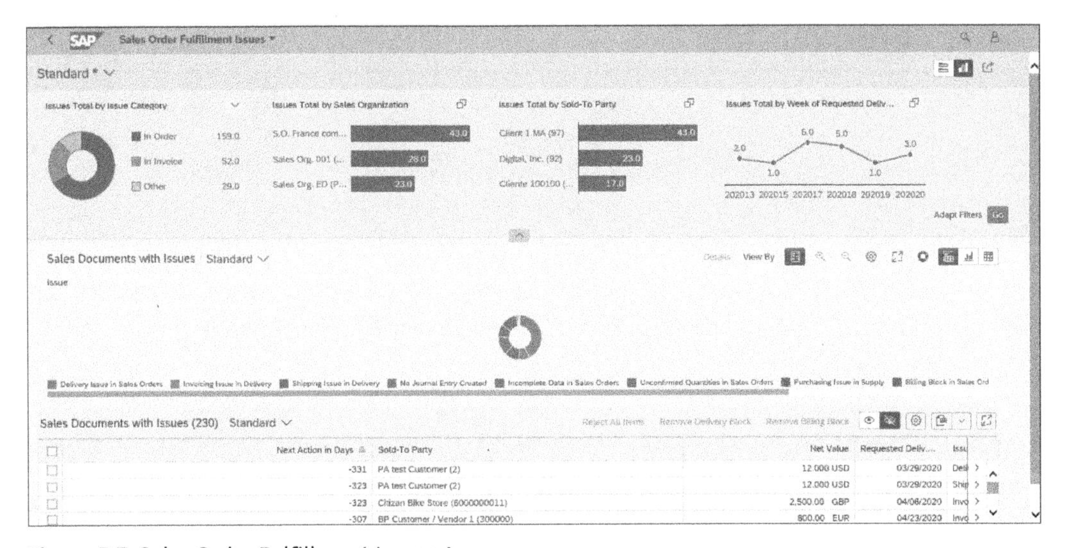

Figure B.7 Sales Order Fulfillment Issues App

- **Predicted Delivery Delay**
  You can configure this cutting-edge app using the Predictive Modeling app. The app uses machine learning capabilities to build on previous delivery performance to predict bottlenecks in deliveries in the supply chain (see Figure B.8).

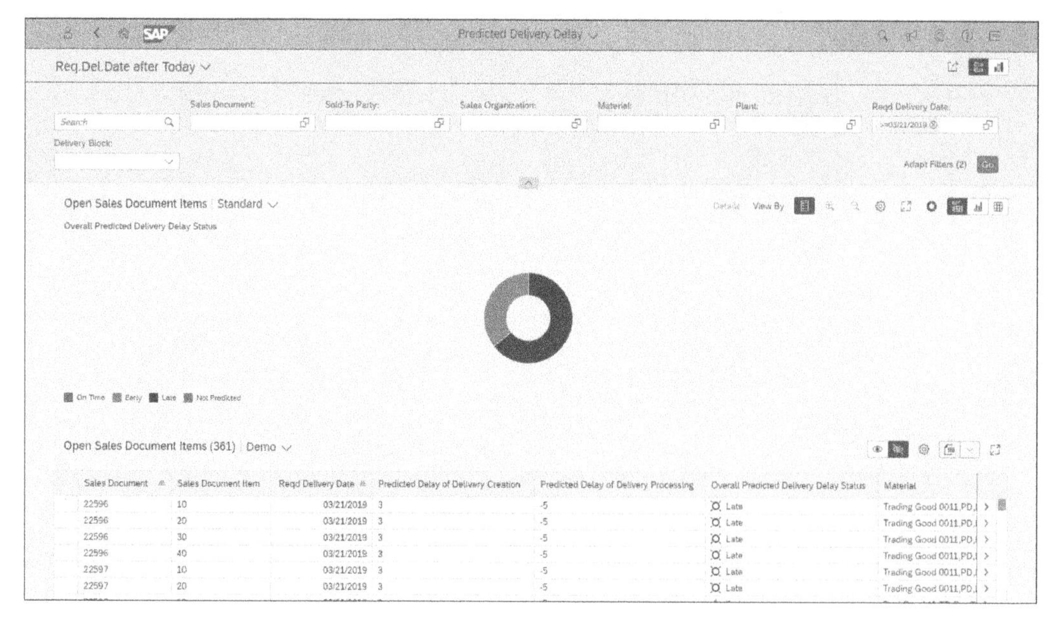

Figure B.8 Predicted Delivery Delay App

B.4 Summary

In Chapter 1, we gave an overview of the concepts of SAP Fiori apps and tiles and how to use them. In this appendix, we've explored some examples of the kind of apps that would be useful in your sales and distribution processes. These cover basic transactional apps, such as Manage Sales Orders, right through to advanced machine learning apps that explore predictive scenarios, such as Predicted Delivery Delay. In the course of your job, you'll likely use all different types of SAP Fiori apps, so it would be advantageous to explore some of the available apps in the SAP Fiori apps reference library, mentioned earlier.

Appendix C
The Authors

James Olcott is a business-savvy and seasoned SAP sales and distribution consultant with more than 20 years' professional experience working primarily in the USA and Canada, with stints in Europe, Asia, Africa, and Australia.

Industries covered include pharmaceutical, medical device, government, aviation, and manufacturing. His technical capabilities include sales and distribution, materials management, MRO, SAP BusinessObjects, and queries in support of data dives, with a particular focus on writing functional specifications.

James' articles have appeared in EURSAP's SAP blog and SAPTips Journal. His background in IT began at a very early age when his father created an IT business in New York City during the 1960s. His extensive account of this can be found on thebernardolcottstory.com.

James is known as a leading SAP evangelist. He has installed confidence in team members through coaching as team lead and trainer in multiple projects. Learning never ends, especially for SAP consultants.

Jon Simmonds is a senior enterprise platform architect for Thermo Fisher Scientific Inc.

As a certified SAP consultant, he has for the last 18 years worked on countless SAP implementations in Europe, the Americas, and APAC. Jon's background is in sales and distribution, but he has practical knowledge of business processes and solutions across a variety of SAP environments (SAP S/4HANA, SAP ERP 6.0 and IS-Media). His technical capabilities include sales and distribution, materials management, ABAP programming, EDI, Smart Forms, SAP Fiori, data migration, business intelligence, and SAP Solution Manager.

Jon's focus is primarily on developing and maintaining an agile approach for ERP strategies and roadmaps within large corporations with a strong focus on innovation. Within this framework, Jon has for many years been actively writing blogs and articles on SAP and IT management for numerous websites and publications.

Contributor

Divyendra Purohit is an entrepreneur and cofounder of SAP consulting start up Insansa Technologies. He has more than 14 years of SAP experience, including multi-country implementations, upgrades, and rollouts. As a logistic solution architect, he worked on multiple initiatives in strategic consulting, digital transformations and process improvements.

Index

I

L

M

O

P

Q

R

S

T

W

- Set up your sales processes: sales order management, shipping and delivery, billing and invoicing, and more
- Configure your SAP S/4HANA system with step-by-step instructions
- Explore key sales reports and analytics

Christian van Helfteren

Configuring Sales in SAP S/4HANA

SAP S/4HANA Sales is here! Business partners, the material master, and critical sales workflows all require careful configuration—this guide has the expertise you need. Learn about key business processes for sales order management, billing and invoicing, available-to-promise, and more. From setup and configuration to your reporting options, this book has you covered!

766 pages, pub. 12/2019
E-Book: $79.99 | **Print:** $89.95 | **Bundle:** $99.99

www.sap-press.com/4907

- Master your core controlling tasks in SAP S/4HANA
- Assess overhead, manufacturing, sales, project, and investment costs
- Streamline your operations with both the new and classic user interfaces

Janet Salmon, Stefan Walz

Controlling with SAP S/4HANA

Business User Guide

SAP S/4HANA brings change to your routine controlling activities. Perform your key tasks in the new environment with this user guide! Get click-by-click instructions for your daily and monthly overhead controlling tasks, and then dive deeper into processes such as make-to-stock/make-to-order scenarios, margin analysis, and investment management. Finally, instructions for intercompany transactions and reporting make this your all-in-one resource!

593 pages, pub. 05/2021
E-Book: $69.99 | **Print:** $79.95 | **Bundle:** $89.99

www.sap-press.com/5282

www.sap-press.com

- Run general ledger accounting, accounts payable and receivable, and asset accounting in SAP S/4HANA Finance
- Get step-by-step instructions for your core accounting tasks
- See how SAP S/4HANA streamlines your operations

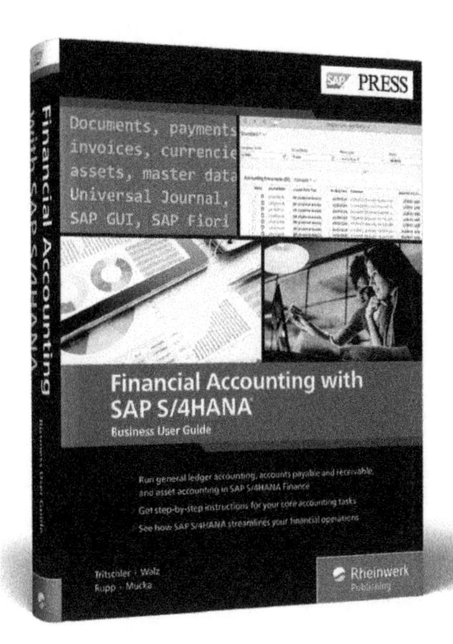

Jonas Tritschler, Stefan Walz, Reinhard Rupp, Nertila Mucka

Financial Accounting with SAP S/4HANA

Business User Guide

Finance professionals, it's time to simplify your day-to-day. This book walks through your financial accounting tasks, whether you're using SAP GUI transactions or SAP Fiori apps in your SAP S/4HANA system. For each of your core FI business processes—general ledger accounting, accounts payable, accounts receivable, and fixed asset accounting—learn how to complete key tasks, click by click. Complete your FI operations smoothly and efficiently!

604 pages, pub. 12/2019
E-Book: $69.99 | **Print:** $79.95 | **Bundle:** $89.99

www.sap-press.com/4938

- Run preventive maintenance, repairs, refurbishment, and more in SAP S/4HANA
- Manage routine plant operations with step-by-step instructions
- Improve your usability and workflows with mobile apps, SAP Fiori, and SAP Intelligent Asset Management

Karl Liebstückel

Plant Maintenance with SAP S/4HANA

Business User Guide

Your company is now on SAP S/4HANA—so how do you run your plant maintenance operations on this new system? Between these pages, you'll find the detailed, step-by-step instructions you need for your routine (and non-routine) functions. Ample screenshots walk you through scheduling repairs, planning maintenance cycles, completing inspections, and all the tasks you perform to keep your assets in shape. With information on new UIs and mobile apps, this guide is the only one you need!

665 pages, pub. 10/2020
E-Book: $69.99 | **Print:** $79.95 | **Bundle:** $89.99

www.sap-press.com/5180

www.sap-press.com

- Learn what SAP S/4HANA offers your company
- Explore key business processes and system architecture
- Consider your deployment options and implementation paths

Devraj Bardhan, Axel Baumgartl, Nga-Sze Choi, Mark Dudgeon, Piotr Górecki, Asidhara Lahiri, Bert Meijerink, Andrew Worsley-Tonks

SAP S/4HANA

An Introduction

Interested in what SAP S/4HANA has to offer? Find out with this big-picture guide! Take a tour of SAP S/4HANA functionality for your key lines of business: finance, manufacturing, supply chain, sales, and more. Preview SAP S/4HANA's architecture, and discover your options for reporting, extensions, and adoption. With insights into the latest intelligent technologies, this is your all-in-one SAP S/4HANA starting point!

648 pages, 4th edition, pub. 03/2021
E-Book: $69.99 | **Print:** $79.95 | **Bundle:** $89.99

www.sap-press.com/5232

- Learn what SAP S/4HANA offers for manufacturing, warehousing, procurement, and beyond
- Explore key SAP Fiori applications for reporting and analytics
- Discover SAP Leonardo technologies for the supply chain

Deb Bhattacharjee, Vadhi Narasimhamurti, Chaitanaya Desai, Guillermo B. Vazquez, Tom Walsh

Logistics with SAP S/4HANA

An Introduction

Transform your logistics operations with SAP S/4HANA! With this introduction, see what SAP has in store for each supply chain line of business: sales order management, manufacturing, inventory management, warehousing, and more. Discover how SAP Fiori apps and embedded analytics improve reporting, and explore the intersection between your supply chain processes and new SAP Leonardo technologies. Take your first look at SAP S/4HANA logistics, and see where it will take your business!

589 pages, 2nd edition, pub. 01/2019
E-Book: $69.99 | **Print:** $79.95 | **Bundle:** $89.99
www.sap-press.com/4785

www.sap-press.com

Interested in reading more?

Please visit our website for all new book and e-book releases from SAP PRESS.

www.sap-press.com